Joel Whitburn Presents

# Songs & Artists 2006

## The Essential Music Guide for Your iPod™ and Other Portable Music Players

ISBN 0-89820-164-0

**Record Research Inc.**
**P.O. Box 200**
**Menomonee Falls, Wisconsin   53052-0200**
**U.S.A.**

Phone:   (262) 251-5408
Fax:   (262) 251-9452
E-Mail:   books@recordresearch.com
Web Site:   www.recordresearch.com

# TABLE OF CONTENTS

## Author's Note.................................................................5
## Artist Section..............................................................7

Lists, in alphabetical order, all the hit songs, by artist — from 1955 to the present

A ★ to the right of a title indicates that the title appears in one of the half-decade Classic Songs Playlists in the back of the book.

## Song Title Section.................................................179

A cross-reference of every song title from the Artist Section

## The Playlists............................................................255

### Classic Songs:

Listings of the 200 essential songs from each half decade:

| | |
|---|---|
| **1955-1959** | **1985-1989** |
| **1960-1964** | **1990-1994** |
| **1965-1969** | **1995-1999** |
| **1970-1974** | **2000-2004** |
| **1975-1979** | **2005** |
| **1980-1984** | |

### Miscellaneous Playlists:

Classic Rock
Road Trip!
The British Invasion 1964-65
We're An American Band '60s & '70s
Retro Radio Early '80s
The Motown Sound Of The '60s
A Classic Christmas:
      A Holly Jolly Christmas (Secular Songs)
      Joy To The World (Sacred Songs)

## Record Research Publications

# Joel Whitburn and Record Research:
# The Undisputed Experts on Recorded Music

What began simply as a teenager's record collection nearly 50 years ago has today grown into the largest and most successful business of its kind anywhere in the world.

Joel Whitburn and his Record Research staff have been highlighting the hits, archiving the artists and tracking the trends in recorded music longer, deeper and more definitively than anyone else in the business. The result: there's no one better qualified or experienced to compile the definitive book of playlists for iPods and other portable music players — the hottest trend in recorded music.

Joel first began collecting records as a teenager growing up in the 1950s. As both his collection and his zeal for record collecting grew through the years, Joel began organizing his records according to the highest positions they reached on *Billboard* magazine's music charts. In 1970, with the encouragement of friends in the music industry, Joel turned his chart-watching hobby into a business with the publication of his first book — a slender volume titled simply *Record Research*.

Over the past 35 years, Joel's company, Record Research Inc., has published 104 reference books, which chronicle well over a century of American music, reaching as far back as 1890. Record Research publications cover virtually every charted music genre, including Pop, Rock, Country, R&B/Hip-Hop, Adult Contemporary, Dance/Disco and more.

These volumes, as well as Joel's books published by Billboard Books, are required reading for virtually anyone with a serious interest in music. Joel has also collaborated with Rhino Records on a series of 150 *Billboard* CD compilations of America's top-charted hits. His own comprehensive charted music collection is the backbone of his research.

Now, with his latest book — *Songs & Artists 2006: The Essential Music Guide for Your iPod and Other Portable Music Players* — Joel and his Record Researchers move into new and somewhat "uncharted" territory.

"While there certainly are many charted hits in the book, *Songs & Artists 2006* looks beyond the charts — past just the commonly played hits," Joel notes. "I've included my personal picks of all the songs a listener needs to hear to fully appreciate the scope and impact of each artist's career and contribution to the legacy of recorded music."

"Here, and only here, are the detailed, 'must-have' playlists that comprehensively capture the essence of each artist, each era and each music genre," he adds.

From an eager record-collecting teenager in the 1950s to a world-renowned musicologist in the 21st century, Joel Whitburn's passion for recorded music is stronger than ever in the digital age.

# AUTHOR'S NOTE

The first thing I bought when I moved into my first home was a Wurlitzer juke box — before drapes, before a couch, before a kitchen table. I had always wanted a juke box, the colored lights, the big speakers and, best of all, the ability to punch two buttons and play any one of my favorite 100 songs! Inside this glowing wonder were a mechanized arm and a turntable that did all the work. This was in 1964, a few weeks before I married Fran. In the four decades since then, we've always had a juke box, from those that play vinyl 45s to those that play CDs.

Last year, I bought the ultimate juke box, an iPod. I am still blown away at the power of this amazing music player. It's a dream to be able to carry over 10,000 songs in the palm of my hand! And best of all, I can take it with me and turn *any* stereo into Joel's juke box!

That little device has inspired many ideas for this record collector and music lover. *Songs & Artists* is the realization of one of those ideas. In the months after I got my iPod, I went crazy downloading songs from my music collection. I wanted my electronic music collection to be as broad and comprehensive as a 40GB portable hard drive would allow. The depth of this collection went beyond the charts and included many genres. I wanted to have a simple checklist of the songs and artists of mainstream popular music, which encompasses Rock, Country, R&B, Adult Contemporary, Rap, Show Tunes, and just about every type of music there is. Thus, came the idea for this book.

In creating this checklist, my staff and I initially came up with a list of the top hits of the Rock Era, which began in 1955. This included the Pop and Rock hits of the Pop singles charts and those that crossed over from the R&B, Country, Adult Contemporary, and Rock charts, and hit big. (Hits that made only the Country chart from 1990-on are included as this is when Country's popularity exploded but was not reflected on the Pop charts.) In compiling over 14,000 songs and 3,700 artists that are in this book, we went beyond the singles charts to include album cuts that are now classics but were never released as singles and thus never charted, such as Led Zeppelin's "Stairway To Heaven" or "Moon River" by Andy Williams.

One of the most fun features of *Songs & Artists* is the Playlist section. The ten half-decade "Classic Songs" playlists, comprising 200 songs each, is especially helpful for planning anniversaries, reunions or birthdays. Songs on these lists have stood the test of time and some became more popular as years went by. An example of this is "La Bamba" by Ritchie Valens; his record "Donna" was a much bigger hit in its time, but "La Bamba," is now remembered as his signature song, even becoming the title of his biopic. You can tell which songs in the Artist section appear in a "Classic Songs" playlist as they are denoted with a ★. We've also included other specialty playlists; however, page constraints of this book would only allow so many. In future editions, we hope to include more playlists. We welcome your suggestions!

The purpose of this book is to help you in organizing and shaping your electronic music collection. Of course, the ultimate song storage device is your memory. You can remember more songs than can possibly be contained in any music player, at least with present technology. May this book stimulate your memory and aid you in further personalizing the songs and artists on your juke box.

JOEL WHITBURN

# ARTIST SECTION

# A

## AALIYAH
- ☐ '98 Are You That Somebody? ★
- ☐ '94 At Your Best (You Are Love)
- ☐ '94 Back & Forth ★
- ☐ '03 Come Over
- ☑ '02 I Care 4 U
- ☐ '00 I Don't Wanna
- ☐ '96 If Your Girl Only Knew
- ☐ '02 Miss You ★
- ☑ '02 More Than A Woman
- ☐ '97 One I Gave My Heart To, The ★
- ☐ '96 One In A Million
- ☑ '01 Rock The Boat
- ☑ '00 Try Again ★

## ABBA
- ☐ '79 Chiquitita
- ☐ '76 Dancing Queen ★
- ☐ '79 Does Your Mother Know
- ☐ '76 Fernando
- ☐ '74 Honey, Honey
- ☐ '76 I Do, I Do, I Do, I Do, I Do
- ☐ '77 Knowing Me, Knowing You
- ☐ '76 Mamma Mia
- ☐ '77 Name Of The Game, The
- ☐ '75 SOS
- ☐ '78 Take A Chance On Me ★
- ☐ '74 Waterloo
- ☐ '82 When All Is Said And Done
- ☐ '80 Winner Takes It All, The

## ABBOTT, Gregory
- ☐ '86 Shake You Down ★

## ABC
- ☐ '85 Be Near Me
- ☐ '86 (How To Be A) Millionaire
- ☐ '82 Look Of Love, The
- ☐ '83 Poison Arrow
- ☐ '87 When Smokey Sings

## ABDUL, Paula
- ☐ '91 Blowing Kisses In The Wind
- ☐ '89 Cold Hearted
- ☐ '89 Forever Your Girl ★
- ☐ '89 (It's Just) The Way That You Love Me
- ☐ '95 My Love Is For Real
- ☐ '89 Opposites Attract ★
- ☐ '91 Promise Of A New Day, The ★
- ☐ '91 Rush, Rush ★
- ☐ '88 Straight Up ★
- ☐ '92 Vibeology
- ☐ '92 Will You Marry Me?

## AC/DC
- ☐ '80 Back In Black
- ☐ '93 Big Gun
- ☐ '81 Dirty Deeds Done Dirt Cheap
- ☐ '81 For Those About To Rock (We Salute You)
- ☐ '95 Hard As A Rock
- ☐ '79 Highway To Hell
- ☐ '90 Moneytalks
- ☐ '00 Stiff Upper Lip
- ☐ '76 T.N.T.
- ☐ '90 Thunderstruck
- ☐ '77 Whole Lotta Rosie
- ☐ '80 You Shook Me All Night Long ★

## ACE
- ☑ '75 How Long

## ACE, Johnny
- ☐ '55 Pledging My Love

## ACE OF BASE
- ☐ '93 All That She Wants ★
- ☐ '95 Beautiful Life
- ☐ '98 Cruel Summer
- ☐ '94 Don't Turn Around
- ☐ '94 Living In Danger
- ☐ '96 Lucky Love
- ☐ '94 Sign, The ★

## ACKLIN, Barbara
- ☐ '68 Love Makes A Woman

## ADAMS, Bryan
- ☐ '93 All For Love ★
  *BRYAN ADAMS  ROD STEWART  STING*
- ☐ '91 Can't Stop This Thing We Started ★
- ☐ '83 Cuts Like A Knife
- ☐ '92 Do I Have To Say The Words?
- ☐ '91 (Everything I Do) I Do It For You ★
- ☐ '95 Have You Ever Really Loved A Woman? ★
- ☐ '87 Hearts On Fire
- ☐ '87 Heat Of The Night
- ☐ '85 Heaven ★
- ☐ '96 I Finally Found Someone
  *BARBRA STREISAND & BRYAN ADAMS*
- ☐ '97 I'll Always Be Right There
- ☐ '85 It's Only Love
  *BRYAN ADAMS & TINA TURNER*
- ☐ '96 Let's Make A Night To Remember
- ☐ '82 Lonely Nights
- ☐ '85 One Night Love Affair
- ☐ '93 Please Forgive Me
- ☐ '84 Run To You
- ☐ '85 Somebody
- ☐ '83 Straight From The Heart
- ☐ '85 Summer Of '69 ★
- ☐ '91 There Will Never Be Another Tonight
- ☐ '83 This Time
- ☐ '92 Thought I'd Died And Gone To Heaven
- ☐ '87 Victim Of Love

## ADAMS, Johnny
- ☐ '69 Reconsider Me

## ADAMS, Oleta
- ☐ '90 Get Here

## ADDERLEY, "Cannonball"
- ☐ '67 Mercy, Mercy, Mercy

## ADDRISI BROTHERS, The
- ☐ '59 Cherrystone
- ☐ '77 Slow Dancin' Don't Turn Me On
- ☐ '72 We've Got To Get It On Again

## ADKINS, Trace
- ☐ '96 Every Light In The House
- ☐ '97 I Left Something Turned On At Home
- ☐ '97 (This Ain't) No Thinkin' Thing

## AD LIBS, The
- ☐ '65 Boy From New York City, The ★

## ADVENTURES OF STEVIE V
- ☐ '90 Dirty Cash (Money Talks)

## AEROSMITH
- ☐ '93 Amazing
- ☐ '88 Angel
- ☐ '77 Back In The Saddle
- ☐ '94 Blind Man
- ☐ '78 Come Together
- ☐ '94 Crazy
- ☐ '93 Cryin'
- ☐ '94 Deuces Are Wild
- ☐ '77 Draw The Line
- ☑ '73 Dream On
- ☑ '87 Dude (Looks Like A Lady)
- ☑ '97 Falling In Love (Is Hard On The Knees)
- ☐ '98 I Don't Want To Miss A Thing ★
- ☑ '01 Jaded
- ☑ '89 Janie's Got A Gun ★
- ☐ '77 Kings And Queens
- ☐ '76 Last Child
- ☐ '93 Livin' On The Edge
- ☑ '89 Love In An Elevator
- ☐ '73 Mama Kin
- ☑ '90 Other Side, The
- ☑ '97 Pink
- ☐ '88 Rag Doll
- ☐ '79 Remember (Walking In The Sand)
- ☐ '74 Same Old Song And Dance
- ☑ '75 Sweet Emotion ★
- ☐ '97 Taste Of India
- ☐ '74 Train Kept A Rollin'
- ☑ '76 Walk This Way ★
- ☑ '90 What It Takes

## AFROMAN
- ☐ '01 Because I Got High

## AFTER 7
- ☑ '90 Can't Stop
- ☑ '89 Heat Of The Moment
- ☐ '91 Nights Like This
- ☐ '90 Ready Or Not
- ☐ '95 'Til You Do Me Right

## AFTER THE FIRE
- ☐ '83 Der Kommissar ★

## AGUILERA, Christina
- ☐ '02 Beautiful ★
- ☐ '03 Can't Hold Us Down
- ☐ '99 Christmas Song (Chestnuts Roasting On An Open Fire)
- ☐ '00 Come On Over Baby (all I want is you) ★
- ☐ '03 Fighter
- ☐ '99 Genie In A Bottle ★
- ☐ '00 I Turn To You
- ☐ '01 Lady Marmalade ★
  *CHRISTINA AGUILERA, LIL' KIM, MYA & P!NK*
- ☐ '01 Nobody Wants To Be Lonely
  *RICKY MARTIN with Christina Aguilera*
- ☐ '03 Voice Within, The
- ☐ '99 What A Girl Wants ★

## A-HA
- ☐ '85 Sun Always Shines On T.V., The
- ☐ '85 Take On Me ★

## AHMAD
- ☐ '94 Back In The Day

## AIKEN, Clay
- ☐ '03 Invisible
- ☐ '04 Solitaire
- ☐ '03 This Is The Night ★

## AIR SUPPLY
- ☐ '80 All Out Of Love ★
- ☐ '82 Even The Nights Are Better
- ☐ '80 Every Woman In The World
- ☐ '81 Here I Am (Just When I Thought I Was Over You)
- ☐ '85 Just As I Am
- ☐ '80 Lost In Love ★
- ☐ '83 Making Love Out Of Nothing At All
- ☐ '81 One That You Love, The
- ☐ '81 Sweet Dreams
- ☐ '82 Two Less Lonely People In The World
- ☐ '82 Young Love

## AKENS, Jewel
- ☐ '65 Birds And The Bees, The ★

## AKINS, Rhett
- ☐ '96 Don't Get Me Started
- ☐ '95 That Ain't My Truck

## AKON
- ☐ '04 Locked Up
- ☐ '05 Lonely ★

## ALABAMA
- ☐ '93 Angels Among Us
- ☐ '92 Born Country
- ☐ '83 Closer You Get, The
- ☐ '97 Dancin', Shaggin' On The Boulevard
- ☐ '91 Down Home
- ☐ '81 Feels So Right
- ☐ '90 Forever's As Far As I'll Go
- ☐ '85 Forty Hour Week (For A Livin')
- ☐ '99 God Must Have Spent A Little More Time On You
- ☐ '91 Here We Are
- ☐ '89 High Cotton
- ☐ '98 How Do You Fall In Love
- ☐ '92 I'm In A Hurry (And Don't Know Why)
- ☐ '84 If You're Gonna Play In Texas (You Gotta Have A Fiddle In The Band)
- ☐ '90 Jukebox In My Mind
- ☐ '81 Love In The First Degree
- ☐ '82 Mountain Music
- ☐ '90 Pass It On Down
- ☐ '93 Reckless
- ☐ '84 Roll On (Eighteen Wheeler)

☐ '97 Sad Lookin' Moon
☐ '95 She Ain't Your Ordinary Girl
☐ '89 Song Of The South
☐ '82 Take Me Down
☐ '85 There's No Way

## ALARM, The
☐ '89 Sold Me Down The River

## ALBERT, Morris
☐ '75 Feelings

## AL B. SURE!
☐ '89 If I'm Not Your Lover
☐ '90 Missunderstanding
☐ '88 Nite And Day
☐ '88 Off On Your Own (Girl)
☐ '88 Rescue Me
☐ '92 Right Now

## ALEXANDER, Arthur
☐ '62 Anna (Go To Him)
☐ '62 You Better Move On

## ALI, Tatyana
☐ '98 Daydreamin'

## ALIAS
☐ '90 More Than Words Can Say ★
☐ '91 Waiting For Love

## ALICE DEEJAY
☐ '00 Better Off Alone

## ALICE IN CHAINS
☐ '95 Heaven Beside You
☐ '94 No Excuses
☐ '93 Rooster

## ALIEN ANT FARM
☐ '01 Smooth Criminal

## ALIVE & KICKING
☐ '70 Tighter, Tighter

## ALLAN, Davie, & The Arrows
☐ '67 Blue's Theme

## ALLAN, Gary
☐ '02 Man To Man
☐ '04 Nothing On But The Radio
☐ '02 One, The
☐ '03 Tough Little Boys

## ALLEN, Deborah
☐ '83 Baby I Lied

## ALLEN, Donna
☐ '89 Joy And Pain
☐ '87 Serious

## ALLEN, Rex
☐ '62 Don't Go Near The Indians

## ALL-4-ONE
☐ '95 I Can Love You Like That
☐ '94 I Swear ★
☐ '94 So Much In Love ★
☐ '96 Someday

## ALLISON, Gene
☐ '57 You Can Make It If You Try

## ALLMAN, Gregg
☐ '87 I'm No Angel
☐ '73 Midnight Rider

## ALLMAN BROTHERS BAND, The
☐ '72 Ain't Wastin' Time No More
☐ '72 Blue Sky
☐ '79 Crazy Love
☐ '70 Dreams
☐ '91 End Of The Line
☐ '90 Good Clean Fun
☐ '70 In Memory Of Elizabeth Reed
☐ '73 Jessica
☐ '72 Melissa
☐ '72 One Way Out
☐ '73 Ramblin Man ★
☐ '70 Revival (Love Is Everywhere)
☐ '71 Statesboro Blues
☐ '81 Straight From The Heart
☐ '70 Whipping Post

## ALL SAINTS
☐ '98 I Know Where It's At
☐ '98 Never Ever ★

## ALLURE
☐ '97 All Cried Out
☐ '97 Head Over Heels

## ALPERT, Herb/The Tijuana Brass
☐ '67 Banda, A
☐ '68 Carmen
☐ '67 Casino Royale
☐ '87 Diamonds
  *HERB ALPERT (with Janet Jackson)*
☐ '66 Flamingo
☐ '67 Happening, The
☐ '87 Keep Your Eye On Me
☐ '62 Lonely Bull, The
☐ '87 Making Love In The Rain
☐ '66 Mame
☐ '64 Mexican Shuffle, The
☐ '79 Rise ★
☐ '79 Rotation
☐ '82 Route 101
☐ '66 Spanish Flea
☐ '65 Taste Of Honey
☐ '68 This Guy's In Love With You ★
☐ '65 Tijuana Taxi
☐ '68 To Wait For Love
☐ '67 Wade In The Water
☐ '66 What Now My Love
☐ '66 Work Song, The
☐ '65 Zorba The Greek

## ALSTON, Gerald
☐ '90 Slow Motion

## ALTER BRIDGE
☐ '04 Open Your Eyes

## AMAZING RHYTHM ACES, The
☐ '75 Third Rate Romance

## AMBER
- ☐ '96  This Is Your Night

## AMBOY DUKES, The
- ☐ '68  Journey To The Center Of The Mind

## AMBROSIA
- ☐ '80  Biggest Part Of Me
- ☐ '75  Holdin' On To Yesterday
- ☐ '78  How Much I Feel
- ☐ '77  Magical Mystery Tour
- ☐ '80  You're The Only Woman (You & I)

## AMERICA
- ☐ '83  Border, The
- ☐ '75  Daisy Jane
- ☐ '73  Don't Cross The River
- ☐ '72  Horse With No Name, A ★
- ☐ '72  I Need You
- ☐ '74  Lonely People
- ☐ '72  Sandman
- ☐ '75  Sister Golden Hair ★
- ☐ '74  Tin Man
- ☐ '76  Today's The Day
- ☐ '72  Ventura Highway
- ☐ '82  You Can Do Magic

## AMERICAN BREED, The
- ☐ '67  Bend Me, Shape Me
- ☐ '68  Green Light
- ☐ '67  Step Out Of Your Mind

## AMERICAN IDOL FINALISTS
- ☐ '03  God Bless The U.S.A.

## AMERICAN IDOL SEASON 4
- ☐ '05  When You Tell Me That You Love Me

## AMERIE
- ☐ '05  1 Thing ★
- ☐ '02  Why Don't We Fall In Love

## AMES, Ed
- ☐ '67  My Cup Runneth Over
- ☐ '67  Time, Time
- ☐ '67  When The Snow Is On The Roses
- ☐ '67  Who Will Answer?

## AMES BROTHERS, The
- ☐ '60  China Doll
- ☐ '56  Forever Darling
- ☐ '56  It Only Hurts For A Little While
- ☐ '57  Melodie D'Amour (Melody of Love)
- ☐ '55  My Bonnie Lassie
- ☐ '58  Pussy Cat
- ☐ '58  Red River Rose
- ☐ '57  Tammy
- ☐ '58  Very Precious Love, A

## AMOS, Tori
- ☐ '94  God
- ☐ '92  Silent All These Years

## ANDERSON, Bill
- ☐ '67  For Loving You
  - *BILL ANDERSON & JAN HOWARD*
- ☐ '63  Still

## ANDERSON, John
- ☐ '93  Money In The Bank
- ☐ '92  Seminole Wind
- ☐ '83  Swingin'
- ☐ '91  Straight Tequila Night

## ANDERSON, Laurie
- ☐ '82  O Superman (For Massenet)
- ☐ '84  Sharkey's Day

## ANDERSON, Lynn
- ☐ '70  Rose Garden ★

## ANDERSON, Sunshine
- ☐ '01  Heard It All Before

## ANDREWS, Jessica
- ☐ '01  Who I Am

## ANDREWS, Julie
- ☐ '56  I Could Have Danced All Night
- ☐ '65  My Favorite Things

## ANDREWS, Lee, & The Hearts
- ☐ '57  Tear Drops
- ☐ '58  Try The Impossible

## ANGELICA
- ☐ '91  Angel Baby

## ANGELS, The
- ☐ '62  Cry Baby Cry
- ☐ '63  I Adore Him
- ☐ '63  My Boyfriend's Back ★
- ☐ '61  'Til

## ANIMALS, The
- ☐ '65  Bring It On Home To Me
- ☐ '66  Don't Bring Me Down
- ☐ '65  Don't Let Me Be Misunderstood
- ☐ '66  Help Me Girl
- ☐ '64  House Of The Rising Sun, The ★
- ☐ '64  I'm Crying
- ☐ '66  Inside-Looking Out
- ☐ '65  It's My Life
- ☐ '67  Monterey
- ☐ '67  San Franciscan Nights
- ☐ '66  See See Rider
- ☐ '68  Sky Pilot
- ☐ '65  We Gotta Get Out Of This Place
- ☐ '67  When I Was Young

## ANIMOTION
- ☐ '85  Let Him Go
- ☐ '85  Obsession
- ☐ '89  Room To Move

## ANKA, Paul
- ☐ '58  (All of a Sudden) My Heart Sings
- ☐ '58  Crazy Love
- ☐ '61  Dance On Little Girl
- ☐ '57  Diana ★
- ☐ '62  Eso Beso (That Kiss!)
- ☐ '69  Goodnight My Love
- ☐ '60  Hello Young Lovers
- ☐ '83  Hold Me 'Til The Mornin' Comes

- ☐ '75 (I Believe) There's Nothing Stronger Than Our Love
- ☐ '75 I Don't Like To Sleep Alone
- ☐ '59 I Miss You So
- ☐ '59 It's Time To Cry
- ☐ '58 Let The Bells Keep Ringing
- ☐ '59 Lonely Boy ★
- ☐ '63 Love (Makes the World Go 'Round)
- ☐ '62 Love Me Warm And Tender
- ☐ '60 My Home Town
- ☐ '74 One Man Woman/One Woman Man
- ☐ '60 Puppy Love ★
- ☐ '59 Put Your Head On My Shoulder ★
- ☐ '62 Steel Guitar And A Glass Of Wine, A
- ☐ '61 Story Of My Love, The
- ☐ '60 Summer's Gone
- ☐ '75 Times Of Your Life
- ☐ '61 Tonight My Love, Tonight
- ☐ '58 You Are My Destiny
- ☐ '74 (You're) Having My Baby ★

## ANNETTE
- ☐ '59 First Name Initial
- ☐ '59 Lonely Guitar
- ☐ '60 O Dio Mio
- ☐ '60 Pineapple Princess
- ☐ '59 Tall Paul
- ☐ '60 Train Of Love

## ANN-MARGRET
- ☐ '61 I Just Don't Understand

## ANOTHER BAD CREATION
- ☐ '91 Iesha
- ☐ '91 Playground

## ANT, Adam
- ☐ '82 Goody Two Shoes ★
- ☐ '90 Room At The Top
- ☐ '95 Wonderful

## ANTHONY, Marc
- ☐ '99 I Need To Know ★
- ☐ '00 You Sang To Me ★

## ANTHONY, Ray
- ☐ '59 Peter Gunn

## APOLLO 100
- ☐ '72 Joy

## APPLE, Fiona
- ☐ '97 Criminal

## APPLEJACKS, The
- ☐ '58 Mexican Hat Rock
- ☐ '58 Rocka-Conga

## APRIL WINE
- ☐ '82 Enough Is Enough
- ☐ '80 I Like To Rock
- ☐ '81 Just Between You And Me
- ☐ '79 Roller
- ☐ '72 You Could Have Been A Lady

## AQUA
- ☐ '97 Barbie Girl

- ☐ '97 Lollipop (Candyman)

## AQUATONES, The
- ☐ '58 You

## ARBORS, The
- ☐ '69 Letter, The
- ☐ '66 Symphony For Susan, A

## ARCADIA
- ☐ '85 Election Day
- ☐ '86 Goodbye Is Forever

## ARC ANGELS
- ☐ '92 Too Many Ways To Fall

## ARCHER, Tasmin
- ☐ '93 Sleeping Satellite

## ARCHIES, The
- ☐ '68 Bang-Shang-A-Lang
- ☐ '69 Jingle Jangle
- ☐ '69 Sugar, Sugar ★

## ARDEN, Jann
- ☐ '96 Insensitive

## ARDEN, Toni
- ☐ '58 Padre

## ARENA, Tina
- ☐ '96 Chains

## ARGENT
- ☐ '72 Hold Your Head Up ★

## ARMS, Russell
- ☐ '57 Cinco Robles (Five Oaks)

## ARMSTRONG, Louis
- ☐ '56 Blueberry Hill
- ☐ '64 Hello, Dolly! ★
- ☐ '56 Theme From The Threepenny Opera (Mack The Knife)
- ☐ '88 What A Wonderful World

## ARNOLD, Eddy
- ☐ '55 Cattle Call, The
- ☐ '66 I Want To Go With You
- ☐ '66 Last Word In Lonesome Is Me, The
- ☐ '65 Make The World Go Away
- ☐ '67 Turn The World Around

## ARRESTED DEVELOPMENT
- ☐ '92 Mr. Wendal ★
- ☐ '92 People Everyday
- ☐ '92 Tennessee ★

## ARTISTS AGAINST AIDS
- ☐ '01 What's Going On

## ARTISTS UNITED AGAINST APARTHEID
- ☐ '85 Sun City

## ART OF NOISE, The
- ☐ '88 Kiss
- ☐ '86 Paranoimia
- ☐ '86 Peter Gunn

## ASHANTI
- ☐ '02 Baby
- ☐ '02 Foolish ★
- ☐ '02 Happy
- ☐ '04 Only U
- ☐ '03 Rain On Me
- ☐ '03 Rock Wit U (Awww Baby) ★

## ASHFORD & SIMPSON
- ☐ '79 Found A Cure
- ☐ '89 I'll Be There For You
- ☐ '78 It Seems To Hang On
- ☐ '84 Solid

## ASHTON, GARDNER & DYKE
- ☐ '71 Resurrection Shuffle

## ASIA
- ☐ '90 Days Like These
- ☐ '83 Don't Cry
- ☐ '82 Heat Of The Moment ★
- ☐ '82 Only Time Will Tell
- ☐ '83 Smile Has Left Your Eyes, The

## ASSEMBLED MULTITUDE, The
- ☐ '70 Overture From Tommy (A Rock Opera)

## ASSOCIATION, The
- ☐ '66 Along Comes Mary
- ☐ '66 Cherish ★
- ☐ '68 Everything That Touches You
- ☐ '67 Never My Love ★
- ☐ '66 Pandora's Golden Heebie Jeebies
- ☐ '68 Time For Livin'
- ☐ '67 Windy ★

## ASTLEY, Jon
- ☐ '88 Put This Love To The Test

## ASTLEY, Rick
- ☐ '91 Cry For Help
- ☐ '89 Giving Up On Love
- ☐ '93 Hopelessly
- ☐ '88 It Would Take A Strong Strong Man
- ☐ '87 Never Gonna Give You Up ★
- ☐ '88 She Wants To Dance With Me
- ☐ '88 Together Forever

## ASTRONAUTS, The
- ☐ '63 Baja

## ATARIS, The
- ☐ '03 Boys Of Summer, The

## ATC
- ☐ '01 Around The World (La La La La La)

## ATLANTA RHYTHM SECTION
- ☐ '81 Alien
- ☐ '78 Champagne Jam
- ☐ '79 Do It Or Die
- ☐ '74 Doraville
- ☐ '78 I'm Not Gonna Let It Bother Me Tonight
- ☐ '78 Imaginary Lover
- ☐ '77 So In To You
- ☐ '79 Spooky

## ATLANTIC STARR
- ☐ '87 Always ★
- ☐ '82 Circles
- ☐ '92 Masterpiece ★
- ☐ '89 My First Love
- ☐ '85 Secret Lovers

## AUDIOSLAVE
- ☐ '05 Be Yourself ★
- ☐ '02 Cochise
- ☐ '03 I Am The Highway
- ☐ '03 Like A Stone
- ☐ '03 Show Me How To Live

## AUSTIN, Patti
- ☐ '82 Baby, Come To Me ★
  - *PATTI AUSTIN (with James Ingram)*

## AUSTIN, Sil
- ☐ '56 Slow Walk

## AUTOGRAPH
- ☐ '84 Turn Up The Radio

## AVALON, Frankie
- ☐ '59 Bobby Sox To Stockings
- ☐ '59 Boy Without A Girl, A
- ☐ '58 DeDe Dinah
- ☐ '60 Don't Throw Away All Those Teardrops
- ☐ '58 Ginger Bread
- ☐ '58 I'll Wait For You
- ☐ '59 Just Ask Your Heart
- ☐ '60 Togetherness
- ☐ '59 Venus ★
- ☐ '60 Where Are You
- ☐ '59 Why
- ☐ '62 You Are Mine

## AVANT
- ☐ '04 Don't Take Your Love Away
- ☐ '02 Makin' Good Love
- ☐ '00 My First Love
- ☐ '03 Read Your Mind
- ☐ '00 Separated

## AVANT-GARDE, The
- ☐ '68 Naturally Stoned

## AWB (AVERAGE WHITE BAND)
- ☐ '75 Cut The Cake
- ☐ '75 If I Ever Lose This Heaven
- ☐ '74 Pick Up The Pieces ★
- ☐ '76 Queen Of My Soul
- ☐ '75 School Boy Crush

## AZ
- ☐ '95 Sugar Hill

## AZAR, Steve
- ☐ '01 I Don't Have To Be Me ('Til Monday)

## AZ YET
- ☐ '97 Hard To Say I'm Sorry
- ☐ '96 Last Night

# B

## BABY
- ☐ '02 Do That...

## BABY BASH
- ☐ '05 Baby I'm Back
- ☐ '03 Suga Suga

## BABYFACE
- ☐ '94 And Our Feelings
- ☐ '97 Every Time I Close My Eyes
- ☐ '92 Give U My Heart
- ☐ '89 It's No Crime
- ☐ '90 My Kinda Girl
- ☐ '93 Never Keeping Secrets
- ☐ '89 Tender Lover
- ☐ '01 There She Goes
- ☐ '96 This Is For The Lover In You ★
- ☐ '94 When Can I See You
- ☐ '90 Whip Appeal

## BABYS, The
- ☐ '80 Back On My Feet Again
- ☐ '79 Every Time I Think Of You
- ☐ '77 Isn't It Time

## BACHELORS, The
- ☐ '65 Chapel In The Moonlight
- ☐ '64 Diane
- ☐ '64 I Believe
- ☐ '66 Love Me With All Of Your Heart
- ☐ '65 Marie
- ☐ '64 No Arms Can Ever Hold You

## BACHMAN, Tal
- ☐ '99 She's So High

## BACHMAN-TURNER OVERDRIVE
- ☐ '73 Blue Collar
- ☐ '75 Hey You
- ☐ '74 Let It Ride
- ☐ '75 Roll On Down The Highway
- ☐ '76 Take It Like A Man
- ☐ '74 Takin' Care Of Business
- ☐ '74 You Ain't Seen Nothing Yet ★

## BACKSTREET BOYS
- ☐ '99 All I Have To Give
- ☐ '97 As Long As You Love Me ★
- ☐ '01 Drowning
- ☐ '98 Everybody (Backstreet's Back) ★
- ☐ '99 I Want It That Way ★
- ☐ '98 I'll Never Break Your Heart ★
- ☐ '05 Incomplete ★
- ☐ '99 Larger Than Life
- ☐ '01 More Than That
- ☐ '00 One, The
- ☐ '97 Quit Playing Games (With My Heart) ★
- ☐ '00 Shape Of My Heart
- ☐ '00 Show Me The Meaning Of Being Lonely ★

## BACKUS, Jim
- ☐ '58 Delicious!

## BAD COMPANY
- ☐ '74 Bad Company
- ☐ '77 Burnin' Sky
- ☐ '74 Can't Get Enough
- ☐ '82 Electricland
- ☐ '75 Feel Like Makin' Love
- ☐ '75 Good Lovin' Gone Bad
- ☐ '90 Holy Water
- ☐ '92 How About That
- ☐ '90 If You Needed Somebody
- ☐ '75 Movin' On
- ☐ '88 No Smoke Without A Fire
- ☐ '74 Ready For Love
- ☐ '79 Rock 'N' Roll Fantasy
- ☐ '76 Run With The Pack
- ☐ '75 Shooting Star
- ☐ '76 Silver, Blue & Gold
- ☐ '91 Walk Through Fire
- ☐ '76 Young Blood

## BAD ENGLISH
- ☐ '89 Forget Me Not
- ☐ '90 Possession
- ☐ '89 Price Of Love
- ☐ '89 When I See You Smile ★

## BADFINGER
- ☐ '72 Baby Blue
- ☐ '70 Come And Get It
- ☐ '71 Day After Day ★
- ☐ '70 No Matter What

## BADU, Erykah
- ☐ '00 Bag Lady
- ☐ '02 Love of My Life (An Ode To Hip Hop)
- ☐ '97 Next Lifetime
- ☐ '97 On&On
- ☐ '97 Tyrone

## BAEZ, Joan
- ☐ '75 Diamonds And Rust
- ☐ '71 Night They Drove Old Dixie Down ★
- ☐ '63 We Shall Overcome

## BAHA MEN
- ☐ '00 Who Let The Dogs Out ★

## BAILEY, Philip
- ☐ '84 Easy Lover
  *PHILIP BAILEY (with Phil Collins)*

## BAINBRIDGE, Merril
- ☐ '96 Mouth ★

## BAKER, Anita
- ☐ '94 Body & Soul
- ☐ '86 Caught Up In The Rapture
- ☐ '88 Giving You The Best That I Got
- ☐ '89 Just Because
- ☐ '86 Sweet Love
- ☐ '90 Talk To Me

## BAKER, George, Selection
- ☐ '70 Little Green Bag
- ☐ '75 Paloma Blanca

## BAKER, LaVern
- ☐ '55 Bop-Ting-A-Ling
- ☐ '60 Bumble Bee
- ☐ '56 I Can't Love You Enough
- ☐ '58 I Cried A Tear
- ☐ '59 I Waited Too Long
- ☐ '56 Jim Dandy ★
- ☐ '55 Play It Fair
- ☐ '61 Saved
- ☐ '62 See See Rider
- ☐ '55 Tweedlee Dee

## BALANCE
- ☐ '81 Breaking Away

## BALIN, Marty
- ☐ '81 Atlanta Lady (Something About Your Love)
- ☐ '81 Hearts

## BALL, David
- ☐ '01 Riding With Private Malone
- ☐ '94 Thinkin' Problem

## BALL, Kenny, & His Jazzmen
- ☐ '62 Midnight In Moscow ★

## BALLARD, Hank, & The Midnighters
- ☐ '61 Continental Walk, The
- ☐ '60 Finger Poppin' Time
- ☐ '60 Hoochi Coochi Coo, The
- ☐ '60 Let's Go, Let's Go, Let's Go
- ☐ '60 Twist, The

## BALLOON FARM, The
- ☐ '68 Question Of Temperature, A

## BALTIMORA
- ☐ '85 Tarzan Boy

## BAMBAATAA, Afrika
- ☐ '82 Planet Rock ★

## BANANARAMA
- ☐ '84 Cruel Summer
- ☐ '87 I Heard A Rumour
- ☐ '84 Robert DeNiro's Waiting
- ☐ '86 Venus ★

## BAND, The
- ☐ '73 Ain't Got No Home
- ☐ '68 Chest Fever
- ☐ '72 Don't Do It
- ☐ '71 Life Is A Carnival
- ☐ '68 I Shall Be Released
- ☐ '69 Night They Drove Old Dixie Down, The
- ☐ '76 Ophelia
- ☐ '69 Rag Mama Rag
- ☐ '70 Shape I'm In
- ☐ '68 This Wheel's On Fire
- ☐ '70 Time To Kill
- ☐ '69 Up On Cripple Creek
- ☐ '68 Weight, The ★

## BAND AID
- ☐ '84 Do They Know It's Christmas?

## B ANGIE B
- ☐ '91 I Don't Want To Lose Your Love
- ☐ '91 So Much Love

## BANGLES
- ☐ '89 Be With You
- ☐ '89 Eternal Flame ★
- ☐ '87 Hazy Shade Of Winter ★
- ☐ '86 If She Knew What She Wants
- ☐ '88 In Your Room
- ☐ '86 Manic Monday ★
- ☐ '86 Walk Like An Egyptian ★
- ☐ '87 Walking Down Your Street

## BANKS, Darrell
- ☐ '66 Open The Door To Your Heart

## BANKS, Lloyd
- ☐ '05 Karma
- ☐ '04 On Fire

## BARBER('S), Chris, Jazz Band
- ☐ '59 Petite Fleur (Little Flower)

## BARBARIANS, The
- ☐ '65 Are You A Boy Or Are You A Girl

## BARBOUR, Keith
- ☐ '69 Echo Park

## BARDEUX
- ☐ '88 When We Kiss

## BARE, Bobby
- ☐ '58 All American Boy, The ★
  *BILL PARSONS*
- ☐ '63 Detroit City
- ☐ '63 500 Miles Away From Home
- ☐ '74 Marie Laveau
- ☐ '64 Miller's Cave
- ☐ '62 Shame On Me

## BARENAKED LADIES
- ☐ '99 It's All Been Done
- ☐ '98 One Week ★
- ☐ '00 Pinch Me

## BAR-KAYS
- ☐ '84 Freakshow On The Dance Floor
- ☐ '79 Move Your Boogie Body
- ☐ '76 Shake Your Rump To The Funk
- ☐ '67 Soul Finger

## BARNES, Jimmy
- ☐ '87 Good Times
  *INXS & JIMMY BARNES*
- ☐ '88 Too Much Ain't Enough Love

## BARNUM, H.B.
- ☐ '61 Lost Love

## BARRETTO, Ray
- ☐ '63 El Watusi

## BARRY, Joe
- ☐ '61 I'm A Fool To Care

## BARRY, Len
- ☐ '66 Like A Baby
- ☐ '65 1-2-3
- ☐ '66 Somewhere

## BARRY & THE TAMERLANES
- ☐ '63 I Wonder What She's Doing Tonight

## BARTLEY, Chris
- ☐ '67 Sweetest Thing This Side Of Heaven

## BASIA
- ☐ '90 Cruising For Bruising
- ☐ '88 Time And Tide

## BASIE, Count
- ☐ '56 April In Paris
- ☐ '55 Every Day

## BASIL, Toni
- ☐ '82 Mickey ★

## BASS, Fontella
- ☐ '65 Don't Mess Up A Good Thing
  - *FONTELLA BASS & BOBBY McCLURE*
- ☐ '65 Recovery
- ☐ '65 Rescue Me

## BASSEY, Shirley
- ☐ '65 Goldfinger

## BAXTER, Les
- ☐ '56 Poor People Of Paris, The ★
- ☐ '55 Unchained Melody
- ☐ '55 Wake The Town And Tell The People

## BAY CITY ROLLERS
- ☐ '76 I Only Want To Be With You
- ☐ '76 Money Honey
- ☐ '76 Rock And Roll Love Letter
- ☐ '75 Saturday Night ★
- ☐ '77 Way I Feel Tonight, The
- ☐ '77 You Made Me Believe In Magic

## BAZUKA
- ☐ '75 Dynomite

## BBMAK
- ☐ '00 Back Here

## B. BUMBLE & THE STINGERS
- ☐ '61 Bumble Boogie
- ☐ '62 Nut Rocker

## BEACH BOYS, The
- ☐ '66 Barbara Ann ★
- ☐ '63 Be True To Your School
- ☐ '81 Beach Boys Medley, The
- ☐ '65 California Girls ★
- ☐ '66 Caroline, No
  - *BRIAN WILSON*
- ☐ '81 Come Go With Me
- ☐ '64 Dance, Dance, Dance
- ☐ '67 Darlin'
- ☐ '68 Do It Again
- ☐ '65 Do You Wanna Dance?
- ☐ '64 Don't Worry Baby
- ☐ '62 409
- ☐ '64 Fun, Fun, Fun ★
- ☐ '85 Getcha Back
- ☐ '66 God Only Knows ★
- ☐ '66 Good Vibrations ★
- ☐ '65 Help Me, Rhonda ★
- ☐ '67 Heroes And Villains
- ☐ '69 I Can Hear Music
- ☐ '64 I Get Around ★
- ☐ '63 In My Room ★
- ☐ '76 It's O.K.
- ☐ '88 Kokomo ★
- ☐ '63 Little Deuce Coupe
- ☐ '65 Little Girl I Once Knew, The
- ☐ '76 Rock And Roll Music
- ☐ '63 Shut Down
- ☐ '66 Sloop John B ★
- ☐ '63 Surfer Girl
- ☐ '62 Surfin' Safari
- ☐ '63 Surfin' U.S.A. ★
- ☐ '63 Ten Little Indians
- ☐ '64 When I Grow Up (To Be A Man)
- ☐ '67 Wild Honey
- ☐ '66 Wouldn't It Be Nice

## BEASTIE BOYS
- ☐ '04 Ch-Check It Out
- ☐ '89 Hey Ladies
- ☐ '98 Intergalactic
- ☐ '94 Sabotage
- ☐ '86 (You Gotta) Fight For Your Right (To Party!) ★

## BEATLES, The
- ☐ '70 Across The Universe
- ☐ '65 Act Naturally
- ☐ '64 Ain't She Sweet
- ☐ '64 All My Loving
- ☐ '67 All You Need Is Love ★
- ☐ '64 And I Love Her
- ☐ '67 Baby You're A Rich Man
- ☐ '68 Back In The U.S.S.R.
- ☐ '69 Ballad Of John And Yoko, The
- ☐ '82 Beatles' Movie Medley, The
- ☐ '68 Birthday
- ☐ '68 Blackbird
- ☐ '64 Can't Buy Me Love ★
- ☐ '69 Come Together ★
- ☐ '67 Day In The Life, A
- ☐ '65 Day Tripper
- ☐ '68 Dear Prudence
- ☐ '64 Do You Want To Know A Secret ★
- ☐ '69 Don't Let Me Down
- ☐ '66 Drive My Car
- ☐ '65 Eight Days A Week ★
- ☐ '66 Eleanor Rigby ★
- ☐ '67 Fool On The Hill
- ☐ '95 Free As A Bird
- ☐ '64 From Me To You
- ☐ '69 Get Back ★
- ☐ '68 Glass Onion
- ☐ '69 Golden Slumbers/Carry That Weight/The End/Her Majesty
- ☐ '66 Good Day Sunshine
- ☐ '76 Got To Get You Into My Life
- ☐ '64 Hard Day's Night, A ★

## BEATLES, The — cont'd
- ☐ '67 Hello Goodbye ★
- ☐ '65 Help! ★
- ☐ '68 Helter Skelter
- ☐ '69 Here Comes The Sun
- ☐ '68 Hey Jude ★
- ☐ '67 I Am The Walrus
- ☐ '65 I Don't Want To Spoil The Party
- ☐ '64 I Feel Fine ★
- ☐ '64 I Saw Her Standing There ★
- ☐ '64 I Should Have Known Better
- ☐ '64 I Want To Hold Your Hand ★
- ☐ '64 I'll Cry Instead
- ☐ '65 I'm A Loser
- ☐ '64 If I Fell
- ☐ '65 In My Life ★
- ☐ '68 Lady Madonna ★
- ☐ '70 Let It Be ★
- ☐ '70 Long And Winding Road, The ★
- ☐ '64 Love Me Do ★
- ☐ '67 Lovely Rita
- ☐ '67 Lucy In The Sky With Diamonds
- ☐ '67 Magical Mystery Tour
- ☐ '64 Matchbox
- ☐ '67 Maxwell's Silver Hammer
- ☐ '65 Michelle
- ☐ '64 My Bonnie (My Bonnie Lies Over The Ocean)
- ☐ '65 No Reply
- ☐ '65 Norwegian Wood (This Bird Has Flown)
- ☐ '66 Nowhere Man ★
- ☐ '68 Ob-La Di, Ob-La-Da
- ☐ '69 Octopus's Garden
- ☐ '69 Oh! Darling
- ☐ '69 Old Brown Shoe
- ☐ '64 P.S. I Love You
- ☐ '66 Paperback Writer ★
- ☐ '67 Penny Lane ★
- ☐ '64 Please Please Me ★
- ☐ '66 Rain
- ☐ '96 Real Love
- ☐ '68 Revolution
- ☐ '64 Rock And Roll Music
- ☐ '68 Rocky Raccoon
- ☐ '64 Roll Over Beethoven
- ☐ '67 Sgt. Pepper's Lonely Hearts Club Band
- ☐ '69 She Came In Through The Bathroom Window
- ☐ '64 She Loves You ★
- ☐ '64 She's A Woman
- ☐ '67 She's Leaving Home
- ☐ '64 Slow Down
- ☐ '69 Something ★
- ☐ '67 Strawberry Fields Forever ★
- ☐ '66 Taxman
- ☐ '64 Thank You Girl
- ☐ '65 Ticket To Ride ★
- ☐ '64 Twist And Shout ★
- ☐ '65 We Can Work It Out ★
- ☐ '67 When I'm Sixty-Four
- ☐ '68 While My Guitar Gently Weeps
- ☐ '67 With A Little Help From My Friends
- ☐ '66 Yellow Submarine ★
- ☐ '65 Yesterday ★

- ☐ '64 You Can't Do That
- ☐ '65 You're Going To Lose That Girl
- ☐ '65 You've Got To Hide Your Love Away

## BEAU BRUMMELS, The
- ☐ '65 Just A Little
- ☐ '65 Laugh, Laugh

## BECK
- ☐ '05 E-Pro
- ☐ '93 Loser ★
- ☐ '96 Where It's At

## BECKHAM, Bob
- ☐ '60 Crazy Arms
- ☐ '59 Just As Much As Ever

## BEDINGFIELD, Daniel
- ☐ '02 Gotta Get Thru This
- ☐ '03 If You're Not The One

## BEE GEES
- ☐ '97 Alone
- ☐ '77 Boogie Child
- ☐ '77 Edge Of The Universe
- ☐ '75 Fanny (Be Tender With My Love)
- ☐ '81 He's A Liar
- ☐ '67 Holiday
- ☐ '71 How Can You Mend A Broken Heart ★
- ☐ '77 How Deep Is Your Love ★
- ☐ '68 I Started A Joke
- ☐ '68 I've Gotta Get A Message To You
- ☐ '75 Jive Talkin' ★
- ☐ '67 (Lights Went Out In) Massachusetts
- ☐ '70 Lonely Days ★
- ☐ '76 Love So Right
- ☐ '79 Love You Inside Out
- ☐ '78 More Than A Woman
- ☐ '72 My World
- ☐ '67 New York Mining Disaster 1941 (Have You Seen My Wife, Mr. Jones)
- ☐ '78 Night Fever ★
- ☐ '75 Nights On Broadway
- ☐ '89 One
- ☐ '72 Run To Me
- ☐ '77 Stayin' Alive ★
- ☐ '67 To Love Somebody
- ☐ '78 Too Much Heaven ★
- ☐ '79 Tragedy ★
- ☐ '83 Woman In You, The
- ☐ '68 Words
- ☐ '76 You Should Be Dancing ★

## BEENIE MAN
- ☐ '04 Dude
- ☐ '02 Feel It Boy
- ☐ '98 Who Am I "Sim Simma"

## BEGA, Lou
- ☐ '99 Mambo No. 5 (A Little Bit Of...) ★

## BEGINNING OF THE END, The
- ☐ '71 Funky Nassau

## BELAFONTE, Harry
- ☐ '57 Banana Boat (Day-O)
- ☐ '57 Cocoanut Woman

- ☐ '57 Island In The Sun
- ☐ '56 Jamaica Farewell
- ☐ '57 Mama Look At Bubu
- ☐ '56 Mary's Boy Child

## BELEW, Adrian
- ☐ '89 Oh Daddy
- ☐ '90 Pretty Pink Rose
  *ADRIAN BELEW & DAVID BOWIE*

## BELL, Archie, & The Drells
- ☐ '68 I Can't Stop Dancing
- ☐ '68 There's Gonna Be A Showdown
- ☐ '68 Tighten Up ★

## BELL, Benny
- ☐ '75 Shaving Cream

## BELL, Madeline
- ☐ '68 I'm Gonna Make You Love Me

## BELL, Vincent
- ☐ '70 Airport Love Theme (Gwen And Vern)

## BELL, William
- ☐ '77 Tryin' To Love Two

## BELLAMY BROTHERS
- ☐ '79 If I Said You Have A Beautiful Body Would You Hold It Against Me
- ☐ '76 Let Your Love Flow ★
- ☐ '85 Old Hippie
- ☐ '82 Redneck Girl

## BELL & JAMES
- ☐ '79 Livin' It Up (Friday Night)

## BELL BIV DeVOE
- ☐ '90 B.B.D. (I Thought It Was Me)?
- ☐ '90 Do Me!
- ☐ '92 Gangsta
- ☐ '90 Poison ★
- ☐ '93 Something In Your Eyes
- ☐ '90 When Will I See You Smile Again?
- ☐ '91 Word To The Mutha!

## BELLE, Regina
- ☐ '89 All I Want Is Forever
  *JAMES "J.T." TAYLOR & REGINA BELLE*
- ☐ '89 Baby Come To Me
- ☐ '89 Make It Like It Was
- ☐ '87 Show Me The Way
- ☐ '90 What Goes Around
- ☐ '92 Whole New World (Aladdin's Theme) ★
  *PEABO BRYSON & REGINA BELLE*

## BELLE STARS, The
- ☐ '89 Iko Iko

## BELL NOTES, The
- ☐ '59 I've Had It

## BELLS, The
- ☐ '71 Stay Awhile

## BELLUS, Tony
- ☐ '59 Robbin' The Cradle

## BELLY
- ☐ '93 Feed The Tree

## BELMONTS, The
- ☐ '62 Come On Little Angel
- ☐ '61 Tell Me Why

## BELVIN, Jesse
- ☐ '59 Guess Who

## BENATAR, Pat
- ☐ '88 All Fired Up
- ☐ '93 Everybody Lay Down
- ☐ '81 Fire And Ice
- ☐ '79 Heartbreaker
- ☐ '80 Hell Is For Children
- ☐ '80 Hit Me With Your Best Shot ★
- ☐ '79 I Need A Lover
- ☐ '85 Invincible
- ☐ '83 Little Too Late
- ☐ '83 Looking For A Stranger
- ☐ '83 Love Is A Battlefield
- ☐ '85 Ooh Ooh Song
- ☐ '81 Promises In The Dark
- ☐ '85 Sex As A Weapon
- ☐ '82 Shadows Of The Night
- ☐ '81 Treat Me Right
- ☐ '84 We Belong ★
- ☐ '80 We Live For Love
- ☐ '80 You Better Run

## BENÉT, Eric
- ☐ '99 Spend My Life With You

## BENNETT, Boyd, & His Rockets
- ☐ '55 My Boy-Flat Top
- ☐ '55 Seventeen

## BENNETT, Joe, & The Sparkletones
- ☐ '57 Black Slacks

## BENNETT, Tony
- ☐ '56 Autumn Waltz, The
- ☐ '56 Can You Find It In Your Heart
- ☐ '60 Climb Ev'ry Mountain
- ☐ '58 Firefly
- ☐ '65 Fly Me To The Moon
- ☐ '67 For Once In My Life
- ☐ '63 Good Life, The
- ☐ '56 Happiness Street (Corner Sunshine Square)
- ☐ '62 I Left My Heart In San Francisco ★
- ☐ '63 I Wanna Be Around
- ☐ '65 If I Ruled The World
- ☐ '56 Just In Time
- ☐ '57 One For My Baby
- ☐ '65 Shadow Of Your Smile, The
- ☐ '59 Smile
- ☐ '68 They Can't Take That Away From Me
- ☐ '63 This Is All I Ask
- ☐ '66 Time For Love, A
- ☐ '64 Who Can I Turn To (When Nobody Needs Me)
- ☐ '68 Yesterday I Heard The Rain
- ☐ '58 Young And Warm And Wonderful

## BENSON, George
- ☐ '80 Give Me The Night
- ☐ '77 Greatest Love Of All, The
- ☐ '83 Inside Love (So Personal)
- ☐ '83 Lady Love Me (One More Time)
- ☐ '79 Love Ballad
- ☐ '78 On Broadway
- ☐ '76 This Masquerade
- ☐ '81 Turn Your Love Around

## BENTLEY, Dierks
- ☐ '03 What Was I Thinkin'

## BENTON, Brook
- ☐ '60 Baby (You've Got What It Takes) ★
  *DINAH WASHINGTON & BROOK BENTON*
- ☐ '61 Boll Weevil Song, The
- ☐ '59 Endlessly
- ☐ '60 Fools Rush In (Where Angels Fear To Tread)
- ☐ '61 For My Baby
- ☐ '61 Frankie And Johnny
- ☐ '64 Going Going Gone
- ☐ '60 Hither And Thither And Yon
- ☐ '62 Hotel Happiness
- ☐ '63 I Got What I Wanted
- ☐ '59 It's Just A Matter Of Time ★
- ☐ '60 Kiddio
- ☐ '62 Lie To Me
- ☐ '63 My True Confession
- ☐ '70 Rainy Night In Georgia ★
- ☐ '61 Revenge
- ☐ '60 Rockin' Good Way (To Mess Around And Fall In Love)
  *DINAH WASHINGTON & BROOK BENTON*
- ☐ '60 Same One, The
- ☐ '62 Shadrack
- ☐ '59 So Many Ways
- ☐ '59 Thank You Pretty Baby
- ☐ '61 Think Twice
- ☐ '60 Ties That Bind, The
- ☐ '63 Two Tickets To Paradise

## BERLIN
- ☐ '83 Metro, The
- ☐ '84 No More Words
- ☐ '86 Take My Breath Away ★

## BERNARD, Rod
- ☐ '59 This Should Go On Forever

## BERRY, Chuck
- ☐ '59 Almost Grown
- ☐ '59 Back In The U.S.A.
- ☐ '56 Brown Eyed Handsome Man
- ☐ '58 Carol
- ☐ '58 Johnny B. Goode ★
- ☐ '55 Maybellene ★
- ☐ '72 My Ding-A-Ling ★
- ☐ '64 Nadine (Is It You?)
- ☐ '64 No Particular Place To Go
- ☐ '58 Reelin' & Rockin'
- ☐ '72 Reelin' & Rockin' [live]
- ☐ '57 Rock & Roll Music ★
- ☐ '56 Roll Over Beethoven ★
- ☐ '57 School Day ★
- ☐ '58 Sweet Little Sixteen ★
- ☐ '55 Thirty Days (To Come Back Home)
- ☐ '64 You Never Can Tell

## BERRY, John
- ☐ '96 She's Taken A Shine
- ☐ '95 Standing On The Edge Of Goodbye
- ☐ '94 Your Love Amazes Me

## BETTER THAN EZRA
- ☐ '95 Good

## BEYONCÉ
- ☐ '03 Baby Boy ★
- ☐ '03 Crazy In Love ★
- ☐ '03 Me, Myself And I
- ☐ '04 Naughty Girl ★

## B-52's, The
- ☐ '89 Channel Z
- ☐ '79 Dance This Mess Around
- ☐ '90 Deadbeat Club
- ☐ '92 Good Stuff
- ☐ '83 Legal Tender
- ☐ '89 Love Shack ★
- ☐ '80 Private Idaho
- ☐ '89 Roam
- ☐ '79 Rock Lobster

## B.G.
- ☐ '99 Bling Bling

## BIG AUDIO DYNAMITE
- ☐ '91 Globe, The
- ☐ '89 James Brown
- ☐ '88 Just Play Music!
- ☐ '91 Rush

## BIG BOPPER
- ☐ '58 Big Bopper's Wedding
- ☐ '58 Chantilly Lace ★

## BIG BROTHER & THE HOLDING COMPANY
— see JOPLIN, Janis

## BIG COUNTRY
- ☐ '83 In A Big Country

## BIG MOUNTAIN
- ☐ '94 Baby, I Love Your Way ★

## BIG PUNISHER
- ☐ '98 Still Not A Player

## BIG STAR
- ☐ '74 September Gurls
- ☐ '72 Thirteen

## BIG TYMERS
- ☐ '02 Still Fly

## BILK, Mr. Acker
- ☐ '62 Stranger On The Shore ★

## BILLY & LILLIE
- ☐ '58 La Dee Dah ★
- ☐ '58 Lucky Ladybug

## BILLY JOE & THE CHECKMATES
- ☐ '62  Percolator (Twist)

## BINGOBOYS
- ☐ '91  How To Dance

## BISHOP, Elvin
- ☐ '76  Fooled Around And Fell In Love ★

## BISHOP, Stephen
- ☐ '78  Everybody Needs Love
- ☐ '83  It Might Be You
- ☐ '77  On And On
- ☐ '76  Save It For A Rainy Day

## BIZ MARKIE
- ☐ '90  Just A Friend ★

## BJÖRK
- ☐ '94  Big Time Sensuality
- ☐ '93  Human Behaviour

## BLACK('S), Bill, Combo
- ☐ '60  Blue Tango
- ☐ '60  Don't Be Cruel
- ☐ '61  Hearts Of Stone
- ☐ '60  Josephine
- ☐ '61  Ole Buttermilk Sky
- ☐ '59  Smokie
- ☐ '60  White Silver Sands

## BLACK, Cilla
- ☐ '64  You're My World

## BLACK, Clint
- ☐ '93  Bad Goodbye, A
  - CLINT BLACK with Wynonna
- ☐ '89  Better Man, A
- ☐ '94  Good Run Of Bad Luck, A
- ☐ '89  Killin' Time
- ☐ '96  Like The Rain
- ☐ '91  Loving Blind
- ☐ '90  Nobody's Home
- ☐ '97  Nothin' But The Taillights
- ☐ '95  One Emotion
- ☐ '98  Shoes You're Wearing, The
- ☐ '97  Something That We Do
- ☐ '93  State Of Mind
- ☐ '95  Summer's Comin'
- ☐ '90  Walkin' Away
- ☐ '92  We Tell Ourselves
- ☐ '99  When I Said I Do
  - CLINT BLACK (with Lisa Hartman Black)
- ☐ '93  When My Ship Comes In
- ☐ '91  Where Are You Now

## BLACK, Jeanne
- ☐ '60  He'll Have To Stay

## BLACK BOX
- ☐ '90  Everybody Everybody
- ☐ '90  I Don't Know Anybody Else
- ☐ '91  Strike It Up

## BLACKBYRDS, The
- ☐ '76  Happy Music
- ☐ '75  Walking In Rhythm

## BLACK CROWES, The
- ☐ '90  Hard To Handle
- ☐ '92  Hotel Illness
- ☐ '98  Kicking My Heart Around
- ☐ '92  Remedy
- ☐ '91  Seeing Things
- ☐ '91  She Talks To Angels
- ☐ '92  Sting Me
- ☐ '92  Thorn In My Pride

## BLACK EYED PEAS
- ☐ '05  Don't Phunk With My Heart ★
- ☐ '04  Hey Mama
- ☐ '04  Let's Get It Started
- ☐ '03  Where Is The Love? ★

## BLACKFLAG
- ☐ '82  TV Party

## BLACKFOOT
- ☐ '79  Highway Song
- ☐ '79  Train, Train

## BLACKHAWK
- ☐ '94  Every Once In A While
- ☐ '95  I'm Not Strong Enough To Say No
- ☐ '95  Like There Ain't No Yesterday

## BLACK OAK ARKANSAS
- ☐ '73  Jim Dandy

## BLACKOUT ALLSTARS, The
- ☐ '96  I Like It

## BLACK ROB
- ☐ '01  Bad Boy For Life
  - P. DIDDY, BLACK ROB & MARK CURRY

## BLACK SABBATH
- ☐ '70  Black Sabbath
- ☐ '71  Children Of The Grave
- ☐ '71  Iron Man
- ☐ '70  N.I.B.
- ☐ '71  Paranoid
- ☐ '98  Psycho Man
- ☐ '71  War Pigs

## BLACKstreet
- ☐ '94  Before I Let You Go
- ☐ '94  Booti Call
- ☐ '97  Don't Leave Me
- ☐ '96  No Diggity ★
- ☐ '98  Take Me There
  - BLACKSTREET & MYA

## BLANCHARD, Jack, & Misty Morgan
- ☐ '70  Tennessee Bird Walk

## BLAND, Billy
- ☐ '60  Let The Little Girl Dance

## BLAND, Bobby
- ☐ '64  Ain't Nothing You Can Do
- ☐ '63  Call On Me
- ☐ '61  Don't Cry No More
- ☐ '57  Farther Up The Road
- ☐ '61  I Pity The Fool

## BLAND, Bobby — cont'd
- ☐ '74 I Wouldn't Treat A Dog (The Way You Treated Me)
- ☐ '59 I'll Take Care Of You
- ☐ '63 That's The Way Love Is
- ☐ '61 Turn On Your Love Light

## BLANE, Marcie
- ☐ '62 Bobby's Girl ★

## BLAQUE
- ☐ '00 Bring It All To Me ★
  BLAQUE Feat. *NSYNC
- ☐ '99 808

## BLESSID UNION OF SOULS
- ☐ '99 Hey Leonardo (She Likes Me For Me)
- ☐ '95 I Believe ★
- ☐ '97 I Wanna Be There
- ☐ '95 Let Me Be The One

## BLIGE, Mary J.
- ☐ '94 Be Happy
- ☐ '97 Everything
- ☐ '01 Family Affair ★
- ☐ '97 I Can Love You
- ☐ '95 I'm Goin' Down
- ☐ '03 Love @ 1st Sight
- ☐ '01 No More Drama
- ☐ '96 Not Gon' Cry ★
- ☐ '03 Ooh!
- ☐ '02 Rainy Dayz
- ☐ '92 Real Love
- ☐ '97 Seven Days
- ☐ '93 Sweet Thing
- ☐ '92 You Remind Me

## BLIND FAITH
- ☐ '69 Can't Find My Way Home

## BLIND MELON
- ☐ '93 No Rain

## BLINK-182
- ☐ '00 Adam's Song
- ☐ '99 All The Small Things ★
- ☐ '03 Feeling This
- ☐ '04 I Miss You
- ☐ '00 Man Overboard
- ☐ '01 Rock Show, The
- ☐ '99 What's My Age Again?

## BLONDIE
- ☐ '80 Atomic
- ☐ '80 Call Me ★
- ☐ '79 Dreaming
- ☐ '79 Heart Of Glass ★
- ☐ '82 Island Of Lost Souls
- ☐ '99 Maria
- ☐ '79 One Way Or Another
- ☐ '81 Rapture ★
- ☐ '80 Tide Is High, The ★

## BLOODROCK
- ☐ '71 D.O.A.

## BLOODSTONE
- ☐ '73 Natural High
- ☐ '74 Outside Woman

## BLOOD, SWEAT & TEARS
- ☐ '69 And When I Die
- ☐ '71 Go Down Gamblin'
- ☐ '70 Hi-De-Ho
- ☐ '70 Lucretia Mac Evil
- ☐ '69 Spinning Wheel ★
- ☐ '69 You've Made Me So Very Happy ★

## BLOOM, Bobby
- ☐ '70 Montego Bay

## BLOW, Kurtis
- ☐ '80 Breaks, The

## BLOW MONKEYS, The
- ☐ '86 Digging Your Scene

## BLUE CHEER
- ☐ '68 Summertime Blues

## BLUE HAZE
- ☐ '72 Smoke Gets In Your Eyes

## BLUE JAYS, The
- ☐ '61 Lover's Island

## BLUE MAGIC
- ☐ '74 Sideshow
- ☐ '74 Three Ring Circus

## BLUE ÖYSTER CULT
- ☐ '81 Burnin' For You
- ☐ '76 (Don't Fear) The Reaper ★
- ☐ '77 Godzilla
- ☐ '79 In Thee

## BLUES BROTHERS
- ☐ '80 Gimme Some Lovin'
- ☐ '79 Hey Bartender
- ☐ '79 Rubber Biscuit
- ☐ '78 Soul Man
- ☐ '80 Who's Making Love

## BLUES IMAGE
- ☐ '70 Ride Captain Ride ★

## BLUES MAGOOS
- ☐ '66 (We Ain't Got) Nothin' Yet

## BLUE STARS
- ☐ '55 Lullaby Of Birdland

## BLUES TRAVELER
- ☐ '96 But Anyway
- ☐ '95 Hook
- ☐ '95 Run-Around ★

## BLUE SWEDE
- ☐ '74 Hooked On A Feeling ★
- ☐ '74 Never My Love

## BLUR
- ☐ '97 Song 2

## BMU (BLACK MEN UNITED)
- ☐ '94 U Will Know

## BOB & EARL
- ☐ '63 Harlem Shuffle

## BOBBETTES, The
- ☐ '57 Mr. Lee ★

## BOB B. SOXX & THE BLUE JEANS
- ☐ '63 Why Do Lovers Break Each Other's Heart?
- ☐ '62 Zip-A-Dee Doo-Dah

## BoDEANS
- ☐ '96 Closer To Free
- ☐ '86 Fadeaway
- ☐ '91 Good Things

## BOGGUSS, Suzy
- ☐ '92 Drive South

## BOLTON, Michael
- ☐ '95 Can I Touch You...There?
- ☐ '97 Go The Distance
- ☐ '89 How Am I Supposed To Live Without You ★
- ☐ '90 How Can We Be Lovers
- ☐ '91 Love Is A Wonderful Thing
- ☐ '92 Missing You Now
- ☐ '93 Said I Loved You...But I Lied
- ☐ '88 (Sittin' On) The Dock Of The Bay
- ☐ '89 Soul Provider
- ☐ '92 Steel Bars
- ☐ '87 That's What Love Is All About
- ☐ '91 Time, Love And Tenderness
- ☐ '92 To Love Somebody
- ☐ '91 When A Man Loves A Woman
- ☐ '90 When I'm Back On My Feet Again

## BOND, Johnny
- ☐ '60 Hot Rod Lincoln

## BONDS, Gary (U.S.)
- ☐ '61 Dear Lady Twist
- ☐ '60 New Orleans
- ☐ '82 Out Of Work
- ☐ '61 Quarter To Three ★
- ☐ '61 School Is In
- ☐ '61 School Is Out
- ☐ '62 Seven Day Weekend
- ☐ '81 This Little Girl
- ☐ '62 Twist, Twist Senora

## BONE CRUSHER
- ☐ '03 Never Scared

## BONE THUGS-N-HARMONY
- ☐ '96 Crossroads, Tha ★
- ☐ '96 Days Of Our Livez
- ☐ '95 1st Of Tha Month
- ☐ '98 Ghetto Cowboy
  *MO THUGS FAMILY & BONE THUGS N HARMONY*
- ☐ '97 If I Could Teach The World

- ☐ '97 Look Into My Eyes ★
- ☐ '94 Thuggish-Ruggish-Bone

## BONEY M
- ☐ '78 Rivers Of Babylon

## BONHAM, Tracy
- ☐ '96 Mother Mother

## BON JOVI
- ☐ '94 Always ★
- ☐ '88 Bad Medicine ★
- ☐ '93 Bed Of Roses
- ☐ '90 Blaze Of Glory ★
- ☐ '88 Born To Be My Baby
- ☐ '87 Edge Of A Broken Heart
- ☐ '89 I'll Be There For You ★
- ☐ '93 In These Arms
- ☐ '00 It's My Life
- ☐ '92 Keep The Faith
- ☐ '89 Lay Your Hands On Me
- ☐ '86 Livin' On A Prayer ★
- ☐ '89 Living In Sin
- ☐ '90 Miracle
- ☐ '87 Never Say Goodbye
- ☐ '84 Runaway
- ☐ '95 This Ain't A Love Song
- ☐ '87 Wanted Dead Or Alive
- ☐ '86 You Give Love A Bad Name ★

## BONNIE LOU
- ☐ '55 Daddy-O

## BONNIE SISTERS
- ☐ '56 Cry Baby

## BONOFF, Karla
- ☐ '82 Personally

## BOOKER, Chuckii
- ☐ '92 Games
- ☐ '89 Turned Away

## BOOKER, James
- ☐ '60 Gonzo

## BOOKER T. & THE MG'S
- ☐ '62 Green Onions ★
- ☐ '67 Groovin'
- ☐ '68 Hang 'Em High
- ☐ '67 Hip Hug-Her
- ☐ '69 Mrs. Robinson
- ☐ '68 Soul-Limbo
- ☐ '69 Time Is Tight

## BOOMTOWN RATS, The
- ☐ '80 I Don't Like Mondays
- ☐ '81 Up All Night

## BOONE, Daniel
- ☐ '72 Beautiful Sunday

## BOONE, Debby
- ☐ '77 You Light Up My Life ★

## BOONE, Pat
- ☐ '55 Ain't That A Shame
- ☐ '57 April Love ★
- ☐ '55 At My Front Door (Crazy Little Mama)
- ☐ '57 Bernardine
- ☐ '61 Big Cold Wind
- ☐ '56 Chains Of Love
- ☐ '56 Don't Forbid Me
- ☐ '59 For A Penny
- ☐ '58 For My Good Fortune
- ☐ '56 Friendly Persuasion (Thee I Love)
- ☐ '58 Gee, But It's Lonely
- ☐ '55 Gee Whittakers!
- ☐ '56 I Almost Lost My Mind ★
- ☐ '56 I'll Be Home
- ☐ '58 I'll Remember Tonight
- ☐ '58 If Dreams Came True
- ☐ '58 It's Too Soon To Know
- ☐ '61 Johnny Will
- ☐ '56 Long Tall Sally
- ☐ '57 Love Letters In The Sand ★
- ☐ '61 Moody River ★
- ☐ '57 Remember You're Mine
- ☐ '62 Speedy Gonzales
- ☐ '58 Sugar Moon
- ☐ '57 There's A Gold Mine In The Sky
- ☐ '56 Tutti' Frutti
- ☐ '59 Twixt Twelve And Twenty
- ☐ '55 Two Hearts
- ☐ '60 (Welcome) New Lovers
- ☐ '57 Why Baby Why
- ☐ '59 With The Wind And The Rain In Your Hair
- ☐ '58 Wonderful Time Up There, A

## BOSTON
- ☐ '86 Amanda ★
- ☐ '87 Can'tcha Say (You Believe In Me)/Still In Love
- ☐ '78 Don't Look Back
- ☐ '78 Feelin' Satisfied
- ☐ '76 Hitch A Ride
- ☐ '76 Let Me Take You Home Tonight
- ☐ '77 Long Time
- ☐ '78 Man I'll Never Be, A
- ☐ '76 More Than A Feeling ★
- ☐ '77 Peace Of Mind
- ☐ '76 Rock & Roll Band
- ☐ '76 Smokin'
- ☐ '76 Something About You
- ☐ '86 We're Ready

## BOURGEOIS TAGG
- ☐ '90 Dare To Fall In Love
  *BRENT BOURGEOIS*
- ☐ '87 I Don't Mind At All

## BOWEN, Jimmy
- ☐ '57 I'm Stickin' With You

## BOWIE, David
- ☐ '80 Ashes To Ashes
- ☐ '84 Blue Jean
- ☐ '72 Changes
- ☐ '83 China Girl
- ☐ '85 Dancing In The Street
  *MICK JAGGER & DAVID BOWIE*
- ☐ '87 Day-In Day-Out
- ☐ '74 Diamond Dogs
- ☐ '75 Fame ★
- ☐ '80 Fashion
- ☐ '75 Golden Years
- ☐ '77 Heroes ★
- ☐ '73 Jean Genie
- ☐ '83 Let's Dance ★
- ☐ '83 Modern Love
- ☐ '87 Never Let Me Down
- ☐ '90 Pretty Pink Rose
  *ADRIAN BELEW & DAVID BOWIE*
- ☐ '74 Rebel Rebel
- ☐ '73 Space Oddity
- ☐ '72 Starman
- ☐ '72 Suffragette City
- ☐ '85 This Is Not America
  *DAVID BOWIE & PAT METHENY GROUP*
- ☐ '76 TVC 15
- ☐ '81 Under Pressure ★
  *QUEEN & DAVID BOWIE*
- ☐ '75 Young Americans
- ☐ '72 Ziggy Stardust

## BOWLING FOR SOUP
- ☐ '04 1985

## BOW WOW WOW
- ☐ '82 I Want Candy ★

## BOX TOPS, The
- ☐ '68 Choo Choo Train
- ☐ '68 Cry Like A Baby ★
- ☐ '68 I Met Her In Church
- ☐ '67 Letter, The ★
- ☐ '67 Neon Rainbow
- ☐ '69 Soul Deep
- ☐ '68 Sweet Cream Ladies, Forward March

## BOYCE, Tommy, & Bobby Hart
- ☐ '68 Alice Long (You're Still My Favorite Girlfriend)
- ☐ '67 I Wonder What She's Doing Tonite

## BOY KRAZY
- ☐ '93 That's What Love Can Do

## BOY MEETS GIRL
- ☐ '88 Waiting For A Star To Fall

## BOYS, The
- ☐ '90 Crazy
- ☐ '88 Dial My Heart
- ☐ '89 Lucky Charm

## BOYS CLUB
- ☐ '88 I Remember Holding You

## BOYS DON'T CRY
- ☐ '86 I Wanna Be A Cowboy

## BOYZ II MEN
- ☐ '92 End Of The Road ★
- ☐ '97 4 Seasons Of Loneliness ★
- ☐ '94 I'll Make Love To You ★
- ☐ '92 In The Still Of The Nite (I'll Remember)

- ☐ '91 It's So Hard To Say Goodbye To Yesterday ★
- ☐ '93 Let It Snow
- ☐ '91 Motownphilly
- ☐ '94 On Bended Knee ★
- ☐ '95 One Sweet Day ★
  *MARIAH CAREY & BOYZ II MEN*
- ☐ '97 Song For Mama, A
- ☐ '95 Water Runs Dry

## BRADLEY, Jan
- ☐ '63 Mama Didn't Lie

## BRADLEY, Owen, Quintet
- ☐ '57 White Silver Sands

## BRAM TCHAIKOVSKY
- ☐ '79 Girl Of My Dreams

## BRANCH, Michelle
- ☐ '02 All You Wanted ★
- ☐ '03 Are You Happy Now?
- ☐ '03 Breathe
- ☐ '01 Everywhere
- ☐ '02 Game Of Love, The ★
  *SANTANA Feat. Michelle Branch*
- ☐ '02 Goodbye To You

## BRAND NEW HEAVIES, The
- ☐ '91 Never Stop

## BRANDT, Paul
- ☐ '96 I Do

## BRANDY
- ☐ '99 Almost Doesn't Count
- ☐ '95 Baby ★
- ☐ '95 Best Friend
- ☐ '98 Boy Is Mine, The ★
  *BRANDY & MONICA*
- ☐ '95 Brokenhearted
- ☐ '02 Full Moon
- ☐ '98 Have You Ever? ★
- ☐ '94 I Wanna Be Down ★
- ☐ '96 Missing You
  *BRANDY, TAMIA, GLADYS KNIGHT & CHAKA KHAN*
- ☐ '95 Sittin' Up In My Room ★
- ☐ '04 Talk About Our Love
- ☐ '02 What About Us?

## BRANIGAN, Laura
- ☐ '82 Gloria ★
- ☐ '83 How Am I Supposed To Live Without You
- ☐ '84 Lucky One, The
- ☐ '87 Power Of Love
- ☐ '84 Self Control
- ☐ '83 Solitaire

## BRASS CONSTRUCTION
- ☐ '76 Movin'

## BRASS RING, The
- ☐ '67 Dis-Advantages Of You, The
- ☐ '66 Phoenix Love Theme (Senza Fine)

## BRAUN, Bob
- ☐ '62 Till Death Do Us Part

## BRAVE COMBO
- ☐ '93 Cielito Lindo
- ☐ '87 Happy Wanderer

## BRAXTON, Toni
- ☐ '93 Another Sad Love Song
- ☐ '93 Breathe Again ★
- ☐ '00 He Wasn't Man Enough ★
- ☐ '94 I Belong To You
- ☐ '97 I Don't Want To
- ☐ '00 Just Be A Man About It
- ☐ '92 Love Shoulda Brought You Home
- ☐ '93 Seven Whole Days
- ☐ '96 Un-Break My Heart ★
- ☐ '94 You Mean The World To Me
- ☐ '96 You're Makin' Me High ★

## BREAD
- ☐ '73 Aubrey
- ☐ '71 Baby I'm - A Want You
- ☐ '72 Diary
- ☐ '72 Everything I Own
- ☐ '72 Guitar Man, The
- ☐ '77 Hooked On You
- ☐ '71 If
- ☐ '70 It Don't Matter To Me
- ☐ '71 Let Your Love Go
- ☐ '76 Lost Without Your Love
- ☐ '70 Make It With You ★
- ☐ '71 Mother Freedom
- ☐ '72 Sweet Surrender

## BREAKFAST CLUB
- ☐ '87 Right On Track

## BREAKING BENJAMIN
- ☐ '04 So Cold
- ☐ '05 Sooner Or Later

## BREATHE
- ☐ '89 Don't Tell Me Lies
- ☐ '88 Hands To Heaven ★
- ☐ '88 How Can I Fall?
- ☐ '90 Say A Prayer

## BREEDERS, The
- ☐ '93 Cannonball

## BREMERS, Beverly
- ☐ '71 Don't Say You Don't Remember

## BRENDA & THE TABULATIONS
- ☐ '67 Dry Your Eyes
- ☐ '71 Right On The Tip Of My Tongue

## BRENNAN, Walter
- ☐ '60 Dutchman's Gold
- ☐ '62 Old Rivers

## BREWER, Teresa
- ☐ '60 Anymore
- ☐ '55 Banjo's Back In Town, The
- ☐ '56 Bo Weevil
- ☐ '57 Empty Arms

## BREWER, Teresa — cont'd
- ☐ '55 Let Me Go, Lover!
- ☐ '55 Pledging My Love
- ☐ '56 Sweet Old Fashioned Girl, A
- ☐ '56 Tear Fell, A
- ☐ '57 You Send Me

## BREWER & SHIPLEY
- ☐ '71 One Toke Over The Line

## BRICK
- ☐ '76 Dazz
- ☐ '77 Dusic

## BRICKELL, Edie
- ☐ '88 What I Am

## BRICKMAN, Jim
- ☐ '97 Gift, The
- ☐ '01 Simple Things

## BRIDGES, Alicia
- ☐ '78 I Love The Nightlife (Disco 'Round)

## BRIGHTER SIDE OF DARKNESS
- ☐ '72 Love Jones

## BRILEY, Martin
- ☐ '83 Salt In My Tears, The

## BRISTOL, Johnny
- ☐ '74 Hang On In There Baby

## BROCK, Chad
- ☐ '99 Ordinary Life
- ☐ '00 Yes!

## B-ROCK & THE BIZZ
- ☐ '97 MyBabyDaddy

## BRONSKI BEAT
- ☐ '86 Hit That Perfect Beat
- ☐ '85 Smalltown Boy

## BROOKLYN BRIDGE
- ☐ '69 Blessed Is The Rain
- ☐ '68 Worst That Could Happen

## BROOKLYN DREAMS — see SUMMER, Donna

## BROOKS, Donnie
- ☐ '60 Doll House
- ☐ '60 Mission Bell

## BROOKS, Garth
- ☐ '93 Ain't Going Down (Til The Sun Comes Up)
- ☐ '93 American Honky-Tonk Bar Association
- ☐ '95 Beaches Of Cheyenne, The
- ☐ '94 Callin' Baton Rouge
- ☐ '90 Dance, The
- ☐ '90 Friends In Low Places ★
- ☐ '89 If Tomorrow Never Comes
- ☐ '97 In Another's Eyes
  *TRISHA YEARWOOD & GARTH BROOKS*
- ☐ '96 It's Midnight Cinderella
- ☐ '93 Learning To Live Again
- ☐ '97 Longneck Bottle
- ☐ '99 Lost In You
  *GARTH BROOKS AS CHRIS GAINES*
- ☐ '89 Much Too Young (To Feel This Damn Old)
- ☐ '90 Not Counting You
- ☐ '92 Papa Loved Mama
- ☐ '92 River, The
- ☐ '91 Rodeo
- ☐ '91 Shameless
- ☐ '95 She's Every Woman
- ☐ '97 She's Gonna Make It
- ☐ '92 Somewhere Other Than The Night
- ☐ '93 Standing Outside The Fire
- ☐ '93 That Summer
- ☐ '91 Thunder Rolls, The
- ☐ '98 To Make You Feel My Love
- ☐ '91 Two Of A Kind, Workin' On A Full House
- ☐ '97 Two Piña Coladas
- ☐ '90 Unanswered Prayers
- ☐ '92 What She's Doing Now
- ☐ '02 Wrapped Up In You
- ☐ '98 You Move Me

## BROOKS, Louis, & His Hi-Toppers
- ☐ '55 It's Love Baby (24 Hours a Day)

## BROOKS, Meredith
- ☐ '97 Bitch ★

## BROOKS & DUNN
- ☐ '01 Ain't Nothing 'Bout You
- ☐ '92 Boot Scootin' Boogie ★
- ☐ '91 Brand New Man
- ☐ '97 He's Got You
- ☐ '97 Honky Tonk Truth
- ☐ '98 How Long Gone
- ☐ '98 Husbands And Wives
- ☐ '96 I Am That Man
- ☐ '98 If You See Him/If You See Her
  *REBA/BROOKS & DUNN*
- ☐ '05 It's Getting Better All The Time
- ☐ '95 Little Miss Honky Tonk
- ☐ '01 Long Goodbye, The
- ☐ '96 Man This Lonely, A
- ☐ '96 My Maria
- ☐ '91 My Next Broken Heart
- ☐ '92 Neon Moon
- ☐ '01 Only In America
- ☐ '03 Red Dirt Road
- ☐ '93 Rock My World (Little Country Girl)
- ☐ '93 She Used To Be Mine
- ☐ '94 She's Not The Cheatin' Kind
- ☐ '94 That Ain't No Way To Go
- ☐ '04 That's What It's All About
- ☐ '93 We'll Burn That Bridge
- ☐ '03 You Can't Take The Honky Tonk Out Of The Girl
- ☐ '95 You're Gonna Miss Me When I'm Gone

## BROTHER CANE
- ☐ '95 And Fools Shine On
- ☐ '93 Got No Shame
- ☐ '98 I Lie In The Bed I Make

## BROTHERHOOD OF MAN, The
- ☐ '76 Save Your Kisses For Me
- ☐ '70 United We Stand

## BROTHERS FOUR, The
- ☐ '61 Frogg
- ☐ '60 Greenfields ★
- ☐ '60 My Tani

## BROTHERS JOHNSON, The
- ☐ '76 Get The Funk Out Ma Face
- ☐ '76 I'll Be Good To You
- ☐ '80 Stomp!
- ☐ '77 Strawberry Letter 23

## BROWN, Al
- ☐ '60 Madison, The

## BROWN, Arthur
- ☐ '68 Fire

## BROWN, Bobby
- ☐ '88 Don't Be Cruel
- ☐ '89 Every Little Step
- ☐ '93 Get Away
- ☐ '86 Girlfriend
- ☐ '92 Good Enough
- ☐ '92 Humpin' Around
- ☐ '88 My Prerogative ★
- ☐ '89 On Our Own ★
- ☐ '89 Rock Wit'cha
- ☐ '89 Roni
- ☐ '93 Something In Common
  *BOBBY BROWN With Whitney Houston*

## BROWN, Buster
- ☐ '60 Fannie Mae

## BROWN, Charles
- ☐ '60 Please Come Home For Christmas

## BROWN, Chuck, & The Soul Searchers
- ☐ '79 Bustin' Loose

## BROWN, Foxy
- ☐ '97 I'll Be

## BROWN, James
- ☐ '69 Ain't It Funky Now
- ☐ '61 Baby, You're Right
- ☐ '61 Bewildered
- ☐ '67 Bring It Up
- ☐ '70 Brother Rapp
- ☐ '67 Cold Sweat
- ☐ '71 Escape-ism
- ☐ '72 Get On The Good Foot
- ☐ '71 Get Up, Get Into It, Get Involved
- ☐ '70 Get Up (I Feel Like Being Like A) Sex Machine
- ☐ '69 Give It Up Or Turnit A Loose
- ☐ '71 Hot Pants (She Got To Use What She Got To Get What She Wants)
- ☐ '67 I Can't Stand Myself (When You Touch Me)
- ☐ '69 I Don't Want Nobody To Give Me Nothing (Open Up The Door, I'll Get It Myself)
- ☐ '72 I Got A Bag Of My Own
- ☐ '73 I Got Ants In My Pants
- ☐ '68 I Got The Feelin'
- ☐ '65 I Got You (I Feel Good) ★
- ☐ '88 I'm Real
- ☐ '66 It's A Man's Man's Man's World
- ☐ '70 It's A New Day
- ☐ '72 King Heroin
- ☐ '69 Let A Man Come In And Do The Popcorn
- ☐ '68 Licking Stick - Licking Stick
- ☐ '85 Living In America
- ☐ '61 Lost Someone
- ☐ '71 Make It Funky
- ☐ '69 Mother Popcorn (You Got To Have A Mother For Me)
- ☐ '74 My Thang
- ☐ '62 Night Train
- ☐ '64 Oh Baby Don't You Weep
- ☐ '64 Out Of Sight
- ☐ '74 Papa Don't Take No Mess
- ☐ '65 Papa's Got A Brand New Bag ★
- ☐ '74 Payback, The
- ☐ '56 Please, Please, Please ★
- ☐ '69 Popcorn, The
- ☐ '63 Prisoner Of Love
- ☐ '68 Say It Loud - I'm Black And I'm Proud
- ☐ '71 Soul Power
- ☐ '70 Super Bad
- ☐ '72 Talking Loud And Saying Nothing
- ☐ '68 There Was A Time
- ☐ '60 Think
- ☐ '58 Try Me

## BROWN, Jocelyn
- ☐ '84 Somebody Else's Guy

## BROWN, Maxine
- ☐ '60 All In My Mind
- ☐ '61 Funny
- ☐ '64 Oh No Not My Baby

## BROWN, Nappy
- ☐ '55 Don't Be Angry
- ☐ '57 Little By Little

## BROWN, Peter
- ☐ '78 Dance With Me
  *PETER BROWN with Betty Wright*
- ☐ '77 Do Ya Wanna Get Funky With Me

## BROWN, Polly
- ☐ '75 Up In A Puff Of Smoke

## BROWN, Roy
- ☐ '57 Let The Four Winds Blow

## BROWN, Ruth
- ☐ '55 I Want To Do More
- ☐ '57 Lucky Lips
- ☐ '58 This Little Girl's Gone Rockin'

## BROWN, Shirley
- ☐ '74 Woman To Woman

## BROWN, Sleepy
- ☐ '04 I Can't Wait

## BROWNE, Jackson
- ☐ '80 Boulevard
- ☐ '72 Doctor My Eyes
- ☐ '83 For A Rocker
- ☐ '86 For America
- ☐ '77 Here Come Those Tears Again
- ☐ '80 Hold On Hold Out
- ☐ '86 In The Shape Of A Heart
- ☐ '74 Late For The Sky
- ☐ '83 Lawyers In Love
- ☐ '78 Load-Out/Stay
- ☐ '76 Pretender, The
- ☐ '72 Redneck Friend
- ☐ '72 Rock Me On The Water
- ☐ '78 Running On Empty
- ☐ '82 Somebody's Baby
- ☐ '83 Tender Is The Night
- ☐ '80 That Girl Could Sing
- ☐ '78 You Love The Thunder
- ☐ '85 You're A Friend Of Mine
  *CLARENCE CLEMONS & JACKSON BROWNE*

## BROWNE, Tom
- ☐ '80 Funkin' For Jamaica (N.Y.)

## BROWNS, The
- ☐ '60 Old Lamplighter, The
- ☐ '59 Scarlet Ribbons (For Her Hair)
- ☐ '59 Three Bells, The ★

## BROWNSTONE
- ☐ '97 5 Miles To Empty
- ☐ '94 If You Love Me

## BROWNSVILLE STATION
- ☐ '74 Kings Of The Party
- ☐ '73 Smokin' In The Boy's Room

## BRUBECK, Dave, Quartet
- ☐ '61 Take Five

## BRYANT, Anita
- ☐ '60 In My Little Corner Of The World
- ☐ '60 Paper Roses
- ☐ '59 Till There Was You
- ☐ '60 Wonderland By Night

## BRYANT, Ray, Combo
- ☐ '60 Madison Time

## BRYNNER, Yul, & Deborah Kerr
- ☐ '56 Shall We Dance

## BRYSON, Peabo
- ☐ '92 Beauty And The Beast ★
  *CELINE DION & PEABO BRYSON*
- ☐ '93 By The Time This Night Is Over
  *KENNY G with Peabo Bryson*
- ☐ '91 Can You Stop The Rain
- ☐ '78 I'm So Into You
- ☐ '84 If Ever You're In My Arms Again
- ☐ '89 Show & Tell
- ☐ '83 Tonight, I Celebrate My Love
  *PEABO BRYSON & ROBERTA FLACK*
- ☐ '92 Whole New World (Aladdin's Theme) ★
  *PEABO BRYSON & REGINA BELLE*

## B.T. EXPRESS
- ☐ '74 Do It ('Til You're Satisfied) ★
- ☐ '75 Express
- ☐ '75 Give It What You Got
- ☐ '75 Peace Pipe

## B2K
- ☐ '02 Bump, Bump, Bump ★
  *B2K & P. DIDDY*
- ☐ '03 Girlfriend
- ☐ '02 Gots Ta Be
- ☐ '02 Uh Huh

## BUBBLE PUPPY, The
- ☐ '69 Hot Smoke & Sasafrass

## BUBLÉ, Michael
- ☐ '05 Home ★

## BUCHANAN & GOODMAN — see GOODMAN, Dickie

## BUCHANAN BROTHERS
- ☐ '69 Medicine Man

## BUCKCHERRY
- ☐ '99 Lit Up

## BUCKINGHAM, Lindsey
- ☐ '84 Go Insane
- ☐ '83 Holiday Road
- ☐ '81 Trouble

## BUCKINGHAMS, The
- ☐ '67 Don't You Care
- ☐ '67 Hey Baby (They're Playing Our Song)
- ☐ '66 Kind Of A Drag ★
- ☐ '67 Mercy, Mercy, Mercy
- ☐ '67 Susan

## BUCKLEY, Jeff
- ☐ '94 Hallelujah

## BUCKNER & GARCIA
- ☐ '82 Pac-Man Fever

## BUDDEN, Joe
- ☐ '03 Pump It Up

## BUFFALO SPRINGFIELD, The
- ☐ '67 Bluebird
- ☐ '67 For What It's Worth ★
- ☐ '67 Mr. Soul
- ☐ '67 Rock 'N' Roll Woman

## BUFFETT, Jimmy
- ☐ '77 Changes In Latitudes, Changes In Attitudes
- ☐ '78 Cheeseburger In Paradise
- ☐ '74 Come Monday
- ☐ '79 Fins
- ☐ '03 It's Five O'Clock Somewhere
  *ALAN JACKSON & JIMMY BUFFETT*
- ☐ '85 Jolly Mon Sing
- ☐ '78 Mañana
- ☐ '77 Margaritaville ★
- ☐ '83 One Particular Harbor
- ☐ '80 Volcano

## BUGGLES, The
- ☐ '79 Video Killed The Radio Star

## BULLET
- ☐ '71 White Lies, Blue Eyes

## BUOYS, The
- ☐ '71 Timothy

## BURDON, Eric, & War
- ☐ '70 Spill The Wine ★

## BURKE, Solomon
- ☐ '62 Cry To Me
- ☐ '64 Everybody Needs Somebody To Love
- ☐ '64 Goodbye Baby (Baby Goodbye)
- ☐ '65 Got To Get You Off My Mind
- ☐ '63 If You Need Me
- ☐ '61 Just Out Of Reach (Of My Two Open Arms)
- ☐ '65 Tonight's The Night
- ☐ '63 You're Good For Me

## BURNETTE, Dorsey
- ☐ '60 (There Was A) Tall Oak Tree

## BURNETTE, Johnny
- ☐ '60 Dreamin'
- ☐ '61 God, Country And My Baby
- ☐ '61 Little Boy Sad
- ☐ '56 Train Kept A-Rollin', The
- ☐ '60 You're Sixteen ★

## BURNETTE, Rocky
- ☐ '80 Tired Of Toein' The Line

## BUSH
- ☐ '99 Chemicals Between Us, The
- ☐ '95 Comedown
- ☐ '94 Everything Zen
- ☐ '95 Glycerine ★
- ☐ '96 Greedy Fly
- ☐ '96 Swallowed

## BUSH, Kate
- ☐ '85 Cloudbusting
- ☐ '87 Don't Give Up
  - *PETER GABRIEL & KATE BUSH*
- ☐ '85 Hounds Of Love
- ☐ '89 Love And Anger
- ☐ '85 Running Up That Hill
- ☐ '78 Wuthering Heights

## BUSTA RHYMES
- ☐ '01 Break Ya Neck
- ☐ '98 Dangerous
- ☐ '03 I Know What You Want ★
  - *BUSTA RHYMES & MARIAH CAREY*
- ☐ '02 Pass The Courvoisier
- ☐ '97 Put Your Hands Where My Eyes Could See
- ☐ '98 Turn It Up [Remix]/Fire It Up
- ☐ '99 What's It Gonna Be?! ★
- ☐ '96 Woo-Hah!! Got You All In Check

## BUSTERS, The
- ☐ '63 Bust Out

## BUTLER, Jerry
- ☐ '71 Ain't Understanding Mellow
  - *JERRY BUTLER & BRENDA LEE EAGER*
- ☐ '68 Are You Happy
- ☐ '61 Find Another Girl
- ☐ '58 For Your Precious Love
  - *JERRY BUTLER & THE IMPRESSIONS*
- ☐ '60 He Will Break Your Heart
- ☐ '68 Hey, Western Union Man
- ☐ '64 I Stand Accused
- ☐ '61 I'm A Telling You
- ☐ '64 Let It Be Me
  - *BETTY EVERETT & JERRY BUTLER*
- ☐ '62 Make It Easy On Yourself
- ☐ '69 Moody Woman
- ☐ '61 Moon River
- ☐ '67 Mr. Dream Merchant
- ☐ '63 Need To Belong
- ☐ '68 Never Give You Up
- ☐ '69 Only The Strong Survive
- ☐ '69 What's The Use Of Breaking Up

## BUTLER, Jonathan
- ☐ '87 Lies

## BUTTHOLE SURFERS
- ☐ '96 Pepper

## BUZZCOCKS, The
- ☐ '78 Ever Fallen In Love
- ☐ '78 What Do I Get?

## B*WITCHED
- ☐ '99 C'est La Vie

## BYRD, Tracy
- ☐ '96 Big Love
- ☐ '93 Holdin' Heaven
- ☐ '98 I'm From The Country
- ☐ '95 Keeper Of The Stars, The
- ☐ '02 Ten Rounds With José Cuervo

## BYRDS, The
- ☐ '65 All I Really Want To Do
- ☐ '66 Eight Miles High ★
- ☐ '65 I'll Feel A Whole Lot Better
- ☐ '66 Mr. Spaceman
- ☐ '65 Mr. Tambourine Man ★
- ☐ '67 My Back Pages
- ☐ '67 So You Want To Be A Rock 'N' Roll Star
- ☐ '65 Turn! Turn! Turn! (To Everything There Is A Season) ★

## BYRNES, Edward
- ☐ '59 Kookie, Kookie (Lend Me Your Comb)
  - *EDWARD BYRNES & CONNIE STEVENS*

# C

## CABRERA, Ryan
- ☐ '04 On The Way Down
- ☐ '04 True

## CADETS, The
- ☐ '56 Stranded In The Jungle

## CADILLACS, The
- '58 Peek-A-Boo
- '55 Speedoo

## CAFFERTY, John
- '85 C-I-T-Y
- '84 On The Dark Side
- '84 Tender Years
- '85 Tough All Over

## CAGLE, Chris
- '02 I Breathe In, I Breathe Out

## CAIOLA, Al, & His Orchestra
- '61 Bonanza
- '60 Magnificent Seven, The

## CAKE
- '96 Distance, The
- '98 Never There

## CALDWELL, Bobby
- '78 What You Won't Do For Love

## CALE, J.J.
- '72 Crazy Mama

## CALL, The
- '89 Let The Day Begin

## CALLING, The
- '01 Wherever You Will Go ★

## CALLOWAY
- '90 I Wanna Be Rich ★

## CAMEO
- '85 Attack Me With Your Love
- '87 Back And Forth
- '86 Candy
- '81 Freaky Dancin'
- '79 I Just Want To Be
- '84 She's Strange
- '85 Single Life
- '86 Word Up ★

## CAMOUFLAGE
- '88 Great Commandment, The

## CAMPBELL, Glen
- '70 All I Have To Do Is Dream
  *BOBBIE GENTRY & GLEN CAMPBELL*
- '67 By The Time I Get To Phoenix
- '75 Country Boy (You Got Your Feet In L.A.)
- '71 Dream Baby (How Long Must I Dream)
- '68 Dreams Of The Everyday Housewife
- '70 Everything A Man Could Ever Need
- '69 Galveston
- '68 Gentle On My Mind
- '70 Honey Come Back
- '68 I Wanna Live
- '70 It's Only Make Believe
- '69 Let It Be Me
  *GLEN CAMPBELL & BOBBIE GENTRY*
- '70 Oh Happy Day
- '75 Rhinestone Cowboy ★
- '77 Southern Nights ★
- '77 Sunflower
- '69 True Grit
- '69 Try A Little Kindness
- '69 Where's The Playground Susie
- '68 Wichita Lineman ★

## CAMPBELL, Jo Ann
- '62 (I'm The Girl On) Wolverton Mountain
- '60 Kookie Little Paradise, A

## CAMPBELL, Tevin
- '92 Alone With You
- '94 Always In My Heart
- '93 Can We Talk
- '92 Goodbye
- '94 I'm Ready
- '90 Round And Round
- '91 Tell Me What You Want Me To Do
- '90 Tomorrow (A Better You, Better Me)
  *QUINCY JONES Feat. Tevin Campbell*

## CAMPER VAN BEETHOVEN
- '89 Pictures Of Matchstick Men

## CAM'RON
- '02 Hey Ma ★
- '02 Oh Boy ★

## C & C MUSIC FACTORY
- '94 Do You Wanna Get Funky
- '90 Gonna Make You Sweat (Everybody Dance Now) ★
- '91 Here We Go
- '91 Things That Make You Go Hmmmm...

## CANDLEBOX
- '94 Far Behind
- '98 It's Alright

## CANDYMAN
- '90 Knockin' Boots

## CANIBUS
- '98 Second Round K.O.

## CANNED HEAT
- '68 Going Up The Country
- '70 Let's Work Together
- '68 On The Road Again

## CANNIBAL & THE HEADHUNTERS
- '65 Land Of 1000 Dances

## CANNON, Ace
- '62 Blues (Stay Away From Me)
- '61 Tuff

## CANNON, Freddy
- '64 Abigail Beecher
- '65 Action
- '61 Buzz Buzz A-Diddle-It
- '60 Chattanooga Shoe Shine Boy
- '60 Jump Over
- '62 Palisades Park ★
- '59 Tallahassee Lassie
- '61 Transistor Sister
- '59 Way Down Yonder In New Orleans

## CANNON, Nick
☐ '03  Gigolo

## CANTRELL, Blu
☐ '01  Hit 'Em Up Style (Oops!)  ★

## CAPALDI, Jim
☐ '83  Living On The Edge
☐ '83  That's Love

## CAPITOLS, The
☐ '66  Cool Jerk

## CAPRIS, The
☐ '60  There's A Moon Out Tonight  ★

## CAPTAIN & TENNILLE
☐ '77  Can't Stop Dancin'
☐ '79  Do That To Me One More Time  ★
☐ '76  Lonely Night (Angel Face)
☐ '75  Love Will Keep Us Together  ★
☐ '76  Muskrat Love
☐ '76  Shop Around
☐ '75  Way I Want To Touch You, The
☐ '78  You Never Done It Like That

## CAPTAIN HOLLYWOOD PROJECT
☐ '93  More And More

## CARA, Irene
☐ '84  Breakdance
☐ '80  Fame  ★
☐ '83  Flashdance...What A Feeling  ★
☐ '80  Out Here On My Own
☐ '83  Why Me?

## CARAVELLES, The
☐ '63  You Don't Have To Be A Baby To Cry

## CARDIGANS, The
☐ '96  Lovefool  ★

## CAREFREES, The
☐ '64  We Love You Beatles

## CAREY, Mariah
☐ '94  All I Want For Christmas Is You
☐ '96  Always Be My Baby  ★
☐ '94  Anytime You Need A Friend
☐ '97  Butterfly
☐ '91  Can't Let Go
☐ '00  Crybaby
☐ '93  Dreamlover  ★
☐ '91  Emotions  ★
☐ '94  Endless Love
   *LUTHER VANDROSS & MARIAH CAREY*
☐ '95  Fantasy  ★
☐ '96  Forever
☐ '99  Heartbreaker
☐ '93  Hero  ★
☐ '97  Honey  ★
☐ '91  I Don't Wanna Cry
☐ '03  I Know What You Want  ★
   *BUSTA RHYMES & MARIAH CAREY*
☐ '99  I Still Believe
☐ '92  I'll Be There  ★
☐ '05  It's Like That
☐ '90  Love Takes Time  ★

☐ '01  Loverboy
☐ '92  Make It Happen
☐ '98  My All  ★
☐ '95  One Sweet Day  ★
   *MARIAH CAREY & BOYZ II MEN*
☐ '91  Someday  ★
☐ '99  Thank God I Found You  ★
☐ '90  Vision Of Love  ★
☐ '05  We Belong Together  ★
☐ '98  When You Believe
   *WHITNEY HOUSTON & MARIAH CAREY*
☐ '94  Without You

## CAREY, Tony
☐ '84  Fine Fine Day, A
☐ '84  First Day Of Summer, The

## CARGILL, Henson
☐ '67  Skip A Rope

## CARLISLE, Belinda
☐ '88  Circle In The Sand
☐ '87  Heaven Is A Place On Earth  ★
☐ '88  I Get Weak
☐ '89  Leave A Light On
☐ '86  Mad About You
☐ '90  Summer Rain

## CARLISLE, Bob
☐ '97  Butterfly Kisses  ★

## CARLTON, Carl
☐ '74  Everlasting Love
☐ '81  She's A Bad Mama Jama (She's Built,
         She's Stacked)

## CARLTON, Vanessa
☐ '02  Ordinary Day
☐ '02  Thousand Miles, A  ★

## CARMEN, Eric
☐ '75  All By Myself  ★
☐ '78  Change Of Heart
☐ '87  Hungry Eyes
☐ '85  I Wanna Hear It From Your Lips
☐ '88  Make Me Lose Control
☐ '76  Never Gonna Fall In Love Again
☐ '77  She Did It
☐ '76  Sunrise

## CARNE, Jean
☐ '86  Closer Than Close

## CARNES, Kim
☐ '81  Bette Davis Eyes  ★
☐ '85  Crazy In The Night (Barking At
         Airplanes)
☐ '82  Does It Make You Remember
☐ '80  Don't Fall In Love With A Dreamer
   *KENNY ROGERS with Kim Carnes*
☐ '81  Draw Of The Cards
☐ '80  More Love
☐ '82  Voyeur
☐ '84  What About Me?
   *KENNY ROGERS with Kim Carnes & James
   Ingram*
☐ '78  You're A Part Of Me
   *GENE COTTON with Kim Carnes*

## CAROSONE, Renato
- ☐ '58 Torero

## CARPENTER, Mary Chapin
- ☐ '91 Down At The Twist And Shout
- ☐ '93 He Thinks He'll Keep Her
- ☐ '92 I Feel Lucky
- ☐ '94 I Take My Chances
- ☐ '93 Passionate Kisses
- ☐ '94 Shut Up And Kiss Me

## CARPENTERS
- ☐ '77 All You Get From Love Is A Love Song
- ☐ '77 Calling Occupants Of Interplanetary Craft
- ☐ '71 For All We Know
- ☐ '72 Goodbye To Love
- ☐ '72 Hurting Each Other
- ☐ '76 I Need To Be In Love
- ☐ '74 I Won't Last A Day Without You
- ☐ '72 It's Going To Take Some Time
- ☐ '70 Merry Christmas Darling
- ☐ '75 Only Yesterday
- ☐ '74 Please Mr. Postman
- ☐ '71 Rainy Days And Mondays ★
- ☐ '73 Sing
- ☐ '75 Solitaire
- ☐ '71 Superstar ★
- ☐ '76 There's A Kind Of Hush (All Over The World)
- ☐ '70 (They Long To Be) Close To You ★
- ☐ '73 Top Of The World ★
- ☐ '81 Touch Me When We're Dancing
- ☐ '70 We've Only Just Begun ★
- ☐ '73 Yesterday Once More

## CARR, Cathy
- ☐ '56 Ivory Tower ★

## CARR, Joe "Fingers"
- ☐ '56 Portuguese Washerwomen

## CARR, Valerie
- ☐ '58 When The Boys Talk About The Girls

## CARR, Vikki
- ☐ '67 It Must Be Him
- ☐ '67 Lesson, The
- ☐ '69 With Pen In Hand

## CARRACK, Paul
- ☐ '87 Don't Shed A Tear
- ☐ '89 I Live By The Groove
- ☐ '82 I Need You
- ☐ '88 One Good Reason

## CARRADINE, Keith
- ☐ '76 I'm Easy

## CARROLL, David, & His Orchestra
- ☐ '55 It's Almost Tomorrow
- ☐ '55 Melody Of Love
- ☐ '62 White Rose Of Athens, The

## CARS, The
- ☐ '78 Bye Bye Love
- ☐ '79 Dangerous Type
- ☐ '84 Drive ★
- ☐ '78 Good Times Roll
- ☐ '84 Hello Again
- ☐ '86 I'm Not The One
- ☐ '79 It's All I Can Do
- ☐ '78 Just What I Needed
- ☐ '79 Let's Go ★
- ☐ '84 Magic
- ☐ '78 Moving In Stereo
- ☐ '78 My Best Friend's Girl
- ☐ '81 Shake It Up ★
- ☐ '82 Since You're Gone
- ☐ '85 Tonight She Comes
- ☐ '80 Touch And Go
- ☐ '85 Why Can't I Have You
- ☐ '87 You Are The Girl
- ☐ '84 You Might Think
- ☐ '78 You're All I've Got Tonight

## CARSON, Jeff
- ☐ '95 Car, The
- ☐ '95 Not On Your Love

## CARSON, Kit
- ☐ '55 Band Of Gold

## CARSON, Mindy
- ☐ '55 Wake The Town And Tell The People

## CARTER, Aaron
- ☐ '00 Aaron's Party (Come Get It)

## CARTER, Carlene
- ☐ '90 Come On Back
- ☐ '93 Every Little Thing
- ☐ '90 I Fell In Love

## CARTER, Clarence
- ☐ '68 Looking For A Fox
- ☐ '70 Patches
- ☐ '68 Slip Away
- ☐ '69 Snatching It Back
- ☐ '89 Strokin'
- ☐ '68 Too Weak To Fight

## CARTER, Deana
- ☐ '97 How Do I Get There
- ☐ '96 Strawberry Wine
- ☐ '96 We Danced Anyway

## CARTER, Mel
- ☐ '66 Band Of Gold
- ☐ '65 Hold Me, Thrill Me, Kiss Me

## CARTWRIGHT, Lionel
- ☐ '91 Leap Of Faith

## CASCADES, The
- ☐ '63 Last Leaf, The
- ☐ '63 Rhythm Of The Rain ★

## CASE
- ☐ '98 Faded Pictures
  *CASE & JOE*
- ☐ '99 Happily Ever After
- ☐ '01 Missing You ★
- ☐ '96 Touch Me Tease Me

## CASH, Alvin, & The Crawlers
- ☐ '65 Twine Time

## CASH, Johnny
- ☐ '58 All Over Again
- ☐ '58 Ballad Of A Teenage Queen
- ☐ '69 Boy Named Sue, A ★
- ☐ '55 Cry! Cry! Cry!
- ☐ '69 Daddy Sang Bass
- ☐ '59 Don't Take Your Guns To Town
- ☐ '56 Folsom Prison Blues
- ☐ '68 Folsom Prison Blues [live]
- ☐ '56 Get Rhythm
- ☐ '79 (Ghost) Riders In The Sky
- ☐ '57 Give My Love To Rose
- ☐ '58 Guess Things Happen That Way
- ☐ '85 Highwayman
  *WAYLON JENNINGS/WILLIE NELSON/*
  *JOHNNY CASH/KRIS KRISTOFFERSON*
- ☐ '03 Hurt
- ☐ '59 I Got Stripes
- ☐ '56 I Walk The Line ★
- ☐ '70 If I Were A Carpenter
- ☐ '67 Jackson
  *JOHNNY CASH & JUNE CARTER (above 2)*
- ☐ '71 Man In Black
- ☐ '76 One Piece At A Time
- ☐ '63 Ring Of Fire ★
- ☐ '72 Thing Called Love, A
- ☐ '64 Understand Your Man
- ☐ '58 Ways Of A Woman In Love, The
- ☐ '70 What Is Truth

## CASH, Rosanne
- ☐ '81 Seven Year Ache

## CASHMAN & WEST
- ☐ '72 American City Suite

## CASINOS, The
- ☐ '67 Then You Can Tell Me Goodbye

## CASSIDY
- ☐ '03 Hotel ★
- ☐ '05 I'm A Hustla

## CASSIDY, David
- ☐ '71 Cherish
- ☐ '72 Could It Be Forever
- ☐ '72 How Can I Be Sure
- ☐ '90 Lyin' To Myself
- ☐ '72 Rock Me Baby

## CASSIDY, Shaun
- ☐ '77 Da Doo Ron Ron
- ☐ '78 Do You Believe In Magic
- ☐ '77 Hey Deanie
- ☐ '77 That's Rock 'N' Roll

## CASTAWAYS, The
- ☐ '65 Liar, Liar

## CASTELLS, The
- ☐ '61 Sacred
- ☐ '62 So This Is Love

## CASTLEMAN, Boomer
- ☐ '75 Judy Mae

## CASTOR, Jimmy
- ☐ '75 Bertha Butt Boogie, The
- ☐ '66 Hey, Leroy, Your Mama's Callin' You
- ☐ '72 Troglodyte (Cave Man)

## CATE BROS.
- ☐ '76 Union Man

## CATES, George, & His Orchestra
- ☐ '56 Moonglow And Theme From "Picnic"

## CATHY JEAN & THE ROOMMATES
- ☐ '61 Please Love Me Forever

## CAT MOTHER & THE ALL NIGHT NEWS BOYS
- ☐ '69 Good Old Rock 'N Roll

## CAUSE & EFFECT
- ☐ '92 You Think You Know Her

## CAVALIERE, Felix
- ☐ '80 Only A Lonely Heart Sees

## C COMPANY Feat. TERRY NELSON
- ☐ '71 Battle Hymn Of Lt. Calley

## CELEBRATION Feat. MIKE LOVE
- ☐ '78 Almost Summer

## CERRONE
- ☐ '77 Love In 'C' Minor

## CETERA, Peter
- ☐ '89 After All
  *CHER & PETER CETERA*
- ☐ '93 Even A Fool Can See
- ☐ '86 Glory Of Love ★
- ☐ '86 Next Time I Fall, The
  *PETER CETERA with Amy Grant*
- ☐ '88 One Good Woman
- ☐ '92 Restless Heart

## CHAD & JEREMY
- ☐ '65 Before And After
- ☐ '66 Distant Shores
- ☐ '65 If I Loved You
- ☐ '64 Summer Song, A
- ☐ '64 Willow Weep For Me
- ☐ '64 Yesterday's Gone

## CHAIRMEN OF THE BOARD
- ☐ '70 Everything's Tuesday
- ☐ '70 Give Me Just A Little More Time
- ☐ '70 Pay To The Piper
- ☐ '70 (You've Got Me) Dangling On A String

## CHAKACHAS, The
- ☐ '72 Jungle Fever

## CHAMBERLAIN, Richard
- ☐ '63 All I Have To Do Is Dream
- ☐ '62 Love Me Tender
- ☐ '62 Theme From Dr. Kildare (Three Stars Will Shine Tonight)

## CHAMBERS BROTHERS, The
- ☐ '68 I Can't Turn You Loose
- ☐ '68 Time Has Come Today

## CHAMPAIGN
- ☐ '81 How 'Bout Us
- ☐ '83 Try Again

## CHAMPS, The
- ☐ '58 El Rancho Rock
- ☐ '62 Limbo Rock
- ☐ '58 Tequila ★
- ☐ '60 Too Much Tequila

## CHANDLER, Gene
- ☐ '64 Bless Our Love
- ☐ '62 Duke Of Earl ★
- ☐ '78 Get Down
- ☐ '70 Groovy Situation
- ☐ '66 I Fooled You This Time
- ☐ '64 Just Be True
- ☐ '65 Nothing Can Stop Me
- ☐ '63 Rainbow
- ☐ '65 Rainbow '65 [live]
- ☐ '64 What Now

## CHANGE
- ☐ '80 Lover's Holiday, A

## CHANGING FACES
- ☐ '94 Foolin' Around
- ☐ '97 G.H.E.T.T.O.U.T.
- ☐ '94 Stroke You Up

## CHANNEL, Bruce
- ☐ '62 Hey! Baby ★

## CHANSON
- ☐ '78 Don't Hold Back

## CHANTAY'S
- ☐ '63 Pipeline ★

## CHANTELS, The
- ☐ '58 Every Night (I Pray)
- ☐ '57 He's Gone
- ☐ '61 Look In My Eyes
- ☐ '58 Maybe ★
- ☐ '61 Well. I Told You

## CHAPIN, Harry
- ☐ '74 Cat's In The Cradle ★
- ☐ '80 Sequel
- ☐ '72 Taxi
- ☐ '74 WOLD

## CHAPMAN, Tracy
- ☐ '88 Fast Car ★
- ☐ '96 Give Me One Reason ★

## CHARLENE
- ☐ '82 I've Never Been To Me

## CHARLES, Jimmy
- ☐ '60 Million To One, A

## CHARLES, Ray
- ☐ '72 America The Beautiful
- ☐ '87 Baby Grand
  - *BILLY JOEL & RAY CHARLES*
- ☐ '62 Born To Lose
- ☐ '63 Busted
- ☐ '65 Crying Time
- ☐ '63 Don't Set Me Free
- ☐ '56 Drown In My Own Tears
- ☐ '68 Eleanor Rigby
- ☐ '55 Fool For You, A
- ☐ '60 Georgia On My Mind ★
- ☐ '67 Here We Go Again
- ☐ '62 Hide 'Nor Hair
- ☐ '61 Hit The Road Jack ★
- ☐ '62 I Can't Stop Loving You ★
- ☐ '66 I Chose To Sing The Blues
- ☐ '59 I'm Movin' On
- ☐ '55 I've Got A Woman
- ☐ '66 Let's Go Get Stoned
- ☐ '63 No One
- ☐ '61 One Mint Julep
- ☐ '60 Ruby
- ☐ '57 Swanee River Rock (Talkin' 'Bout That River)
- ☐ '63 Take These Chains From My Heart
- ☐ '63 That Lucky Old Sun
- ☐ '66 Together Again
- ☐ '61 Unchain My Heart
- ☐ '59 What'd I Say ★
- ☐ '63 Without Love (There Is Nothing)
- ☐ '67 Yesterday
- ☐ '62 You Are My Sunshine
- ☐ '62 You Don't Know Me
- ☐ '62 Your Cheating Heart

## CHARLES, Ray, Singers
- ☐ '64 Al-Di-La
- ☐ '64 Love Me With All Your Heart (Cuando Calienta El Sol)

## CHARLES, Sonny
- ☐ '69 Black Pearl
  - *SONNY CHARLES & THE CHECKMATES, LTD.*
- ☐ '83 Put It In A Magazine

## CHARLES & EDDIE
- ☐ '92 Would I Lie To You?

## CHARLIE
- ☐ '83 It's Inevitable

## CHARMS, The
- ☐ '55 Hearts Of Stone
- ☐ '56 Ivory Tower
- ☐ '55 Ling, Ting, Tong

## CHARTBUSTERS, The
- ☐ '64 She's The One

## CHASE
- ☐ '71 Get It On

## CHASEZ, JC
- ☐ '03 Blowin' Me Up (With Her Love)

## CHEAP TRICK
- ☐ '79 Ain't That A Shame
- ☐ '90 Can't Stop Fallin' Into Love
- ☐ '88 Don't Be Cruel
- ☐ '79 Dream Police
- ☐ '88 Flame, The ★
- ☐ '88 Ghost Town
- ☐ '79 I Want You To Want Me ★
- ☐ '78 Surrender
- ☐ '79 Voices

## CHECKER, Chubby
- ☐ '63 Birdland
- ☐ '59 Class, The
- ☐ '61 (Dance The) Mess Around
- ☐ '62 Dancin' Party
- ☐ '61 Fly, The
- ☐ '64 Hey, Bobba Needle
- ☐ '63 Hooka Tooka
- ☐ '60 Hucklebuck, The
- ☐ '61 Jingle Bell Rock
  *BOBBY RYDELL & CHUBBY CHECKER*
- ☐ '63 Let's Limbo Some More
- ☐ '61 Let's Twist Again
- ☐ '62 Limbo Rock ★
- ☐ '63 Loddy Lo
- ☐ '61 Pony Time ★
- ☐ '62 Popeye (The Hitchhiker)
- ☐ '62 Slow Twistin'
  *CHUBBY CHECKER (with Dee Dee Sharp)*
- ☐ '63 Twenty Miles
- ☐ '60 Twist, The ★
- ☐ '63 Twist It Up

## CHEECH & CHONG
- ☐ '73 Basketball Jones Featuring Tyrone Shoelaces
- ☐ '74 Black Lassie
- ☐ '71 Dave
- ☐ '74 Earache My Eye (Featuring Alice Bowie)
- ☐ '73 Sister Mary Elephant (Shudd-Up!)
- ☐ '74 Three Little Pigs

## CHEERS, The
- ☐ '55 Black Denim Trousers ★

## CHER
- ☐ '89 After All
  *CHER & PETER CETERA*
- ☐ '66 Alfie
- ☐ '65 All I Really Want To Do
- ☐ '66 Bang Bang (My Baby Shot Me Down)
- ☐ '98 Believe ★
- ☐ '74 Dark Lady
- ☐ '71 Gypsys, Tramps & Thieves ★
- ☐ '73 Half-Breed
- ☐ '90 Heart Of Stone
- ☐ '87 I Found Someone
- ☐ '89 If I Could Turn Back Time ★
- ☐ '89 Just Like Jesse James
- ☐ '72 Living In A House Divided
- ☐ '91 Love And Understanding
- ☐ '90 Shoop Shoop Song (It's In His Kiss)
- ☐ '79 Take Me Home
- ☐ '74 Train Of Thought

- ☐ '72 Way Of Love, The
- ☐ '88 We All Sleep Alone
- ☐ '65 Where Do You Go
- ☐ '67 You Better Sit Down Kids

## CHERRELLE
- ☐ '88 Everything I Miss At Home
- ☐ '88 Never Knew Love Like This
  *ALEXANDER O'NEAL Feat. Cherrelle*
- ☐ '86 Saturday Love
  *CHERRELLE with Alexander O'Neal*

## CHERRY, Don
- ☐ '55 Band Of Gold ★
- ☐ '56 Ghost Town
- ☐ '56 Wild Cherry

## CHERRY, Eagle-Eye
- ☐ '98 Save Tonight ★

## CHERRY, Neneh
- ☐ '89 Buffalo Stance ★
- ☐ '89 Kisses On The Wind

## CHESNEY, Kenny
- ☐ '05 Anything But Mine ★
- ☐ '03 Big Star
- ☐ '01 Don't Happen Twice
- ☐ '02 Good Stuff, The
- ☐ '99 How Forever Feels
- ☐ '04 I Go Back
- ☐ '00 I Lost It
- ☐ '96 Me And You
- ☐ '03 No Shoes, No Shirt, No Problems
- ☐ '00 She Thinks My Tractor's Sexy
- ☐ '97 She's Got It All
- ☐ '98 That's Why I'm Here
- ☐ '03 There Goes My Life
- ☐ '96 When I Close My Eyes
- ☐ '04 When The Sun Goes Down
  *KENNY CHESNEY & UNCLE KRACKER*
- ☐ '04 Woman With You, The
- ☐ '99 You Had Me From Hello
- ☐ '01 Young

## CHESNUTT, Mark
- ☐ '93 Almost Goodbye
- ☐ '90 Brother Jukebox
- ☐ '92 Bubba Shot The Jukebox
- ☐ '94 Goin' Through The Big D
- ☐ '95 Gonna Get A Life
- ☐ '98 I Don't Want To Miss A Thing
- ☐ '93 I Just Wanted You To Know
- ☐ '92 I'll Think Of Something
- ☐ '93 It Sure Is Monday
- ☐ '96 It's A Little Too Late
- ☐ '97 Thank God For Believers
- ☐ '90 Too Cold At Home
- ☐ '91 Your Love Is A Miracle

## CHEVALIER, Maurice
- ☐ '58 Thank Heaven For Little Girls

## CHEVELLE
- ☐ '02 Red, The
- ☐ '03 Send The Pain Below
- ☐ '04 Vitamin R (Leading Us Along)

## CHIC
- [ ] '77 Dance, Dance, Dance (Yowsah, Yowsah, Yowsah)
- [ ] '79 Good Times ★
- [ ] '79 I Want Your Love
- [ ] '78 Le Freak ★

## CHICAGO
- [ ] '78 Alive Again
- [ ] '85 Along Comes A Woman
- [ ] '77 Baby, What A Big Surprise
- [ ] '71 Beginnings
- [ ] '74 Call On Me
- [ ] '71 Colour My World
- [ ] '72 Dialogue
- [ ] '70 Does Anybody Really Know What Time It Is?
- [ ] '73 Feelin' Stronger Every Day
- [ ] '71 Free
- [ ] '84 Hard Habit To Break
- [ ] '82 Hard To Say I'm Sorry ★
- [ ] '75 Harry Truman
- [ ] '97 Here In My Heart
- [ ] '88 I Don't Wanna Live Without Your Love
- [ ] '69 I'm A Man
- [ ] '74 (I've Been) Searchin' So Long
- [ ] '87 If She Would Have Been Faithful...
- [ ] '76 If You Leave Me Now ★
- [ ] '73 Just You 'N' Me
- [ ] '88 Look Away
- [ ] '82 Love Me Tomorrow
- [ ] '71 Lowdown
- [ ] '70 Make Me Smile
- [ ] '78 No Tell Lover
- [ ] '75 Old Days
- [ ] '71 Questions 67 And 68
- [ ] '72 Saturday In The Park ★
- [ ] '84 Stay The Night
- [ ] '70 25 Or 6 To 4 ★
- [ ] '89 What Kind Of Man Would I Be?
- [ ] '86 Will You Still Love Me?
- [ ] '74 Wishing You Were Here
- [ ] '89 You're Not Alone
- [ ] '84 You're The Inspiration ★

## CHICAGO BEARS SHUFFLIN' CREW
- [ ] '86 Superbowl Shuffle

## CHICAGO LOOP, The
- [ ] '66 (When She Needs Good Lovin') She Comes To Me

## CHIFFONS, The
- [ ] '63 He's So Fine ★
- [ ] '63 I Have A Boyfriend
- [ ] '63 Love So Fine, A
- [ ] '63 One Fine Day
- [ ] '66 Sweet Talkin' Guy

## CHILD, Jane
- [ ] '90 Don't Wanna Fall In Love

## CHI-LITES, The
- [ ] '71 (For God's Sake) Give More Power To The People
- [ ] '71 Have You Seen Her ★

- [ ] '73 Letter To Myself, A
- [ ] '72 Oh Girl ★
- [ ] '73 Stoned Out Of My Mind

## CHILLIWACK
- [ ] '82 I Believe
- [ ] '81 My Girl (Gone, Gone, Gone)

## CHIMES, The
- [ ] '61 I'm In The Mood For Love
- [ ] '60 Once In Awhile

## CHINGY
- [ ] '04 Balla Baby
- [ ] '03 Holidae In ★
- [ ] '04 One Call Away ★
- [ ] '03 Right Thurr ★

## CHIPMUNKS, The
- [ ] '62 Alvin Twist, The
- [ ] '59 Alvin's Harmonica
- [ ] '60 Alvin's Orchestra
- [ ] '58 Chipmunk Song, The
- [ ] '59 Ragtime Cowboy Joe
- [ ] '60 Rudolph The Red Nosed Reindeer

## CHORDETTES, The
- [ ] '56 Born To Be With You
- [ ] '56 Eddie My Love
- [ ] '57 Just Between You And Me
- [ ] '56 Lay Down Your Arms
- [ ] '58 Lollipop ★
- [ ] '55 Mr. Sandman ★
- [ ] '61 Never On Sunday
- [ ] '59 No Other Arms, No Other Lips
- [ ] '58 Zorro

## CHORDS, The
- [ ] '54 Sh-Boom

## CHRISTIE
- [ ] '70 Yellow River

## CHRISTIE, Lou
- [ ] '63 Gypsy Cried, The
- [ ] '69 I'm Gonna Make You Mine
- [ ] '65 Lightnin' Strikes ★
- [ ] '66 Rhapsody In The Rain
- [ ] '63 Two Faces Have I

## CHRISTOPHER, Gavin
- [ ] '86 One Step Closer To You

## CHUMBAWAMBA
- [ ] '97 Tubthumping ★

## CHURCH, The
- [ ] '90 Metropolis
- [ ] '88 Under The Milky Way

## CHURCH, Eugene
- [ ] '58 Pretty Girls Everywhere

## CIARA
- [ ] '04 Goodies ★
- [ ] '05 Oh ★
- [ ] '05 1,2 Step ★

## CINDERELLA
- ☐ '89 Coming Home
- ☐ '88 Don't Know What You Got (Till It's Gone)
- ☐ '89 Last Mile, The
- ☐ '86 Nobody's Fool
- ☐ '90 Shelter Me

## CITIZEN KING
- ☐ '99 Better Days (And The Bottom Drops Out)

## CITY BOY
- ☐ '78 5.7.0.5.

## CITY HIGH
- ☐ '01 Caramel
- ☐ '01 What Would You Do?

## C.J. & CO.
- ☐ '77 Devil's Gun

## CLANTON, Jimmy
- ☐ '60 Another Sleepless Night
- ☐ '60 Come Back
- ☐ '59 Go, Jimmy, Go
- ☐ '58 Just A Dream
- ☐ '58 Letter To An Angel, A
- ☐ '59 My Own True Love
- ☐ '58 Part Of Me, A
- ☐ '62 Venus In Blue Jeans
- ☐ '61 What Am I Gonna Do

## CLAPTON, Eric
- ☐ '70 After Midnight
- ☐ '89 Bad Love
- ☐ '70 Bell Bottom Blues
  - *DEREK & THE DOMINOS*
- ☐ '70 Blues Power
- ☐ '96 Change The World ★
- ☐ '77 Cocaine
- ☐ '80 Cocaine [live]
- ☐ '85 Forever Man
- ☐ '76 Hello Old Friend
- ☐ '81 I Can't Stand It
- ☐ '74 I Shot The Sheriff ★
- ☐ '83 I've Got A Rock N' Roll Heart
- ☐ '86 It's In The Way That You Use It
- ☐ '78 Lay Down Sally ★
- ☐ '72 Layla ★
  - *DEREK & THE DOMINOS*
- ☐ '92 Layla [live]
- ☐ '70 Let It Rain
- ☐ '98 My Father's Eyes
- ☐ '89 Pretending
- ☐ '78 Promises
- ☐ '85 See What Love Can Do
- ☐ '85 She's Waiting
- ☐ '92 Tears In Heaven ★
- ☐ '80 Tulsa Time
- ☐ '79 Watch Out For Lucy
- ☐ '74 Willie And The Hand Jive
- ☐ '78 Wonderful Tonight

## CLARK, Claudine
- ☐ '62 Party Lights

## CLARK, Dave, Five
- ☐ '64 Any Way You Want It
- ☐ '66 At The Scene
- ☐ '64 Because
- ☐ '64 Bits And Pieces
- ☐ '64 Can't You See That She's Mine
- ☐ '65 Catch Us If You Can
- ☐ '65 Come Home
- ☐ '64 Do You Love Me
- ☐ '67 Everybody Knows
- ☐ '64 Everybody Knows (I Still Love You)
- ☐ '64 Glad All Over
- ☐ '65 I Like It Like That
- ☐ '65 Over And Over ★
- ☐ '66 Please Tell Me Why
- ☐ '65 Reelin' And Rockin'
- ☐ '66 Try Too Hard
- ☐ '67 You Got What It Takes
- ☐ '67 You Must Have Been A Beautiful Baby

## CLARK, Dee
- ☐ '59 Hey Little Girl
- ☐ '59 How About That
- ☐ '59 Just Keep It Up
- ☐ '58 Nobody But You
- ☐ '61 Raindrops ★
- ☐ '61 Your Friends

## CLARK, Petula
- ☐ '66 Color My World
- ☐ '67 Don't Sleep In The Subway
- ☐ '64 Downtown ★
- ☐ '66 I Couldn't Live Without Your Love
- ☐ '65 I Know A Place
- ☐ '68 Kiss Me Goodbye
- ☐ '65 My Love ★
- ☐ '65 Round Every Corner
- ☐ '66 Sign Of The Times, A
- ☐ '67 This Is My Song
- ☐ '66 Who Am I
- ☐ '65 You'd Better Come Home

## CLARK, Roy
- ☐ '73 Come Live With Me
- ☐ '69 Yesterday, When I Was Young

## CLARK, Sanford
- ☐ '56 Fool, The ★

## CLARK, Terri
- ☐ '95 Better Things To Do
- ☐ '97 Emotional Girl
- ☐ '04 Girls Lie Too
- ☐ '02 I Just Wanna Be Mad
- ☐ '03 I Wanna Do It All
- ☐ '98 Now That I Found You
- ☐ '96 Poor, Poor Pitiful Me
- ☐ '95 When Boy Meets Girl
- ☐ '98 You're Easy On The Eyes

## CLARKE, Stanley
- ☐ '81 Sweet Baby
  - *STANLEY CLARKE/GEORGE DUKE*

## CLARKSON, Kelly
- ☐ '05 Behind These Hazel Eyes ★
- ☐ '04 Breakaway ★
- ☐ '03 Miss Independent
- ☐ '02 Moment Like This, A ★
- ☐ '05 Since U Been Gone ★

## CLASH, The
- ☐ '79 Complete Control
- ☐ '80 London Calling ★
- ☐ '82 Rock The Casbah ★
- ☐ '82 Should I Stay Or Should I Go
- ☐ '80 Train In Vain (Stand By Me)
- ☐ '79 White Man In Hammersmith Palais
- ☐ '79 White Riot

## CLASSICS, The
- ☐ '63 Till Then

## CLASSICS IV
- ☐ '69 Everyday With You Girl
- ☐ '67 Spooky ★
- ☐ '68 Stormy
- ☐ '69 Traces
- ☐ '72 What Am I Crying For?

## CLAY, Judy
- ☐ '68 Country Girl - City Man
  *BILLY VERA & JUDY CLAY*

## CLAY, Tom
- ☐ '71 What The World Needs Now Is Love/Abraham, Martin and John

## CLAYTON, Adam, & Larry Mullen
- ☐ '96 Theme From Mission: Impossible

## CLEFTONES, The
- ☐ '61 Heart And Soul
- ☐ '56 Little Girl Of Mine

## CLEMONS, Clarence
- ☐ '85 You're A Friend Of Mine
  *CLARENCE CLEMONS & JACKSON BROWNE*

## CLEOPATRA
- ☐ '98 Cleopatra's Theme

## CLIBURN, Van
- ☐ '58 Tchaikovsky: Piano Concerto No. 1

## CLIFF, Jimmy
- ☐ '75 Harder They Come, The
- ☐ '93 I Can See Clearly Now
- ☐ '69 Many Rivers To Cross
- ☐ '69 Wonderful World, Beautiful People
- ☐ '75 You Can Get It If You Really Want It

## CLIFFORD, Buzz
- ☐ '61 Baby Sittin' Boogie

## CLIFFORD, Linda
- ☐ '78 Runaway Love

## CLIFFORD, Mike
- ☐ '62 Close To Cathy

## CLIMAX
- ☐ '72 Precious And Few

## CLIMAX BLUES BAND
- ☐ '77 Couldn't Get It Right
- ☐ '81 I Love You

## CLIMIE FISHER
- ☐ '88 Love Changes (Everything)

## CLINE, Patsy
- ☐ '61 Crazy ★
- ☐ '61 I Fall To Pieces ★
- ☐ '62 She's Got You
- ☐ '63 Sweet Dreams (Of You)
- ☐ '57 Walkin' After Midnight

## CLINTON, George
- ☐ '83 Atomic Dog

## CLIPSE
- ☐ '02 Grindin'
- ☐ '02 When The Last Time

## CLIQUE, The
- ☐ '69 Sugar On Sunday

## CLOONEY, Rosemary
- ☐ '54 Hey There
- ☐ '54 Mambo Italiano
- ☐ '57 Mangos
- ☐ '56 Memories Of You
- ☐ '54 This Ole House

## CLOVERS, The
- ☐ '56 Devil Or Angel
- ☐ '56 Love, Love, Love
- ☐ '59 Love Potion No. 9

## CLUB NOUVEAU
- ☐ '87 Lean On Me ★
- ☐ '87 Why You Treat Me So Bad

## COASTERS, The
- ☐ '59 Along Came Jones
- ☐ '59 Charlie Brown ★
- ☐ '59 I'm A Hog For You
- ☐ '61 Little Egypt (Ying-Yang)
- ☐ '59 Poison Ivy
- ☐ '59 Run Red Run
- ☐ '57 Searchin' ★
- ☐ '61 Wait A Minute
- ☐ '58 Yakety Yak ★
- ☐ '57 Young Blood ★

## COCHRAN, Anita
- ☐ '97 What If I Said
  *ANITA COCHRAN with Steve Wariner*

## COCHRAN, Eddie
- ☐ '58 C'mon Everybody ★
- ☐ '59 Cut Across Shorty
- ☐ '57 Drive In Show
- ☐ '58 Jeannie Jeannie Jeannie
- ☐ '57 Sittin' In The Balcony
- ☐ '59 Somethin Else
- ☐ '58 Summertime Blues ★
- ☐ '59 Teenage Heaven
- ☐ '60 Three Steps To Heaven
- ☐ '57 Twenty Flight Rock

## COCHRANE, Tom
- ☐ '92 Life Is A Highway
- ☐ '92 No Regrets

## COCKBURN, Bruce
- ☐ '80 Wondering Where The Lions Are

## COCKER, Joe
- ☐ '70 Cry Me A River
- ☐ '69 Delta Lady
- ☐ '72 Feeling Alright
- ☐ '71 High Time We Went
- ☐ '70 Letter, The
- ☐ '72 Midnight Rider
- ☐ '69 She Came In Through The Bathroom Window
- ☐ '82 Up Where We Belong ★
  *JOE COCKER & JENNIFER WARNES*
- ☐ '89 When The Night Comes
- ☐ '69 With A Little Help From My Friends
- ☐ '75 You Are So Beautiful

## COCK ROBIN
- ☐ '85 When Your Heart Is Weak

## COFFEY, Dennis
- ☐ '71 Scorpio
- ☐ '72 Taurus

## COHN, Marc
- ☐ '91 Walking In Memphis

## COLDPLAY
- ☐ '03 Clocks ★
- ☐ '02 Scientist, The
- ☐ '05 Speed Of Sound ★
- ☐ '01 Yellow

## COLE, Cozy
- ☐ '58 Topsy II ★
- ☐ '58 Turvy II

## COLE, Jude
- ☐ '90 Baby, It's Tonight
- ☐ '92 Start The Car
- ☐ '90 Time For Letting Go

## COLE, Nat "King"
- ☐ '58 Angel Smile
- ☐ '56 Ask Me
- ☐ '57 Ballerina
- ☐ '55 Blossom Fell, A ★
- ☐ '58 Come Closer To Me
- ☐ '55 Darling Je Vous Aime Beaucoup
- ☐ '62 Dear Lonely Hearts
- ☐ '55 Forgive My Heart
- ☐ '64 I Don't Want To Be Hurt Anymore
- ☐ '64 I Don't Want To See Tomorrow
- ☐ '55 If I May
  *NAT "KING" COLE & THE FOUR KNIGHTS*
- ☐ '58 Looking Back
- ☐ '57 My Personal Possession
  *NAT "KING" COLE & THE FOUR KNIGHTS*
- ☐ '56 Night Lights
- ☐ '62 Ramblin' Rose ★
- ☐ '55 Sand And The Sea, The

- ☐ '57 Send For Me
- ☐ '55 Someone You Love
- ☐ '57 Stardust
- ☐ '63 That Sunday, That Summer
- ☐ '56 That's All There Is To That
  *NAT "KING" COLE & THE FOUR KNIGHTS*
- ☐ '63 Those Lazy-Hazy-Crazy Days Of Summer
- ☐ '60 Time And The River
- ☐ '56 To The Ends Of The Earth
- ☐ '56 Too Young To Go Steady
- ☐ '91 Unforgettable
  *NATALIE COLE with Nat "King" Cole*
- ☐ '57 With You On My Mind

## COLE, Natalie
- ☐ '87 I Live For Your Love
- ☐ '77 I've Got Love On My Mind
- ☐ '75 Inseparable
- ☐ '87 Jump Start
- ☐ '89 Miss You Like Crazy
- ☐ '78 Our Love
- ☐ '88 Pink Cadillac
- ☐ '80 Someone That I Used To Love
- ☐ '76 Sophisticated Lady (She's A Different Lady)
- ☐ '75 This Will Be
- ☐ '91 Unforgettable
  *NATALIE COLE with Nat "King" Cole*
- ☐ '90 Wild Women Do

## COLE, Paula
- ☐ '97 I Don't Want To Wait
- ☐ '98 Me
- ☐ '97 Where Have All The Cowboys Gone?

## COLLECTIVE SOUL
- ☐ '95 December
- ☐ '95 Gel
- ☐ '99 Heavy
- ☐ '97 Listen
- ☐ '97 Precious Declaration
- ☐ '94 Shine
- ☐ '95 Smashing Young Man
- ☐ '96 Where The River Flows
- ☐ '00 Why
- ☐ '95 World I Know, The

## COLLIER, Mitty
- ☐ '64 I Had A Talk With My Man

## COLLINS, Dave & Ansil
- ☐ '71 Double Barrel

## COLLINS, Dorothy
- ☐ '55 My Boy - Flat Top
- ☐ '56 Seven Days

## COLLINS, Edwyn
- ☐ '95 Girl Like You, A

## COLLINS, Judy
- ☐ '70 Amazing Grace ★
- ☐ '68 Both Sides Now
- ☐ '73 Cook With Honey
- ☐ '75 Send In The Clowns

## COLLINS, Phil
- [ ] '84 Against All Odds (Take A Look At Me Now) ★
- [ ] '89 Another Day In Paradise ★
- [ ] '93 Both Sides Of The Story
- [ ] '02 Can't Stop Loving You
- [ ] '90 Do You Remember?
- [ ] '85 Don't Lose My Number
- [ ] '84 Easy Lover
  *PHILIP BAILEY (with Phil Collins)*
- [ ] '94 Everyday
- [ ] '88 Groovy Kind Of Love ★
- [ ] '90 Hang In Long Enough
- [ ] '93 Hero
  *DAVID CROSBY & PHIL COLLINS*
- [ ] '81 I Missed Again
- [ ] '90 I Wish It Would Rain Down ★
- [ ] '81 In The Air Tonight
- [ ] '85 One More Night ★
- [ ] '85 Separate Lives ★
  *PHIL COLLINS & MARILYN MARTIN*
- [ ] '90 Something Happened On The Way To Heaven
- [ ] '85 Sussudio ★
- [ ] '86 Take Me Home
- [ ] '98 True Colors
- [ ] '88 Two Hearts ★
- [ ] '82 You Can't Hurry Love
- [ ] '99 You'll Be In My Heart

## COLLINS, Tyler
- [ ] '90 Girls Nite Out

## COLLINS, William "Bootsy"
- [ ] '78 Bootzilla

## COLOR ME BADD
- [ ] '91 All 4 Love ★
- [ ] '94 Choose
- [ ] '96 Earth, The Sun, The Rain, The
- [ ] '92 Forever Love
- [ ] '91 I Adore Mi Amor ★
- [ ] '91 I Wanna Sex You Up
- [ ] '92 Slow Motion
- [ ] '92 Thinkin' Back
- [ ] '93 Time And Chance

## COLTER, Jessi
- [ ] '75 I'm Not Lisa

## COLTRANE, Chi
- [ ] '72 Thunder And Lightning

## COLVIN, Shawn
- [ ] '97 Sunny Came Home ★

## COMMANDER CODY & HIS LOST PLANET AIRMEN
- [ ] '72 Hot Rod Lincoln

## COMMODORES
- [ ] '77 Brick House
- [ ] '77 Easy
- [ ] '76 Just To Be Close To You
- [ ] '81 Lady (You Bring Me Up)
- [ ] '74 Machine Gun
- [ ] '85 Nightshift

- [ ] '81 Oh No
- [ ] '80 Old-Fashion Love
- [ ] '79 Sail On
- [ ] '75 Slippery When Wet
- [ ] '79 Still
- [ ] '75 Sweet Love
- [ ] '78 Three Times A Lady ★
- [ ] '77 Too Hot Ta Trot
- [ ] '79 Wonderland

## COMMUNARDS
- [ ] '87 Never Can Say Goodbye

## COMO, Perry
- [ ] '55 All At Once You Love Her
- [ ] '73 And I Love You So
- [ ] '58 Catch A Falling Sta ★
- [ ] '62 Caterina
- [ ] '60 Delaware
- [ ] '65 Dream On Little Dreamer
- [ ] '57 Girl With The Golden Braids, The
- [ ] '56 Glendora
- [ ] '56 Hot Diggity (Dog Ziggity Boom) ★
- [ ] '63 (I Love You) Don't You Forget It
- [ ] '70 It's Impossible
- [ ] '57 Ivy Rose
- [ ] '56 Juke Box Baby
- [ ] '57 Just Born (To Be Your Baby)
- [ ] '58 Kewpie Doll
- [ ] '55 Ko Ko Mo (I Love You So)
- [ ] '58 Love Makes The World Go 'Round
- [ ] '58 Magic Moments
- [ ] '58 Moon Talk
- [ ] '56 More
- [ ] '54 Papa Loves Mambo
- [ ] '57 Round And Round ★
- [ ] '69 Seattle
- [ ] '56 Somebody Up There Likes Me
- [ ] '67 Stop! And Think It Over
- [ ] '55 Tina Marie
- [ ] '67 You Made It That Way (Watermelon Summer)

## COMPANY B
- [ ] '87 Fascinated

## CONCRETE BLONDE
- [ ] '90 Joey ★

## CONFEDERATE RAILROAD
- [ ] '92 Queen Of Memphis
- [ ] '93 Trashy Woman

## CON FUNK SHUN
- [ ] '77 Ffun
- [ ] '81 Too Tight

## CONLEY, Arthur
- [ ] '68 Funky Street
- [ ] '67 Shake, Rattle & Roll
- [ ] '67 Sweet Soul Music ★

## CONNIFF, Ray, Sinters
- [ ] '66 Lookin' For Love
- [ ] '66 Somewhere, My Love

## CONNOR, Chris
- ☐ '56 I Miss You So

## CONNORS, Norman
- ☐ '76 You Are My Starship

## CONTI, Bill
- ☐ '77 Gonna Fly Now

## CONTOURS, The
- ☐ '62 Do You Love Me ★

## CONWELL, Tommy, & The Young Rumblers
- ☐ '88 I'm Not Your Man
- ☐ '88 If We Never Meet Again

## COOKE, Sam
- ☐ '63 Another Saturday Night
- ☐ '62 Bring It On Home To Me
- ☐ '60 Chain Gang ★
- ☐ '65 Change Is Gonna Come, A ★
- ☐ '64 Cousin Of Mine
- ☐ '61 Cupid
- ☐ '59 Everybody Likes To Cha Cha Cha
- ☐ '61 Feel It
- ☐ '63 Frankie And Johnny
- ☐ '64 Good News
- ☐ '64 Good Times
- ☐ '62 Having A Party
- ☐ '57 (I Love You) For Sentimental Reasons
- ☐ '57 I'll Come Running Back To You
- ☐ '63 Little Red Rooster
- ☐ '58 Lonely Island
- ☐ '58 Love You Most Of All
- ☐ '62 Nothing Can Change This Love
- ☐ '59 Only Sixteen
- ☐ '60 Sad Mood
- ☐ '63 Send Me Some Lovin'
- ☐ '65 Shake
- ☐ '62 Somebody Have Mercy
- ☐ '65 Sugar Dumpling
- ☐ '57 Summertime
- ☐ '61 That's It - I Quit - I'm Movin' On
- ☐ '62 Twistin' The Night Away
- ☐ '58 Win Your Love For Me
- ☐ '60 Wonderful World
- ☐ '57 You Send Me ★
- ☐ '58 You Were Made For Me

## COOKIES, The
- ☐ '62 Chains
- ☐ '63 Don't Say Nothin' Bad (About My Baby)
- ☐ '63 Girls Grow Up Faster Than Boys

## COOLEY, Eddie, & The Dimples
- ☐ '56 Priscilla

## COOLIDGE, Rita
- ☐ '83 All Time High
- ☐ '79 I'd Rather Leave While I'm In Love
- ☐ '78 Way You Do The Things You Do, The
- ☐ '77 We're All Alone
- ☐ '78 You
- ☐ '77 (Your Love Has Lifted Me) Higher And Higher

## COOLIO
- ☐ '97 C U When U Get There
- ☐ '94 Fantastic Voyage ★
- ☐ '95 Gangsta's Paradise ★
- ☐ '96 It's All The Way Live (Now)
- ☐ '96 1,2,3,4 (Sumpin' New)
- ☐ '95 Too Hot

## COOPER, Alice
- ☐ '72 Be My Lover
- ☐ '73 Billion Dollar Babies
- ☐ '80 Clones (We're All)
- ☐ '71 Eighteen
- ☐ '72 Elected
- ☐ '73 Hello Hurray
- ☐ '78 How You Gonna See Me Now
- ☐ '76 I Never Cry
- ☐ '73 No More Mr. Nice Guy
- ☐ '75 Only Women
- ☐ '89 Poison
- ☐ '72 School's Out
- ☐ '72 Under My Wheels
- ☐ '75 Welcome To My Nightmare
- ☐ '77 You And Me

## COOPER, Les, & The Soul Rockers
- ☐ '62 Wiggle Wobble

## COOPER, Michael
- ☐ '87 To Prove My Love

## COPE, Julian
- ☐ '87 World Shut Your Mouth

## COPELAND, Ken
- ☐ '57 Pledge Of Love

## COPPOLA, Imani
- ☐ '97 Legend Of A Cowgirl

## COREY, Jill
- ☐ '56 I Love My Baby (My Baby Loves Me)
- ☐ '57 Love Me To Pieces

## CORINA
- ☐ '91 Temptation

## CORNELIUS BROTHERS & SISTER ROSE
- ☐ '72 Don't Ever Be Lonely (A Poor Little Fool Like Me)
- ☐ '72 I'm Never Gonna Be Alone Anymore
- ☐ '72 Too Late To Turn Back Now ★
- ☐ '71 Treat Her Like A Lady ★

## CORNELL, Don
- ☐ '55 Bible Tells Me So, The
- ☐ '55 Love Is A Many-Splendored Thing
- ☐ '55 Most Of All
- ☐ '55 Young Abe Lincoln

## CORONA
- ☐ '94 Rhythm Of The Night, The ★

## CORRS, The
- ☐ '01 Breathless

## CORSAIRS, The
- ☐ '61 Smoky Places

## CORTEZ, Dave "Baby"
- ☐ '59 Happy Organ, The ★
- ☐ '62 Rinky Dink

## COSBY, Bill
- ☐ '67 Little Ole Man (Uptight-Everything's Alright)

## COSTA, Don, & His Orchestra
- ☐ '60 Never On Sunday
- ☐ '60 Theme From "The Unforgiven" (The Need For Love)

## COSTELLO, Elvis
- ☐ '79 Accidents Will Happen
- ☐ '77 Alison
- ☐ '83 Everyday I Write The Book
- ☐ '80 I Can't Stand Up For Falling Down
- ☐ '79 Oliver's Army
- ☐ '91 Other Side Of Summer, The
- ☐ '78 Pump It Up
- ☐ '78 Radio, Radio
- ☐ '89 Veronica
- ☐ '77 Watching The Detectives ★
- ☐ '79 (What's So Funny 'Bout) Peace, Love And Understanding

## COTTON, Gene
- ☐ '78 Before My Heart Finds Out
- ☐ '78 Like A Sunday In Salem (The Amos & Andy Song)
- ☐ '78 You're A Part Of Me
  - *GENE COTTON with Kim Carnes*
- ☐ '76 You've Got Me Runnin'

## COUNT FIVE
- ☐ '66 Psychotic Reaction

## COUNTING CROWS
- ☐ '04 Accidentally In Love
- ☐ '96 Angels Of The Silences
- ☐ '94 Einstein On The Beach (For An Eggman)
- ☐ '99 Hanginaround
- ☐ '96 Long December, A ★
- ☐ '93 Mr. Jones ★
- ☐ '94 Round Here

## COUNTRY JOE & THE FISH
- ☐ '67 I-Feel-Like-I'm-Fixin'-To-Die-Rag
- ☐ '67 Not So Sweet Martha Lorraine
- ☐ '68 Rock And Soul Music

## COVAY, Don
- ☐ '73 I Was Checkin' Out She Was Checkin' In
- ☐ '64 Mercy, Mercy

## COVEN
- ☐ '71 One Tin Soldier, The Legend of Billy Jack

## COVERDALE•PAGE
- ☐ '93 Pride And Joy

## COVER GIRLS, The
- ☐ '87 Because Of You
- ☐ '89 My Heart Skips A Beat
- ☐ '88 Promise Me
- ☐ '89 We Can't Go Wrong
- ☐ '92 Wishing On A Star

## COWBOY CHURCH SUNDAY SCHOOL
- ☐ '55 Open Up Your Heart (And Let The Sunshine In)

## COWSILLS, The
- ☐ '69 Hair
- ☐ '68 Indian Lake
- ☐ '67 Rain, The Park & Other Things, The ★
- ☐ '68 We Can Fly

## COX, Deborah
- ☐ '98 Nobody's Supposed To Be Here ★
- ☐ '95 Sentimental
- ☐ '99 We Can't Be Friends
- ☐ '96 Who Do U Love

## COZIER, Jimmy
- ☐ '01 She's All I Got

## CRABBY APPLETON
- ☐ '70 Go Back

## CRACKER
- ☐ '93 Low

## CRADDOCK, Billy "Crash"
- ☐ '74 Rub It In
- ☐ '74 Ruby, Baby

## CRAMER, Floyd
- ☐ '62 Chattanooga Choo Choo
- ☐ '60 Last Date ★
- ☐ '61 On The Rebound
- ☐ '61 San Antonio Rose

## CRANBERRIES, The
- ☐ '93 Linger ★
- ☐ '95 Ode To My Family
- ☐ '96 Salvation
- ☐ '96 When You're Gone
- ☐ '94 Zombie

## CRANE, Les
- ☐ '71 Desiderata

## CRASH TEST DUMMIES
- ☐ '94 Mmm Mmm Mmm Mmm ★

## CRAWFORD, Johnny
- ☐ '62 Cindy's Birthday
- ☐ '63 Proud
- ☐ '62 Rumors
- ☐ '62 Your Nose Is Gonna Grow

## CRAY, Robert, Band
- ☐ '86 Smoking Gun

## CRAZY ELEPHANT
- ☐ '69 Gimme Gimme Good Lovin'

## CRAZY TOWN
- ☐ '00 Butterfly ★

## CREAM
- ☐ '69 Badge
- ☐ '69 Crossroads
- ☐ '67 I Feel Free
- ☐ '68 Spoonful
- ☐ '67 Strange Brew
- ☐ '68 Sunshine Of Your Love ★
- ☐ '68 White Room

## CREED
- ☐ '99 Higher ★
- ☐ '97 My Own Prison
- ☐ '01 My Sacrifice ★
- ☐ '98 One
- ☐ '02 One Last Breath
- ☐ '98 Torn
- ☐ '00 What If
- ☐ '98 What's This Life For
- ☐ '00 With Arms Wide Open ★

## CREEDENCE CLEARWATER REVIVAL
- ☐ '69 Bad Moon Rising ★
- ☐ '69 Born On The Bayou
- ☐ '69 Commotion
- ☐ '69 Down On The Corner ★
- ☐ '69 Fortunate Son
- ☐ '69 Green River ★
- ☐ '71 Have You Ever Seen The Rain ★
- ☐ '71 Hey Tonight
- ☐ '70 I Heard It Through The Grapevine
- ☐ '68 I Put A Spell On You
- ☐ '69 Lodi
- ☐ '70 Long As I Can See The Light
- ☐ '70 Lookin' Out My Back Door ★
- ☐ '69 Proud Mary ★
- ☐ '70 Run Through The Jungle
- ☐ '72 Someday Never Comes
- ☐ '68 Suzie Q.
- ☐ '71 Sweet Hitch-Hiker
- ☐ '70 Travelin' Band ★
- ☐ '70 Up Around The Bend ★
- ☐ '70 Who'll Stop The Rain ★

## CRENSHAW, Marshall
- ☐ '82 Someday, Someway

## CRESCENDOS, The
- ☐ '58 Oh Julie

## CRESTS, The
- ☐ '59 Angels Listened In, The
- ☐ '61 Model Girl
- ☐ '59 Six Nights A Week
- ☐ '58 16 Candles ★
- ☐ '60 Step By Step
- ☐ '60 Trouble In Paradise
- ☐ '61 What A Surprise

## CREW-CUTS, The
- ☐ '55 Angels In The Sky
- ☐ '55 Chop Chop Boom
- ☐ '55 Don't Be Angry
- ☐ '55 Earth Angel
- ☐ '55 Gum Drop
- ☐ '55 Ko Ko Mo (I Love You So)
- ☐ '55 Mostly Martha
- ☐ '56 Seven Days
- ☐ '55 Story Untold, A
- ☐ '57 Young Love

## CREWE, Bob
- ☐ '66 Music To Watch Girls By

## CRICKETS, The — see HOLLY, Buddy

## CRITTERS, The
- ☐ '67 Don't Let The Rain Fall Down On Me
- ☐ '66 Mr. Dieingly Sad
- ☐ '66 Younger Girl

## CROCE, Jim
- ☐ '73 Bad, Bad Leroy Brown ★
- ☐ '73 I Got A Name
- ☐ '74 I'll Have To Say I Love You In A Song
- ☐ '73 One Less Set Of Footsteps
- ☐ '72 Operator (That's Not the Way it Feels)
- ☐ '73 Time In A Bottle ★
- ☐ '74 Workin' At The Car Wash Blues
- ☐ '72 You Don't Mess Around With Jim

## CROSBY, Bing
- ☐ '57 Around The World
- ☐ '56 True Love ★
  - *BING CROSBY & GRACE KELLY*
- ☐ '55 White Christmas

## CROSBY, David
- ☐ '93 Hero
  - *DAVID CROSBY & PHIL COLLINS*
- ☐ '72 Immigration Man
  - *GRAHAM NASH & DAVID CROSBY*

## CROSBY, STILLS & NASH (& YOUNG)
- ☐ '70 Almost Cut My Hair
- ☐ '88 American Dream
- ☐ '70 Carry On
- ☐ '77 Dark Star
- ☐ '77 Fair Game
- ☐ '88 Got It Made
- ☐ '70 Helpless
- ☐ '69 Helplessly Hoping
- ☐ '77 Just A Song Before I Go
- ☐ '69 Marrakesh Express
- ☐ '70 Ohio ★
- ☐ '70 Our House
- ☐ '82 Southern Cross
- ☐ '69 Suite: Judy Blue Eyes
- ☐ '70 Teach Your Children
- ☐ '82 Wasted On The Way
- ☐ '69 Wooden Ships
- ☐ '70 Woodstock

## CROSS, Christopher
- ☐ '83 All Right
- ☐ '81 Arthur's Theme (Best That You Can Do) ★
- ☐ '80 Never Be The Same
- ☐ '80 Ride Like The Wind ★
- ☐ '80 Sailing ★
- ☐ '81 Say You'll Be Mine
- ☐ '83 Think Of Laura

## CROSS COUNTRY
- ☐ '73 In The Midnight Hour

## CROSSFADE
- ☐ '04 Cold

## CROW
- ☐ '69 Evil Woman Don't Play Your Games With Me

## CROW, Sheryl
- ☐ '94 All I Wanna Do ★
- ☐ '95 Can't Cry Anymore
- ☐ '97 Change Would Do You Good, A
- ☐ '97 Everyday Is A Winding Road
- ☐ '03 First Cut Is The Deepest, The
- ☐ '96 If It Makes You Happy ★
- ☐ '94 Leaving Las Vegas
- ☐ '98 My Favorite Mistake
- ☐ '02 Picture ★
  *KID ROCK Feat. Sheryl Crow*
- ☐ '02 Soak Up The Sun
- ☐ '02 Steve McQueen
- ☐ '94 Strong Enough ★

## CROWDED HOUSE
- ☐ '87 Don't Dream It's Over ★
- ☐ '87 Something So Strong

## CROWELL, Rodney
- ☐ '80 Ashes By Now

## CRUCIAL CONFLICT
- ☐ '96 Hay

## CRUSADERS, The
- ☐ '79 Street Life

## CRYSTALS, The
- ☐ '63 Da Doo Ron Ron ★
- ☐ '62 He's A Rebel ★
- ☐ '62 He's Sure The Boy I Love
- ☐ '63 Then He Kissed Me
- ☐ '61 There's No Other (Like My Baby)
- ☐ '62 Uptown

## CUFF LINKS, The
- ☐ '69 Tracy

## CULT, The
- ☐ '89 Fire Woman

## CULTURE BEAT
- ☐ '93 Mr. Vain

## CULTURE CLUB
- ☐ '83 Church Of The Poison Mind
- ☐ '93 Crying Game, The
- ☐ '82 Do You Really Want To Hurt Me ★
- ☐ '83 I'll Tumble 4 Ya
- ☐ '84 It's A Miracle
- ☐ '83 Karma Chameleon ★
- ☐ '87 Live My Life
- ☐ '84 Miss Me Blind
- ☐ '84 Mistake No. 3
- ☐ '86 Move Away
- ☐ '83 Time (Clock Of The Heart)
- ☐ '84 War Song, The

## CUMMINGS, Burton
- ☐ '76 Stand Tall
- ☐ '81 You Saved My Soul

## CURB, Mike, Congregation
- ☐ '70 Burning Bridges

## CURE, The
- ☐ '85 Boys Don't Cry
- ☐ '89 Fascination Street
- ☐ '92 Friday I'm In Love
- ☐ '92 High
- ☐ '87 Just Like Heaven
- ☐ '92 Letter To Elise, A
- ☐ '89 Love Song
- ☐ '90 Never Enough
- ☐ '90 Pictures Of You
- ☐ '93 Purple Haze

## CUTTING CREW
- ☐ '87 (I Just) Died In Your Arms ★
- ☐ '87 I've Been In Love Before
- ☐ '87 One For The Mockingbird

## CYMARRON
- ☐ '71 Rings ★

## CYMBAL, Johnny
- ☐ '63 Mr. Bass Man
- ☐ '63 Teenage Heaven

## CYPRESS HILL
- ☐ '93 Insane In The Brain

## CYRKLE, The
- ☐ '66 Red Rubber Ball ★
- ☐ '66 Turn-Down Day

## CYRUS, Billy Ray
- ☐ '92 Achy Breaky Heart ★
- ☐ '98 Busy Man
- ☐ '92 Could've Been Me
- ☐ '93 In The Heart Of A Woman

# D

## DA BRAT
- ☐ '94 Fa All Y'all
- ☐ '94 Funkdafied
- ☐ '97 Ghetto Love
- ☐ '95 Give It 2 You
- ☐ '98 Party Continues, The
  *JD & DA BRAT*
- ☐ '96 Sittin' On Top Of The World
- ☐ '00 What'Chu Like

## DADDY DEWDROP
- ☐ '71 Chick-A-Boom (Don't Ya Jes' Love It)

## DADDY-O'S, The
- ☐ '58 Got A Match?

## DADDY YANKEE
- ☐ '04 Gasolina

## DALE, Alan
- ☐ '55 Cherry Pink (And Apple Blossom White)
- ☐ '55 Sweet And Gentle

## DALE, Dick
- ☐ '61 Let's Go Trippin'
- ☐ '62 Misirlou

## DALE & GRACE
- ☐ '63 I'm Leaving It Up To You
- ☐ '64 Stop And Think It Over

## DALTREY, Roger
- ☐ '85 After The Fire
- ☐ '80 Without Your Love

## DAMIAN, Michael
- ☐ '89 Cover Of Love
- ☐ '89 Rock On
- ☐ '89 Was It Nothing At All

## DAMIAN DAME
- ☐ '91 Exclusivity
- ☐ '91 Right Down To It

## DAMITA JO
- ☐ '61 I'll Be There
- ☐ '60 I'll Save The Last Dance For You

## DAMN YANKEES
- ☐ '90 Coming Of Age
- ☐ '92 Don't Tread On Me
- ☐ '90 High Enough ★
- ☐ '92 Mister Please
- ☐ '92 Where You Goin' Now

## DAMON('S), Liz, Orient Express
- ☐ '70 1900 Yesterday

## DAMONE, Vic
- ☐ '57 Affair To Remember (Our Love Affair)
- ☐ '56 On The Street Where You Live ★
- ☐ '65 You Were Only Fooling (While I Was Falling In Love)

## DANA, Vic
- ☐ '66 I Love You Drops
- ☐ '70 If I Never Knew Your Name
- ☐ '65 Red Roses For A Blue Lady
- ☐ '64 Shangri-La

## DANCER, PRANCER & NERVOUS
- ☐ '59 Happy Reindeer, The

## D'ANGELO
- ☐ '95 Brown Sugar
- ☐ '96 Lady
- ☐ '00 Untitled (How Does It Feel)

## DANIELS, Charlie, Band
- ☐ '79 Devil Went Down To Georgia, The ★
- ☐ '80 In America
- ☐ '80 Legend Of Wooley Swamp, The
- ☐ '75 Long Haired Country Boy
- ☐ '75 South's Gonna Do It, The
- ☐ '82 Still In Saigon
- ☐ '73 Uneasy Rider

## DANLEERS, The
- ☐ '58 One Summer Night

## DANNY & THE JUNIORS
- ☐ '57 At The Hop ★
- ☐ '58 Dottie
- ☐ '58 Rock And Roll Is Here To Stay
- ☐ '60 Twistin' U.S.A.

## DANNY WILSON
- ☐ '87 Mary's Prayer

## DANTÉ & THE EVERGREENS
- ☐ '60 Alley-Oop

## D'ARBY, Terence Trent
- ☐ '88 Dance Little Sister
- ☐ '88 Sign Your Name
- ☐ '88 Wishing Well ★

## DARIN, Bobby
- ☐ '60 Artificial Flowers
- ☐ '60 Beyond The Sea
- ☐ '60 Clementine
- ☐ '59 Dream Lover ★
- ☐ '58 Early In The Morning
- ☐ '63 18 Yellow Roses
- ☐ '62 If A Man Answers
- ☐ '66 If I Were A Carpenter
- ☐ '61 Irresistible You
- ☐ '61 Lazy River
- ☐ '59 Mack The Knife ★
- ☐ '66 Mame
- ☐ '61 Multiplication
- ☐ '61 Nature Boy
- ☐ '59 Plain Jane
- ☐ '58 Queen Of The Hop ★
- ☐ '58 Splish Splash ★
- ☐ '62 Things
- ☐ '62 What'd I Say
- ☐ '60 Won't You Come Home Bill Bailey
- ☐ '61 You Must Have Been A Beautiful Baby
- ☐ '63 You're The Reason I'm Living

## DARREN, James
- ☐ '67 All
- ☐ '62 Conscience
- ☐ '59 Gidget
- ☐ '61 Goodbye Cruel World
- ☐ '62 Her Royal Majesty
- ☐ '62 Mary's Little Lamb

## DARTELLS, The
- ☐ '63 Hot Pastrami

## DARUDE
- ☐ '01 Sandstorm

## DAS EFX
- ☐ '92 They Want EFX

## DASHBOARD CONFESSIONAL
- ☐ '04 Vindicated

## DAVID, Craig
- ☐ '01 Fill Me In
- ☐ '01 7 Days

## DAVID & DAVID
- ☐ '86 Welcome To The Boomtown

## DAVID & JONATHAN
- ☐ '66 Michelle

## DAVIDSON, Clay
- ☐ '00 Unconditional

## DAVIS, Alana
- ☐ '97 32 Flavors

## DAVIS, Mac
- ☐ '72 Baby Don't Get Hooked On Me ★
- ☐ '80 It's Hard To Be Humble
- ☐ '74 One Hell Of A Woman
- ☐ '74 Rock N' Roll (I Gave You The Best Years Of My Life)
- ☐ '74 Stop And Smell The Roses

## DAVIS, Paul
- ☐ '81 Cool Night
- ☐ '80 Do Right
- ☐ '77 I Go Crazy
- ☐ '74 Ride 'Em Cowboy
- ☐ '82 '65 Love Affair
- ☐ '76 Superstar
- ☐ '78 Sweet Life

## DAVIS, Sammy Jr.
- ☐ '72 Candy Man, The ★
- ☐ '67 Don't Blame The Children
- ☐ '68 I've Gotta Be Me
- ☐ '55 Love Me Or Leave Me
- ☐ '63 Shelter Of Your Arms, The
- ☐ '55 Something's Gotta Give
- ☐ '55 That Old Black Magic
- ☐ '62 What Kind Of Fool Am I

## DAVIS, Skeeter
- ☐ '63 End Of The World, The ★
- ☐ '60 (I Can't Help You) I'm Falling Too
- ☐ '63 I Can't Stay Mad At You
- ☐ '60 My Last Date (With You)

## DAVIS, Spencer, Group
- ☐ '66 Gimme Some Lovin' ★
- ☐ '67 I'm A Man

## DAVIS, Tyrone
- ☐ '82 Are You Serious
- ☐ '68 Can I Change My Mind
- ☐ '76 Give It Up (Turn It Loose)
- ☐ '69 Is It Something You've Got
- ☐ '73 There It Is
- ☐ '70 Turn Back The Hands Of Time
- ☐ '75 Turning Point

## DAWN — see ORLANDO, Tony

## DAY, Bobby
- ☐ '58 Over And Over
- ☐ '58 Rock-in Robin ★

## DAY, Doris
- ☐ '58 Everybody Loves A Lover
- ☐ '55 I'll Never Stop Loving You
- ☐ '55 Love Me Or Leave Me
- ☐ '56 Whatever Will Be, Will Be (Que Sera, Sera) ★

## DAY, Howie
- ☐ '05 Collide

## DAY, Morris
- ☐ '88 Fishnet
- ☐ '85 Oak Tree, The

## DAYNE, Taylor
- ☐ '93 Can't Get Enough Of Your Love
- ☐ '88 Don't Rush Me
- ☐ '90 Heart Of Stone
- ☐ '88 I'll Always Love You
- ☐ '90 I'll Be Your Shelter
- ☐ '90 Love Will Lead You Back ★
- ☐ '88 Prove Your Love
- ☐ '87 Tell It To My Heart
- ☐ '89 With Every Beat Of My Heart

## DAYS OF THE NEW
- ☐ '98 Down Town, The
- ☐ '99 Enemy
- ☐ '98 Shelf In The Room
- ☐ '97 Touch, Peel And Stand

## DAZZ BAND
- ☐ '82 Let It Whip ★

## DC TALK
- ☐ '95 Jesus Freak
- ☐ '96 Just Between You And Me

## DEADEYE DICK
- ☐ '94 New Age Girl

## DEAD OR ALIVE
- ☐ '86 Brand New Lover
- ☐ '85 You Spin Me Round (Like A Record)

## DEAL, Bill, & The Rhondels
- ☐ '69 I've Been Hurt
- ☐ '69 May I
- ☐ '69 What Kind Of Fool Do You Think I Am

## DEAN, Billy
- ☐ '92 If There Hadn't Been You
- ☐ '05 Let Them Be Little
- ☐ '90 Only Here For A Little While
- ☐ '91 Somewhere In My Broken Heart

## DEAN, Jimmy
- ☐ '61 Big Bad John ★
- ☐ '62 Cajun Queen, The
- ☐ '62 Dear Ivan
- ☐ '76 I.O.U.
- ☐ '62 Little Black Book
- ☐ '62 P.T. 109
- ☐ '62 Steel Men
- ☐ '62 To A Sleeping Beauty

## DEAN & JEAN
- ☐ '64 Hey Jean, Hey Dean
- ☐ '63 Tra La La La Suzy

## DeBARGE
- ☐ '83 All This Love
- ☐ '83 I Like It
- ☐ '85 Rhythm Of The Night ★

- □ '83 Time Will Reveal
- □ '85 Who's Holding Donna Now

## DeBARGE, Chico
- □ '86 Talk To Me

## DeBARGE, El
- □ '86 Who's Johnny

## DeBURGH, Chris
- □ '83 Don't Pay The Ferryman
- □ '84 High On Emotion
- □ '87 Lady In Red, The ★

## DeCASTRO SISTERS, The
- □ '55 Boom Boom Boomerang
- □ '55 Teach Me Tonight

## DEE, Jimmy
- □ '58 Henrietta

## DEE, Joey, & the Starliters
- □ '62 Hey, Let's Twist
- □ '61 Peppermint Twist ★
- □ '62 Shout
- □ '62 What Kind Of Love Is This

## DEE, Kiki
- □ '76 Don't Go Breaking My Heart ★
  *ELTON JOHN & KIKI DEE*
- □ '74 I've Got The Music In Me

## DEE, Lenny
- □ '55 Plantation Boogie

## DEE, Tommy
- □ '59 Three Stars

## DEEE-LITE
- □ '90 Groove Is In The Heart

## DEELE, The
- □ '83 Body Talk
- □ '88 Two Occasions

## DEEP BLUE SOMETHING
- □ '95 Breakfast At Tiffany's ★

## DEEP PURPLE
- □ '70 Black Night
- □ '72 Highway Star
- □ '68 Hush
- □ '68 Kentucky Woman
- □ '74 Might Just Take Your Life
- □ '69 River Deep-Mountain High
- □ '73 Smoke On The Water ★
- □ '72 Space Truckin'
- □ '71 Strange Kind Of Woman
- □ '73 Woman From Tokyo

## DEES, Rick
- □ '76 Disco Duck

## DEFAULT
- □ '01 Wasting My Time

## DEF LEPPARD
- □ '87 Animal
- □ '88 Armageddon It
- □ '84 Bringin' On The Heartbreak
- □ '83 Foolin'
- □ '92 Have You Ever Needed Someone So Bad
- □ '88 Hysteria
- □ '92 Let's Get Rocked ★
- □ '88 Love Bites
- □ '92 Make Love Like A Man
- □ '93 Miss You In A Heartbeat
- □ '83 Photograph
- □ '88 Pour Some Sugar On Me ★
- □ '99 Promises
- □ '83 Rock Of Ages
- □ '89 Rocket
- □ '92 Stand Up (Kick Love Into Motion)
- □ '93 Two Steps Behind

## DeFRANCO FAMILY
- □ '73 Abra-Ca-Dabra
- □ '73 Heartbeat - It's A Lovebeat
- □ '74 Save The Last Dance For Me

## DEFTONES
- □ '00 Change (In The House Of Flies)

## DeGARMO, Diana
- □ '04 Dreams

## DEGRAW, Gavin
- □ '05 I Don't Want To Be ★

## DÉJA
- □ '87 You And Me Tonight

## DeJOHN SISTERS
- □ '55 (My Baby Don't Love Me) No More

## DEKKER, Desmond, & The Aces
- □ '69 Israelites

## DEL AMITRI
- □ '92 Always The Last To Know
- □ '90 Kiss This Thing Goodbye
- □ '95 Roll To Me

## DELANEY & BONNIE
- □ '70 Comin' Home
- □ '71 Never Ending Song Of Love
- □ '71 Only You Know And I Know
- □ '70 Soul Shake

## DE LA SOUL
- □ '89 Me Myself And I

## DELEGATES, The
- □ '72 Convention '72

## DELFONICS, The
- □ '68 Break Your Promise
- □ '70 Didn't I (Blow Your Mind This Time)
- □ '68 La - La - Means I Love You
- □ '68 Ready Or Not Here I Come (Can't Hide From Love)
- □ '70 Trying To Make A Fool Of Me
- □ '69 You Got Yours And I'll Get Mine

## DELINQUENT HABITS
- □ '96 Tres Delinquentes

## DELLS, The
- ☐ '68 Always Together
- ☐ '68 Does Anybody Know I'm Here
- ☐ '73 Give Your Baby A Standing Ovation
- ☐ '69 I Can Sing A Rainbow/Love Is Blue
- ☐ '71 Love We Had (Stays On My Mind)
- ☐ '69 Oh, What A Night
- ☐ '68 Stay In My Corner
- ☐ '68 There Is

## DELL-VIKINGS, The
- ☐ '57 Come Go With Me ★
- ☐ '57 Cool Shake
- ☐ '57 Whispering Bells

## DEMENSIONS, The
- ☐ '60 Over The Rainbow

## DENNIS, Cathy
- ☐ '89 C'mon And Get My Love
  *D MOB Introducing Cathy Dennis*
- ☐ '90 Just Another Dream
- ☐ '91 Too Many Walls
- ☐ '91 Touch Me (All Night Long)
- ☐ '92 You Lied To Me

## DENNY, Martin
- ☐ '59 Enchanted Sea, The
- ☐ '59 Quiet Village

## DENVER, John
- ☐ '74 Annie's Song ★
- ☐ '74 Back Home Again
- ☐ '75 Calypso
- ☐ '75 Fly Away
- ☐ '77 How Can I Leave You Again
- ☐ '75 I'm Sorry
- ☐ '76 Looking For Space
- ☐ '77 My Sweet Lady
- ☐ '72 Rocky Mountain High
- ☐ '82 Shanghai Breezes
- ☐ '81 Some Days Are Diamonds (Some Days Are Stone)
- ☐ '74 Sunshine On My Shoulders ★
- ☐ '74 Sweet Surrender
- ☐ '71 Take Me Home, Country Roads ★
- ☐ '75 Thank God I'm A Country Boy ★

## DEODATO
- ☐ '73 Also Sprach Zarathustra (2001)

## DEPECHE MODE
- ☐ '90 Enjoy The Silence
- ☐ '93 I Feel You
- ☐ '97 It's No Good
- ☐ '87 Never Let Me Down Again
- ☐ '85 People Are People ★
- ☐ '89 Personal Jesus ★
- ☐ '90 Policy Of Truth
- ☐ '87 Strangelove
- ☐ '93 Walking In My Shoes

## DEREK
- ☐ '68 Cinnamon

## DEREK & THE DOMINOS — see CLAPTON, Eric

## DERRINGER, Rick
- ☐ '74 Rock And Roll, Hoochie Koo

## DeSARIO, Teri
- ☐ '79 Yes, I'm Ready
  *TERI DeSARIO with K.C.*

## DeSHANNON, Jackie
- ☐ '69 Love Will Find A Way
- ☐ '69 Put A Little Love In Your Heart
- ☐ '65 What The World Needs Now Is Love

## DESMOND, Johnny
- ☐ '55 Play Me Hearts And Flowers (I Wanna Cry)
- ☐ '55 Sixteen Tons
- ☐ '55 Yellow Rose Of Texas, The

## DES'REE
- ☐ '94 You Gotta Be ★

## DESTINY'S CHILD
- ☐ '99 Bills, Bills, Bills ★
- ☐ '01 Bootylicious ★
- ☐ '99 Bug A Boo
- ☐ '01 Emotion
- ☐ '05 Girl
- ☐ '00 Independent Women ★
- ☐ '00 Jumpin', Jumpin' ★
- ☐ '04 Lose My Breath ★
- ☐ '97 No, No, No ★
- ☐ '99 Say My Name ★
- ☐ '05 Soldier ★
- ☐ '01 Survivor ★

## DETERGENTS, The
- ☐ '64 Leader Of The Laundromat

## DETROIT EMERALDS
- ☐ '72 Baby Let Me Take You (In My Arms)
- ☐ '71 Do Me Right
- ☐ '72 You Want It, You Got It

## DeVAUGHN, William
- ☐ '74 Be Thankful For What You Got

## DEVICE
- ☐ '86 Hanging On A Heart Attack

## DEVO
- ☐ '80 Whip It ★
- ☐ '81 Working In The Coal Mine

## DeVORZON, Barry, & Perry Botkin, Jr.
- ☐ '76 Nadia's Theme (The Young And The Restless)

## DEVOTIONS, The
- ☐ '64 Rip Van Winkle

## DEXYS MIDNIGHT RUNNERS
- ☐ '83 Come On Eileen ★

## DeYOUNG, Cliff
- ☐ '74 My Sweet Lady

## DeYOUNG, Dennis
- ☐ '84 Desert Moon

## DIAMOND, Neil
- ☐ '81 America
- ☐ '73 Be
- ☐ '69 Brother Love's Travelling Salvation Show
- ☐ '66 Cherry, Cherry
- ☐ '73 "Cherry Cherry" from Hot August Night
- ☐ '70 Cracklin' Rosie ★
- ☐ '77 Desirée
- ☐ '70 Do It
- ☐ '71 Done Too Soon
- ☐ '79 Forever In Blue Jeans
- ☐ '67 Girl, You'll Be A Woman Soon
- ☐ '70 He Ain't Heavy...He's My Brother
- ☐ '82 Heartlight
- ☐ '81 Hello Again
- ☐ '69 Holly Holy
- ☐ '71 I Am...I Said
- ☐ '66 I Got The Feelin' (Oh No No)
- ☐ '67 I Thank The Lord For The Night Time
- ☐ '83 I'm Alive
- ☐ '75 I've Been This Way Before
- ☐ '76 If You Know What I Mean
- ☐ '67 Kentucky Woman
- ☐ '74 Longfellow Serenade
- ☐ '80 Love On The Rocks ★
- ☐ '82 On The Way To The Sky
- ☐ '72 Play Me
- ☐ '68 Red Red Wine
- ☐ '79 Say Maybe
- ☐ '79 September Morn'
- ☐ '70 Shilo
- ☐ '66 Solitary Man
- ☐ '72 Song Sung Blue ★
- ☐ '70 Soolaimón (African Trilogy II)
- ☐ '71 Stones
- ☐ '69 Sweet Caroline ★
- ☐ '72 Walk On Water
- ☐ '81 Yesterday's Songs
- ☐ '78 You Don't Bring Me Flowers ★
  *BARBRA STREISAND & NEIL DIAMOND*
- ☐ '67 You Got To Me

## DIAMOND RIO
- ☐ '02 Beautiful Mess
- ☐ '97 How Your Love Makes Me Feel
- ☐ '02 I Believe
- ☐ '98 Imagine That
- ☐ '92 In A Week Or Two
- ☐ '94 Love A Little Stronger
- ☐ '91 Meet In The Middle
- ☐ '92 Norma Jean Riley
- ☐ '01 One More Day
- ☐ '98 Unbelievable
- ☐ '95 Walkin' Away

## DIAMONDS, The
- ☐ '56 Church Bells May Ring, The
- ☐ '58 High Sign
- ☐ '56 Ka-Ding-Dong
- ☐ '58 Kathy-O
- ☐ '57 Little Darlin' ★
- ☐ '56 Love, Love, Love
- ☐ '61 One Summer Night

- ☐ '59 She Say (Oom Dooby Doom)
- ☐ '57 Silhouettes
- ☐ '56 Soft Summer Breeze
- ☐ '57 Stroll, The
- ☐ '58 Walking Along
- ☐ '56 Why Do Fools Fall In Love
- ☐ '57 Words Of Love
- ☐ '57 Zip Zip

## DIBANGO, Manu
- ☐ '73 Soul Makossa

## DICK & DEEDEE
- ☐ '61 Mountain's High, The ★
- ☐ '62 Tell Me
- ☐ '64 Thou Shalt Not Steal
- ☐ '63 Turn Around
- ☐ '63 Young And In Love

## DICKENS, "Little" Jimmy
- ☐ '65 May The Bird Of Paradise Fly Up Your Nose

## DICKY DOO & THE DON'TS
- ☐ '58 Click-Clack
- ☐ '58 Nee Nee Na Na Na Na Nu Nu

## DIDDLEY, Bo
- ☐ '55 Bo Diddley ★
- ☐ '55 I'm A Man
- ☐ '60 Road Runner
- ☐ '59 Say Man
- ☐ '57 Who Do You Love?
- ☐ '62 You Can't Judge A Book By The Cover

## DIDO
- ☐ '01 Thankyou ★
- ☐ '03 White Flag

## DIESEL
- ☐ '81 Sausalito Summernight

## DIFFIE, Joe
- ☐ '95 Bigger Than The Beatles
- ☐ '90 Home
- ☐ '91 If The Devil Danced (In Empty Pockets)
- ☐ '90 If You Want Me To
- ☐ '00 It's Always Somethin'
- ☐ '91 New Way (To Light Up An Old Flame)
- ☐ '99 Night To Remember, A
- ☐ '94 Pickup Man
- ☐ '93 Prop Me Up Beside The Jukebox (If I Die)
- ☐ '95 So Help Me Girl
- ☐ '94 Third Rock From The Sun

## DIGABLE PLANETS
- ☐ '93 Rebirth Of Slick (Cool Like Dat)

## DIGITAL UNDERGROUND
- ☐ '90 Humpty Dance, The ★
- ☐ '91 Kiss You Back

## DINNING, Mark
- ☐ '59 Teen Angel ★

## DINO
- ☐ '90 Gentle
- ☐ '89 I Like It
- ☐ '93 Ooh Child
- ☐ '90 Romeo
- ☐ '89 Sunshine

## DINO, Kenny
- ☐ '61 Your Ma Said You Cried In Your Sleep Last Night

## DINO, Paul
- ☐ '61 Ginnie Bell

## DINO, DESI & BILLY
- ☐ '65 I'm A Fool
- ☐ '65 Not The Lovin' Kind
- ☐ '65 Rebel Kind, The

## DINOSAUR JR.
- ☐ '94 Feel The Pain

## DION
- ☐ '68 Abraham, Martin And John
- ☐ '63 Be Careful Of Stones That You Throw
- ☐ '63 Donna The Prima Donna
- ☐ '63 Drip Drop
- ☐ '61 Havin' Fun
- ☐ '62 (I Was) Born To Cry
- ☐ '62 Little Diane
- ☐ '60 Lonely Teenager
- ☐ '62 Love Came To Me
- ☐ '62 Lovers Who Wander
- ☐ '61 Majestic, The
- ☐ '63 Ruby Baby ★
- ☐ '61 Runaround Sue ★
- ☐ '63 Sandy
- ☐ '63 This Little Girl
- ☐ '61 Wanderer, The ★

## DION & THE BELMONTS
- ☐ '58 Don't Pity Me
- ☐ '59 Every Little Thing I Do
- ☐ '58 I Wonder Why
- ☐ '60 In The Still Of The Night
- ☐ '58 No One Knows
- ☐ '59 Teenager In Love, A ★
- ☐ '60 When You Wish Upon A Star
- ☐ '59 Where Or When

## DION, Celine
- ☐ '97 All By Myself
- ☐ '92 Beauty And The Beast ★
  *CELINE DION & PEABO BRYSON*
- ☐ '96 Because You Loved Me ★
- ☐ '03 Have You Ever Been In Love
- ☐ '98 I'm Your Angel ★
  *R. KELLY & CELINE DION*
- ☐ '91 (If There Was) Any Other Way
- ☐ '92 If You Asked Me To ★
- ☐ '96 It's All Coming Back To Me Now ★
- ☐ '92 Love Can Move Mountains
- ☐ '94 Misled
- ☐ '98 My Heart Will Go On (Love Theme From 'Titanic') ★
- ☐ '02 New Day Has Come, A

- ☐ '92 Nothing Broken But My Heart
- ☐ '93 Power Of Love, The ★
- ☐ '99 That's The Way It Is
- ☐ '98 To Love You More
- ☐ '93 When I Fall In Love
  *CELINE DION & CLIVE GRIFFIN*
- ☐ '90 Where Does My Heart Beat Now ★

## DIRE STRAITS
- ☐ '91 Calling Elvis
- ☐ '91 Heavy Fuel
- ☐ '85 Money For Nothing ★
- ☐ '86 So Far Away
- ☐ '79 Sultans Of Swing ★
- ☐ '85 Walk Of Life ★

## DIRKSEN, Senator Everett McKinley
- ☐ '66 Gallant Men

## DIRTY VEGAS
- ☐ '02 Days Go By ★

## DISCO TEX & HIS SEX-O-LETTES
- ☐ '74 Get Dancin'
- ☐ '75 I Wanna Dance Wit' Choo (Doo Dat Dance)

## DISHWALLA
- ☐ '96 Counting Blue Cars

## DISTURBED
- ☐ '02 Prayer

## DIVINE
- ☐ '98 Lately ★
- ☐ '99 One More Try

## DIVINYLS
- ☐ '91 I Touch Myself

## DIXIEBELLES, The
- ☐ '63 (Down At) Papa Joe's
- ☐ '64 Southtown, U.S.A.

## DIXIE CHICKS
- ☐ '99 Cowboy Take Me Away
- ☐ '00 Goodbye Earl
- ☐ '01 If I Fall You're Going Down With Me
- ☐ '02 Landslide
- ☐ '02 Long Time Gone
- ☐ '99 Ready To Run
- ☐ '98 There's Your Trouble
- ☐ '02 Travelin' Soldier
- ☐ '98 Wide Open Spaces
- ☐ '00 Without You
- ☐ '99 You Were Mine

## DIXIE CUPS, The
- ☐ '64 Chapel Of Love ★
- ☐ '65 Iko Iko
- ☐ '64 People Say
- ☐ '64 You Should Have Seen The Way He Looked At Me

## D.J. JAZZY JEFF & THE FRESH PRINCE
- ☐ '93 Boom! Shake The Room
- ☐ '88 Nightmare On My Street, A

□ '88 Parents Just Don't Understand
□ '91 Ring My Bell
□ '91 Summertime

## DJ KOOL
□ '97 Let Me Clear My Throat

## DJ SAMMY & YANOU
□ '02 Heaven ★

## DMX
□ '98 Get At Me Dog
□ '00 Party Up (Up In Here)
□ '99 Ruff Ryders' Anthem

## DOBKINS, Carl Jr.
□ '59 Lucky Devil
□ '59 My Heart Is An Open Book

## DR. BUZZARD'S ORIGINAL SAVANNAH BAND
□ '76 Whispering/Cherchez La Femme/Se Si Bon

## DR. DRE
□ '93 Dre Day
  *DR. DRE/SNOOP DOGGY DOGG*
□ '00 Forgot About Dre
□ '95 Keep Their Heads Ringin'
□ '93 Let Me Ride
□ '00 Next Episode, The
□ '93 Nuthin' But A "G" Thang ★
  *DR. DRE/SNOOP DOGGY DOGG (above 2)*

## DR. HOOK
□ '82 Baby Makes Her Blue Jeans Talk
□ '79 Better Love Next Time
□ '72 Cover Of "Rolling Stone", The
□ '80 Girls Can Get It
□ '76 Little Bit More, A
□ '76 Only Sixteen
□ '80 Sexy Eyes
□ '78 Sharing The Night Together
□ '72 Sylvia's Mother
□ '79 When You're In Love With A Beautiful Woman

## DR. JOHN
□ '73 Right Place Wrong Time

## DOGGETT, Bill
□ '58 Hold It
□ '56 Honky Tonk ★
□ '56 Slow Walk
□ '57 Soft

## DOG'S EYE VIEW
□ '96 Everything Falls Apart

## DOKKEN
□ '83 Breaking The Chains

## DOLBY, Thomas
□ '83 She Blinded Me With Science

## DOMINO
□ '93 Getto Jam
□ '94 Sweet Potatoe Pie

## DOMINO, Fats
□ '55 Ain't That A Shame ★
□ '61 Ain't That Just Like A Woman
□ '55 All By Myself
□ '59 Be My Guest
□ '57 Big Beat, The
□ '57 Blue Monday ★
□ '56 Blueberry Hill ★
□ '56 Bo Weevil
□ '60 Country Boy
□ '60 Don't Come Knockin'
□ '61 Fell In Love On Monday
□ '56 Honey Chile
□ '59 I Want To Walk You Home
□ '57 I Want You To Know
□ '59 I'm Gonna Be A Wheel Some Day
□ '56 I'm In Love Again
□ '59 I'm Ready
□ '57 I'm Walkin'
□ '61 It Keeps Rainin'
□ '57 It's You I Love
□ '61 Let The Four Winds Blow
□ '56 My Blue Heaven
□ '60 My Girl Josephine
□ '60 Natural Born Lover
□ '55 Poor Me
□ '60 Put Your Arms Around Me Honey
□ '63 Red Sails In The Sunset
□ '61 Shu Rah
□ '58 Sick And Tired
□ '60 Three Nights A Week
□ '57 Valley Of Tears
□ '57 Wait And See
□ '60 Walking To New Orleans ★
□ '61 What A Party
□ '61 What A Price
□ '57 When I See You
□ '56 When My Dreamboat Comes Home
□ '58 Whole Lotta Loving
□ '62 You Win Again

## DONALDS, Andru
□ '94 Mishale

## DONALDSON, Bo, & The Heywoods
□ '74 Billy, Don't Be A Hero ★
□ '74 Heartbreak Kid, The
□ '74 Who Do You Think You Are

## DON & JUAN
□ '62 What's Your Name

## DONEGAN, Lonnie, & His Skiffle Group
□ '61 Does Your Chewing Gum Lose It's Flavor (On The Bedpost Over Night)
□ '56 Rock Island Line ★

## DONNER, Ral
□ '61 Girl Of My Best Friend
□ '61 Please Don't Go
□ '61 She's Everything (I Wanted You To Be)
□ '62 (What A Sad Way) To Love Someone
□ '61 You Don't Know What You've Got (Until You Lose It)

## DONNIE & THE DREAMERS
- ☐ '61 Count Every Star

## DONOVAN
- ☐ '69 Atlantis
- ☐ '65 Catch The Wind
- ☐ '67 Epistle To Dippy
- ☐ '69 Goo Goo Barabajagal (Love Is Hot)
- ☐ '68 Hurdy Gurdy Man
- ☐ '68 Jennifer Juniper
- ☐ '68 Lalena
- ☐ '66 Mellow Yellow ★
- ☐ '66 Sunshine Superman ★
- ☐ '67 There Is A Mountain
- ☐ '69 To Susan On The West Coast Waiting
- ☐ '67 Wear Your Love Like Heaven

## DOOBIE BROTHERS, The
- ☐ '74 Another Park, Another Sunday
- ☐ '74 Black Water ★
- ☐ '73 China Grove ★
- ☐ '91 Dangerous
- ☐ '79 Dependin' On You
- ☐ '89 Doctor, The
- ☐ '74 Eyes Of Silver
- ☐ '76 It Keeps You Runnin'
- ☐ '72 Jesus Is Just Alright
- ☐ '72 Listen To The Music
- ☐ '73 Long Train Runnin'
- ☐ '79 Minute By Minute
- ☐ '89 Need A Little Taste Of Love
- ☐ '80 One Step Closer
- ☐ '80 Real Love
- ☐ '72 Rockin' Down The Highway
- ☐ '73 South City Midnight Lady
- ☐ '75 Sweet Maxine
- ☐ '75 Take Me In Your Arms (Rock Me)
- ☐ '76 Takin' It To The Streets
- ☐ '79 What A Fool Believes ★
- ☐ '77 You Belong To Me

## DO OR DIE
- ☐ '96 Po Pimp

## DOORS, The
- ☐ '67 Alabama Song (Whiskey Bar)
- ☐ '67 Back Door Man
- ☐ '67 Break On Through (To The Other Side)
- ☐ '67 Crystal Ship
- ☐ '67 End, The
- ☐ '68 Five To One
- ☐ '68 Hello, I Love You ★
- ☐ '71 L.A. Woman
- ☐ '67 Light My Fire ★
- ☐ '71 Love Her Madly
- ☐ '67 Love Me Two Times
- ☐ '67 Moonlight Drive
- ☐ '67 People Are Strange
- ☐ '71 Riders On The Storm
- ☐ '70 Roadhouse Blues
- ☐ '67 Strange Days
- ☐ '69 Tell All The People
- ☐ '68 Touch Me
- ☐ '68 Unknown Soldier, The
- ☐ '67 When The Music's Over

- ☐ '69 Wishful Sinful

## DORE, Charlie
- ☐ '80 Pilot Of The Airwaves

## DORMAN, Harold
- ☐ '60 Mountain Of Love

## DORSEY, Jimmy, Orchestra
- ☐ '57 June Night
- ☐ '57 So Rare ★

## DORSEY, Lee
- ☐ '61 Do-Re-Mi
- ☐ '66 Holy Cow
- ☐ '65 Ride Your Pony
- ☐ '66 Working In The Coal Mine
- ☐ '61 Ya Ya

## DORSEY, Tommy, Orchestra
- ☐ '58 Tea For Two Cha Cha

## DOUBLE
- ☐ '86 Captain Of Her Heart, The

## DOUGLAS, Carl
- ☐ '74 Kung Fu Fighting ★

## DOUGLAS, Carol
- ☐ '74 Doctor's Orders

## DOUGLAS, Mike
- ☐ '65 Men In My Little Girl's Life, The

## DOVE, Ronnie
- ☐ '66 Cry
- ☐ '66 Happy Summer Days
- ☐ '66 I Really Don't Want To Know
- ☐ '65 I'll Make All Your Dreams Come True
- ☐ '65 Kiss Away
- ☐ '66 Let's Start All Over Again
- ☐ '65 Little Bit Of Heaven, A
- ☐ '65 One Kiss For Old Times' Sake
- ☐ '64 Right Or Wrong
- ☐ '64 Say You
- ☐ '66 When Liking Turns To Loving

## DOVELLS, The
- ☐ '61 Bristol Stomp ★
- ☐ '62 Bristol Twistin' Annie
- ☐ '62 (Do The New) Continental
- ☐ '62 Hully Gully Baby
- ☐ '63 You Can't Sit Down

## DOWELL, Joe
- ☐ '62 Little Red Rented Rowboat
- ☐ '61 Wooden Heart ★

## DOZIER, Lamont
- ☐ '74 Fish Ain't Bitin'
- ☐ '73 Trying To Hold On To My Woman

## DRAKE, Charlie
- ☐ '62 My Boomerang Won't Come Back

## DRAKE, Pete
- ☐ '64 Forever

## DRAMATICS, The
- ☐ '76  Be My Girl
- ☐ '72  In The Rain
- ☐ '71  Whatcha See Is Whatcha Get ★

## DRAPER, Rusty
- ☐ '55  Are You Satisfied?
- ☐ '57  Freight Train
- ☐ '56  In The Middle Of The House
- ☐ '57  Let's Go Calypso
- ☐ '55  Seventeen
- ☐ '55  Shifting, Whispering Sands, The

## DREAM
- ☐ '00  He Loves U Not ★
- ☐ '01  This Is Me

## DREAM ACADEMY, The
- ☐ '85  Life In A Northern Town ★
- ☐ '86  Love Parade, The

## DREAMLOVERS, The
- ☐ '61  When We Get Married

## DREAM WEAVERS, The
- ☐ '55  It's Almost Tomorrow

## DRIFTERS, The
- ☐ '55  Adorable
- ☐ '59  Dance With Me
- ☐ '60  I Count The Tears
- ☐ '63  I'll Take You Home
- ☐ '64  I've Got Sand In My Shoes
- ☐ '59  (If You Cry) True Love, True Love
- ☐ '63  On Broadway
- ☐ '61  Please Stay
- ☐ '64  Saturday Night At The Movies
- ☐ '60  Save The Last Dance For Me ★
- ☐ '61  Some Kind Of Wonderful
- ☐ '61  Sweets For My Sweet
- ☐ '59  There Goes My Baby ★
- ☐ '60  This Magic Moment
- ☐ '64  Under The Boardwalk
- ☐ '62  Up On The Roof ★
- ☐ '55  What'cha Gonna Do
- ☐ '62  When My Little Girl Is Smiling
- ☐ '54  White Christmas

## D.R.S.
- ☐ '93  Gangsta Lean

## DRU HILL
- ☐ '98  How Deep Is Your Love ★
- ☐ '02  I Should Be...
- ☐ '97  In My Bed
- ☐ '97  Never Make A Promise
- ☐ '96  Tell Me
- ☐ '98  These Are The Times
- ☐ '97  We're Not Making Love No More

## DRUSKY, Roy
- ☐ '61  Three Hearts In A Tangle

## D12
- ☐ '04  How Come
- ☐ '04  My Band ★ ,
- ☐ '01  Purple Hills

## DUALS
- ☐ '61  Stick Shift

## DUBS, The
- ☐ '57  Could This Be Magic

## DUDLEY, Dave
- ☐ '63  Six Days On The Road

## DUFF, Hilary
- ☐ '04  Come Clean

## DUICE
- ☐ '93  Dazzey Duks

## DUKE, George
- ☐ '77  Reach For It
- ☐ '81  Sweet Baby
  - *STANLEY CLARKE/GEORGE DUKE*

## DUKE, Patty
- ☐ '65  Don't Just Stand There
- ☐ '65  Say Something Funny

## DUNDAS, David
- ☐ '76  Jeans On

## DUNN, Holly
- ☐ '86  Daddy's Hands
- ☐ '90  You Really Had Me Going

## DUPREE, Robbie
- ☐ '80  Hot Rod Hearts
- ☐ '80  Steal Away

## DUPREES, The
- ☐ '63  Have You Heard
- ☐ '62  My Own True Love
- ☐ '63  Why Don't You Believe Me
- ☐ '62  You Belong To Me

## DUPRI, Jermaine
- ☐ '98  Party Continues, The
  - *JD & DA BRAT*
- ☐ '01  Welcome To Atlanta
  - *JERMAINE DUPRI • LUDACRIS*

## DURAN DURAN
- ☐ '88  All She Wants Is
- ☐ '93  Come Undone
- ☐ '83  Girls On Film
- ☐ '82  Hungry Like The Wolf ★
- ☐ '88  I Don't Want Your Love
- ☐ '83  Is There Something I Should Know
- ☐ '84  New Moon On Monday
- ☐ '86  Notorious ★
- ☐ '92  Ordinary World ★
- ☐ '84  Reflex, The ★
- ☐ '83  Rio
- ☐ '85  Save A Prayer
- ☐ '87  Skin Trade
- ☐ '83  Union Of The Snake
- ☐ '85  View To A Kill, A ★
- ☐ '84  Wild Boys, The ★

## DYKE & THE BLAZERS
- ☐ '69 Let A Woman Be A Woman - Let A Man Be A Man
- ☐ '69 We Got More Soul

## DYLAN, Bob
- ☐ '68 All Along The Watchtower
- ☐ '65 Ballad Of A Thin Man
- ☐ '63 Blowin' In The Wind ★
- ☐ '66 Can You Please Crawl Out Your Window?
- ☐ '65 Desolation Row
- ☐ '63 Don't Think Twice, It's All Right
- ☐ '89 Everything Is Broken
- ☐ '73 Fool Such As I
- ☐ '74 Forever Young
- ☐ '71 George Jackson
- ☐ '79 Gotta Serve Somebody
- ☐ '65 Highway 61 Revisited
- ☐ '75 Hurricane
- ☐ '69 I Threw It All Away
- ☐ '66 I Want You
- ☐ '76 Isis
- ☐ '64 It Ain't Me Babe
- ☐ '65 It's All Over Now, Baby Blue
- ☐ '66 Just Like A Woman
- ☐ '73 Knockin' On Heaven's Door
- ☐ '69 Lay Lady Lay
- ☐ '67 Leopard-Skin Pill-Box Hat
- ☐ '65 Like A Rolling Stone ★
- ☐ '65 Maggie's Farm
- ☐ '74 Most Likely You Go Your Way (And I'll Go Mine)
- ☐ '76 Mozambique
- ☐ '65 Mr. Tambourine Man
- ☐ '64 My Back Pages
- ☐ '74 On A Night Like This
- ☐ '65 Positively 4th Street
- ☐ '66 Rainy Day Women #12 & 35 ★
- ☐ '66 Stuck Inside Of Mobile With The Memphis Blues Again
- ☐ '65 Subterranean Homesick Blues
- ☐ '75 Tangled Up In Blue
- ☐ '64 Times They Are A-Changin', The ★
- ☐ '66 Visions Of Johanna
- ☐ '71 Watching The River Flow
- ☐ '74 You Angel You

## DYSON, Ronnie
- ☐ '70 (If You Let Me Make Love To You Then) Why Can't I Touch You?
- ☐ '73 One Man Band (Plays All Alone)

# E

## EAGLES
- ☐ '75 After The Thrill Is Gone
- ☐ '74 Already Gone
- ☐ '74 Best Of My Love ★
- ☐ '73 Desperado
- ☐ '73 Doolin-Dalton
- ☐ '94 Get Over It
- ☐ '79 Heartache Tonight ★
- ☐ '77 Hotel California ★
- ☐ '80 I Can't Tell You Why ★
- ☐ '79 In The City
- ☐ '74 James Dean
- ☐ '77 Life In The Fast Lane
- ☐ '79 Long Run, The
- ☐ '94 Love Will Keep Us Alive
- ☐ '75 Lyin' Eyes ★
- ☐ '76 New Kid In Town ★
- ☐ '75 One Of These Nights ★
- ☐ '73 Outlaw Man
- ☐ '72 Peaceful Easy Feeling
- ☐ '78 Please Come Home For Christmas
- ☐ '79 Sad Café
- ☐ '80 Seven Bridges Road
- ☐ '72 Take It Easy
- ☐ '75 Take It To The Limit ★
- ☐ '73 Tequila Sunrise
- ☐ '79 Those Shoes
- ☐ '77 Victim Of Love
- ☐ '77 Wasted Time
- ☐ '72 Witchy Woman

## EAMON
- ☐ '03 F**k It (I Don't Want You Back)

## EARL, Stacy
- ☐ '91 Love Me All Up
- ☐ '92 Romeo & Juliet

## EARL-JEAN
- ☐ '64 I'm Into Somethin' Good

## EARLS, The
- ☐ '62 Remember Then

## EARTH, WIND & FIRE
- ☐ '79 After The Love Has Gone ★
- ☐ '79 Boogie Wonderland
  *EARTH, WIND & FIRE WITH THE EMOTIONS*
- ☐ '74 Devotion
- ☐ '83 Fall In Love With Me
- ☐ '78 Fantasy
- ☐ '76 Getaway
- ☐ '78 Got To Get You Into My Life
- ☐ '81 Let's Groove ★
- ☐ '74 Mighty Mighty
- ☐ '76 Saturday Nite
- ☐ '78 September
- ☐ '77 Serpentine Fire
- ☐ '75 Shining Star ★
- ☐ '75 Sing A Song
- ☐ '87 System Of Survival
- ☐ '75 That's The Way Of The World
- ☐ '88 Thinking Of You

## EASTON, Sheena
- ☐ '83 Almost Over You
- ☐ '89 Arms Of Orion, The
  *PRINCE with Sheena Easton*
- ☐ '85 Do It For Love
- ☐ '81 For Your Eyes Only ★
- ☐ '88 Lover In Me, The
- ☐ '81 Modern Girl
- ☐ '81 Morning Train (Nine To Five) ★
- ☐ '84 Strut
- ☐ '84 Sugar Walls
- ☐ '83 Telefone (Long Distance Love Affair)
- ☐ '83 We've Got Tonight
  *KENNY ROGERS & SHEENA EASTON*

- ☐ '91 What Comes Naturally
- ☐ '82 When He Shines
- ☐ '81 You Could Have Been With Me

## EASYBEATS, The
- ☐ '67 Friday On My Mind

## ECHO & THE BUNNYMEN
- ☐ '86 Bring On The Dancing Horses
- ☐ '84 Killing Moon, The

## ECHOES, The
- ☐ '61 Baby Blue

## EDDY, Duane
- ☐ '62 Ballad Of Paladin, The
- ☐ '60 Because They're Young ★
- ☐ '59 Bonnie Came Back
- ☐ '63 Boss Guitar
- ☐ '58 Cannonball
- ☐ '62 (Dance With The) Guitar Man
- ☐ '59 Forty Miles Of Bad Road
- ☐ '59 Lonely One, The
- ☐ '58 Moovin' N' Groovin'
- ☐ '60 "Pepe"
- ☐ '60 Peter Gunn
- ☐ '58 Ramrod
- ☐ '58 Rebel-'Rouser ★
- ☐ '61 Ring Of Fire
- ☐ '60 Shazam!
- ☐ '59 Some Kind-A Earthquake
- ☐ '61 Theme From Dixie
- ☐ '59 "Yep!"

## EDEN'S CRUSH
- ☐ '01 Get Over Yourself

## EDISON LIGHTHOUSE
- ☐ '70 Love Grows (Where My Rosemary Goes)

## EDMONDS, Kevon
- ☐ '99 24/7

## EDMUNDS, Dave
- ☐ '70 I Hear You Knocking
- ☐ '83 Slipping Away

## EDSELS, The
- ☐ '61 Rama Lama Ding Dong

## EDWARD BEAR
- ☐ '73 Close Your Eyes
- ☐ '72 Last Song

## EDWARDS, Bobby
- ☐ '61 You're The Reason

## EDWARDS, Dennis
- ☐ '84 Don't Look Any Further

## EDWARDS, Jonathan
- ☐ '71 Sunshine

## EDWARDS, Tommy
- ☐ '60 I Really Don't Want To Know
- ☐ '58 It's All In The Game ★

- ☐ '58 Love Is All We Need
- ☐ '59 Morning Side Of The Mountain, The
- ☐ '59 My Melancholy Baby
- ☐ '59 Please Mr. Sun

## EELS
- ☐ '96 Novocaine For The Soul

## E-40
- ☐ '97 Rappers' Ball
- ☐ '97 Things'll Never Change

## EGAN, Walter
- ☐ '78 Magnet And Steel

## EIFFEL 65
- ☐ '99 Blue (Da Ba Dee) ★

## 8TH DAY, The
- ☐ '71 She's Not Just Another Woman
- ☐ '71 You've Got To Crawl (Before You Walk)

## ELASTICA
- ☐ '95 Connection

## ELBERT, Donnie
- ☐ '72 I Can't Help Myself (Sugar Pie, Honey Bunch)
- ☐ '71 Where Did Our Love Go

## EL CHICANO
- ☐ '73 Tell Her She's Lovely
- ☐ '70 Viva Tirado

## EL DORADOS, The
- ☐ '55 At My Front Door

## ELECTRIC INDIAN, The
- ☐ '69 Keem-O-Sabe

## ELECTRIC LIGHT ORCHESTRA
- ☐ '80 All Over The World
- ☐ '86 Calling America
- ☐ '74 Can't Get It Out Of My Head
- ☐ '79 Confusion
- ☐ '77 Do Ya
- ☐ '79 Don't Bring Me Down ★
- ☐ '75 Evil Woman
- ☐ '75 Fire On High
- ☐ '81 Hold On Tight
- ☐ '80 I'm Alive
- ☐ '79 Last Train To London
- ☐ '76 Livin' Thing
- ☐ '78 Mr. Blue Sky
- ☐ '83 Rock 'N' Roll Is King
- ☐ '73 Roll Over Beethoven
- ☐ '79 Shine A Little Love
- ☐ '73 Showdown
- ☐ '76 Strange Magic
- ☐ '78 Sweet Talkin' Woman
- ☐ '77 Telephone Line
- ☐ '77 Turn To Stone
- ☐ '81 Twilight
- ☐ '80 Xanadu ★

*OLIVIA NEWTON-JOHN/ELECTRIC LIGHT ORCHESTRA*

## ELECTRIC PRUNES, The
- ☐ '67 Get Me To The World On Time
- ☐ '66 I Had Too Much To Dream (Last Night)

## ELECTRONIC
- ☐ '91 Get The Message
- ☐ '90 Getting Away With It

## ELEGANTS, The
- ☐ '58 Little Star ★

## ELGART, Larry
- ☐ '82 Hooked On Swing

## ELLEDGE, Jimmy
- ☐ '61 Funny How Time Slips Away

## ELLIMAN, Yvonne
- ☐ '77 Hello Stranger
- ☐ '71 I Don't Know How To Love Him
- ☐ '78 If I Can't Have You ★
- ☐ '76 Love Me
- ☐ '79 Love Pains

## ELLIOTT, Missy "Misdemeanor"
- ☐ '01 Get Ur Freak On ★
- ☐ '02 Gossip Folks
- ☐ '99 Hot Boyz ★
- ☐ '01 One Minute Man
- ☐ '03 Pass That Dutch
- ☐ '97 Rain (Supa Dupa Fly)
- ☐ '97 Sock It 2 Me
- ☐ '02 Work It ★

## ELLIS, Shirley
- ☐ '65 Clapping Song, The
- ☐ '64 Name Game, The
- ☐ '63 Nitty Gritty, The

## ELLISON, Lorraine
- ☐ '66 Stay With Me

## EMERSON DRIVE
- ☐ '02 Fall Into Me
- ☐ '02 I Should Be Sleeping

## EMERSON, LAKE & PALMER
- ☐ '77 Fanfare For The Common Man
- ☐ '72 From The Beginning
- ☐ '72 Hoedown
- ☐ '73 Karn Evil 9
- ☐ '71 Lucky Man

## EMF
- ☐ '91 Lies.
- ☐ '91 Unbelievable ★

## EMINEM
- ☐ '02 Cleanin' Out My Closet ★
- ☐ '05 Encore
- ☐ '04 Just Lose It ★
- ☐ '05 Like Toy Soldiers
- ☐ '02 Lose Yourself ★
- ☐ '05 Mockingbird ★
- ☐ '99 My Name Is
- ☐ '00 Real Slim Shady, The ★
- ☐ '03 Sing For The Moment

- ☐ '00 Stan ★
- ☐ '03 Superman
- ☐ '02 Without Me ★

## EMOTIONS, The
- ☐ '77 Best Of My Love ★
- ☐ '79 Boogie Wonderland
  - *EARTH, WIND & FIRE WITH THE EMOTIONS*
- ☐ '69 So I Can Love You

## ENCHANTMENT
- ☐ '77 Gloria
- ☐ '78 It's You That I Need
- ☐ '77 Sunshine

## ENGLAND, Ty
- ☐ '95 Should've Asked Her Faster

## ENGLAND DAN & JOHN FORD COLEY
- ☐ '77 Gone Too Far
- ☐ '76 I'd Really Love To See You Tonight ★
- ☐ '77 It's Sad To Belong
- ☐ '79 Love Is The Answer
- ☐ '76 Nights Are Forever Without You
- ☐ '78 We'll Never Have To Say Goodbye Again

## ENGLISH BEAT
- ☐ '80 Ranking Full Stop
- ☐ '82 Save It For Later

## ENGLISH CONGREGATION, The
- ☐ '72 Softly Whispering I Love You

## ENIGMA
- ☐ '94 Return To Innocence ★
- ☐ '91 Sadeness

## EN VOGUE
- ☐ '91 Don't Go
- ☐ '96 Don't Let Go (Love) ★
- ☐ '92 Free Your Mind
- ☐ '92 Give It Up, Turn It Loose
- ☐ '92 Giving Him Something He Can Feel
- ☐ '90 Hold On
- ☐ '90 Lies
- ☐ '93 Love Don't Love You
- ☐ '92 My Lovin' (You're Never Gonna Get It) ★
- ☐ '97 Too Gone, Too Long
- ☐ '94 Whatta Man ★
  - *SALT 'N' PEPA with En Vogue*
- ☐ '97 Whatever
- ☐ '90 You Don't Have To Worry

## ENYA
- ☐ '91 Caribbean Blue
- ☐ '94 Oíche Chiún (Silent Night)
- ☐ '01 Only Time ★
- ☐ '89 Orinoco Flow (Sail Away) ★

## EPPS, Preston
- ☐ '59 Bongo Rock

## EQUALS, The
- ☐ '68 Baby, Come Back

## ERASURE
- ☐ '94 Always
- ☐ '88 Chains Of Love
- ☐ '88 Little Respect, A

## ERIC B & RAKIM
- ☐ '87 I Know You Got Soul
- ☐ '88 Paid In Full

## ERUPTION
- ☐ '78 I Can't Stand The Rain

## ESCAPE CLUB, The
- ☐ '91 I'll Be There
- ☐ '88 Shake For The Sheik
- ☐ '88 Wild, Wild West ★

## ESPN Presents
- ☐ '97 Jock Jam, The

## ESQUIRES, The
- ☐ '67 And Get Away
- ☐ '67 Get On Up

## ESSEX, The
- ☐ '63 Easier Said Than Done ★
- ☐ '63 Walkin' Miracle, A

## ESSEX, David
- ☐ '73 Rock On

## ESTEFAN, Gloria/Miami Sound Machine
- ☐ '88 Anything For You ★
- ☐ '86 Bad Boy
- ☐ '87 Betcha Say That
- ☐ '91 Can't Forget You
- ☐ '87 Can't Stay Away From You
- ☐ '91 Coming Out Of The Dark ★
- ☐ '85 Conga
- ☐ '90 Cuts Both Ways
- ☐ '89 Don't Wanna Lose You ★
- ☐ '95 Everlasting Love
- ☐ '86 Falling In Love (Uh-Oh)
- ☐ '89 Get On Your Feet
- ☐ '98 Heaven's What I Feel
- ☐ '89 Here We Are
- ☐ '93 I See Your Smile
- ☐ '96 I'm Not Giving You Up
- ☐ '91 Live For Loving You
- ☐ '99 Music Of My Heart ★
  - *NSYNC & GLORIA ESTEFAN*
- ☐ '88 1-2-3
- ☐ '87 Rhythm Is Gonna Get You
- ☐ '94 Turn The Beat Around
- ☐ '86 Words Get In The Way

## ESTUS, Deon
- ☐ '89 Heaven Help Me
  - *DEON ESTUS (with George Michael)*

## ETERNAL
- ☐ '94 Stay

## ETHERIDGE, Melissa
- ☐ '94 Come To My Window
- ☐ '05 Cry Baby/Piece Of My Heart
- ☐ '96 I Want To Come Over
- ☐ '94 I'm The Only One ★

- ☐ '95 If I Wanted To
- ☐ '96 Nowhere To Go

## E.U.
- ☐ '88 Da'Butt

## EUROPE
- ☐ '87 Carrie
- ☐ '87 Final Countdown, The ★
- ☐ '87 Rock The Night
- ☐ '88 Superstitious

## EURYTHMICS
- ☐ '89 Don't Ask Me Why
- ☐ '84 Here Comes The Rain Again ★
- ☐ '83 Love Is A Stranger
- ☐ '86 Missionary Man
- ☐ '84 Right By Your Side
- ☐ '85 Sisters Are Doin' It For Themselves
  - *EURYTHMICS & ARETHA FRANKLIN*
- ☐ '83 Sweet Dreams (Are Made of This) ★
- ☐ '85 There Must Be An Angel (Playing With My Heart)
- ☐ '84 Who's That Girl?
- ☐ '85 Would I Lie To You?

## EVAN & JARON
- ☐ '00 Crazy For This Girl

## EVANESCENCE
- ☐ '03 Bring Me To Life ★
- ☐ '04 My Immortal ★

## EVANS, Faith
- ☐ '99 All Night Long
- ☐ '02 I Love You
- ☐ '97 I'll Be Missing You ★
  - *PUFF DADDY & FAITH EVANS*
- ☐ '98 Love Like This
- ☐ '99 Never Gonna Let You Go
- ☐ '95 Soon As I Get Home
- ☐ '01 You Gets No Love
- ☐ '95 You Used To Love Me

## EVANS, Paul
- ☐ '60 Happy-Go-Lucky-Me
- ☐ '60 Midnite Special
- ☐ '59 (Seven Little Girls) Sitting In The Back Seat

## EVANS, Sara
- ☐ '00 Born To Fly
- ☐ '01 I Could Not Ask For More
- ☐ '02 I Keep Looking
- ☐ '98 No Place That Far
- ☐ '03 Perfect
- ☐ '04 Suds In The Bucket

## EVE
- ☐ '02 Gangsta Lovin' ★
- ☐ '99 Gotta Man
- ☐ '01 Let Me Blow Ya Mind ★
- ☐ '00 Love Is Blind
- ☐ '02 Satisfaction
- ☐ '99 What Ya Want
  - *EVE & NOKIO*

## EVERCLEAR
- ☐ '97 Everything To Everyone
- ☐ '98 I Will Buy You A New Life
- ☐ '95 Santa Monica (Watch The World Die)
- ☐ '00 Wonderful

## EVERETT, Betty
- ☐ '64 Let It Be Me
  *BETTY EVERETT & JERRY BUTLER*
- ☐ '64 Shoop Shoop Song (It's In His Kiss)
- ☐ '69 There'll Come A Time

## EVERLAST
- ☐ '98 What It's Like

## EVERLY BROTHERS, The
- ☐ '58 All I Have To Do Is Dream ★
- ☐ '60 Always It's You
- ☐ '58 Bird Dog ★
- ☐ '67 Bowling Green
- ☐ '57 Bye Bye Love ★
- ☐ '60 Cathy's Clown ★
- ☐ '58 Claudette
- ☐ '62 Crying In The Rain
- ☐ '58 Devoted To You
- ☐ '61 Don't Blame Me
- ☐ '61 Ebony Eyes
- ☐ '64 Gone, Gone, Gone
- ☐ '60 Let It Be Me
- ☐ '60 Like Strangers
- ☐ '60 Love Hurts
- ☐ '60 Lucille
- ☐ '60 Memories Are Made Of This
- ☐ '59 Poor Jenny
- ☐ '58 Problems ★
- ☐ '60 So Sad (To Watch Good Love Go Bad)
- ☐ '61 Stick With Me Baby
- ☐ '59 Take A Message To Mary
- ☐ '61 Temptation
- ☐ '62 That's Old Fashioned (That's The Way Love Should Be)
- ☐ '58 This Little Girl Of Mine
- ☐ '59 ('Til) I Kissed You ★
- ☐ '57 Wake Up Little Susie ★
- ☐ '61 Walk Right Back
- ☐ '60 When Will I Be Loved

## EVERY MOTHERS' SON
- ☐ '67 Come On Down To My Boat ★

## EVERYTHING
- ☐ '98 Hooch

## EVERYTHING BUT THE GIRL
- ☐ '95 Missing ★

## EVE 6
- ☐ '01 Here's To The Night
- ☐ '98 Inside Out
- ☐ '00 Promise

## EXCITERS, The
- ☐ '62 Tell Him

## EXILE
- ☐ '78 Kiss You All Over ★
- ☐ '78 You Thrill Me

## EXPOSÉ
- ☐ '87 Come Go With Me
- ☐ '92 I Wish The Phone Would Ring
- ☐ '93 I'll Never Get Over You (Getting Over Me)
- ☐ '87 Let Me Be The One
- ☐ '87 Point Of No Return
- ☐ '87 Seasons Change ★
- ☐ '89 Tell Me Why
- ☐ '89 What You Don't Know
- ☐ '89 When I Looked At Him
- ☐ '90 Your Baby Never Looked Good In Blue

## EXTREME
- ☐ '91 Hole Hearted
- ☐ '91 More Than Words ★
- ☐ '92 Rest In Peace

## EYE TO EYE
- ☐ '82 Nice Girls

# F

## FABARES, Shelley
- ☐ '62 Johnny Angel ★
- ☐ '62 Johnny Loves Me

## FABIAN
- ☐ '60 About This Thing Called Love
- ☐ '59 Come On And Get Me
- ☐ '59 Hound Dog Man
- ☐ '59 I'm A Man
- ☐ '60 String Along
- ☐ '59 This Friendly World
- ☐ '59 Tiger ★
- ☐ '59 Turn Me Loose

## FABIAN, Lara
- ☐ '00 I Will Love Again

## FABOLOUS
- ☐ '04 Breathe
- ☐ '01 Can't Deny It
- ☐ '03 Can't Let You Go ★
- ☐ '03 Into You ★
- ☐ '02 Trade It All
- ☐ '01 Young'n (Holla Back)

## FABRIC, Bent, & His Piano
- ☐ '62 Alley Cat

## FABULOUS THUNDERBIRDS, The
- ☐ '88 Powerful Stuff
- ☐ '86 Tuff Enuff
- ☐ '86 Wrap It Up

## FACENDA, Tommy
- ☐ '59 High School U.S.A.

## FACES
- ☐ '71 (I Know) I'm Losing You
  *ROD STEWART With Faces*
- ☐ '73 Ooh La La
- ☐ '72 Stay With Me

## FACE TO FACE
- ☐ '84 10-9-8

## FACTS OF LIFE
- ☐ '77 Sometimes

## FAGEN, Donald
- ☐ '82 I.G.Y. (What A Beautiful World)
- ☐ '83 New Frontier

## FAIRCHILD, Barbara
- ☐ '73 Teddy Bear Song

## FAITH, Adam
- ☐ '65 It's Alright

## FAITH, Percy, & His Orchestra
- ☐ '60 Theme For Young Lovers
- ☐ '60 Theme From "A Summer Place" ★

## FAITHFULL, Marianne
- ☐ '64 As Tears Go By
- ☐ '65 Come And Stay With Me
- ☐ '65 Summer Nights
- ☐ '65 This Little Bird

## FAITH, HOPE & CHARITY
- ☐ '75 To Each His Own

## FAITH NO MORE
- ☐ '90 Epic

## FALCO
- ☐ '86 Rock Me Amadeus ★
- ☐ '86 Vienna Calling

## FALCON, Billy
- ☐ '91 Power Windows

## FALCONS, The
- ☐ '59 You're So Fine

## FALTERMEYER, Harold
- ☐ '85 Axel F ★

## FÄLTSKOG, Agnetha
- ☐ '83 Can't Shake Loose

## FAME, Georgie
- ☐ '68 Ballad Of Bonnie And Clyde, The
- ☐ '65 Yeh, Yeh

## FANCY
- ☐ '74 Touch Me
- ☐ '74 Wild Thing

## FANNY
- ☐ '75 Butter Boy
- ☐ '71 Charity Ball

## FANTASIA
- ☐ '04 I Believe ★
- ☐ '05 Truth Is ★

## FANTASTIC JOHNNY C, The
- ☐ '67 Boogaloo Down Broadway
- ☐ '68 Hitch It To The Horse

## FARDON, Don
- ☐ '68 (The Lament Of The Cherokee) Indian Reservation

## FARGO, Donna
- ☐ '72 Funny Face
- ☐ '72 Happiest Girl In The Whole U.S.A., The

## FARRIS, Dionne
- ☐ '95 I Know ★

## FASTBALL
- ☐ '99 Out Of My Head
- ☐ '98 Way, The ★

## FASTER PUSSYCAT
- ☐ '90 House Of Pain

## FATBACK
- ☐ '80 Backstrokin'
- ☐ '78 I Like Girls

## FAT BOYS
- ☐ '84 Jail House Rap
- ☐ '88 Twist (Yo, Twist!)
   *FAT BOYS (with Chubby Checker)*
- ☐ '87 Wipeout
   *FAT BOYS (with The Beach Boys)*

## FATBOY SLIM
- ☐ '99 Praise You
- ☐ '98 Rockafeller Skank, The

## FATHER MC
- ☐ '92 Everything's Gonna Be Alright
- ☐ '91 I'll Do 4 U

## FAT JOE
- ☐ '01 We Thuggin
- ☐ '02 What's Luv? ★

## FELDER, Wilton
- ☐ '85 (No Matter How High I Get) I'll Still Be Lookin' Up To You

## FELICIANO, José
- ☐ '70 Feliz Navidad
- ☐ '68 Hi-Heel Sneakers
- ☐ '68 Light My Fire

## FELONY
- ☐ '83 Fanatic, The

## FENDER, Freddy
- ☐ '75 Before The Next Teardrop Falls ★
- ☐ '75 Secret Love
- ☐ '75 Wasted Days And Wasted Nights
- ☐ '76 You'll Lose A Good Thing

## FENDERMEN, The
- ☐ '60 Mule Skinner Blues ★

## FERGUSON, Jay
- ☐ '79 Shakedown Cruise
- ☐ '77 Thunder Island

## FERGUSON, Johnny
- ☐ '60 Angela Jones

## FERGUSON, Maynard
- ☐ '77 Gonna Fly Now (Theme From "Rocky")

## FERKO STRING BAND
- ☐ '55  Alabama Jubilee

## FERRANTE & TEICHER
- ☐ '60  Exodus ★
- ☐ '61  (Love Theme From) One Eyed Jacks
- ☐ '69  Midnight Cowboy
- ☐ '60  Theme From The Apartment
- ☐ '61  Tonight

## FERRY, Bryan
- ☐ '88  Kiss And Tell
- ☐ '85  Slave To Love

## FEVER TREE
- ☐ '68  San Francisco Girls (Return Of The Native)

## FIELD MOB
- ☐ '02  Sick Of Being Lonely

## FIELDS, Ernie, Orch.
- ☐ '59  In The Mood

## FIELDS, Richard "Dimples"
- ☐ '82  If It Ain't One Thing...It's Another

## FIESTAS, The
- ☐ '59  So Fine

## 5TH DIMENSION, The
- ☐ '69  Aquarius/Let The Sunshine In ★
- ☐ '70  Blowing Away
- ☐ '68  California Soul
- ☐ '68  Carpet Man
- ☐ '67  Go Where You Wanna Go
- ☐ '72  If I Could Reach You
- ☐ '72  (Last Night) I Didn't Get To Sleep At All
- ☐ '73  Living Together, Growing Together
- ☐ '71  Love's Lines, Angles And Rhymes
- ☐ '71  Never My Love
- ☐ '70  One Less Bell To Answer ★
- ☐ '67  Paper Cup
- ☐ '70  Puppet Man
- ☐ '70  Save The Country
- ☐ '68  Stoned Soul Picnic
- ☐ '68  Sweet Blindness
- ☐ '72  Together Let's Find Love
- ☐ '67  Up -- Up And Away
- ☐ '69  Wedding Bell Blues ★
- ☐ '69  Workin' On A Groovy Thing

## FIFTH ESTATE, The
- ☐ '67  Ding Dong! The Witch Is Dead

## 50 CENT
- ☐ '05  Candy Shop ★
- ☐ '05  Disco Inferno ★
- ☐ '03  In Da Club ★
- ☐ '05  Just A Lil Bit ★
- ☐ '03  P.I.M.P. ★
- ☐ '03  21 Questions ★
- ☐ '02  Wanksta

## FILTER
- ☐ '95  Hey Man Nice Shot
- ☐ '99  Take A Picture

## FINE YOUNG CANNIBALS
- ☐ '89  Don't Look Back
- ☐ '89  Good Thing ★
- ☐ '89  She Drives Me Crazy ★

## FINGER ELEVEN
- ☐ '04  One Thing

## FINNEGAN, Larry
- ☐ '62  Dear One

## FIORILLO, Elisa
- ☐ '90  On The Way Up
- ☐ '87  Who Found Who
  - *JELLYBEAN/Elisa Fiorillo*

## FIREBALLS, The/GILMER, Jimmy
- ☐ '67  Bottle Of Wine
- ☐ '60  Bulldog
- ☐ '63  Daisy Petal Pickin'
- ☐ '61  Quite A Party
- ☐ '63  Sugar Shack ★
- ☐ '59  Torquay
- ☐ '60  Vaquero

## FIREFALL
- ☐ '77  Cinderella
- ☐ '80  Headed For A Fall
- ☐ '77  Just Remember I Love You
- ☐ '81  Staying With It
- ☐ '78  Strange Way
- ☐ '76  You Are The Woman

## FIREFLIES
- ☐ '59  You Were Mine

## FIREHOUSE
- ☐ '91  Don't Treat Me Bad
- ☐ '95  I Live My Life For You
- ☐ '91  Love Of A Lifetime
- ☐ '92  When I Look Into Your Eyes

## FIRM, The
- ☐ '86  All The Kings Horses
- ☐ '85  Radioactive

## FIRST CHOICE
- ☐ '73  Armed And Extremely Dangerous

## FIRST CLASS
- ☐ '74  Beach Baby

## FISCHER, Lisa
- ☐ '91  How Can I Ease The Pain

## FISHER, Eddie
- ☐ '56  Cindy, Oh Cindy
- ☐ '55  Dungaree Doll
- ☐ '55  Everybody's Got A Home But Me
- ☐ '66  Games That Lovers Play
- ☐ '55  Heart
- ☐ '54  I Need You Now
- ☐ '55  (I'm Always Hearing) Wedding Bells
- ☐ '55  Man Chases A Girl (Until She Catches Him)
- ☐ '56  On The Street Where You Live
- ☐ '55  Song Of The Dreamer

## FISHER, Miss Toni
- ☐ '59 Big Hurt, The ★
- ☐ '62 West Of The Wall

## FITZGERALD, Ella
- ☐ '60 How High The Moon
- ☐ '60 Mack The Knife

## FIVE
- ☐ '98 When The Lights Go Out

## FIVE AMERICANS, The
- ☐ '66 I See The Light
- ☐ '67 Sound Of Love
- ☐ '67 Western Union
- ☐ '67 Zip Code

## FIVE BLOBS, The
- ☐ '58 Blob, The

## FIVE FLIGHTS UP
- ☐ '70 Do What You Wanna Do

## FIVE FOR FIGHTING
- ☐ '04 100 Years
- ☐ '04 Silent Night
- ☐ '01 Superman (It's Not Easy)

## FIVE KEYS, The
- ☐ '55 Ling, Ting, Tong
- ☐ '56 Out Of Sight, Out Of Mind
- ☐ '56 Wisdom Of A Fool

## FIVE MAN ELECTRICAL BAND
- ☐ '71 Absolutely Right
- ☐ '71 Signs ★

## 504 BOYZ
- ☐ '00 Wobble Wobble

## FIVE SATINS, The
- ☐ '56 In The Still Of The Nite ★
- ☐ '57 To The Aisle

## FIVE STAIRSTEPS, The
- ☐ '70 O-o-h Child ★

## FIVE STAR
- ☐ '85 Let Me Be The One

## 5000 VOLTS
- ☐ '75 I'm On Fire

## FIXX, The
- ☐ '84 Are We Ourselves?
- ☐ '84 Deeper And Deeper
- ☐ '89 Driven Out
- ☐ '91 How Much Is Enough
- ☐ '83 One Thing Leads To Another ★
- ☐ '83 Saved By Zero
- ☐ '86 Secret Separation
- ☐ '83 Sign Of Fire, The

## FLACK, Roberta
- ☐ '78 Closer I Get To You, The
  *ROBERTA FLACK with Donny Hathaway*
- ☐ '74 Feel Like Makin' Love
- ☐ '72 First Time Ever I Saw Your Face ★

- ☐ '78 If Ever I See You Again
- ☐ '73 Jesse
- ☐ '73 Killing Me Softly With His Song ★
- ☐ '82 Making Love
- ☐ '88 Oasis
- ☐ '91 Set The Night To Music
  *ROBERTA FLACK with Maxi Priest*
- ☐ '83 Tonight, I Celebrate My Love
- ☐ '72 Where Is The Love
  *ROBERTA FLACK & DONNY HATHAWAY*
- ☐ '71 You've Got A Friend

## FLAMING EMBER, The
- ☐ '70 I'm Not My Brothers Keeper
- ☐ '69 Mind, Body and Soul
- ☐ '70 Westbound #9

## FLAMING LIPS, The
- ☐ '94 She Don't Use Jelly

## FLAMINGOS, The
- ☐ '59 I Only Have Eyes For You ★
- ☐ '59 Lovers Never Say Goodbye
- ☐ '60 Nobody Loves Me Like You
- ☐ '60 Your Other Love

## FLARES, The
- ☐ '61 Foot Stomping

## FLASH
- ☐ '72 Small Beginnings

## FLASH CADILLAC & THE CONTINENTAL KIDS
- ☐ '76 Did You Boogie (With Your Baby)

## FLEETWOOD MAC
- ☐ '69 Albatross
- ☐ '88 As Long As You Follow
- ☐ '87 Big Love
- ☐ '69 Black Magic Woman
- ☐ '77 Chain, The
- ☐ '77 Don't Stop ★
- ☐ '77 Dreams ★
- ☐ '87 Everywhere
- ☐ '77 Go Your Own Way ★
- ☐ '77 Gold Dust Woman
- ☐ '82 Gypsy
- ☐ '82 Hold Me ★
- ☐ '73 Hypnotized
- ☐ '77 I Don't Want To Know
- ☐ '75 Landslide
- ☐ '87 Little Lies
- ☐ '82 Love In Store
- ☐ '75 Monday Morning
- ☐ '77 Never Going Back Again
- ☐ '70 Oh Well
- ☐ '75 Over My Head
- ☐ '76 Rhiannon (Will You Ever Win)
- ☐ '79 Sara
- ☐ '90 Save Me
- ☐ '76 Say You Love Me
- ☐ '77 Second Hand News
- ☐ '87 Seven Wonders
- ☐ '77 Silver Springs
- ☐ '80 Think About Me

## FLEETWOOD MAC — cont'd
- [ ] '79 Tusk ★
- [ ] '77 You Make Loving Fun

## FLEETWOODS, The
- [ ] '59 Come Softly To Me ★
- [ ] '63 Goodnight My Love
- [ ] '59 Graduation's Here
- [ ] '61 (He's) The Great Impostor
- [ ] '62 Lovers By Night, Strangers By Day
- [ ] '59 Mr. Blue ★
- [ ] '60 Outside My Window
- [ ] '60 Runaround
- [ ] '61 Tragedy

## FLINT, Shelby
- [ ] '60 Angel On My Shoulder

## FLIRTATIONS, The
- [ ] '69 Nothing But A Heartache

## FLOATERS, The
- [ ] '77 Float On ★

## FLOCK OF SEAGULLS, A
- [ ] '82 I Ran (So Far Away) ★
- [ ] '82 Space Age Love Song
- [ ] '83 Wishing (If I Had A Photograph Of You)

## FLOETRY
- [ ] '03 Say Yes

## FLOYD, Eddie
- [ ] '68 Bring It On Home To Me
- [ ] '68 I've Never Found A Girl (To Love Me Like You Do)
- [ ] '66 Knock On Wood

## FLOYD, King
- [ ] '71 Baby Let Me Kiss You
- [ ] '70 Groove Me
- [ ] '72 Woman Don't Go Astray

## FLYING LIZARDS
- [ ] '80 Money

## FLYING MACHINE, The
- [ ] '69 Smile A Little Smile For Me

## FOCUS
- [ ] '73 Hocus Pocus

## FOGELBERG, Dan
- [ ] '84 Believe In Me
- [ ] '81 Hard To Say
- [ ] '80 Heart Hotels
- [ ] '84 Language Of Love, The
- [ ] '81 Leader Of The Band
- [ ] '87 Lonely In Love
- [ ] '79 Longer
- [ ] '83 Make Love Stay
- [ ] '82 Missing You
- [ ] '77 Nether Lands
- [ ] '75 Part Of The Plan
- [ ] '78 Power Of Gold, The
  *DAN FOGELBERG/TIM WEISBERG*
- [ ] '90 Rhythm Of The Rain/Rain
- [ ] '82 Run For The Roses

- [ ] '80 Same Old Lang Syne

## FOGERTY, John
- [ ] '75 Almost Saturday Night
- [ ] '85 Centerfield
- [ ] '86 Change In The Weather
- [ ] '86 Eye Of The Zombie
- [ ] '73 Hearts Of Stone
- [ ] '72 Jambalaya (On the Bayou)
  *THE BLUE RIDGE RANGERS (above 2)*
- [ ] '84 Old Man Down The Road, The
- [ ] '85 Rock And Roll Girls
- [ ] '75 Rockin' All Over The World

## FOGHAT
- [ ] '76 Drivin' Wheel
- [ ] '75 Fool For The City
- [ ] '77 I Just Want To Make Love To You [live]
- [ ] '75 Slow Ride
- [ ] '78 Stone Blue
- [ ] '79 Third Time Lucky (First Time I Was A Fool)

## FOLDS, Ben, Five
- [ ] '97 Brick

## FOLK IMPLOSION
- [ ] '95 Natural One

**FONTANA, Wayne — see MINDBENDERS**

## FONTANE SISTERS, The
- [ ] '56 Banana Boat Song, The
- [ ] '58 Chanson D'Amour (Song Of Love)
- [ ] '55 Daddy-O
- [ ] '56 Eddie My Love
- [ ] '55 Hearts Of Stone
- [ ] '55 Rock Love
- [ ] '55 Rollin' Stone
- [ ] '55 Seventeen

## FOO FIGHTERS
- [ ] '02 All My Life
- [ ] '05 Best Of You ★
- [ ] '96 Big Me
- [ ] '97 Everlong
- [ ] '99 Learn To Fly
- [ ] '95 This Is A Call

## FORBERT, Steve
- [ ] '79 Romeo's Tune

## FORCE M.D.'S
- [ ] '87 Love Is A House
- [ ] '86 Tender Love

## FORD, Frankie
- [ ] '59 Sea Cruise

## FORD, Lita
- [ ] '89 Close My Eyes Forever
  *LITA FORD (with Ozzy Osbourne)*
- [ ] '88 Kiss Me Deadly

## FORD, "Tennessee" Ernie
- [ ] '55 Ballad Of Davy Crockett
- [ ] '57 In The Middle Of An Island
- [ ] '55 Sixteen Tons ★
- [ ] '56 That's All

## FORD, Willa
- ☐ '01 I Wanna Be Bad

## FOREIGNER
- ☐ '78 Blue Morning, Blue Day
- ☐ '82 Break It Up
- ☐ '77 Cold As Ice
- ☐ '79 Dirty White Boy
- ☐ '78 Double Vision
- ☐ '77 Feels Like The First Time
- ☐ '79 Head Games
- ☐ '78 Hot Blooded ★
- ☐ '88 I Don't Want To Live Without You
- ☐ '84 I Want To Know What Love Is ★
- ☐ '81 Juke Box Hero
- ☐ '77 Long, Long Way From Home
- ☐ '87 Say You Will
- ☐ '85 That Was Yesterday
- ☐ '81 Urgent
- ☐ '81 Waiting For A Girl Like You ★

## FORTUNES, The
- ☐ '71 Here Comes That Rainy Day Feeling Again
- ☐ '65 Here It Comes Again
- ☐ '65 You've Got Your Troubles

## FOSTER, David
- ☐ '85 Love Theme From St. Elmo's Fire

## FOSTER, Radney
- ☐ '93 Nobody Wins

## FOUNDATIONS, The
- ☐ '67 Baby, Now That I've Found You
- ☐ '69 Build Me Up Buttercup

## FOUNTAINS OF WAYNE
- ☐ '03 Stacy's Mom

## FOUR ACES
- ☐ '55 Heart
- ☐ '56 I Only Know I Love You
- ☐ '55 Love Is A Many-Splendored Thing ★
- ☐ '55 Melody Of Love
- ☐ '55 Mister Sandman
- ☐ '55 Woman In Love, A
- ☐ '56 You Can't Run Away From It

## FOUR COINS, The
- ☐ '55 I Love You Madly
- ☐ '55 Memories Of You
- ☐ '57 My One Sin
- ☐ '57 Shangri-La
- ☐ '58 World Outside, The

## FOUR ESQUIRES, The
- ☐ '58 Hideaway
- ☐ '57 Love Me Forever

## FOUR FRESHMEN, The
- ☐ '56 Graduation Day

## FOUR JACKS & A JILL
- ☐ '68 Master Jack

## FOUR LADS, The
- ☐ '56 Bus Stop Song (A Paper Of Pins)
- ☐ '58 Enchanted Island
- ☐ '56 House With Love In It, A
- ☐ '57 I Just Don't Know
- ☐ '58 Mocking Bird, The
- ☐ '55 Moments To Remember ★
- ☐ '56 My Little Angel
- ☐ '56 No, Not Much! ★
- ☐ '57 Put A Light In The Window
- ☐ '56 Standing On The Corner ★
- ☐ '58 There's Only One Of You
- ☐ '57 Who Needs You

## 4 NON BLONDES
- ☐ '93 What's Up ★

## FOURPLAY
- ☐ '91 After The Dance

## 4 P.M. (For Positive Music)
- ☐ '94 Sukiyaki

## FOUR PREPS, The
- ☐ '62 Big Draft, The
- ☐ '58 Big Man
- ☐ '59 Down By The Station
- ☐ '56 Dreamy Eyes
- ☐ '60 Got A Girl
- ☐ '58 Lazy Summer Night
- ☐ '61 More Money For You And Me
- ☐ '58 26 Miles (Santa Catalina) ★

## 4 SEASONS, The
- ☐ '63 Ain't That A Shame!
- ☐ '64 Alone
- ☐ '67 Beggin'
- ☐ '62 Big Girls Don't Cry ★
- ☐ '64 Big Man In Town
- ☐ '65 Bye, Bye, Baby (Baby, Goodbye)
- ☐ '63 Candy Girl
- ☐ '67 C'mon Marianne
- ☐ '64 Dawn (Go Away) ★
- ☐ '75 December, 1963 (Oh, What a Night) ★
- ☐ '65 Don't Think Twice
- ☐ '66 I've Got You Under My Skin
- ☐ '65 Let's Hang On!
- ☐ '63 Marlena
- ☐ '63 New Mexican Rose
- ☐ '66 Opus 17 (Don't You Worry 'Bout Me)
- ☐ '64 Rag Doll ★
- ☐ '64 Ronnie
- ☐ '62 Santa Claus Is Coming To Town
- ☐ '64 Save It For Me
- ☐ '62 Sherry ★
- ☐ '64 Stay
- ☐ '66 Tell It To The Rain
- ☐ '63 Walk Like A Man ★
- ☐ '67 Watch The Flowers Grow
- ☐ '75 Who Loves You ★
- ☐ '68 Will You Love Me Tomorrow
- ☐ '66 Working My Way Back To You

## FOUR TOPS
- ☐ '73 Ain't No Woman (Like The One I've Got)
- ☐ '73 Are You Man Enough
- ☐ '65 Ask The Lonely
- ☐ '64 Baby I Need Your Loving
- ☐ '67 Bernadette
- ☐ '65 I Can't Help Myself ★
- ☐ '68 If I Were A Carpenter
- ☐ '88 Indestructible
- ☐ '70 It's All In The Game
- ☐ '65 It's The Same Old Song
- ☐ '72 Keeper Of The Castle
- ☐ '74 One Chain Don't Make No Prison
- ☐ '66 Reach Out I'll Be There ★
- ☐ '70 River Deep - Mountain High
  *THE SUPREMES & FOUR TOPS*
- ☐ '67 7 Rooms Of Gloom
- ☐ '66 Shake Me, Wake Me (When It's Over)
- ☐ '65 Something About You
- ☐ '66 Standing In The Shadows Of Love
- ☐ '70 Still Water (Love)
- ☐ '73 Sweet Understanding Love
- ☐ '68 Walk Away Renee
- ☐ '81 When She Was My Girl
- ☐ '67 You Keep Running Away

## FOUR VOICES, The
- ☐ '58 Dancing With My Shadow
- ☐ '56 Lovely One

## FOX, Samantha
- ☐ '89 I Only Wanna Be With You
- ☐ '88 I Wanna Have Some Fun
- ☐ '88 Naughty Girls (Need Love Too)
- ☐ '86 Touch Me (I Want Your Body)

## FOXX, Inez, with Charlie Foxx
- ☐ '63 Mockingbird

## FOXY
- ☐ '78 Get Off
- ☐ '79 Hot Number

## FRAMPTON, Peter
- ☐ '76 Baby, I Love Your Way
- ☐ '76 Do You Feel Like We Do
- ☐ '79 I Can't Stand It No More
- ☐ '77 I'm In You ★
- ☐ '76 Show Me The Way ★
- ☐ '77 Signed, Sealed, Delivered (I'm Yours)

## FRANCIS, Connie
- ☐ '59 Among My Souvenirs
- ☐ '61 Baby's First Christmas
- ☐ '64 Blue Winter
- ☐ '61 Breakin' In A Brand New Broken Heart
- ☐ '62 Don't Break The Heart That Loves You ★
- ☐ '60 Everybody's Somebody's Fool ★
- ☐ '63 Follow The Boys
- ☐ '59 Frankie
- ☐ '59 God Bless America
- ☐ '61 (He's My) Dreamboat
- ☐ '62 I'm Gonna' Be Warm This Winter
- ☐ '59 If I Didn't Care

- ☐ '63 If My Pillow Could Talk
- ☐ '60 Jealous Of You (Tango Della Gelosia)
- ☐ '59 Lipstick On Your Collar
- ☐ '60 Mama
- ☐ '60 Many Tears Ago
- ☐ '58 My Happiness ★
- ☐ '60 My Heart Has A Mind Of Its Own
- ☐ '62 Second Hand Love
- ☐ '58 Stupid Cupid
- ☐ '60 Teddy
- ☐ '61 Together
- ☐ '62 Vacation
- ☐ '61 When The Boy In Your Arms (Is The Boy In Your Heart)
- ☐ '61 Where The Boys Are
- ☐ '58 Who's Sorry Now
- ☐ '63 Your Other Love

## FRANKE & THE KNOCKOUTS
- ☐ '81 Sweetheart
- ☐ '82 Without You (Not Another Lonely Night)
- ☐ '81 You're My Girl

## FRANKIE GOES TO HOLLYWOOD
- ☐ '84 Relax ★
- ☐ '84 Two Tribes

## FRANKIE J
- ☐ '03 Don't Wanna Try
- ☐ '05 Obsession [No Es Amor] ★

## FRANKLIN, Aretha
- ☐ '68 Ain't No Way
- ☐ '72 All The King's Horses
- ☐ '73 Angel
- ☐ '86 Another Night
- ☐ '67 Baby I Love You
- ☐ '77 Break It To Me Gently
- ☐ '71 Bridge Over Troubled Water
- ☐ '70 Call Me
- ☐ '67 Chain Of Fools ★
- ☐ '72 Day Dreaming
- ☐ '67 Do Right Woman-Do Right Man
- ☐ '70 Don't Play That Song
- ☐ '69 Eleanor Rigby
- ☐ '85 Freeway Of Love
- ☐ '83 Get It Right
- ☐ '68 House That Jack Built, The
- ☐ '87 I Knew You Were Waiting (For Me) ★
  *ARETHA FRANKLIN & GEORGE MICHAEL*
- ☐ '67 I Never Loved A Man (The Way I Love You)
- ☐ '68 I Say A Little Prayer
- ☐ '74 I'm In Love
- ☐ '86 Jimmy Lee
- ☐ '82 Jump To It
- ☐ '86 Jumpin' Jack Flash
- ☐ '67 Natural Woman (You Make Me Feel Like)
- ☐ '67 Respect ★
- ☐ '61 Rock-A-Bye Your Baby With A Dixie Melody
- ☐ '71 Rock Steady
- ☐ '98 Rose Is Still A Rose, A
- ☐ '68 See Saw
- ☐ '69 Share Your Love With Me

- ☐ '85 Sisters Are Doin' It For Themselves
  *EURYTHMICS & ARETHA FRANKLIN*
- ☐ '71 Spanish Harlem
- ☐ '70 Spirit In The Dark
- ☐ '68 (Sweet Sweet Baby) Since You've Been Gone
- ☐ '68 Think
- ☐ '89 Through The Storm
  *ARETHA FRANKLIN & ELTON JOHN*
- ☐ '80 United Together
- ☐ '73 Until You Come Back To Me (That's What I'm Gonna Do)
- ☐ '69 Weight, The
- ☐ '85 Who's Zoomin' Who
- ☐ '94 Willing To Forgive
- ☐ '71 You're All I Need To Get By

## FRANZ FERDINAND
- ☐ '04 Take Me Out

## FREAK NASTY
- ☐ '97 Da' Dip

## FREBERG, Stan
- ☐ '57 Banana Boat (Day-O)
- ☐ '56 Heartbreak Hotel
- ☐ '57 Wun'erful, Wun'erful!
- ☐ '55 Yellow Rose Of Texas, The

## FRED, John, & His Playboy Band
- ☐ '67 Judy In Disguise (With Glasses) ★

## FREDDIE & THE DREAMERS
- ☐ '65 Do The Freddie
- ☐ '65 I Understand (Just How You Feel)
- ☐ '65 I'm Telling You Now ★
- ☐ '65 You Were Made For Me

## FREE
- ☐ '70 All Right Now

## FREEMAN, Bobby
- ☐ '58 Betty Lou Got A New Pair Of Shoes
- ☐ '64 C'mon And Swim
- ☐ '58 Do You Want To Dance
- ☐ '60 (I Do The) Shimmy Shimmy

## FREEMAN, Ernie
- ☐ '57 Raunchy

## FREE MOVEMENT, The
- ☐ '71 I've Found Someone Of My Own

## FREHLEY, Ace
- ☐ '78 New York Groove

## FRENCH, Nicki
- ☐ '95 Total Eclipse Of The Heart ★

## FREY, Glenn
- ☐ '84 Heat Is On, The ★
- ☐ '82 I Found Somebody
- ☐ '82 One You Love, The
- ☐ '84 Sexy Girl
- ☐ '85 Smuggler's Blues
- ☐ '88 True Love
- ☐ '85 You Belong To The City ★

## FRIDA
- ☐ '82 I Know There's Something Going On

## FRIEDMAN, Dean
- ☐ '77 Ariel

## FRIEND & LOVER
- ☐ '68 Reach Out Of The Darkness

## FRIENDS OF DISTINCTION, The
- ☐ '69 Going In Circles
- ☐ '69 Grazing In The Grass
- ☐ '70 Love Or Let Me Be Lonely

## FRIJID PINK
- ☐ '70 House Of The Rising Sun

## FROST, Max, & The Troopers
- ☐ '68 Shape Of Things To Come

## FUEL
- ☐ '00 Hemorrhage (In My Hands)
- ☐ '98 Shimmer

## FUGEES
- ☐ '95 Fu-Gee-La
- ☐ '96 Killing Me Softly ★
- ☐ '96 No Woman, No Cry
- ☐ '96 Ready Or Not
- ☐ '97 Sweetest Thing, The

## FULLER, Bobby, Four
- ☐ '66 I Fought The Law ★
- ☐ '66 Love's Made A Fool Of You

## FUNKADELIC
- ☐ '71 Maggot Brain
- ☐ '79 (not just) Knee Deep
- ☐ '78 One Nation Under A Groove

## FUNKY 4 + 1
- ☐ '01 That's The Joint

## FURTADO, Nelly
- ☐ '01 I'm Like A Bird
- ☐ '01 Turn Off The Light ★

## FU-SCHNICKENS
- ☐ '93 What's Up Doc? (Can We Rock?)

## FUZZ, The
- ☐ '71 I Love You For All Seasons

# G

## GABLE, Eric
- ☐ '89 Remember (The First Time)

## GABRIEL, Peter
- ☐ '86 Big Time
- ☐ '92 Digging In The Dirt
- ☐ '87 Don't Give Up
  *PETER GABRIEL & KATE BUSH*
- ☐ '80 Games Without Frontiers
- ☐ '86 In Your Eyes
- ☐ '86 Red Rain
- ☐ '82 Shock The Monkey
- ☐ '86 Sledgehammer ★
- ☐ '77 Solsbury Hill
- ☐ '92 Steam

## GABRIELLE
- ☐ '93  Dreams

## GADABOUTS, The
- ☐ '56  Stranded In The Jungle

## GALLERY
- ☐ '72  Big City Miss Ruth Ann
- ☐ '72  I Believe In Music
- ☐ '72  Nice To Be With You

## GALLOP, Frank
- ☐ '66  Ballad Of Irving, The

## GAME, The
- ☐ '05  Hate It Or Love It ★
- ☐ '05  How We Do ★

## GAP BAND, The
- ☐ '89  All Of My Love
- ☐ '84  Beep A Freak
- ☐ '80  Burn Rubber (Why You Wanna Hurt Me)
- ☐ '82  Early In The Morning
- ☐ '86  Going In Circles
- ☐ '82  Outstanding
- ☐ '83  Party Train
- ☐ '82  You Dropped A Bomb On Me

## GARBAGE
- ☐ '96  #1 Crush
- ☐ '96  Stupid Girl

## GARDNER, Don, & Dee Dee Ford
- ☐ '62  I Need Your Loving

## GARFUNKEL, Art
- ☐ '73  All I Know
- ☐ '75  Break Away
- ☐ '75  I Only Have Eyes For You
- ☐ '73  I Shall Sing
- ☐ '74  Second Avenue
- ☐ '78  (What A) Wonderful World
  *ART GARFUNKEL with James Taylor & Paul Simon*

## GARI, Frank
- ☐ '61  Lullaby Of Love
- ☐ '61  Princess
- ☐ '60  Utopia

## GARLAND, Judy
- ☐ '61  For Me And My Gal [live]
- ☐ '61  Over The Rainbow [live]
- ☐ '61  Trolley Song, The [live]
- ☐ '61  You Made Me Love You [live]

## GARNETT, Gale
- ☐ '64  We'll Sing In The Sunshine

## GARRETT, Leif
- ☐ '78  I Was Made For Dancin'
- ☐ '77  Runaround Sue
- ☐ '77  Surfin' USA

## GARY, John
- ☐ '67  Cold

## GATES, David
- ☐ '73  Clouds
- ☐ '77  Goodbye Girl
- ☐ '75  Never Let Her Go
- ☐ '78  Took The Last Train

## GAYE, Marvin
- ☐ '67  Ain't No Mountain High Enough
- ☐ '68  Ain't Nothing Like The Real Thing
  *MARVIN GAYE & TAMMI TERRELL (above 2)*
- ☐ '65  Ain't That Peculiar
- ☐ '63  Can I Get A Witness
- ☐ '68  Chained
- ☐ '73  Come Get To This
- ☐ '74  Distant Lover
- ☐ '69  Good Lovin' Ain't Easy To Come By
  *MARVIN GAYE & TAMMI TERRELL*
- ☐ '77  Got To Give It Up ★
- ☐ '63  Hitch Hike
- ☐ '64  How Sweet It Is To Be Loved By You
- ☐ '68  I Heard It Through The Grapevine ★
- ☐ '76  I Want You
- ☐ '65  I'll Be Doggone
- ☐ '67  If I Could Build My Whole World Around You
  *MARVIN GAYE & TAMMI TERRELL*
- ☐ '71  Inner City Blues (Make Me Wanna Holler)
- ☐ '67  It Takes Two
  *MARVIN GAYE & KIM WESTON*
- ☐ '68  Keep On Lovin' Me Honey
  *MARVIN GAYE & TAMMI TERRELL*
- ☐ '73  Let's Get It On ★
- ☐ '71  Mercy Mercy Me (The Ecology)
- ☐ '74  My Mistake (Was To Love You)
- ☐ '64  Once Upon A Time
  *MARVIN GAYE & MARY WELLS*
- ☐ '63  Pride And Joy
- ☐ '85  Sanctified Lady
- ☐ '82  Sexual Healing ★
- ☐ '62  Stubborn Kind Of Fellow
- ☐ '69  That's The Way Love Is
- ☐ '69  Too Busy Thinking About My Baby
- ☐ '72  Trouble Man
- ☐ '64  Try It Baby
- ☐ '71  What's Going On ★
- ☐ '64  What's The Matter With You Baby
  *MARVIN GAYE & MARY WELLS*
- ☐ '73  You're A Special Part Of Me
  *DIANA ROSS & MARVIN GAYE*
- ☐ '64  You're A Wonderful One
- ☐ '68  You're All I Need To Get By
- ☐ '67  Your Precious Love
  *MARVIN GAYE & TAMMI TERRELL (above 2)*

## GAYLE, Crystal
- ☐ '77  Don't It Make My Brown Eyes Blue ★
- ☐ '79  Half The Way
- ☐ '78  Ready For The Times To Get Better
- ☐ '78  Talking In Your Sleep
- ☐ '82  You And I
  *EDDIE RABBITT with Crystal Gayle*

## GAYNOR, Gloria
- ☐ '78  I Will Survive ★
- ☐ '74  Never Can Say Goodbye

## G-CLEFS, The
- ☐ '61 I Understand (Just How You Feel)
- ☐ '56 Ka-Ding Dong

## GEDDES, David
- ☐ '75 Last Game Of The Season (A Blind Man In The Bleachers)
- ☐ '75 Run Joey Run

## GEILS, J., Band
- ☐ '82 Angel In Blue
- ☐ '81 Centerfold ★
- ☐ '80 Come Back
- ☐ '82 Freeze-Frame ★
- ☐ '73 Give It To Me
- ☐ '82 I Do
- ☐ '71 Looking For A Love
- ☐ '80 Love Stinks
- ☐ '74 Must Of Got Lost
- ☐ '78 One Last Kiss

## GENE & DEBBE
- ☐ '68 Playboy

## GENE LOVES JEZEBEL
- ☐ '90 Jealous

## GENERAL PUBLIC
- ☐ '94 I'll Take You There
- ☐ '84 Tenderness

## GENESIS
- ☐ '81 Abacab
- ☐ '78 Follow You Follow Me
- ☐ '92 Hold On My Heart
- ☐ '91 I Can't Dance
- ☐ '87 In Too Deep
- ☐ '86 Invisible Touch ★
- ☐ '92 Jesus He Knows Me
- ☐ '83 Just A Job To Do
- ☐ '75 Lamb Lies Down On Broadway
- ☐ '86 Land Of Confusion
- ☐ '83 Mama
- ☐ '82 Man On The Corner
- ☐ '80 Misunderstanding
- ☐ '92 Never A Time
- ☐ '81 No Reply At All
- ☐ '91 No Son Of Mine
- ☐ '82 Paperlate
- ☐ '83 That's All!
- ☐ '86 Throwing It All Away
- ☐ '87 Tonight, Tonight, Tonight
- ☐ '80 Turn It On Again

## GENTRY, Bobbie
- ☐ '70 All I Have To Do Is Dream
  *BOBBIE GENTRY & GLEN CAMPBELL*
- ☐ '69 Fancy
- ☐ '69 Let It Be Me
  *GLEN CAMPBELL & BOBBIE GENTRY*
- ☐ '67 Ode To Billie Joe ★

## GENTRYS, The
- ☐ '65 Keep On Dancing

## GEORGE, Barbara
- ☐ '61 I Know (You Don't Love Me No More)

## GEORGIA SATELLITES
- ☐ '86 Keep Your Hands To Yourself ★

## GERARDO
- ☐ '91 Rico Suave
- ☐ '91 We Want The Funk

## GERRY & THE PACEMAKERS
- ☐ '64 Don't Let The Sun Catch You Crying
- ☐ '65 Ferry Cross The Mersey
- ☐ '66 Girl On A Swing
- ☐ '64 How Do You Do It?
- ☐ '64 I Like It
- ☐ '64 I'll Be There
- ☐ '65 It's Gonna Be Alright

## GETO BOYS, The
- ☐ '91 Mind Playing Tricks On Me
- ☐ '93 Six Feet Deep

## GETZ, Stan
- ☐ '62 Desafinado
  *STAN GETZ/CHARLIE BYRD*
- ☐ '64 Girl From Ipanema, The
  *GETZ/GILBERTO*

## GHOST TOWN DJ'S
- ☐ '96 My Boo

## GIANT
- ☐ '90 I'll See You In My Dreams

## GIANT STEPS
- ☐ '88 Another Lover

## GIBB, Andy
- ☐ '80 Desire
- ☐ '78 Everlasting Love, An
- ☐ '80 I Can't Help It
  *ANDY GIBB & OLIVIA NEWTON-JOHN*
- ☐ '77 I Just Want To Be Your Everything ★
- ☐ '77 (Love Is) Thicker Than Water ★
- ☐ '78 (Our Love) Don't Throw It All Away
- ☐ '78 Shadow Dancing ★
- ☐ '80 Time Is Time

## GIBB, Barry — see STREISAND, Barbra

## GIBB, Robin
- ☐ '84 Boys Do Fall In Love
- ☐ '78 Oh! Darling

## GIBBS, Georgia
- ☐ '55 Dance With Me Henry (Wallflower)
- ☐ '56 Happiness Street
- ☐ '58 Hula Hoop Song, The
- ☐ '55 I Want You To Be My Baby
- ☐ '56 Kiss Me Another
- ☐ '56 Rock Right
- ☐ '55 Sweet And Gentle
- ☐ '56 Tra La La
- ☐ '55 Tweedle Dee

## GIBBS, Terri
- ☐ '81 Somebody's Knockin'

## GIBSON, Debbie
- ☐ '90 Anything Is Possible
- ☐ '89 Electric Youth
- ☐ '88 Foolish Beat
- ☐ '89 Lost In Your Eyes ★
- ☐ '89 No More Rhyme
- ☐ '87 Only In My Dreams
- ☐ '88 Out Of The Blue
- ☐ '87 Shake Your Love
- ☐ '88 Staying Together

## GIBSON, Don
- ☐ '58 Blue Blue Day
- ☐ '60 Just One Time
- ☐ '58 Oh Lonesome Me ★
- ☐ '61 Sea Of Heartbreak

## GILDER, Nick
- ☐ '78 Hot Child In The City ★

## GILKYSON, Terry, & The Easy Riders
- ☐ '57 Marianne

## GILL, Johnny
- ☐ '90 Fairweather Friend
- ☐ '90 My, My, My
- ☐ '90 Rub You The Right Way
- ☐ '92 Silent Prayer
  *SHANICE Feat. Johnny Gill*
- ☐ '92 Slow And Sexy
  *SHABBA RANKS Feat. Johnny Gill*
- ☐ '89 Where Do We Go From Here
  *STACY LATTISAW with Johnny Gill*
- ☐ '91 Wrap My Body Tight

## GILL, Vince
- ☐ '92 Don't Let Our Love Start Slippin' Away
- ☐ '93 Heart Won't Lie, The
  *REBA McENTIRE & VINCE GILL*
- ☐ '95 Go Rest High On That Mountain
- ☐ '94 House Of Love
  *AMY GRANT with Vince Gill*
- ☐ '92 I Still Believe In You
- ☐ '95 I Will Always Love You
  *DOLLY PARTON with Vince Gill*
- ☐ '97 Little More Love, A
- ☐ '90 Never Knew Lonely
- ☐ '93 No Future In The Past
- ☐ '93 One More Last Chance
- ☐ '96 Pretty Little Adriana
- ☐ '92 Take Your Memory With You
- ☐ '94 Tryin' To Get Over You
- ☐ '94 What The Cowgirls Do
- ☐ '90 When I Call Your Name
- ☐ '94 When Love Finds You
- ☐ '94 Whenever You Come Around
- ☐ '95 You Better Think Twice

## GILLEY, Mickey
- ☐ '80 Stand By Me

## GILMAN, Billy
- ☐ '00 One Voice

## GILMER, Jimmy — see FIREBALLS

## GILREATH, James
- ☐ '63 Little Band Of Gold

## GINA G
- ☐ '96 Ooh Aah...Just A Little Bit

## GIN BLOSSOMS
- ☐ '94 Allison Road
- ☐ '96 Follow You Down ★
- ☐ '93 Found Out About You
- ☐ '93 Hey Jealousy
- ☐ '96 Til I Hear It From You
- ☐ '94 Until I Fall Away

## GINO & GINA
- ☐ '58 (It's Been A Long Time) Pretty Baby

## GINUWINE
- ☐ '01 Differences
- ☐ '03 Hell Yeah
- ☐ '02 I Need A Girl (Part Two) ★
  *P. DIDDY & GINUWINE*
- ☐ '03 In Those Jeans
- ☐ '96 Pony ★
- ☐ '99 So Anxious
- ☐ '02 Stingy

## GIUFFRIA
- ☐ '84 Call To The Heart

## GLADIOLAS, The
- ☐ '57 Little Darlin'

## GLAHÉ, Will, & His Orchestra
- ☐ '57 Liechtensteiner Polka

## GLASS BOTTLE, The
- ☐ '71 I Ain't Got Time Anymore

## GLASS TIGER
- ☐ '86 Don't Forget Me (When I'm Gone) ★
- ☐ '87 I Will Be There
- ☐ '88 I'm Still Searching
- ☐ '86 Someday

## GLAZER, Tom
- ☐ '63 On Top Of Spaghetti

## GLENCOVES, The
- ☐ '63 Hootenanny

## GLITTER, Gary
- ☐ '72 Rock And Roll Part 2 ★

## GODLEY & CREME
- ☐ '85 Cry

## GODSMACK
- ☐ '00 Awake
- ☐ '01 Greed
- ☐ '02 I Stand Alone
- ☐ '03 Re-Align
- ☐ '04 Running Blind
- ☐ '03 Straight Out Of Line

## GODSPELL
- ☐ '72 Day By Day

## GOD'S PROPERTY
- ☐ '97 Stomp

## GO-GO'S
- ☐ '84 Head Over Heels
- ☐ '81 Our Lips Are Sealed ★
- ☐ '84 Turn To You
- ☐ '82 Vacation
- ☐ '82 We Got The Beat ★

## GOLD, Andrew
- ☐ '77 Lonely Boy
- ☐ '78 Thank You For Being A Friend

## GOLDEN EARRING
- ☐ '74 Radar Love
- ☐ '82 Twilight Zone

## GOLDSBORO, Bobby
- ☐ '68 Autumn Of My Life
- ☐ '66 Blue Autumn
- ☐ '68 Honey ★
- ☐ '66 It's Too Late
- ☐ '65 Little Things
- ☐ '64 See The Funny Little Clown
- ☐ '68 Straight Life, The
- ☐ '73 Summer (The First Time)
- ☐ '65 Voodoo Woman
- ☐ '70 Watching Scotty Grow
- ☐ '64 Whenever He Holds You

## GOMM, Ian
- ☐ '79 Hold On

## GONE ALL STARS
- ☐ '58 "7-11" (Mambo No. 5)

## GONZALEZ
- ☐ '79 Haven't Stopped Dancing Yet

## GOOD CHARLOTTE
- ☐ '02 Lifestyles Of The Rich And Famous

## GOODIE MOB
- ☐ '95 Cell Therapy

## GOODMAN, Dickie
- ☐ '66 Batman & His Grandmother
- ☐ '74 Energy Crisis '74
- ☐ '56 Flying Saucer, The
- ☐ '57 Flying Saucer The 2nd
- ☐ '75 Mr. Jaws
- ☐ '57 Santa And The Satellite
- ☐ '61 Touchables In Brooklyn, The

## GOO GOO DOLLS
- ☐ '99 Black Balloon
- ☐ '00 Broadway
- ☐ '04 Give A Little Bit
- ☐ '02 Here Is Gone
- ☐ '98 Iris ★
- ☐ '95 Name ★
- ☐ '98 Slide ★

## GORDON, Barry
- ☐ '55 Nuttin' For Christmas

## GORDON, Rosco
- ☐ '60 Just A Little Bit

## GORE, Lesley
- ☐ '67 California Nights
- ☐ '64 I Don't Wanna Be A Loser
- ☐ '63 It's My Party ★
- ☐ '63 Judy's Turn To Cry
- ☐ '64 Look Of Love
- ☐ '64 Maybe I Know
- ☐ '65 My Town, My Guy And Me
- ☐ '63 She's A Fool
- ☐ '65 Sunshine, Lollipops And Rainbows
- ☐ '64 That's The Way Boys Are
- ☐ '63 You Don't Own Me

## GORILLAZ
- ☐ '01 Clint Eastwood

## GORME, Eydie
- ☐ '63 Blame It On The Bossa Nova
- ☐ '63 I Can't Stop Talking About You
- ☐ '63 I Want To Stay Here
  - *STEVE & EYDIE (above 2)*
- ☐ '64 I Want You To Meet My Baby
- ☐ '57 Love Me Forever
- ☐ '56 Mama, Teach Me To Dance
- ☐ '56 Too Close For Comfort
- ☐ '58 You Need Hands

## GOULET, Robert
- ☐ '64 My Love, Forgive Me (Amore, Scusami)

## GO WEST
- ☐ '87 Don't Look Down - The Sequel
- ☐ '92 Faithful
- ☐ '90 King Of Wishful Thinking
- ☐ '85 We Close Our Eyes
- ☐ '93 What You Won't Do For Love

## GQ
- ☐ '79 Disco Nights (Rock-Freak)
- ☐ '79 I Do Love You

## GRACIE, Charlie
- ☐ '57 Butterfly ★
- ☐ '57 Fabulous

## GRACIN, Josh
- ☐ '04 Nothin' To Lose

## GRAHAM, Larry
- ☐ '80 One In A Million You

## GRAMM, Lou
- ☐ '89 Just Between You And Me
- ☐ '87 Midnight Blue
- ☐ '90 True Blue Love

## GRAMMER, Billy
- ☐ '58 Gotta Travel On

## GRANAHAN, Gerry
- ☐ '58 No Chemise, Please

## GRANATA, Rocco
- ☐ '59 Marina

## GRAND FUNK RAILROAD
- ☐ '75 Bad Time
- ☐ '70 Closer To Home/I'm Your Captain
- ☐ '72 Footstompin' Music
- ☐ '74 Loco-Motion, The
- ☐ '72 Rock 'N Roll Soul
- ☐ '74 Shinin' On
- ☐ '74 Some Kind Of Wonderful
- ☐ '73 Walk Like A Man
- ☐ '73 We're An American Band ★

## GRANDMASTER FLASH & THE FURIOUS FIVE
- ☐ '82 Message, The ★
- ☐ '83 White Lines (Don't Don't Do It)
  *GRANDMASTER & MELLE MEL*

## GRANT, Amy
- ☐ '85 Angles
- ☐ '91 Baby Baby ★
- ☐ '86 El Shaddai
- ☐ '91 Every Heartbeat ★
- ☐ '85 Find A Way
- ☐ '92 Good For Me
- ☐ '94 House Of Love
  *AMY GRANT with Vince Gill*
- ☐ '92 I Will Remember You
- ☐ '88 Lead Me On
- ☐ '94 Lucky One
- ☐ '86 Next Time I Fall, The
  *PETER CETERA with Amy Grant*
- ☐ '97 Takes A Little Time
- ☐ '91 That's What Love Is For
- ☐ '85 Thy Word

## GRANT, Earl
- ☐ '58 End, The
- ☐ '62 Swingin' Gently

## GRANT, Eddy
- ☐ '83 Electric Avenue ★
- ☐ '84 Romancing The Stone

## GRANT, Gogi
- ☐ '55 Suddenly There's A Valley
- ☐ '56 Wayward Wind, The ★

## GRANT, Janie
- ☐ '61 Triangle

## GRASS ROOTS, The
- ☐ '70 Baby Hold On
- ☐ '68 Bella Linda
- ☐ '72 Glory Bound
- ☐ '69 Heaven Knows
- ☐ '69 I'd Wait A Million Years
- ☐ '67 Let's Live For Today
- ☐ '68 Midnight Confessions
- ☐ '69 River Is Wide, The
- ☐ '72 Runway, The
- ☐ '71 Sooner Or Later
- ☐ '70 Temptation Eyes
- ☐ '67 Things I Should Have Said
- ☐ '71 Two Divided By Love
- ☐ '66 Where Were You When I Needed You

## GRATEFUL DEAD
- ☐ '80 Alabama Getaway
- ☐ '71 Bertha
- ☐ '70 Box Of Rain
- ☐ '70 Casey Jones
- ☐ '70 Dark Star
- ☐ '75 Franklin's Tower
- ☐ '70 Friend Of The Devil
- ☐ '87 Hell In A Bucket
- ☐ '75 Music Never Stopped
- ☐ '72 One More Saturday Night
- ☐ '71 Playing In The Band
- ☐ '70 Ripple
- ☐ '78 Shakedown Street
- ☐ '69 St. Stephen
- ☐ '70 Sugar Magnolia
- ☐ '77 Terrapin Station
- ☐ '87 Touch Of Grey ★
- ☐ '70 Truckin'
- ☐ '70 Turn On Your Love Light
- ☐ '70 Uncle John's Band

## GRAY, Dobie
- ☐ '73 Drift Away
- ☐ '65 "In" Crowd, The
- ☐ '78 You Can Do It

## GRAY, Macy
- ☐ '00 I Try ★

## GREAN, Charles Randolph, Sounde
- ☐ '69 Quentin's Theme

## GREAT WHITE
- ☐ '89 Angel Song, The
- ☐ '89 Once Bitten Twice Shy

## GREAVES, R.B.
- ☐ '70 Always Something There To Remind Me
- ☐ '69 Take A Letter Maria ★

## GRECCO, Cyndi
- ☐ '76 Making Our Dreams Come True

## GREEN, Al
- ☐ '73 Call Me (Come Back Home)
- ☐ '75 Full Of Fire
- ☐ '73 Here I Am (Come And Take Me)
- ☐ '72 I'm Still In Love With You
- ☐ '76 Keep Me Cryin'
- ☐ '75 L-O-V-E (Love)
- ☐ '74 Let's Get Married
- ☐ '71 Let's Stay Together ★
- ☐ '73 Livin' For You
- ☐ '72 Look What You Done For Me
- ☐ '72 Love And Happiness
- ☐ '88 Put A Little Love In Your Heart
  *ANNIE LENNOX & AL GREEN*
- ☐ '74 Sha-La-La (Make Me Happy)
- ☐ '74 Take Me To The River
- ☐ '71 Tired Of Being Alone
- ☐ '72 You Ought To Be With Me

## GREEN, Garland
- ☐ '69 Jealous Kind Of Fella

## GREEN, Pat
- [ ] '03  Wave On Wave

## GREEN, Vivian
- [ ] '03  Emotional Rollercoaster

## GREENBAUM, Norman
- [ ] '70  Spirit In The Sky ★

## GREEN DAY
- [ ] '04  American Idiot
- [ ] '94  Basket Case ★
- [ ] '05  Boulevard Of Broken Dreams ★
- [ ] '95  Brain Stew/Jaded
- [ ] '95  Geek Stink Breath
- [ ] '97  Good Riddance (Time Of Your Life)
- [ ] '05  Holiday ★
- [ ] '95  J.A.R. (Jason Andrew Relva)
- [ ] '94  Long View
- [ ] '00  Minority
- [ ] '00  Warning
- [ ] '94  When I Come Around ★

## GREENE, Lorne
- [ ] '64  Ringo

## GREEN JELLY
- [ ] '93  Three Little Pigs

## GREENWOOD, Lee
- [ ] '84  God Bless The USA

## GREGG, Bobby
- [ ] '62  Jam, The

## GRIFFITHS, Marcia
- [ ] '89  Electric Slide (Boogie) ★

## GRIGGS, Andy
- [ ] '05  If Heaven
- [ ] '00  She's More
- [ ] '99  You Won't Ever Be Lonely

## GROBAN, Josh
- [ ] '04  Believe
- [ ] '02  O Holy Night
- [ ] '02  To Where You Are
- [ ] '03  You Raise Me Up

## GROCE, Larry
- [ ] '76  Junk Food Junkie

## GROOVE THEORY
- [ ] '95  Tell Me

## GROSS, Henry
- [ ] '76  Shannon
- [ ] '76  Springtime Mama

## GTR
- [ ] '86  When The Heart Rules The Mind

## GUARALDI, Vince, Trio
- [ ] '62  Cast Your Fate To The Wind

## GUESS WHO, The
- [ ] '71  Albert Flasher
- [ ] '70  American Woman ★
- [ ] '74  Clap For The Wolfman
- [ ] '74  Dancin' Fool
- [ ] '70  Hand Me Down World
- [ ] '69  Laughing
- [ ] '70  No Sugar Tonight/New Mother Nature
- [ ] '69  No Time
- [ ] '71  Rain Dance
- [ ] '65  Shakin' All Over
- [ ] '70  Share The Land
- [ ] '74  Star Baby
- [ ] '69  These Eyes
- [ ] '69  Undun

## GUIDRY, Greg
- [ ] '82  Goin' Down

## GUITAR, Bonnie
- [ ] '57  Dark Moon

## GUNHILL ROAD
- [ ] '73  Back When My Hair Was Short

## G-UNIT
- [ ] '03  Stunt 101
- [ ] '04  Wanna Get To Know You

## GUNS N' ROSES
- [ ] '91  Don't Cry
- [ ] '90  Knockin' On Heaven's Door
- [ ] '91  Live And Let Die
- [ ] '92  November Rain ★
- [ ] '89  Paradise City
- [ ] '89  Patience ★
- [ ] '88  Sweet Child O' Mine ★
- [ ] '88  Welcome To The Jungle
- [ ] '91  You Could Be Mine

## GUTHRIE, Arlo
- [ ] '72  City Of New Orleans, The

## GUTHRIE, Gwen
- [ ] '86  Ain't Nothin' Goin' On But The Rent

## GUY
- [ ] '99  Dancin'
- [ ] '91  Do Me Right
- [ ] '89  I Like
- [ ] '91  Let's Chill

## GUY, Jasmine
- [ ] '91  Just Want To Hold You

# H

## HADDAWAY
- [ ] '93  What Is Love ★

## HAGAR, Sammy
- [ ] '87  Give To Live
- [ ] '84  I Can't Drive 55
- [ ] '82  I'll Fall In Love Again
- [ ] '97  Little White Lie
- [ ] '97  Marching To Mars
- [ ] '99  Mas Tequila
- [ ] '84  Two Sides Of Love
- [ ] '87  Winner Takes It All
- [ ] '82  Your Love Is Driving Me Crazy

## HAGGARD, Merle
- ☐ '66 Bottle Let Me Down, The
- ☐ '66 Fugitive, The
- ☐ '73 If We Make It Through December
- ☐ '68 Mama Tried
- ☐ '69 Okie From Muskogee
- ☐ '83 Pancho And Lefty
  *WILLIE NELSON & MERLE HAGGARD*
- ☐ '66 Swinging Doors

## HAIRCUT ONE HUNDRED
- ☐ '82 Love Plus One

## HALEY, Bill, & His Comets
- ☐ '55 Birth Of The Boogie
- ☐ '55 Burn That Candle
- ☐ '55 Dim, Dim The Lights
- ☐ '55 Mambo Rock
- ☐ '55 Razzle-Dazzle
- ☐ '56 Rip It Up
- ☐ '56 R-O-C-K
- ☐ '55 Rock-A-Beatin' Boogie
- ☐ '55 Rock Around The Clock ★
- ☐ '56 Rudy's Rock
- ☐ '56 Saints Rock 'N Roll, The
- ☐ '56 See You Later, Alligator ★
- ☐ '54 Shake, Rattle And Roll
- ☐ '58 Skinny Minnie

## HALL, Aaron
- ☐ '98 All The Places (I Will Kiss You)
- ☐ '92 Don't Be Afraid
- ☐ '94 I Miss You

## HALL, Daryl
- ☐ '86 Dreamtime
- ☐ '86 Foolish Pride

## HALL, Daryl, & John Oates
- ☐ '84 Adult Education
- ☐ '77 Back Together Again
- ☐ '82 Did It In A Minute
- ☐ '02 Do It For Love
- ☐ '76 Do What You Want, Be What You Are
- ☐ '88 Downtown Life
- ☐ '88 Everything Your Heart Desires
- ☐ '83 Family Man
- ☐ '80 How Does It Feel To Be Back
- ☐ '81 I Can't Go For That (No Can Do)
- ☐ '78 It's A Laugh
- ☐ '82 Italian Girls
- ☐ '81 Kiss On My List ★
- ☐ '82 Maneater ★
- ☐ '84 Method Of Modern Love
- ☐ '88 Missed Opportunity
- ☐ '85 Nite At The Apollo Live! The Way You Do The Things You Do/My Girl
- ☐ '83 One On One
- ☐ '84 Out Of Touch ★
- ☐ '85 Possession Obsession
- ☐ '81 Private Eyes ★
- ☐ '77 Rich Girl ★
- ☐ '76 Sara Smile
- ☐ '83 Say It Isn't So
- ☐ '74 She's Gone
- ☐ '90 So Close

- ☐ '85 Some Things Are Better Left Unsaid
- ☐ '79 Wait For Me
- ☐ '81 You Make My Dreams
- ☐ '80 You've Lost That Lovin' Feeling
- ☐ '82 Your Imagination

## HALL, Jimmy
- ☐ '80 I'm Happy That Love Has Found You

## HALL, Larry
- ☐ '59 Sandy

## HALL, Tom T.
- ☐ '73 I Love

## HALOS, The
- ☐ '61 "Nag"

## HAMILTON, Anthony
- ☐ '04 Charlene

## HAMILTON, Bobby
- ☐ '58 Crazy Eyes For You

## HAMILTON, George IV
- ☐ '63 Abilene
- ☐ '58 Now And For Always
- ☐ '57 Only One Love
- ☐ '56 Rose And A Baby Ruth, A
- ☐ '57 Why Don't They Understand

## HAMILTON, Roy
- ☐ '58 Don't Let Go
- ☐ '55 Unchained Melody
- ☐ '61 You Can Have Her

## HAMILTON, Russ
- ☐ '57 Rainbow

## HAMILTON, JOE FRANK & REYNOLDS
- ☐ '71 Don't Pull Your Love
- ☐ '75 Fallin' In Love ★
- ☐ '75 Winners And Losers

## HAMLISCH, Marvin
- ☐ '74 Entertainer, The

## HAMMER, Jan
- ☐ '85 Miami Vice Theme ★

## HAMMOND, Albert
- ☐ '74 I'm A Train
- ☐ '72 It Never Rains In Southern California
- ☐ '75 99 Miles From L.A.

## HANCOCK, Herbie
- ☐ '83 Rockit

## HANSON
- ☐ '97 I Will Come To You
- ☐ '97 MMMBop ★
- ☐ '00 This Time Around
- ☐ '97 Where's The Love

## HAPPENINGS, The
- ☐ '66 Go Away Little Girl
- ☐ '67 I Got Rhythm
- ☐ '67 My Mammy
- ☐ '66 See You In September

## HARDCASTLE, Paul
- ☐ '85 19

## HARNELL, Joe, & His Orchestra
- ☐ '62 Fly Me To The Moon - Bossa Nova

## HARPERS BIZARRE
- ☐ '67 Chattanooga Choo Choo
- ☐ '67 Come To The Sunshine
- ☐ '67 59th Street Bridge Song (Feelin' Groovy)

## HARPO, Slim
- ☐ '66 Baby Scratch My Back
- ☐ '57 I'm A King Bee
- ☐ '61 Rainin' In My Heart

## HARPTONES, The
- ☐ '56 Life Is But A Dream

## HARRIS, Betty
- ☐ '63 Cry To Me

## HARRIS, Eddie
- ☐ '61 Exodus

## HARRIS, Emmylou
- ☐ '81 Mister Sandman

## HARRIS, Major
- ☐ '75 Love Won't Let Me Wait

## HARRIS, Richard
- ☐ '68 MacArthur Park

## HARRIS, Rolf
- ☐ '63 Tie Me Kangaroo Down, Sport

## HARRIS, Sam
- ☐ '84 Sugar Don't Bite

## HARRIS, Thurston
- ☐ '57 Little Bitty Pretty One

## HARRISON, George
- ☐ '81 All Those Years Ago ★
- ☐ '71 Bangla-Desh
- ☐ '79 Blow Away
- ☐ '77 Crackerbox Palace
- ☐ '74 Dark Horse
- ☐ '75 Ding Dong; Ding Dong
- ☐ '73 Give Me Love - (Give Me Peace On Earth) ★
- ☐ '87 Got My Mind Set On You ★
- ☐ '70 Isn't It A Pity
- ☐ '70 My Sweet Lord ★
- ☐ '76 This Song
- ☐ '71 What Is Life
- ☐ '87 When We Was Fab
- ☐ '75 You

## HARRISON, Wilbert
- ☐ '59 Kansas City ★
- ☐ '69 Let's Work Together

## HART, Corey
- ☐ '85 Boy In The Box
- ☐ '86 Can't Help Falling In Love
- ☐ '85 Everything In My Heart
- ☐ '86 I Am By Your Side
- ☐ '88 In Your Soul
- ☐ '84 It Ain't Enough
- ☐ '90 Little Love, A
- ☐ '85 Never Surrender
- ☐ '84 Sunglasses At Night

## HART, Freddie
- ☐ '71 Easy Loving

## HARTMAN, Dan
- ☐ '84 I Can Dream About You
- ☐ '78 Instant Replay
- ☐ '85 Second Nature
- ☐ '84 We Are The Young

## HARVEY, PJ
- ☐ '95 Down By The Water

## HARVEY DANGER
- ☐ '98 Flagpole Sitta

## HATFIELD, Juliana, Three
- ☐ '93 My Sister

## HATHAWAY, Donny — see FLACK, Roberta

## HATHAWAY, Lalah
- ☐ '90 Heaven Knows

## HAVENS, Richie
- ☐ '71 Here Comes The Sun

## HAWKES, Chesney
- ☐ '91 One And Only, The

## HAWKINS, Dale
- ☐ '58 La-Do-Dada
- ☐ '57 Susie-Q
- ☐ '59 Yea-Yea (Class Cutter)

## HAWKINS, Edwin, Singers
- ☐ '70 Lay Down (Candles In The Rain)
  *MELANIE with The Edwin Hawkins Singers*
- ☐ '69 Oh Happy Day

## HAWKINS, Ronnie
- ☐ '59 Forty Days
- ☐ '59 Mary Lou

## HAWKINS, Screamin' Jay
- ☐ '56 I Put A Spell On You

## HAWKINS, Sophie B.
- ☐ '95 As I Lay Me Down ★
- ☐ '92 Damn I Wish I Was Your Lover

## HAYES, Bill
- ☐ '55 Ballad Of Davy Crockett, The ★
- ☐ '57 Wringle, Wrangle

## HAYES, Isaac
- [ ] '69 By The Time I Get To Phoenix
- [ ] '72 Do Your Thing
- [ ] '79 Don't Let Go
- [ ] '73 "Joy"
- [ ] '71 Never Can Say Goodbye
- [ ] '71 Theme From Shaft ★
- [ ] '72 Theme From The Men
- [ ] '69 Walk On By

## HAYES, Wade
- [ ] '94 Old Enough To Know Better
- [ ] '96 On A Good Night

## HAYMAN, Richard
- [ ] '56 Theme from "The Three Penny Opera" (Moritat)
  *RICHARD HAYMAN & JAN AUGUST*

## HAYWOOD, Leon
- [ ] '80 Don't Push It Don't Force It
- [ ] '75 I Want'a Do Something Freaky To You

## HAZELWOOD, Lee — see SINATRA, Nancy

## HEAD, Murray
- [ ] '85 One Night In Bangkok ★
- [ ] '70 Superstar

## HEAD, Roy
- [ ] '65 Apple Of My Eye
- [ ] '65 Just A Little Bit
- [ ] '65 Treat Her Right ★

## HEAD EAST
- [ ] '75 Never Been Any Reason
- [ ] '78 Since You've Been Gone

## HEALEY, Jeff, Band
- [ ] '89 Angel Eyes

## HEART
- [ ] '90 All I Wanna Do Is Make Love To You ★
- [ ] '87 Alone ★
- [ ] '77 Barracuda
- [ ] '76 Crazy On You
- [ ] '79 Dog & Butterfly
- [ ] '76 Dreamboat Annie
- [ ] '80 Even It Up
- [ ] '78 Heartless
- [ ] '83 How Can I Refuse
- [ ] '90 I Didn't Want To Need You
- [ ] '77 Kick It Out
- [ ] '77 Little Queen
- [ ] '76 Magic Man
- [ ] '85 Never
- [ ] '86 Nothin' At All
- [ ] '78 Straight On
- [ ] '90 Stranded
- [ ] '80 Tell It Like It Is
- [ ] '87 There's The Girl
- [ ] '86 These Dreams ★
- [ ] '82 This Man Is Mine
- [ ] '85 What About Love?
- [ ] '87 Who Will You Run To
- [ ] '93 Will You Be There (In The Morning)

## HEARTBEATS, The
- [ ] '56 Thousand Miles Away, A

## HEATHERTON, Joey
- [ ] '72 Gone

## HEATWAVE
- [ ] '78 Always And Forever
- [ ] '77 Boogie Nights ★
- [ ] '78 Groove Line, The

## HEAVY D & THE BOYZ
- [ ] '97 Big Daddy
- [ ] '94 Got Me Waiting
- [ ] '91 Is It Good To You
- [ ] '91 Now That We Found Love
- [ ] '94 Nuttin' But Love

## HEBB, Bobby
- [ ] '66 Satisfied Mind, A
- [ ] '66 Sunny ★

## HEFTI, Neal
- [ ] '66 Batman Theme

## HEIGHTS, The
- [ ] '92 How Do You Talk To An Angel ★

## HELMS, Bobby
- [ ] '57 Fraulein
- [ ] '57 Jingle Bell Rock
- [ ] '57 My Special Angel

## HENDERSON, Joe
- [ ] '62 Snap Your Fingers

## HENDERSON, Michael
- [ ] '78 Take Me I'm Yours

## HENDRICKS, Bobby
- [ ] '58 Itchy Twitchy Feeling

## HENDRIX, Jimi
- [ ] '68 All Along The Watchtower ★
- [ ] '71 Angel
- [ ] '67 Are You Experienced?
- [ ] '68 Burning Of The Midnight Lamp
- [ ] '68 Crosstown Traffic
- [ ] '71 Dolly Dagger
- [ ] '67 Fire
- [ ] '67 Foxey Lady
- [ ] '71 Freedom
- [ ] '67 Hey Joe
- [ ] '68 If 6 Was 9
- [ ] '68 Little Wing
- [ ] '67 Manic Depression
- [ ] '67 Purple Haze ★
- [ ] '69 Red House
- [ ] '71 Star Spangled Banner
- [ ] '69 Stone Free
- [ ] '67 Third Stone From The Sun
- [ ] '68 Up From The Skies
- [ ] '68 Voodoo Child (Slight Return)
- [ ] '67 Wind Cries Mary, The

## HENLEY, Don
- ☐ '85 All She Wants To Do Is Dance
- ☐ '84 Boys Of Summer, The ★
- ☐ '82 Dirty Laundry ★
- ☐ '89 End Of The Innocence, The
- ☐ '90 Heart Of The Matter, The
- ☐ '89 I Will Not Go Quietly
- ☐ '89 Last Worthless Evening, The
- ☐ '81 Leather And Lace
  *STEVIE NICKS (with Don Henley)*
- ☐ '90 New York Minute
- ☐ '85 Not Enough Love In The World
- ☐ '92 Sometimes Love Just Ain't Enough ★
  *PATTY SMYTH with Don Henley*
- ☐ '85 Sunset Grill
- ☐ '00 Taking You Home
- ☐ '92 Walkaway Joe
  *TRISHA YEARWOOD with Don Henley*
- ☐ '86 Who Owns This Place

## HENRY, Clarence
- ☐ '56 Ain't Got No Home
- ☐ '61 But I Do
- ☐ '61 You Always Hurt The One You Love

## HENSON, Jim
- ☐ '79 Rainbow Connection
- ☐ '70 Rubber Duckie

## HERMAN'S HERMITS
- ☐ '65 Can't You Hear My Heartbeat
- ☐ '66 Dandy
- ☐ '67 Don't Go Out Into The Rain (You're Going To Melt)
- ☐ '66 East West
- ☐ '68 I Can Take Or Leave Your Loving
- ☐ '65 I'm Henry VIII, I Am ★
- ☐ '64 I'm Into Something Good
- ☐ '65 Just A Little Bit Better
- ☐ '66 Leaning On The Lamp Post
- ☐ '66 Listen People
- ☐ '65 Mrs. Brown You've Got A Lovely Daughter ★
- ☐ '65 Must To Avoid, A
- ☐ '67 No Milk Today
- ☐ '65 Silhouettes
- ☐ '67 There's A Kind Of Hush
- ☐ '66 This Door Swings Both Ways
- ☐ '65 Wonderful World

## HERNANDEZ, Patrick
- ☐ '79 Born To Be Alive ★

## HERNDON, Ty
- ☐ '98 It Must Be Love
- ☐ '96 Living In A Moment
- ☐ '97 Loved Too Much
- ☐ '95 What Mattered Most

## HESITATIONS, The
- ☐ '68 Born Free

## HEWETT, Howard
- ☐ '86 I'm For Real
- ☐ '90 Show Me

## HEYWOOD, Eddie
- ☐ '56 Canadian Sunset ★
  *HUGO WINTERHALTER with Eddie Heywood*
- ☐ '56 Soft Summer Breeze

## HIBBLER, Al
- ☐ '56 After The Lights Go Down Low
- ☐ '56 11th Hour Melody
- ☐ '55 He
- ☐ '56 Never Turn Back
- ☐ '55 Unchained Melody ★

## HI-FIVE
- ☐ '91 I Can't Wait Another Minute
- ☐ '91 I Like The Way (The Kissing Game) ★
- ☐ '93 Never Should've Let You Go
- ☐ '92 Quality Time
- ☐ '92 She's Playing Hard To Get

## HIGGINS, Bertie
- ☐ '81 Key Largo

## HIGH INERGY
- ☐ '77 You Can't Turn Me Off (In The Middle Of Turning Me On)

## HIGHLIGHTS, The
- ☐ '56 City Of Angels

## HIGHWAYMEN, The
- ☐ '61 Cotton Fields
- ☐ '61 Michael ★

## HILL, Bunker
- ☐ '62 Hide & Go Seek

## HILL, Dan
- ☐ '87 Can't We Try
  *DAN HILL (with Vonda Sheppard)*
- ☐ '87 Never Thought (That I Could Love)
- ☐ '77 Sometimes When We Touch ★
- ☐ '89 Unborn Heart

## HILL, Faith
- ☐ '99 Breathe ★
- ☐ '02 Cry
- ☐ '01 If My Heart Had Wings
- ☐ '95 It Matters To Me
- ☐ '97 It's Your Love ★
  *TIM McGRAW with Faith Hill*
- ☐ '98 Just To Hear You Say That You Love Me
  *FAITH HILL (With Tim McGraw)*
- ☐ '98 Let Me Let Go
- ☐ '94 Piece Of My Heart
- ☐ '96 Someone Else's Dream
- ☐ '94 Take Me As I Am
- ☐ '01 There You'll Be
- ☐ '98 This Kiss ★
- ☐ '00 Way You Love Me, The ★
- ☐ '93 Wild One

## HILL, Jessie
- ☐ '60 Ooh Poo Pah Doo

## HILL, Lauryn
- ☐ '98 Can't Take My Eyes Off Of You
- ☐ '98 Doo Wop (That Thing) ★
- ☐ '99 Everything Is Everything
- ☐ '99 Ex-Factor

## HILLSIDE SINGERS, The
- ☐ '71 I'd Like To Teach The World To Sing

## HILLTOPPERS, The
- ☐ '57 Joker (That's What They Call Me)
- ☐ '56 Ka-Ding-Dong
- ☐ '55 Kentuckian Song, The
- ☐ '57 Marianne
- ☐ '55 My Treasure
- ☐ '55 Only You (And You Alone)

## HINTON, Joe
- ☐ '64 Funny

## HIPSWAY
- ☐ '87 Honeythief, The

## HIRT, Al
- ☐ '64 Cotton Candy
- ☐ '64 Java
- ☐ '64 Sugar Lips

## HITCHCOCK, Robyn, & The Egyptians
- ☐ '89 Madonna Of The Wasps
- ☐ '91 So You Think You're In Love

## HODGES, Eddie
- ☐ '62 (Girls, Girls, Girls) Made To Love
- ☐ '61 I'm Gonna Knock On Your Door

## HOFFS, Susanna
- ☐ '91 My Side Of The Bed

## HOKU
- ☐ '00 Another Dumb Blonde

## HOLDEN, Ron
- ☐ '60 Love You So

## HOLE
- ☐ '98 Celebrity Skin
- ☐ '94 Doll Parts
- ☐ '98 Malibu

## HOLLAND, Amy
- ☐ '80 How Do I Survive

## HOLLAND, Eddie
- ☐ '62 Jamie

## HOLLIDAY, Jennifer
- ☐ '82 And I Am Telling You I'm Not Going
- ☐ '83 I Am Love

## HOLLIES, The
- ☐ '74 Air That I Breathe, The ★
- ☐ '66 Bus Stop
- ☐ '67 Carrie-Anne
- ☐ '69 He Ain't Heavy, He's My Brother
- ☐ '68 Jennifer Eccles
- ☐ '64 Just One Look
- ☐ '72 Long Cool Woman (In A Black Dress) ★
- ☐ '72 Long Dark Road
- ☐ '65 Look Through Any Window
- ☐ '67 On A Carousel
- ☐ '67 Pay You Back With Interest
- ☐ '83 Stop In The Name Of Love
- ☐ '66 Stop Stop Stop

## HOLLISTER, Dave
- ☐ '99 My Favorite Girl

## HOLLOWAY, Brenda
- ☐ '64 Every Little Bit Hurts
- ☐ '65 When I'm Gone
- ☐ '67 You've Made Me So Very Happy

## HOLLY, Buddy/The Crickets
- ☐ '58 Early In The Morning
- ☐ '57 Everyday
- ☐ '58 Heartbeat
- ☐ '58 I'm Gonna Love You, Too
- ☐ '59 It Doesn't Matter Anymore
- ☐ '58 It's So Easy
- ☐ '58 Maybe Baby
- ☐ '57 Not Fade Away
- ☐ '57 Oh, Boy! ★
- ☐ '57 Peggy Sue ★
- ☐ '59 Raining In My Heart
- ☐ '58 Rave On ★
- ☐ '58 Real Wild Child
      *IVAN*
- ☐ '57 That'll Be The Day ★
- ☐ '58 Think It Over
- ☐ '59 True Love Ways
- ☐ '57 Words Of Love

## HOLLYWOOD ARGYLES
- ☐ '60 Alley-Oop ★

## HOLLYWOOD FLAMES
- ☐ '57 Buzz-Buzz-Buzz

## HOLMAN, Eddie
- ☐ '69 Hey There Lonely Girl ★

## HOLMES, Clint
- ☐ '73 Playground In My Mind ★

## HOLMES, Rupert
- ☐ '80 Answering Machine
- ☐ '79 Escape (The Pina Colada Song) ★
- ☐ '80 Him

## HOLY, Steve
- ☐ '01 Good Morning Beautiful

## HOMBRES, The
- ☐ '67 Let It Out (Let It All Hang Out)

## HOMER & JETHRO
- ☐ '59 Battle Of Kookamonga, The

## HONDELLS, The
- ☐ '64 Little Honda ★

## HONEYCOMBS, The
- ☐ '64 Have I The Right?

## HONEY CONE, The
- [ ] '72 Day I Found Myself, The
- [ ] '71 One Monkey Don't Stop No Show
- [ ] '71 Stick-Up
- [ ] '71 Want Ads ★

## HONEYDRIPPERS, The
- [ ] '85 Rockin' At Midnight
- [ ] '84 Sea Of Love ★

## HONEYMOON SUITE
- [ ] '86 Feel It Again

## HOOBASTANK
- [ ] '01 Crawling In The Dark
- [ ] '04 Reason, The ★
- [ ] '02 Running Away

## HOODOO GURUS
- [ ] '89 Come Anytime

## HOOKER, John Lee
- [ ] '62 Boom Boom

## HOOTERS
- [ ] '85 All You Zombies
- [ ] '85 And We Danced
- [ ] '85 Day By Day
- [ ] '87 Johnny B
- [ ] '86 Where Do The Children Go

## HOOTIE & THE BLOWFISH
- [ ] '94 Hold My Hand ★
- [ ] '96 I Go Blind
- [ ] '98 I Will Wait
- [ ] '95 Let Her Cry
- [ ] '96 Old Man & Me (When I Get To Heaven)
- [ ] '95 Only Wanna Be With You ★
- [ ] '95 Time
- [ ] '96 Tucker's Town

## HOPKIN, Mary
- [ ] '69 Goodbye
- [ ] '70 Temma Harbour
- [ ] '68 Those Were The Days ★

## HORNE, Jimmy "Bo"
- [ ] '78 Dance Across The Floor

## HORNE, Lena
- [ ] '55 Love Me Or Leave Me

## HORNSBY, Bruce, & The Range
- [ ] '90 Across The River
- [ ] '86 Every Little Kiss
- [ ] '88 Look Out Any Window
- [ ] '87 Mandolin Rain
- [ ] '88 Valley Road, The
- [ ] '86 Way It Is, The ★

## HORTON, Johnny
- [ ] '59 Battle Of New Orleans, The ★
- [ ] '60 North To Alaska ★
- [ ] '60 Sink The Bismarck

## HOT
- [ ] '77 Angel In Your Arms

## HOT BUTTER
- [ ] '72 Popcorn

## HOT CHOCOLATE
- [ ] '75 Disco Queen
- [ ] '75 Emma
- [ ] '78 Every 1's A Winner
- [ ] '77 So You Win Again
- [ ] '75 You Sexy Thing ★

## HOTLEGS
- [ ] '70 Neanderthal Man

## HOUSE OF PAIN
- [ ] '92 Jump Around ★

## HOUSTON
- [ ] '04 I Like That

## HOUSTON, David
- [ ] '66 Almost Persuaded
- [ ] '67 My Elusive Dreams
  *DAIVD HOUSTON & TAMMY WYNETTE*

## HOUSTON, Marques
- [ ] '03 Clubbin

## HOUSTON, Thelma
- [ ] '76 Don't Leave Me This Way ★
- [ ] '79 Saturday Night, Sunday Morning

## HOUSTON, Whitney
- [ ] '90 All The Man That I Need ★
- [ ] '96 Count On Me
  *WHITNEY HOUSTON & CECE WINANS*
- [ ] '87 Didn't We Almost Have It All ★
- [ ] '95 Exhale (Shoop Shoop) ★
- [ ] '86 Greatest Love Of All ★
- [ ] '98 Heartbreak Hotel ★
- [ ] '85 How Will I Know ★
- [ ] '96 I Believe In You And Me
- [ ] '93 I Have Nothing
- [ ] '00 I Learned From The Best
- [ ] '87 I Wanna Dance With Somebody (Who Loves Me) ★
- [ ] '92 I Will Always Love You ★
- [ ] '93 I'm Every Woman
- [ ] '90 I'm Your Baby Tonight ★
- [ ] '99 It's Not Right But It's Okay ★
- [ ] '88 Love Will Save The Day
- [ ] '91 Miracle
- [ ] '99 My Love Is Your Love ★
- [ ] '91 My Name Is Not Susan
- [ ] '88 One Moment In Time
- [ ] '93 Queen Of The Night
- [ ] '93 Run To You
- [ ] '85 Saving All My Love For You ★
- [ ] '87 So Emotional
- [ ] '93 Something In Common
  *BOBBY BROWN With Whitney Houston*
- [ ] '91 Star Spangled Banner, The
- [ ] '97 Step By Step
- [ ] '98 When You Believe
  *WHITNEY HOUSTON & MARIAH CAREY*
- [ ] '88 Where Do Broken Hearts Go ★
- [ ] '96 Why Does It Hurt So Bad
- [ ] '85 You Give Good Love

## HOWARD, Adina
- ☐ '95 Freak Like Me ★

## HOWARD, Miki
- ☐ '92 Ain't Nobody Like You
- ☐ '89 Ain't Nuthin' In The World
- ☐ '90 Love Under New Management
- ☐ '90 Until You Come Back To Me (That's What I'm Gonna Do)

## HOWLIN' WOLF
- ☐ '61 Back Door Man
- ☐ '61 Red Rooster
- ☐ '65 Killing Floor
- ☐ '56 Smoke Stack Lightning
- ☐ '60 Spoonful

## H-TOWN
- ☐ '93 Knockin' Da Boots
- ☐ '97 They Like It Slow
- ☐ '96 Thin Line Between Love & Hate, A

## HUDSON BROTHERS
- ☐ '75 Rendezvous
- ☐ '74 So You Are A Star

## HUES CORPORATION, The
- ☐ '74 Rock The Boat ★
- ☐ '74 Rockin' Soul

## HUGH, Grayson
- ☐ '89 Talk It Over

## HUGHES, Fred
- ☐ '65 Oo Wee Baby, I Love You

## HUGHES, Jimmy
- ☐ '64 Steal Away

## HUGO & LUIGI
- ☐ '59 Just Come Home

## HUMAN BEINZ, The
- ☐ '67 Nobody But Me

## HUMAN LEAGUE, The
- ☐ '82 Don't You Want Me ★
- ☐ '90 Heart Like A Wheel
- ☐ '86 Human ★
- ☐ '83 (Keep Feeling) Fascination
- ☐ '83 Mirror Man
- ☐ '95 Tell Me When

## HUMBLE PIE
- ☐ '72 Hot 'N' Nasty
- ☐ '71 I Don't Need No Doctor
- ☐ '71 Stone Cold Fever
- ☐ '72 30 Days In The Hole

## HUMPERDINCK, Engelbert
- ☐ '76 After The Lovin'
- ☐ '67 Am I That Easy To Forget
- ☐ '69 I'm A Better Man
- ☐ '67 Last Waltz, The
- ☐ '68 Les Bicyclettes De Belsize
- ☐ '68 Man Without Love, A
- ☐ '70 My Marie
- ☐ '68 Quando, Quando, Quando

- ☐ '67 Release Me (And Let Me Love Again)
- ☐ '70 Sweetheart
- ☐ '67 There Goes My Everything
- ☐ '78 This Moment In Time
- ☐ '71 When There's No You
- ☐ '69 Winter World Of Love

## HUMPHREY, Paul
- ☐ '71 Cool Aid

## HUNT, Tommy
- ☐ '63 I Am A Witness

## HUNTER, Ivory Joe
- ☐ '57 Empty Arms
- ☐ '56 Since I Met You Baby ★

## HUNTER, John
- ☐ '84 Tragedy

## HUNTER, Tab
- ☐ '59 (I'll Be With You In) Apple Blossom Time
- ☐ '57 Ninety-Nine Ways
- ☐ '57 Young Love

## HUSKY, Ferlin
- ☐ '57 Gone
- ☐ '60 Wings Of A Dove

## HYLAND, Brian
- ☐ '62 Ginny Come Lately
- ☐ '70 Gypsy Woman
- ☐ '60 Itsy Bitsy Teenie Weenie Yellow Polkadot Bikini ★
- ☐ '66 Joker Went Wild, The
- ☐ '61 Let Me Belong To You
- ☐ '66 Run, Run, Look And See
- ☐ '62 Sealed With A Kiss
- ☐ '62 Warmed Over Kisses (Left Over Love)

## HYMAN, Dick
- ☐ '69 Minotaur, The
- ☐ '56 Moritat (A Theme from "The Three Penny Opera")

## HYMAN, Phyllis
- ☐ '91 Don't Wanna Change The World

# I

## IAN, Janis
- ☐ '75 At Seventeen
- ☐ '67 Society's Child (Baby I've Been Thinking)

## ICE CUBE
- ☐ '94 Bop Gun (One Nation)
- ☐ '93 Check Yo Self
- ☐ '93 It Was A Good Day
- ☐ '98 Pushin' Weight
- ☐ '99 You Can Do It
- ☐ '94 You Know How We Do It

## ICEHOUSE
- ☐ '87 Crazy
- ☐ '88 Electric Blue

## ICICLE WORKS
- ☐ '84 Whisper To A Scream (Birds Fly)

## IDEAL
- ☐ '99 Get Gone

## IDES OF MARCH, The
- ☐ '70 Vehicle ★

## IDOL, Billy
- ☐ '90 Cradle Of Love ★
- ☐ '81 Dancing With Myself
- ☐ '87 Don't Need A Gun
- ☐ '84 Eyes Without A Face ★
- ☐ '84 Flesh For Fantasy
- ☐ '82 Hot In The City
- ☐ '81 Mony Mony
- ☐ '87 Mony Mony "Live" ★
- ☐ '83 Rebel Yell ★
- ☐ '87 Sweet Sixteen
- ☐ '86 To Be A Lover
- ☐ '83 White Wedding

## IFIELD, Frank
- ☐ '62 I Remember You

## IGLESIAS, Enrique
- ☐ '99 Bailamos ★
- ☐ '00 Be With You ★
- ☐ '02 Escape
- ☐ '01 Hero ★
- ☐ '99 Rhythm Divine

## IGLESIAS, Julio
- ☐ '84 All Of You
  - *JULIO IGLESIAS & DIANA ROSS*
- ☐ '84 To All The Girls I've Loved Before ★
  - *JULIO IGLESIAS & WILLIE NELSON*

## IKETTES, The
- ☐ '62 I'm Blue (The Gong-Gong Song)
- ☐ '65 Peaches "N" Cream

## ILLUSION, The
- ☐ '69 Did You See Her Eyes

## IMAJIN
- ☐ '98 Shorty (You Keep Playin' With My Mind)

## IMBRUGLIA, Natalie
- ☐ '98 Torn ★
- ☐ '98 Wishing I Was There

## IMMATURE
- ☐ '94 Constantly
- ☐ '94 Never Lie
- ☐ '96 Please Don't Go
- ☐ '99 Stay The Night
- ☐ '97 Watch Me Do My Thing
- ☐ '95 We Got It

## IMPALAS, The
- ☐ '59 Sorry (I Ran All the Way Home) ★

## IMPRESSIONS, The
- ☐ '64 Amen
- ☐ '70 Check Out Your Mind
- ☐ '69 Choice Of Colors
- ☐ '74 Finally Got Myself Together (I'm A Changed Man)
- ☐ '68 Fool For You
- ☐ '58 For Your Precious Love
  - *JERRY BUTLER & THE IMPRESSIONS*
- ☐ '61 Gypsy Woman
- ☐ '64 I'm So Proud
- ☐ '63 It's All Right
- ☐ '64 Keep On Pushing
- ☐ '65 People Get Ready ★
- ☐ '75 Same Thing It Took
- ☐ '75 Sooner Or Later
- ☐ '64 Talking About My Baby
- ☐ '68 This Is My Country
- ☐ '67 We're A Winner
- ☐ '65 Woman's Got Soul
- ☐ '64 You Must Believe Me
- ☐ '65 You've Been Cheatin'

## INC., The
- ☐ '02 Down 4 U

## INCUBUS
- ☐ '00 Drive
- ☐ '04 Megalomaniac
- ☐ '99 Pardon Me
- ☐ '00 Stellar
- ☐ '04 Talk Shows On Mute
- ☐ '02 Warning
- ☐ '01 Wish You Were Here

## INDECENT OBSESSION
- ☐ '90 Tell Me Something

## INDEPENDENTS, The
- ☐ '73 Leaving Me

## INDIA.ARIE
- ☐ '01 Video

## INDIGO GIRLS
- ☐ '89 Closer To Fine

## INFORMATION SOCIETY
- ☐ '90 Think
- ☐ '88 Walking Away
- ☐ '88 What's On Your Mind (Pure Energy)

## INGMANN, Jorgen, & His Guitar
- ☐ '61 Apache ★

## INGRAM, James
- ☐ '82 Baby, Come To Me ★
  - *PATTI AUSTIN (with James Ingram)*
- ☐ '90 I Don't Have The Heart ★
- ☐ '81 Just Once
- ☐ '81 One Hundred Ways
  - *QUINCY JONES Feat. James Ingram (above 2)*
- ☐ '86 Somewhere Out There ★
  - *LINDA RONSTADT & JAMES INGRAM*
- ☐ '84 What About Me?
  - *KENNY ROGERS with Kim Carnes & James Ingram*
- ☐ '83 Yah Mo B There
  - *JAMES INGRAM (with Michael McDonald)*

## INGRAM, Luther
- ☐ '72 I'll Be Your Shelter (In Time Of Storm)
- ☐ '72 (If Loving You Is Wrong) I Don't Want To Be Right

## INNER CIRCLE
- ☐ '93 Bad Boys ★
- ☐ '93 Sweat (A La La La La Long)

## INNOCENTS, The
- ☐ '60 Gee Whiz
- ☐ '60 Honest I Do

## INOJ
- ☐ '98 Love You Down
- ☐ '98 Time After Time

## INSTANT FUNK
- ☐ '79 I Got My Mind Made Up (You Can Get It Girl)

## INTRIGUES, The
- ☐ '69 In A Moment

## INTRO
- ☐ '93 Come Inside

## INTRUDERS, The
- ☐ '68 Cowboys To Girls
- ☐ '73 I'll Always Love My Mama
- ☐ '68 (Love Is Like A) Baseball Game

## INXS
- ☐ '87 Devil Inside ★
- ☐ '90 Disappear
- ☐ '97 Elegantly Wasted
- ☐ '87 Good Times
  - *INXS & JIMMY BARNES*
- ☐ '92 Heaven Sent
- ☐ '87 Need You Tonight ★
- ☐ '88 Never Tear Us Apart
- ☐ '88 New Sensation
- ☐ '92 Not Enough Time
- ☐ '83 One Thing, The
- ☐ '90 Suicide Blonde
- ☐ '86 What You Need

## IRBY, Joyce "Fenderella"
- ☐ '89 Mr. D.J.

## IRIS, Donnie
- ☐ '80 Ah! Leah!
- ☐ '81 Love Is Like A Rock
- ☐ '82 My Girl

## IRISH ROVERS, The
- ☐ '68 Unicorn, The
- ☐ '81 Wasn't That A Party

## IRON BUTTERFLY
- ☐ '68 In-A-Gadda-Da-Vida ★

## IRONHORSE
- ☐ '79 Sweet Lui-Louise

## IRWIN, Big Dee
- ☐ '63 Swinging On A Star
  - *BIG DEE IRWIN (with Little Eva)*

## IRWIN, Russ
- ☐ '91 My Heart Belongs To You

## ISAAK, Chris
- ☐ '90 Wicked Game ★

## ISLANDERS, The
- ☐ '59 Enchanted Sea, The

## ISLEY BROTHERS, The
- ☐ '83 Between The Sheets
- ☐ '01 Contagious
- ☐ '80 Don't Say Goodnight (It's Time For Love)
- ☐ '75 Fight The Power
- ☐ '75 For The Love Of You
- ☐ '69 I Turned You On
- ☐ '79 I Wanna Be With You
- ☐ '69 It's Your Thing ★
- ☐ '77 Livin' In The Life
- ☐ '71 Love The One You're With
- ☐ '72 Pop That Thang
- ☐ '77 Pride, The
- ☐ '59 Shout ★
- ☐ '78 Take Me To The Next Phase
- ☐ '73 That Lady
- ☐ '66 This Old Heart Of Mine (Is Weak For You)
- ☐ '62 Twist And Shout
- ☐ '76 Who Loves You Better

## ISLEY, JASPER, ISLEY
- ☐ '85 Caravan Of Love

## IT'S A BEAUTIFUL DAY
- ☐ '69 White Bird

## IVAN — see HOLLY, Buddy

## IVES, Burl
- ☐ '62 Call Me Mr. In-Between
- ☐ '62 Funny Way Of Laughin'
- ☐ '61 Little Bitty Tear, A
- ☐ '62 Mary Ann Regrets

## IVY THREE, The
- ☐ '60 Yogi

# J

## JACKS, The
- ☐ '55 Why Don't You Write Me?

## JACKS, Terry
- ☐ '74 Seasons In The Sun ★

## JACKSON, Alan
- ☐ '97 Between The Devil And Me
- ☐ '90 Chasin' That Neon Rainbow
- ☐ '93 Chattahoochee ★
- ☐ '92 Dallas
- ☐ '91 Don't Rock The Jukebox
- ☐ '02 Drive (For Daddy Gene)
- ☐ '94 Gone Country
- ☐ '90 Here In The Real World
- ☐ '96 Home
- ☐ '95 I Don't Even Know Your Name
- ☐ '91 I'd Love You All Over Again

'98 I'll Go On Loving You
'95 I'll Try
'00 It Must Be Love
'03 It's Five O'Clock Somewhere
    *ALAN JACKSON & JIMMY BUFFETT*
'96 Little Bitty
'99 Little Man
'94 Livin' On Love
'92 Love's Got A Hold On You
'93 Mercury Blues
'92 Midnight In Montgomery
'99 Pop A Top
'03 Remember When
'98 Right On The Money
'92 She's Got The Rhythm (And I Got The Blues)
'91 Someday
'94 Summertime Blues
'95 Tall, Tall Trees
'02 That'd Be Alright
'97 There Goes
'90 Wanted
'01 Where I Come From
'01 Where Were You (When The World Stopped Turning)
'97 Who's Cheatin' Who
'02 Work In Progress

## JACKSON, Chuck
'62 Any Day Now (My Wild Beautiful Bird)
'61 I Don't Want To Cry

## JACKSON, Deon
'66 Love Makes The World Go Round

## JACKSON, Freddie
'91 Do Me Again
'86 Have You Ever Loved Somebody
'85 He'll Never Love You (Like I Do)
'88 Hey Lover
'92 I Could Use A Little Love (Right Now)
'87 I Don't Want To Lose Your Love
'87 Jam Tonight
'86 Little Bit More, A
'90 Love Me Down
'91 Main Course
'88 Nice 'N' Slow
'85 Rock Me Tonight (For Old Times Sake)
'86 Tasty Love
'85 You Are My Lady

## JACKSON, J.J.
'66 But It's Alright

## JACKSON, Janet
'93 Again ★
'01 All For You ★
'90 Alright
'94 And On And On
'94 Any Time, Any Place
'94 Because Of Love
'92 Best Things In Life Are Free, The
    *LUTHER VANDROSS & JANET JACKSON*
'90 Black Cat ★
'90 Come Back To Me
'86 Control

'87 Diamonds
    *HERB ALPERT (with Janet Jackson)*
'00 Doesn't Really Matter ★
'90 Escapade ★
'98 Go Deep
'97 Got 'Til It's Gone
'98 I Get Lonely
'93 If
'87 Let's Wait Awhile
'90 Love Will Never Do (Without You) ★
'89 Miss You Much ★
'86 Nasty
'87 Pleasure Principle, The
'89 Rhythm Nation ★
'95 Runaway ★
'95 Scream
    *MICHAEL JACKSON & JANET JACKSON*
'01 Someone To Call My Lover ★
'01 Son Of A Gun (I Betcha Think This Song Is About You)
'91 State Of The World
'93 That's The Way Love Goes ★
'97 Together Again ★
'86 What Have You Done For Me Lately
'86 When I Think Of You ★
'93 Where Are You Now
'94 You Want This

## JACKSON, Jermaine
'72 Daddy's Home
'84 Do What You Do
'89 Don't Take It Personal
'84 Dynamite
'86 I Think It's Love
'82 Let Me Tickle Your Fancy
'80 Let's Get Serious
'84 Tell Me I'm Not Dreamin' (Too Good To Be True)
    *JERMAINE & MICHAEL JACKSON*
'80 You're Supposed To Keep Your Love For Me

## JACKSON, Joe
'83 Breaking Us In Two
'79 Is She Really Going Out With Him?
'82 Steppin' Out
'84 You Can't Get What You Want (Till You Know What You Want)

## JACKSON, Michael
'88 Another Part Of Me
'87 Bad ★
'83 Beat It ★
'72 Ben
'83 Billie Jean ★
'91 Black Or White ★
'01 Butterflies
'88 Dirty Diana ★
'79 Don't Stop 'Til You Get Enough ★
'84 Farewell My Summer Love
'82 Girl Is Mine, The ★
    *MICHAEL JACKSON & PAUL McCARTNEY*
'71 Got To Be There
'92 Heal The World
'83 Human Nature
'87 I Just Can't Stop Loving You ★

## JACKSON, Michael — cont'd

- ☐ '72 I Wanna Be Where You Are
- ☐ '92 In The Closet
- ☐ '92 Jam
- ☐ '75 Just A Little Bit Of You
- ☐ '88 Man In The Mirror ★
- ☐ '80 Off The Wall
- ☐ '83 P.Y.T. (Pretty Young Thing)
- ☐ '92 Remember The Time ★
- ☐ '79 Rock With You ★
- ☐ '72 Rockin' Robin
- ☐ '83 Say Say Say ★
  PAUL McCARTNEY & MICHAEL JACKSON
- ☐ '95 Scream
  MICHAEL JACKSON & JANET JACKSON
- ☐ '80 She's Out Of My Life
- ☐ '88 Smooth Criminal
- ☐ '84 Tell Me I'm Not Dreamin' (Too Good To Be True)
  JERMAINE & MICHAEL JACKSON
- ☐ '96 They Don't Care About Us
- ☐ '84 Thriller ★
- ☐ '83 Wanna Be Startin' Somethin'
- ☐ '87 Way You Make Me Feel, The ★
- ☐ '93 Who Is It
- ☐ '93 Will You Be There
- ☐ '95 You Are Not Alone
- ☐ '01 You Rock My World

## JACKSON, Millie

- ☐ '72 Ask Me What You Want
- ☐ '73 Hurts So Good

## JACKSON, Rebbie

- ☐ '84 Centipede

## JACKSON, Stonewall

- ☐ '59 Waterloo

## JACKSON, Wanda

- ☐ '61 In The Middle Of A Heartache
- ☐ '60 Let's Have A Party
- ☐ '61 Right Or Wrong

## JACKSON 5, The

- ☐ '70 ABC ★
- ☐ '78 Blame It On The Boogie
- ☐ '72 Corner Of The Sky
- ☐ '74 Dancing Machine
- ☐ '76 Enjoy Yourself
- ☐ '73 Get It Together
- ☐ '73 Hallelujah Day
- ☐ '80 Heartbreak Hotel
- ☐ '75 I Am Love
- ☐ '69 I Want You Back ★
- ☐ '70 I'll Be There ★
- ☐ '72 Little Bitty Pretty One
- ☐ '72 Lookin' Through The Windows
- ☐ '70 Love You Save, The ★
- ☐ '80 Lovely One
- ☐ '71 Mama's Pearl
- ☐ '71 Maybe Tomorrow
- ☐ '71 Never Can Say Goodbye
- ☐ '79 Shake Your Body (Down To The Ground)

- ☐ '77 Show You The Way To Go
- ☐ '84 State Of Shock
- ☐ '71 Sugar Daddy
- ☐ '84 Torture
- ☐ '74 Whatever You Got, I Want

## JACOBS, Dick, & His Orchestra

- ☐ '57 Fascination
- ☐ '56 "Main Title" And "Molly-O"
- ☐ '56 Petticoats Of Portugal

## JADAKISS

- ☐ '04 U Make Me Wanna
- ☐ '04 Why?

## JADE

- ☐ '92 Don't Walk Away
- ☐ '94 Every Day Of The Week
- ☐ '92 I Wanna Love You
- ☐ '93 One Woman

## JAGGED EDGE

- ☐ '98 Gotta Be
- ☐ '99 He Can't Love U
- ☐ '00 Let's Get Married
- ☐ '00 Promise
- ☐ '03 Walked Outta Heaven ★
- ☐ '01 Where The Party At ★

## JAGGER, Mick

- ☐ '85 Dancing In The Street
  MICK JAGGER & DAVID BOWIE
- ☐ '93 Don't Tear Me Up
- ☐ '85 Just Another Night
- ☐ '87 Let's Work
- ☐ '85 Lucky In Love

## JAGGERZ, The

- ☐ '70 Rapper, The ★

## JAHEIM

- ☐ '02 Anything
- ☐ '00 Could It Be
- ☐ '02 Fabulous
- ☐ '03 Put That Woman First

## JAM, The

- ☐ '83 In The City
- ☐ '81 That's Entertainment

## JAMES

- ☐ '93 Laid

## JAMES, Etta

- ☐ '60 All I Could Do Was Cry
- ☐ '61 At Last
- ☐ '61 Don't Cry, Baby
- ☐ '60 My Dearest Darling
- ☐ '63 Pushover
- ☐ '68 Security
- ☐ '62 Something's Got A Hold On Me
- ☐ '62 Stop The Wedding
- ☐ '67 Tell Mama
- ☐ '61 Trust In Me
- ☐ '55 Wallflower, The

## JAMES, Joni
- ☐ '56 Give Us This Day
- ☐ '55 How Important Can It Be?
- ☐ '59 Little Things Mean A Lot
- ☐ '60 My Last Date (With You)
- ☐ '58 There Goes My Heart
- ☐ '59 There Must Be A Way
- ☐ '55 You Are My Love

## JAMES, Rick
- ☐ '83 Cold Blooded
- ☐ '82 Dance Wit' Me
- ☐ '81 Give It To Me Baby
- ☐ '88 Loosey's Rap
- ☐ '78 Mary Jane
- ☐ '84 17
- ☐ '81 Super Freak
- ☐ '78 You And I

## JAMES, Sonny
- ☐ '57 First Date, First Kiss, First Love
- ☐ '56 Young Love ★

## JAMES, Tommy
- ☐ '71 Draggin' The Line
- ☐ '71 I'm Comin' Home
- ☐ '80 Three Times In Love

## JAMES, Tommy, & The Shondells
- ☐ '69 Ball Of Fire
- ☐ '68 Crimson And Clover ★
- ☐ '69 Crystal Blue Persuasion
- ☐ '68 Do Something To Me
- ☐ '67 Gettin' Together
- ☐ '66 Hanky Panky ★
- ☐ '67 I Like The Way
- ☐ '67 I Think We're Alone Now
- ☐ '66 It's Only Love
- ☐ '67 Mirage
- ☐ '68 Mony Mony ★
- ☐ '66 Say I Am (What I Am)
- ☐ '69 She
- ☐ '69 Sweet Cherry Wine

## JAMES GANG
- ☐ '70 Funk #49
- ☐ '71 Walk Away

## JAMIES, The
- ☐ '58 Summertime, Summertime

## JAN & DEAN
- ☐ '59 Baby Talk
- ☐ '64 Dead Man's Curve
- ☐ '63 Drag City
- ☐ '61 Heart And Soul
- ☐ '63 Honolulu Lulu
- ☐ '65 I Found A Girl
- ☐ '58 Jennie Lee
- ☐ '63 Linda
- ☐ '64 Little Old Lady (From Pasadena) ★
- ☐ '64 New Girl In School, The
- ☐ '66 Popsicle
- ☐ '64 Ride The Wild Surf
- ☐ '64 Sidewalk Surfin'
- ☐ '63 Surf City ★
- ☐ '60 We Go Together
- ☐ '65 You Really Know How To Hurt A Guy

## JANE'S ADDICTION
- ☐ '90 Been Caught Stealing
- ☐ '88 Jane Says
- ☐ '03 Just Because
- ☐ '90 Stop!

## JANKOWSKI, Horst
- ☐ '65 Walk In The Black Forest, A ★

## JARMELS, The
- ☐ '61 Little Bit Of Soap, A

## JARREAU, Al
- ☐ '87 Moonlighting (Theme)
- ☐ '83 Mornin'
- ☐ '88 So Good
- ☐ '81 We're In This Love Together

## JARS OF CLAY
- ☐ '96 Flood
- ☐ '02 I Need You
- ☐ '95 Love Song For A Savior

## JA RULE
- ☐ '01 Always On Time ★
- ☐ '00 Between Me And You
- ☐ '02 Down A** Chick
- ☐ '99 Holla Holla
- ☐ '01 I Cry
- ☐ '01 Livin' It Up ★
- ☐ '02 Mesmerize ★
- ☐ '04 New York
- ☐ '00 Put It On Me
- ☐ '04 Wonderful ★

## JAY & THE AMERICANS
- ☐ '65 Cara, Mia
- ☐ '64 Come A Little Bit Closer
- ☐ '66 Crying
- ☐ '64 Let's Lock The Door (And Throw Away The Key)
- ☐ '63 Only In America
- ☐ '62 She Cried
- ☐ '65 Some Enchanted Evening
- ☐ '65 Sunday And Me
- ☐ '68 This Magic Moment
- ☐ '69 Walkin' In The Rain

## JAY & THE TECHNIQUES
- ☐ '67 Apples, Peaches, Pumpkin Pie
- ☐ '67 Keep The Ball Rollin'
- ☐ '68 Strawberry Shortcake

## JAYE, Jerry
- ☐ '67 My Girl Josephine

## JAYHAWKS, The
- ☐ '56 Stranded In The Jungle

## JAYNETTS, The
- ☐ '63 Sally, Go 'Round The Roses ★

## JAY-Z

- ☐ '04 Big Chips
  *R. KELLY & JAY-Z*
- ☐ '00 Big Pimpin'
- ☐ '98 Can I Get A...
- ☐ '03 Change Clothes
- ☐ '04 Dirt Off Your Shoulder
- ☐ '03 Excuse Me Miss
- ☐ '01 Girls, Girls, Girls
- ☐ '98 Hard Knock Life (Ghetto Anthem)
- ☐ '00 I Just Wanna Love U (Give It 2 Me)
- ☐ '01 Izzo (H.O.V.A.) ★
- ☐ '99 Jigga My Nigga
- ☐ '04 99 Problems
- ☐ '04 Numb/Encore
  *JAY-Z & LINKIN PARK*
- ☐ '02 '03 Bonnie & Clyde ★

## JB's, The

- ☐ '73 Doing It To Death
  *FRED WESLEY & THE J.B's*

## JEAN, Wyclef

- ☐ '98 Gone Till November
- ☐ '00 911
- ☐ '02 Two Wrongs

## JEFFERSON

- ☐ '69 Baby Take Me In Your Arms

## JEFFERSON AIRPLANE/STARSHIP

- ☐ '82 Be My Lady
- ☐ '78 Count On Me
- ☐ '68 Crown Of Creation
- ☐ '81 Find Your Way Back
- ☐ '68 Greasy Heart
- ☐ '89 It's Not Enough
- ☐ '87 It's Not Over ('Til It's Over)
- ☐ '79 Jane
- ☐ '75 Miracles
- ☐ '84 No Way Out
- ☐ '87 Nothing's Gonna Stop Us Now ★
- ☐ '67 Plastic Fantastic Lover
- ☐ '75 Play On Love
- ☐ '71 Pretty As You Feel
- ☐ '74 Ride The Tiger
- ☐ '78 Runaway
- ☐ '85 Sara
- ☐ '67 Somebody To Love
- ☐ '86 Tomorrow Doesn't Matter Tonight
- ☐ '69 Volunteers
- ☐ '85 We Built This City ★
- ☐ '67 White Rabbit ★
- ☐ '83 Winds Of Change
- ☐ '76 With Your Love

## JEFFREY, Joe, Group

- ☐ '69 My Pledge Of Love

## JELLYBEAN

- ☐ '85 Sidewalk Talk
- ☐ '87 Who Found Who
  *JELLYBEAN/Elisa Fiorillo*

## JELLY BEANS, The

- ☐ '64 I Wanna Love Him So Bad

## JENNINGS, Waylon

- ☐ '76 Good Hearted Woman
  *WAYLON & WILLIE*
- ☐ '85 Highwayman
  *WAYLON JENNINGS/WILLIE NELSON/
  JOHNNY CASH/KRIS KRISTOFFERSON*
- ☐ '77 Luckenbach, Texas (Back to the Basics of Love)
- ☐ '78 Mammas Don't Let Your Babies Grow Up To Be Cowboys
  *WAYLON & WILLIE*
- ☐ '80 Theme From The Dukes Of Hazzard (Good Ol' Boys)

## JENSEN, Kris

- ☐ '62 Torture

## JESUS & MARY CHAIN, The

- ☐ '89 Blues From A Gun
- ☐ '90 Head On

## JESUS JONES

- ☐ '91 Real, Real, Real
- ☐ '91 Right Here, Right Now ★

## JET

- ☐ '03 Are You Gonna Be My Girl
- ☐ '04 Cold Hard Bitch
- ☐ '04 Look What You've Done

## JETHRO TULL

- ☐ '71 Aqualung
- ☐ '69 Bouree
- ☐ '74 Bungle In The Jungle
- ☐ '71 Cross-Eyed Mary
- ☐ '71 Hymn 43
- ☐ '72 Living In The Past
- ☐ '71 Locomotive Breath
- ☐ '75 Minstrel In The Gallery
- ☐ '69 New Day Yesterday
- ☐ '74 Skating Away On The Thin Ice Of A New Day
- ☐ '70 Teacher
- ☐ '72 Thick As A Brick
- ☐ '76 Too Old To Rock 'N' Roll: Too Young To Die

## JETS, The

- ☐ '87 Cross My Broken Heart
- ☐ '86 Crush On You
- ☐ '87 I Do You
- ☐ '88 Make It Real
- ☐ '88 Rocket 2 U
- ☐ '86 You Got It All

## JETT, Joan, & The Blackhearts

- ☐ '82 Crimson And Clover
- ☐ '90 Dirty Deeds
- ☐ '82 Do You Wanna Touch Me (Oh Yeah)
- ☐ '83 Everyday People
- ☐ '83 Fake Friends
- ☐ '88 I Hate Myself For Loving You
- ☐ '81 I Love Rock 'N Roll ★
- ☐ '87 Light Of Day
- ☐ '88 Little Liar

## JEWEL
- ☐ '97 Foolish Games
- ☐ '98 Hands ★
- ☐ '03 Intuition
- ☐ '01 Standing Still
- ☐ '96 Who Will Save Your Soul
- ☐ '96 You Were Meant For Me ★

## JEWELL, Buddy
- ☐ '03 Help Pour Out The Rain (Lacey's Song)
- ☐ '03 Sweet Southern Comfort

## JIGSAW
- ☐ '76 Love Fire
- ☐ '75 Sky High

## JIMENEZ, Jose
- ☐ '61 Astronaut, The

## JIMMY EAT WORLD
- ☐ '01 Middle, The ★
- ☐ '04 Pain
- ☐ '02 Sweetness

## JINKINS, Gus, & Orchestra
- ☐ '56 Tricky

## JIVE BOMBERS, The
- ☐ '57 Bad Boy

## JIVE BUNNY & THE MASTERMIXERS
- ☐ '89 Swing The Mood

## JIVE FIVE, The
- ☐ '65 I'm A Happy Man
- ☐ '61 My True Story ★

## J.J. FAD
- ☐ '88 Supersonic

## J-KWON
- ☐ '04 Tipsy ★

## JoBOXERS
- ☐ '83 Just Got Lucky

## JODECI
- ☐ '92 Come & Talk To Me
- ☐ '93 Cry For You
- ☐ '94 Feenin'
- ☐ '91 Forever My Lady
- ☐ '95 Freek 'n You
- ☐ '96 Get On Up
- ☐ '93 Lately ★
- ☐ '95 Love U 4 Life
- ☐ '91 Stay

## JOE
- ☐ '96 All The Things (Your Man Won't Do)
- ☐ '97 Don't Wanna Be A Player
- ☐ '98 Faded Pictures
  - *CASE & JOE*
- ☐ '00 I Wanna Know ★
- ☐ '01 Stutter ★

## JOEL, Billy
- ☐ '93 All About Soul
- ☐ '80 All For Leyna
- ☐ '82 Allentown
- ☐ '90 And So It Goes
- ☐ '87 Baby Grand
  - *BILLY JOEL & RAY CHARLES*
- ☐ '74 Ballad Of Billy The Kid
- ☐ '79 Big Shot
- ☐ '74 Captain Jack
- ☐ '80 Close To The Borderline
- ☐ '80 Don't Ask Me Why
- ☐ '74 Entertainer, The
- ☐ '79 Honesty
- ☐ '90 I Go To Extremes
- ☐ '83 Innocent Man, An
- ☐ '80 It's Still Rock And Roll To Me ★
- ☐ '77 Just The Way You Are ★
- ☐ '85 Keeping The Faith
- ☐ '84 Leave A Tender Moment Alone
- ☐ '84 Longest Time, The
- ☐ '86 Matter Of Trust, A
- ☐ '86 Modern Woman
- ☐ '78 Movin' Out (Anthony's Song)
- ☐ '78 My Life ★
- ☐ '76 New York State Of Mind
- ☐ '85 Night Is Still Young, The
- ☐ '78 Only The Good Die Young
- ☐ '74 Piano Man
- ☐ '82 Pressure
- ☐ '93 River Of Dreams, The ★
- ☐ '78 Rosalinda's Eyes
- ☐ '81 Say Goodbye To Hollywood
- ☐ '77 Scenes From An Italian Restaurant
- ☐ '78 She's Always A Woman
- ☐ '81 She's Got A Way
- ☐ '80 Sometimes A Fantasy
- ☐ '77 Stranger, The
- ☐ '83 Tell Her About It ★
- ☐ '86 This Is The Time
- ☐ '83 Uptown Girl ★
- ☐ '89 We Didn't Start The Fire ★
- ☐ '80 You May Be Right
- ☐ '85 You're Only Human (Second Wind)

## JOE PUBLIC
- ☐ '92 Live And Learn ★

## JOHN, Elton
- ☐ '95 Believe
- ☐ '74 Bennie And The Jets ★
- ☐ '74 Bitch Is Back, The
- ☐ '77 Bite Your Lip (Get up and dance!)
- ☐ '95 Blessed
- ☐ '82 Blue Eyes
- ☐ '70 Border Song
- ☐ '71 Burn Down The Mission
- ☐ '94 Can You Feel The Love Tonight ★
- ☐ '73 Candle In The Wind
- ☐ '87 Candle In The Wind [live]
- ☐ '97 Candle In The Wind 1997 ★
- ☐ '81 Chloe
- ☐ '94 Circle Of Life
- ☐ '90 Club At The End Of The Street
- ☐ '72 Crocodile Rock ★
- ☐ '73 Daniel ★
- ☐ '76 Don't Go Breaking My Heart ★
  - *ELTON JOHN & KIKI DEE*

## JOHN, Elton — cont'd

- ☐ '74 Don't Let The Sun Go Down On Me ★
- ☐ '91 Don't Let The Sun Go Down On Me [live] ★
  *GEORGE MICHAEL & ELTON JOHN*
- ☐ '78 Ego
- ☐ '82 Empty Garden (Hey Hey Johnny)
- ☐ '87 Flames Of Paradise
  *JENNIFER RUSH (with Elton John)*
- ☐ '71 Friends
- ☐ '73 Funeral For A Friend/Love Lies Bleeding
- ☐ '73 Goodbye Yellow Brick Road ★
- ☐ '73 Grey Seal
- ☐ '76 Grow Some Funk Of Your Own
- ☐ '73 Harmony
- ☐ '89 Healing Hands
- ☐ '72 Hercules
- ☐ '72 Honky Cat
- ☐ '88 I Don't Wanna Go On With You Like That
- ☐ '83 I Guess That's Why They Call It The Blues
- ☐ '83 I'm Still Standing
- ☐ '84 In Neon
- ☐ '75 Island Girl ★
- ☐ '83 Kiss The Bride
- ☐ '92 Last Song, The
- ☐ '71 Levon
- ☐ '80 Little Jeannie ★
- ☐ '74 Lucy In The Sky With Diamonds ★
- ☐ '71 Madman Across The Water
- ☐ '79 Mama Can't Buy You Love
- ☐ '72 Mona Lisas And Mad Hatters
- ☐ '86 Nikita
- ☐ '81 Nobody Wins
- ☐ '92 One, The
- ☐ '78 Part-Time Love
- ☐ '75 Philadelphia Freedom ★
- ☐ '75 Pinball Wizard
- ☐ '72 Rocket Man ★
- ☐ '90 Sacrifice
- ☐ '84 Sad Songs (Say So Much)
- ☐ '80 (Sartorial Eloquence) Don't Ya Wanna Play This Game No More?
- ☐ '73 Saturday Night's Alright For Fighting
- ☐ '93 Simple Life
- ☐ '75 Someone Saved My Life Tonight
- ☐ '97 Something About The Way You Look Tonight ★
- ☐ '76 Sorry Seems To Be The Hardest Word
- ☐ '73 Step Into Christmas
- ☐ '70 Take Me To The Pilot
- ☐ '89 Through The Storm
  *ARETHA FRANKLIN & ELTON JOHN*
- ☐ '71 Tiny Dancer
- ☐ '79 Victim Of Love
- ☐ '84 Who Wears These Shoes?
- ☐ '88 Word In Spanish, A
- ☐ '85 Wrap Her Up
- ☐ '99 Written In The Stars
  *ELTON JOHN & LEANN RIMES*
- ☐ '90 You Gotta Love Someone
- ☐ '70 Your Song ★

## JOHN, Little Willie

- ☐ '56 Fever
- ☐ '60 Heartbreak (It's Hurtin' Me)
- ☐ '59 Leave My Kitten Alone
- ☐ '60 Sleep
- ☐ '58 Talk To Me, Talk To Me

## JOHN, Robert

- ☐ '80 Hey There Lonely Girl
- ☐ '72 Lion Sleeps Tonight, The
- ☐ '79 Sad Eyes

## JOHN & ERNEST

- ☐ '73 Super Fly Meets Shaft

## JOHNNIE & JOE

- ☐ '57 Over The Mountain; Across The Sea

## JOHNNY & THE HURRICANES

- ☐ '60 Beatnik Fly
- ☐ '59 Crossfire
- ☐ '60 Down Yonder
- ☐ '59 Red River Rock ★
- ☐ '59 Reveille Rock
- ☐ '60 Rocking Goose

## JOHNNY HATES JAZZ

- ☐ '88 I Don't Want To Be A Hero
- ☐ '88 Shattered Dreams

## JOHNS, Sammy

- ☐ '75 Chevy Van

## JOHNSON, Betty

- ☐ '58 Dream
- ☐ '56 I Dreamed
- ☐ '58 Little Blue Man, The
- ☐ '57 Little White Lies

## JOHNSON, Don

- ☐ '86 Heartbeat
- ☐ '88 Till I Loved You
  *BARBRA STREISAND & DON JOHNSON*

## JOHNSON, Jesse

- ☐ '86 Crazay

## JOHNSON, Marv

- ☐ '59 Come To Me
- ☐ '60 I Love The Way You Love
- ☐ '59 You Got What It Takes
- ☐ '60 (You've Got To) Move Two Mountains

## JOHNSON, Michael

- ☐ '78 Almost Like Being In Love
- ☐ '78 Bluer Than Blue
- ☐ '79 This Night Won't Last Forever

## JOHNSTON, Tom

- ☐ '79 Savannah Nights

## JOJO

- ☐ '04 Baby It's You
- ☐ '04 Leave (Get Out)

## JO JO GUNNE

- ☐ '72 Run Run Run

## JOLI, France
- [ ] '79 Come To Me

## JOMANDA
- [ ] '91 Got A Love For You

## JON & ROBIN & The In Crowd
- [ ] '67 Do It Again A Little Bit Slower

## JON B
- [ ] '98 Are U Still Down
- [ ] '95 Pretty Girl
- [ ] '95 Someone To Love
- [ ] '98 They Don't Know

## JONES, Donell
- [ ] '99 U Know What's Up
- [ ] '00 Where I Wanna Be

## JONES, Etta
- [ ] '60 Don't Go To Strangers

## JONES, George
- [ ] '80 He Stopped Loving Her Today ★
- [ ] '62 She Thinks I Still Care
- [ ] '61 Tender Years
- [ ] '59 White Lightning

## JONES, Glenn
- [ ] '92 Here I Go Again
- [ ] '84 Show Me
- [ ] '87 We've Only Just Begun (The Romance Is Not Over)

## JONES, Howard
- [ ] '89 Everlasting Love
- [ ] '85 Life In One Day
- [ ] '92 Lift Me Up
- [ ] '84 New Song
- [ ] '86 No One Is To Blame
- [ ] '89 Prisoner, The
- [ ] '85 Things Can Only Get Better
- [ ] '84 What Is Love?
- [ ] '86 You Know I Love You...Don't You?

## JONES, Jack
- [ ] '63 Call Me Irresponsible
- [ ] '66 Day In The Life Of A Fool, A
- [ ] '64 Dear Heart
- [ ] '66 Impossible Dream, The
- [ ] '67 Lady
- [ ] '62 Lollipops And Roses
- [ ] '67 Now I Know
- [ ] '65 Race Is On, The
- [ ] '63 Wives And Lovers

## JONES, Jimmy
- [ ] '60 Good Timin' ★
- [ ] '59 Handy Man ★

## JONES, Joe
- [ ] '60 You Talk Too Much

## JONES, Linda
- [ ] '67 Hypnotized

## JONES, Norah
- [ ] '02 Don't Know Why

## JONES, Oran "Juice"
- [ ] '86 Rain, The

## JONES, Quincy
- [ ] '81 Ai No Corrida (I-No-Ko-ree-da)
- [ ] '89 I'll Be Good To You
  - QUINCY JONES Ft. Ray Charles & Chaka Khan
- [ ] '81 Just Once
- [ ] '81 One Hundred Ways
  - QUINCY JONES & JAMES INGRAM
- [ ] '90 Secret Garden (Sweet Seduction Suite)
  - QUINCY JONES/Al B. Sure!/James Ingram/ El DeBarge/Barry White
- [ ] '78 Stuff Like That
- [ ] '90 Tomorrow (A Better You, Better Me)
  - QUINCY JONES Feat. Tevin Campbell

## JONES, Rickie Lee
- [ ] '79 Chuck E.'s In Love
- [ ] '79 Young Blood

## JONES, Shirley
- [ ] '86 Do You Get Enough Love

## JONES, Tom
- [ ] '70 Can't Stop Loving You
- [ ] '70 Daughter Of Darkness
- [ ] '68 Delilah
- [ ] '67 Detroit City
- [ ] '66 Green, Green Grass Of Home
- [ ] '68 Help Yourself
- [ ] '70 I (Who Have Nothing)
- [ ] '67 I'll Never Fall In Love Again
- [ ] '65 It's Not Unusual
- [ ] '69 Love Me Tonight
- [ ] '71 Puppet Man
- [ ] '71 Resurrection Shuffle
- [ ] '77 Say You'll Stay Until Tomorrow
- [ ] '71 She's A Lady ★
- [ ] '65 Thunderball
- [ ] '65 What's New Pussycat? ★
- [ ] '65 With These Hands
- [ ] '69 Without Love (There Is Nothing)

## JONES GIRLS, The
- [ ] '79 You Gonna Make Me Love Somebody Else

## JOPLIN, Janis/BIG BROTHER & THE HOLDING COMPANY
- [ ] '68 Ball And Chain
- [ ] '71 Cry Baby
- [ ] '68 Down On Me
- [ ] '71 Get It While You Can
- [ ] '69 Kozmic Blues
- [ ] '71 Me And Bobby McGee ★
- [ ] '71 Mercedes Benz
- [ ] '71 Move Over
- [ ] '68 Piece Of My Heart ★
- [ ] '69 Try (Just A Little Bit Harder)

## JORDAN, Jeremy
- [ ] '92 Right Kind Of Love, The
- [ ] '93 Wannagirl

## JORDAN, Montell
- ☐ '96  Falling
- ☐ '99  Get It On...Tonite ★
- ☐ '98  I Can Do That
- ☐ '96  I Like
- ☐ '98  Let's Ride ★
- ☐ '95  Somethin' 4 Da Honeyz
- ☐ '95  This Is How We Do It ★
- ☐ '97  What's On Tonight

## JOURNEY
- ☐ '83  After The Fall
- ☐ '80  Any Way You Want It
- ☐ '78  Anytime
- ☐ '83  Ask The Lonely
- ☐ '86  Be Good To Yourself
- ☐ '81  Don't Stop Believin'
- ☐ '83  Faithfully
- ☐ '86  Girl Can't Help It
- ☐ '86  I'll Be Alright Without You
- ☐ '79  Just The Same Way
- ☐ '78  Lights
- ☐ '79  Lovin', Touchin', Squeezin'
- ☐ '85  Only The Young
- ☐ '82  Open Arms ★
- ☐ '81  Party's Over (Hopelessly In Love)
- ☐ '83  Send Her My Love
- ☐ '83  Separate Ways (Worlds Apart)
- ☐ '82  Still They Ride
- ☐ '86  Suzanne
- ☐ '80  Walks Like A Lady
- ☐ '78  Wheel In The Sky
- ☐ '96  When You Love A Woman
- ☐ '81  Who's Crying Now

## JOY DIVISION
- ☐ '80  Love Will Tear Us Apart

## J-SHIN
- ☐ '99  One Night Stand

## JUDAS PRIEST
- ☐ '80  Breaking The Law
- ☐ '80  Living After Midnight
- ☐ '82  You've Got Another Thing Comin'

## JUNIOR
- ☐ '86  Grandpa (Tell Me 'Bout The Good Old Days)
- ☐ '85  Have Mercy
- ☐ '84  Why Not Me

## JUMP 'N THE SADDLE
- ☐ '83  Curly Shuffle, The

## JUNIOR
- ☐ '82  Mama Used To Say

## JUNIOR M.A.F.I.A.
- ☐ '96  Get Money
- ☐ '95  Player's Anthem

## JUSTIS, Bill
- ☐ '57  Raunchy ★

## JUST US
- ☐ '66  I Can't Grow Peaches On A Cherry Tree

## JUVENILE
- ☐ '99  Back That Azz Up
- ☐ '04  Nolia Clap
  - JUVENILE • WACKO • SKIP
- ☐ '04  Slow Motion

# K

## KADISON, Joshua
- ☐ '94  Beautiful In My Eyes
- ☐ '93  Jessie

## KAEMPFERT, Bert, & His Orchestra
- ☐ '62  Afrikaan Beat
- ☐ '65  Moon Over Naples
- ☐ '65  Red Roses For A Blue Lady
- ☐ '61  Tenderly
- ☐ '65  Three O'Clock In The Morning
- ☐ '60  Wonderland By Night ★

## KAJAGOOGOO
- ☐ '83  Too Shy

## KALIN TWINS
- ☐ '58  Forget Me Not
- ☐ '59  It's Only The Beginning
- ☐ '58  When

## KALLEN, Kitty
- ☐ '56  Go On With The Wedding
  - KITTY KALLEN & GEORGIE SHAW
- ☐ '59  If I Give My Heart To You
- ☐ '62  My Coloring Book
- ☐ '60  That Old Feeling

## KALLMANN, Gunter, Chorus
- ☐ '66  Wish Me A Rainbow

## KAMOZE, Ini
- ☐ '94  Here Comes The Hotstepper ★

## KANDI
- ☐ '00  Don't Think I'm Not

## KANE, Big Daddy
- ☐ '88  Ain't No Half-Steppin'
- ☐ '93  Very Special

## KANE GANG, The
- ☐ '87  Motortown

## KANSAS
- ☐ '86  All I Wanted
- ☐ '76  Carry On Wayward Son
- ☐ '78  Dust In The Wind
- ☐ '83  Fight Fire With Fire
- ☐ '80  Hold On
- ☐ '79  People Of The South Wind
- ☐ '82  Play The Game Tonight
- ☐ '77  Point Of Know Return
- ☐ '77  Portait (He Knew)

## KASENETZ-KATZ SINGING ORCHESTRAL CIRCUS
- ☐ '68 Quick Joey Small (Run Joey Run)

## KASHIF
- ☐ '87 Love Changes
  *KASHIF & MELI'SA MORGAN*

## KATRINA & THE WAVES
- ☐ '85 Do You Want Crying
- ☐ '89 That's The Way
- ☐ '85 Walking On Sunshine

## KC & THE SUNSHINE BAND
- ☐ '76 Boogie Shoes
- ☐ '75 Get Down Tonight ★
- ☐ '83 Give It Up
- ☐ '76 I Like To Do It
- ☐ '77 I'm Your Boogie Man ★
- ☐ '78 It's The Same Old Song
- ☐ '77 Keep It Comin' Love
- ☐ '79 Please Don't Go ★
- ☐ '76 (Shake, Shake, Shake) Shake Your Booty ★
- ☐ '75 That's The Way (I Like It) ★
- ☐ '79 Yes, I'm Ready
  *TERI DeSARIO with K.C.*

## K-CI & JOJO
- ☐ '98 All My Life ★
- ☐ '00 Crazy
- ☐ '95 If You Think You're Lonely Now
- ☐ '99 Tell Me It's Real ★
- ☐ '97 You Bring Me Up

## K-DOE, Ernie
- ☐ '61 Mother-In-Law ★

## KEEDY
- ☐ '91 Save Some Love

## KEITH
- ☐ '66 Ain't Gonna Lie
- ☐ '66 98.6
- ☐ '67 Tell Me To My Face

## KEITH, Lisa
- ☐ '93 Better Than You

## KEITH, Toby
- ☐ '03 American Soldier
- ☐ '02 Beer For My Horses
  *TOBY KEITH with Willie Nelson*
- ☐ '02 Courtesy Of The Red, White And Blue (The Angry American)
- ☐ '96 Does That Blue Moon Ever Shine On You
- ☐ '00 How Do You Like Me Now?!
- ☐ '03 I Love This Bar
- ☐ '01 I Wanna Talk About Me
- ☐ '01 I'm Just Talkin' About Tonight
- ☐ '97 I'm So Happy I Can't Stop Crying
  *TOBY KEITH with Sting*
- ☐ '93 Little Less Talk And A Lot More Action
- ☐ '96 Me Too
- ☐ '02 My List
- ☐ '93 Should've Been A Cowboy

- ☐ '04 Stays In Mexico
- ☐ '97 We Were In Love
- ☐ '04 Whiskey Girl
- ☐ '94 Who's That Man
- ☐ '02 Who's Your Daddy?
- ☐ '94 Wish I Didn't Know Now
- ☐ '95 You Ain't Much Fun
- ☐ '00 You Shouldn't Kiss Me Like This

## KELIS
- ☐ '03 Milkshake ★

## KELLER, Jerry
- ☐ '59 Here Comes Summer

## KELLY, Monty, & His Orchestra
- ☐ '60 Summer Set

## KELLY, R.
- ☐ '04 Big Chips
  *R. KELLY & JAY-Z*
- ☐ '94 Bump N' Grind ★
- ☐ '93 Dedicated
- ☐ '99 Did You Ever Think
- ☐ '96 Down Low (Nobody Has To Know)
- ☐ '01 Feelin' On Yo Booty
- ☐ '01 Fiesta Remix ★
- ☐ '97 Gotham City
- ☐ '04 Happy People
- ☐ '92 Honey Love
- ☐ '96 I Believe I Can Fly ★
- ☐ '96 I Can't Sleep Baby (If I) ★
- ☐ '00 I Wish
- ☐ '98 I'm Your Angel ★
  *R. KELLY & CELINE DION*
- ☐ '99 If I Could Turn Back The Hands Of Time ★
- ☐ '02 Ignition ★
- ☐ '93 Sex Me
- ☐ '92 Slow Dance (Hey Mr. DJ)
- ☐ '03 Snake
- ☐ '03 Step In The Name Of Love
- ☐ '03 Thoia Thoing
- ☐ '98 When A Woman's Fed Up
- ☐ '01 World's Greatest, The
- ☐ '95 You Remind Me Of Something
- ☐ '94 Your Body's Callin'

## KEMP, Johnny
- ☐ '89 Birthday Suit
- ☐ '88 Just Got Paid

## KEMP, Tara
- ☐ '91 Hold You Tight ★
- ☐ '91 Piece Of My Heart

## KENDRICKS, Eddie
- ☐ '74 Boogie Down ★
- ☐ '76 He's A Friend
- ☐ '73 Keep On Truckin' ★
- ☐ '75 Shoeshine Boy
- ☐ '74 Son Of Sagittarius

## KENNEDY, Joyce — see OSBORNE, Jeffrey

## KENNER, Chris
- ☐ '61 I Like It Like That ★

## KENNY G
- ☐ '99 Auld Lang Syne
- ☐ '93 By The Time This Night Is Over
  *KENNY G with Peabo Bryson*
- ☐ '87 Don't Make Me Wait For Love
- ☐ '92 Forever In Love
- ☐ '88 Silhouette
- ☐ '87 Songbird

## KERSH, David
- ☐ '97 Another You
- ☐ '97 If I Never Stop Loving You

## KERSHAW, Sammy
- ☐ '91 Cadillac Style
- ☐ '94 I Can't Reach Her Anymore
- ☐ '97 Love Of My Life
- ☐ '94 National Working Woman's Holiday
- ☐ '93 She Don't Know She's Beautiful
- ☐ '94 Third Rate Romance

## KETCHUM, Hal
- ☐ '93 Hearts Are Gonna Roll
- ☐ '92 Past The Point Of Rescue
- ☐ '91 Small Town Saturday Night
- ☐ '92 Sure Love

## KEYS, Alicia
- ☐ '04 Diary ★
- ☐ '01 Fallin'
- ☐ '04 If I Ain't Got You ★
- ☐ '05 Karma ★
- ☐ '04 My Boo ★
  *USHER & ALICIA KEYS*
- ☐ '01 Woman's Worth, A
- ☐ '03 You Don't Know My Name ★

## KHAN, Chaka/RUFUS
- ☐ '83 Ain't Nobody
- ☐ '84 I Feel For You ★
- ☐ '78 I'm Every Woman
- ☐ '96 Missing You
  *BRANDY, TAMIA, GLADYS KNIGHT & CHAKA KHAN*
- ☐ '75 Once You Get Started
- ☐ '76 Sweet Thing
- ☐ '74 Tell Me Something Good
- ☐ '81 What Cha' Gonna Do For Me
- ☐ '74 You Got The Love

## KIARA
- ☐ '88 This Time
  *KIARA (with Shanice)*

## KID ROCK
- ☐ '99 Bawitdaba
- ☐ '99 Cowboy
- ☐ '00 Only God Knows Why
- ☐ '02 Picture ★
  *KID ROCK Feat. Sheryl Crow*

## KIHN, Greg, Band
- ☐ '81 Breakup Song (They Don't Write 'Em)
- ☐ '83 Jeopardy ★
- ☐ '85 Lucky

## KILGORE, Theola
- ☐ '63 Love Of My Man, The

## KILLERS, The
- ☐ '05 Mr. Brightside ★
- ☐ '04 Somebody Told Me

## KIM, Andy
- ☐ '69 Baby, I Love You
- ☐ '70 Be My Baby
- ☐ '74 Fire, Baby I'm On Fire
- ☐ '68 How'd We Ever Get This Way
- ☐ '74 Rock Me Gently ★
- ☐ '68 Shoot'em Up, Baby
- ☐ '69 So Good Together

## KIMBERLY, Adrian
- ☐ '61 The Graduation Song... Pomp And Circumstance

## KING, B.B.
- ☐ '71 Ask Me No Questions
- ☐ '56 Bad Luck
- ☐ '66 Don't Answer The Door
- ☐ '55 Every Day I Have The Blues
- ☐ '73 I Like To Live The Love
- ☐ '56 On My Word Of Honor
- ☐ '68 Paying The Cost To Be The Boss
- ☐ '64 Rock Me Baby
- ☐ '60 Sweet Sixteen
- ☐ '69 Thrill Is Gone, The ★
- ☐ '73 To Know You Is To Love You
- ☐ '88 When Love Comes To Town
  *U2 with B.B. King*

## KING, Ben E.
- ☐ '61 Amor
- ☐ '62 Don't Play That Song (You Lied)
- ☐ '63 I (Who Have Nothing)
- ☐ '60 Spanish Harlem ★
- ☐ '61 Stand By Me ★
- ☐ '75 Supernatural Thing

## KING, Carole
- ☐ '72 Been To Canaan
- ☐ '73 Believe In Humanity
- ☐ '73 Corazón
- ☐ '77 Hard Rock Cafe
- ☐ '71 I Feel The Earth Move
- ☐ '62 It Might As Well Rain Until September
- ☐ '71 It's Too Late ★
- ☐ '74 Jazzman
- ☐ '75 Nightingale
- ☐ '80 One Fine Day
- ☐ '76 Only Love Is Real
- ☐ '71 So Far Away
- ☐ '72 Sweet Seasons

## KING, Claude
- ☐ '62 Wolverton Mountain

## KING, Diana
- ☐ '97 I Say A Little Prayer
- ☐ '95 Shy Guy

## KING, Evelyn "Champagne"
- ☐ '82  Betcha She Don't Love You
- ☐ '88  Flirt
- ☐ '79  I Don't Know If It's Right
- ☐ '81  I'm In Love
- ☐ '82  Love Come Down
- ☐ '78  Shame

## KING, Freddy
- ☐ '61  Hide Away

## KING, Jonathan
- ☐ '65  Everyone's Gone To The Moon

## KING, Teddi
- ☐ '56  Mr. Wonderful

## KING CRIMSON
- ☐ '69  Court Of The Crimson King

## KING CURTIS
- ☐ '67  Memphis Soul Stew
- ☐ '67  Ode To Billie Joe
- ☐ '62  Soul Twist

## KING HARVEST
- ☐ '72  Dancing In The Moonlight

## KINGS, The
- ☐ '80  This Beat Goes On/Switchin' To Glide ★

## KINGSMEN, The
- ☐ '65  Jolly Green Giant, The
- ☐ '63  Louie Louie ★
- ☐ '64  Money

## KINGSTON TRIO, The
- ☐ '60  Bad Man Blunder
- ☐ '63  Desert Pete
- ☐ '60  El Matador
- ☐ '60  Everglades
- ☐ '63  Greenback Dollar
- ☐ '59  M.T.A.
- ☐ '63  Reverend Mr. Black
- ☐ '62  Scotch And Soda
- ☐ '59  Tijuana Jail, The
- ☐ '58  Tom Dooley ★
- ☐ '62  Where Have All The Flowers Gone
- ☐ '59  Worried Man, A

## KINKS, The
- ☐ '64  All Day And All Of The Night
- ☐ '70  Apeman
- ☐ '72  Celluloid Heroes
- ☐ '83  Come Dancing ★
- ☐ '66  Dedicated Follower Of Fashion
- ☐ '81  Destroyer
- ☐ '85  Do It Again
- ☐ '83  Don't Forget To Dance
- ☐ '77  Father Christmas
- ☐ '85  Living On A Thin Line
- ☐ '70  Lola ★
- ☐ '79  Low Budget
- ☐ '78  Rock 'N' Roll Fantasy, A
- ☐ '65  Set Me Free
- ☐ '77  Sleepwalker
- ☐ '66  Sunny Afternoon
- ☐ '65  Tired Of Waiting For You
- ☐ '70  Victoria
- ☐ '68  Waterloo Sunset
- ☐ '65  Well Respected Man, A
- ☐ '65  Who'll Be The Next In Line
- ☐ '79  (Wish I Could Fly Like) Superman
- ☐ '64  You Really Got Me ★

## KISS
- ☐ '76  Beth
- ☐ '77  Calling Dr. Love
- ☐ '77  Christine Sixteen
- ☐ '74  Cold Gin
- ☐ '76  Detroit Rock City
- ☐ '74  Deuce
- ☐ '76  Flaming Youth
- ☐ '90  Forever
- ☐ '76  Hard Luck Woman
- ☐ '74  Hotter Than Hell
- ☐ '79  I Was Made For Lovin' You
- ☐ '77  Love Gun
- ☐ '74  Nothin' To Lose
- ☐ '98  Psycho Circus
- ☐ '75  Rock And Roll All Nite [live] ★
- ☐ '78  Rocket Ride
- ☐ '76  Shout It Out Loud
- ☐ '74  Strutter
- ☐ '79  Sure Know Something

## KISSOON, Mac & Katie
- ☐ '71  Chirpy Chirpy Cheep Cheep

## KIX
- ☐ '89  Don't Close Your Eyes

## KLF, The
- ☐ '92  Justified & Ancient ★
- ☐ '91  3 A.M. Eternal

## KLIQUE
- ☐ '83  Stop Doggin' Me Around

## KLYMAXX
- ☐ '85  I Miss You
- ☐ '87  I'd Still Say Yes
- ☐ '86  Man Size Love
- ☐ '84  Men All Pause, The

## KNACK, The
- ☐ '80  Baby Talks Dirty
- ☐ '79  Frustrated
- ☐ '79  Good Girls Don't
- ☐ '79  My Sharona ★

## KNICKERBOCKERS, The
- ☐ '65  Lies

## KNIGHT, Frederick
- ☐ '72  I've Been Lonely For So Long

## KNIGHT, Gladys, & The Pips
- ☐ '74  Best Thing That Ever Happened To Me
- ☐ '73  Daddy Could Swear, I Declare
- ☐ '68  End Of Our Road, The
- ☐ '61  Every Beat Of My Heart
- ☐ '67  Everybody Needs Love

## KNIGHT, Gladys, & The Pips — cont'd
- ☐ '69 Friendship Train
- ☐ '64 Giving Up
- ☐ '72 Help Me Make It Through The Night
- ☐ '71 I Don't Want To Do Wrong
- ☐ '74 I Feel A Song (In My Heart)
- ☐ '67 I Heard It Through The Grapevine
- ☐ '73 I've Got To Use My Imagination
- ☐ '70 If I Were Your Woman
- ☐ '68 It Should Have Been Me
- ☐ '80 Landlord
- ☐ '61 Letter Full Of Tears
- ☐ '75 Love Finds It's Own Way
- ☐ '88 Love Overboard
- ☐ '88 Lovin' On Next To Nothin'
- ☐ '71 Make Me The Woman That You Go Home To
- ☐ '91 Men
- ☐ '73 Midnight Train To Georgia ★
- ☐ '96 Missing You
  *BRANDY, TAMIA, GLADYS KNIGHT & CHAKA KHAN*
- ☐ '73 Neither One Of Us (Wants To Be The First To Say Goodbye)
- ☐ '69 Nitty Gritty, The
- ☐ '74 On And On
- ☐ '75 Part Time Love
- ☐ '83 Save The Overtime (For Me)
- ☐ '76 So Sad The Song
- ☐ '75 Way We Were/Try To Remember
- ☐ '73 Where Peaceful Waters Flow
- ☐ '70 You Need Love Like I Do (Don't You)

## KNIGHT, Jean
- ☐ '71 Mr. Big Stuff ★

## KNIGHT, Jordan
- ☐ '99 Give It To You

## KNIGHT, Robert
- ☐ '67 Everlasting Love

## KNIGHT, Sonny
- ☐ '56 Confidential

## KNOBLOCK, Fred
- ☐ '80 Killin' Time
  *FRED KNOBLOCK & SUSAN ANTON*
- ☐ '80 Why Not Me

## KNOCKOUTS, The
- ☐ '59 Darling Lorraine

## KNOX, Buddy
- ☐ '57 Hula Love
- ☐ '59 I Think I'm Gonna Kill Myself
- ☐ '60 Lovey Dovey
- ☐ '57 Party Doll ★
- ☐ '57 Rock Your Little Baby To Sleep
- ☐ '58 Somebody Touched Me
- ☐ '59 Teasable, Pleasable You

## KOFFMAN, Moe, Quartette
- ☐ '58 Swingin' Shepherd Blues, The

## KOKOMO
- ☐ '61 Asia Minor

## KON KAN
- ☐ '88 I Beg Your Pardon

## KOOL & THE GANG
- ☐ '82 Big Fun
- ☐ '80 Celebration ★
- ☐ '85 Cherish ★
- ☐ '85 Emergency
- ☐ '85 Fresh
- ☐ '73 Funky Stuff
- ☐ '82 Get Down On It
- ☐ '74 Higher Plane
- ☐ '74 Hollywood Swinging
- ☐ '83 Joanna ★
- ☐ '81 Jones Vs. Jones
- ☐ '73 Jungle Boogie
- ☐ '79 Ladies Night
- ☐ '82 Let's Go Dancin' (Ooh La, La, La)
- ☐ '84 Misled
- ☐ '74 Rhyme Tyme People
- ☐ '75 Spirit Of The Boogie
- ☐ '87 Stone Love
- ☐ '81 Take My Heart (You Can Have It If You Want It)
- ☐ '84 Tonight
- ☐ '80 Too Hot
- ☐ '86 Victory

## KOOL MOE DEE
- ☐ '89 They Want Money

## KORGIS, The
- ☐ '80 Everybody's Got To Learn Sometime

## KORN
- ☐ '03 Did My Time

## K.P. & ENVYI
- ☐ '97 Swing My Way

## KRAFTWERK
- ☐ '75 Autobahn

## KRAMER, Billy J.
- ☐ '64 Bad To Me
- ☐ '64 From A Window
- ☐ '64 I'll Keep You Satisfied
- ☐ '64 Little Children

## KRANZ, George
- ☐ '85 Trommeltanz (Din Daa Daa)

## KRAUSS, Alison, & Union Station
- ☐ '95 When You Say Nothing At All

## KRAVITZ, Lenny
- ☐ '00 Again ★
- ☐ '99 American Woman
- ☐ '93 Are You Gonna Go My Way
- ☐ '01 Dig In
- ☐ '98 Fly Away
- ☐ '91 It Ain't Over 'Til It's Over ★
- ☐ '04 Lady

## KRIS KROSS
- ☐ '93 Alright
- ☐ '92 Jump ★

☐ '95 Tonite's Tha Night
☐ '92 Warm It Up

## KRISTOFFERSON, Kris
☐ '85 Highwayman
*WAYLON JENNINGS/WILLIE NELSON/*
*JOHNNY CASH/KRIS KRISTOFFERSON*
☐ '71 Loving Her Was Easier (Than Anything I'll Ever Do Again)
☐ '73 Why Me

## KROEGER, Chad
☐ '02 Hero ★
☐ '03 Why Don't You & I
*SANTANA Feat. Alex Band or Chad Kroeger*

## K7
☐ '93 Come Baby Come

## KUBAN, Bob, & The In-Men
☐ '66 Cheater, The

## KUT KLOSE
☐ '95 I Like

## K.W.S.
☐ '92 Please Don't Go

## KYPER
☐ '90 Tic-Tac-Toe

# L

## LaBELLE, Patti/THE BLUE-BELLES
☐ '63 Down The Aisle (Wedding Song)
☐ '62 I Sold My Heart To The Junkman
☐ '83 If Only You Knew
☐ '75 Lady Marmalade ★
☐ '84 Love Has Finally Come At Last
*BOBBY WOMACK & PATTI LaBELLE*
☐ '85 New Attitude
☐ '86 Oh, People
☐ '86 On My Own ★
*PATTI LaBELLE & MICHAEL McDONALD*
☐ '91 Somebody Loves You Baby (You Know Who It Is)
☐ '64 You'll Never Walk Alone

## LA BOUCHE
☐ '95 Be My Lover ★
☐ '96 Fallin' In Love
☐ '96 Sweet Dreams

## LADD, Cheryl
☐ '78 Think It Over

## LADY FLASH
☐ '76 Street Singin'

## L.A. GUNS
☐ '90 Ballad of Jayne, The

## LAI, Francis, & His Orchestra
☐ '71 Theme From Love Story

## LAID BACK
☐ '84 White Horse

## LAINE, Frankie
☐ '55 Humming Bird

☐ '67 I'll Take Care Of Your Cares
☐ '57 Love Is A Golden Ring
☐ '67 Making Memories
☐ '56 Moonlight Gambler ★
☐ '68 To Each His Own
☐ '55 Woman In Love, A
☐ '69 You Gave Me A Mountain

## LAKESIDE
☐ '80 Fantastic Voyage

## LaMOND, George
☐ '90 Bad Of The Heart

## LANCE, Major
☐ '65 Come See
☐ '63 Hey Little Girl
☐ '64 Matador, The
☐ '63 Monkey Time, The
☐ '64 Rhythm
☐ '64 Um, Um, Um, Um, Um, Um

## LANE, Mickey Lee
☐ '64 Shaggy Dog

## lang, k.d.
☐ '93 Calling All Angels
*JANE SIBERRY with k.d. lang*
☐ '92 Constant Craving

## LARKS, The
☐ '64 Jerk, The

## LaROSA, Julius
☐ '55 Domani (Tomorrow)
☐ '56 Lipstick And Candy And Rubbersole Shoes
☐ '55 Suddenly There's A Valley
☐ '58 Torero

## LARSEN-FEITEN BAND
☐ '80 Who'll Be The Fool Tonight

## LARSON, Nicolette
☐ '80 Let Me Go, Love
☐ '78 Lotta Love

## LA'S, The
☐ '91 There She Goes

## LaSALLE, Denise
☐ '72 Now Run And Tell That
☐ '71 Trapped By A Thing Called Love

## LASGO
☐ '02 Something

## LASLEY, David
☐ '82 If I Had My Wish Tonight

## LAST, James, Band
☐ '80 Seduction (Love Theme)
☐ '72 Music From Across The Way

## LATIMORE
☐ '74 Let's Straighten It Out
☐ '77 Somethin' 'Bout 'Cha

## LaTOUR
- ☐ '91 People Are Still Having Sex

## LATTIMORE, Kenny
- ☐ '97 For You

## LATTISAW, Stacy
- ☐ '80 Let Me Be Your Angel
- ☐ '81 Love On A Two Way Street
- ☐ '83 Miracles
- ☐ '89 Where Do We Go From Here
  *STACY LATTISAW with Johnny Gill*

## LAUPER, Cyndi
- ☐ '84 All Through The Night
- ☐ '86 Change Of Heart
- ☐ '83 Girls Just Want To Have Fun ★
- ☐ '85 Goonies 'R' Good Enough, The
- ☐ '89 I Drove All Night
- ☐ '84 Money Changes Everything
- ☐ '84 She Bop
- ☐ '84 Time After Time ★
- ☐ '86 True Colors ★
- ☐ '87 What's Going On

## LAUREN, Rod
- ☐ '59 If I Had A Girl

## LAURIE, Annie
- ☐ '57 It Hurts To Be In Love

## LAURIE SISTERS, The
- ☐ '55 Dixie Danny

## LAVIGNE, Avril
- ☐ '02 Complicated ★
- ☐ '04 Don't Tell Me
- ☐ '02 I'm With You ★
- ☐ '04 My Happy Ending
- ☐ '02 Sk8er Boi

## LAW, The
- ☐ '91 Laying Down The Law

## LAWRENCE, Eddie
- ☐ '56 Old Philosopher, The

## LAWRENCE, Joey
- ☐ '93 Nothin' My Love Can't Fix

## LAWRENCE, Steve
- ☐ '63 Don't Be Afraid, Little Darlin'
- ☐ '60 Footsteps
- ☐ '62 Go Away Little Girl ★
- ☐ '63 I Can't Stop Talking About You
- ☐ '63 I Want To Stay Here
  *STEVE & EYDIE (above 2)*
- ☐ '57 Party Doll
- ☐ '63 Poor Little Rich Girl
- ☐ '61 Portrait Of My Love
- ☐ '59 Pretty Blue Eyes
- ☐ '63 Walking Proud

## LAWRENCE, Tracy
- ☐ '93 Alibis
- ☐ '94 As Any Fool Can See
- ☐ '97 Better Man, Better Off
- ☐ '93 Can't Break It To My Heart
- ☐ '94 I See It Now
- ☐ '94 If The Good Die Young
- ☐ '95 If The World Had A Front Porch
- ☐ '96 Is That A Tear
- ☐ '00 Lessons Learned
- ☐ '93 My Second Home
- ☐ '96 Stars Over Texas
- ☐ '91 Sticks And Stones
- ☐ '95 Texas Tornado
- ☐ '96 Time Marches On

## LAWRENCE, Vicki
- ☐ '73 Night The Lights Went Out In Georgia ★

## LAYNE, Joy
- ☐ '57 Your Wild Heart

## LEAPY LEE
- ☐ '68 Little Arrows

## LEAVES, The
- ☐ '66 Hey Joe

## LeBLANC & CARR
- ☐ '77 Falling

## LE CLICK
- ☐ '97 Call Me

## LED ZEPPELIN
- ☐ '79 All My Love
- ☐ '69 Babe I'm Gonna Leave You
- ☐ '71 Black Dog
- ☐ '69 Communication Breakdown
- ☐ '73 Crunge, The
- ☐ '73 Dancing Days
- ☐ '69 Dazed And Confused
- ☐ '73 D'yer Mak'er
- ☐ '79 Fool In The Rain ★
- ☐ '70 Gallows Pole
- ☐ '71 Going To California
- ☐ '69 Good Times Bad Times
- ☐ '69 Heartbreaker
- ☐ '79 Hot Dog
- ☐ '75 Houses Of The Holy
- ☐ '69 How Many More Times
- ☐ '69 I Can't Quit You Baby
- ☐ '70 Immigrant Song ★
- ☐ '79 In The Evening
- ☐ '75 Kashmir
- ☐ '69 Living Loving Maid (She's Just A Woman)
- ☐ '71 Misty Mountain Hop
- ☐ '76 Nobody's Fault But Mine
- ☐ '73 Ocean, The
- ☐ '73 Over The Hills And Far Away
- ☐ '73 Rain Song
- ☐ '69 Ramble On
- ☐ '71 Rock And Roll
- ☐ '70 Since I've Been Loving You
- ☐ '73 Song Remains The Same
- ☐ '71 Stairway To Heaven ★
- ☐ '69 Thank You
- ☐ '75 Trampled Under Foot
- ☐ '69 What Is And What Should Never Be

□ '71 When The Levee Breaks
□ '69 Whole Lotta Love ★

## LEE, Brenda
□ '62 All Alone Am I
□ '61 Anybody But Me
□ '63 As Usual
□ '62 Break It To Me Gently
□ '66 Coming On Strong
□ '61 Dum Dum
□ '60 Emotions
□ '62 Everybody Loves Me But You
□ '61 Fool #1
□ '63 Grass Is Greener, The
□ '62 Heart In Hand
□ '60 I Want To Be Wanted ★
□ '63 I Wonder
□ '61 I'm Learning About Love
□ '60 I'm Sorry ★
□ '64 Is It True
□ '62 It Started All Over Again
□ '69 Johnny One Time
□ '60 Just A Little
□ '63 Losing You
□ '63 My Whole World Is Falling Down
□ '67 Ride, Ride, Ride
□ '60 Rockin' Around The Christmas Tree
□ '65 Rusty Bells
□ '62 So Deep
□ '59 Sweet Nothin's
□ '60 That's All You Gotta Do
□ '64 Think
□ '65 Too Many Rivers
□ '61 You Can Depend On Me
□ '63 Your Used To Be

## LEE, Curtis
□ '61 Pretty Little Angel Eyes

## LEE, Dickey
□ '62 I Saw Linda Yesterday
□ '65 Laurie (Strange Things Happen)
□ '62 Patches

## LEE, Jackie
□ '65 Duck, The

## LEE, Johnny
□ '82 Cherokee Fiddle
□ '80 Lookin' For Love

## LEE, Laura
□ '72 Rip Off
□ '71 Women's Love Rights

## LEE, Murphy
□ '03 Shake Ya Tailfeather ★
       *NELLY/P. DIDDY/MURPHY LEE*
□ '03 Wat Da Hook Gon Be

## LEE, Peggy
□ '58 Fever ★
□ '69 Is That All There Is
□ '56 Mr. Wonderful

## LEFEVRE, Raymond, & His Orchestra
□ '68 Ame Caline (Soul Coaxing)
□ '58 Day The Rains Came, The

## LEFT BANKE, The
□ '67 Pretty Ballerina
□ '66 Walk Away Renee

## LEGEND, John
□ '05 Ordinary People

## LEMONHEADS, The
□ '93 Into Your Arms

## LEMON PIPERS, The
□ '67 Green Tambourine ★

## LEN
□ '99 Steal My Sunshine

## LENNON, John
□ '80 Beautiful Boy (Darling Boy)
□ '69 Cold Turkey
□ '69 Give Peace A Chance
□ '70 God
□ '71 Happy Xmas (War Is Over)
□ '71 Imagine ★
□ '70 Instant Karma (We All Shine On) ★
□ '80 (Just Like) Starting Over ★
□ '73 Mind Games
□ '70 Mother
□ '84 Nobody Told Me
□ '74 #9 Dream
□ '71 Power To The People
□ '75 Stand By Me
□ '81 Watching The Wheels
□ '74 Whatever Gets You Thru The Night ★
□ '81 Woman ★
□ '72 Woman Is The Nigger Of The World

## LENNON, Julian
□ '89 Now You're In Heaven
□ '85 Say You're Wrong
□ '86 Stick Around
□ '85 Too Late For Goodbyes
□ '84 Valotte

## LENNON SISTERS, The
□ '56 Tonight You Belong To Me

## LENNOX, Annie
□ '95 No More "I Love You's"
□ '88 Put A Little Love In Your Heart
       *ANNIE LENNOX & AL GREEN*
□ '92 Walking On Broken Glass ★
□ '92 Why

## LEONETTI, Tommy
□ '56 Free
□ '69 Kum Ba Yah

## LE ROUX
□ '82 Nobody Said It Was Easy (Lookin' For The Lights)

## LESTER, Ketty
□ '62 Love Letters

## LETTERMEN, The
- ☐ '62 Come Back Silly Girl
- ☐ '67 Goin' Out Of My Head/Can't Take My Eyes Off You
- ☐ '62 How Is Julie?
- ☐ '69 Hurt So Bad
- ☐ '71 Love
- ☐ '65 Theme From "A Summer Place"
- ☐ '69 Traces/Memories Medley
- ☐ '61 Way You Look Tonight, The
- ☐ '61 When I Fall In Love

## LEVEL 42
- ☐ '87 Lessons In Love
- ☐ '86 Something About You

## LEVERT
- ☐ '88 Addicted To You
- ☐ '91 Baby I'm Ready
- ☐ '87 Casanova
- ☐ '89 Just Coolin'
- ☐ '87 My Forever Love
- ☐ '86 (Pop, Pop, Pop, Pop) Goes My Mind
- ☐ '88 Pull Over

## LEVERT, Gerald
- ☐ '92 Baby Hold On To Me
- ☐ '94 I'd Give Anything
- ☐ '91 Private Line
- ☐ '92 School Me
- ☐ '99 Taking Everything
- ☐ '98 Thinkin' Bout It

## LEWIS, Aaron
- ☐ '00 Outside
  - *AARON LEWIS with Fred Durst*

## LEWIS, Barbara
- ☐ '65 Baby, I'm Yours
- ☐ '63 Hello Stranger
- ☐ '66 Make Me Belong To You
- ☐ '65 Make Me Your Baby
- ☐ '64 Puppy Love

## LEWIS, Bobby
- ☐ '61 One Track Mind
- ☐ '61 Tossin' And Turnin' ★

## LEWIS, Donna
- ☐ '97 At The Beginning
  - *DONNA LEWIS & RICHARD MARX*
- ☐ '96 I Love You Always Forever ★

## LEWIS, Gary, & The Playboys
- ☐ '65 Count Me In
- ☐ '65 Everybody Loves A Clown
- ☐ '67 Girls In Love
- ☐ '66 Green Grass
- ☐ '66 My Heart's Symphony
- ☐ '65 Save Your Heart For Me
- ☐ '68 Sealed With A Kiss
- ☐ '65 She's Just My Style ★
- ☐ '66 Sure Gonna Miss Her
- ☐ '65 This Diamond Ring ★
- ☐ '66 Where Will The Words Come From
- ☐ '66 (You Don't Have To) Paint Me A Picture

## LEWIS, Glenn
- ☐ '01 Don't You Forget It

## LEWIS, Huey, & The News
- ☐ '85 Back In Time
- ☐ '91 Couple Days Off
- ☐ '00 Cruisin'
- ☐ '82 Do You Believe In Love
- ☐ '87 Doing It All For My Baby
- ☐ '83 Heart And Soul
- ☐ '84 Heart Of Rock & Roll, The
- ☐ '86 Hip To Be Square
- ☐ '82 Hope You Love Me Like You Say You Do
- ☐ '87 I Know What I Like
- ☐ '84 I Want A New Drug
- ☐ '84 If This Is It
- ☐ '91 It Hit Me Like A Hammer
- ☐ '93 It's Alright
- ☐ '87 Jacob's Ladder ★
- ☐ '88 Perfect World
- ☐ '85 Power Of Love, The ★
- ☐ '88 Small World
- ☐ '86 Stuck With You
- ☐ '84 Walking On A Thin Line
- ☐ '82 Workin' For A Livin'

## LEWIS, Jerry
- ☐ '56 Rock-A-Bye Your Baby With A Dixie Melody

## LEWIS, Jerry Lee
- ☐ '58 Breathless
- ☐ '72 Chantilly Lace
- ☐ '73 Drinking Wine Spo-Dee O'Dee
- ☐ '57 Great Balls Of Fire ★
- ☐ '58 High School Confidential
- ☐ '71 Me And Bobby McGee
- ☐ '61 What'd I Say
- ☐ '57 Whole Lot Of Shakin' Going On ★
- ☐ '58 You Win Again

## LEWIS, Ramsey
- ☐ '65 Hang On Sloopy
- ☐ '66 Hard Day's Night, A
- ☐ '65 "In" Crowd, The
- ☐ '66 Wade In The Water

## LEWIS, Smiley
- ☐ '55 I Hear You Knocking

## LFO
- ☐ '99 Girl On TV
- ☐ '99 Summer Girls ★

## LIA, Orsa
- ☐ '79 I Never Said I Love You

## LIFEHOUSE
- ☐ '00 Hanging By A Moment ★
- ☐ '05 You And Me

## LIGHTER SHADE OF BROWN, A
- ☐ '91 On A Sunday Afternoon

## LIGHTFOOT, Gordon
- ☐ '82 Baby Step Back
- ☐ '74 Carefree Highway
- ☐ '78 Circle Is Small (I Can See It In Your Eyes)
- ☐ '70 If You Could Read My Mind
- ☐ '75 Rainy Day People
- ☐ '74 Sundown ★
- ☐ '76 Wreck Of The Edmund Fitzgerald ★

## LIGHTHOUSE
- ☐ '71 One Fine Morning
- ☐ '72 Sunny Days

## LIGHTNING SEEDS, The
- ☐ '92 Life Of Riley, The
- ☐ '90 Pure

## LIL BOW WOW
- ☐ '00 Bounce With Me
- ☐ '00 Bow Wow (That's My Name)
- ☐ '03 Let's Get Down

## LIL' FLIP
- ☐ '04 Game Over (Flip)
- ☐ '04 Sunshine ★

## LIL JON & THE EAST SIDE BOYZ
- ☐ '03 Get Low ★
- ☐ '05 Lovers And Friends ★
- ☐ '04 What U Gon' Do

## LIL' KIM
- ☐ '03 Jump Off, The
- ☐ '01 Lady Marmalade ★
  - *CHRISTINA AGUILERA, LIL' KIM, MYA & P!NK*
- ☐ '03 Magic Stick ★
- ☐ '96 No Time
- ☐ '97 Not Tonight

## LIL' MO
- ☐ '03 4 Ever
- ☐ '01 Superwoman

## LIL' ROMEO
- ☐ '01 My Baby ★

## LIL SCRAPPY
- ☐ '04 No Problem

## LIL WAYNE
- ☐ '04 Go D.J.

## LIL' ZANE
- ☐ '00 Callin' Me

## LIMAHL
- ☐ '85 Never Ending Story

## LIMP BIZKIT
- ☐ '01 My Way
- ☐ '99 Nookie
- ☐ '99 Re-Arranged
- ☐ '00 Rollin'

## LIND, Bob
- ☐ '66 Elusive Butterfly

## LINDEN, Kathy
- ☐ '58 Billy
- ☐ '59 Goodbye Jimmy, Goodbye

## LINDISFARNE
- ☐ '78 Run For Home

## LINDSAY, Mark
- ☐ '69 Arizona
- ☐ '70 Silver Bird

## LINEAR
- ☐ '90 Sending All My Love
- ☐ '92 T.L.C.

## LINES, Aaron
- ☐ '02 You Can't Hide Beautiful

## LINK
- ☐ '98 Whatcha Gone Do?

## LINKIN PARK
- ☐ '04 Breaking The Habit
- ☐ '01 Crawling
- ☐ '03 Faint
- ☐ '01 In The End ★
- ☐ '04 Lying From You
- ☐ '03 Numb
- ☐ '04 Numb/Encore
  - *JAY-Z & LINKIN PARK*
- ☐ '03 Somewhere I Belong

## LIPPS, INC.
- ☐ '80 Funkytown ★

## LISA LISA & CULT JAM
- ☐ '86 All Cried Out
- ☐ '87 Head To Toe ★
- ☐ '85 I Wonder If I Take You Home
- ☐ '91 Let The Beat Hit 'Em
- ☐ '89 Little Jackie Wants To Be A Star
- ☐ '87 Lost In Emotion ★

## LIT
- ☐ '99 Miserable
- ☐ '99 My Own Worst Enemy

## LITTLE ANTHONY & THE IMPERIALS
- ☐ '64 Goin' Out Of My Head
- ☐ '65 Hurt So Bad
- ☐ '65 I Miss You So
- ☐ '64 I'm On The Outside (Looking In)
- ☐ '59 Shimmy, Shimmy, Ko-Ko-Bop
- ☐ '65 Take Me Back
- ☐ '58 Tears On My Pillow ★

## LITTLE BEAVER
- ☐ '74 Party Down

## LITTLE CAESAR & THE ROMANS
- ☐ '61 Those Oldies But Goodies (Remind Me Of You)

## LITTLE DIPPERS, The
- ☐ '60 Forever

## LITTLE EVA
- ☐ '62 Keep Your Hands Off My Baby
- ☐ '63 Let's Turkey Trot
- ☐ '62 Loco-Motion, The ★
- ☐ '63 Swinging On A Star
  - *BIG DEE IRWIN (with Little Eva)*

## LITTLE FEAT
- ☐ '78 Dixie Chicken
- ☐ '88 Hate To Lose Your Lovin'
- ☐ '88 Let It Roll
- ☐ '90 Texas Twister

## LITTLE JOE & THE THRILLERS
- ☐ '57 Peanuts

## LITTLE JOEY & THE FLIPS
- ☐ '62 Bongo Stomp

## LITTLE MILTON
- ☐ '65 We're Gonna Make It

## LITTLE RICHARD
- ☐ '58 Baby Face
- ☐ '57 Girl Can't Help It, The
- ☐ '58 Good Golly, Miss Molly ★
- ☐ '56 Heebie-Jeebies
- ☐ '57 Jenny, Jenny
- ☐ '57 Keep A Knockin'
- ☐ '56 Long Tall Sally ★
- ☐ '57 Lucille ★
- ☐ '58 Ooh! My Soul
- ☐ '56 Ready Teddy
- ☐ '56 Rip It Up
- ☐ '57 Send Me Some Lovin'
- ☐ '56 Slippin' And Slidin'
- ☐ '56 Tutti-Frutti ★

## LITTLE RIVER BAND
- ☐ '79 Cool Change
- ☐ '77 Happy Anniversary
- ☐ '77 Help Is On Its Way
- ☐ '76 It's A Long Way There
- ☐ '79 Lady
- ☐ '79 Lonesome Loser
- ☐ '82 Man On Your Mind
- ☐ '81 Night Owls, The
- ☐ '82 Other Guy, The
- ☐ '78 Reminiscing
- ☐ '81 Take It Easy On Me
- ☐ '83 We Two
- ☐ '83 You're Driving Me Out Of My Mind

## LITTLE SISTER
- ☐ '70 Somebody's Watching You
- ☐ '70 You're The One

## LITTLE TEXAS
- ☐ '93 God Blessed Texas
- ☐ '94 Kick A Little
- ☐ '94 My Love
- ☐ '93 What Might Have Been

## LITTLE WALTER & HIS JUKES
- ☐ '55 My Babe

## LIVE
- ☐ '95 All Over You
- ☐ '99 Dolphin's Cry, The
- ☐ '94 I Alone
- ☐ '97 Lakini's Juice
- ☐ '95 Lightning Crashes
- ☐ '94 Selling The Drama
- ☐ '97 Turn My Head

## LIVING COLOUR
- ☐ '89 Cult Of Personality
- ☐ '89 Glamour Boys
- ☐ '90 Type

## LIVING IN A BOX
- ☐ '87 Living In A Box

## LL COOL J
- ☐ '90 Around The Way Girl
- ☐ '96 Doin It
- ☐ '98 Father
- ☐ '88 Going Back To Cali
- ☐ '04 Headsprung
- ☐ '95 Hey Lover
- ☐ '04 Hush
- ☐ '87 I Need Love
- ☐ '89 I'm That Type Of Guy
- ☐ '96 Loungin ★
- ☐ '02 Luv U Better
- ☐ '91 Mama Said Knock You Out
- ☐ '02 Paradise
- ☐ '86 Rock The Bells

## LLOYD
- ☐ '04 Southside

## LOBO
- ☐ '72 Don't Expect Me To Be Your Friend
- ☐ '75 Don't Tell Me Goodnight
- ☐ '73 How Can I Tell Her
- ☐ '72 I'd Love You To Want Me ★
- ☐ '73 It Sure Took A Long, Long Time
- ☐ '71 Me And You And A Dog Named Boo
- ☐ '74 Standing At The End Of The Line
- ☐ '79 Where Were You When I Was Falling In Love

## LOCKLIN, Hank
- ☐ '60 Please Help Me, I'm Falling

## LOEB, Lisa
- ☐ '95 Do You Sleep?
- ☐ '97 I Do
- ☐ '94 Stay (I Missed You) ★

## LOGGINS, Dave
- ☐ '74 Please Come To Boston

## LOGGINS, Kenny
- ☐ '86 Danger Zone ★
- ☐ '82 Don't Fight It
  - *KENNY LOGGINS with Steve Perry*
- ☐ '84 Footloose ★
- ☐ '97 For The First Time
- ☐ '85 Forever
- ☐ '82 Heart To Heart
- ☐ '80 I'm Alright

- ☐ '84 I'm Free (Heaven Helps The Man)
- ☐ '80 Keep The Fire
- ☐ '87 Meet Me Half Way
- ☐ '88 Nobody's Fool
- ☐ '79 This Is It
- ☐ '85 Vox Humana
- ☐ '83 Welcome To Heartlight
- ☐ '78 Whenever I Call You "Friend"

## LOGGINS & MESSINA
- ☐ '72 Danny's Song
- ☐ '72 House At Pooh Corner
- ☐ '73 My Music
- ☐ '73 Thinking Of You
- ☐ '72 Your Mama Don't Dance

## LO-KEY?
- ☐ '92 I Got A Thang 4 Ya!

## LOLITA
- ☐ '60 Sailor (Your Home Is The Sea)

## LONDON, Julie
- ☐ '55 Cry Me A River

## LONDON, Laurie
- ☐ '58 He's Got The Whole World (In His Hands) ★

## LONDONBEAT
- ☐ '91 Better Love, A
- ☐ '91 I've Been Thinking About You ★

## LONESTAR
- ☐ '99 Amazed ★
- ☐ '97 Come Cryin' To Me
- ☐ '98 Everything's Changed
- ☐ '01 I'm Already There
- ☐ '04 Let's Be Us Again
- ☐ '04 Mr. Mom
- ☐ '03 My Front Porch Looking In
- ☐ '96 No News
- ☐ '02 Not A Day Goes By
- ☐ '99 Smile
- ☐ '00 Tell Her
- ☐ '00 What About Now

## LONG, Shorty
- ☐ '68 Here Comes The Judge

## LOOKING GLASS
- ☐ '72 Brandy (You're A Fine Girl) ★
- ☐ '73 Jimmy Loves Mary-Anne

## LOOSE ENDS
- ☐ '85 Hangin' On A String (Contemplating)
- ☐ '86 Slow Down
- ☐ '88 Watching You

## LOPEZ, Denise
- ☐ '88 Sayin' Sorry (Don't Make It Right)

## LOPEZ, Jennifer
- ☐ '01 Ain't It Funny
- ☐ '02 All I Have ★
- ☐ '05 Get Right ★
- ☐ '03 I'm Glad
- ☐ '02 I'm Gonna Be Alright

- ☐ '01 I'm Real ★
- ☐ '99 If You Had My Love ★
- ☐ '02 Jenny From The Block ★
- ☐ '00 Love Don't Cost A Thing
- ☐ '01 Play
- ☐ '99 Waiting For Tonight

## LOPEZ, Trini
- ☐ '66 I'm Comin' Home, Cindy
- ☐ '63 If I Had A Hammer
- ☐ '63 Kansas City
- ☐ '65 Lemon Tree

## LORAIN, A'Me
- ☐ '90 Whole Wide World

## LORBER, Jeff
- ☐ '86 Facts Of Love
  *JEFF LORBER Feat. Karyn White*

## LORD TARIQ & PETER GUNZ
- ☐ '97 Deja Vu (Uptown Baby)

## LORENZ, Trey
- ☐ '92 Someone To Hold

## LORING, Gloria
- ☐ '86 Friends And Lovers
  *GLORIA LORING & CARL ANDERSON*

## LOS BRAVOS
- ☐ '66 Black Is Black
- ☐ '68 Bring A Little Lovin'

## LOS DEL RIO
- ☐ '95 Macarena (bayside boys mix) ★

## LOS INDIOS TABAJARAS
- ☐ '63 Maria Elena

## LOS LOBOS
- ☐ '87 Come On, Let's Go
- ☐ '87 La Bamba ★

## LOS LONELY BOYS
- ☐ '04 Heaven

## LOST BOYZ
- ☐ '96 Renee

## LOST GENERATION, The
- ☐ '70 Sly, Slick, And The Wicked, The

## LOSTPROPHETS
- ☐ '03 Last Train Home

## LOUDERMILK, John D.
- ☐ '61 Language Of Love
- ☐ '57 Sittin' In The Balcony

## LOUIE LOUIE
- ☐ '90 Sittin' In The Lap Of Luxury

## LOVE
- ☐ '68 Alone Again Or
- ☐ '66 My Little Red Book
- ☐ '66 7 And 7 Is

## LOVE, Darlene
- ☐ '63 (Today I Met) The Boy I'm Gonna Marry
- ☐ '63 Wait Til' My Bobby Gets Home

## LOVE, Monie
- ☐ '91 It's A Shame (My Sister)

## LOVE & KISSES
- ☐ '78 Thank God It's Friday

## LOVE & ROCKETS
- ☐ '89 So Alive

## LOVELESS, Patty
- ☐ '93 Blame It On Your Heart
- ☐ '90 Chains
- ☐ '94 I Try To Think About Elvis
- ☐ '96 Lonely Too Long
- ☐ '89 Timber, I'm Falling In Love
- ☐ '95 You Can Feel Bad

## LOVERBOY
- ☐ '86 Heaven In Your Eyes
- ☐ '83 Hot Girls In Love
- ☐ '85 Lovin' Every Minute Of It
- ☐ '82 Lucky Ones
- ☐ '87 Notorious
- ☐ '83 Queen Of The Broken Hearts
- ☐ '86 This Could Be The Night
- ☐ '81 Turn Me Loose
- ☐ '82 When It's Over
- ☐ '81 Working For The Weekend ★

## LOVE UNLIMITED
- ☐ '74 I Belong To You
- ☐ '72 Walkin' In The Rain With The One I Love

## LOVE UNLIMITED ORCHESTRA
- ☐ '73 Love's Theme ★
- ☐ '75 Satin Soul

## LOVIN' SPOONFUL, The
- ☐ '67 Darling Be Home Soon
- ☐ '66 Daydream ★
- ☐ '66 Did You Ever Have To Make Up Your Mind?
- ☐ '65 Do You Believe In Magic ★
- ☐ '66 Nashville Cats
- ☐ '66 Rain On The Roof
- ☐ '67 She Is Still A Mystery
- ☐ '67 Six O'Clock
- ☐ '66 Summer In The City ★
- ☐ '65 You Didn't Have To Be So Nice

## LOWE, Jim
- ☐ '57 Four Walls
- ☐ '56 Green Door, The ★
- ☐ '57 Talkin' To The Blues

## LOWE, Nick
- ☐ '79 Cruel To Be Kind

## LOX, The
- ☐ '98 If You Think I'm Jiggy
- ☐ '98 Money, Power & Respect

## LSG
- ☐ '97 My Body ★

## L.T.D.
- ☐ '77 (Every Time I Turn Around) Back In Love Again
- ☐ '78 Holding On (When Love Is Gone)
- ☐ '76 Love Ballad
- ☐ '80 Shine On

## LUCAS
- ☐ '94 Lucas With The Lid Off

## LUCY PEARL
- ☐ '00 Dance Tonight

## LUDACRIS
- ☐ '03 Act A Fool
- ☐ '01 Area Codes
- ☐ '04 Get Back
- ☐ '02 Move B***h
- ☐ '05 Number One Spot
- ☐ '01 Rollout (My Business)
- ☐ '02 Saturday (Oooh! Ooooh!)
- ☐ '01 Southern Hospitality
- ☐ '04 Splash Waterfalls
- ☐ '03 Stand Up ★
- ☐ '01 Welcome To Atlanta
  *JERMAINE DUPRI • LUDACRIS*
- ☐ '00 What's Your Fantasy

## LUKE, Robin
- ☐ '58 Susie Darlin'

## LULU
- ☐ '67 Best Of Both Worlds
- ☐ '68 Morning Dew
- ☐ '81 I Could Never Miss You (More Than I Do)
- ☐ '69 Oh Me Oh My (I'm A Fool For You Baby)
- ☐ '67 To Sir With Love ★

## LUMAN, Bob
- ☐ '60 Let's Think About Living

## LUMIDEE
- ☐ '03 Never Leave You - Uh Oooh, Uh Oooh! ★

## LUNDBERG, Victor
- ☐ '67 Open Letter To My Teenage Son, An

## LUNIZ
- ☐ '95 I Got 5 On It

## LUSCIOUS JACKSON
- ☐ '96 Naked Eye

## LYMAN, Arthur, Group
- ☐ '61 Yellow Bird ★

## LYMON, Frankie, & The Teenagers
- ☐ '57 Goody Goody
- ☐ '56 I Want You To Be My Girl
- ☐ '56 Why Do Fools Fall In Love ★

## LYNN, Barbara
☐ '62  You'll Lose A Good Thing

## LYNN, Cheryl
☐ '83  Encore
☐ '78  Got To Be Real

## LYNN, Loretta
☐ '70  Coal Miner's Daughter
☐ '71  One's On The Way

## LYNNE, Gloria
☐ '64  I Wish You Love

## LYNYRD SKYNYRD
☐ '74  Call Me The Breeze
☐ '74  Don't Ask Me No Questions
☐ '76  Double Trouble
☐ '74  Free Bird ★
☐ '76  Gimme Back My Bullets
☐ '73  Gimme Three Steps
☐ '73  I Ain't The One
☐ '75  Saturday Night Special
☐ '91  Smokestack Lightning
☐ '74  Sweet Home Alabama ★
☐ '77  That Smell
☐ '77  What's Your Name
☐ '74  Workin' For MCA
☐ '77  You Got That Right

## LYTTLE, Kevin
☐ '04  Turn Me On ★

# M

## M
☐ '79  Pop Muzik ★

## MABLEY, Moms
☐ '69  Abraham, Martin And John

## MacGREGOR, Byron
☐ '74  Americans

## MacGREGOR, Mary
☐ '79  Good Friend
☐ '76  Torn Between Two Lovers ★

## MACK, Craig
☐ '94  Flava In Ya Ear
☐ '94  Get Down

## MACK, Lonnie
☐ '63  Memphis
☐ '63  Wham!

## MACK 10
☐ '97  Backyard Boogie
☐ '96  Nothin' But The Cavi Hit
       *MACK 10 & THA DOGG POUND*

## MacKENZIE, Gisele
☐ '55  Hard To Get

## MacRAE, Gordon
☐ '55  Oklahoma!
☐ '58  Secret, The

## MAD COBRA
☐ '92  Flex

## MADDOX, Johnny
☐ '55  Crazy Otto, The

## MADIGAN, Betty
☐ '58  Dance Everyone Dance

## MADNESS
☐ '83  It Must Be Love
☐ '83  Our House

## MADONNA
☐ '03  American Life
☐ '00  American Pie
☐ '85  Angel
☐ '93  Bad Girl
☐ '99  Beautiful Stranger
☐ '84  Borderline
☐ '87  Causing A Commotion ★
☐ '89  Cherish
☐ '85  Crazy For You ★
☐ '92  Deeper And Deeper
☐ '02  Die Another Day
☐ '97  Don't Cry For Me Argentina
☐ '00  Don't Tell Me
☐ '85  Dress You Up
☐ '92  Erotica
☐ '89  Express Yourself ★
☐ '98  Frozen
☐ '90  Hanky Panky
☐ '83  Holiday
☐ '94  I'll Remember
☐ '85  Into The Groove
☐ '90  Justify My Love ★
☐ '90  Keep It Together
☐ '87  La Isla Bonita
☐ '89  Like A Prayer ★
☐ '84  Like A Virgin ★
☐ '86  Live To Tell
☐ '84  Lucky Star
☐ '85  Material Girl ★
☐ '03  Me Against The Music
☐ '00  Music ★
☐ '89  Oh Father
☐ '86  Open Your Heart
☐ '86  Papa Don't Preach ★
☐ '98  Power Of Good-Bye, The
☐ '93  Rain
☐ '98  Ray Of Light ★
☐ '91  Rescue Me
☐ '94  Secret
☐ '88  Spotlight
☐ '94  Take A Bow ★
☐ '92  This Used To Be My Playground ★
☐ '86  True Blue
☐ '90  Vogue ★
☐ '01  What It Feels Like For A Girl
☐ '87  Who's That Girl
☐ '96  You Must Love Me
☐ '95  You'll See

## MAD SEASON
☐ '95  River Of Deceit

## MAGGARD, Cledus
- ☐ '75  White Knight, The

## MAGIC LANTERNS
- ☐ '68  Shame, Shame

## MAHARIS, George
- ☐ '62  Teach Me Tonight

## MAIN INGREDIENT, The
- ☐ '72  Everybody Plays The Fool
- ☐ '74  Happiness Is Just Around The Bend
- ☐ '74  Just Don't Want To Be Lonely

## MAJORS, The
- ☐ '62  Wonderful Dream, A

## MAKEBA, Miriam
- ☐ '67  Pata Pata

## MALO
- ☐ '72  Suavecito

## MALTBY, Richard, & His Orchestra
- ☐ '56  Themes From "The Man With The Golden Arm"

## MAMA CASS
- ☐ '68  Dream A Little Dream Of Me
- ☐ '69  It's Getting Better
- ☐ '69  Make Your Own Kind Of Music

## MAMAS & THE PAPAS, The
- ☐ '66  California Dreamin' ★
- ☐ '67  Creeque Alley
- ☐ '67  Dedicated To The One I Love
- ☐ '67  Glad To Be Unhappy
- ☐ '66  I Saw Her Again
- ☐ '66  Look Through My Window
- ☐ '66  Monday, Monday ★
- ☐ '67  Twelve Thirty (Young Girls Are Coming To The Canyon)
- ☐ '66  Words Of Love

## MANCHESTER, Melissa
- ☐ '78  Don't Cry Out Loud
- ☐ '80  Fire In The Morning
- ☐ '75  Just Too Many People
- ☐ '76  Just You And I
- ☐ '75  Midnight Blue
- ☐ '79  Pretty Girls
- ☐ '82  You Should Hear How She Talks About You ★

## MANCINI, Henry, & His Orchestra
- ☐ '63  Charade
- ☐ '63  Days Of Wine And Roses
- ☐ '64  Dear Heart
- ☐ '69  Love Theme From Romeo & Juliet ★
- ☐ '61  Moon River ★
- ☐ '60  Mr. Lucky
- ☐ '64  Pink Panther Theme, The
- ☐ '71  Theme From Love Story

## MANDRELL, Barbara
- ☐ '81  I Was Country When Country Wasn't Cool

## [continued]
- ☐ '79  (If Loving You Is Wrong) I Don't Want To Be Right
- ☐ '78  Sleeping Single In A Double Bed

## MANFRED MANN
- ☐ '76  Blinded By The Light ★
- ☐ '64  Do Wah Diddy Diddy ★
- ☐ '81  For You
- ☐ '68  Mighty Quinn (Quinn The Eskimo)
- ☐ '66  Pretty Flamingo
- ☐ '84  Runner
- ☐ '64  Sha La La
- ☐ '77  Spirit In The Night

## MANGIONE, Chuck
- ☐ '78  Feels So Good
- ☐ '80  Give It All You Got
- ☐ '71  Hill Where The Lord Hides

## MANHATTANS, The
- ☐ '75  Don't Take Your Love
- ☐ '76  Kiss And Say Goodbye ★
- ☐ '72  One Life To Live
- ☐ '80  Shining Star ★
- ☐ '73  There's No Me Without You

## MANHATTAN TRANSFER, The
- ☐ '79  Birdland
- ☐ '81  Boy From New York City
- ☐ '75  Operator
- ☐ '83  Spice Of Life
- ☐ '80  Trickle Trickle
- ☐ '80  Twilight Zone/Twilight Tone

## MANILOW, Barry
- ☐ '78  Can't Smile Without You
- ☐ '78  Copacabana (At The Copa)
- ☐ '75  Could It Be Magic
- ☐ '77  Daybreak
- ☐ '78  Even Now
- ☐ '80  I Don't Want To Walk Without You
- ☐ '80  I Made It Through The Rain
- ☐ '75  I Write The Songs ★
- ☐ '75  It's A Miracle
- ☐ '89  Keep Each Other Warm
- ☐ '82  Let's Hang On
- ☐ '77  Looks Like We Made It
- ☐ '74  Mandy ★
- ☐ '82  Memory
- ☐ '82  Oh Julie
- ☐ '81  Old Songs, The
- ☐ '83  Read 'Em And Weep
- ☐ '78  Ready To Take A Chance Again
- ☐ '79  Ships
- ☐ '83  Some Kind Of Friend
- ☐ '81  Somewhere Down The Road
- ☐ '78  Somewhere In The Night
- ☐ '76  This One's For You
- ☐ '76  Tryin' To Get The Feeling Again
- ☐ '76  Weekend In New England
- ☐ '79  When I Wanted You

## MANN, Barry
- ☐ '61  Who Put The Bomp (In The Bomp, Bomp, Bomp)

## MANN, Carl
- ☐ '59  Mona Lisa

## MANN, Gloria
- ☐ '55  Earth Angel Will You Be Mine
- ☐ '55  Teen Age Prayer

## MANN, Herbie
- ☐ '75  Hijack
- ☐ '69  Memphis Underground
- ☐ '79  Superman

## MANTOVANI & His Orchestra
- ☐ '57  Around The World
- ☐ '60  Jamaica Farewell
- ☐ '60  Main Theme from Exodus

## MARATHONS, The
- ☐ '61  Peanut Butter

## MARCELS, The
- ☐ '61  Blue Moon ★
- ☐ '61  Heartaches

## MARCH, Little Peggy
- ☐ '63  Hello Heartache, Goodbye Love
- ☐ '63  I Will Follow Him ★
- ☐ '63  I Wish I Were A Princess

## MARCHAN, Bobby
- ☐ '60  There's Something On Your Mind

## MARCY PLAYGROUND
- ☐ '97  Sex and Candy

## MARDONES, Benny
- ☐ '80  Into The Night

## MARESCA, Ernie
- ☐ '62  Shout! Shout! (Knock Yourself Out)

## MARIE, Teena
- ☐ '80  I Need Your Lovin'
- ☐ '84  Lovergirl
- ☐ '88  Ooo La La La
- ☐ '81  Square Biz

## MARIO
- ☐ '02  Just A Friend 2002 ★
- ☐ '05  Let Me Love You ★

## MARKETTS, The
- ☐ '62  Balboa Blue
- ☐ '66  Batman Theme
- ☐ '63  Out Of Limits ★
- ☐ '62  Surfer's Stomp

## MAR-KEYS
- ☐ '61  Last Night

## MARKHAM, Pigmeat
- ☐ '68  Here Comes The Judge

## MARK IV, The
- ☐ '59  I Got A Wife

## MARKY MARK & The Funky Bunch
- ☐ '91  Good Vibrations ★
- ☐ '91  Wildside

## MARLEY, Bob
- ☐ '80  Could You Be Loved
- ☐ '77  Exodus
- ☐ '75  Get Up, Stand Up ★
- ☐ '73  I Shot The Sheriff
- ☐ '78  Is This Love
- ☐ '77  Jamming
- ☐ '75  Lively Up Yourself
- ☐ '75  No Woman No Cry [live] ★
- ☐ '77  One Love
- ☐ '80  Redemption Song ★
- ☐ '76  Roots, Rock, Reggae
- ☐ '77  Three Little Birds

## MARLEY, Ziggy, & The Melody Makers
- ☐ '88  Tomorrow People
- ☐ '88  Tumblin' Down

## MARLOWE, Marion
- ☐ '55  Man In The Raincoat, The

## MARMALADE, The
- ☐ '70  Reflections Of My Life

## MAROON5
- ☐ '03  Harder To Breathe
- ☐ '04  She Will Be Loved ★
- ☐ '05  Sunday Morning
- ☐ '04  This Love ★

## M/A/R/R/S
- ☐ '87  Pump Up The Volume ★

## MARSHALL TUCKER BAND, The
- ☐ '73  Can't You See
- ☐ '75  Fire On The Mountain
- ☐ '77  Heard It In A Love Song

## MARTERIE, Ralph, & His Orchestra
- ☐ '57  Shish-Kebab
- ☐ '57  Tricky

## MARTHA & THE VANDELLAS
- ☐ '63  Come And Get These Memories
- ☐ '64  Dancing In The Street ★
- ☐ '63  Heat Wave
- ☐ '67  Honey Chile
- ☐ '66  I'm Ready For Love
- ☐ '67  Jimmy Mack
- ☐ '67  Love Bug Leave My Heart Alone
- ☐ '66  My Baby Loves Me
- ☐ '65  Nowhere To Run
- ☐ '63  Quicksand
- ☐ '64  Wild One
- ☐ '65  You've Been In Love Too Long

## MARTIKA
- ☐ '89  I Feel The Earth Move
- ☐ '91  Love...Thy Will Be Done
- ☐ '88  More Than You Know
- ☐ '89  Toy Soldiers ★

## MARTIN, Bobbi
- ☐ '64  Don't Forget I Still Love You
- ☐ '70  For The Love Of Him

## MARTIN, Dean
- ☐ '58 Angel Baby
- ☐ '66 Come Running Back
- ☐ '64 Door Is Still Open To My Heart, The
- ☐ '64 Everybody Loves Somebody ★
- ☐ '65 Houston
- ☐ '65 I Will
- ☐ '67 In The Chapel In The Moonlight
- ☐ '67 In The Misty Moonlight
- ☐ '56 Innamorata
- ☐ '67 Little Ole Wine Drinker, Me
- ☐ '55 Memories Are Made Of This ★
- ☐ '68 Not Enough Indians
- ☐ '65 (Remember Me) I'm The One Who Loves You
- ☐ '58 Return To Me
- ☐ '65 Send Me The Pillow You Dream On
- ☐ '66 Somewhere There's A Someone
- ☐ '56 Standing On The Corner
- ☐ '58 Volare (Nel Blu Dipinto Di Blu)
- ☐ '64 You're Nobody Till Somebody Loves You

## MARTIN, Marilyn
- ☐ '86 Night Moves
- ☐ '85 Separate Lives ★
  *PHIL COLLINS & MARILYN MARTIN*

## MARTIN, Moon
- ☐ '79 Rolene

## MARTIN, Ricky
- ☐ '98 Cup Of Life, The
- ☐ '99 Livin' La Vida Loca ★
- ☐ '01 Nobody Wants To Be Lonely
  *RICKY MARTIN with Christina Aguilera*
- ☐ '99 Shake Your Bon-Bon
- ☐ '00 She Bangs
- ☐ '99 She's All I Ever Had ★

## MARTIN, Steve
- ☐ '78 King Tut

## MARTIN, Tony
- ☐ '56 Walk Hand In Hand

## MARTIN, Trade
- ☐ '62 That Stranger Used To Be My Girl

## MARTIN, Vince
- ☐ '56 Cindy, Oh Cindy

## MARTINDALE, Wink
- ☐ '59 Deck Of Cards

## MARTINEZ, Angie
- ☐ '02 If I Could Go!

## MARTINEZ, Nancy
- ☐ '86 For Tonight

## MARTINO, Al
- ☐ '64 Always Together
- ☐ '67 Daddy's Little Girl
- ☐ '63 I Love You Because
- ☐ '64 I Love You More And More Every Day
- ☐ '63 Living A Lie
- ☐ '68 Love Is Blue
- ☐ '67 Mary In The Morning
- ☐ '67 More Than The Eye Can See
- ☐ '63 Painted, Tainted Rose
- ☐ '65 Spanish Eyes
- ☐ '64 Tears And Roses
- ☐ '66 Think I'll Go Somewhere And Cry Myself To Sleep
- ☐ '74 To The Door Of The Sun (Alle Porte Del Sole)
- ☐ '75 Volare
- ☐ '66 Wiederseh'n

## MARVELETTES, The
- ☐ '63 As Long As I Know He's Mine
- ☐ '62 Beechwood 4-5789
- ☐ '66 Don't Mess With Bill
- ☐ '67 Hunter Gets Captured By The Game
- ☐ '65 I'll Keep Holding On
- ☐ '67 My Baby Must Be A Magician
- ☐ '62 Playboy
- ☐ '61 Please Mr. Postman ★
- ☐ '64 Too Many Fish In The Sea
- ☐ '62 Twistin' Postman
- ☐ '67 When You're Young And In Love

## MARVELOWS, The
- ☐ '65 I Do

## MARX, Richard
- ☐ '89 Angelia
- ☐ '97 At The Beginning
  *DONNA LEWIS & RICHARD MARX*
- ☐ '90 Children Of The Night
- ☐ '87 Don't Mean Nothing
- ☐ '88 Endless Summer Nights
- ☐ '92 Hazard ★
- ☐ '88 Hold On To The Nights ★
- ☐ '91 Keep Coming Back
- ☐ '94 Now and Forever ★
- ☐ '89 Right Here Waiting ★
- ☐ '89 Satisfied
- ☐ '87 Should've Known Better
- ☐ '92 Take This Heart
- ☐ '90 Too Late To Say Goodbye
- ☐ '97 Until I Find You Again
- ☐ '94 Way She Loves Me, The

## MARY JANE GIRLS
- ☐ '85 In My House

## MARYMARY
- ☐ '00 Shackles (Praise You)

## MASE
- ☐ '04 Breathe, Stretch, Shake
- ☐ '97 Feel So Good ★
- ☐ '98 Lookin' At Me
- ☐ '04 Welcome Back
- ☐ '98 What You Want

## MASEKELA, Hugh
- ☐ '68 Grazing In The Grass ★

## MASHMAKHAN
- ☐ '70 As The Years Go By

## MASON, Barbara
- ☐ '74 From His Woman To You
- ☐ '73 Give Me Your Love
- ☐ '65 Sad, Sad Girl
- ☐ '65 Yes, I'm Ready

## MASON, Dave
- ☐ '77 Let It Go, Let It Flow
- ☐ '70 Only You Know And I Know
- ☐ '77 So High (Rock Me Baby And Roll Me Away)
- ☐ '77 We Just Disagree
- ☐ '78 Will You Still Love Me Tomorrow

## MASTA ACE INCORPORATED
- ☐ '94 Born To Roll

## MASTER P
- ☐ '98 Goodbye To My Homies
- ☐ '98 I Got The Hook Up!
- ☐ '97 I Miss My Homies
- ☐ '98 Make Em' Say Uhh!

## MATCHBOX TWENTY
- ☐ '98 Back 2 Good
- ☐ '00 Bent ★
- ☐ '03 Bright Lights
- ☐ '02 Disease
- ☐ '00 If You're Gone ★
- ☐ '97 Push ★
- ☐ '98 Real World ★
- ☐ '97 3 AM ★
- ☐ '03 Unwell ★

## MATHEWS, Tobin, & Co.
- ☐ '60 Ruby Duby Du

## MATHIS, Johnny
- ☐ '58 All The Time
- ☐ '58 Call Me
- ☐ '58 Certain Smile, A
- ☐ '57 Chances Are ★
- ☐ '58 Come To Me
- ☐ '63 Every Step Of The Way
- ☐ '82 Friends In Love
  *DIONNE WARWICK & JOHNNY MATHIS*
- ☐ '62 Gina
- ☐ '73 I'm Coming Home
- ☐ '57 It's Not For Me To Say
- ☐ '60 Maria
- ☐ '59 Misty
- ☐ '60 My Love For You
- ☐ '57 No Love (But Your Love)
- ☐ '59 Small World
- ☐ '59 Someone
- ☐ '60 Starbright
- ☐ '58 Teacher, Teacher
- ☐ '78 Too Much, Too Little, Too Late ★
  *JOHNNY MATHIS/DENIECE WILLIAMS*
- ☐ '57 Twelfth Of Never, The
- ☐ '63 What Will Mary Say
- ☐ '57 Wild Is The Wind
- ☐ '57 Wonderful! Wonderful! ★

## MATTEA, Kathy
- ☐ '88 Eighteen Wheels And A Dozen Roses

- ☐ '94 Walking Away A Winner

## MATTHEWS, Dave, Band
- ☐ '05 American Baby ★
- ☐ '95 Ants Marching
- ☐ '97 Crash Into Me ★
- ☐ '98 Don't Drink The Water
- ☐ '01 I Did It
- ☐ '01 Space Between, The
- ☐ '98 Stay (Wasting Time)
- ☐ '96 Too Much
- ☐ '95 What Would You Say
- ☐ '02 Where Are You Going

## MATTHEWS, Ian
- ☐ '78 Shake It
- ☐ '71 Woodstock

## MAURIAT, Paul, & His Orchestra
- ☐ '68 Love Is Blue ★

## MAXWELL
- ☐ '96 Ascension (Don't Ever Wonder)
- ☐ '99 Fortunate
- ☐ '01 Lifetime

## MAXWELL, Robert, Orchestra
- ☐ '59 Little Dipper
  *THE MICKEY MOZART QUINTET*
- ☐ '64 Shangri-La

## MAYALL, John
- ☐ '70 Don't Waste My Time
- ☐ '69 Room To Move

## MAYE, Marilyn
- ☐ '67 Step To The Rear

## MAYER, John
- ☐ '03 Bigger Than My Body
- ☐ '05 Daughters ★
- ☐ '02 No Such Thing
- ☐ '02 Your Body Is A Wonderland

## MAYER, Nathaniel
- ☐ '62 Village Of Love

## MAYFIELD, Curtis
- ☐ '70 (Don't Worry) If There's A Hell Below We're All Going To Go
- ☐ '72 Freddie's Dead (Theme From "Superfly")
- ☐ '73 Future Shock
- ☐ '74 Kung Fu
- ☐ '72 Superfly

## MAZE Featuring Frankie Beverly
- ☐ '85 Back In Stride
- ☐ '89 Can't Get Over You

## MC BRAINS
- ☐ '92 Oochie Coochie

## MC5
- ☐ '69 Kick Out The Jams

## M.C. HAMMER
- ☐ '91 Addams Groove
- ☐ '90 Have You Seen Her
- ☐ '90 Pray ★
- ☐ '94 Pumps And A Bump
- ☐ '91 2 Legit 2 Quit ★
- ☐ '90 U Can't Touch This ★

## MC LYTE
- ☐ '96 Cold Rock A Party
- ☐ '96 Keep On, Keepin' On
- ☐ '93 RuffNeck

## McANALLY, Mac
- ☐ '77 It's A Crazy World

## McBRIDE, Martina
- ☐ '02 Blessed
- ☐ '97 Broken Wing, A
- ☐ '05 God's Will
- ☐ '98 Happy Girl
- ☐ '99 I Love You
- ☐ '04 In My Daughter's Eyes
- ☐ '99 Love's The Only House
- ☐ '93 My Baby Loves Me
- ☐ '03 This One's For The Girls
- ☐ '97 Valentine
- ☐ '99 Whatever You Say
- ☐ '02 Where Would You Be
- ☐ '95 Wild Angels
- ☐ '98 Wrong Again

## McCAIN, Edwin
- ☐ '99 I Could Not Ask For More
- ☐ '98 I'll Be

## McCALL, C.W.
- ☐ '75 Convoy ★

## McCANN, Lila
- ☐ '97 I Wanna Fall In Love

## McCANN, Peter
- ☐ '77 Do You Wanna Make Love

## McCARTNEY, Jesse
- ☐ '05 Beautiful Soul ★

## McCARTNEY, Paul/Wings
- ☐ '71 Another Day
- ☐ '79 Arrow Through Me
- ☐ '74 Band On The Run ★
- ☐ '71 Bip Bop
- ☐ '80 Coming Up (Live At Glasgow) ★
- ☐ '82 Ebony And Ivory ★
  *PAUL McCARTNEY (with Stevie Wonder)*
- ☐ '79 Getting Closer
- ☐ '82 Girl Is Mine, The ★
  *MICHAEL JACKSON & PAUL McCARTNEY*
- ☐ '77 Girls' School
- ☐ '72 Give Ireland Back To The Irish
- ☐ '79 Goodnight Tonight
- ☐ '73 Helen Wheels
- ☐ '72 Hi, Hi, Hi
- ☐ '78 I've Had Enough
- ☐ '74 Jet
- ☐ '74 Junior's Farm ★

- ☐ '76 Let 'Em In
- ☐ '75 Letting Go
- ☐ '75 Listen To What The Man Said ★
- ☐ '73 Live And Let Die ★
- ☐ '78 London Town
- ☐ '72 Mary Had A Little Lamb
- ☐ '70 Maybe I'm Amazed
- ☐ '77 Maybe I'm Amazed [live]
- ☐ '77 Mull Of Kintyre
- ☐ '89 My Brave Face
- ☐ '73 My Love ★
- ☐ '74 Nineteen Hundred And Eighty Five
- ☐ '84 No More Lonely Nights
- ☐ '86 Press
- ☐ '74 Sally G
- ☐ '83 Say Say Say ★
  *PAUL McCARTNEY & MICHAEL JACKSON*
- ☐ '76 Silly Love Songs ★
- ☐ '83 So Bad
- ☐ '85 Spies Like Us
- ☐ '82 Take It Away
- ☐ '71 Uncle Albert/Admiral Halsey ★
- ☐ '75 Venus And Mars Rock Show
- ☐ '78 With A Little Luck ★

## McCLAIN, Alton, & Destiny
- ☐ '79 It Must Be Love

## McCLINTON, Delbert
- ☐ '80 Giving It Up For Your Love

## McCLURE, Bobby
- ☐ '65 Don't Mess Up A Good Thing
  *FONTELLA BASS & BOBBY McCLURE*

## McCOO, Marilyn, & Billy Davis, Jr.
- ☐ '76 You Don't Have To Be A Star (To Be In My Show)
- ☐ '77 Your Love

## McCOY, Neal
- ☐ '93 No Doubt About It
- ☐ '97 Shake, The
- ☐ '94 Wink

## McCOY, Van
- ☐ '75 Hustle, The ★

## McCOYS, The
- ☐ '66 Come On Let's Go
- ☐ '65 Fever
- ☐ '65 Hang On Sloopy ★

## McCRACKLIN, Jimmy
- ☐ '61 Just Got To Know
- ☐ '58 Walk, The

## McCRAE, George
- ☐ '75 I Get Lifted
- ☐ '74 Rock Your Baby ★

## McCRAE, Gwen
- ☐ '75 Rockin' Chair

## McCREADY, Mindy
- ☐ '97 Girl's Gotta Do (What A Girl's Gotta Do)
- ☐ '96 Guys Do It All The Time

## McDANIELS, Gene
- ☐ '62 Chip Chip
- ☐ '61 Hundred Pounds Of Clay, A ★
- ☐ '62 Point Of No Return
- ☐ '62 Spanish Lace
- ☐ '61 Tear, A
- ☐ '61 Tower Of Strength

## McDEVITT, Chas., Skiffle Group
- ☐ '57 Freight Train

## McDONALD, Michael
- ☐ '82 I Keep Forgettin' (Every Time You're Near)
- ☐ '85 No Lookin' Back
- ☐ '86 On My Own ★
  *PATTI LaBELLE & MICHAEL McDONALD*
- ☐ '86 Sweet Freedom
- ☐ '83 Yah Mo B There
  *JAMES INGRAM (with Michael McDonald)*

## McDOWELL, Ronnie
- ☐ '77 King Is Gone, The

## McENTIRE, Reba
- ☐ '95 And Still
- ☐ '93 Does He Love You
- ☐ '91 Fancy
- ☐ '96 Fear Of Being Alone, The
- ☐ '91 For My Broken Heart
- ☐ '92 Greatest Man I Never Knew, The
- ☐ '95 Heart Is A Lonely Hunter, The
- ☐ '93 Heart Won't Lie, The
  *REBA McENTIRE & VINCE GILL*
- ☐ '96 How Was I To Know
- ☐ '97 I'd Rather Ride Around With You
- ☐ '01 I'm A Survivor
- ☐ '98 If You See Him/If You See Her
  *REBA/BROOKS & DUNN*
- ☐ '92 Is There Life Out There
- ☐ '86 Little Rock
- ☐ '90 Rumor Has It
- ☐ '04 Somebody
- ☐ '94 Till You Love Me
- ☐ '90 Walk On
- ☐ '99 What Do You Say
- ☐ '86 Whoever's In New England
- ☐ '90 You Lie

## McFADDEN, Bob, & Dor
- ☐ '59 Mummy, The

## McFADDEN & WHITEHEAD
- ☐ '79 Ain't No Stoppin' Us Now

## McFERRIN, Bobby
- ☐ '88 Don't Worry Be Happy ★

## McGOVERN, Maureen
- ☐ '79 Different Worlds
- ☐ '73 Morning After, The

## McGRAW, Tim
- ☐ '01 Angry All The Time
- ☐ '04 Back When
- ☐ '01 Bring On The Rain
  *JO DEE MESSINA with Tim McGraw*
- ☐ '02 Cowboy In Me, The
- ☐ '94 Don't Take The Girl ★
- ☐ '94 Down On The Farm
- ☐ '97 Everywhere
- ☐ '01 Grown Men Don't Cry
- ☐ '95 I Like It, I Love It
- ☐ '94 Indian Outlaw ★
- ☐ '97 It's Your Love ★
  *TIM McGRAW with Faith Hill*
- ☐ '98 Just To Hear You Say That You Love Me
  *FAITH HILL (With Tim McGraw)*
- ☐ '97 Just To See You Smile
- ☐ '04 Live Like You Were Dying
- ☐ '99 My Best Friend
- ☐ '00 My Next Thirty Years
- ☐ '94 Not A Moment Too Soon
- ☐ '98 One Of These Days
- ☐ '99 Please Remember Me ★
- ☐ '03 Real Good Man
- ☐ '02 Red Rag Top
- ☐ '96 She Never Lets It Go To Her Heart
- ☐ '02 She's My Kind Of Rain
- ☐ '99 Something Like That
- ☐ '02 Unbroken
- ☐ '03 Watch The Wind Blow By
- ☐ '98 Where The Green Grass Grows

## McGRIFF, Jimmy
- ☐ '62 I've Got A Woman

## McGUINN, CLARK & HILLMAN
- ☐ '79 Don't You Write Her Off

## McGUIRE, Barry
- ☐ '65 Eve Of Destruction ★

## McGUIRE SISTERS, The
- ☐ '56 Delilah Jones
- ☐ '58 Ding Dong
- ☐ '56 Ev'ry Day Of My Life
- ☐ '56 Goodnight My Love, Pleasant Dreams
- ☐ '55 He
- ☐ '55 It May Sound Silly
- ☐ '61 Just For Old Time's Sake
- ☐ '59 May You Always
- ☐ '55 No More
- ☐ '56 Picnic
- ☐ '55 Sincerely
- ☐ '55 Something's Gotta Give
- ☐ '57 Sugartime ★
- ☐ '56 Weary Blues

## McINTYRE, Joey
- ☐ '99 Stay The Same

## McKENNITT, Loreena
- ☐ '98 Mummers' Dance, The

## McKENZIE, Bob & Doug
- ☐ '82 Take Off

## McKENZIE, Scott
- ☐ '67 Like An Old Time Movie
- ☐ '67 San Francisco (Be Sure To Wear Flowers In Your Hair)

## McKNIGHT, Brian
- ☐ '98 Anytime
- ☐ '99 Back At One ★
- ☐ '98 Hold Me
- ☐ '93 Love Is ★
  *VANESSA WILLIAMS & BRIAN McKNIGHT*
- ☐ '93 One Last Cry
- ☐ '97 You Should Be Mine (Don't Waste Your Time)

## McLACHLAN, Sarah
- ☐ '98 Adia ★
- ☐ '98 Angel ★
- ☐ '97 Building A Mystery
- ☐ '99 I Will Remember You [live]
- ☐ '98 Sweet Surrender

## McLAIN, Tommy
- ☐ '66 Sweet Dreams

## McLEAN, Don
- ☐ '71 American Pie ★
- ☐ '72 Castles In The Air
- ☐ '81 Crying
- ☐ '72 Dreidel
- ☐ '81 Since I Don't Have You
- ☐ '72 Vincent
- ☐ '75 Wonderful Baby

## McLEAN, Phil
- ☐ '61 Small Sad Sam

## McNAMARA, Robin
- ☐ '70 Lay A Little Lovin' On Me

## McPHATTER, Clyde
- ☐ '58 Come What May
- ☐ '57 Just To Hold My Hand
- ☐ '62 Little Bitty Pretty One
- ☐ '57 Long Lonely Nights
- ☐ '62 Lover Please
- ☐ '58 Lover's Question, A ★
- ☐ '56 Seven Days
- ☐ '59 Since You've Been Gone
- ☐ '60 Ta Ta
- ☐ '56 Treasure Of Love
- ☐ '57 Without Love (There Is Nothing)

## McSHANN, Jay, Orchestra
- ☐ '55 Hands Off

## McVIE, Christine
- ☐ '84 Got A Hold On Me
- ☐ '84 Love Will Show Us How

## MEAD, Sister Janet
- ☐ '74 Lord's Prayer, The

## MEAT LOAF
- ☐ '77 Bat Out Of Hell
- ☐ '93 I'd Do Anything For Love (But I Won't Do That)
- ☐ '95 I'd Lie For You (And That's The Truth)
- ☐ '94 Objects In The Rear View Mirror May Appear Closer Than They Are
- ☐ '78 Paradise By The Dashboard Light
- ☐ '94 Rock And Roll Dreams Come Through
- ☐ '78 Two Out Of Three Ain't Bad
- ☐ '78 You Took The Words Right Out Of My Mouth

## MEAT PUPPETS
- ☐ '94 Backwater

## MECO
- ☐ '80 Empire Strikes Back (Medley)
- ☐ '82 Pop Goes The Movies
- ☐ '77 Star Wars Theme/Cantina Band ★
- ☐ '78 Theme From Close Encounters
- ☐ '78 Themes From The Wizard Of Oz

## MEDEIROS, Glenn
- ☐ '90 All I'm Missing Is You
- ☐ '87 Nothing's Gonna Change My Love For You
- ☐ '90 She Ain't Worth It ★

## MEDLEY, Bill
- ☐ '68 Brown Eyed Woman
- ☐ '87 (I've Had) The Time Of My Life ★
  *BILL MEDLEY & JENNIFER WARNES*

## MEISNER, Randy
- ☐ '80 Deep Inside My Heart
- ☐ '81 Hearts On Fire
- ☐ '82 Never Been In Love

## MEL & TIM
- ☐ '69 Backfield In Motion
- ☐ '72 Starting All Over Again

## MELANIE
- ☐ '73 Bitter Bad
- ☐ '71 Brand New Key ★
- ☐ '70 Lay Down (Candles In The Rain)
  *MELANIE with The Edwin Hawkins Singers*
- ☐ '72 Nickel Song, The
- ☐ '70 Peace Will Come (According To Plan)
- ☐ '72 Ring The Living Bell

## MELENDEZ, Lisette
- ☐ '91 Together Forever

## MELLENCAMP, John Cougar
- ☐ '92 Again Tonight
- ☐ '81 Ain't Even Done With The Night
- ☐ '84 Authority Song
- ☐ '88 Check It Out
- ☐ '87 Cherry Bomb
- ☐ '83 Crumblin' Down
- ☐ '91 Get A Leg Up
- ☐ '82 Hand To Hold On To
- ☐ '93 Human Wheels
- ☐ '82 Hurts So Good ★
- ☐ '79 I Need A Lover
- ☐ '99 I'm Not Running Anymore
- ☐ '82 Jack & Diane ★
- ☐ '96 Key West Intermezzo (I Saw You First)
- ☐ '85 Lonely Ol' Night
- ☐ '92 Now More Than Ever
- ☐ '87 Paper In Fire
- ☐ '01 Peaceful World
- ☐ '83 Pink Houses
- ☐ '89 Pop Singer

□ '86 R.O.C.K. In The U.S.A. (A Salute To 60's Rock) ★
□ '86 Rain On The Scarecrow
□ '87 Real Life, The
□ '86 Rumbleseat
□ '85 Small Town
□ '80 This Time
□ '93 What If I Came Knocking
□ '94 Wild Night ★
  *JOHN MELLENCAMP & ME'SHELL NDEGÉOCELLO*
□ '98 Your Life Is Now

## MELLO-KINGS, The
□ '57 Tonite, Tonite

## MELLO-TONES, The
□ '57 Rosie Lee

## MELLOW MAN ACE
□ '90 Mentirosa

## MELVIN, Harold, & The Blue Notes
□ '75 Bad Luck
□ '75 Hope That We Can Be Together Soon
□ '72 If You Don't Know Me By Now ★
□ '73 Love I Lost, The
□ '75 Wake Up Everybody

## MEN AT LARGE
□ '93 So Alone

## MEN AT WORK
□ '83 Be Good Johnny
□ '82 Down Under ★
□ '83 Dr. Heckyll & Mr. Jive
□ '83 It's A Mistake
□ '83 Overkill
□ '82 Who Can It Be Now? ★

## MENDES, Sergio
□ '84 Alibis
□ '68 Fool On The Hill, The
□ '68 Look Of Love, The
□ '83 Never Gonna Let You Go
□ '68 Scarborough Fair

## MEN WITHOUT HATS
□ '87 Pop Goes The World
□ '83 Safety Dance, The ★

## MERCHANT, Natalie
□ '95 Carnival
□ '96 Jealousy
□ '98 Kind & Generous
□ '95 Wonder

## MERCY
□ '69 Love (Can Make You Happy)

## MERCYME
□ '01 I Can Only Imagine
□ '04 Word Of God Speak

## MESSINA, Jo Dee
□ '01 Bring On The Rain
  *JO DEE MESSINA with Tim McGraw*
□ '00 Burn

□ '98 Bye-Bye
□ '96 Heads Carolina, Tails California
□ '98 I'm Alright
□ '99 Lesson In Leavin'
□ '05 My Give A Damn's Busted ★
□ '98 Stand Beside Me
□ '00 That's The Way

## METALLICA
□ '91 Enter Sandman
□ '96 Hero Of The Day
□ '00 I Disappear
□ '86 Master Of Puppets
□ '97 Memory Remains, The
□ '99 No Leaf Clover
□ '92 Nothing Else Matters
□ '89 One
□ '98 Turn The Page
□ '91 Unforgiven, The
□ '97 Unforgiven II, The
□ '96 Until It Sleeps
□ '99 Whiskey In The Jar

## METERS, The
□ '69 Cissy Strut
□ '69 Sophisticated Cissy

## METHOD MAN
□ '95 How High
  *REDMAN/METHOD MAN*
□ '95 I'll Be There For You/You're All I Need To Get By ★

## MFSB
□ '74 TSOP (The Sound Of Philadelphia) ★
  *MFSB Feat. The Three Degrees*

## MICHAEL, George/Wham!
□ '84 Careless Whisper ★
□ '86 Different Corner, A
□ '91 Don't Let The Sun Go Down On Me [live] ★
  *GEORGE MICHAEL & ELTON JOHN*
□ '86 Edge Of Heaven, The
□ '85 Everything She Wants ★
□ '87 Faith ★
□ '96 Fastlove
□ '88 Father Figure ★
□ '85 Freedom
□ '90 Freedom ★
□ '87 I Knew You Were Waiting (For Me) ★
  *ARETHA FRANKLIN & GEORGE MICHAEL*
□ '87 I Want Your Sex
□ '85 I'm Your Man
□ '96 Jesus To A Child
□ '88 Kissing A Fool
□ '88 Monkey ★
□ '88 One More Try ★
□ '90 Praying For Time ★
□ '93 Somebody To Love
  *GEORGE MICHAEL & QUEEN*
□ '92 Too Funky
□ '91 Waiting For That Day
□ '84 Wake Me Up Before You Go-Go ★

## MICHAELS, Lee
- ☐ '71 Can I Get A Witness
- ☐ '71 Do You Know What I Mean

## MICHEL, Pras
- ☐ '98 Ghetto Supastar (That Is What You Are)

## MICHEL'LE
- ☐ '90 Nicety
- ☐ '89 No More Lies
- ☐ '91 Something In My Heart

## MICKEY & SYLVIA
- ☐ '57 Love Is Strange ★

## MIDLER, Bette
- ☐ '73 Boogie Woogie Bugle Boy
- ☐ '72 Do You Want To Dance?
- ☐ '73 Friends
- ☐ '90 From A Distance ★
- ☐ '79 Married Men
- ☐ '80 My Mother's Eyes
- ☐ '80 Rose, The ★
- ☐ '80 When A Man Loves A Woman
- ☐ '89 Wind Beneath My Wings ★

## MIDNIGHT OIL
- ☐ '88 Beds Are Burning
- ☐ '90 Blue Sky Mine

## MIDNIGHT STAR
- ☐ '88 Don't Rock The Boat
- ☐ '83 Freak-A-Zoid
- ☐ '86 Headlines
- ☐ '84 Operator

## MIGHTY MIGHTY BOSSTONES, The
- ☐ '97 Impression That I Get, The

## MIKAILA
- ☐ '00 So In Love With Two

## MIKE + THE MECHANICS
- ☐ '86 All I Need Is A Miracle
- ☐ '89 Living Years, The ★
- ☐ '88 Nobody's Perfect
- ☐ '85 Silent Running (On Dangerous Ground)
- ☐ '86 Taken In

## MILES, Garry
- ☐ '60 Look For A Star

## MILES, John
- ☐ '77 Slowdown

## MILES, Robert
- ☐ '96 Children

## MILESTONE
- ☐ '97 I Care 'Bout You

## MILIAN, Christina
- ☐ '01 AM To PM
- ☐ '04 Dip It Low

## MILLER, Chuck
- ☐ '55 House Of Blue Lights, The

## MILLER, Jody
- ☐ '71 He's So Fine
- ☐ '65 Home Of The Brave
- ☐ '65 Queen Of The House

## MILLER, Mitch, Orchestra
- ☐ '59 Children's Marching Song (Nick Nack Paddy Whack)
- ☐ '56 Lisbon Antigua (In Old Lisbon)
- ☐ '58 March From The River Kwai and Colonel Bogey
- ☐ '56 Theme Song From "Song For A Summer Night"
- ☐ '55 Yellow Rose Of Texas, The ★

## MILLER, Ned
- ☐ '62 From A Jack To A King

## MILLER, Roger
- ☐ '64 Chug-A-Lug
- ☐ '64 Dang Me
- ☐ '64 Do-Wacka-Do
- ☐ '65 Engine Engine #9
- ☐ '65 England Swings
- ☐ '66 Husbands And Wives
- ☐ '65 Kansas City Star
- ☐ '65 King Of The Road ★
- ☐ '68 Little Green Apples
- ☐ '65 One Dyin' And A Buryin'
- ☐ '67 Walkin' In The Sunshine
- ☐ '66 You Can't Roller Skate In A Buffalo Herd

## MILLER, Steve, Band
- ☐ '82 Abracadabra ★
- ☐ '76 Dance, Dance, Dance
- ☐ '76 Fly Like An Eagle ★
- ☐ '68 Gangster Of Love
- ☐ '70 Going To The Country
- ☐ '81 Heart Like A Wheel
- ☐ '86 I Want To Make The World Turn Around
- ☐ '77 Jet Airliner
- ☐ '73 Joker, The ★
- ☐ '77 Jungle Love
- ☐ '68 Living In The U.S.A.
- ☐ '76 Rock'n Me ★
- ☐ '69 Space Cowboy
- ☐ '77 Swingtown
- ☐ '76 Take The Money And Run ★
- ☐ '93 Wide River
- ☐ '73 Your Cash Ain't Nothin' But Trash

## MILLI VANILLI
- ☐ '90 All Or Nothing
- ☐ '89 Baby Don't Forget My Number ★
- ☐ '89 Blame It On The Rain ★
- ☐ '89 Girl I'm Gonna Miss You ★
- ☐ '89 Girl You Know It's True

## MILLS, Frank
- ☐ '79 Music Box Dancer ★

## MILLS, Garry
- ☐ '60 Look For A Star

## MILLS, Hayley
- ☐ '62 Johnny Jingo
- ☐ '61 Let's Get Together

## MILLS, Stephanie
- ☐ '89 Home
- ☐ '87 I Feel Good All Over
- ☐ '86 I Have Learned To Respect The Power Of Love
- ☐ '80 Never Knew Love Like This Before ★
- ☐ '89 Something In The Way (You Make Me Feel)
- ☐ '80 Sweet Sensation
- ☐ '81 Two Hearts
  *STEPHANIE MILLS Feat. Teddy Pendergrass*
- ☐ '79 What Cha Gonna Do With My Lovin'
- ☐ '87 (You're Puttin') A Rush On Me

## MILLS BROTHERS, The
- ☐ '68 Cab Driver
- ☐ '58 Get A Job
- ☐ '57 Queen Of The Senior Prom

## MILSAP, Ronnie
- ☐ '82 Any Day Now
- ☐ '81 I Wouldn't Have Missed It For The World
- ☐ '77 It Was Almost Like A Song
- ☐ '85 Lost In The Fifties Tonight (In The Still Of The Night)
- ☐ '88 Old Folks
  *RONNIE MILSAP & MIKE REID*
- ☐ '80 Smoky Mountain Rain
- ☐ '83 Stranger In My House
- ☐ '81 (There's) No Gettin' Over Me

## MIMMS, Garnet, & The Enchanters
- ☐ '63 Baby Don't You Weep
- ☐ '63 Cry Baby
- ☐ '63 For Your Precious Love
- ☐ '66 I'll Take Good Care Of You

## MINDBENDERS, The
- ☐ '65 Game Of Love ★
- ☐ '66 Groovy Kind Of Love, A ★

## MINEO, Sal
- ☐ '57 Lasting Love
- ☐ '57 Start Movin' (In My Direction)

## MINIATURE MEN
- ☐ '62 Baby Elephant Walk

## MINOGUE, Kylie
- ☐ '02 Can't Get You Out Of My Head
- ☐ '88 I Should Be So Lucky
- ☐ '88 It's No Secret
- ☐ '88 Loco-Motion, The
- ☐ '02 Love At First Sight

## MINT CONDITION
- ☐ '92 Breakin' My Heart (Pretty Brown Eyes)
- ☐ '99 If You Love Me
- ☐ '94 U Send Me Swingin'
- ☐ '96 What Kind Of Man Would I Be
- ☐ '97 You Don't Have To Hurt No More

## MIRACLES, The
- ☐ '69 Abraham, Martin And John
- ☐ '69 Baby, Baby Don't Cry
- ☐ '66 (Come 'Round Here) I'm The One You Need
- ☐ '74 Do It Baby
- ☐ '69 Doggone Right
- ☐ '65 Going To A Go-Go
- ☐ '69 Here I Go Again
- ☐ '71 I Don't Blame You At All
- ☐ '63 I Gotta Dance To Keep From Crying
- ☐ '64 I Like It Like That
- ☐ '67 I Second That Emotion
- ☐ '62 I'll Try Something New
- ☐ '68 If You Can Want
- ☐ '67 Love I Saw In You Was Just A Mirage
- ☐ '75 Love Machine ★
- ☐ '63 Love She Can Count On, A
- ☐ '63 Mickey's Monkey
- ☐ '67 More Love
- ☐ '65 My Girl Has Gone
- ☐ '65 Ooo Baby Baby
- ☐ '69 Point It Out
- ☐ '60 Shop Around ★
- ☐ '68 Special Occasion
- ☐ '70 Tears Of A Clown, The ★
- ☐ '64 That's What Love Is Made Of
- ☐ '65 Tracks Of My Tears, The
- ☐ '62 What's So Good About Good-by
- ☐ '68 Yester Love
- ☐ '62 You've Really Got A Hold On Me

## MISSING PERSONS
- ☐ '82 Destination Unknown
- ☐ '82 Words

## MIS-TEEQ
- ☐ '04 Scandalous

## MR. BIG
- ☐ '92 Just Take My Heart
- ☐ '91 To Be With You ★
- ☐ '93 Wild World

## MR. CHEEKS
- ☐ '01 Lights, Camera, Action!

## MR. MISTER
- ☐ '85 Broken Wings ★
- ☐ '86 Is It Love
- ☐ '85 Kyrie ★
- ☐ '87 Something Real (Inside Me/Inside You)

## MR. PRESIDENT
- ☐ '97 Coco Jamboo

## MITCHELL, Guy
- ☐ '59 Heartaches By The Number
- ☐ '57 Knee Deep In The Blues
- ☐ '56 Ninety Nine Years (Dead Or Alive)
- ☐ '57 Rock-A-Billy
- ☐ '56 Singing The Blues ★

## MITCHELL, Joni
- ☐ '70 Big Yellow Taxi
- ☐ '74 Big Yellow Taxi [live]
- ☐ '69 Both Sides Now
- ☐ '71 Carey
- ☐ '69 Chelsea Morning
- ☐ '74 Free Man In Paris
- ☐ '74 Help Me
- ☐ '70 Woodstock
- ☐ '72 You Turn Me On, I'm A Radio

## MITCHELL, Kim
- ☐ '85 Go For Soda

## MITCHELL, Willie
- ☐ '68 Soul Serenade
- ☐ '64 20-75

## MOBY
- ☐ '99 Natural Blues
- ☐ '00 South Side

## MOBY GRAPE
- ☐ '67 Hey Grandma
- ☐ '67 Omaha

## MOCEDADES
- ☐ '74 Eres Tu (Touch The Wind)

## MODELS
- ☐ '86 Out Of Mind Out Of Sight

## MODERN ENGLISH
- ☐ '83 I Melt With You ★

## MODERN LOVERS, The
- ☐ '76 Roadrunner

## MODEST MOUSE
- ☐ '04 Float On

## MODUGNO, Domenico
- ☐ '58 Nel Blu Dipinto Di Blu (Volaré) ★

## MOJO MEN, The
- ☐ '67 Sit Down, I Think I Love You

## MOKENSTEF
- ☐ '95 He's Mine

## MOLLY HATCHET
- ☐ '79 Flirtin' With Disaster

## MOMENTS, The
- ☐ '75 Look At Me (I'm In Love)
- ☐ '70 Love On A Two-Way Street ★
- ☐ '74 Sexy Mama
- ☐ '80 Special Lady
  *RAY, GOODMAN & BROWN*

## MONEY, Eddie
- ☐ '78 Baby Hold On
- ☐ '87 Endless Nights
- ☐ '79 Gimme Some Water
- ☐ '86 I Wanna Go Back
- ☐ '91 I'll Get By
- ☐ '88 Love In Your Eyes, The
- ☐ '79 Maybe I'm A Fool
- ☐ '89 Peace In Our Time
- ☐ '82 Shakin'
- ☐ '86 Take Me Home Tonight
- ☐ '82 Think I'm In Love
- ☐ '78 Two Tickets To Paradise
- ☐ '88 Walk On Water

## MONEY, JT
- ☐ '99 Who Dat ★

## MONICA
- ☐ '96 Ain't Nobody
- ☐ '98 Angel Of Mine ★
- ☐ '95 Before You Walk Out Of My Life
- ☐ '98 Boy Is Mine, The ★
  *BRANDY & MONICA*
- ☐ '95 Don't Take It Personal (just one of dem days) ★
- ☐ '98 First Night, The ★
- ☐ '97 For You I Will
- ☐ '95 Like This And Like That
- ☐ '03 So Gone
- ☐ '04 U Should've Known Better
- ☐ '96 Why I Love You So Much

## MONIFAH
- ☐ '98 Touch It
- ☐ '96 You

## MONKEES, The
- ☐ '68 D. W. Washburn
- ☐ '67 Daydream Believer ★
- ☐ '67 Girl I Knew Somewhere, The
- ☐ '66 I'm A Believer ★
- ☐ '66 (I'm Not Your) Steppin' Stone
- ☐ '68 It's Nice To Be With You
- ☐ '66 Last Train To Clarksville ★
- ☐ '69 Listen To The Band
- ☐ '67 Little Bit Me, A Little Bit You, A
- ☐ '67 Mary, Mary
- ☐ '67 Pleasant Valley Sunday
- ☐ '67 Randy Scouse Git
- ☐ '67 She
- ☐ '68 Tapioca Tundra
- ☐ '86 That Was Then, This Is Now
- ☐ '66 Theme From The Monkees
- ☐ '68 Valleri
- ☐ '67 Words

## MONOTONES, The
- ☐ '58 Book Of Love ★

## MONRO, Matt
- ☐ '61 My Kind Of Girl
- ☐ '64 Walk Away

## MONROE, Vaughn
- ☐ '56 Don't Go To Strangers
- ☐ '56 In The Middle Of The House

## MONSTER MAGNET
- ☐ '98 Space Lord

## MONTE, Lou
- ☐ '58 Lazy Mary
- ☐ '62 Pepino The Italian Mouse

## MONTENEGRO, Hugo, Orchestra
- ☐ '68 Good, The Bad And The Ugly, The ★

## MONTEZ, Chris
- ☐ '66 Call Me
- ☐ '62 Let's Dance ★
- ☐ '66 More I See You, The
- ☐ '66 There Will Never Be Another You
- ☐ '66 Time After Time

## MONTGOMERY, John Michael
- ☐ '94 Be My Baby Tonight
- ☐ '98 Cover You In Kisses
- ☐ '98 Hold On To Me
- ☐ '99 Home To You
- ☐ '97 How Was I To Know
- ☐ '95 I Can Love You Like That
- ☐ '93 I Love The Way You Love Me
- ☐ '93 I Swear
- ☐ '94 If You've Got Love
- ☐ '04 Letters From Home
- ☐ '92 Life's A Dance
- ☐ '00 Little Girl, The
- ☐ '95 Sold (The Grundy County Auction Incident)

## MONTGOMERY, Melba
- ☐ '74 No Charge

## MONTGOMERY GENTRY
- ☐ '05 Gone
- ☐ '04 If You Ever Stop Loving Me
- ☐ '99 Lonely And Gone
- ☐ '02 My Town
- ☐ '01 She Couldn't Change Me

## MOODY BLUES, The
- ☐ '78 Driftwood
- ☐ '70 Eyes Of A Child
- ☐ '81 Gemini Dream
- ☐ '65 Go Now!
- ☐ '75 I Dreamed Last Night
- ☐ '88 I Know You're Out There Somewhere
- ☐ '73 I'm Just A Singer (In A Rock And Roll Band)
- ☐ '72 Isn't Life Strange
- ☐ '68 Legend Of A Mind
- ☐ '69 Never Comes The Day
- ☐ '72 Nights In White Satin ★
- ☐ '70 Question
- ☐ '68 Ride My See-Saw
- ☐ '83 Sitting At The Wheel
- ☐ '78 Steppin' In A Slide Zone
- ☐ '71 Story In Your Eyes, The
- ☐ '68 Tuesday Afternoon (Forever Afternoon)
- ☐ '81 Voice, The
- ☐ '86 Your Wildest Dreams

## MOONEY, Art, & His Orchestra
- ☐ '55 Honey-Babe

## MOONGLOWS, The
- ☐ '56 See Saw
- ☐ '55 Sincerely ★
- ☐ '58 Ten Commandments Of Love
- ☐ '56 We Go Together

## MOORE, Bob, & His Orch.
- ☐ '61 Mexico

## MOORE, Bobby, & The Rhythm Aces
- ☐ '66 Searching For My Love

## MOORE, Chanté
- ☐ '99 Chanté's Got A Man

## MOORE, Dorothy
- ☐ '77 I Believe You
- ☐ '76 Misty Blue

## MOORE, Jackie
- ☐ '70 Precious, Precious

## MOORE, Mandy
- ☐ '99 Candy
- ☐ '00 I Wanna Be With You

## MOORE, Melba
- ☐ '86 Falling
- ☐ '86 Little Bit More, A

## MORALES, Michael
- ☐ '89 What I Like About You
- ☐ '89 Who Do You Give Your Love To?

## MORGAN, Craig
- ☐ '02 Almost Home
- ☐ '05 That's What I Love About Sunday ★

## MORGAN, Debelah
- ☐ '00 Dance With Me ★

## MORGAN, Jane
- ☐ '58 Day The Rains Came, The
- ☐ '57 Fascination
- ☐ '59 With Open Arms

## MORGAN, Jaye P.
- ☐ '55 Danger! Heartbreak Ahead
- ☐ '55 If You Don't Want My Love
- ☐ '55 Longest Walk, The
- ☐ '55 Pepper-Hot Baby
- ☐ '55 Softly, Softly
- ☐ '55 That's All I Want From You

## MORGAN, Lorrie
- ☐ '90 Five Minutes
- ☐ '97 Go Away
- ☐ '95 I Didn't Know My Own Strength
- ☐ '92 Watch Me
- ☐ '92 What Part Of No

## MORGAN, Meli'sa
- ☐ '85 Do Me Baby
- ☐ '87 If You Can Do It: I Can Too!!
- ☐ '87 Love Changes
  *KASHIF & MELI'SA MORGAN*

## MORGAN, Russ, & His Orchestra
- ☐ '55 Dogface Soldier
- ☐ '56 Poor People Of Paris, The

## MORISSETTE, Alanis
- ☐ '95 Hand In My Pocket
- ☐ '02 Hands Clean
- ☐ '96 Head Over Feet
- ☐ '96 Ironic ★
- ☐ '98 Thank U ★
- ☐ '98 Uninvited
- ☐ '96 You Learn
- ☐ '95 You Oughta Know ★

## MORMON TABERNACLE CHOIR
- ☐ '59 Battle Hymn Of The Republic

## MORODER, Giorgio
- ☐ '79 Chase
- ☐ '72 Son Of My Father

## MORRISON, Mark
- ☐ '97 Return Of The Mack ★

## MORRISON, Van
- ☐ '71 Blue Money
- ☐ '67 Brown Eyed Girl ★
- ☐ '71 Call Me Up In Dreamland
- ☐ '70 Come Running
- ☐ '70 Crazy Love
- ☐ '70 Domino
- ☐ '70 Into The Mystic
- ☐ '72 Jackie Wilson Said (I'm In Heaven When You Smile)
- ☐ '70 Moondance
- ☐ '72 Redwood Tree
- ☐ '71 Tupelo Honey
- ☐ '78 Wavelength
- ☐ '71 Wild Night

## MORRISSEY
- ☐ '89 Last Of The Famous International Playboys, The
- ☐ '94 More You Ignore Me, The Closer I Get
- ☐ '89 Ouija Board, Ouija Board
- ☐ '91 Our Frank
- ☐ '90 Piccadilly Palare
- ☐ '92 Tomorrow
- ☐ '92 We Hate It When Our Friends Become Successful

## MOTELS, The
- ☐ '82 Only The Lonely
- ☐ '83 Remember The Nights
- ☐ '85 Shame
- ☐ '83 Suddenly Last Summer

## MOTHERLODE
- ☐ '69 When I Die

## MÖTLEY CRÜE
- ☐ '90 Don't Go Away Mad (Just Go Away)
- ☐ '89 Dr. Feelgood
- ☐ '87 Girls, Girls, Girls
- ☐ '85 Home Sweet Home
- ☐ '89 Kickstart My Heart
- ☐ '85 Smokin' In The Boys Room
- ☐ '90 Without You

## MOTT THE HOOPLE
- ☐ '72 All The Young Dudes

- ☐ '74 Golden Age Of Rock 'N' Roll, The

## MOUNTAIN
- ☐ '70 Mississippi Queen

## MOUTH & MACNEAL
- ☐ '72 How Do You Do?

## MOVING PICTURES
- ☐ '82 What About Me

## MOYET, Alison
- ☐ '85 Invisible

## M PEOPLE
- ☐ '94 Moving On Up

## MRAZ, Jason
- ☐ '03 Remedy (I Won't Worry)

## MTUME
- ☐ '83 Juicy Fruit

## M2M
- ☐ '99 Don't Say You Love Me

## MUDVAYNE
- ☐ '05 Happy?

## MULDAUR, Maria
- ☐ '74 I'm A Woman
- ☐ '74 Midnight At The Oasis

## MULLINS, Shawn
- ☐ '98 Lullaby ★

## MUMBA, Samantha
- ☐ '00 Gotta Tell You ★

## MUNGO JERRY
- ☐ '70 In The Summertime ★

## MURDOCK, Shirley
- ☐ '87 As We Lay

## MURMAIDS, The
- ☐ '63 Popsicles And Icicles ★

## MURPHEY, Michael
- ☐ '75 Carolina In The Pines
- ☐ '72 Geronimo's Cadillac
- ☐ '76 Renegade
- ☐ '82 What's Forever For
- ☐ '75 Wildfire

## MURPHY, David Lee
- ☐ '95 Dust On The Bottle
- ☐ '04 Loco

## MURPHY, Eddie
- ☐ '85 Party All The Time
- ☐ '89 Put Your Mouth On Me

## MURPHY, Peter
- ☐ '90 Cuts You Up

## MURPHY, Walter
- ☐ '76 Fifth Of Beethoven, A

## MURRAY, Anne
- ☐ '81 Blessed Are The Believers
- ☐ '79 Broken Hearted Me
- ☐ '80 Could I Have This Dance
- ☐ '73 Danny's Song
- ☐ '79 Daydream Believer
- ☐ '79 I Just Fall In Love Again
- ☐ '83 Little Good News, A
- ☐ '73 Love Song
- ☐ '79 Shadows In The Moonlight
- ☐ '70 Snowbird
- ☐ '78 You Needed Me ★
- ☐ '74 You Won't See Me

## MUSICAL YOUTH
- ☐ '82 Pass The Dutchie

## MUSIC EXPLOSION, The
- ☐ '67 Little Bit O' Soul ★

## MUSIC MACHINE, The
- ☐ '66 Talk Talk

## MUSIQ
- ☐ '02 Dontchange
- ☐ '02 Halfcrazy
- ☐ '00 Just Friends (Sunny)
- ☐ '01 Love

## MYA
- ☐ '00 Case Of The Ex (Whatcha Gonna Do) ★
- ☐ '98 It's All About Me
  *MYA With Sisqo*
- ☐ '01 Lady Marmalade ★
  *CHRISTINA AGUILERA, LIL' KIM, MYA & P!NK*
- ☐ '98 Movin' On
- ☐ '99 My First Night With You
- ☐ '03 My Love Is Like...WO
- ☐ '98 Take Me There
  *BLACKSTREET & MYA*

## MYERS, Billie
- ☐ '97 Kiss The Rain

## MYLES, Alannah
- ☐ '89 Black Velvet ★

## MYLES, Billy
- ☐ '57 Joker (That's What They Call Me)

## MYSTICS, The
- ☐ '59 Hushabye

## MYSTIKAL
- ☐ '01 Bouncin' Back (Bumpin' Me Against The Wall)
- ☐ '00 Danger (Been So Long)
- ☐ '99 It Ain't My Fault 2
  *SILKK THE SHOCKER & MYSTIKAL*
- ☐ '00 Shake Ya Ass

# N

## NAKED EYES
- ☐ '83 Always Something There To Remind Me
- ☐ '83 Promises, Promises
- ☐ '84 (What) In The Name Of Love
- ☐ '83 When The Lights Go Out

## NAPOLEON XIV
- ☐ '66 They're Coming To Take Me Away, Ha-Haaa!

## NAPPY ROOTS
- ☐ '02 Po' Folks

## NAS
- ☐ '03 I Can
- ☐ '02 Made You Look
- ☐ '96 Street Dreams

## NASH, Graham
- ☐ '71 Chicago
- ☐ '72 Immigration Man
  *GRAHAM NASH & DAVID CROSBY*

## NASH, Johnny
- ☐ '69 Cupid
- ☐ '68 Hold Me Tight
- ☐ '72 I Can See Clearly Now ★
- ☐ '73 Stir It Up
- ☐ '57 Very Special Love, A

## NASHVILLE TEENS, The
- ☐ '64 Tobacco Road

## NATALIE
- ☐ '05 Goin' Crazy ★

## NATE DOGG
- ☐ '96 Never Leave Me Alone
- ☐ '98 Nobody Does It Better
- ☐ '94 Regulate ★
  *WARREN G. & NATE DOGG*

## NATURAL FOUR
- ☐ '74 Can This Be Real

## NATURAL SELECTION
- ☐ '91 Do Anything ★
- ☐ '91 Hearts Don't Think (They Feel)!

## NAUGHTON, David
- ☐ '79 Makin' It

## NAUGHTY BY NATURE
- ☐ '95 Feel Me Flow
- ☐ '93 Hip Hop Hooray
- ☐ '99 Jamboree
- ☐ '91 O.P.P. ★

## NAZARETH
- ☐ '75 Hair Of The Dog
- ☐ '75 Love Hurts
- ☐ '74 This Flight Tonight

## NAZZ
- ☐ '69 Hello It's Me

## NDEGÉOCELLO, Me'Shell — see MELLENCAMP, JoHN

## NEELY, Sam
- ☐ '72 Loving You Just Crossed My Mind
- ☐ '74 You Can Have Her

## NEIGHBORHOOD, The
- ☐ '70 Big Yellow Taxi

## NELLY
- ☐ '02 Air Force Ones ★
- ☐ '02 Dilemma ★
- ☐ '00 E.I.
- ☐ '02 Hot In Herre ★
- ☐ '00 (Hot S**t) Country Grammar
- ☐ '04 My Place
- ☐ '01 #1
- ☐ '04 Over And Over ★
- ☐ '01 Ride Wit Me ★
- ☐ '03 Shake Ya Tailfeather ★
  *NELLY/P. DIDDY/MURPHY LEE*

## NELSON
- ☐ '90 After The Rain
- ☐ '90 (Can't Live Without Your) Love And Affection ★
- ☐ '91 More Than Ever
- ☐ '91 Only Time Will Tell

## NELSON, Marc
- ☐ '99 15 Minutes

## NELSON, Ricky
- ☐ '57 Be-Bop Baby
- ☐ '58 Believe What You Say ★
- ☐ '61 Everlovin'
- ☐ '63 Fools Rush In
- ☐ '63 For You
- ☐ '72 Garden Party
- ☐ '61 Hello Mary Lou ★
- ☐ '58 I Got A Feeling
- ☐ '59 I Wanna Be Loved
- ☐ '60 I'm Not Afraid
- ☐ '57 I'm Walking
- ☐ '59 It's Late
- ☐ '62 It's Up To You
- ☐ '59 Just A Little Too Much
- ☐ '58 Lonesome Town
- ☐ '58 My Bucket's Got A Hole In It
- ☐ '59 Never Be Anyone Else But You
- ☐ '58 Poor Little Fool ★
- ☐ '69 She Belongs To Me
- ☐ '57 Stood Up ★
- ☐ '63 String Along
- ☐ '59 Sweeter Than You
- ☐ '62 Teen Age Idol
- ☐ '57 Teenager's Romance, A
- ☐ '61 Travelin' Man ★
- ☐ '57 Waitin' In School
- ☐ '61 Wonder Like You, A
- ☐ '60 You Are The Only One
- ☐ '57 You're My One And Only Love
- ☐ '60 Young Emotions
- ☐ '62 Young World

## NELSON, Sandy
- ☐ '61 Let There Be Drums
- ☐ '59 Teen Beat

## NELSON, Willie
- ☐ '82 Always On My Mind ★
- ☐ '02 Beer For My Horses
  *TOBY KEITH with Willie Nelson*
- ☐ '75 Blue Eyes Crying In The Rain ★
- ☐ '84 City Of New Orleans
- ☐ '78 Georgia On My Mind
- ☐ '76 Good Hearted Woman
  *WAYLON & WILLIE*
- ☐ '85 Highwayman
  *WAYLON JENNINGS/WILLIE NELSON/
  JOHNNY CASH/KRIS KRISTOFFERSON*
- ☐ '82 Let It Be Me
- ☐ '78 Mammas Don't Let Your Babies Grow Up To Be Cowboys
  *WAYLON & WILLIE*
- ☐ '80 My Heroes Have Always Been Cowboys
- ☐ '76 Night Life
- ☐ '80 On The Road Again ★
- ☐ '83 Pancho And Lefty
  *WILLIE NELSON & MERLE HAGGARD*
- ☐ '84 To All The Girls I've Loved Before ★
  *JULIO IGLESIAS & WILLIE NELSON*

## NENA
- ☐ '83 99 Luftballons ★

## NEON PHILHARMONIC, The
- ☐ '69 Morning Girl

## NERO, Peter
- ☐ '71 Theme From "Summer Of '42"

## NERVOUS NORVUS
- ☐ '56 Ape Call
- ☐ '56 Transfusion

## NESMITH, Michael
- ☐ '70 Joanne

## NEVIL, Robbie
- ☐ '88 Back On Holiday
- ☐ '86 C'est La Vie
- ☐ '87 Dominoes
- ☐ '91 Just Like You
- ☐ '87 Wot's It To Ya

## NEVILLE, Aaron
- ☐ '90 All My Life
- ☐ '89 Don't Know Much ★
  *LINDA RONSTADT Ft. Aaron Neville (above 2)*
- ☐ '91 Everybody Plays The Fool
- ☐ '66 Tell It Like It Is ★

## NEVILLE, Ivan
- ☐ '88 Not Just Another Girl

## NEWBEATS, The
- ☐ '64 Bread And Butter ★
- ☐ '64 Everything's Alright
- ☐ '65 Run, Baby Run (Back Into My Arms)

## NEW BIRTH, The
- ☐ '75 Dream Merchant
- ☐ '73 I Can Understand It

## NEWBURY, Mickey
- ☐ '71 American Trilogy, An

## NEW CHRISTY MINSTRELS, The
- ☐ '63 Green, Green
- ☐ '63 Saturday Night
- ☐ '64 Today

## NEW COLONY SIX, The
- ☐ '66 I Confess
- ☐ '68 I Will Always Think About You
- ☐ '68 Things I'd Like To Say

## NEW EDITION
- ☐ '88 Can You Stand The Rain
- ☐ '83 Candy Girl
- ☐ '84 Cool It Now
- ☐ '85 Count Me Out
- ☐ '86 Earth Angel
- ☐ '96 Hit Me Off
- ☐ '96 I'm Still In Love With You
- ☐ '88 If It Isn't Love
- ☐ '86 Little Bit Of Love (Is All It Takes)
- ☐ '85 Lost In Love
- ☐ '84 Mr. Telephone Man

## NEW ENGLAND
- ☐ '79 Don't Ever Wanna Lose Ya

## NEW KIDS ON THE BLOCK
- ☐ '89 Cover Girl
- ☐ '89 Didn't I (Blow Your Mind)
- ☐ '89 Hangin' Tough ★
- ☐ '89 I'll Be Loving You (Forever) ★
- ☐ '92 If You Go Away
- ☐ '88 Please Don't Go Girl
- ☐ '90 Step By Step ★
- ☐ '89 This One's For The Children
- ☐ '90 Tonight
- ☐ '88 You Got It (The Right Stuff)

## NEWMAN, Jimmy
- ☐ '57 Fallen Star, A

## NEWMAN, Randy
- ☐ '88 It's Money That Matters
- ☐ '72 Political Science
- ☐ '72 Sail Away
- ☐ '77 Short People ★

## NEW ORDER
- ☐ '86 Bizarre Love Triangle
- ☐ '83 Blue Monday
- ☐ '85 Perfect Kiss
- ☐ '93 Regret
- ☐ '87 True Faith

## NEW RADICALS
- ☐ '98 You Get What You Give

## NEW SEEKERS, The
- ☐ '71 I'd Like To Teach The World To Sing (In Perfect Harmony)
- ☐ '70 Look What They've Done To My Song Ma
- ☐ '73 Pinball Wizard/See Me, Feel Me

## NEWSONG
- ☐ '00 Christmas Shoes, The

## NEWTON, Juice
- ☐ '81 Angel Of The Morning
- ☐ '82 Break It To Me Gently
- ☐ '82 Heart Of The Night

- ☐ '82 Love's Been A Little Bit Hard On Me
- ☐ '81 Queen Of Hearts ★
- ☐ '81 Sweetest Thing (I've Ever Known)
- ☐ '83 Tell Her No

## NEWTON, Wayne
- ☐ '72 Can't You Hear The Song?
- ☐ '72 Daddy Don't You Walk So Fast
- ☐ '63 Danke Schoen
- ☐ '65 Red Roses For A Blue Lady
- ☐ '80 Years

## NEWTON-JOHN, Olivia
- ☐ '76 Come On Over
- ☐ '79 Deeper Than The Night
- ☐ '76 Don't Stop Believin'
- ☐ '96 Grease Megamix, The
  *JOHN TRAVOLTA & OLIVIA NEWTON-JOHN*
- ☐ '75 Have You Never Been Mellow ★
- ☐ '82 Heart Attack
- ☐ '78 Hopelessly Devoted To You ★
- ☐ '80 I Can't Help It
  *ANDY GIBB & OLIVIA NEWTON-JOHN*
- ☐ '74 I Honestly Love You ★
- ☐ '71 If Not For You
- ☐ '74 If You Love Me (Let Me Know)
- ☐ '75 Let It Shine
- ☐ '73 Let Me Be There
- ☐ '78 Little More Love, A
- ☐ '84 Livin' In Desperate Times
- ☐ '80 Magic ★
- ☐ '82 Make A Move On Me
- ☐ '81 Physical ★
- ☐ '75 Please Mr. Please
- ☐ '77 Sam
- ☐ '75 Something Better To Do
- ☐ '85 Soul Kiss
- ☐ '80 Suddenly
  *OLIVIA NEWTON-JOHN & CLIFF RICHARD*
- ☐ '78 Summer Nights
  *JOHN TRAVOLTA & OLIVIA NEWTON-JOHN*
- ☐ '83 Twist Of Fate
- ☐ '80 Xanadu ★
  *OLIVIA NEWTON-JOHN/ELECTRIC LIGHT ORCHESTRA*
- ☐ '78 You're The One That I Want ★
  *JOHN TRAVOLTA & OLIVIA NEWTON-JOHN*

## NEW VAUDEVILLE BAND, The
- ☐ '66 Winchester Cathedral ★

## NEW YORK CITY
- ☐ '73 I'm Doin' Fine Now

## NEW YORK DOLLS
- ☐ '73 Personality Crisis

## NEXT
- ☐ '97 Butta Love
- ☐ '98 I Still Love You
- ☐ '98 Too Close ★
- ☐ '00 Wifey

## NICHOLAS, Paul
- ☐ '77 Heaven On The 7th Floor

## NICHOLS, Joe
- ☐ '02 Brokenheartsville
- ☐ '02 Impossible, The
- ☐ '05 What's A Guy Gotta Do

## NICKELBACK
- ☐ '04 Feelin' Way Too Damn Good
- ☐ '03 Figured You Out
- ☐ '01 How You Remind Me ★
- ☐ '02 Never Again
- ☐ '03 Someday ★
- ☐ '01 Too Bad

## NICKS, Stevie
- ☐ '82 After The Glitter Fades
- ☐ '82 Edge Of Seventeen (Just Like The White Winged Dove)
- ☐ '86 I Can't Wait
- ☐ '83 If Anyone Falls
- ☐ '81 Leather And Lace
  *STEVIE NICKS (with Don Henley)*
- ☐ '86 Needles And Pins
  *TOM PETTY with Stevie Nicks*
- ☐ '83 Nightbird
  *STEVIE NICKS (with Sandy Stewart)*
- ☐ '89 Rooms On Fire
- ☐ '83 Stand Back
- ☐ '81 Stop Draggin' My Heart Around ★
  *STEVIE NICKS with Tom Petty*
- ☐ '85 Talk To Me

## NICOLE
- ☐ '98 Make It Hot

## NIELSEN/PEARSON
- ☐ '80 If You Should Sail

## NIGHT
- ☐ '79 Hot Summer Nights
- ☐ '79 If You Remember Me
  *CHRIS THOMPSON & NIGHT*

## NIGHTINGALE, Maxine
- ☐ '79 Lead Me On
- ☐ '76 Right Back Where We Started From ★

## NIGHT RANGER
- ☐ '83 Don't Tell Me You Love Me
- ☐ '85 Four In The Morning (I Can't Take Any More)
- ☐ '85 Goodbye
- ☐ '85 Sentimental Street
- ☐ '84 Sister Christian ★
- ☐ '84 When You Close Your Eyes

## NIKKI
- ☐ '90 Notice Me

## NILSSON
- ☐ '72 Coconut
- ☐ '74 Daybreak
- ☐ '69 Everybody's Talkin'
- ☐ '69 I Guess The Lord Must Be In New York City
- ☐ '72 Jump Into The Fire
- ☐ '71 Me And My Arrow
- ☐ '72 Spaceman
- ☐ '71 Without You ★

## NINA SKY
- ☐ '04 Move Ya Body ★

## NINEDAYS
- ☐ '00 Absolutely (Story Of A Girl) ★

## NINE INCH NAILS
- ☐ '94 Closer
- ☐ '99 Day The World Went Away, The
- ☐ '05 Hand That Feeds, The
- ☐ '95 Hurt
- ☐ '94 March Of The Pigs

## 1910 FRUITGUM CO.
- ☐ '69 Indian Giver
- ☐ '68 1, 2, 3, Red Light
- ☐ '68 Simon Says

## 98°
- ☐ '98 Because Of You ★
- ☐ '00 Give Me Just One Night (Una Noche) ★
- ☐ '99 Hardest Thing, The
- ☐ '99 I Do (Cherish You)
- ☐ '97 Invisible Man
- ☐ '00 My Everything

## 95 SOUTH
- ☐ '93 Whoot, There It Is

## NIRVANA
- ☐ '94 About A Girl
- ☐ '93 All Apologies
- ☐ '92 Come As You Are
- ☐ '93 Heart-Shaped Box
- ☐ '91 In Bloom
- ☐ '95 Man Who Sold The World, The
- ☐ '91 Smells Like Teen Spirit ★
- ☐ '02 You Know You're Right

## NITEFLYTE
- ☐ '79 If You Want It

## NITTY GRITTY DIRT BAND
- ☐ '79 American Dream, An
- ☐ '87 Fishin' In The Dark
- ☐ '80 Make A Little Magic
- ☐ '70 Mr. Bojangles ★

## NITZSCHE, Jack
- ☐ '63 Lonely Surfer, The

## NIVEA
- ☐ '02 Don't Mess With My Man
- ☐ '05 Okay

## NOBLE, Nick
- ☐ '55 Bible Tells Me So, The
- ☐ '57 Fallen Star, A
- ☐ '57 Moonlight Swim
- ☐ '56 To You, My Love

## NOBLES, Cliff, & Co.
- ☐ '68 Horse, The ★

## NO DOUBT
- ☐ '96 Don't Speak ★
- ☐ '00 Ex-Girlfriend
- ☐ '02 Hella Good

- [ ] '01 Hey Baby ★
- [ ] '03 It's My Life
- [ ] '95 Just A Girl
- [ ] '00 Simple Kind Of Life
- [ ] '96 Spiderwebs
- [ ] '02 Underneath It All ★

## NOGUEZ, Jacky, & His Orchestra
- [ ] '59 Ciao, Ciao Bambina

## NOLAN, Kenny
- [ ] '76 I Like Dreamin'
- [ ] '77 Love's Grown Deep

## NO MERCY
- [ ] '97 Please Don't Go
- [ ] '96 Where Do You Go ★

## NONCHALANT
- [ ] '96 5 O'Clock

## N.O.R.E. /NOREAGA
- [ ] '02 Nothin'
- [ ] '04 Oye Mi Canto
- [ ] '98 SuperThug (What What)

## NORTH, Freddie
- [ ] '71 She's All I Got

## NOTORIOUS B.I.G., The
- [ ] '95 Big Poppa ★
- [ ] '97 Going Back To Cali
- [ ] '97 Hypnotize ★
- [ ] '94 Juicy
- [ ] '97 Mo Money Mo Problems ★
- [ ] '95 One More Chance/Stay With Me ★

## NOVA, Aldo
- [ ] '82 Fantasy

## *NSYNC
- [ ] '00 Bring It All To Me ★
  BLAQUE Feat. *NSYNC
- [ ] '00 Bye Bye Bye ★
- [ ] '02 Girlfriend ★
- [ ] '98 (God Must Have Spent) A Little More Time On You ★
- [ ] '01 Gone
- [ ] '98 I Want You Back
- [ ] '00 It's Gonna Be Me ★
- [ ] '99 Music Of My Heart ★
  *NSYNC & GLORIA ESTEFAN
- [ ] '01 Pop
- [ ] '98 Tearin' Up My Heart
- [ ] '00 This I Promise You ★

## N2DEEP
- [ ] '92 Back To The Hotel

## NIIU
- [ ] '94 I Miss You

## NU FLAVOR
- [ ] '97 Heaven

## NUGENT, Ted
- [ ] '77 Cat Scratch Fever
- [ ] '76 Dog Eat Dog

- [ ] '95 Fred Bear
- [ ] '76 Free-For-All
- [ ] '75 Hey Baby
- [ ] '77 Home Bound
- [ ] '78 Need You Bad
- [ ] '77 Wang Dang Sweet Poontang
- [ ] '80 Wango Tango
- [ ] '78 Yank Me, Crank Me

## NUMAN, Gary
- [ ] '80 Cars ★

## NU SHOOZ
- [ ] '86 I Can't Wait
- [ ] '86 Point Of No Return

## NUTMEGS, The
- [ ] '55 Story Untold

## NU TORNADOS, The
- [ ] '58 Philadelphia U.S.A.

## NUTTY SQUIRRELS, The
- [ ] '59 Uh! Oh!

## N.W.A.
- [ ] '89 F*** Tha Police

## NYLONS, The
- [ ] '87 Kiss Him Goodbye

## NYRO, Laura
- [ ] '68 Stoned Soul Picnic
- [ ] '66 Wedding Bell Blues

# O

## OAK RIDGE BOYS
- [ ] '83 American Made
- [ ] '82 Bobbie Sue
- [ ] '81 Elvira ★

## OASIS
- [ ] '96 Champagne Supernova
- [ ] '97 Don't Go Away
- [ ] '95 Live Forever
- [ ] '95 Wonderwall ★

## O'BANION, John
- [ ] '81 Love You Like I Never Loved Before

## O'BRYAN
- [ ] '82 Gigolo, The
- [ ] '84 Lovelite

## OCASEK, Ric
- [ ] '86 Emotion In Motion
- [ ] '86 Something To Grab For

## OCEAN
- [ ] '71 Put Your Hand In The Hand ★

## OCEAN, Billy
- [ ] '84 Caribbean Queen (No More Love On The Run) ★
- [ ] '88 Colour Of Love, The
- [ ] '88 Get Outta My Dreams, Get Into My Car ★
- [ ] '89 Licence To Chill

## OCEAN, Billy — cont'd

- ☐ '86 Love Is Forever
- ☐ '76 Love Really Hurts Without You
- ☐ '86 Love Zone
- ☐ '84 Loverboy ★
- ☐ '85 Mystery Lady
- ☐ '85 Suddenly
- ☐ '86 There'll Be Sad Songs (To Make You Cry) ★
- ☐ '85 When The Going Gets Tough, The Tough Get Going

## OCEAN BLUE, The

- ☐ '91 Ballerina Out Of Control
- ☐ '89 Between Something And Nothing
- ☐ '93 Sublime

## O'CONNOR, Sinéad

- ☐ '90 Emperor's New Clothes, The
- ☐ '90 Nothing Compares 2 U ★

## O'DAY, Alan

- ☐ '77 Undercover Angel ★

## O'DELL, Kenny

- ☐ '67 Beautiful People

## ODYSSEY

- ☐ '77 Native New Yorker

## OFFSPRING, The

- ☐ '94 Come Out And Play
- ☐ '97 Gone Away
- ☐ '03 Hit That
- ☐ '00 Original Prankster
- ☐ '98 Pretty Fly (For A White Guy)
- ☐ '94 Self Esteem
- ☐ '99 Why Don't You Get A Job?

## OHIO EXPRESS

- ☐ '67 Beg, Borrow And Steal
- ☐ '68 Chewy Chewy
- ☐ '68 Down At Lulu's
- ☐ '68 Yummy Yummy Yummy

## OHIO PLAYERS

- ☐ '73 Ecstasy
- ☐ '74 Fire
- ☐ '76 Fopp
- ☐ '73 Funky Worm
- ☐ '75 Love Rollercoaster ★
- ☐ '74 Skin Tight
- ☐ '75 Sweet Sticky Thing
- ☐ '76 Who'd She Coo?

## O'JAYS, The

- ☐ '72 Back Stabbers ★
- ☐ '76 Darlin' Darlin' Baby (Sweet, Tender, Love)
- ☐ '74 For The Love Of Money
- ☐ '79 Forever Mine
- ☐ '80 Girl, Don't Let It Get You Down
- ☐ '75 Give The People What They Want
- ☐ '89 Have You Had Your Love Today
- ☐ '75 I Love Music
- ☐ '76 Livin' For The Weekend
- ☐ '73 Love Train ★

- ☐ '87 Lovin' You
- ☐ '76 Message In Our Music
- ☐ '73 Put Your Hands Together
- ☐ '73 Time To Get Down
- ☐ '78 Use Ta Be My Girl

## O'KAYSIONS, The

- ☐ '68 Girl Watcher

## O'KEEFE, Danny

- ☐ '72 Good Time Charlie's Got The Blues

## OLDFIELD, Mike

- ☐ '74 Tubular Bells

## OL DIRTY BASTARD

- ☐ '99 Got Your Money

## OLEANDER

- ☐ '99 Why I'm Here

## OLIVER

- ☐ '69 Good Morning Starshine ★
- ☐ '69 Jean

## OLIVIA

- ☐ '01 Bizounce

## OLLIE & JERRY

- ☐ '84 Breakin'...There's No Stopping Us

## OL SKOOL

- ☐ '98 Am I Dreaming

## OLSSON, Nigel

- ☐ '78 Dancin' Shoes
- ☐ '79 Little Bit Of Soap

## OLYMPICS, The

- ☐ '60 Big Boy Pete
- ☐ '63 Bounce, The
- ☐ '58 Western Movies

## OMARION

- ☐ '05 O

## OMC

- ☐ '97 How Bizarre ★

## O'NEAL, Alexander

- ☐ '87 Fake
- ☐ '88 Never Knew Love Like This
  *ALEXANDER O'NEAL feat. Cherrelle*
- ☐ '86 Saturday Love
  *CHERRELLE with Alexander O'Neal*

## O'NEAL, Jamie

- ☐ '00 There Is No Arizona
- ☐ '01 When I Think About Angels

## O'NEAL, Shaquille

- ☐ '93 (I Know I Got) Skillz

## 100 PROOF AGED IN SOUL

- ☐ '70 Somebody's Been Sleeping

## ONE 2 MANY

- ☐ '89 Downtown

## 112
- ☐ '99 Anywhere
- ☐ '96 Come See Me
- ☐ '97 Cupid
- ☐ '01 Dance With Me
- ☐ '00 It's Over Now
- ☐ '98 Love Me
- ☐ '96 Only You
- ☐ '01 Peaches & Cream ★
- ☐ '05 U Already Know

## ONYX
- ☐ '93 Slam

## OPUS
- ☐ '86 Live Is Life

## ORBISON, Roy
- ☐ '60 Blue Angel
- ☐ '63 Blue Bayou
- ☐ '66 Breakin' Up Is Breakin' My Heart
- ☐ '61 Candy Man
- ☐ '62 Crowd, The
- ☐ '61 Crying ★
- ☐ '62 Dream Baby (How Long Must I Dream)
- ☐ '63 Falling
- ☐ '65 Goodnight
- ☐ '60 I'm Hurtin'
- ☐ '63 In Dreams
- ☐ '64 Indian Wedding
- ☐ '64 It's Over
- ☐ '62 Léah
- ☐ '63 Mean Woman Blues
- ☐ '64 Oh, Pretty Woman ★
- ☐ '60 Only The Lonely ★
- ☐ '56 Ooby Dooby
- ☐ '63 Pretty Paper
- ☐ '65 Ride Away
- ☐ '61 Running Scared ★
- ☐ '65 (Say) You're My Girl
- ☐ '66 Twinkle Toes
- ☐ '60 Up Town
- ☐ '62 Workin' For The Man
- ☐ '89 You Got It

## ORCHESTRAL MANOEUVRES IN THE DARK
- ☐ '88 Dreaming
- ☐ '86 (Forever) Live And Die
- ☐ '86 If You Leave ★
- ☐ '85 So In Love

## ORIGINAL CASTE, The
- ☐ '69 One Tin Soldier

## ORIGINALS, The
- ☐ '69 Baby, I'm For Real
- ☐ '70 Bells, The

## ORLANDO, Tony (& DAWN)
- ☐ '61 Bless You
- ☐ '70 Candida
- ☐ '76 Cupid
- ☐ '61 Halfway To Paradise
- ☐ '75 He Don't Love You (Like I Love You) ★
- ☐ '71 I Play And Sing
- ☐ '70 Knock Three Times ★
- ☐ '74 Look In My Eyes Pretty Woman
- ☐ '69 Make Believe
- ☐ '75 Mornin' Beautiful
- ☐ '73 Say, Has Anybody Seen My Sweet Gypsy Rose
- ☐ '74 Steppin' Out (Gonna Boogie Tonight)
- ☐ '71 Summer Sand
- ☐ '73 Tie A Yellow Ribbon Round The Ole Oak Tree ★
- ☐ '73 Who's In The Strawberry Patch With Sally

## ORLEANS
- ☐ '75 Dance With Me
- ☐ '79 Love Takes Time
- ☐ '76 Still The One

## ORLONS, The
- ☐ '63 Cross Fire!
- ☐ '62 Don't Hang Up
- ☐ '63 Not Me
- ☐ '63 South Street
- ☐ '62 Wah Watusi, The ★

## ORR, Benjamin
- ☐ '86 Stay The Night

## ORRICO, Stacie
- ☐ '03 (there's gotta be) More To Life

## OSBORNE, Jeffrey
- ☐ '85 Borderlines, The
- ☐ '83 Don't You Get So Mad
- ☐ '82 I Really Don't Need No Light
- ☐ '84 Last Time I Made Love, The
  *JOYCE KENNEDY & JEFFREY OSBORNE*
- ☐ '87 Love Power
  *DIONNE WARWICK & JEFFREY OSBORNE*
- ☐ '82 On The Wings Of Love
- ☐ '90 Only Human
- ☐ '88 She's On The Left
- ☐ '83 Stay With Me Tonight
- ☐ '86 You Should Be Mine (The Woo Woo Song)

## OSBORNE, Joan
- ☐ '95 One Of Us ★

## OSBOURNE, Ozzy
- ☐ '89 Close My Eyes Forever
  *LITA FORD (with Ozzy Osbourne)*
- ☐ '81 Crazy Train
- ☐ '81 Flying High Again
- ☐ '01 Gets Me Through
- ☐ '91 Mama, I'm Coming Home
- ☐ '95 Perry Mason
- ☐ '92 Road To Nowhere
- ☐ '86 Shot In The Dark

## OSLIN, K.T.
- ☐ '90 Come Next Monday
- ☐ '87 Do Ya'
- ☐ '87 80's Ladies

## OSMOND, Donny
- ☐ '73 Are You Lonesome Tonight
- ☐ '76 C'mon Marianne
- ☐ '71 Go Away Little Girl
- ☐ '71 Hey Girl
- ☐ '73 Million To One, A
- ☐ '90 My Love Is A Fire
- ☐ '72 Puppy Love
- ☐ '89 Sacred Emotion
- ☐ '89 Soldier Of Love
- ☐ '71 Sweet And Innocent
- ☐ '72 Too Young
- ☐ '73 Twelfth Of Never, The
- ☐ '72 Why
- ☐ '73 Young Love

## OSMOND, Donny & Marie
- ☐ '76 Ain't Nothing Like The Real Thing
- ☐ '75 Deep Purple
- ☐ '74 I'm Leaving It (All) Up To You
- ☐ '74 Morning Side Of The Mountain
- ☐ '78 On The Shelf
- ☐ '77 (You're My) Soul And Inspiration

## OSMOND, Little Jimmy
- ☐ '72 Long Haired Lover From Liverpool

## OSMOND, Marie
- ☐ '85 Meet Me In Montana
    *MARIE OSMOND with Dan Seals*
- ☐ '73 Paper Roses
- ☐ '77 This Is The Way That I Feel
- ☐ '75 Who's Sorry Now

## OSMONDS, The
- ☐ '72 Crazy Horses
- ☐ '71 Double Lovin'
- ☐ '72 Down By The Lazy River
- ☐ '72 Hold Her Tight
- ☐ '74 Love Me For A Reason
- ☐ '71 One Bad Apple ★
- ☐ '75 Proud One, The
- ☐ '71 Yo-Yo

## O'SULLIVAN, Gilbert
- ☐ '72 Alone Again (Naturally) ★
- ☐ '72 Clair
- ☐ '73 Get Down
- ☐ '73 Ooh Baby
- ☐ '73 Out Of The Question

## OTHER ONES, The
- ☐ '87 Holiday

## OTIS, Johnny, Show
- ☐ '58 Willie And The Hand Jive

## O-TOWN
- ☐ '01 All Or Nothing ★
- ☐ '00 Liquid Dreams

## OUTFIELD, The
- ☐ '86 All The Love In The World
- ☐ '90 For You
- ☐ '85 Say It Isn't So
- ☐ '87 Since You've Been Gone
- ☐ '89 Voices Of Babylon

- ☐ '86 Your Love

## OUTKAST
- ☐ '96 ATLiens
- ☐ '96 Elevators (me & you)
- ☐ '03 Hey Ya! ★
- ☐ '00 Ms. Jackson ★
- ☐ '94 Player's Ball
- ☐ '04 Roses ★
- ☐ '01 So Fresh, So Clean
- ☐ '03 Way You Move, The ★
- ☐ '01 Whole World, The

## OUTLAWS
- ☐ '80 (Ghost) Riders In The Sky
- ☐ '75 Green Grass & High Tides
- ☐ '75 There Goes Another Love Song

## OUTSIDERS, The
- ☐ '66 Girl In Love
- ☐ '66 Help Me Girl
- ☐ '66 Respectable
- ☐ '66 Time Won't Let Me

## OVERSTREET, Paul
- ☐ '90 Daddy's Come Around
- ☐ '90 Seein' My Father In Me

## OWEN, Reg, & His Orchestra
- ☐ '58 Manhattan Spiritual

## OWENS, Buck
- ☐ '63 Act Naturally
- ☐ '65 Buckaroo
- ☐ '65 I've Got A Tiger By The Tail
- ☐ '63 Love's Gonna Live Here
- ☐ '64 My Heart Skips A Beat
- ☐ '88 Streets Of Bakersfield
    *DWIGHT YOAKAM & BUCK OWENS*
- ☐ '64 Together Again

## OWENS, Donnie
- ☐ '58 Need You

## OXO
- ☐ '83 Whirly Girl

## OZARK MOUNTAIN DAREDEVILS
- ☐ '74 If You Wanna Get To Heaven
- ☐ '75 Jackie Blue

# P

## PABLO, Petey
- ☐ '04 Freek-A-Leek ★
- ☐ '01 Raise Up

## PABLO CRUISE
- ☐ '81 Cool Love
- ☐ '78 Don't Want To Live Without It
- ☐ '79 I Go To Rio
- ☐ '79 I Want You Tonight
- ☐ '78 Love Will Find A Way
- ☐ '77 Whatcha Gonna Do?

## PACIFIC GAS & ELECTRIC
- ☐ '70 Are You Ready?

## PAGE, Jimmy
- ☐ '94 Gallows Pole
- ☐ '98 Most High
  *JIMMY PAGE & ROBERT PLANT* (above 2)
- ☐ '93 Pride And Joy
  *COVERDALE•PAGE*

## PAGE, Martin
- ☐ '94 In The House Of Stone And Light

## PAGE, Patti
- ☐ '56 Allegheny Moon ★
- ☐ '58 Another Time, Another Place
- ☐ '58 Belonging To Someone
- ☐ '55 Croce Di Oro (Cross Of Gold)
- ☐ '56 Go On With The Wedding
- ☐ '65 Hush, Hush, Sweet Charlotte ★
- ☐ '57 I'll Remember Today
- ☐ '58 Left Right Out Of Your Heart
- ☐ '55 Let Me Go, Lover!
- ☐ '56 Mama From The Train
- ☐ '62 Most People Get Married
- ☐ '57 Old Cape Cod ★
- ☐ '60 One Of Us (Will Weep Tonight)
- ☐ '57 Poor Man's Roses (Or A Rich Man's Gold)
- ☐ '57 Wondering

## PAGE, Tommy
- ☐ '90 I'll Be Your Everything ★
- ☐ '89 Shoulder To Cry On, A

## PAIGE, Jennifer
- ☐ '98 Crush ★

## PAIGE, Kevin
- ☐ '90 Anything I Want
- ☐ '89 Don't Shut Me Out

## PAISLEY, Brad
- ☐ '03 Celebrity
- ☐ '99 He Didn't Have To Be
- ☐ '02 I'm Gonna Miss Her (The Fishin' Song)
- ☐ '03 Little Moments
- ☐ '05 Mud On The Tires ★
- ☐ '01 Two People Fell In Love
- ☐ '00 We Danced
- ☐ '04 Whiskey Lullaby
- ☐ '01 Wrapped Around

## PALMER, Robert
- ☐ '86 Addicted To Love ★
- ☐ '79 Bad Case Of Loving You (Doctor, Doctor)
- ☐ '79 Can We Still Be Friends
- ☐ '88 Early In The Morning
- ☐ '78 Every Kinda People
- ☐ '86 Hyperactive
- ☐ '86 I Didn't Mean To Turn You On
- ☐ '91 Mercy Mercy Me (The Ecology)/I Want You
- ☐ '88 Simply Irresistible ★
- ☐ '90 You're Amazing

## PAN'JABI MC
- ☐ '03 Beware Of The Boys

## PAPA ROACH
- ☐ '04 Getting Away With Murder
- ☐ '00 Last Resort
- ☐ '04 Scars
- ☐ '02 She Loves Me Not

## PAPERBOY
- ☐ '92 Ditty

## PAPER LACE
- ☐ '74 Night Chicago Died, The ★

## PARADE, The
- ☐ '67 Sunshine Girl

## PARADONS, The
- ☐ '60 Diamonds And Pearls

## PARIS SISTERS, The
- ☐ '61 Be My Boy
- ☐ '62 He Knows I Love Him Too Much
- ☐ '61 I Love How You Love Me ★

## PARKER, Fess
- ☐ '55 Ballad Of Davy Crockett
- ☐ '57 Wringle Wrangle

## PARKER, Graham
- ☐ '77 Hold Back The Night
- ☐ '85 Wake Up (Next To You)
  *GRAHAM PARKER & THE SHOT*

## PARKER, Ray Jr./Raydio
- ☐ '82 Bad Boy
- ☐ '84 Ghostbusters ★
- ☐ '85 Girls Are More Fun
- ☐ '83 I Still Can't Get Over Loving You
- ☐ '78 Jack And Jill
- ☐ '84 Jamie
- ☐ '82 Other Woman, The
- ☐ '81 That Old Song
- ☐ '80 Two Places At The Same Time
- ☐ '81 Woman Needs Love (Just Like You Do)
- ☐ '79 You Can't Change That

## PARKER, Robert
- ☐ '66 Barefootin'

## PARKS, Michael
- ☐ '70 Long Lonesome Highway

## PARLIAMENT
- ☐ '78 Aqua Boogie (A Psychoalphadisco-betabioaquadoloop)
- ☐ '78 Flash Light
- ☐ '67 (I Wanna) Testify
  *THE PARLIAMENTS*
- ☐ '76 Tear The Roof Off The Sucker (Give Up The Funk)

## PARR, John
- ☐ '84 Naughty Naughty
- ☐ '85 St. Elmo's Fire (Man In Motion) ★

## PARSONS, Alan, Project
- ☐ '77 Breakdown
- ☐ '79 Damned If I Do
- ☐ '84 Don't Answer Me
- ☐ '77 Don't Let It Show
- ☐ '82 Eye In The Sky ★
- ☐ '80 Games People Play
- ☐ '77 I Robot
- ☐ '77 I Wouldn't Want To Be Like You
- ☐ '84 Prime Time
- ☐ '76 Raven, The
- ☐ '87 Standing On Higher Ground
- ☐ '76 (System Of) Doctor Tarr And Professor Fether
- ☐ '81 Time
- ☐ '78 What Goes Up

## PARSONS, Bill — see BARE, Bobby

## PARTLAND BROTHERS
- ☐ '87 Soul City

## PARTNERS IN KRYME
- ☐ '90 Turtle Power!

## PARTON, Dolly
- ☐ '78 Baby I'm Burnin'
- ☐ '04 Baby, It's Cold Outside
- ☐ '71 Coat Of Many Colors
- ☐ '78 Heartbreaker
- ☐ '77 Here You Come Again ★
- ☐ '74 I Will Always Love You
- ☐ '95 I Will Always Love You
  *DOLLY PARTON with Vince Gill*
- ☐ '83 Islands In The Stream ★
  *KENNY ROGERS with Dolly Parton*
- ☐ '74 Jolene
- ☐ '70 Joshua
- ☐ '80 9 To 5 ★
- ☐ '91 Rockin' Years
  *DOLLY PARTON & RICKY VAN SHELTON*
- ☐ '80 Starting Over Again
- ☐ '78 Two Doors Down

## PARTRIDGE FAMILY, The
- ☐ '72 Breaking Up Is Hard To Do
- ☐ '71 Doesn't Somebody Want To Be Wanted
- ☐ '70 I Think I Love You ★
- ☐ '71 I Woke Up In Love This Morning
- ☐ '71 I'll Meet You Halfway
- ☐ '71 It's One Of Those Nights (Yes Love)
- ☐ '72 Looking Through The Eyes Of Love

## PARTY, The
- ☐ '91 In My Dreams
- ☐ '90 Summer Vacation

## PASTELS, The
- ☐ '58 Been So Long

## PASTEL SIX, The
- ☐ '62 Cinnamon Cinder (It's A Very Nice Dance)

## PATIENCE & PRUDENCE
- ☐ '56 Gonna Get Along Without Ya Now
- ☐ '56 Tonight You Belong To Me

## PATTON, Robbie
- ☐ '81 Don't Give It Up
- ☐ '83 Smiling Islands

## PATTY & THE EMBLEMS
- ☐ '64 Mixed-Up, Shook-Up, Girl

## PAUL, Billy
- ☐ '72 Me And Mrs. Jones ★
- ☐ '74 Thanks For Saving My Life

## PAUL, Les, & Mary Ford
- ☐ '55 Amukiriki (The Lord Willing)
- ☐ '57 Cinco Robles (Five Oaks)
- ☐ '55 Hummingbird
- ☐ '61 Jura (I Swear I Love You)
- ☐ '58 Put A Ring On My Finger

## PAUL, Sean
- ☐ '03 Get Busy ★
- ☐ '02 Gimme The Light ★
- ☐ '04 I'm Still In Love With You
- ☐ '03 Like Glue

## PAUL & PAULA
- ☐ '63 First Quarrel
- ☐ '62 Hey Paula ★
- ☐ '63 Young Lovers

## PAVEMENT
- ☐ '97 Shady Lane
- ☐ '92 Summer Babe

## PAVONE, Rita
- ☐ '64 Remember Me

## PAYNE, Freda
- ☐ '70 Band Of Gold ★
- ☐ '71 Bring The Boys Home
- ☐ '70 Deeper & Deeper

## PEACHES & HERB
- ☐ '67 Close Your Eyes
- ☐ '67 For Your Love
- ☐ '80 I Pledge My Love
- ☐ '66 Let's Fall In Love
- ☐ '67 Love Is Strange
- ☐ '79 Reunited ★
- ☐ '78 Shake Your Groove Thing
- ☐ '67 Two Little Kids

## PEACH UNION
- ☐ '97 On My Own

## PEARL, Leslie
- ☐ '82 If The Love Fits Wear It

## PEARL JAM
- ☐ '92 Alive
- ☐ '94 Better Man ★
- ☐ '92 Black
- ☐ '93 Daughter
- ☐ '94 Dissident
- ☐ '92 Even Flow
- ☐ '98 Given To Fly
- ☐ '93 Go

☐ '95 I Got Id
☐ '92 Jeremy ★
☐ '99 Last Kiss ★
☐ '00 Nothing As It Seems
☐ '94 Spin The Black Circle
☐ '94 Tremor Christ
☐ '96 Who You Are
☐ '00 Yellow Ledbetter

## PEBBLES
☐ '88 Girlfriend
☐ '90 Giving You The Benefit
☐ '90 Love Makes Things Happen
☐ '88 Mercedes Boy ★
☐ '88 Take Your Time

## PEEBLES, Ann
☐ '73 I Can't Stand The Rain

## PEEPLES, Nia
☐ '91 Street Of Dreams
☐ '88 Trouble

## PENDERGRASS, Teddy
☐ '80 Can't We Try
☐ '78 Close The Door
☐ '91 It Should've Been You
☐ '88 Joy
☐ '80 Love T.K.O.
☐ '79 Turn Off The Lights
☐ '88 2 A.M.
☐ '81 Two Hearts
*STEPHANIE MILLS Feat. Teddy Pendergrass*

## PENGUINS, The
☐ '55 Earth Angel ★

## PENISTON, Ce Ce
☐ '91 Finally
☐ '94 I'm In The Mood
☐ '92 Keep On Walkin'
☐ '92 We Got A Love Thang

## PENN, Michael
☐ '90 No Myth

## PEOPLE
☐ '68 I Love You

## PEOPLE'S CHOICE
☐ '75 Do It Any Way You Wanna
☐ '71 I Likes To Do It

## PEPPERMINT RAINBOW, The
☐ '69 Will You Be Staying After Sunday

## PEREZ, Amanda
☐ '03 Angel

## PERFECT CIRCLE, A
☐ '00 Judith
☐ '03 Outsider, The
☐ '03 Weak And Powerless

## PERFECT GENTLEMEN
☐ '90 Ooh La La (I Can't Get Over You)

## PERICOLI, Emilio
☐ '62 Al Di La'

## PERKINS, Carl
☐ '56 Blue Suede Shoes ★
☐ '56 Boppin' The Blues
☐ '56 Honey Don't
☐ '57 Matchbox

## PERKINS, Tony
☐ '57 Moon-Light Swim

## PERRY, Phil
☐ '91 Call Me

## PERRY, Steve
☐ '82 Don't Fight It
*KENNY LOGGINS with Steve Perry*
☐ '84 Foolish Heart
☐ '84 Oh Sherrie ★
☐ '84 She's Mine
☐ '84 Strung Out
☐ '94 You Better Wait

## PERSUADERS, The
☐ '73 Some Guys Have All The Luck
☐ '71 Thin Line Between Love & Hate

## PETER & GORDON
☐ '64 I Don't Want To See You Again
☐ '65 I Go To Pieces
☐ '66 Knight In Rusty Armour
☐ '66 Lady Godiva
☐ '64 Nobody I Know
☐ '67 Sunday For Tea
☐ '65 To Know You Is To Love You
☐ '65 True Love Ways
☐ '66 Woman
☐ '64 World Without Love, A ★

## PETER, PAUL & MARY
☐ '63 Blowin' In The Wind
☐ '69 Day Is Done
☐ '63 Don't Think Twice, It's All Right
☐ '65 For Lovin' Me
☐ '67 I Dig Rock And Roll Music
☐ '62 If I Had A Hammer
☐ '69 Leaving On A Jet Plane ★
☐ '62 Lemon Tree
☐ '63 Puff (The Magic Dragon) ★
☐ '63 Stewball
☐ '67 Too Much Of Nothing

## PETERS, Bernadette
☐ '80 Gee Whiz

## PETERSEN, Paul
☐ '62 My Dad
☐ '62 She Can't Find Her Keys

## PETERSON, Michael
☐ '97 Drink, Swear, Steal & Lie
☐ '97 From Here To Eternity

## PETERSON, Ray
- [ ] '60 Corinna, Corinna
- [ ] '59 Goodnight My Love
- [ ] '61 Missing You
- [ ] '60 Tell Laura I Love Her ★
- [ ] '59 Wonder Of You, The

## PETS, The
- [ ] '58 Cha-Hua-Hua

## PET SHOP BOYS
- [ ] '88 Always On My Mind
- [ ] '88 Domino Dancing
- [ ] '87 It's A Sin
- [ ] '86 Opportunities (Let's Make Lots Of Money)
- [ ] '86 West End Girls ★
- [ ] '87 What Have I Done To Deserve This? ★
    *PET SHOP BOYS (& Dusty Springfield)*

## PETTY, Tom, & The Heartbreakers
- [ ] '77 American Girl
- [ ] '77 Breakdown
- [ ] '83 Change Of Heart
- [ ] '85 Don't Come Around Here No More ★
- [ ] '79 Don't Do Me Like That
- [ ] '79 Even The Losers
- [ ] '89 Free Fallin' ★
- [ ] '79 Here Comes My Girl
- [ ] '78 I Need To Know
- [ ] '89 I Won't Back Down
- [ ] '91 Into The Great Wide Open
- [ ] '87 Jammin' Me
- [ ] '91 Learning To Fly
- [ ] '78 Listen To Her Heart
- [ ] '93 Mary Jane's Last Dance
- [ ] '86 Needles And Pins
    *TOM PETTY with Stevie Nicks*
- [ ] '91 Out In The Cold
- [ ] '80 Refugee
- [ ] '89 Runnin' Down A Dream
- [ ] '81 Stop Draggin' My Heart Around ★
    *STEVIE NICKS with Tom Petty*
- [ ] '81 Waiting, The
- [ ] '94 You Don't Know How It Feels
- [ ] '82 You Got Lucky
- [ ] '94 You Wreck Me

## PHAIR, Liz
- [ ] '94 Supernova
- [ ] '03 Why Can't I?

## PHARRELL
- [ ] '03 Frontin' ★

## PHILLIPS, Esther
- [ ] '62 Release Me
- [ ] '75 What A Diff'rence A Day Makes

## PHILLIPS, Phil, With The Twilights
- [ ] '59 Sea Of Love ★

## PHOTOGLO, Jim
- [ ] '81 Fool In Love With You
- [ ] '80 We Were Meant To Be Lovers

## PICKETT, Bobby "Boris", & The Crypt-Kickers
- [ ] '62 Monster Mash ★
- [ ] '62 Monsters' Holiday

## PICKETT, Wilson
- [ ] '71 Don't Knock My Love
- [ ] '71 Don't Let The Green Grass Fool You
- [ ] '70 Engine Number 9
- [ ] '67 Everybody Needs Somebody To Love
- [ ] '71 Fire And Water
- [ ] '67 Funky Broadway
- [ ] '68 Hey Jude
- [ ] '67 I Found A Love
- [ ] '68 I'm A Midnight Mover
- [ ] '65 In The Midnight Hour ★
- [ ] '66 Land Of 1000 Dances
- [ ] '66 Mustang Sally
- [ ] '68 She's Lookin' Good
- [ ] '66 634-5789 (Soulsville, U.S.A.)
- [ ] '67 Stag-O-Lee
- [ ] '70 Sugar Sugar

## PIERCE, Webb
- [ ] '59 I Ain't Never
- [ ] '55 In The Jailhouse Now
- [ ] '55 Love, Love, Love

## PILOT
- [ ] '75 Magic

## P!NK
- [ ] '02 Don't Let Me Get Me
- [ ] '02 Family Portrait
- [ ] '01 Get The Party Started ★
- [ ] '02 Just Like A Pill
- [ ] '01 Lady Marmalade ★
    *CHRISTINA AGUILERA, LIL' KIM, MYA & P!NK*
- [ ] '00 Most Girls ★
- [ ] '00 There You Go ★
- [ ] '01 You Make Me Sick

## PINK FLOYD
- [ ] '80 Another Brick In The Wall ★
- [ ] '73 Brain Damage/Eclipse
- [ ] '80 Comfortably Numb
- [ ] '73 Great Gig In The Sky
- [ ] '75 Have A Cigar
- [ ] '80 Hey You
- [ ] '94 Keep Talking
- [ ] '87 Learning To Fly
- [ ] '73 Money ★
- [ ] '87 On The Turning Away
- [ ] '71 One Of These Days
- [ ] '80 Run Like Hell
- [ ] '67 See Emily Play
- [ ] '75 Shine On You Crazy Diamond
- [ ] '75 Speak To Me/Breathe
- [ ] '73 Time
- [ ] '73 Us And Them
- [ ] '75 Welcome To The Machine
- [ ] '75 Wish You Were Here
- [ ] '80 Young Lust

## PINK LADY
- [ ] '79 Kiss In The Dark

## PIPKINS, The
- ☐ '70 Gimme Dat Ding

## PITBULL
- ☐ '04 Culo

## PITNEY, Gene
- ☐ '66 Backstage
- ☐ '61 Every Breath I Take
- ☐ '62 Half Heaven - Half Heartache
- ☐ '65 I Must Be Seeing Things
- ☐ '61 (I Wanna) Love My Life Away
- ☐ '64 I'm Gonna Be Strong
- ☐ '62 If I Didn't Have A Dime (To Play The Jukebox)
- ☐ '64 It Hurts To Be In Love
- ☐ '65 Last Chance To Turn Around
- ☐ '65 Looking Through The Eyes Of Love
- ☐ '62 (Man Who Shot) Liberty Valance ★
- ☐ '63 Mecca
- ☐ '62 Only Love Can Break A Heart ★
- ☐ '68 She's A Heartbreaker
- ☐ '61 Town Without Pity
- ☐ '63 True Love Never Runs Smooth
- ☐ '63 Twenty Four Hours From Tulsa

## PIXIES
- ☐ '89 Here Comes Your Man
- ☐ '89 Monkey Gone To Heaven

## PIXIES THREE, The
- ☐ '63 Birthday Party

## PLANET SOUL
- ☐ '95 Set U Free

## PLANT, Robert
- ☐ '83 Big Log
- ☐ '82 Burning Down One Side
- ☐ '93 Calling To You
- ☐ '94 Gallows Pole
  - *JIMMY PAGE & ROBERT PLANT*
- ☐ '88 Heaven Knows
- ☐ '90 Hurting Kind (I've Got My Eyes On You)
- ☐ '83 In The Mood
- ☐ '85 Little By Little
- ☐ '98 Most High
  - *JIMMY PAGE & ROBERT PLANT*
- ☐ '83 Other Arms
- ☐ '88 Ship Of Fools
- ☐ '88 Tall Cool One

## PLATTERS, The
- ☐ '59 Enchanted
- ☐ '55 Great Pretender, The ★
- ☐ '60 Harbor Lights
- ☐ '57 He's Mine
- ☐ '66 I Love You 1000 Times
- ☐ '61 I'll Never Smile Again
- ☐ '57 I'm Sorry
- ☐ '61 If I Didn't Care
- ☐ '56 It Isn't Right
- ☐ '57 My Dream
- ☐ '56 My Prayer ★
- ☐ '56 On My Word Of Honor
- ☐ '56 One In A Million

- ☐ '55 Only You (And You Alone) ★
- ☐ '60 Red Sails In The Sunset
- ☐ '59 Remember When
- ☐ '58 Smoke Gets In Your Eyes ★
- ☐ '60 To Each His Own
- ☐ '58 Twilight Time ★
- ☐ '59 Where
- ☐ '67 With This Ring
- ☐ '56 You'll Never Never Know
- ☐ '56 (You've Got) The Magic Touch

## PLAYA
- ☐ '98 Cheers 2 U

## PLAYER
- ☐ '77 Baby Come Back ★
- ☐ '78 Prisoner Of Your Love
- ☐ '78 This Time I'm In It For Love

## PLAYMATES, The
- ☐ '58 Beep Beep
- ☐ '58 Don't Go Home
- ☐ '58 Jo-Ann
- ☐ '60 Wait For Me
- ☐ '59 What Is Love?

## PM DAWN
- ☐ '92 I'd Die Without You ★
- ☐ '93 Looking Through Patient Eyes ★
- ☐ '92 Paper Doll
- ☐ '91 Set Adrift On Memory Bliss ★

## POCO
- ☐ '89 Call It Love
- ☐ '79 Crazy Love
- ☐ '79 Heart Of The Night
- ☐ '89 Nothin' To Hide

## P.O.D.
- ☐ '01 Alive
- ☐ '99 Set Your Eyes To Zion
- ☐ '01 Youth Of The Nation

## POETS, The
- ☐ '66 She Blew A Good Thing

## POINDEXTER, Buster
- ☐ '88 Hot Hot Hot

## POINT BLANK
- ☐ '81 Nicole

## POINTER, Bonnie
- ☐ '79 Heaven Must Have Sent You
- ☐ '79 I Can't Help Myself (Sugar Pie, Honey Bunch)

## POINTER SISTERS
- ☐ '82 American Music
- ☐ '84 Automatic
- ☐ '85 Dare Me
- ☐ '74 Fairytale
- ☐ '78 Fire ★
- ☐ '86 Goldmine
- ☐ '79 Happiness
- ☐ '80 He's So Shy ★

## POINTER SISTERS — cont'd
- ☐ '75 How Long (Betcha' Got A Chick On The Side)
- ☐ '84 I'm So Excited
- ☐ '84 Jump (For My Love) ★
- ☐ '84 Neutron Dance
- ☐ '82 Should I Do It
- ☐ '81 Slow Hand ★
- ☐ '73 Yes We Can Can

## POISON
- ☐ '88 Every Rose Has Its Thorn ★
- ☐ '88 Fallen Angel
- ☐ '87 I Won't Forget You
- ☐ '91 Life Goes On
- ☐ '88 Nothin' But A Good Time
- ☐ '91 Ride The Wind
- ☐ '90 Something To Believe In
- ☐ '87 Talk Dirty To Me
- ☐ '90 Unskinny Bop ★
- ☐ '89 Your Mama Don't Dance

## POLICE, The
- ☐ '80 De Do Do Do, De Da Da Da ★
- ☐ '81 Don't Stand So Close To Me
- ☐ '83 Every Breath You Take ★
- ☐ '81 Every Little Thing She Does Is Magic ★
- ☐ '83 King Of Pain ★
- ☐ '79 Message In A Bottle
- ☐ '79 Roxanne ★
- ☐ '82 Spirits In The Material World
- ☐ '83 Synchronicity II
- ☐ '84 Wrapped Around Your Finger

## PONI-TAILS
- ☐ '58 Born Too Late

## POP, Iggy
- ☐ '90 Candy
- ☐ '90 Home
- ☐ '77 Lust For Life

## POPPY FAMILY, The
- ☐ '70 That's Where I Went Wrong
- ☐ '70 Which Way You Goin' Billy? ★

## PORNO FOR PYROS
- ☐ '93 Pets

## PORTRAIT
- ☐ '92 Here We Go Again!

## POSEY, Sandy
- ☐ '66 Born A Woman
- ☐ '67 I Take It Back
- ☐ '66 Single Girl
- ☐ '67 What A Woman In Love Won't Do

## POSITIVE K
- ☐ '92 I Got A Man

## POST, Mike
- ☐ '75 Rockford Files, The
- ☐ '81 Theme From Hill Street Blues, The
- ☐ '82 (Theme From) Magnum P.I.

## POURCEL, Franck
- ☐ '59 Only You

## POWELL, Jane
- ☐ '56 True Love

## POWELL, Jesse
- ☐ '99 You

## POWERS, Joey
- ☐ '63 Midnight Mary

## POWER STATION, The
- ☐ '85 Communication
- ☐ '85 Get It On
- ☐ '85 Some Like It Hot

## POZO-SECO SINGERS
- ☐ '66 I Can Make It With You
- ☐ '66 Look What You've Done
- ☐ '66 Time

## PRADO, Perez, & His Orchestra
- ☐ '55 Cherry Pink And Apple Blossom White ★
- ☐ '58 Patricia ★

## PRATT & McCLAIN
- ☐ '76 Happy Days

## PRELUDE
- ☐ '74 After The Goldrush

## PREMIERS, The
- ☐ '64 Farmer John

## PRESIDENTS, The
- ☐ '70 5-10-15-20 (25-30 Years Of Love)

## PRESIDENTS OF THE UNITED STATES OF AMERICA, The
- ☐ '95 Lump
- ☐ '96 Peaches

## PRESLEY, Elvis
- ☐ '64 Ain't That Loving You Baby
- ☐ '57 All Shook Up ★
- ☐ '72 American Trilogy, An
- ☐ '62 Anything That's Part Of You
- ☐ '56 Anyway You Want Me (That's How I Will Be)
- ☐ '60 Are You Lonesome To-night? ★
- ☐ '64 Ask Me
- ☐ '67 Big Boss Man
- ☐ '59 Big Hunk O' Love, A ★
- ☐ '57 Blue Christmas
- ☐ '61 Blue Hawaii
- ☐ '56 Blue Suede Shoes
- ☐ '63 Bossa Nova Baby
- ☐ '72 Burning Love ★
- ☐ '61 Can't Help Falling In Love ★
- ☐ '69 Clean Up Your Own Back Yard
- ☐ '65 Crying In The Chapel ★
- ☐ '65 Do The Clam
- ☐ '58 Don't ★
- ☐ '58 Don't Ask Me Why
- ☐ '56 Don't Be Cruel ★

- ☐ '69 Don't Cry Daddy
- ☐ '58 Doncha' Think It's Time
- ☐ '60 Fame And Fortune
- ☐ '61 Flaming Star
- ☐ '62 Follow That Dream
- ☐ '59 Fool Such As I, A
- ☐ '66 Frankie And Johnny
- ☐ '62 Good Luck Charm ★
- ☐ '68 Guitar Man
- ☐ '58 Hard Headed Woman ★
- ☐ '56 Heartbreak Hotel ★
- ☐ '56 Hound Dog ★
- ☐ '76 Hurt
- ☐ '58 I Beg Of You
- ☐ '61 I Feel So Bad
- ☐ '58 I Got Stung
- ☐ '60 I Gotta Know
- ☐ '59 I Need Your Love Tonight
- ☐ '70 I Really Don't Want To Know
- ☐ '56 I Want You, I Need You, I Love You
- ☐ '56 I Was The One
- ☐ '65 I'm Yours
- ☐ '74 I've Got A Thing About You Baby
- ☐ '70 I've Lost You
- ☐ '66 If Every Day Was Like Christmas
- ☐ '68 If I Can Dream
- ☐ '74 If You Talk In Your Sleep
- ☐ '69 In The Ghetto ★
- ☐ '67 Indescribably Blue
- ☐ '64 It Hurts Me
- ☐ '60 It's Now Or Never ★
- ☐ '57 Jailhouse Rock ★
- ☐ '70 Kentucky Rain
- ☐ '58 King Creole
- ☐ '62 King Of The Whole Wide World
- ☐ '64 Kiss Me Quick
- ☐ '64 Kissin' Cousins
- ☐ '68 Little Less Conversation, A
- ☐ '61 Little Sister
- ☐ '61 Lonely Man
- ☐ '66 Love Letters
- ☐ '56 Love Me ★
- ☐ '56 Love Me Tender ★
- ☐ '57 Loving You
- ☐ '61 (Marie's the Name) His Latest Flame
- ☐ '69 Memories
- ☐ '60 Mess Of Blues, A
- ☐ '76 Moody Blue
- ☐ '56 My Baby Left Me
- ☐ '75 My Boy
- ☐ '77 My Way
- ☐ '59 My Wish Came True
- ☐ '55 Mystery Train ★
- ☐ '63 One Broken Heart For Sale
- ☐ '58 One Night
- ☐ '57 Peace In The Valley
- ☐ '57 Playing For Keeps
- ☐ '56 Poor Boy
- ☐ '74 Promised Land
- ☐ '65 Puppet On A String
- ☐ '62 Return To Sender ★
- ☐ '61 Rock-A-Hula Baby
- ☐ '69 Rubberneckin'
- ☐ '61 Sentimental Me

- ☐ '72 Separate Ways
- ☐ '62 She's Not You
- ☐ '66 Spinout
- ☐ '73 Steamroller Blues
- ☐ '60 Stuck On You ★
- ☐ '64 Such A Night
- ☐ '65 (Such An) Easy Question
- ☐ '61 Surrender ★
- ☐ '62 Suspicion
- ☐ '69 Suspicious Minds ★
- ☐ '57 Teddy Bear ★
- ☐ '66 Tell Me Why
- ☐ '54 That's All Right
- ☐ '57 That's When Your Heartaches Begin
- ☐ '70 There Goes My Everything
- ☐ '57 Too Much ★
- ☐ '57 Treat Me Nice
- ☐ '75 T-R-O-U-B-L-E
- ☐ '68 U.S. Male
- ☐ '72 Until It's Time For You To Go
- ☐ '64 Viva Las Vegas
- ☐ '77 Way Down
- ☐ '58 Wear My Ring Around Your Neck
- ☐ '64 What'd I Say
- ☐ '56 When My Blue Moon Turns To Gold Again
- ☐ '71 Where Did They Go, Lord
- ☐ '61 Wild In The Country
- ☐ '63 Witchcraft
- ☐ '70 Wonder Of You, The
- ☐ '60 Wooden Heart
- ☐ '70 You Don't Have To Say You Love Me
- ☐ '63 (You're the) Devil In Disguise ★
- ☐ '68 Your Time Hasn't Come Yet, Baby

## PRESSHA
- ☐ '98 Splackavellie

## PRESTON, Billy
- ☐ '74 Nothing From Nothing ★
- ☐ '72 Outa-Space
- ☐ '73 Space Race
- ☐ '74 Struttin'
- ☐ '73 Will It Go Round In Circles ★
- ☐ '79 With You I'm Born Again
  *BILLY PRESTON & SYREETA*

## PRESTON, Johnny
- ☐ '60 Cradle Of Love
- ☐ '60 Feel So Fine
- ☐ '59 Running Bear ★

## PRESTON, Robert
- ☐ '62 Seventy Six Trombones

## PRETENDERS, The
- ☐ '82 Back On The Chain Gang ★
- ☐ '80 Brass In Pocket (I'm Special)
- ☐ '86 Don't Get Me Wrong
- ☐ '94 I'll Stand By You ★
- ☐ '81 Message Of Love
- ☐ '83 Middle Of The Road
- ☐ '86 My Baby
- ☐ '82 My City Was Gone
- ☐ '94 Night In My Veins
- ☐ '84 Show Me

## PRETENDERS, The — cont'd
- ☐ '80 Stop Your Sobbing
- ☐ '84 2000 Miles

## PRETTY POISON
- ☐ '87 Catch Me (I'm Falling)
- ☐ '88 Nightime

## PRICE, Kelly
- ☐ '98 Friend of Mine

## PRICE, Lloyd
- ☐ '59 Come Into My Heart
- ☐ '59 I'm Gonna Get Married ★
- ☐ '57 Just Because
- ☐ '60 Lady Luck
- ☐ '63 Misty
- ☐ '59 Personality ★
- ☐ '60 Question
- ☐ '58 Stagger Lee ★
- ☐ '59 Where Were You (On Our Wedding Day)?

## PRICE, Ray
- ☐ '58 City Lights
- ☐ '56 Crazy Arms
- ☐ '67 Danny Boy
- ☐ '70 For The Good Times

## PRIDE, Charley
- ☐ '67 Crystal Chandelier
- ☐ '67 Does My Ring Hurt Your Finger
- ☐ '70 Is Anybody Goin' To San Antone
- ☐ '69 Kaw-Liga [live]
- ☐ '71 Kiss An Angel Good Mornin'

## PRIEST, Maxi
- ☐ '90 Close To You ★
- ☐ '91 Set The Night To Music
  ROBERTA FLACK with Maxi Priest
- ☐ '96 That Girl
- ☐ '88 Wild World

## PRIMA, Louis, & Keely Smith
- ☐ '56 Just A Gigolo/I Ain't Got Nobody
- ☐ '58 That Old Black Magic
- ☐ '60 Wonderland By Night
  LOUIS PRIMA

## PRIMITIVE RADIO GODS
- ☐ '96 Standing Outside A Broken Phone Booth With Money In My Hand

## PRINCE
- ☐ '88 Alphabet St.
- ☐ '89 Arms Of Orion, The
  PRINCE with Sheena Easton
- ☐ '89 Batdance ★
- ☐ '81 Controversy
- ☐ '91 Cream ★
- ☐ '83 Delirious
- ☐ '91 Diamonds And Pearls ★
- ☐ '91 Gett Off
- ☐ '87 I Could Never Take The Place Of Your Man
- ☐ '95 I Hate U

- ☐ '79 I Wanna Be Your Lover
- ☐ '84 I Would Die 4 U
- ☐ '86 Kiss ★
- ☐ '84 Let's Go Crazy ★
- ☐ '94 Letitgo
- ☐ '83 Little Red Corvette ★
- ☐ '92 Money Don't Matter 2 Night
- ☐ '94 Most Beautiful Girl In The World, The ★
- ☐ '86 Mountains
- ☐ '92 My Name Is Prince
- ☐ '82 **1999**
- ☐ '89 Partyman
- ☐ '85 Pop Life
- ☐ '84 Purple Rain ★
- ☐ '85 Raspberry Beret ★
- ☐ '92 7 ★
- ☐ '87 Sign 'O' The Times
- ☐ '85 Take Me With U
- ☐ '90 Thieves In The Temple
- ☐ '87 U Got The Look
- ☐ '84 When Doves Cry ★

## PRISM
- ☐ '82 Don't Let Him Know

## PROBY, P.J.
- ☐ '67 Niki Hoeky

## PROCLAIMERS, The
- ☐ '93 I'm Gonna Be (500 Miles) ★

## PROCOL HARUM
- ☐ '72 Conquistador [live]
- ☐ '67 Homburg
- ☐ '72 Salty Dog, A [live]
- ☐ '67 Whiter Shade Of Pale, A ★

## PRODIGY
- ☐ '97 Firestarter

## PRODUCERS, The
- ☐ '81 What's He Got?

## PRODUCT G&B, The — see SANTANA

## PROFYLE
- ☐ '00 Liar

## PRUETT, Jeanne
- ☐ '73 Satin Sheets

## PSEUDO ECHO
- ☐ '87 Funky Town

## PSYCHEDELIC FURS
- ☐ '88 All That Money Wants
- ☐ '84 Ghost In You
- ☐ '87 Heartbreak Beat
- ☐ '89 House
- ☐ '83 Love My Way
- ☐ '81 Pretty In Pink
- ☐ '91 Until She Comes

## PUBLIC ANNOUNCEMENT
- ☐ '98 Body Bumpin' Yippie-Yi-Yo
- ☐ '00 Mamacita

## PUBLIC ENEMY
- ☐ '88 Bring The Noise
- ☐ '91 Can't Truss It
- ☐ '88 Don't Believe The Hype
- ☐ '89 Fight The Power
- ☐ '94 Give It Up
- ☐ '90 911 Is A Joke

## PUBLIC IMAGE LTD.
- ☐ '89 Disappointed
- ☐ '90 Don't Ask Me
- ☐ '84 This Is Not A Love Song

## PUCKETT, Gary, & The Union Gap
- ☐ '69 Don't Give In To Him
- ☐ '68 Lady Willpower
- ☐ '68 Over You
- ☐ '69 This Girl Is A Woman Now
- ☐ '67 Woman, Woman ★
- ☐ '68 Young Girl

## PUDDLE OF MUDD
- ☐ '03 Away From Me
- ☐ '01 Blurry ★
- ☐ '01 Control
- ☐ '02 Drift & Die
- ☐ '02 She Hates Me

## PUFF DADDY/P. DIDDY
- ☐ '01 Bad Boy For Life
  *P. DIDDY, BLACK ROB & MARK CURRY*
- ☐ '98 Been Around The World
- ☐ '02 Bump, Bump, Bump ★
  *B2K & P. DIDDY*
- ☐ '97 Can't Nobody Hold Me Down ★
- ☐ '98 Come With Me ★
- ☐ '02 I Need A Girl (Part One) ★
- ☐ '02 I Need A Girl (Part Two) ★
  *P. DIDDY & GINUWINE*
- ☐ '97 I'll Be Missing You ★
  *PUFF DADDY & FAITH EVANS*
- ☐ '97 It's All About The Benjamins ★
- ☐ '99 Satisfy You ★
- ☐ '03 Shake Ya Tailfeather ★
  *NELLY/P. DIDDY/MURPHY LEE*
- ☐ '98 Victory

## PUPPIES, The
- ☐ '94 Funky Y-2-C

## PURE PRAIRIE LEAGUE
- ☐ '75 Amie
- ☐ '80 I'm Almost Ready
- ☐ '80 Let Me Love You Tonight
- ☐ '81 Still Right Here In My Heart

## PURIFY, James & Bobby
- ☐ '66 I'm Your Puppet
- ☐ '67 Let Love Come Between Us
- ☐ '67 Shake A Tail Feather

## PURSELL, Bill
- ☐ '63 Our Winter Love

## PYRAMIDS, The
- ☐ '64 Penetration

# Q

## Q
- ☐ '77 Dancin' Man

## QB FINEST
- ☐ '01 Oochie Wally

## Q-TIP
- ☐ '99 Vivrant Thing

## QUAD CITY DJ'S
- ☐ '96 C'Mon N' Ride It (The Train) ★
- ☐ '96 Space Jam

## QUARTERFLASH
- ☐ '82 Find Another Fool
- ☐ '81 Harden My Heart ★
- ☐ '83 Take Me To Heart

## QUATRO, Suzi
- ☐ '79 Stumblin' In
  *SUZI QUATRO & CHRIS NORMAN*

## QUEEN
- ☐ '80 Another One Bites The Dust ★
- ☐ '78 Bicycle Race
- ☐ '82 Body Language
- ☐ '76 Bohemian Rhapsody ★
- ☐ '79 Crazy Little Thing Called Love ★
- ☐ '78 Don't Stop Me Now
- ☐ '80 Don't Try Suicide
- ☐ '78 Fat Bottomed Girls
- ☐ '89 I Want It All
- ☐ '75 Killer Queen
- ☐ '80 Play The Game
- ☐ '84 Radio Ga-Ga
- ☐ '76 Somebody To Love
- ☐ '93 Somebody To Love [live]
  *GEORGE MICHAEL & QUEEN*
- ☐ '77 Tie Your Mother Down
- ☐ '81 Under Pressure ★
  *QUEEN & DAVID BOWIE*
- ☐ '77 We Will Rock You/We Are The Champions ★
- ☐ '76 You're My Best Friend

## QUEEN LATIFAH
- ☐ '90 Ladies First
- ☐ '93 U.N.I.T.Y.

## QUEEN PEN
- ☐ '98 All My Love

## QUEENS OF THE STONE AGE
- ☐ '05 Little Sister
- ☐ '02 No One Knows

## QUEENSRYCHE
- ☐ '93 Real World
- ☐ '97 Sign Of The Times
- ☐ '91 Silent Lucidity

## ? (QUESTION MARK) & THE MYSTERIANS
- ☐ '66 96 Tears ★
- ☐ '66 I Need Somebody

## QUICKSILVER MESSENGER SERVICE
- ☐ '70 Fresh Air

## QUIET RIOT
- ☐ '84 Bang Your Head (Metal Health)
- ☐ '83 Cum On Feel The Noize ★

## QUIN-TONES, The
- ☐ '58 Down The Aisle Of Love

# R

## RABBITT, Eddie
- ☐ '80 Drivin' My Life Away ★
- ☐ '79 Every Which Way But Loose ★
- ☐ '82 I Don't Know Where To Start
- ☐ '80 I Love A Rainy Night ★
- ☐ '89 On Second Thought
- ☐ '81 Someone Could Lose A Heart Tonight
- ☐ '81 Step By Step
- ☐ '79 Suspicions
- ☐ '82 You And I
  - *EDDIE RABBITT with Crystal Gayle*
- ☐ '83 You Can't Run From Love

## RADIOHEAD
- ☐ '93 Creep
- ☐ '95 Fake Plastic Trees
- ☐ '97 Paranoid Android

## RAEKWON
- ☐ '95 Ice Cream

## RAFFERTY, Gerry
- ☐ '78 Baker Street ★
- ☐ '79 Days Gone Down (Still Got The Light In Your Eyes)
- ☐ '79 Get It Right Next Time
- ☐ '78 Home And Dry
- ☐ '78 Right Down The Line

## RAGE AGAINST THE MACHINE
- ☐ '96 Bulls On Parade

## RAINBOW
- ☐ '79 Since You Been Gone
- ☐ '82 Stone Cold
- ☐ '83 Street Of Dreams

## RAINDROPS, The
- ☐ '63 Kind Of Boy You Can't Forget, The
- ☐ '63 What A Guy

## RAINWATER, Marvin
- ☐ '57 Gonna Find Me A Bluebird

## RAITT, Bonnie
- ☐ '90 Have A Heart
- ☐ '91 I Can't Make You Love Me
- ☐ '94 Love Sneakin' Up On You
- ☐ '92 Not The Only One
- ☐ '91 Something To Talk About ★
- ☐ '95 You Got It

## RAMBEAU, Eddie
- ☐ '65 Concrete And Clay

## RAM JAM
- ☐ '77 Black Betty

## RAMONES
- ☐ '76 Blitzkrieg Bop ★
- ☐ '80 Do You Remember Rock 'N' Roll Radio
- ☐ '78 Do You Wanna Dance
- ☐ '95 I Don't Want To Grow Up
- ☐ '78 I Wanna Be Sedated
- ☐ '80 Rock 'N' Roll High School
- ☐ '78 Rockaway Beach
- ☐ '77 Sheena Is A Punk Rocker

## RAMPAGE
- ☐ '97 Take It To The Streets

## RAMRODS
- ☐ '61 (Ghost) Riders In The Sky

## RAN-DELLS, The
- ☐ '63 Martian Hop

## RANDOLPH, Boots
- ☐ '63 Yakety Sax

## RANDY & THE RAINBOWS
- ☐ '63 Denise

## RANKS, Shabba
- ☐ '91 Housecall (Your Body Can't Lie To Me)
- ☐ '92 Mr. Loverman
- ☐ '92 Slow And Sexy
  - *SHABBA RANKS Feat. Johnny Gill*

## RAPPIN' 4-TAY
- ☐ '95 I'll Be Around
- ☐ '94 Playaz Club

## RARE EARTH
- ☐ '70 Born To Wander
- ☐ '70 Get Ready
- ☐ '71 Hey Big Brother
- ☐ '71 I Just Want To Celebrate
- ☐ '70 (I Know) I'm Losing You
- ☐ '78 Warm Ride

## RASCAL FLATTS
- ☐ '05 Bless The Broken Road ★
- ☐ '03 I Melt
- ☐ '03 Love You Out Loud
- ☐ '04 Mayberry
- ☐ '00 Prayin' For Daylight
- ☐ '02 These Days

## RASCALS, The
- ☐ '68 Beautiful Morning, A
- ☐ '69 Carry Me Back
- ☐ '67 Girl Like You, A
- ☐ '66 Good Lovin' ★
- ☐ '67 Groovin' ★
- ☐ '69 Heaven
- ☐ '67 How Can I Be Sure
- ☐ '66 I Ain't Gonna Eat Out My Heart Anymore
- ☐ '67 I've Been Lonely Too Long
- ☐ '67 It's Wonderful
- ☐ '68 People Got To Be Free ★
- ☐ '68 Ray Of Hope, A
- ☐ '69 See
- ☐ '66 You Better Run

## RASPBERRIES
- ☐ '72  Go All The Way ★
- ☐ '72  I Wanna Be With You
- ☐ '73  Let's Pretend
- ☐ '74  Overnight Sensation (Hit Record)

## RATT
- ☐ '85  Lay It Down
- ☐ '84  Round And Round

## RAWLS, Lou
- ☐ '67  Dead End Street
- ☐ '78  Lady Love
- ☐ '66  Love Is A Hurtin' Thing
- ☐ '71  Natural Man, A
- ☐ '76  You'll Never Find Another Love Like Mine ★
- ☐ '69  Your Good Thing (Is About To End)

## RAY, Diane
- ☐ '63  Please Don't Talk To The Lifeguard

## RAY, James
- ☐ '61  If You Gotta Make A Fool Of Somebody

## RAY, Jimmy
- ☐ '98  Are You Jimmy Ray?

## RAY, Johnnie
- ☐ '56  Just Walking In The Rain ★
- ☐ '57  Look Homeward, Angel
- ☐ '57  Yes Tonight, Josephine
- ☐ '57  You Don't Owe Me A Thing

## RAYBON BROS.
- ☐ '97  Butterfly Kisses

## RAYBURN, Margie
- ☐ '57  I'm Available

## RAYE, Collin
- ☐ '99  Anyone Else
- ☐ '00  Couldn't Last A Moment
- ☐ '97  Gift, The
- ☐ '98  I Can Still Feel You
- ☐ '92  In This Life
- ☐ '97  Little Red Rodeo
- ☐ '94  Little Rock
- ☐ '91  Love, Me
- ☐ '94  My Kind Of Girl
- ☐ '95  Not That Different
- ☐ '95  One Boy, One Girl
- ☐ '94  That's My Story

## RAY, GOODMAN & BROWN — see MOMENTS

## RAY J
- ☐ '97  Let It Go
- ☐ '01  Wait A Minute

## RAYS, The
- ☐ '57  Silhouettes ★

## REA, Chris
- ☐ '78  Fool (If You Think It's Over)

## READY FOR THE WORLD
- ☐ '85  Digital Display
- ☐ '86  Love You Down
- ☐ '85  Oh Sheila ★

## REAL LIFE
- ☐ '84  Catch Me I'm Falling
- ☐ '83  Send Me An Angel

## REAL McCOY
- ☐ '94  Another Night ★
- ☐ '95  Come And Get Your Love
- ☐ '97  One More Time
- ☐ '95  Run Away ★

## REBELS, The
- ☐ '62  Wild Weekend

## REDBONE
- ☐ '74  Come And Get Your Love
- ☐ '71  Witch Queen Of New Orleans, The

## REDDING, Gene
- ☐ '74  This Heart

## REDDING, Otis
- ☐ '68  Amen
- ☐ '66  Fa-Fa-Fa-Fa-Fa (Sad Song)
- ☐ '68  Happy Song, The
- ☐ '65  I've Been Loving You Too Long
- ☐ '67  Knock On Wood
  - *OTIS & CARLA*
- ☐ '63  Pain In My Heart
- ☐ '68  Papa's Got A Brand New Bag
- ☐ '65  Respect
- ☐ '66  Satisfaction
- ☐ '68  (Sittin' On) The Dock Of The Bay ★
- ☐ '63  These Arms Of Mine
- ☐ '67  Tramp
  - *OTIS & CARLA*
- ☐ '66  Try A Little Tenderness

## REDDY, Helen
- ☐ '75  Ain't No Way To Treat A Lady
- ☐ '74  Angie Baby ★
- ☐ '75  Bluebird
- ☐ '73  Delta Dawn
- ☐ '75  Emotion
- ☐ '72  I Am Woman ★
- ☐ '76  I Can't Hear You No More
- ☐ '71  I Don't Know How To Love Him
- ☐ '74  Keep On Singing
- ☐ '73  Leave Me Alone (Ruby Red Dress)
- ☐ '73  Peaceful
- ☐ '75  Somewhere In The Night
- ☐ '74  You And Me Against The World
- ☐ '77  You're My World

## REDEYE
- ☐ '70  Games

## RED HOT CHILI PEPPERS
- ☐ '02  By The Way
- ☐ '00  Californication
- ☐ '02  Can't Stop
- ☐ '91  Give It Away
- ☐ '89  Higher Ground

## RED HOT CHILI PEPPERS — cont'd
- ☐ '96  Love Rollercoaster
- ☐ '95  My Friends
- ☐ '00  Otherside
- ☐ '99  Scar Tissue ★
- ☐ '93  Soul To Squeeze
- ☐ '92  Under The Bridge ★

## REDMAN
- ☐ '95  How High
  *REDMAN/METHOD MAN*

## REDNEX
- ☐ '95  Cotton Eye Joe ★

## REED, Dan, Network
- ☐ '88  Ritual

## REED, Jerry
- ☐ '70  Amos Moses
- ☐ '71  When You're Hot, You're Hot

## REED, Jimmy
- ☐ '56  Ain't That Lovin' You Baby
- ☐ '60  Baby What You Want Me To Do
- ☐ '61  Big Boss Man
- ☐ '61  Bright Lights Big City
- ☐ '57  Honest I Do
- ☐ '56  You've Got Me Dizzy

## REED, Lou
- ☐ '76  Coney Island Baby
- ☐ '89  Dirty Blvd.
- ☐ '72  Perfect Day
- ☐ '74  Sally Can't Dance
- ☐ '73  Satellite Of Love
- ☐ '78  Street Hassle
- ☐ '74  Sweet Jane
- ☐ '73  Walk On The Wild Side
- ☐ '74  White Light/White Heat

## REESE, Della
- ☐ '57  And That Reminds Me
- ☐ '59  Don't You Know ★
- ☐ '59  Not One Minute More

## REEVES, Jim
- ☐ '62  Adios Amigo
- ☐ '60  Am I Losing You
- ☐ '58  Billy Bayou
- ☐ '66  Distant Drums
- ☐ '57  Four Walls
- ☐ '59  He'll Have To Go ★
- ☐ '60  I Missed Me
- ☐ '60  I'm Gettin' Better

## REFLECTIONS, The
- ☐ '64  (Just Like) Romeo & Juliet

## RE-FLEX
- ☐ '83  Politics Of Dancing, The

## REGENTS, The
- ☐ '61  Barbara-Ann
- ☐ '61  Runaround

## REGINA
- ☐ '86  Baby Love

## REID, Clarence
- ☐ '69  Nobody But You Babe

## REID, Mike
- ☐ '88  Old Folks
  *RONNIE MILSAP & MIKE REID*
- ☐ '90  Walk On Faith

## R.E.M.
- ☐ '94  Bang And Blame
- ☐ '92  Drive
- ☐ '96  E-Bow The Letter
- ☐ '93  Everybody Hurts
- ☐ '91  Losing My Religion ★
- ☐ '93  Man On The Moon
- ☐ '87  One I Love, The
- ☐ '88  Orange Crush
- ☐ '83  Radio Free Europe
- ☐ '91  Shiny Happy People
- ☐ '88  Stand
- ☐ '94  What's The Frequency, Kenneth?

## REMBRANDTS, The
- ☐ '95  I'll Be There For You (Theme from "Friends")
- ☐ '91  Just The Way It Is, Baby

## RENAY, Diane
- ☐ '64  Kiss Me Sailor
- ☐ '64  Navy Blue

## RENÉ & ANGELA
- ☐ '85  Save Your Love (For #1)
- ☐ '86  You Don't Have To Cry
- ☐ '85  Your Smile

## RENE & RENE
- ☐ '68  Lo Mucho Que Te Quiero

## REO SPEEDWAGON
- ☐ '85  Can't Fight This Feeling ★
- ☐ '81  Don't Let Him Go
- ☐ '88  Here With Me
- ☐ '84  I Do'wanna Know
- ☐ '87  In My Dreams
- ☐ '81  In Your Letter
- ☐ '80  Keep On Loving You ★
- ☐ '82  Keep The Fire Burnin'
- ☐ '85  Live Every Moment
- ☐ '85  One Lonely Night
- ☐ '74  Ridin' The Storm Out
- ☐ '78  Roll With The Changes
- ☐ '82  Sweet Time
- ☐ '81  Take It On The Run ★
- ☐ '87  That Ain't Love
- ☐ '78  Time For Me To Fly

## REPLACEMENTS, The
- ☐ '84  I Will Dare
- ☐ '89  I'll Be You
- ☐ '90  Merry Go Round

## RESTLESS HEART
- ☐ '87  I'll Still Be Loving You
- ☐ '93  Tell Me What You Dream
- ☐ '92  When She Cries
- ☐ '91  You Can Depend On Me

## REUNION
- ☐ '74  Life Is A Rock (But The Radio Rolled Me)

## REVELS, The
- ☐ '59  Midnight Stroll

## REVERE, Paul, & The Raiders
- ☐ '71  Birds Of A Feather
- ☐ '68  Don't Take It So Hard
- ☐ '66  Good Thing
- ☐ '66  Great Airplane Strike, The
- ☐ '67  Him Or Me - What's It Gonna Be?
- ☐ '66  Hungry
- ☐ '67  I Had A Dream
- ☐ '71  Indian Reservation ★
- ☐ '65  Just Like Me
- ☐ '66  Kicks ★
- ☐ '69  Let Me
- ☐ '61  Like, Long Hair
- ☐ '69  Mr. Sun, Mr. Moon
- ☐ '68  Too Much Talk
- ☐ '67  Ups And Downs

## REYNOLDS, Debbie
- ☐ '60  Am I That Easy To Forget
- ☐ '57  Tammy ★
- ☐ '58  Very Special Love, A

## REYNOLDS, Jody
- ☐ '58  Endless Sleep ★

## REYNOLDS, Lawrence
- ☐ '69  Jesus Is A Soul Man

## RHYTHM HERITAGE
- ☐ '76  Baretta's Theme ("Keep Your Eye On The Sparrow")
- ☐ '75  Theme From S.W.A.T. ★

## RHYTHM SYNDICATE
- ☐ '91  Hey Donna
- ☐ '91  P.A.S.S.I.O.N

## RICH, Charlie
- ☐ '73  Behind Closed Doors
- ☐ '75  Every Time You Touch Me (I Get High)
- ☐ '74  I Love My Friend
- ☐ '60  Lonely Weekends
- ☐ '65  Mohair Sam
- ☐ '73  Most Beautiful Girl, The ★
- ☐ '77  Rollin' With The Flow
- ☐ '74  There Won't Be Anymore
- ☐ '74  Very Special Love Song, A

## RICH, Tony, Project
- ☐ '95  Nobody Knows ★

## RICHARD, Cliff
- ☐ '80  Carrie
- ☐ '82  Daddy's Home
- ☐ '76  Devil Woman
- ☐ '80  Dreaming
- ☐ '63  It's All In The Game
- ☐ '80  Little In Love, A
- ☐ '59  Living Doll
  *CLIFF RICHARD & The Drifters*
- ☐ '80  Suddenly
  *OLIVIA NEWTON-JOHN & CLIFF RICHARD*
- ☐ '79  We Don't Talk Anymore

## RICHARDS, Keith
- ☐ '88  Take It So Hard
- ☐ '92  Wicked As It Seems

## RICHIE, Lionel
- ☐ '83  All Night Long (All Night) ★
- ☐ '86  Ballerina Girl
- ☐ '86  Dancing On The Ceiling ★
- ☐ '92  Do It To Me
- ☐ '96  Don't Wanna Lose You
- ☐ '81  Endless Love ★
  *DIANA ROSS & LIONEL RICHIE*
- ☐ '84  Hello
- ☐ '86  Love Will Conquer All
- ☐ '83  My Love
- ☐ '84  Penny Lover
- ☐ '83  Running With The Night
- ☐ '85  Say You, Say Me ★
- ☐ '87  Se La
- ☐ '84  Stuck On You
- ☐ '82  Truly ★
- ☐ '83  You Are

## RICOCHET
- ☐ '96  Daddy's Money

## RIDDLE, Nelson, & His Orchestra
- ☐ '55  Lisbon Antigua ★
- ☐ '56  Port Au Prince
- ☐ '62  Route 66 Theme
- ☐ '56  Theme From "The Proud Ones"

## RIFF
- ☐ '91  My Heart Is Failing Me

## RIGHTEOUS BROTHERS, The
- ☐ '74  Dream On
- ☐ '65  Ebb Tide
- ☐ '74  Give It To The People
- ☐ '66  Go Ahead And Cry
- ☐ '66  He
- ☐ '65  Hung On You
- ☐ '65  Just Once In My Life
- ☐ '63  Little Latin Lupe Lu
- ☐ '74  Rock And Roll Heaven
- ☐ '65  Unchained Melody ★
- ☐ '66  (You're My) Soul And Inspiration ★
- ☐ '64  You've Lost That Lovin' Feelin' ★

## RIGHT SAID FRED (R*S*F)
- ☐ '91  I'm Too Sexy ★

## RILEY, Cheryl Pepsii
- ☐ '88  Thanks For My Child

## RILEY, Jeannie C.
- ☐ '68  Harper Valley P.T.A. ★

## RILEY, Teddy
- ☐ '89  My Fantasy

## RIMES, LeAnn
- [ ] '99 Big Deal
- [ ] '96 Blue
- [ ] '00 Can't Fight The Moonlight
- [ ] '97 How Do I Live ★
- [ ] '00 I Need You
- [ ] '98 Looking Through Your Eyes
- [ ] '96 One Way Ticket (Because I Can)
- [ ] '96 Unchained Melody
- [ ] '99 Written In The Stars
      *ELTON JOHN & LEANN RIMES*
- [ ] '97 You Light Up My Life

## RIOS, Miguel
- [ ] '70 Song Of Joy, A

## RIP CHORDS, The
- [ ] '63 Hey Little Cobra ★
- [ ] '64 Three Window Coupe

## RIPERTON, Minnie
- [ ] '75 Lovin' You ★

## RITCHIE FAMILY, The
- [ ] '76 Best Disco In Town, The
- [ ] '75 Brazil

## RITENOUR, Lee
- [ ] '81 Is It You

## RITTER, Tex
- [ ] '61 I Dreamed Of A Hill-Billy Heaven

## RIVERA, Chita
- [ ] '61 America

## RIVERS, Johnny
- [ ] '67 Baby I Need Your Lovin'
- [ ] '73 Blue Suede Shoes
- [ ] '75 Help Me Rhonda
- [ ] '66 (I Washed My Hands In) Muddy Water
- [ ] '64 Maybelline
- [ ] '64 Memphis ★
- [ ] '65 Midnight Special
- [ ] '64 Mountain Of Love
- [ ] '69 Muddy River
- [ ] '66 Poor Side Of Town ★
- [ ] '72 Rockin' Pneumonia - Boogie Woogie Flu
- [ ] '66 Secret Agent Man ★
- [ ] '65 Seventh Son
- [ ] '67 Summer Rain
- [ ] '77 Swayin' To The Music (Slow Dancin')
- [ ] '67 Tracks Of My Tears, The
- [ ] '65 Under Your Spell Again
- [ ] '65 Where Have All The Flowers Gone

## RIVIERAS, The
- [ ] '64 California Sun

## RIVINGTONS, The
- [ ] '62 Papa-Oom-Mow-Mow

## ROACHFORD
- [ ] '89 Cuddly Toy (Feel For Me)

## ROAD APPLES, The
- [ ] '75 Let's Live Together

## ROB BASE & D.J. E-Z ROCK
- [ ] '88 It Takes Two

## ROBBINS, Marty
- [ ] '60 Ballad Of The Alamo
- [ ] '60 Big Iron
- [ ] '62 Devil Woman
- [ ] '61 Don't Worry ★
- [ ] '59 El Paso ★
- [ ] '59 Hanging Tree, The
- [ ] '60 Is There Any Chance
- [ ] '58 Just Married
- [ ] '62 Ruby Ann
- [ ] '58 She Was Only Seventeen (He Was One Year More)
- [ ] '56 Singing The Blues
- [ ] '57 Story Of My Life, The
- [ ] '57 White Sport Coat (And A Pink Carnation) ★

## ROBERT & JOHNNY
- [ ] '58 We Belong Together

## ROBERTS, Austin
- [ ] '75 Rocky
- [ ] '72 Something's Wrong With Me

## ROBERTSON, Don
- [ ] '56 Happy Whistler, The

## ROBERTSON, Robbie
- [ ] '87 Showdown At Big Sky

## ROBIC, Ivo
- [ ] '59 Morgen

## ROBIN S
- [ ] '93 Show Me Love ★

## ROBINS, The
- [ ] '55 Smokey Joe's Café

## ROBINSON, Floyd
- [ ] '59 Makin' Love

## ROBINSON, Smokey
- [ ] '75 Agony And The Ecstasy, The
- [ ] '73 Baby Come Close
- [ ] '75 Baby That's Backatcha
- [ ] '81 Being With You
- [ ] '79 Cruisin'
- [ ] '87 Just To See Her
- [ ] '80 Let Me Be The Clock
- [ ] '87 One Heartbeat
- [ ] '82 Tell Me Tomorrow

## ROBINSON, Vicki Sue
- [ ] '76 Turn The Beat Around

## ROBYN
- [ ] '97 Do You Know (What It Takes)
- [ ] '98 Do You Really Want Me (Show Respect)
- [ ] '97 Show Me Love

## ROCHELL & THE CANDLES
- [ ] '61 Once Upon A Time

## ROCK-A-TEENS
- ☐ '59  Woo-Hoo

## ROCKETS
- ☐ '79  Oh Well

## ROCKWELL
- ☐ '84  Obscene Phone Caller
- ☐ '84  Somebody's Watching Me

## ROCKY FELLERS, The
- ☐ '63  Killer Joe

## RODGERS, Eileen
- ☐ '56  Miracle Of Love
- ☐ '58  Treasure Of Your Love

## RODGERS, Jimmie
- ☐ '58  Are You Really Mine
- ☐ '58  Bimbombey
- ☐ '67  Child Of Clay
- ☐ '57  Honeycomb ★
- ☐ '59  I'm Never Gonna Tell
- ☐ '66  It's Over
- ☐ '57  Kisses Sweeter Than Wine ★
- ☐ '58  Make Me A Miracle
- ☐ '58  Oh-Oh, I'm Falling In Love Again
- ☐ '59  Ring-A-Ling-A-Lario
- ☐ '58  Secretly
- ☐ '60  T.L.C. Tender Love And Care
- ☐ '59  Tucumcari
- ☐ '60  Waltzing Matilda

## ROE, Tommy
- ☐ '64  Come On
- ☐ '69  Dizzy ★
- ☐ '63  Everybody
- ☐ '69  Heather Honey
- ☐ '66  Hooray For Hazel
- ☐ '66  It's Now Winters Day
- ☐ '69  Jam Up Jelly Tight
- ☐ '62  Sheila ★
- ☐ '71  Stagger Lee
- ☐ '62  Susie Darlin'
- ☐ '66  Sweet Pea

## ROGER
- ☐ '81  I Heard It Through The Grapevine
- ☐ '87  I Want To Be Your Man

## ROGERS, Julie
- ☐ '64  Wedding, The

## ROGERS, Kenny/First Edition
- ☐ '83  All My Life
- ☐ '69  But You Know I Love You
- ☐ '00  Buy Me A Rose
  *KENNY ROGERS With Alison Krauss & Billy Dean*
- ☐ '79  Coward Of The County ★
- ☐ '77  Daytime Friends
- ☐ '80  Don't Fall In Love With A Dreamer
  *KENNY ROGERS with Kim Carnes*
- ☐ '78  Gambler, The
- ☐ '99  Greatest, The
- ☐ '70  Heed The Call
- ☐ '81  I Don't Need You

- ☐ '83  Islands In The Stream ★
  *KENNY ROGERS with Dolly Parton*
- ☐ '68  Just Dropped In (To See What Condition My Condition Was In)
- ☐ '80  Lady ★
- ☐ '78  Love Or Something Like It
- ☐ '80  Love The World Away
- ☐ '82  Love Will Turn You Around
- ☐ '77  Lucille ★
- ☐ '69  Ruben James
- ☐ '69  Ruby, Don't Take Your Love To Town
- ☐ '81  Share Your Love With Me
- ☐ '79  She Believes In Me
- ☐ '70  Something's Burning
- ☐ '70  Tell It All Brother
- ☐ '84  This Woman
- ☐ '81  Through The Years
- ☐ '83  We've Got Tonight
  *KENNY ROGERS & SHEENA EASTON*
- ☐ '84  What About Me?
  *KENNY ROGERS with Kim Carnes & James Ingram*
- ☐ '81  What Are We Doin' In Love
  *DOTTIE WEST (with Kenny Rogers)*
- ☐ '79  You Decorated My Life

## ROLLING STONES, The
- ☐ '74  Ain't Too Proud To Beg
- ☐ '90  Almost Hear You Sigh
- ☐ '73  Angie ★
- ☐ '97  Anybody Seen My Baby?
- ☐ '65  As Tears Go By
- ☐ '78  Beast Of Burden
- ☐ '71  Bitch
- ☐ '71  Brown Sugar ★
- ☐ '67  Dandelion
- ☐ '74  Doo Doo Doo Doo Doo (Heartbreaker)
- ☐ '80  Emotional Rescue ★
- ☐ '78  Far Away Eyes
- ☐ '76  Fool To Cry
- ☐ '65  Get Off Of My Cloud ★
- ☐ '69  Gimme Shelter
- ☐ '82  Going To A Go-Go
- ☐ '81  Hang Fire
- ☐ '72  Happy
- ☐ '86  Harlem Shuffle
- ☐ '66  Have You Seen Your Mother, Baby, Standing In The Shadow?
- ☐ '65  Heart Of Stone
- ☐ '91  Highwire
- ☐ '69  Honky Tonk Women ★
- ☐ '65  (I Can't Get No) Satisfaction ★
- ☐ '64  It's All Over Now
- ☐ '74  It's Only Rock 'N Roll (But I Like It)
- ☐ '68  Jumpin' Jack Flash ★
- ☐ '66  Lady Jane
- ☐ '65  Last Time, The
- ☐ '67  Let's Spend The Night Together
- ☐ '94  Love Is Strong
- ☐ '78  Miss You ★
- ☐ '89  Mixed Emotions
- ☐ '66  Mothers Little Helper
- ☐ '66  19th Nervous Breakdown ★
- ☐ '64  Not Fade Away
- ☐ '86  One Hit (To The Body)
- ☐ '66  Paint It, Black ★

## ROLLING STONES, The — cont'd
- ☐ '89 Rock And A Hard Place
- ☐ '67 Ruby Tuesday ★
- ☐ '78 Shattered
- ☐ '67 She's A Rainbow
- ☐ '80 She's So Cold
- ☐ '81 Start Me Up ★
- ☐ '68 Street Fighting Man
- ☐ '68 Sympathy For The Devil ★
- ☐ '64 Tell Me (You're Coming Back)
- ☐ '64 Time Is On My Side
- ☐ '72 Tumbling Dice
- ☐ '66 Under My Thumb
- ☐ '83 Undercover Of The Night
- ☐ '81 Waiting On A Friend
- ☐ '71 Wild Horses
- ☐ '69 You Can't Always Get What You Want
- ☐ '94 You Got Me Rocking

## ROMANTICS, The
- ☐ '84 One In A Million
- ☐ '83 Talking In Your Sleep ★
- ☐ '80 What I Like About You

## ROME
- ☐ '97 Do You Like This
- ☐ '97 I Belong To You (Every Time I See Your Face)

## ROMEO VOID
- ☐ '84 Girl In Trouble (Is A Temporary Thing)

## RONDO, Don
- ☐ '56 Two Different Worlds
- ☐ '57 White Silver Sands

## RONETTES, The
- ☐ '63 Baby, I Love You
- ☐ '63 Be My Baby ★
- ☐ '64 Do I Love You?
- ☐ '64 Walking In The Rain

## RONNIE & THE HI-LITES
- ☐ '62 I Wish That We Were Married

## RONNY & THE DAYTONAS
- ☐ '64 G.T.O. ★
- ☐ '65 Sandy

## RONSTADT, Linda
- ☐ '90 All My Life
  *LINDA RONSTADT Ft. Aaron Neville*
- ☐ '78 Back In The U.S.A.
- ☐ '77 Blue Bayou
- ☐ '67 Different Drum
- ☐ '89 Don't Know Much ★
  *LINDA RONSTADT Ft. Aaron Neville*
- ☐ '82 Get Closer
- ☐ '75 Heat Wave
- ☐ '80 How Do I Make You
- ☐ '80 Hurt So Bad
- ☐ '80 I Can't Let Go
- ☐ '82 I Knew You When
- ☐ '77 It's So Easy
- ☐ '70 Long Long Time
- ☐ '78 Ooh Baby Baby
- ☐ '78 Poor Poor Pitiful Me

- ☐ '86 Somewhere Out There ★
  *LINDA RONSTADT & JAMES INGRAM*
- ☐ '76 That'll Be The Day
- ☐ '75 Tracks Of My Tears
- ☐ '78 Tumbling Dice
- ☐ '75 When Will I Be Loved ★
- ☐ '74 You're No Good ★

## ROOFTOP SINGERS, The
- ☐ '63 Tom Cat
- ☐ '63 Walk Right In ★

## ROOTS, The
- ☐ '97 What They Do
- ☐ '99 You Got Me

## ROSE, David, & His Orchestra
- ☐ '62 Stripper, The ★

## ROSE GARDEN, The
- ☐ '67 Next Plane To London

## ROSE ROYCE
- ☐ '76 Car Wash ★
- ☐ '77 I Wanna Get Next To You
- ☐ '78 Love Don't Live Here Anymore
- ☐ '77 Ooh Boy

## ROSIE & THE ORIGINALS
- ☐ '60 Angel Baby

## ROSS, Diana
- ☐ '70 Ain't No Mountain High Enough ★
- ☐ '84 All Of You
  *JULIO IGLESIAS & DIANA ROSS*
- ☐ '79 Boss, The
- ☐ '81 Endless Love ★
  *DIANA ROSS & LIONEL RICHIE*
- ☐ '77 Gettin' Ready For Love
- ☐ '73 Good Morning Heartache
- ☐ '80 I'm Coming Out
- ☐ '80 It's My Turn
- ☐ '74 Last Time I Saw Him
- ☐ '76 Love Hangover ★
- ☐ '82 Mirror, Mirror
- ☐ '84 Missing You
- ☐ '82 Muscles
- ☐ '74 My Mistake (Was To Love You)
  *DIANA ROSS & MARVIN GAYE*
- ☐ '76 One Love In My Lifetime
- ☐ '83 Pieces Of Ice
- ☐ '70 Reach Out And Touch (Somebody's Hand)
- ☐ '71 Reach Out I'll Be There
- ☐ '70 Remember Me
- ☐ '71 Surrender
- ☐ '84 Swept Away
- ☐ '75 Theme From Mahogany (Do You Know Where You're Going To) ★
- ☐ '73 Touch Me In The Morning
- ☐ '80 Upside Down ★
- ☐ '81 Why Do Fools Fall In Love
- ☐ '73 You're A Special Part Of Me
  *DIANA ROSS & MARVIN GAYE*

## ROSS, Jack
- ☐ '62 Cinderella

## ROSS, Jackie
- ☐ '64 Selfish One

## ROSS, Spencer
- ☐ '60 Tracy's Theme

## ROTH, David Lee
- ☐ '85 California Girls
- ☐ '85 Just A Gigolo/I Ain't Got Nobody
- ☐ '88 Just Like Paradise
- ☐ '86 Yankee Rose

## ROUTERS, The
- ☐ '62 Let's Go

## ROVER BOYS, The
- ☐ '56 Graduation Day

## ROWLAND, Kelly
- ☐ '02 Stole

## ROXETTE
- ☐ '92 Church Of Your Heart
- ☐ '89 Dangerous ★
- ☐ '89 Dressed For Success
- ☐ '91 Fading Like A Flower (Every Time You Leave)
- ☐ '90 It Must Have Been Love ★
- ☐ '91 Joyride ★
- ☐ '89 Listen To Your Heart ★
- ☐ '89 Look, The ★
- ☐ '91 Spending My Time

## ROXY MUSIC
- ☐ '82 Avalon
- ☐ '75 Love Is The Drug
- ☐ '83 More Than This

## ROYAL, Billy Joe
- ☐ '69 Cherry Hill Park
- ☐ '65 Down In The Boondocks
- ☐ '65 I Knew You When
- ☐ '65 I've Got To Be Somebody

## ROYAL GUARDSMEN, The
- ☐ '68 Baby Let's Wait
- ☐ '67 Return Of The Red Baron, The
- ☐ '66 Snoopy Vs. The Red Baron ★
- ☐ '67 Snoopy's Christmas

## ROYAL PHILHARMONIC ORCHESTRA
- ☐ '81 Hooked On Classics

## ROYAL SCOTS DRAGOON GUARDS
- ☐ '72 Amazing Grace

## ROYAL TEENS
- ☐ '59 Believe Me
- ☐ '58 Short Shorts ★

## ROYALTONES, The
- ☐ '58 Poor Boy

## ROZALLA
- ☐ '92 Everybody's Free (To Feel Good)

## RTZ
- ☐ '92 Until Your Love Comes Back Around

## RUBETTES, The
- ☐ '74 Sugar Baby Love

## RUBICON
- ☐ '78 I'm Gonna Take Care Of Everything

## RUBY & THE ROMANTICS
- ☐ '63 Hey There Lonely Boy
- ☐ '63 My Summer Love
- ☐ '63 Our Day Will Come ★

## RUDE BOYS
- ☐ '91 Are You Lonely For Me
- ☐ '91 Written All Over Your Face

## RUFF ENDZ
- ☐ '00 No More

## RUFFIN, David
- ☐ '69 My Whole World Ended (The Moment You Left Me)
- ☐ '75 Walk Away From Love

## RUFFIN, Jimmy
- ☐ '67 Gonna Give Her All The Love I've Got
- ☐ '80 Hold On To My Love
- ☐ '66 I've Passed This Way Before
- ☐ '66 What Becomes Of The Brokenhearted

## RUFUS — see KHAN, Chaka

## RUGBYS, The
- ☐ '69 You, I

## RUNDGREN, Todd
- ☐ '83 Bang The Drum All Day
- ☐ '78 Can We Still Be Friends
- ☐ '76 Good Vibrations
- ☐ '73 Hello It's Me
- ☐ '72 I Saw The Light
- ☐ '70 We Gotta Get You A Woman

## RUN-D.M.C.
- ☐ '93 Down With The King
- ☐ '84 It's Like That
- ☐ '85 King Of Rock
- ☐ '86 My Adidas
- ☐ '86 Walk This Way ★
- ☐ '86 You Be Illin'

## RUPEE
- ☐ '04 Tempted To Touch

## RUSH
- ☐ '85 Big Money, The
- ☐ '77 Closer To The Heart
- ☐ '93 Cold Fire
- ☐ '84 Distant Early Warning
- ☐ '91 Dreamline
- ☐ '75 Fly By Night
- ☐ '80 Freewill
- ☐ '91 Ghost Of A Chance
- ☐ '82 New World Man
- ☐ '81 Red Barchetta
- ☐ '89 Show Don't Tell
- ☐ '80 Spirit Of Radio
- ☐ '93 Stick It Out

## RUSH — cont'd
- ☐ '96 Test For Echo
- ☐ '81 Tom Sawyer

## RUSH, Jennifer
- ☐ '87 Flames Of Paradise
  *JENNIFER RUSH (with Elton John)*

## RUSH, Merrilee
- ☐ '68 Angel Of The Morning

## RUSHEN, Patrice
- ☐ '84 Feels So Real (Won't Let Go)
- ☐ '82 Forget Me Nots

## RUSSELL, Andy
- ☐ '67 It's Such A Pretty World Today

## RUSSELL, Bobby
- ☐ '68 1432 Franklin Pike Circle Hero
- ☐ '71 Saturday Morning Confusion

## RUSSELL, Brenda
- ☐ '88 Piano In The Dark
- ☐ '79 So Good, So Right

## RUSSELL, Leon
- ☐ '75 Lady Blue
- ☐ '72 Tight Rope

## RYAN, Charlie
- ☐ '60 Hot Rod Lincoln

## RYDELL, Bobby
- ☐ '63 Butterfly Baby
- ☐ '62 Cha-Cha-Cha, The
- ☐ '60 Ding-A-Ling
- ☐ '61 Fish, The
- ☐ '63 Forget Him
- ☐ '61 Good Time Baby
- ☐ '61 I Wanna Thank You
- ☐ '62 I'll Never Dance Again
- ☐ '62 (I've Got) Bonnie
- ☐ '61 Jingle Bell Rock
  *BOBBY RYDELL & CHUBBY CHECKER*
- ☐ '59 Kissin' Time
- ☐ '60 Little Bitty Girl
- ☐ '60 Sway
- ☐ '60 Swingin' School
- ☐ '61 That Old Black Magic
- ☐ '60 Volare
- ☐ '59 We Got Love
- ☐ '60 Wild One ★
- ☐ '63 Wildwood Days

## RYDER, Mitch, & The Detroit Wheels
- ☐ '66 Devil With A Blue Dress On & Good Golly Miss Molly ★
- ☐ '65 Jenny Take A Ride!
- ☐ '66 Little Latin Lupe Lu ★
- ☐ '67 Sock It To Me-Baby!
- ☐ '67 Too Many Fish In The Sea & Three Little Fishes

# S

## SAADIQ, Raphael
- ☐ '95 Ask Of You

## SADE
- ☐ '86 Never As Good As The First Time
- ☐ '92 No Ordinary Love
- ☐ '88 Nothing Can Come Between Us
- ☐ '88 Paradise
- ☐ '85 Smooth Operator ★
- ☐ '85 Sweetest Taboo, The

## SADLER, SSgt Barry
- ☐ '66 Ballad Of The Green Berets, The ★

## SAFARIS
- ☐ '60 Image Of A Girl

## SA-FIRE
- ☐ '89 Thinking Of You

## SAGA
- ☐ '82 On The Loose
- ☐ '83 Wind Him Up

## SAGER, Carole Bayer
- ☐ '81 Stronger Than Before

## SAIGON KICK
- ☐ '92 Love Is On The Way

## SAILCAT
- ☐ '72 Motorcycle Mama

## SAINTE-MARIE, Buffy
- ☐ '72 Mister Can't You See

## ST. PETERS, Crispian
- ☐ '66 Pied Piper, The ★
- ☐ '67 You Were On My Mind

## SAKAMOTO, Kyu
- ☐ '63 Sukiyaki ★

## SALIVA
- ☐ '02 Always
- ☐ '01 Your Disease

## SALSOUL ORCHESTRA, The
- ☐ '76 Nice 'N' Naasty
- ☐ '76 Tangerine

## SALT-N-PEPA
- ☐ '95 Ain't Nuthin' But A She Thing
- ☐ '91 Do You Want Me
- ☐ '90 Expression
- ☐ '91 Let's Talk About Sex
- ☐ '94 None Of Your Business
- ☐ '87 Push It
- ☐ '93 Shoop ★
- ☐ '94 Whatta Man ★
  *SALT 'N' PEPA with En Vogue*

## SAM & DAVE
- ☐ '66 Hold On! I'm A Comin'
- ☐ '68 I Thank You
- ☐ '67 Soul Man ★
- ☐ '67 When Something Is Wrong With My Baby

## SAMI JO
- ☐ '74 Tell Me A Lie

## SAMMIE
- ☐ '00  I Like It

## SAM THE SHAM & THE PHARAOHS
- ☐ '66  Hair On My Chinny Chin Chin, The
- ☐ '66  How Do You Catch A Girl
- ☐ '65  Ju Ju Hand
- ☐ '66  Lil' Red Riding Hood ★
- ☐ '65  Ring Dang Doo
- ☐ '65  Wooly Bully ★

## SAMUELLE
- ☐ '90  So You Like What You See

## SANDLER, Adam
- ☐ '95  Chanukah Song, The

## SANDPEBBLES, The
- ☐ '67  Love Power

## SANDPIPERS, The
- ☐ '69  Come Saturday Morning
- ☐ '67  Cuando Sali De Cuba
- ☐ '66  Guantanamera
- ☐ '66  Louie, Louie

## SANDS, Jodie
- ☐ '57  With All My Heart

## SANDS, Tommy
- ☐ '57  Goin' Steady
- ☐ '58  Sing Boy Sing
- ☐ '57  Teen-Age Crush ★
- ☐ '59  Worryin' Kind, The

## SANFORD/TOWNSEND BAND, The
- ☐ '77  Smoke From A Distant Fire

## SANG, Samantha
- ☐ '77  Emotion

## SANTA ESMERALDA
- ☐ '77  Don't Let Me Be Misunderstood

## SANTAMARIA, Mongo
- ☐ '63  Watermelon Man

## SANTANA
- ☐ '70  Black Magic Woman/Gypsy Queen ★
- ☐ '71  Everybody's Everything
- ☐ '70  Evil Ways
- ☐ '02  Game Of Love, The ★
  *SANTANA Feat. Michelle Branch*
- ☐ '82  Hold On
- ☐ '69  Jingo
- ☐ '76  Let It Shine
- ☐ '00  Maria Maria ★
  *SANTANA Feat. The Product G&B*
- ☐ '72  No One To Depend On
- ☐ '78  One Chain (Don't Make No Prison)
- ☐ '71  Oye Como Va
- ☐ '77  She's Not There
- ☐ '99  Smooth ★
  *SANTANA Feat. Rob Thomas*
- ☐ '79  Stormy
- ☐ '03  Why Don't You & I
  *SANTANA Feat. Alex Band or Chad Kroeger*
- ☐ '81  Winning

## SANTO & JOHNNY
- ☐ '79  You Know That I Love You
- ☐ '59  Sleep Walk ★
- ☐ '59  Tear Drop

## SANTOS, Larry
- ☐ '76  We Can't Hide It Anymore

## SAPPHIRES, The
- ☐ '64  Who Do You Love

## SATRIANI, Joe
- ☐ '92  Summer Song

## SAVAGE, Chantay
- ☐ '96  I Will Survive

## SAVAGE GARDEN
- ☐ '99  Animal Song, The
- ☐ '00  Crash And Burn
- ☐ '99  I Knew I Loved You ★
- ☐ '97  I Want You ★
- ☐ '97  To The Moon And Back
- ☐ '97  Truly Madly Deeply ★

## SAWYER BROWN
- ☐ '91  Dirt Road, The
- ☐ '89  Race Is On, The
- ☐ '97  Six Days On The Road
- ☐ '92  Some Girls Do
- ☐ '85  Step That Step
- ☐ '93  Thank God For You
- ☐ '97  This Night Won't Last Forever
- ☐ '94  This Time
- ☐ '96  Treat Her Right
- ☐ '91  Walk, The

## SAYER, Leo
- ☐ '77  Easy To Love
- ☐ '77  How Much Love
- ☐ '81  Living In A Fantasy
- ☐ '75  Long Tall Glasses (I Can Dance)
- ☐ '80  More Than I Can Say ★
- ☐ '77  Thunder In My Heart
- ☐ '77  When I Need You ★
- ☐ '76  You Make Me Feel Like Dancing ★

## SCAGGS, Boz
- ☐ '80  Breakdown Dead Ahead
- ☐ '72  Dinah Flo
- ☐ '76  Georgia
- ☐ '88  Heart Of Mine
- ☐ '76  It's Over
- ☐ '80  JoJo
- ☐ '77  Lido Shuffle
- ☐ '80  Look What You've Done To Me
- ☐ '76  Lowdown
- ☐ '80  Miss Sun

## SCANDAL/SMYTH, Patty
- ☐ '92  No Mistakes
- ☐ '92  Sometimes Love Just Ain't Enough ★
  *PATTY SMYTH with Don Henley*
- ☐ '84  Warrior, The

## SCARBURY, Joey
- ☐ '81 Theme From "Greatest American Hero" (Believe It or Not)

## SCARFACE
- ☐ '94 I Never Seen A Man Cry (aka I Seen A Man Die)
- ☐ '97 Smile

## SCARLETT & BLACK
- ☐ '88 You Don't Know

## SCHILLING, Peter
- ☐ '83 Major Tom (Coming Home)

## SCHMIT, Timothy B.
- ☐ '87 Boys Night Out

## SCHWARTZ, Eddie
- ☐ '81 All Our Tomorrows

## S CLUB 7
- ☐ '01 Never Had A Dream Come True

## SCORPIONS
- ☐ '82 No One Like You
- ☐ '84 Rock You Like A Hurricane
- ☐ '91 Wind Of Change

## SCOTT, Bobby
- ☐ '56 Chain Gang

## SCOTT, Freddie
- ☐ '66 Are You Lonely For Me
- ☐ '63 Hey, Girl

## SCOTT, Jack
- ☐ '60 Burning Bridges ★
- ☐ '58 Goodbye Baby
- ☐ '60 It Only Happened Yesterday
- ☐ '58 Leroy
- ☐ '58 My True Love ★
- ☐ '60 Oh, Little One
- ☐ '59 Way I Walk, The
- ☐ '60 What In The World's Come Over You ★
- ☐ '58 With Your Love

## SCOTT, Linda
- ☐ '61 Don't Bet Money Honey
- ☐ '61 I Don't Know Why
- ☐ '61 I've Told Every Little Star ★
- ☐ '61 It's All Because

## SCOTT, Peggy, & Jo Jo Benson
- ☐ '68 Lover's Holiday
- ☐ '68 Pickin' Wild Mountain Berries
- ☐ '69 Soulshake

## SCRITTI POLITTI
- ☐ '85 Perfect Way

## SEA, Johnny
- ☐ '66 Day For Decision

## SEAL
- ☐ '91 Crazy ★
- ☐ '96 Don't Cry
- ☐ '96 Fly Like An Eagle

- ☐ '95 Kiss From A Rose ★
- ☐ '04 Love's Divine
- ☐ '94 Prayer For The Dying

## SEALS, Dan
- ☐ '86 Bop
- ☐ '90 Good Times
- ☐ '90 Love On Arrival
- ☐ '85 Meet Me In Montana
  *MARIE OSMOND with Dan Seals*

## SEALS & CROFTS
- ☐ '73 Diamond Girl
- ☐ '76 Get Closer
- ☐ '73 Hummingbird
- ☐ '75 I'll Play For You
- ☐ '77 My Fair Share
- ☐ '72 Summer Breeze
- ☐ '73 We May Never Pass This Way (Again)
- ☐ '78 You're The Love

## SEARCHERS, The
- ☐ '65 Bumble Bee
- ☐ '64 Don't Throw Your Love Away
- ☐ '64 Love Potion Number Nine
- ☐ '64 Needles And Pins
- ☐ '64 Some Day We're Gonna Love Again
- ☐ '65 What Have They Done To The Rain
- ☐ '64 When You Walk In The Room

## SEBASTIAN, John
- ☐ '76 Welcome Back ★

## SECADA, Jon
- ☐ '93 Angel
- ☐ '92 Do You Believe In Us
- ☐ '93 I'm Free
- ☐ '94 If You Go
- ☐ '92 Just Another Day ★
- ☐ '94 Mental Picture

## SECRETS, The
- ☐ '63 Boy Next Door, The

## SEDAKA, Neil
- ☐ '63 Alice In Wonderland
- ☐ '75 Bad Blood
- ☐ '63 Bad Girl
- ☐ '62 Breaking Up Is Hard To Do ★
- ☐ '75 Breaking Up Is Hard To Do [slow version]
- ☐ '60 Calendar Girl
- ☐ '58 Diary, The
- ☐ '61 Happy Birthday, Sweet Sixteen
- ☐ '75 Immigrant, The
- ☐ '74 Laughter In The Rain ★
- ☐ '63 Let's Go Steady Again
- ☐ '61 Little Devil
- ☐ '76 Love In The Shadows
- ☐ '62 Next Door To An Angel
- ☐ '59 Oh! Carol
- ☐ '60 Run Samson Run
- ☐ '80 Should've Never Let You Go
  *NEIL SEDAKA & DARA SEDAKA*
- ☐ '60 Stairway To Heaven
- ☐ '76 Steppin' Out

☐ '75 That's When The Music Takes Me
☐ '60 You Mean Everything To Me

## SEDUCTION
☐ '90 Could This Be Love
☐ '90 Heartbeat
☐ '89 Two To Make It Right ★
☐ '89 You're My One And Only (True Love)

## SEEDS, The
☐ '66 Pushin' Too Hard

## SEEKERS, The
☐ '66 Georgy Girl ★
☐ '65 I'll Never Find Another You
☐ '65 World Of Our Own, A

## SEETHER
☐ '04 Broken
☐ '02 Fine Again

## SEGER, Bob
☐ '80 Against The Wind ★
☐ '86 American Storm
☐ '75 Beautiful Loser
☐ '80 Betty Lou's Gettin' Out Tonight
☐ '83 Even Now
☐ '78 Feel Like A Number
☐ '77 Fire Down Below
☐ '80 Fire Lake
☐ '76 Get Out Of Denver
☐ '80 Her Strut
☐ '78 Hollywood Nights
☐ '80 Horizontal Bop
☐ '75 Katmandu
☐ '86 Like A Rock
☐ '77 Mainstreet
☐ '76 Night Moves ★
☐ '79 Old Time Rock & Roll
☐ '68 Ramblin' Gamblin' Man
☐ '91 Real Love, The
☐ '77 Rock And Roll Never Forgets
☐ '83 Roll Me Away
☐ '87 Shakedown ★
☐ '82 Shame On The Moon ★
☐ '78 Still The Same
☐ '75 Travelin' Man
☐ '81 Tryin' To Live My Life Without You
☐ '76 Turn The Page
☐ '84 Understanding
☐ '78 We've Got Tonite
☐ '80 You'll Accomp'ny Me

## SELENA
☐ '95 Dreaming Of You
☐ '95 I Could Fall In Love ★

## SELF, Ronnie
☐ '58 Bop-A-Lena

## SELLARS, Marilyn
☐ '74 One Day At A Time

## SEMBELLO, Michael
☐ '83 Automatic Man
☐ '83 Maniac ★

## SEMISONIC
☐ '98 Closing Time

## SENATOR BOBBY
☐ '67 Wild Thing

## SENSATIONS, The
☐ '62 Let Me In

## SERENDIPITY SINGERS, The
☐ '64 Beans In My Ears
☐ '64 Don't Let The Rain Come Down
(Crooked Little Man)

## SERMON, Erick
☐ '01 Music
☐ '02 React

## SETZER, Brian, Orchestra
☐ '98 Jump Jive An' Wail

## SEVEN MARY THREE
☐ '95 Cumbersome

## 702
☐ '97 All I Want
☐ '97 Get It Together
☐ '96 Steelo
☐ '99 Where My Girls At? ★

## SEVILLE, David
☐ '58 Bird On My Head, The
☐ '58 Witch Doctor ★

## SEX PISTOLS
☐ '77 Anarchy In The U.K.
☐ '77 God Save The Queen
☐ '77 Pretty Vacant

## SEXTON, Charlie
☐ '85 Beat's So Lonely

## SEYMOUR, Phil
☐ '81 Precious To Me

## SHADES OF BLUE
☐ '66 Oh How Happy

## SHADOWS OF KNIGHT, The
☐ '66 Gloria
☐ '66 Oh Yeah

## SHAGGY
☐ '00 Angel ★
☐ '95 Boombastic ★
☐ '00 It Wasn't Me ★
☐ '95 Summer Time

## SHAI
☐ '93 Baby I'm Yours
☐ '93 Comforter
☐ '92 If I Ever Fall In Love ★
☐ '94 Place Where You Belong, The

## SHAKESPEAR'S SISTER
☐ '92 Stay ★

## SHAKIRA
- ☐ '02 Underneath Your Clothes
- ☐ '01 Whenever, Wherever ★

## SHALAMAR
- ☐ '84 Dancing In The Sheets
- ☐ '83 Dead Giveaway
- ☐ '79 Second Time Around, The
- ☐ '77 Uptown Festival

## SHAMEN, The
- ☐ '91 Move Any Mountain (Progen 91)

## SHANA
- ☐ '89 I Want You

## SHANGRI-LAS, The
- ☐ '64 Give Him A Great Big Kiss
- ☐ '65 Give Us Your Blessings
- ☐ '65 I Can Never Go Home Anymore
- ☐ '64 Leader Of The Pack ★
- ☐ '66 Long Live Our Love
- ☐ '64 Remember (Walkin' in the Sand)

## SHANICE
- ☐ '91 I Love Your Smile ★
- ☐ '92 Saving Forever For You
- ☐ '92 Silent Prayer
  *SHANICE Feat. Johnny Gill*
- ☐ '99 When I Close My Eyes

## SHANNON
- ☐ '83 Let The Music Play

## SHANNON, Del
- ☐ '63 From Me To You
- ☐ '64 Handy Man
- ☐ '61 Hats Off To Larry
- ☐ '61 Hey! Little Girl
- ☐ '64 Keep Searchin' (We'll Follow The Sun)
- ☐ '62 Little Town Flirt
- ☐ '61 Runaway ★
- ☐ '81 Sea Of Love
- ☐ '61 So Long Baby
- ☐ '65 Stranger In Town
- ☐ '62 Swiss Maid, The

## SHARP, Dee Dee
- ☐ '63 Do The Bird
- ☐ '62 Gravy (For My Mashed Potatoes)
- ☐ '62 Mashed Potato Time ★
- ☐ '62 Ride!
- ☐ '62 Slow Twistin'
  *CHUBBY CHECKER (with Dee Dee Sharp)*
- ☐ '63 Wild!

## SHARP, Kevin
- ☐ '96 Nobody Knows

## SHAW, Tommy
- ☐ '84 Girls With Guns

## SHeDAISY
- ☐ '00 I Will...But
- ☐ '99 Little Good-Byes
- ☐ '04 Passenger Seat

## SHEIK, Duncan
- ☐ '96 Barely Breathing

## SHEILA E.
- ☐ '84 Belle Of St. Mark, The
- ☐ '84 Glamorous Life, The
- ☐ '85 Love Bizarre, A

## SHELLS, The
- ☐ '60 Baby Oh Baby

## SHELTON, Blake
- ☐ '01 Austin
- ☐ '02 Baby, The
- ☐ '02 Ol' Red
- ☐ '04 Some Beach

## SHELTON, Ricky Van
- ☐ '91 I Am A Simple Man
- ☐ '88 I'll Leave This World Loving You
- ☐ '90 I've Cried My Last Tear For You
- ☐ '91 Keep It Between The Lines
- ☐ '88 Life Turned Her That Way
- ☐ '91 Rockin' Years
  *DOLLY PARTON & RICKY VAN SHELTON*

## SHE MOVES
- ☐ '97 Breaking All The Rules

## SHENANDOAH
- ☐ '89 Church On Cumberland Road, The
- ☐ '94 If Bubba Can Dance (I Can Too)
- ☐ '90 Next To You, Next To Me

## SHEP & THE LIMELITES
- ☐ '61 Daddy's Home ★

## SHEPARD, Vonda
- ☐ '87 Can't We Try
  *DAN HILL (with Vonda Sheppard)*
- ☐ '98 Searchin' My Soul (Theme from "Ally McBeal")

## SHEPHERD, Kenny Wayne
- ☐ '98 Blue On Black

## SHEPHERD SISTERS
- ☐ '57 Alone (Why Must I Be Alone)

## SHEPPARD, T.G.
- ☐ '75 Devil In The Bottle
- ☐ '81 I Loved 'Em Every One
- ☐ '79 Last Cheater's Waltz
- ☐ '81 Party Time
- ☐ '82 War Is Hell (On The Homefront Too)

## SHERIFF
- ☐ '83 When I'm With You ★

## SHERMAN, Allan
- ☐ '63 Hello Mudduh, Hello Fadduh! ★

## SHERMAN, Bobby
- ☐ '71 Cried Like A Baby
- ☐ '71 Drum, The
- ☐ '70 Easy Come, Easy Go
- ☐ '70 Hey, Mister Sun
- ☐ '70 Julie, Do Ya Love Me

- ☐ '69 La La La (If I Had You)
- ☐ '69 Little Woman

## SHERRYS, The
- ☐ '62 Pop Pop Pop - Pie

## SHIELDS, The
- ☐ '58 You Cheated

## SHINEDOWN
- ☐ '04 Burning Bright
- ☐ '03 45

## SHIRELLES, The
- ☐ '61 Baby It's You
- ☐ '61 Big John
- ☐ '59 Dedicated To The One I Love ★
- ☐ '63 Don't Say Goodnight And Mean Goodbye
- ☐ '62 Everybody Loves A Lover
- ☐ '63 Foolish Little Girl
- ☐ '58 I Met Him On A Sunday
- ☐ '61 Mama Said
- ☐ '62 Soldier Boy ★
- ☐ '62 Stop The Music
- ☐ '60 Tonights The Night
- ☐ '62 Welcome Home Baby
- ☐ '60 Will You Love Me Tomorrow ★

## SHIRLEY, Don, Trio
- ☐ '61 Water Boy

## SHIRLEY (& COMPANY)
- ☐ '75 Shame, Shame, Shame

## SHIRLEY & LEE
- ☐ '55 Feel So Good
- ☐ '56 I Feel Good
- ☐ '56 Let The Good Times Roll

## SHOCKING BLUE, The
- ☐ '69 Venus ★

## SHONDELL, Troy
- ☐ '61 This Time

## SHORE, Dinah
- ☐ '57 Chantez-Chantez
- ☐ '57 Fascination
- ☐ '55 Love And Marriage
- ☐ '55 Whatever Lola Wants (Lola Gets)

## SHOWMEN, The
- ☐ '61 It Will Stand

## SIBERRY, Jane
- ☐ '93 Calling All Angels
  *JANE SIBERRY with k.d. lang*
- ☐ '89 Everything Reminds Me Of My Dog

## SIGLER, Bunny
- ☐ '67 Let The Good Times Roll & Feel So Good

## SILHOUETTES, The
- ☐ '58 Get A Job ★

## SILK
- ☐ '93 Freak Me

- ☐ '93 Girl U For Me
- ☐ '99 If You (Lovin' Me)

## SILKIE, The
- ☐ '65 You've Got To Hide Your Love Away

## SILKK THE SHOCKER
- ☐ '99 It Ain't My Fault 2
  *SILKK THE SHOCKER & MYSTIKAL*

## SILVER
- ☐ '76 Wham Bam (Shang-A-Lang)

## SILVERCHAIR
- ☐ '95 Tomorrow

## SILVER CONDOR
- ☐ '81 You Could Take My Heart Away

## SILVER CONVENTION
- ☐ '75 Fly, Robin, Fly ★
- ☐ '76 Get Up And Boogie (That's Right)

## SIMEONE, Harry, Chorale
- ☐ '58 Little Drummer Boy, The

## SIMMONS, Gene
- ☐ '64 Haunted House

## SIMMONS, Patrick
- ☐ '83 So Wrong

## SIMON, Carly
- ☐ '71 Anticipation
- ☐ '75 Attitude Dancing
- ☐ '86 Coming Around Again
- ☐ '78 Devoted To You
  *CARLY SIMON & JAMES TAYLOR*
- ☐ '74 Haven't Got Time For The Pain
- ☐ '80 Jesse
- ☐ '74 Mockingbird
  *CARLY SIMON & JAMES TAYLOR*
- ☐ '77 Nobody Does It Better ★
- ☐ '73 Right Thing To Do, The
- ☐ '71 That's The Way I've Always Heard It Should Be
- ☐ '78 You Belong To Me
- ☐ '72 You're So Vain ★

## SIMON, Joe
- ☐ '69 Chokin' Kind, The
- ☐ '71 Drowning In The Sea Of Love
- ☐ '75 Get Down, Get Down (Get On The Floor)
- ☐ '72 Power Of Love
- ☐ '73 Step By Step
- ☐ '73 Theme From Cleopatra Jones
- ☐ '68 (You Keep Me) Hangin' On
- ☐ '70 Your Time To Cry

## SIMON, Paul
- ☐ '73 American Tune
- ☐ '75 50 Ways To Leave Your Lover ★
- ☐ '75 Gone At Last
  *PAUL SIMON/PHOEBE SNOW*
- ☐ '87 Graceland ★
- ☐ '73 Kodachrome ★
- ☐ '80 Late In The Evening

## SIMON, Paul — cont'd

- ☐ '73  Loves Me Like A Rock
  *PAUL SIMON (with The Dixie Hummingbirds)*
- ☐ '72  Me And Julio Down By The Schoolyard
- ☐ '72  Mother And Child Reunion
- ☐ '80  One-Trick Pony
- ☐ '77  Slip Slidin' Away
- ☐ '76  Still Crazy After All These Years
- ☐ '78  (What A) Wonderful World
  *ART GARFUNKEL with JAMES TAYLOR & PAUL SIMON*
- ☐ '86  You Can Call Me Al

## SIMON & GARFUNKEL

- ☐ '68  America
- ☐ '67  At The Zoo
- ☐ '69  Boxer, The
- ☐ '70  Bridge Over Troubled Water ★
- ☐ '70  Cecilia
- ☐ '66  Dangling Conversation, The
- ☐ '70  El Condor Pasa
- ☐ '67  Fakin' It
- ☐ '66  Hazy Shade Of Winter, A
- ☐ '66  Homeward Bound
- ☐ '66  I Am A Rock
- ☐ '68  Mrs. Robinson ★
- ☐ '75  My Little Town
- ☐ '68  Scarborough Fair
- ☐ '65  Sounds Of Silence, The ★
- ☐ '82  Wake Up Little Susie

## SIMONE, Nina

- ☐ '59  I Loves You, Porgy

## SIMPLE MINDS

- ☐ '85  Alive & Kicking
- ☐ '86  All The Things She Said
- ☐ '85  Don't You (Forget About Me) ★
- ☐ '85  Sanctify Yourself
- ☐ '91  See The Lights

## SIMPLE PLAN

- ☐ '03  Perfect
- ☐ '04  Welcome To My Life

## SIMPLY RED

- ☐ '86  Holding Back The Years ★
- ☐ '89  If You Don't Know Me By Now ★
- ☐ '86  Money$ Too Tight (To Mention)
- ☐ '87  Right Thing, The
- ☐ '91  Something Got Me Started

## SIMPSON, Ashlee

- ☐ '04  Pieces Of Me ★

## SIMPSON, Jessica

- ☐ '00  I Think I'm In Love With You
- ☐ '99  I Wanna Love You Forever ★
- ☐ '01  Irresistible
- ☐ '04  Take My Breath Away
- ☐ '03  With You

## SIMPSONS, The

- ☐ '90  Do The Bartman

## SINATRA, Frank

- ☐ '57  All The Way ★
- ☐ '64  Best Is Yet To Come, The
- ☐ '57  Chicago
- ☐ '57  Can I Steal A Little Love
- ☐ '58  Come Fly With Me
- ☐ '68  Cycles
- ☐ '64  Fly Me To The Moon
- ☐ '56  Hey! Jealous Lover ★
- ☐ '59  High Hopes
- ☐ '56  (How Little It Matters) How Little We Know
- ☐ '75  I Believe I'm Gonna Love You
- ☐ '62  I Get A Kick Out Of You
- ☐ '56  I've Got The World On A String
- ☐ '56  I've Got You Under My Skin
- ☐ '65  It Was A Very Good Year
- ☐ '55  Learnin' The Blues ★
- ☐ '55  Love And Marriage ★
- ☐ '55  (Love Is) The Tender Trap
- ☐ '65  My Kind Of Town
- ☐ '69  My Way
- ☐ '60  Nice 'N' Easy
- ☐ '61  Pocketful Of Miracles
- ☐ '58  Put Your Dreams Away
- ☐ '68  Rain In My Heart
- ☐ '55  Same Old Saturday Night
- ☐ '61  Second Time Around, The
- ☐ '64  Softly, As I Leave You
- ☐ '67  Somethin' Stupid ★
  *NANCY SINATRA & FRANK SINATRA*
- ☐ '64  Somewhere In Your Heart
- ☐ '66  Strangers In The Night ★
- ☐ '66  Summer Wind
- ☐ '59  Talk To Me
- ☐ '66  That's Life
- ☐ '80  Theme From New York, New York ★
- ☐ '58  Witchcraft
- ☐ '67  World We Knew (Over And Over)
- ☐ '56  You Make Me Feel So Young

## SINATRA, Nancy

- ☐ '66  Friday's Child
- ☐ '66  How Does That Grab You, Darlin'?
- ☐ '67  Jackson
  *NANCY SINATRA & LEE HAZLEWOOD*
- ☐ '67  Lady Bird
  *NANCY SINATRA & LEE HAZLEWOOD*
- ☐ '67  Lightning's Girl
- ☐ '67  Love Eyes
- ☐ '68  Some Velvet Morning
  *NANCY SINATRA & LEE HAZLEWOOD*
- ☐ '67  Somethin' Stupid ★
  *NANCY SINATRA & FRANK SINATRA*
- ☐ '66  Sugar Town
- ☐ '69  Summer Wine
  *NANCY SINATRA with Lee Hazlewood*
- ☐ '66  These Boots Are Made For Walkin' ★
- ☐ '67  You Only Live Twice

## SINCLAIR, Gordon

- ☐ '74  Americans (A Canadian's Opinion)

## SINGING DOGS, The

- ☐ '55  Oh! Susanna
- ☐ '55  Jingle Bells

## SINGING NUN, The

- ☐ '63  Dominique ★

## SIOUXSIE & THE BANSHEES
- ☐ '91 Kiss Them For Me
- ☐ '88 Peek-A-Boo

## SIR DOUGLAS QUINTET
- ☐ '69 Mendocino
- ☐ '66 Rains Came, The
- ☐ '65 She's About A Mover

## SIR MIX-A-LOT
- ☐ '92 Baby Got Back ★

## SISQÓ
- ☐ '99 Got To Get It
- ☐ '00 Incomplete ★
- ☐ '98 It's All About Me
  - *MYA With Sisqo*
- ☐ '00 Thong Song ★

## SISTER HAZEL
- ☐ '97 All For You

## SISTER SLEDGE
- ☐ '81 All American Girls
- ☐ '79 He's The Greatest Dancer
- ☐ '82 My Guy
- ☐ '79 We Are Family ★

## SIXPENCE NONE THE RICHER
- ☐ '02 Breathe Your Name
- ☐ '98 Kiss Me ★
- ☐ '99 There She Goes

## SIX TEENS, The
- ☐ '56 Casual Look, A

## 69 BOYZ
- ☐ '94 Tootsee Roll
- ☐ '98 Woof Woof

## SKEE-LO
- ☐ '95 I Wish

## SKID ROW
- ☐ '89 18 And Life
- ☐ '89 I Remember You

## SKIP & FLIP
- ☐ '60 Cherry Pie
- ☐ '59 It Was I

## SKYLARK
- ☐ '73 Wildflower

## SKYLINERS, The
- ☐ '60 Pennies From Heaven
- ☐ '59 Since I Don't Have You
- ☐ '59 This I Swear

## SKYY
- ☐ '82 Call Me
- ☐ '89 Real Love
- ☐ '89 Start Of A Romance

## SLADE
- ☐ '73 Cum On Feel The Noize
- ☐ '72 Mama Weer All Crazee Now
- ☐ '84 My Oh My
- ☐ '84 Run Runaway

## SLAUGHTER
- ☐ '90 Fly To The Angels
- ☐ '90 Spend My Life
- ☐ '90 Up All Night

## SLAVE
- ☐ '77 Slide

## SLEDGE, Percy
- ☐ '66 It Tears Me Up
- ☐ '67 Love Me Tender
- ☐ '68 Take Time To Know Her
- ☐ '66 Warm And Tender Love
- ☐ '66 When A Man Loves A Woman ★

## SLY & THE FAMILY STONE
- ☐ '68 Dance To The Music ★
- ☐ '68 Everyday People ★
- ☐ '71 Family Affair ★
- ☐ '69 Hot Fun In The Summertime ★
- ☐ '69 I Want To Take You Higher
- ☐ '73 If You Want Me To Stay
- ☐ '72 Runnin' Away
- ☐ '69 Stand!
- ☐ '70 Thank You (Falettinme Be Mice Elf Agin) ★
- ☐ '74 Time For Livin'

## SLY FOX
- ☐ '85 Let's Go All The Way

## SMALL, Millie
- ☐ '64 My Boy Lollipop ★

## SMALL FACES
- ☐ '67 Itchycoo Park

## SMASHING PUMPKINS, The
- ☐ '98 Ava Adore
- ☐ '95 Bullet With Butterfly Wings
- ☐ '94 Landslide
- ☐ '95 1979
- ☐ '98 Perfect
- ☐ '00 Stand Inside Your Love
- ☐ '96 Thirty-Three
- ☐ '93 Today
- ☐ '96 Tonight, Tonight

## SMASH MOUTH
- ☐ '99 All Star ★
- ☐ '98 Can't Get Enough Of You Baby
- ☐ '01 I'm A Believer
- ☐ '99 Then The Morning Comes
- ☐ '97 Walkin' On The Sun ★

## SMITH
- ☐ '69 Baby It's You

## SMITH, Connie
- ☐ '64 Once A Day

## SMITH, Frankie
- ☐ '81 Double Dutch Bus

## SMITH, Huey (Piano)
- ☐ '58 Don't You Just Know It
- ☐ '57 Rocking Pneumonia And The Boogie Woogie Flu

## SMITH, Hurricane
- ☐ '72 Oh, Babe, What Would You Say?

## SMITH, Jimmy
- ☐ '66 Got My Mojo Working
- ☐ '62 Walk On The Wild Side

## SMITH, Michael W.
- ☐ '03 Above All
- ☐ '92 Friends
- ☐ '92 I Will Be Here For You
- ☐ '04 Lord Have Mercy
- ☐ '98 Love Me Good
- ☐ '91 Place In This World
- ☐ '99 This Is Your Time

## SMITH, O.C.
- ☐ '69 Daddy's Little Man
- ☐ '68 Little Green Apples
- ☐ '68 Son Of Hickory Holler's Tramp, The

## SMITH, Patti, Group
- ☐ '78 Because The Night
- ☐ '79 Dancing Barefoot
- ☐ '75 Gloria
- ☐ '88 People Have The Power

## SMITH, Ray
- ☐ '60 Rockin' Little Angel

## SMITH, Rex
- ☐ '81 Everlasting Love
  - *REX SMITH/RACHEL SWEET*
- ☐ '79 You Take My Breath Away

## SMITH, Sammi
- ☐ '71 Help Me Make It Through The Night

## SMITH, Somethin', & The Redheads
- ☐ '56 In A Shanty In Old Shanty Town
- ☐ '55 It's A Sin To Tell A Lie

## SMITH, Verdelle
- ☐ '66 Tar And Cement

## SMITH, Whistling Jack
- ☐ '67 I Was Kaiser Bill's Batman

## SMITH, Will
- ☐ '98 Gettin' Jiggy Wit It ★
- ☐ '98 Just The Two Of Us
- ☐ '97 Men In Black ★
- ☐ '98 Miami
- ☐ '05 Switch ★
- ☐ '99 Wild Wild West ★
- ☐ '99 Will 2K

## SMITHEREENS, The
- ☐ '87 Behind The Wall Of Sleep
- ☐ '89 Girl Like You, A
- ☐ '88 House We Used To Live In
- ☐ '88 Only A Memory
- ☐ '92 Too Much Passion

- ☐ '91 Top Of The Pops

## SMITHS, The
- ☐ '85 How Soon Is Now?
- ☐ '84 William, It Was Really Nothing

## SMOKIE
- ☐ '76 Living Next Door To Alice

## SMYTH, Patty — see SCANDAL

## SNAP!
- ☐ '90 Ooops Up
- ☐ '90 Power, The ★
- ☐ '92 Rhythm Is A Dancer ★

## SNEAKER
- ☐ '81 More Than Just The Two Of Us

## SNIFF 'N' THE TEARS
- ☐ '79 Driver's Seat

## SNOOP DOGG
- ☐ '03 Beautiful
- ☐ '93 Dre Day
  - *DR. DRE/SNOOP DOGGY DOGG*
- ☐ '04 Drop It Like It's Hot ★
- ☐ '94 Gin & Juice
- ☐ '93 Next Episode, The
- ☐ '93 Nuthin' But A "G" Thang ★
  - *DR. DRE/SNOOP DOGGY DOGG (above 2)*
- ☐ '98 Still A G Thang
- ☐ '93 What's My Name?

## SNOW
- ☐ '93 Girl, I've Been Hurt
- ☐ '93 Informer ★

## SNOW, Hank
- ☐ '62 I've Been Everywhere

## SNOW, Phoebe
- ☐ '75 Gone At Last
  - *PAUL SIMON/PHOEBE SNOW*
- ☐ '75 Poetry Man

## SOFT CELL
- ☐ '82 Tainted Love ★

## SOHO
- ☐ '90 Hippychick ★

## SOLÉ
- ☐ '99 4,5,6

## SOMETHIN' FOR THE PEOPLE
- ☐ '97 My Love Is The Shhh! ★

## SOMMERS, Joanie
- ☐ '62 Johnny Get Angry

## SON BY FOUR
- ☐ '00 Purest Of Pain (A Puro Dolor)

## SONIQUE
- ☐ '00 It Feels So Good

## SONNY & CHER
- ☐ '71 All I Ever Need Is You
- ☐ '65 Baby Don't Go

☐ '67 Beat Goes On, The
☐ '65 But You're Mine
☐ '72 Cowboys Work Is Never Done, A
☐ '65 I Got You Babe ★
☐ '65 Just You
☐ '65 Laugh At Me
    *SONNY*
☐ '66 Little Man
☐ '66 What Now My Love
☐ '72 When You Say Love

## SOPWITH "CAMEL", The
☐ '66 Hello Hello

## S.O.S. BAND, The
☐ '86 Finest, The
☐ '83 Just Be Good To Me
☐ '80 Take Your Time (Do It Right) ★

## SOUL, David
☐ '77 Don't Give Up On Us

## SOUL, Jimmy
☐ '63 If You Wanna Be Happy ★
☐ '62 Twistin' Matilda

## SOUL ASYLUM
☐ '95 Misery
☐ '93 Runaway Train ★
☐ '92 Somebody To Shove

## SOUL CHILDREN, The
☐ '74 I'll Be The Other Woman

## SOULDECISION
☐ '00 Faded

## SOUL FOR REAL
☐ '95 Candy Rain ★
☐ '95 Every Little Thing I Do

## SOUL SURVIVORS
☐ '67 Explosion In Your Soul
☐ '67 Expressway To Your Heart

## S.O.U.L. S.Y.S.T.E.M., The
☐ '92 It's Gonna Be A Lovely Day

## SOUL II SOUL
☐ '89 Back To Life ★
☐ '89 Keep On Movin'

## SOUNDGARDEN
☐ '94 Black Hole Sun
☐ '96 Blow Up The Outside World
☐ '96 Burden In My Hand
☐ '94 Fell On Black Days
☐ '96 Pretty Noose
☐ '94 Spoonman

## SOUNDS OF BLACKNESS
☐ '94 I Believe
☐ '91 Optimistic

## SOUNDS OF SUNSHINE
☐ '71 Love Means (You Never Have To Say You're Sorry)

## SOUNDS ORCHESTRAL
☐ '65 Cast Your Fate To The Wind

## SOUP DRAGONS, The
☐ '92 Divine Thing
☐ '90 I'm Free

## SOUTH, Joe
☐ '69 Don't It Make You Want To Go Home
☐ '69 Games People Play
☐ '70 Walk A Mile In My Shoes

## SOUTHER, J.D.
☐ '74 Fallin' In Love
    *SOUTHER, HILLMAN, FURAY BAND*
☐ '81 Her Town Too
    *JAMES TAYLOR & J.D. SOUTHER*
☐ '79 You're Only Lonely

## SOVINE, Red
☐ '65 Giddyup Go
☐ '76 Teddy Bear

## SPACEHOG
☐ '95 In The Meantime

## SPACEMEN, The
☐ '59 Clouds, The

## SPANDAU BALLET
☐ '83 Gold
☐ '84 Only When You Leave
☐ '83 True ★

## SPANIELS, The
☐ '54 Goodnite Sweetheart, Goodnite

## SPANKY & OUR GANG
☐ '67 Lazy Day
☐ '68 Like To Get To Know You
☐ '67 Making Every Minute Count
☐ '68 Sunday Mornin'
☐ '67 Sunday Will Never Be The Same

## SPARKLE
☐ '98 Be Careful

## SPARXXX, Bubba
☐ '01 Ugly

## SPEARS, Britney
☐ '98 ...Baby One More Time ★
☐ '04 Everytime
☐ '00 From The Bottom Of My Broken Heart
☐ '01 I'm A Slave 4 U
☐ '00 Lucky
☐ '03 Me Against The Music
☐ '00 Oops!...I Did It Again
☐ '99 Sometimes
☐ '00 Stronger
☐ '04 Toxic ★
☐ '99 (You Drive Me) Crazy

## SPENCE, Judson
☐ '88 Yeah, Yeah, Yeah

## SPENCER, Tracie
- ☐ '99 It's All About You (Not About Me)
- ☐ '92 Love Me
- ☐ '88 Symptoms Of True Love
- ☐ '91 Tender Kisses
- ☐ '90 This House

## SPICE GIRLS
- ☐ '98 Goodbye
- ☐ '97 Say You'll Be There
- ☐ '97 Spice Up Your Life
- ☐ '98 Stop
- ☐ '98 Too Much
- ☐ '97 2 Become 1 ★
- ☐ '97 Wannabe ★

## SPIDER
- ☐ '80 New Romance (It's A Mystery)

## SPIN DOCTORS
- ☐ '92 Little Miss Can't Be Wrong
- ☐ '93 Two Princes

## SPINNERS
- ☐ '72 Could It Be I'm Falling In Love
- ☐ '80 Cupid/I've Loved You For A Long Time
- ☐ '73 Ghetto Child
- ☐ '65 I'll Always Love You
- ☐ '72 I'll Be Around
- ☐ '74 I'm Coming Home
- ☐ '70 It's A Shame
- ☐ '75 Living A Little, Laughing A Little
- ☐ '74 Love Don't Love Nobody
- ☐ '75 Love Or Leave
- ☐ '74 Mighty Love
- ☐ '73 One Of A Kind (Love Affair)
- ☐ '76 Rubberband Man, The ★
- ☐ '61 That's What Girls Are Made For
- ☐ '74 Then Came You ★
  *DIONNE WARWICK & SPINNERS*
- ☐ '75 "They Just Can't Stop It" the (Games People Play)
- ☐ '79 Working My Way Back To You/Forgive Me, Girl

## SPIRAL STARECASE
- ☐ '69 More Today Than Yesterday

## SPIRIT
- ☐ '69 I Got A Line On You
- ☐ '71 Nature's Way

## SPLIT ENZ
- ☐ '80 I Got You
- ☐ '82 Six Months In A Leaky Boat

## SPOKESMEN, The
- ☐ '65 Dawn Of Correction, The

## SPONGE
- ☐ '95 Molly (Sixteen Candles)

## SPORTY THIEVZ
- ☐ '99 No Pigeons

## SPRINGFIELD, Dusty
- ☐ '66 All I See Is You
- ☐ '69 Brand New Me, A
- ☐ '64 I Only Want To Be With You
- ☐ '67 I'll Try Anything
- ☐ '67 Look Of Love, The
- ☐ '62 Silver Threads And Golden Needles
- ☐ '68 Son-Of-A Preacher Man
- ☐ '64 Stay Awhile
- ☐ '87 What Have I Done To Deserve This? ★
  *PET SHOP BOYS (& Dusty Springfield)*
- ☐ '69 Windmills Of Your Mind, The
- ☐ '64 Wishin' And Hopin'
- ☐ '66 You Don't Have To Say You Love Me

## SPRINGFIELD, Rick
- ☐ '83 Affair Of The Heart
- ☐ '84 Bop 'Til You Drop
- ☐ '84 Bruce
- ☐ '85 Celebrate Youth
- ☐ '82 Don't Talk To Strangers ★
- ☐ '84 Don't Walk Away
- ☐ '83 Human Touch
- ☐ '82 I Get Excited
- ☐ '81 I've Done Everything For You
- ☐ '81 Jessie's Girl ★
- ☐ '81 Love Is Alright Tonite
- ☐ '84 Love Somebody
- ☐ '88 Rock Of Life
- ☐ '83 Souls
- ☐ '72 Speak To The Sky
- ☐ '85 State Of The Heart
- ☐ '82 What Kind Of Fool Am I

## SPRINGSTEEN, Bruce
- ☐ '78 Badlands
- ☐ '92 Better Days
- ☐ '73 Blinded By The Light
- ☐ '84 Born In The U.S.A. ★
- ☐ '75 Born To Run ★
- ☐ '87 Brilliant Disguise
- ☐ '81 Cadillac Ranch
- ☐ '84 Cover Me
- ☐ '84 Dancing In The Dark ★
- ☐ '78 Darkness On The Edge Of Town
- ☐ '81 Fade Away
- ☐ '73 For You
- ☐ '73 4th Of July, Asbury Park (Sandy)
- ☐ '85 Glory Days
- ☐ '92 Human Touch
- ☐ '80 Hungry Heart ★
- ☐ '85 I'm Goin' Down
- ☐ '85 I'm On Fire
- ☐ '75 Jungleland
- ☐ '85 My Hometown ★
- ☐ '87 One Step Up
- ☐ '84 Pink Cadillac
- ☐ '78 Promised Land
- ☐ '78 Prove It All Night
- ☐ '02 Rising, The
- ☐ '73 Rosalita (Come Out Tonight)
- ☐ '75 Santa Claus Is Comin' To Town
- ☐ '95 Secret Garden
- ☐ '73 Spirit In The Night
- ☐ '94 Streets Of Philadelphia ★
- ☐ '75 Tenth Avenue Freeze-Out
- ☐ '75 Thunder Road ★

'85 Trapped
'87 Tunnel Of Love
'86 War

## SPYRO GYRA
'79 Morning Dance

## SQUEEZE
'82 Black Coffee In Bed
'87 853-5937
'87 Hourglass
'81 Tempted

## SQUIER, Billy
'82 Everybody Wants You
'81 In The Dark
'84 Rock Me Tonite
'81 Stroke, The

## SR-71
'00 Right Now

## STACEY Q
'86 Two Of Hearts
'86 We Connect

## STAFFORD, Jim
'75 I Got Stoned And I Missed It
'74 My Girl Bill
'73 Spiders & Snakes
'73 Swamp Witch
'74 Wildwood Weed
'74 Your Bulldog Drinks Champagne

## STAFFORD, Jo
'55 It's Almost Tomorrow
'56 On London Bridge
'55 Suddenly There's A Valley
'55 Teach Me Tonight
'57 Wind In The Willow

## STAFFORD, Terry
'64 I'll Touch A Star
'64 Suspicion ★

## STAIND
'01 Fade
'01 For You
'01 It's Been Awhile ★
'03 Price To Play
'03 So Far Away

## STALLION
'77 Old Fashioned Boy (You're The One)

## STALLONE, Frank
'83 Far From Over

## STAMPEDERS
'76 Hit The Road Jack
'71 Sweet City Woman

## STAMPLEY, Joe
'73 Soul Song

## STANDELLS, The
'66 Dirty Water

## STANLEY, Michael, Band
'80 He Can't Love You
'83 My Town

## STANSFIELD, Lisa
'90 All Around The World
'92 All Woman
'91 Change
'90 This Is The Right Time
'90 You Can't Deny It

## STAPLE SINGERS, The
'71 Heavy Makes You Happy
(Sha-Na-Boom Boom)
'72 I'll Take You There ★
'73 If You're Ready (Come Go With Me)
'75 Let's Do It Again ★
'73 Oh La De Da
'71 Respect Yourself
'72 This World
'74 Touch A Hand, Make A Friend

## STAPLETON, Cyril, & His Orchestra
'59 Children's Marching Song, The
'56 Italian Theme, The

## STARBUCK
'77 Everybody Be Dancin'
'76 Moonlight Feels Right

## STARCHER, Buddy
'66 History Repeats Itself

## STARGARD
'78 Theme Song From "Which Way Is Up"

## STARLAND VOCAL BAND
'76 Afternoon Delight ★

## STARLETS, The
'61 Better Tell Him No

## STARPOINT
'85 Object Of My Desire

## STARR, Brenda K.
'88 I Still Believe
'88 What You See Is What You Get

## STARR, Edwin
'65 Agent Double-O-Soul
'70 Stop The War Now
'69 Twenty-Five Miles
'70 War ★

## STARR, Kay
'57 My Heart Reminds Me
'55 Rock And Roll Waltz ★
'56 Second Fiddle

## STARR, Randy
'57 After School

## STARR, Ringo
'72 Back Off Boogaloo
'76 Dose Of Rock 'N' Roll, A
'71 Early 1970
'71 It Don't Come Easy

## STARR, Ringo — cont'd
- ☐ '75 It's All Down To Goodnight Vienna
- ☐ '75 No No Song
- ☐ '74 Oh My My
- ☐ '74 Only You
- ☐ '73 Photograph ★
- ☐ '81 Wrack My Brain
- ☐ '73 You're Sixteen ★

## STARS on 45
- ☐ '81 Medley

## STARSHIP — see JEFFERSON AIRPLANE

## STARZ
- ☐ '77 Cherry Baby

## STATLER BROTHERS, The
- ☐ '71 Bed Of Roses
- ☐ '78 Do You Know You Are My Sunshine
- ☐ '72 Do You Remember These
- ☐ '65 Flowers On The Wall

## STATON, Candi
- ☐ '70 Stand By Your Man
- ☐ '76 Young Hearts Run Free

## STATUS QUO, The
- ☐ '68 Pictures Of Matchstick Men

## STEALERS WHEEL
- ☐ '74 Star
- ☐ '73 Stuck In The Middle With You

## STEAM
- ☐ '69 Na Na Hey Hey Kiss Him Goodbye ★

## STEEL BREEZE
- ☐ '83 Dreamin' Is Easy
- ☐ '82 You Don't Want Me Anymore

## STEELHEART
- ☐ '91 I'll Never Let You Go (Angel Eyes) ★

## STEELY DAN
- ☐ '77 Aja
- ☐ '74 Any Major Dude Will Tell You
- ☐ '80 Babylon Sisters
- ☐ '77 Black Cow
- ☐ '75 Black Friday
- ☐ '73 Bodhisattva
- ☐ '00 Cousin Dupree
- ☐ '78 Deacon Blues
- ☐ '72 Dirty Work
- ☐ '72 Do It Again
- ☐ '78 FM (No Static At All)
- ☐ '76 Fez, The
- ☐ '80 Hey Nineteen
- ☐ '78 Josie
- ☐ '76 Kid Charlemagne
- ☐ '73 My Old School
- ☐ '77 Peg
- ☐ '74 Pretzel Logic
- ☐ '73 Reeling In The Years
- ☐ '74 Rikki Don't Lose That Number
- ☐ '81 Time Out Of Mind

## STEFANI, Gwen
- ☐ '05 Hollaback Girl ★
- ☐ '05 Rich Girl ★

## STEINER, Tommy Shane
- ☐ '01 What If She's An Angel

## STEINMAN, Jim
- ☐ '81 Rock And Roll Dreams Come Through

## STEPHENSON, Van
- ☐ '84 Modern Day Delilah

## STEPPENWOLF
- ☐ '68 Born To Be Wild ★
- ☐ '70 Hey Lawdy Mama
- ☐ '68 Magic Carpet Ride
- ☐ '69 Monster
- ☐ '69 Move Over
- ☐ '68 Pusher, The
- ☐ '69 Rock Me
- ☐ '74 Straight Shootin' Woman

## STEREO MC'S
- ☐ '93 Connected
- ☐ '91 Elevate My Mind

## STEREOS, The
- ☐ '61 I Really Love You

## STEVENS, Cat
- ☐ '74 Another Saturday Night
- ☐ '73 Hurt, The
- ☐ '71 Moon Shadow
- ☐ '72 Morning Has Broken ★
- ☐ '74 Oh Very Young
- ☐ '71 Peace Train
- ☐ '74 Ready
- ☐ '77 (Remember The Days Of The) Old Schoolyard
- ☐ '72 Sitting
- ☐ '75 Two Fine People
- ☐ '71 Wild World

## STEVENS, Connie
- ☐ '59 Kookie, Kookie (Lend Me Your Comb)
  *EDWARD BYRNES & CONNIE STEVENS*
- ☐ '60 Sixteen Reasons

## STEVENS, Dodie
- ☐ '59 Pink Shoe Laces ★

## STEVENS, Ray
- ☐ '62 Ahab, The Arab
- ☐ '69 Along Came Jones
- ☐ '70 Everything Is Beautiful ★
- ☐ '69 Gitarzan
- ☐ '63 Harry The Hairy Ape
- ☐ '77 In The Mood
- ☐ '61 Jeremiah Peabody's Poly Unsaturated Quick Dissolving Fast Acting Pleasant Tasting Green And Purple Pills
- ☐ '75 Misty
- ☐ '68 Mr. Businessman
- ☐ '74 Streak, The ★

## STEVENSON, B.W.
- ☐ '73 My Maria

## STEVIE B
- ☐ '90 Because I Love You (The Postman Song) ★
- ☐ '95 Dream About You
- ☐ '89 I Wanna Be The One
- ☐ '91 I'll Be By Your Side
- ☐ '89 In My Eyes
- ☐ '90 Love & Emotion
- ☐ '90 Love Me For Life

## STEWART, Al
- ☐ '80 Midnight Rocks
- ☐ '77 On The Border
- ☐ '79 Song On The Radio
- ☐ '78 Time Passages
- ☐ '76 Year Of The Cat

## STEWART, Amii
- ☐ '79 Knock On Wood ★

## STEWART, Billy
- ☐ '65 I Do Love You
- ☐ '66 Secret Love
- ☐ '65 Sitting In The Park
- ☐ '66 Summertime

## STEWART, David A.
- ☐ '91 Lily Was Here

## STEWART, Jermaine
- ☐ '88 Say It Again
- ☐ '86 We Don't Have To Take Our Clothes Off

## STEWART, John
- ☐ '79 Gold
- ☐ '79 Lost Her In The Sun
- ☐ '79 Midnight Wind

## STEWART, Rod
- ☐ '79 Ain't Love A Bitch
- ☐ '93 All For Love ★
  *BRYAN ADAMS  ROD STEWART  STING*
- ☐ '72 Angel
- ☐ '04 Baby, It's Cold Outside
- ☐ '83 Baby Jane
- ☐ '91 Broken Arrow
- ☐ '89 Crazy About Her
- ☐ '70 Cut Across Shorty
- ☐ '78 Da Ya Think I'm Sexy? ★
- ☐ '89 Downtown Train ★
- ☐ '71 Every Picture Tells A Story
- ☐ '77 First Cut Is The Deepest, The
- ☐ '88 Forever Young
- ☐ '69 Handbags And Gladrags
- ☐ '93 Have I Told You Lately [live] ★
- ☐ '94 Having A Party
  *ROD STEWART With Ronnie Wood*
- ☐ '78 Hot Legs
- ☐ '71 (I Know) I'm Losing You
  *ROD STEWART With Faces*
- ☐ '78 I Was Only Joking
- ☐ '84 Infatuation

- ☐ '77 Killing Of Georgie, The
- ☐ '88 Lost In You
- ☐ '86 Love Touch
- ☐ '71 Maggie May ★
- ☐ '74 Mine For Me
- ☐ '91 Motown Song, The
  *ROD STEWART (with The Temptations)*
- ☐ '88 My Heart Can't Tell You No
- ☐ '80 Passion
- ☐ '71 Reason To Believe
- ☐ '93 Reason To Believe [live]
  *ROD STEWART (with Ronnie Wood)*
- ☐ '91 Rhythm Of My Heart ★
- ☐ '75 Sailing
- ☐ '96 So Far Away
- ☐ '84 Some Guys Have All The Luck
- ☐ '90 This Old Heart Of Mine (1989 Version)
  *ROD STEWART (with Ronald Isley)*
- ☐ '82 Tonight I'm Yours (Don't Hurt Me)
- ☐ '76 Tonight's The Night (Gonna Be Alright) ★
- ☐ '83 What Am I Gonna Do (I'm So In Love With You)
- ☐ '72 You Wear It Well
- ☐ '77 You're In My Heart (The Final Acclaim) ★
- ☐ '81 Young Turks ★

## STEWART, Sandy
- ☐ '62 My Coloring Book

## STIGERS, Curtis
- ☐ '91 I Wonder Why

## STILLS, Stephen
- ☐ '71 Change Partners
- ☐ '70 Love The One You're With
- ☐ '71 Sit Yourself Down

## STING
- ☐ '93 All For Love ★
  *BRYAN ADAMS  ROD STEWART  STING*
- ☐ '91 All This Time
- ☐ '88 Be Still My Beating Heart
- ☐ '00 Desert Rose
- ☐ '93 Fields Of Gold ★
- ☐ '85 Fortress Around Your Heart
- ☐ '96 I'm So Happy I Can't Stop Crying
- ☐ '93 If I Ever Lose My Faith In You
- ☐ '85 If You Love Somebody Set Them Free ★
- ☐ '85 Love Is The Seventh Wave
- ☐ '86 Russians
- ☐ '87 We'll Be Together
- ☐ '94 When We Dance

## STITES, Gary
- ☐ '59 Lonely For You

## STOLOFF, Morris
- ☐ '56 Moonglow and Theme From "Picnic" ★

## STONE, Cliffie, & His Orchestra
- ☐ '55 Popcorn Song, The

## STONE, Doug
- ☐ '93 I Never Knew Love
- ☐ '91 In A Different Light
- ☐ '91 Jukebox With A Country Song, A
- ☐ '92 Too Busy Being In Love
- ☐ '93 Why Didn't I Think Of That

## STONE, Joss
- ☐ '05 Cry Baby/Piece Of My Heart

## STONE, Kirby, Four
- ☐ '58 Baubles, Bangles And Beads

## STONEBOLT
- ☐ '78 I Will Still Love You

## STONE ROSES, The
- ☐ '94 Love Spreads

## STONE SOUR
- ☐ '02 Bother

## STONE TEMPLE PILOTS
- ☐ '96 Big Bang Baby
- ☐ '94 Big Empty
- ☐ '93 Creep
- ☐ '95 Dancing Days
- ☐ '94 Interstate Love Song
- ☐ '96 Lady Picture Show
- ☐ '93 Plush
- ☐ '00 Sour Girl
- ☐ '96 Trippin' On A Hole In A Paper Heart
- ☐ '94 Vasoline

## STOOGES, The
- ☐ '69 I Wanna Be Your Dog
- ☐ '73 Search And Destroy

## STOOKEY, Paul
- ☐ '71 Wedding Song (There Is Love)

## STORIES
- ☐ '73 Brother Louie ★

## STORM, The
- ☐ '91 I've Got A Lot To Learn About Love

## STORM, Billy
- ☐ '59 I've Come Of Age

## STORM, Gale
- ☐ '57 Dark Moon
- ☐ '55 I Hear You Knocking
- ☐ '56 Ivory Tower
- ☐ '55 Memories Are Made Of This
- ☐ '55 Teen Age Prayer
- ☐ '56 Why Do Fools Fall In Love

## STRAIT, George
- ☐ '87 All My Ex's Live In Texas
- ☐ '00 Best Day, The
- ☐ '94 Big One, The
- ☐ '96 Blue Clear Sky
- ☐ '96 Carried Away
- ☐ '97 Carrying Your Love With Me
- ☐ '95 Check Yes Or No
- ☐ '03 Cowboys Like Us
- ☐ '84 Does Fort Worth Ever Cross Your Mind

- ☐ '93 Easy Come, Easy Go
- ☐ '93 Heartland
- ☐ '92 I Cross My Heart
- ☐ '04 I Hate Everything
- ☐ '98 I Just Want To Dance With You
- ☐ '90 I've Come To Expect It From You
- ☐ '91 If I Know Me
- ☐ '02 Living And Living Well
- ☐ '90 Love Without End, Amen
- ☐ '87 Ocean Front Property
- ☐ '97 One Night At A Time
- ☐ '97 Round About Way
- ☐ '01 Run
- ☐ '02 She'll Leave You With A Smile
- ☐ '99 Write This Down
- ☐ '94 You Can't Make A Heart Love Somebody
- ☐ '91 You Know Me Better Than That

## STRANGELOVES, The
- ☐ '65 Cara-Lin
- ☐ '65 I Want Candy
- ☐ '66 Night Time

## STRAWBERRY ALARM CLOCK
- ☐ '67 Incense And Peppermints ★
- ☐ '67 Tomorrow

## STRAY CATS
- ☐ '83 I Won't Stand In Your Way
- ☐ '82 Rock This Town ★
- ☐ '83 (She's) Sexy + 17
- ☐ '82 Stray Cat Strut ★

## STREET PEOPLE
- ☐ '70 Jennifer Tomkins

## STREISAND, Barbra
- ☐ '81 Comin' In And Out Of Your Life
- ☐ '64 Don't Rain On My Parade
- ☐ '64 Funny Girl
- ☐ '80 Guilty
  *BARBRA STREISAND & BARRY GIBB*
- ☐ '63 Happy Days Are Here Again
- ☐ '65 He Touched Me
- ☐ '96 I Finally Found Someone
  *BARBRA STREISAND & BRYAN ADAMS*
- ☐ '80 Kiss Me In The Rain
- ☐ '76 Love Theme From "A Star Is Born" (Evergreen) ★
- ☐ '78 Love Theme From "Eyes Of Laura Mars" (Prisoner)
- ☐ '79 Main Event/Fight, The
- ☐ '82 Memory
- ☐ '77 My Heart Belongs To Me
- ☐ '65 My Man
- ☐ '79 No More Tears (Enough Is Enough) ★
  *BARBRA STREISAND & DONNA SUMMER*
- ☐ '83 Papa, Can You Hear Me?
- ☐ '64 People
- ☐ '65 Second Hand Rose
- ☐ '85 Somewhere
- ☐ '78 Songbird
- ☐ '70 Stoney End
- ☐ '67 Stout-Hearted Men
- ☐ '72 Sweet Inspiration/Where You Lead

'88 Till I Loved You
*BARBRA STREISAND & DON JOHNSON*
'71 Time And Love
'83 Way He Makes Me Feel, The
'73 Way We Were, The ★
'81 What Kind Of Fool
*BARBRA STREISAND & BARRY GIBB*
'71 Where You Lead
'80 Woman In Love ★
'78 You Don't Bring Me Flowers ★
*BARBRA STREISAND & NEIL DIAMOND*

## STRING-A-LONGS, The
'61 Wheels ★

## STROKES, The
'01 Last Night

## STRONG, Barrett
'60 Money (That's what I want)

## STRUNK, Jud
'73 Daisy A Day

## STRYPER
'87 Honestly

## STUDDARD, Ruben
'03 Flying Without Wings ★
'04 Sorry 2004
'03 Superstar

## STYLE COUNCIL, The
'84 My Ever Changing Moods

## STYLES
'02 Good Times

## STYLISTICS, The
'72 Betcha By Golly, Wow
'73 Break Up To Make Up
'72 I'm Stone In Love With You
'74 Let's Put It All Together
'72 People Make The World Go Round
'73 Rockin' Roll Baby
'71 Stop, Look, Listen (To Your Heart)
'71 You Are Everything
'74 You Make Me Feel Brand New ★
'73 You'll Never Get To Heaven (If You Break My Heart)

## STYX
'79 Babe ★
'81 Best Of Times, The ★
'78 Blue Collar Man (Long Nights)
'77 Come Sail Away
'76 Crystal Ball
'83 Don't Let It End
'78 Fooling Yourself (The Angry Young Man)
'77 Grand Illusion, The
'74 Lady
'76 Lorelei
'91 Love At First Sight
'76 Mademoiselle
'83 Mr. Roboto ★
'79 Renegade
'90 Show Me The Way ★

'78 Sing For The Day
'76 Suite Madame Blue
'81 Too Much Time On My Hands
'79 Why Me

## SUAVE'
'88 My Girl

## SUBLIME
'97 Santeria
'96 What I Got
'97 Wrong Way

## SUBWAY
'95 This Lil' Game We Play

## SUGARCUBES, The
'88 Coldsweat
'92 Hit
'89 Regina

## SUGARHILL GANG
'79 Rapper's Delight ★

## SUGARLAND
'05 Baby Girl

## SUGARLOAF
'74 Don't Call Us, We'll Call You
'70 Green-Eyed Lady ★

## SUGAR RAY
'98 Every Morning ★
'00 Falls Apart (Run Away)
'97 Fly ★
'99 Someday
'01 When It's Over

## SUM 41
'01 Fat Lip

## SUMMER, Donna
'79 Bad Girls ★
'80 Cold Love
'79 Dim All The Lights
'79 Heaven Knows ★
*DONNA SUMMER with Brooklyn Dreams*
'79 Hot Stuff ★
'77 I Feel Love
'77 I Love You
'78 Last Dance ★
'82 Love Is In Control (Finger On The Trigger)
'75 Love To Love You Baby ★
'78 MacArthur Park ★
'79 No More Tears (Enough Is Enough) ★
*BARBRA STREISAND & DONNA SUMMER*
'80 On The Radio
'83 She Works Hard For The Money ★
'84 There Goes My Baby
'89 This Time I Know It's For Real
'80 Walk Away
'80 Wanderer, The ★
'82 Woman In Me, The

## SUMMER, Henry Lee
'89 Hey Baby
'88 I Wish I Had A Girl

## SUNDAYS, The
- '90  Here's Where The Story Ends
- '92  Love

## SUNNY & THE SUNGLOWS
- '63  Talk To Me

## SUNNYSIDERS, The
- '55  Hey, Mr. Banjo

## SUNSCREEM
- '92  Love U More

## SUNSHINE COMPANY, The
- '67  Back On The Street Again

## SUPERNAW, Doug
- '93  I Don't Call Him Daddy

## SUPERTRAMP
- '75  Bloody Well Right
- '79  Breakfast In America
- '85  Cannonball
- '75  Dreamer
- '80  Dreamer [live]
- '77  Give A Little Bit
- '79  Goodbye Stranger
- '82  It's Raining Again  ★
- '79  Logical Song, The  ★
- '83  My Kind Of Lady
- '75  Rudy
- '75  School
- '79  Take The Long Way Home

## SUPREMES, The
- '64  Baby Love  ★
- '65  Back In My Arms Again
- '64  Come See About Me  ★
- '69  Composer, The
- '70  Everybody's Got The Right To Love
- '72  Floy Joy
- '68  Forever Came Today
- '67  Happening, The
- '65  I Hear A Symphony
- '69  I'll Try Something New
- '68  I'm Gonna Make You Love Me
     THE SUPREMES & TEMPTATIONS (above 2)
- '69  I'm Livin' In Shame
- '67  In And Out Of Love
- '68  Love Child  ★
- '67  Love Is Here And Now You're Gone
- '66  Love Is Like An Itching In My Heart
- '66  My World Is Empty Without You
- '71  Nathan Jones
- '69  No Matter What Sign You Are
- '65  Nothing But Heartaches
- '67  Reflections
- '70  River Deep - Mountain High
     THE SUPREMES & FOUR TOPS
- '68  Some Things You Never Get Used To
- '69  Someday We'll Be Together
- '70  Stoned Love
- '65  Stop! In The Name Of Love  ★
- '70  Up The Ladder To The Roof
- '63  When The Lovelight Starts Shining Through His Eyes

- '64  Where Did Our Love Go  ★
- '66  You Can't Hurry Love  ★
- '66  You Keep Me Hangin' On  ★

## SURFACE
- '89  Closer Than Friends
- '90  First Time, The  ★
- '87  Happy
- '91  Never Gonna Let You Down
- '89  Shower Me With Your Love
- '89  You Are My Everything

## SURFARIS, The
- '63  Wipe Out  ★

## SURVIVOR
- '82  American Heartbeat
- '85  Burning Heart
- '82  Eye Of The Tiger  ★
- '85  High On You
- '84  I Can't Hold Back
- '86  Is This Love
- '81  Poor Man's Son
- '85  Search Is Over, The

## SWAN, Billy
- '74  I Can Help  ★

## SWANN, Bettye
- '69  Don't Touch Me
- '67  Make Me Yours

## SWAYZE, Patrick
- '87  She's Like The Wind

## SWEAT, Keith
- '98  Come And Get With Me
- '88  I Want Her
- '90  I'll Give All My Love To You
- '99  I'm Not Ready
- '91  Keep It Comin'
- '88  Make It Last Forever
- '90  Make You Sweat
- '90  Merry Go Round
- '96  Nobody  ★
- '88  Something Just Ain't Right
- '96  Twisted  ★
- '92  Why Me Baby?

## SWEATHOG
- '71  Hallelujah

## SWEET
- '76  Action
- '75  Ballroom Blitz
- '75  Fox On The Run  ★
- '73  Little Willy
- '78  Love Is Like Oxygen

## SWEET, Matthew
- '95  Sick Of Myself

## SWEET INSPIRATIONS, The
- '68  Sweet Inspiration

## SWEET SENSATION
- '75  Sad Sweet Dreamer

## SWEET SENSATION
- ☐ '89 Hooked On You [remix]
- ☐ '90 If Wishes Came True ★
- ☐ '90 Love Child
- ☐ '89 Sincerely Yours

## SWINGING BLUE JEANS, The
- ☐ '64 Hippy Hippy Shake

## SWINGIN' MEDALLIONS
- ☐ '66 Double Shot (Of My Baby's Love)

## SWING OUT SISTER
- ☐ '92 Am I The Same Girl
- ☐ '87 Breakout
- ☐ '87 Twilight World

## SWITCH
- ☐ '78 There'll Never Be

## SWITCHFOOT
- ☐ '04 Dare You To Move
- ☐ '04 Meant To Live
- ☐ '04 This Is Your Life

## SWV (Sisters With Voices)
- ☐ '94 Anything
- ☐ '93 I'm So Into You
- ☐ '98 Rain
- ☐ '93 Right Here/Human Nature ★
- ☐ '97 Someone
- ☐ '96 Use Your Heart
- ☐ '93 Weak ★
- ☐ '96 You're The One

## SYBIL
- ☐ '89 Don't Make Me Over
- ☐ '89 Walk On By

## SYLK-E. FYNE
- ☐ '98 Romeo And Juliet

## SYLVERS, Foster
- ☐ '73 Misdemeanor

## SYLVERS, The
- ☐ '76 Boogie Fever ★
- ☐ '77 High School Dance
- ☐ '76 Hot Line

## SYLVESTER
- ☐ '78 Dance (Disco Heat)
- ☐ '79 I (Who Have Nothing)
- ☐ '79 You Make Me Feel (Mighty Real)

## SYLVIA
- ☐ '73 Pillow Talk

## SYLVIA
- ☐ '82 Nobody

## SYMS, Sylvia
- ☐ '56 English Muffins And Irish Stew
- ☐ '56 I Could Have Danced All Night

## SYNCH
- ☐ '86 Where Are You Now?

## SYNDICATE OF SOUND
- ☐ '66 Little Girl ★

## SYSTEM, The
- ☐ '87 Don't Disturb This Groove

## SYSTEM OF A DOWN
- ☐ '02 Aerials
- ☐ '02 Toxicity

# T

## TACO
- ☐ '83 Puttin' On The Ritz ★

## TAG TEAM
- ☐ '93 Whoomp! (There It Is) ★

## TAKE THAT
- ☐ '95 Back For Good ★

## TALKING HEADS
- ☐ '85 And She Was
- ☐ '83 Burning Down The House ★
- ☐ '79 Life During Wartime
- ☐ '80 Once In A Lifetime
- ☐ '77 Psycho Killer
- ☐ '85 Road To Nowhere
- ☐ '91 Sax And Violins
- ☐ '78 Take Me To The River ★
- ☐ '86 Wild Wild Life

## TALK TALK
- ☐ '84 It's My Life

## TA MARA & THE SEEN
- ☐ '85 Everybody Dance

## TAMIA
- ☐ '98 Imagination
- ☐ '96 Missing You
  - *BRANDY, TAMIA, GLADYS KNIGHT & CHAKA KHAN*
- ☐ '98 So Into You
- ☐ '01 Stranger In My House

## TAMI SHOW
- ☐ '91 Truth, The

## TAMS, The
- ☐ '63 What Kind Of Fool (Do You Think I Am)

## TANEGA, Norma
- ☐ '66 Walkin' My Cat Named Dog

## TANK
- ☐ '01 Maybe I Deserve

## TANTRIC
- ☐ '01 Breakdown

## TARRIERS, The
- ☐ '56 Banana Boat Song, The ★
- ☐ '56 Cindy, Oh Cindy

## TASTE OF HONEY, A
- ☐ '78 Boogie Oogie Oogie ★
- ☐ '81 Sukiyaki ★

## t.A.T.u.
- ☐ '03 All The Things She Said

## TAVARES
- ☐ '73 Check It Out
- ☐ '76 Don't Take Away The Music
- ☐ '76 Heaven Must Be Missing An Angel
- ☐ '75 It Only Takes A Minute
- ☐ '77 More Than A Woman
- ☐ '82 Penny For Your Thoughts, A
- ☐ '75 Remember What I Told You To Forget
- ☐ '74 She's Gone
- ☐ '77 Whodunit

## TAYLOR, Andy
- ☐ '86 Take It Easy

## TAYLOR, Bobby, & The Vancouvers
- ☐ '68 Does Your Mama Know About Me

## TAYLOR, James
- ☐ '69 Carolina In My Mind
- ☐ '71 Country Road
- ☐ '78 Devoted To You
  *CARLY SIMON & JAMES TAYLOR*
- ☐ '72 Don't Let Me Be Lonely Tonight
- ☐ '85 Everyday
- ☐ '70 Fire And Rain ★
- ☐ '77 Handy Man
- ☐ '81 Her Town Too
  *JAMES TAYLOR & J.D. SOUTHER*
- ☐ '75 How Sweet It Is (To Be Loved By You)
- ☐ '97 Little More Time With You
- ☐ '71 Long Ago And Far Away
- ☐ '74 Mockingbird
  *CARLY SIMON & JAMES TAYLOR*
- ☐ '88 Never Die Young
- ☐ '76 Shower The People
- ☐ '79 Up On The Roof
- ☐ '78 (What A) Wonderful World
  *ART GARFUNKEL with JAMES TAYLOR & PAUL SIMON*
- ☐ '71 You've Got A Friend ★
- ☐ '77 Your Smiling Face

## TAYLOR, James "J.T."
- ☐ '89 All I Want Is Forever
  *JAMES "J.T." TAYLOR & REGINA BELLE*

## TAYLOR, Johnnie
- ☐ '73 Cheaper To Keep Her
- ☐ '76 Disco Lady ★
- ☐ '70 I Am Somebody
- ☐ '73 I Believe In You (You Believe In Me)
- ☐ '71 Jody's Got Your Girl And Gone
- ☐ '76 Somebody's Gettin' It
- ☐ '70 Steal Away
- ☐ '69 Take Care Of Your Homework
- ☐ '69 Testify (I Wonna)
- ☐ '74 We're Getting Careless With Our Love
- ☐ '68 Who's Making Love

## TAYLOR, Little Johnny
- ☐ '63 Part Time Love

## TAYLOR, Livingston
- ☐ '80 First Time Love
- ☐ '78 I Will Be In Love With You

## TAYLOR, R. Dean
- ☐ '70 Indiana Wants Me

## T-BONES, The
- ☐ '65 No Matter What Shape (Your Stomach's In)

## TEARS FOR FEARS
- ☐ '93 Break It Down Again
- ☐ '85 Everybody Wants To Rule The World ★
- ☐ '85 Head Over Heels
- ☐ '86 Mothers Talk
- ☐ '85 Shout ★
- ☐ '89 Sowing The Seeds Of Love
- ☐ '89 Woman In Chains

## TECHNIQUES
- ☐ '57 Hey! Little Girl

## TECHNOTRONIC
- ☐ '90 Get Up! (Before The Night Is Over)
- ☐ '92 Move This
- ☐ '89 Pump Up The Jam ★

## TEDDY BEARS, The
- ☐ '58 To Know Him, Is To Love Him ★

## TEEGARDEN & VAN WINKLE
- ☐ '70 God, Love And Rock & Roll

## TEEN QUEENS, The
- ☐ '56 Eddie My Love

## TEE SET, The
- ☐ '70 Ma Belle Amie

## TELEVISION
- ☐ '77 Marquee Moon

## TEMPO, Nino, & April Stevens
- ☐ '66 All Strung Out
- ☐ '63 Deep Purple
- ☐ '64 Stardust
- ☐ '63 Whispering

## TEMPOS, The
- ☐ '59 See You In September

## TEMPTATIONS, The
- ☐ '60 Barbara

## TEMPTATIONS, The
- ☐ '66 Ain't Too Proud To Beg
- ☐ '67 All I Need
- ☐ '70 Ball Of Confusion (That's What The World Is Today)
- ☐ '66 Beauty Is Only Skin Deep
- ☐ '68 Cloud Nine
- ☐ '69 Don't Let The Joneses Get You Down
- ☐ '66 Get Ready
- ☐ '64 Girl (Why You Wanna Make Me Blue)
- ☐ '74 Happy People
- ☐ '73 Hey Girl (I Like Your Style)
- ☐ '69 I Can't Get Next To You ★
- ☐ '68 I Could Never Love Another (After Loving You)
- ☐ '66 (I Know) I'm Losing You

- ☐ '68 I Wish It Would Rain
- ☐ '69 I'll Try Something New
- ☐ '68 I'm Gonna Make You Love Me
  THE SUPREMES & TEMPTATIONS (above 2)
- ☐ '65 It's Growing
- ☐ '71 Just My Imagination (Running Away With Me) ★
- ☐ '76 Keep Holding On
- ☐ '73 Let Your Hair Down
- ☐ '67 (Loneliness Made Me Realize) It's You That I Need
- ☐ '73 Masterpiece
- ☐ '91 Motown Song, The
  ROD STEWART (with The Temptations)
- ☐ '65 My Baby
- ☐ '65 My Girl ★
- ☐ '72 Papa Was A Rollin' Stone ★
- ☐ '68 Please Return Your Love To Me
- ☐ '70 Psychedelic Shack
- ☐ '69 Run Away Child, Running Wild
- ☐ '75 Shakey Ground
- ☐ '65 Since I Lost My Baby
- ☐ '71 Superstar (Remember How You Got Where You Are)
- ☐ '84 Treat Her Like A Lady
- ☐ '64 Way You Do The Things You Do, The
- ☐ '67 You're My Everything

## 10cc
- ☐ '75 I'm Not In Love ★
- ☐ '77 Things We Do For Love, The

## 10,000 MANIACS
- ☐ '93 Because The Night
- ☐ '97 More Than This
- ☐ '92 These Are Days
- ☐ '89 Trouble Me

## TEN YEARS AFTER
- ☐ '71 I'd Love To Change The World

## TEPPER, Robert
- ☐ '86 No Easy Way Out

## TERRELL, Tammi — see GAYE, Marvin

## TERROR SQUAD
- ☐ '04 Lean Back ★

## TERRY, Tony
- ☐ '91 With You

## TESLA
- ☐ '89 Love Song
- ☐ '90 Signs

## TEX, Joe
- ☐ '77 Ain't Gonna Bump No More (With No Big Fat Woman)
- ☐ '64 Hold What You've Got
- ☐ '72 I Gotcha ★
- ☐ '65 I Want To (Do Everything For You)
- ☐ '66 Love You Save (May Be Your Own)
- ☐ '68 Men Are Gettin' Scarce
- ☐ '66 S.Y.S.L.J.F.M. (The Letter Song)
- ☐ '67 Show Me

- ☐ '67 Skinny Legs And All
- ☐ '65 Sweet Woman Like You, A

## THALIA
- ☐ '03 I Want You

## THEM
- ☐ '65 Gloria ★
- ☐ '65 Here Comes The Night
- ☐ '65 Mystic Eyes

## THEY MIGHT BE GIANTS
- ☐ '88 Ana Ng
- ☐ '90 Birdhouse In Your Soul
- ☐ '87 Don't Let's Start

## THINK
- ☐ '71 Once You Understand

## THIN LIZZY
- ☐ '76 Boys Are Back In Town, The

## 3RD BASS
- ☐ '91 Pop Goes The Weasel

## THIRD EYE BLIND
- ☐ '97 How's It Going To Be ★
- ☐ '98 Jumper ★
- ☐ '00 Never Let You Go
- ☐ '97 Semi-Charmed Life ★

## THIRD WORLD
- ☐ '79 Now That We Found Love

## 38 SPECIAL
- ☐ '84 Back Where You Belong
- ☐ '82 Caught Up In You
- ☐ '81 Hold On Loosely
- ☐ '83 If I'd Been The One
- ☐ '86 Like No Other Night
- ☐ '80 Rockin' Into The Night
- ☐ '89 Second Chance
- ☐ '91 Sound Of Your Voice, The
- ☐ '84 Teacher Teacher
- ☐ '82 You Keep Runnin' Away

## THOMAS, B.J.
- ☐ '66 Billy And Sue
- ☐ '77 Don't Worry Baby
- ☐ '78 Everybody Loves A Rain Song
- ☐ '70 Everybody's Out Of Town
- ☐ '68 Eyes Of A New York Woman, The
- ☐ '75 (Hey Won't You Play) Another Somebody Done Somebody Wrong Song
- ☐ '68 Hooked On A Feeling
- ☐ '70 I Just Can't Help Believing
- ☐ '66 I'm So Lonesome I Could Cry
- ☐ '66 Mama
- ☐ '71 Mighty Clouds Of Joy
- ☐ '71 No Love At All
- ☐ '69 Raindrops Keep Fallin' On My Head ★
- ☐ '72 Rock And Roll Lullaby

## THOMAS, Carl
- ☐ '00 I Wish

## THOMAS, Carla
- ☐ '66 B-A-B-Y
- ☐ '61 Gee Whiz (Look At His Eyes)
- ☐ '67 Knock On Wood
- ☐ '67 Tramp
  - OTIS & CARLA (above 2)

## THOMAS, Ian
- ☐ '73 Painted Ladies

## THOMAS, Irma
- ☐ '64 Wish Someone Would Care

## THOMAS, Rob
- ☐ '05 Lonely No More ★
- ☐ '99 Smooth ★
  - SANTANA Feat. Rob Thomas

## THOMAS, Rufus
- ☐ '71 Breakdown, The
- ☐ '70 Do The Funky Chicken
- ☐ '70 (Do The) Push And Pull
- ☐ '63 Walking The Dog

## THOMAS, Timmy
- ☐ '72 Why Can't We Live Together

## THOMPSON, Kay
- ☐ '56 Eloise

## THOMPSON, Sue
- ☐ '62 Have A Good Time
- ☐ '62 James (Hold The Ladder Steady)
- ☐ '61 Norman
- ☐ '65 Paper Tiger
- ☐ '61 Sad Movies (Make Me Cry)

## THOMPSON TWINS
- ☐ '84 Doctor! Doctor!
- ☐ '87 Get That Love
- ☐ '84 Hold Me Now ★
- ☐ '86 King For A Day
- ☐ '85 Lay Your Hands On Me
- ☐ '83 Lies
- ☐ '89 Sugar Daddy

## THOMSON, Ali
- ☐ '80 Take A Little Rhythm

## THOMSON, Cyndi
- ☐ '01 What I Really Meant To Say

## THOROGOOD, George, & The Destroyers
- ☐ '82 Bad To The Bone
- ☐ '93 Get A Haircut
- ☐ '85 I Drink Alone

## THREE DAYS GRACE
- ☐ '05 Home
- ☐ '03 (I Hate) Everything About You
- ☐ '04 Just Like You

## THREE DEGREES, The
- ☐ '70 Maybe
- ☐ '74 TSOP (The Sound Of Philadelphia) ★
  - MFSB Feat. The Three Degrees

- ☐ '74 When Will I See You Again

## THREE DOG NIGHT
- ☐ '72 Black & White ★
- ☐ '70 Celebrate
- ☐ '69 Easy To Be Hard
- ☐ '69 Eli's Coming
- ☐ '72 Family Of Man, The
- ☐ '71 Joy To The World ★
- ☐ '73 Let Me Serenade You
- ☐ '71 Liar
- ☐ '70 Mama Told Me (Not To Come) ★
- ☐ '71 Never Been To Spain
- ☐ '71 Old Fashioned Love Song, An
- ☐ '69 One
- ☐ '70 One Man Band
- ☐ '70 Out In The Country
- ☐ '72 Pieces Of April
- ☐ '73 Shambala
- ☐ '74 Show Must Go On, The
- ☐ '74 Sure As I'm Sittin' Here
- ☐ '69 Try A Little Tenderness

## 3 DOORS DOWN
- ☐ '01 Be Like That
- ☐ '01 Duck And Run
- ☐ '03 Here Without You ★
- ☐ '00 Kryptonite ★
- ☐ '05 Let Me Go ★
- ☐ '00 Loser
- ☐ '02 When I'm Gone ★

## 311
- ☐ '96 All Mixed Up
- ☐ '03 Creatures (For A While)
- ☐ '96 Down
- ☐ '04 Love Song

## 3LW
- ☐ '00 No More (Baby I'ma Do Right)

## 3T
- ☐ '95 Anything

## THUNDER, Johnny
- ☐ '62 Loop De Loop

## THUNDERCLAP NEWMAN
- ☐ '69 Something In The Air

## T.I.
- ☐ '05 Bring Em Out ★
- ☐ '04 Let's Get Away
- ☐ '04 Rubber Band Man
- ☐ '05 U Don't Know Me

## TIERRA
- ☐ '80 Together

## TIFFANY
- ☐ '88 All This Time
- ☐ '87 Could've Been
- ☐ '88 I Saw Him Standing There
- ☐ '87 I Think We're Alone Now ★
- ☐ '89 Radio Romance

## TILLIS, Pam
- ☐ '91 Maybe It Was Memphis
- ☐ '94 Mi Vida Loca (My Crazy Life)
- ☐ '94 When You Walk In The Room

## TILLOTSON, Johnny
- ☐ '58 Dreamy Eyes
- ☐ '65 Heartaches By The Number
- ☐ '62 I Can't Help It (If I'm Still In Love With You)
- ☐ '64 I Rise, I Fall
- ☐ '62 It Keeps Right On A-Hurtin'
- ☐ '61 Jimmy's Girl
- ☐ '63 Out Of My Mind
- ☐ '60 Poetry In Motion ★
- ☐ '62 Send Me The Pillow You Dream On
- ☐ '64 She Understands Me
- ☐ '63 Talk Back Trembling Lips
- ☐ '60 Why Do I Love You So
- ☐ '61 Without You
- ☐ '64 Worried Guy
- ☐ '63 You Can Never Stop Me Loving You

## 'TIL TUESDAY
- ☐ '85 Voices Carry
- ☐ '86 What About Love

## TIMBALAND & MAGOO
- ☐ '98 Clock Strikes
- ☐ '98 Luv 2 Luv U
- ☐ '97 Up Jumps Da Boogie

## TIMBERLAKE, Justin
- ☐ '02 Cry Me A River ★
- ☐ '02 Like I Love You
- ☐ '03 Rock Your Body
- ☐ '03 Señorita

## TIMBUK 3
- ☐ '86 Future's So Bright, I Gotta Wear Shades, The

## TIME, The
- ☐ '85 Bird, The
- ☐ '90 Jerk-Out
- ☐ '84 Jungle Love
- ☐ '82 777-9311

## TIMES TWO
- ☐ '88 Strange But True

## TIMEX SOCIAL CLUB
- ☐ '86 Rumors

## TIMMY -T-
- ☐ '90 One More Try ★
- ☐ '90 Time After Time

## TIN MACHINE
- ☐ '91 Baby Universal
- ☐ '91 One Shot

## TIN TIN
- ☐ '71 Toast And Marmalade For Tea

## TINY TIM
- ☐ '68 Tip-Toe Thru' The Tulips With Me

## TIPPIN, Aaron
- ☐ '00 Kiss This
- ☐ '95 That's As Close As I'll Get To Loving You
- ☐ '92 There Ain't Nothin' Wrong With The Radio
- ☐ '01 Where The Stars And Stripes And The Eagle Fly
- ☐ '90 You've Got To Stand For Something

## TLC
- ☐ '92 Ain't 2 Proud 2 Beg
- ☐ '92 Baby-Baby-Baby ★
- ☐ '94 Creep ★
- ☐ '95 Diggin' On You
- ☐ '02 Girl Talk
- ☐ '93 Hat 2 Da Back
- ☐ '99 No Scrubs ★
- ☐ '95 Red Light Special
- ☐ '99 Unpretty ★
- ☐ '95 Waterfalls ★
- ☐ '92 What About Your Friends

## TOADIES
- ☐ '95 Possum Kingdom

## TOAD THE WET SPROCKET
- ☐ '92 All I Want
- ☐ '94 Fall Down
- ☐ '95 Good Intentions
- ☐ '92 Walk On The Ocean

## TOBY BEAU
- ☐ '78 My Angel Baby

## TODAY
- ☐ '89 Girl I Got My Eyes On You

## TODD, Art & Dotty
- ☐ '58 Chanson D'Amour (Song Of Love)

## TOKENS, The
- ☐ '66 I Hear Trumpets Blow
- ☐ '61 Lion Sleeps Tonight, The ★
- ☐ '67 Portrait Of My Love
- ☐ '61 Tonight I Fell In Love

## TOMMY TUTONE
- ☐ '80 Angel Say No
- ☐ '81 867-5309/Jenny ★

## TOM TOM CLUB
- ☐ '82 Genius Of Love

## TONE LOC
- ☐ '89 Funky Cold Medina
- ☐ '88 Wild Thing ★

## TONEY, Oscar Jr.
- ☐ '67 For Your Precious Love

## TONIC
- ☐ '97 If You Could Only See
- ☐ '96 Open Up Your Eyes

## TONY & JOE
- ☐ '58 Freeze, The

## TONY! TONI! TONÉ!
- ☐ '93 Anniversary
- ☐ '90 Blues, The
- ☐ '90 Feels Good
- ☐ '93 If I Had No Loot ★
- ☐ '90 It Never Rains (In Southern California)
- ☐ '94 (Lay Your Head On My) Pillow
- ☐ '96 Let's Get Down
- ☐ '88 Little Walter
- ☐ '97 Thinking Of You
- ☐ '91 Whatever You Want

## TOOL
- ☐ '01 Schism

## TOOTS & THE MAYTALS
- ☐ '73 Pressure Drop

## TOPOL
- ☐ '71 If I Were A Rich Man

## TORME, Mel
- ☐ '62 Comin' Home Baby

## TORNADOES, The
- ☐ '62 Telstar ★

## TOROK, Mitchell
- ☐ '59 Caribbean
- ☐ '60 Pink Chiffon
- ☐ '57 Pledge Of Love

## TOSH, Peter
- ☐ '83 Johnny B. Goode
- ☐ '73 Stepping Razor

## TOTAL
- ☐ '95 Can't You See
- ☐ '96 Kissin' You
- ☐ '95 No One Else
- ☐ '98 Trippin'
- ☐ '97 What About Us

## TOTAL COELO
- ☐ '83 I Eat Cannibals

## TOTO
- ☐ '82 Africa ★
- ☐ '78 Hold The Line
- ☐ '83 I Won't Hold You Back
- ☐ '86 I'll Be Over You
- ☐ '78 I'll Supply The Love
- ☐ '82 Make Believe
- ☐ '79 99
- ☐ '88 Pamela
- ☐ '82 Rosanna ★
- ☐ '84 Stranger In Town
- ☐ '86 Without Your Love

## TOWER OF POWER
- ☐ '74 Don't Change Horses (In The Middle Of A Stream)
- ☐ '73 So Very Hard To Go
- ☐ '72 You're Still A Young Man

## TOWNSELL, Lidell, & M.T.F.
- ☐ '92 Nu Nu

## TOWNSEND, Ed
- ☐ '58 For Your Love

## TOWNSHEND, Pete
- ☐ '85 Face The Face
- ☐ '89 Friend Is A Friend, A
- ☐ '80 Let My Love Open The Door
- ☐ '80 Rough Boys

## TOYA
- ☐ '01 I Do!!

## TOYS, The
- ☐ '65 Attack
- ☐ '65 Lover's Concerto, A ★

## T'PAU
- ☐ '87 Heart And Soul

## TQ
- ☐ '98 Westside

## TRADE WINDS, The
- ☐ '65 New York's A Lonely Town

## TRAFFIC
- ☐ '68 Dear Mr. Fantasy
- ☐ '70 Empty Pages
- ☐ '68 Feelin' Alright?
- ☐ '68 Forty Thousand Headmen
- ☐ '70 Freedom Rider
- ☐ '68 Hole In My Shoe
- ☐ '70 John Barleycorn
- ☐ '71 Low Spark Of High Heeled Boys
- ☐ '68 Paper Sun
- ☐ '71 Rock & Roll Stew
- ☐ '68 You Can All Join In

## TRAIN
- ☐ '03 Calling All Angels
- ☐ '01 Drops Of Jupiter (Tell Me) ★
- ☐ '99 Meet Virginia

## TRAMMPS, The
- ☐ '77 Disco Inferno
- ☐ '76 Hold Back The Night
- ☐ '76 That's Where The Happy People Go

## TRANS-SIBERIAN ORCHESTRA
- ☐ '95 Christmas Eve (Sarajevo 12/24)

## TRAPT
- ☐ '02 Headstrong
- ☐ '03 Still Frame

## TRASHMEN, The
- ☐ '64 Bird Dance Beat
- ☐ '63 Surfin' Bird

## TRAVELING WILBURYS
- ☐ '89 End Of The Line
- ☐ '88 Handle With Care
- ☐ '90 She's My Baby

## TRAVERS, Pat, Band
- ☐ '79 Boom Boom (Out Go The Lights)

## TRAVIS, Randy
- ☐ '94 Before You Kill Us All
- ☐ '91 Better Class Of Losers
- ☐ '88 Deeper Than The Holler
- ☐ '87 Forever And Ever, Amen
- ☐ '91 Forever Together
- ☐ '90 Hard Rock Bottom Of Your Heart
- ☐ '90 He Walked On Water
- ☐ '92 If I Didn't Have You
- ☐ '92 Look Heart, No Hands
- ☐ '86 On The Other Hand
- ☐ '98 Out Of My Bones
- ☐ '98 Spirit Of A Boy - Wisdom Of A Man
- ☐ '02 Three Wooden Crosses
- ☐ '94 Whisper My Name

## TRAVIS & BOB
- ☐ '59 Tell Him No

## TRAVOLTA, John
- ☐ '77 All Strung Out On You
- ☐ '96 Grease Megamix, The
  *JOHN TRAVOLTA & OLIVIA NEWTON-JOHN*
- ☐ '76 Let Her In
- ☐ '78 Summer Nights
- ☐ '78 You're The One That I Want ★
  *JOHN TRAVOLTA & OLIVIA NEWTON-JOHN*
  (above 2)

## TREMELOES, The
- ☐ '67 Even The Bad Times Are Good
- ☐ '67 Here Comes My Baby
- ☐ '67 Silence Is Golden

## TRESVANT, Ralph
- ☐ '92 Money Can't Buy You Love
- ☐ '90 Sensitivity
- ☐ '91 Stone Cold Gentleman

## TREVINO, Rick
- ☐ '96 Running Out Of Reasons To Run

## T. REX
- ☐ '72 Bang A Gong (Get It On)

## TRICK DADDY
- ☐ '01 I'm A Thug
- ☐ '04 Let's Go

## TRILLVILLE
- ☐ '05 Some Cut

## TRIO
- ☐ '82 Da Da Da I Don't Love You You Don't Love Me

## TRIPLETS, The
- ☐ '91 You Don't Have To Go Home Tonight

## TRITT, Travis
- ☐ '91 Anymore
- ☐ '00 Best Of Intentions
- ☐ '92 Can I Trust You With My Heart
- ☐ '94 Foolish Pride
- ☐ '90 Help Me Hold On
- ☐ '91 Here's A Quarter (Call Someone Who Cares)
- ☐ '01 It's A Great Day To Be Alive

- ☐ '01 Love Of A Woman
- ☐ '93 Take It Easy

## TRIUMPH
- ☐ '83 All The Way
- ☐ '79 Hold On
- ☐ '80 I Can Survive
- ☐ '80 I Live For The Weekend
- ☐ '79 Lay It On The Line
- ☐ '78 Rock & Roll Machine
- ☐ '86 Somebody's Out There

## TROCCOLI, Kathy
- ☐ '92 Everything Changes

## TROGGS, The
- ☐ '68 Love Is All Around
- ☐ '66 Wild Thing ★
- ☐ '66 With A Girl Like You

## TROOP
- ☐ '90 All I Do Is Think Of You
- ☐ '88 Mamacita
- ☐ '90 Spread My Wings
- ☐ '92 Sweet November

## TROWER, Robin
- ☐ '74 Bridge Of Sighs
- ☐ '76 Caledonia
- ☐ '74 Day Of The Eagle
- ☐ '74 Little Bit Of Sympathy
- ☐ '74 Too Rolling Stoned
- ☐ '80 Victims Of The Fury

## TROY, Doris
- ☐ '63 Just One Look

## TRUE, Andrea, Connection
- ☐ '76 More, More, More
- ☐ '77 N.Y., You Got Me Dancing

## TRUTH HURTS
- ☐ '02 Addictive ★

## TUBES, The
- ☐ '81 Don't Want To Wait Anymore
- ☐ '83 She's A Beauty
- ☐ '81 Talk To Ya Later

## TUCKER, Tanya
- ☐ '73 Blood Red And Goin' Down
- ☐ '72 Delta Dawn
- ☐ '91 Down To My Last Teardrop
- ☐ '93 It's A Little Too Late
- ☐ '75 Lizzie And The Rainman
- ☐ '93 Soon
- ☐ '92 Two Sparrows In A Hurricane
- ☐ '73 What's Your Mama's Name
- ☐ '91 (Without You) What Do I Do With Me
- ☐ '74 Would You Lay With Me (In A Field Of Stone)

## TUCKER, Tommy
- ☐ '64 Hi-Heel Sneakers

## TUNE WEAVERS, The
- ☐ '57 Happy, Happy Birthday Baby ★

## TURBANS, The
- [ ] '55 When You Dance

## TURNER, Ike & Tina
- [ ] '60 Fool In Love, A
- [ ] '70 I Want To Take You Higher
- [ ] '61 It's Gonna Work Out Fine
- [ ] '73 Nutbush City Limits
- [ ] '61 Poor Fool
- [ ] '71 Proud Mary ★
- [ ] '66 River Deep-Mountain High ★

## TURNER, Jesse Lee
- [ ] '59 Little Space Girl, The

## TURNER, Joe
- [ ] '56 Corrine Corrina
- [ ] '55 Flip Flop And Fly
- [ ] '55 Hide And Seek
- [ ] '54 Shake, Rattle & Roll

## TURNER, Ruby
- [ ] '89 It's Gonna Be Alright

## TURNER, Sammy
- [ ] '59 Always
- [ ] '59 Lavender-Blue

## TURNER, Spyder
- [ ] '66 Stand By Me

## TURNER, Tina
- [ ] '89 Best, The
- [ ] '84 Better Be Good To Me
- [ ] '93 I Don't Wanna Fight
- [ ] '85 It's Only Love
  *BRYAN ADAMS & TINA TURNER*
- [ ] '84 Let's Stay Together
- [ ] '85 One Of The Living
- [ ] '85 Private Dancer
- [ ] '85 Show Some Respect
- [ ] '89 Steamy Windows
- [ ] '86 Two People
- [ ] '86 Typical Male
- [ ] '85 We Don't Need Another Hero (Thunderdome) ★
- [ ] '87 What You Get Is What You See
- [ ] '84 What's Love Got To Do With It ★

## TURTLES, The
- [ ] '68 Elenore
- [ ] '67 Happy Together ★
- [ ] '65 It Ain't Me Babe
- [ ] '65 Let Me Be
- [ ] '67 She'd Rather Be With Me
- [ ] '67 She's My Girl
- [ ] '66 You Baby
- [ ] '67 You Know What I Mean
- [ ] '69 You Showed Me

## TUXEDO JUNCTION
- [ ] '78 Chattanooga Choo Choo

## TWAIN, Shania
- [ ] '95 Any Man Of Mine
- [ ] '99 Come On Over
- [ ] '97 Don't Be Stupid (You Know I Love You)
- [ ] '03 Forever And For Always
- [ ] '98 From This Moment On ★
- [ ] '97 Honey, I'm Home
- [ ] '02 I'm Gonna Getcha Good!
- [ ] '95 (If You're Not In It For Love) I'm Outta Here!
- [ ] '97 Love Gets Me Every Time
- [ ] '99 Man! I Feel Like A Woman!
- [ ] '96 No One Needs To Know
- [ ] '99 That Don't Impress Me Much
- [ ] '95 Whose Bed Have Your Boots Been Under?
- [ ] '96 You Win My Love
- [ ] '98 You're Still The One ★

## TWEET
- [ ] '02 Call Me
- [ ] '02 Oops (Oh My)

## 12 GAUGE
- [ ] '94 Dunkie Butt (Please Please Please)

## TWENNYNINE
- [ ] '79 Peanut Butter

## 20 FINGERS FEAT. GILLETTE
- [ ] '94 Short Dick Man

## TWILLEY, Dwight
- [ ] '84 Girls
- [ ] '75 I'm On Fire

## TWISTA
- [ ] '05 Hope
- [ ] '04 Overnight Celebrity
- [ ] '03 Slow Jamz ★
- [ ] '04 So Sexy

## TWISTED SISTER
- [ ] '84 We're Not Gonna Take It

## TWITTY, Conway
- [ ] '60 C'est Si Bon (It's So Good)
- [ ] '59 Danny Boy
- [ ] '70 Hello Darlin'
- [ ] '60 Is A Blue Bird Blue
- [ ] '58 It's Only Make Believe ★
- [ ] '59 Lonely Blue Boy
- [ ] '59 Mona Lisa
- [ ] '82 Slow Hand
- [ ] '59 Story Of My Love, The
- [ ] '87 That's My Job
- [ ] '60 What Am I Living For
- [ ] '73 You've Never Been This Far Before

## 2 IN A ROOM
- [ ] '90 Wiggle It

## 2 LIVE CREW/LUKE
- [ ] '90 Banned In The U.S.A.
- [ ] '89 Me So Horny
- [ ] '98 Raise The Roof

## 2PAC
- [ ] '96 California Love ★
- [ ] '98 Changes
- [ ] '95 Dear Mama

- ☐ '98 Do For Love
- ☐ '96 How Do U Want It ★
- ☐ '93 I Get Around
- ☐ '93 Keep Ya Head Up
- ☐ '03 Runnin (Dying To Live)
- ☐ '02 Thugz Mansion

## 2 UNLIMITED
- ☐ '92 Get Ready For This

## TYCOON
- ☐ '79 Such A Woman

## TYLER, Bonnie
- ☐ '84 Holding Out For A Hero
- ☐ '78 It's A Heartache ★
- ☐ '83 Total Eclipse Of The Heart ★

## TYMES, The
- ☐ '68 People
- ☐ '63 So Much In Love ★
- ☐ '63 Somewhere
- ☐ '63 Wonderful! Wonderful!
- ☐ '74 You Little Trustmaker

## TYRESE
- ☐ '03 How You Gonna Act Like That
- ☐ '98 Nobody Else
- ☐ '99 Sweet Lady

# U

## UB40
- ☐ '93 Can't Help Falling In Love ★
- ☐ '91 Here I Am (Come And Take Me)
- ☐ '85 I Got You Babe
  *UB40 WITH CHRISSIE HYNDE*
- ☐ '88 Red Red Wine [rap by Astro] ★
- ☐ '90 Way You Do The Things You Do, The

## UGLY KID JOE
- ☐ '93 Cats In The Cradle
- ☐ '92 Everything About You ★

## U-KREW, The
- ☐ '90 If U Were Mine

## ULLMAN, Tracey
- ☐ '84 They Don't Know

## UNCLE KRACKER
- ☐ '03 Drift Away ★
  *UNCLE KRACKER with Dobie Gray*
- ☐ '01 Follow Me ★
- ☐ '04 When The Sun Goes Down
  *KENNY CHESNEY & UNCLE KRACKER*

## UNCLE SAM
- ☐ '97 I Don't Ever Want To See You Again

## UNDERGROUND SUNSHINE
- ☐ '69 Birthday

## UNDISPUTED TRUTH, The
- ☐ '71 Smiling Faces Sometimes ★

## UNIFICS, The
- ☐ '68 Beginning Of My End, The
- ☐ '68 Court Of Love

## UNV
- ☐ '93 Something's Goin' On

## UNWRITTEN LAW
- ☐ '02 Seein' Red

## UPCHURCH, Philip, Combo
- ☐ '61 You Can't Sit Down

## URBAN, Keith
- ☐ '00 But For The Grace Of God
- ☐ '04 Days Go By
- ☐ '05 Making Memories Of Us
- ☐ '02 Raining On Sunday
- ☐ '02 Somebody Like You
- ☐ '01 Where The Blacktop Ends
- ☐ '03 Who Wouldn't Wanna Be Me
- ☐ '03 You'll Think Of Me
- ☐ '04 You're My Better Half

## URBAN DANCE SQUAD
- ☐ '90 Deeper Shade Of Soul

## URIAH HEEP
- ☐ '72 Easy Livin
- ☐ '73 Stealin'

## USA FOR AFRICA
- ☐ '85 We Are The World ★

## USHER
- ☐ '04 Burn ★
- ☐ '05 Caught Up ★
- ☐ '04 Confessions Part II ★
- ☐ '04 My Boo ★
  *USHER & ALICIA KEYS*
- ☐ '98 My Way ★
- ☐ '98 Nice & Slow ★
- ☐ '02 U Don't Have To Call
- ☐ '01 U Got It Bad ★
- ☐ '01 U Remind Me ★
- ☐ '04 Yeah! ★
- ☐ '97 You Make Me Wanna... ★

## US3
- ☐ '93 Cantaloop

## UTOPIA
- ☐ '80 Set Me Free

## U2
- ☐ '89 All I Want Is You
- ☐ '88 Angel Of Harlem
- ☐ '00 Beautiful Day ★
- ☐ '87 Bullet The Blue Sky
- ☐ '88 Desire
- ☐ '97 Discothéque
- ☐ '92 Even Better Than The Real Thing
- ☐ '91 Fly, The
- ☐ '83 40
- ☐ '95 Hold Me, Thrill Me, Kiss Me, Kill Me
- ☐ '87 I Still Haven't Found What I'm Looking For ★
- ☐ '81 I Will Follow
- ☐ '83 I Will Follow [live]
- ☐ '91 Mysterious Ways
- ☐ '83 New Year's Day ★

## U2 — cont'd
- ☐ '90 Night And Day
- ☐ '93 Numb
- ☐ '92 One ★
- ☐ '84 Pride (In The Name Of Love)
- ☐ '97 Staring At The Sun
- ☐ '83 Sunday Bloody Sunday
- ☐ '98 Sweetest Thing
- ☐ '83 Two Hearts Beat As One
- ☐ '05 Vertigo
- ☐ '88 When Love Comes To Town
  *U2 with B.B. King*
- ☐ '87 Where The Streets Have No Name
- ☐ '92 Who's Gonna Ride Your Wild Horses
- ☐ '87 With Or Without You ★

# V

## VALE, Jerry
- ☐ '58 Go Chase A Moonbeam
- ☐ '64 Have You Looked Into Your Heart
- ☐ '56 Innamorata (Sweetheart)
- ☐ '56 You Don't Know Me

## VALENS, Ritchie
- ☐ '58 Come On Let's Go
- ☐ '58 Donna ★
- ☐ '58 La Bamba ★
- ☐ '59 That's My Little Suzie

## VALENTE, Caterina
- ☐ '55 Breeze And I, The

## VALENTINE, Brooke
- ☐ '05 Girlfight

## VALENTINO, Bobby
- ☐ '05 Slow Down ★

## VALENTINO, Mark
- ☐ '62 Push And Kick, The

## VALINO, Joe
- ☐ '56 Garden Of Eden

## VALJEAN
- ☐ '62 Theme From Ben Casey

## VALLI, Frankie
- ☐ '67 Can't Take My Eyes Off You
- ☐ '76 Fallen Angel
- ☐ '78 Grease ★
- ☐ '67 I Make A Fool Of Myself
- ☐ '74 My Eyes Adored You ★
- ☐ '75 Our Day Will Come
- ☐ '75 Swearin' To God
- ☐ '67 To Give (The Reason I Live)

## VALLI, June
- ☐ '60 Apple Green

## VANDENBERG
- ☐ '83 Burning Heart

## VANDROSS, Luther
- ☐ '88 Any Love
- ☐ '82 Bad Boy/Having A Party
- ☐ '92 Best Things In Life Are Free, The
  *LUTHER VANDROSS & JANET JACKSON*
- ☐ '03 Dance With My Father
- ☐ '91 Don't Want To Be A Fool
- ☐ '94 Endless Love
  *LUTHER VANDROSS & MARIAH CAREY*
- ☐ '86 Give Me The Reason
- ☐ '89 Here And Now
- ☐ '83 How Many Times Can We Say Goodbye
  *DIONNE WARWICK & LUTHER VANDROSS*
- ☐ '81 Never Too Much
- ☐ '91 Power Of Love/Love Power
- ☐ '86 Stop To Love
- ☐ '01 Take You Out
- ☐ '87 There's Nothing Better Than Love
  *LUTHER VANDROSS with Gregory Hines*
- ☐ '85 'Til My Baby Comes Home

## VAN DYKE, Leroy
- ☐ '56 Auctioneer
- ☐ '61 Walk On By ★

## VANGELIS
- ☐ '81 Chariots Of Fire ★

## VAN HALEN
- ☐ '78 Ain't Talkin' 'Bout Love
- ☐ '80 And The Cradle Will Rock...
- ☐ '79 Beautiful Girls
- ☐ '86 Best Of Both Worlds
- ☐ '88 Black And Blue
- ☐ '95 Can't Stop Lovin' You
- ☐ '79 Dance The Night Away
- ☐ '82 Dancing In The Street
- ☐ '95 Don't Tell Me (What Love Can Do)
- ☐ '86 Dreams
- ☐ '89 Feels So Good
- ☐ '88 Finish What Ya Started
- ☐ '84 Hot For Teacher
- ☐ '96 Humans Being
- ☐ '84 I'll Wait
- ☐ '78 Ice Cream Man
- ☐ '78 Jamie's Cryin'
- ☐ '84 Jump ★
- ☐ '86 Love Walks In
- ☐ '96 Me Wise Magic
- ☐ '82 (Oh) Pretty Woman
- ☐ '84 Panama
- ☐ '91 Poundcake
- ☐ '91 Right Now
- ☐ '91 Runaround
- ☐ '78 Runnin' With The Devil
- ☐ '91 Top Of The World
- ☐ '81 Unchained
- ☐ '88 When It's Love
- ☐ '86 Why Can't This Be Love ★
- ☐ '78 You Really Got Me

## VANILLA FUDGE
- ☐ '68 Take Me For A Little While
- ☐ '67 You Keep Me Hangin' On

## VANILLA ICE
- ☐ '90 Ice Ice Baby ★
- ☐ '90 Play That Funky Music

## VANITY FARE
- ☐ '69 Early In The Morning
- ☐ '70 Hitchin' A Ride

## VANNELLI, Gino
- ☐ '85 Black Cars
- ☐ '78 I Just Wanna Stop
- ☐ '81 Living Inside Myself
- ☐ '74 People Gotta Move
- ☐ '87 Wild Horses

## VANWARMER, Randy
- ☐ '79 Just When I Needed You Most ★

## VAPORS, The
- ☐ '80 Turning Japanese

## VARIOUS ARTISTS
- ☐ '05 Across The Universe

## VASSAR, Phil
- ☐ '04 In A Real Love
- ☐ '00 Just Another Day In Paradise
- ☐ '01 Six-Pack Summer
- ☐ '02 That's When I Love You

## VAUGHAN, Sarah
- ☐ '56 Banana Boat Song, The
- ☐ '59 Broken-Hearted Melody
- ☐ '55 C'est La Vie
- ☐ '60 Eternally
- ☐ '55 Experience Unnecessary
- ☐ '56 Fabulous Character
- ☐ '55 How Important Can It Be?
- ☐ '55 Make Yourself Comfortable
- ☐ '56 Mr. Wonderful
- ☐ '59 Smooth Operator
- ☐ '55 Whatever Lola Wants

## VAUGHAN, Stevie Ray
- ☐ '84 Cold Shot
- ☐ '89 Crossfire
- ☐ '83 Pride And Joy
- ☐ '91 Sky Is Crying, The
- ☐ '87 Superstition
- ☐ '87 Willie The Wimp

## VAUGHN, Billy, & His Orchestra
- ☐ '58 Blue Hawaii
- ☐ '58 Cimarron (Roll On)
- ☐ '58 La Paloma
- ☐ '60 Look For A Star
- ☐ '55 Melody Of Love
- ☐ '57 Raunchy
- ☐ '57 Sail Along Silvery Moon
- ☐ '55 Shifting Whispering Sands, The ★
- ☐ '62 Swingin' Safari, A
- ☐ '58 Tumbling Tumbleweeds
- ☐ '56 When The White Lilacs Bloom Again

## VEE, Bobby
- ☐ '67 Beautiful People
- ☐ '63 Charms
- ☐ '67 Come Back When You Grow Up
- ☐ '60 Devil Or Angel
- ☐ '62 Night Has A Thousand Eyes, The
- ☐ '62 Please Don't Ask About Barbara
- ☐ '62 Punish Her
- ☐ '60 Rubber Ball
- ☐ '61 Run To Him
- ☐ '62 Sharing You
- ☐ '61 Stayin' In
- ☐ '59 Suzie Baby
- ☐ '61 Take Good Care Of My Baby ★
- ☐ '61 Walkin' With My Angel

## VEGA, Suzanne
- ☐ '87 Luka ★
- ☐ '90 Tom's Diner
  - *D.N.A. Feat. SUZANNE VEGA*

## VELVET REVOLVER
- ☐ '04 Fall To Pieces
- ☐ '04 Slither

## VELVETS, The
- ☐ '61 Tonight (Could Be The Night)

## VELVET UNDERGROUND, The
- ☐ '67 Heroin
- ☐ '67 I'm Waiting For The Man
- ☐ '69 Pale Blue Eyes
- ☐ '69 Rock 'N' Roll
- ☐ '67 Sunday Morning
- ☐ '70 Sweet Jane

## VENGABOYS
- ☐ '99 We Like To Party!

## VENTURES, The
- ☐ '65 Diamond Head
- ☐ '69 Hawaii Five-O
- ☐ '61 Lullaby Of The Leaves
- ☐ '60 Perfidia
- ☐ '61 Ram-Bunk-Shush
- ☐ '66 Secret Agent Man
- ☐ '64 Slaughter On Tenth Avenue
- ☐ '60 Walk -- Don't Run ★
- ☐ '64 Walk-Don't Run '64

## VERA, Billy, & The Beaters
- ☐ '81 At This Moment ★
- ☐ '68 Country Girl - City Man
  - *BILLY VERA & JUDY CLAY*
- ☐ '81 I Can Take Care Of Myself

## VERNE, Larry
- ☐ '60 Mr. Custer ★

## VERTICAL HORIZON
- ☐ '00 Everything You Want ★
- ☐ '00 You're A God

## VERVE, The
- ☐ '98 Bitter Sweet Symphony

## VERVE PIPE, The
- ☐ '97 Freshmen, The ★

## VIBRATIONS, The
- ☐ '64 My Girl Sloopy
- ☐ '61 Watusi, The

## VILLAGE PEOPLE
- ☐ '79 In The Navy ★
- ☐ '78 Macho Man ★
- ☐ '78 Y.M.C.A. ★

## VILLAGE STOMPERS, The
- ☐ '63 Washington Square ★

## VINCENT, Gene, & His Blue Caps
- ☐ '56 Be-Bop-A-Lula ★
- ☐ '56 Bluejean Bop
- ☐ '57 Dance To The Bop
- ☐ '57 Lotta Lovin'
- ☐ '56 Race With The Devil

## VINTON, Bobby
- ☐ '75 Beer Barrel Polka
- ☐ '63 Blue On Blue
- ☐ '63 Blue Velvet ★
- ☐ '64 Clinging Vine
- ☐ '66 Coming Home Soldier
- ☐ '69 Days Of Sand And Shovels, The
- ☐ '72 Every Day Of My Life
- ☐ '68 Halfway To Paradise
- ☐ '68 I Love How You Love Me
- ☐ '67 Just As Much As Ever
- ☐ '65 L-O-N-E-L-Y
- ☐ '65 Long Lonely Nights
- ☐ '64 Mr. Lonely ★
- ☐ '64 My Heart Belongs To Only You
- ☐ '74 My Melody Of Love
- ☐ '63 Over The Mountain (Across The Sea)
- ☐ '67 Please Love Me Forever
- ☐ '62 Rain Rain Go Away
- ☐ '62 Roses Are Red (My Love) ★
- ☐ '65 Satin Pillows
- ☐ '72 Sealed With A Kiss
- ☐ '68 Take Good Care Of My Baby
- ☐ '64 Tell Me Why
- ☐ '63 There! I've Said It Again
- ☐ '69 To Know You Is To Love You

## VIOLENT FEMMES
- ☐ '91 American Music
- ☐ '82 Blister In The Sun
- ☐ '82 Gone Daddy Gone
- ☐ '89 Nightmares

## VIRTUES, The
- ☐ '59 Guitar Boogie Shuffle

## VISCOUNTS, The
- ☐ '59 Harlem Nocturne

## VITAMIN C
- ☐ '00 Graduation (Friends Forever)
- ☐ '99 Smile

## VIXEN
- ☐ '89 Cryin'
- ☐ '88 Edge Of A Broken Heart

## VOGUES, The
- ☐ '65 Five O'Clock World
- ☐ '66 Land Of Milk And Honey, The
- ☐ '66 Magic Town
- ☐ '68 My Special Angel

- ☐ '69 No, Not Much
- ☐ '68 Till
- ☐ '68 Turn Around, Look At Me
- ☐ '65 You're The One

## VOICES OF THEORY
- ☐ '98 Say It
- ☐ '98 Wherever You Go

## VOICES THAT CARE
- ☐ '91 Voices That Care

## VOLUME'S, The
- ☐ '62 I Love You

## VOUDOURIS, Roger
- ☐ '79 Get Used To It

## VOXPOPPERS, The
- ☐ '58 Wishing For Your Love

# W

## WADE, Adam
- ☐ '61 As If I Didn't Know
- ☐ '61 Take Good Care Of Her
- ☐ '61 Writing On The Wall, The

## WADSWORTH MANSION
- ☐ '70 Sweet Mary

## WAGNER, Jack
- ☐ '84 All I Need ★

## WAIKIKIS, The
- ☐ '64 Hawaii Tattoo

## WAILERS, The
- ☐ '59 Tall Cool One

## WAINWRIGHT, Loudon III
- ☐ '73 Dead Skunk

## WAITE, John
- ☐ '85 Every Step Of The Way
- ☐ '84 Missing You ★
- ☐ '84 Tears

## WAKELIN, Johnny
- ☐ '75 Black Superman - "Muhammad Ali"

## WALKER, Chris
- ☐ '92 Take Time

## WALKER, Clay
- ☐ '99 Chain Of Love, The
- ☐ '94 Dreaming With My Eyes Open
- ☐ '96 Hypnotize The Moon
- ☐ '94 If I Could Make A Living
- ☐ '93 Live Until I Die
- ☐ '97 Rumor Has It
- ☐ '97 Then What?
- ☐ '95 This Woman And This Man
- ☐ '93 What's It To You
- ☐ '98 You're Beginning To Get To Me

## WALKER, Jr., & The All Stars
- ☐ '67 Come See About Me
- ☐ '65 Do The Boomerang

'70 Do You See My Love (For You Growing)
'70 Gotta Hold On To This Feeling
'68 Hip City
'66 How Sweet It Is (To Be Loved By You)
'66 (I'm A) Road Runner
'67 Pucker Up Buttercup
'65 Shake And Fingerpop
'65 Shotgun
'69 These Eyes
'69 What Does It Take (To Win Your Love)

## WALKER BROS., The
'65 Make It Easy On Yourself
'66 Sun Ain't Gonna Shine (Anymore)

## WALLACE, Jerry
'58 How The Time Flies
'72 If You Leave Me Tonight I'll Cry
'64 In The Misty Moonlight
'60 Little Coco Palm
'59 Primrose Lane
'62 Shutters And Boards
'60 There She Goes

## WALLFLOWERS, The
'97 Difference, The
'98 Heroes
'96 One Headlight ★
'96 6th Avenue Heartache

## WALL OF VOODOO
'83 Mexican Radio

## WALSH, Joe
'80 All Night Long
'81 Life Of Illusion, A
'78 Life's Been Good
'73 Meadows
'73 Rocky Mountain Way

## WALTERS, Jamie
'95 Hold On

## WAMMACK, Travis
'64 Scratchy
'75 (Shu-Doo-Pa-Poo-Poop) Love Being Your Fool

## WANDERLEY, Walter
'66 Summer Samba (So Nice)

## WANG CHUNG
'84 Dance Hall Days ★
'84 Don't Let Go
'86 Everybody Have Fun Tonight ★
'87 Hypnotize Me
'87 Let's Go!

## WAR
'71 All Day Music
'74 Ballero
'73 Cisco Kid, The ★
'73 Gypsy Man
'77 L.A. Sunshine
'75 Low Rider
'73 Me And Baby Brother

'72 Slippin' Into Darkness
'70 Spill The Wine ★
*ERIC BURDON & WAR*
'76 Summer
'75 Why Can't We Be Friends? ★
'72 World Is A Ghetto, The

## WARD, Anita
'79 Ring My Bell ★

## WARD, Billy, & His Dominoes
'57 Deep Purple
'56 St. Therese Of The Roses
'57 Star Dust

## WARD, Dale
'63 Letter From Sherry

## WARD, Joe
'55 Nuttin For Xmas

## WARD, Robin
'63 Wonderful Summer

## WARINER, Steve
'98 Holes In The Floor Of Heaven
'99 I'm Already Taken
'99 Two Teardrops
'97 What If I Said
*ANITA COCHRAN with Steve Wariner*

## WARNES, Jennifer
'79 I Know A Heartache When I See One
'87 (I've Had) The Time Of My Life ★
*BILL MEDLEY & JENNIFER WARNES*
'77 Right Time Of The Night
'82 Up Where We Belong ★
*JOE COCKER & JENNIFER WARNES*

## WARRANT
'90 Cherry Pie
'89 Down Boys
'89 Heaven
'90 I Saw Red
'90 Sometimes She Cries

## WARREN G
'97 I Shot The Sheriff
'99 I Want It All
'94 Regulate ★
*WARREN G. & NATE DOGG*
'97 Smokin' Me Out
'94 This DJ
'96 What's Love Got To Do With It

## WARWICK, Dionne
'67 Alfie
'63 Anyone Who Had A Heart
'79 Deja Vu
'68 Do You Know The Way To San José
'62 Don't Make Me Over
'82 Friends In Love
*DIONNE WARWICK & JOHNNY MATHIS*
'70 Green Grass Starts To Grow, The
'82 Heartbreaker
'83 How Many Times Can We Say Goodbye
*DIONNE WARWICK & LUTHER VANDROSS*

## WARWICK, Dionne — cont'd
- ☐ '66 I Just Don't Know What To Do With Myself
- ☐ '67 I Say A Little Prayer
- ☐ '69 I'll Never Fall In Love Again
- ☐ '79 I'll Never Love This Way Again
- ☐ '87 Love Power
  *DIONNE WARWICK & JEFFREY OSBORNE*
- ☐ '70 Make It Easy On Yourself
- ☐ '66 Message To Michael
- ☐ '80 No Night So Long
- ☐ '68 Promises, Promises
- ☐ '64 Reach Out For Me
- ☐ '85 That's What Friends Are For ★
- ☐ '68 (Theme From) Valley Of The Dolls ★
- ☐ '74 Then Came You ★
  *DIONNE WARWICK & SPINNERS*
- ☐ '69 This Girl's In Love With You
- ☐ '66 Trains And Boats And Planes
- ☐ '64 Walk On By ★
- ☐ '67 Windows Of The World, The
- ☐ '64 You'll Never Get To Heaven (If You Break My Heart)
- ☐ '69 You've Lost That Lovin' Feeling

## WASHINGTON, Baby
- ☐ '63 That's How Heartaches Are Made

## WASHINGTON, Dinah
- ☐ '60 Baby (You've Got What It Takes) ★
  *DINAH WASHINGTON & BROOK BENTON*
- ☐ '60 Love Walked In
- ☐ '60 Rockin' Good Way (To Mess Around And Fall In Love)
  *DINAH WASHINGTON & BROOK BENTON*
- ☐ '61 September In The Rain
- ☐ '60 This Bitter Earth
- ☐ '59 Unforgettable
- ☐ '59 What A Diff'rence A Day Makes
- ☐ '62 Where Are You

## WASHINGTON, Grover Jr.
- ☐ '81 Just The Two Of Us ★
  *GROVER WASHINGTON, JR. (with Bill Withers)*

## WASHINGTON, Keith
- ☐ '91 Kissing You

## WAS (NOT WAS)
- ☐ '88 Spy In The House Of Love
- ☐ '89 Walk The Dinosaur

## WATERBOYS, The
- ☐ '88 Fisherman's Blues

## WATERFRONT
- ☐ '89 Cry

## WATERS, Crystal
- ☐ '91 Gypsy Woman (She's Homeless)
- ☐ '94 100% Pure Love
- ☐ '97 Say...If You Feel Alright

## WATERS, Muddy
- ☐ '57 Got My Mojo Working
- ☐ '54 Hoochie Coochie Man
- ☐ '55 Manish Boy

## WATLEY, Jody
- ☐ '87 Don't You Want Me
- ☐ '89 Everything
- ☐ '89 Friends
  *JODY WATLEY (With Eric B. & Rakim)*
- ☐ '92 I'm The One You Need
- ☐ '87 Looking For A New Love ★
- ☐ '89 Real Love
- ☐ '88 Some Kind Of Lover
- ☐ '87 Still A Thrill

## WAYNE, Jimmy
- ☐ '03 Stay Gone

## WAYNE, Thomas
- ☐ '59 Tragedy

## WEATHER GIRLS, The
- ☐ '83 It's Raining Men

## WEATHERLY, Jim
- ☐ '74 Need To Be, The

## WEBER, Joan
- ☐ '55 Let Me Go, Lover! ★

## WEEZER
- ☐ '05 Beverly Hills ★
- ☐ '94 Buddy Holly ★
- ☐ '01 Hash Pipe
- ☐ '94 Undone-The Sweater Song

## WE FIVE
- ☐ '65 Let's Get Together
- ☐ '65 You Were On My Mind ★

## WEISSBERG, Eric, & Steve Mandell
- ☐ '73 Dueling Banjos ★

## WELCH, Bob
- ☐ '78 Ebony Eyes
- ☐ '78 Hot Love, Cold World
- ☐ '79 Precious Love
- ☐ '77 Sentimental Lady

## WELCH, Lenny
- ☐ '70 Breaking Up Is Hard To Do
- ☐ '64 Ebb Tide
- ☐ '63 Since I Fell For You
- ☐ '60 You Don't Know Me

## WELK, Lawrence, & His Orchestra
- ☐ '60 Calcutta
- ☐ '60 Last Date
- ☐ '56 Moritat (A Theme From "The Threepenny Opera")
- ☐ '56 Poor People Of Paris, The

## WELLS, Mary
- ☐ '61 I Don't Want To Take A Chance
- ☐ '63 Laughing Boy
- ☐ '64 My Guy ★
- ☐ '64 Once Upon A Time
  *MARVIN GAYE & MARY WELLS*
- ☐ '62 One Who Really Loves You, The
- ☐ '62 Two Lovers
- ☐ '65 Use Your Head

☐ '63 What's Easy For Two Is So Hard For One
☐ '64 What's The Matter With You Baby
*MARVIN GAYE & MARY WELLS*
☐ '62 You Beat Me To The Punch
☐ '63 You Lost The Sweetest Boy
☐ '63 Your Old Stand By

**WESLEY, Fred — see J.B.'s**

## WEST, Dottie
☐ '81 What Are We Doin' In Love
*DOTTIE WEST (with Kenny Rogers)*

## WEST, Kanye
☐ '04 All Falls Down
☐ '04 Jesus Walks ★
☐ '03 Through The Wire

## WEST COAST RAP ALL-STARS, The
☐ '90 We're All In The Same Gang

## WESTLIFE
☐ '00 Swear It Again

**WESTON, Kim — see GAYE, Marvin**

## WESTSIDE CONNECTION
☐ '96 Bow Down
☐ '03 Gangsta Nation
☐ '97 Gangstas Make The World Go Round

## WET WILLIE
☐ '74 Keep On Smilin'
☐ '77 Street Corner Serenade
☐ '79 Weekend

## WHEN IN ROME
☐ '88 Promise, The

## WHISPERS, The
☐ '80 And The Beat Goes On
☐ '81 It's A Love Thing
☐ '80 Lady
☐ '87 Rock Steady

## WHISTLE
☐ '90 Always And Forever

## WHITCOMB, Ian
☐ '65 You Turn Me On

## WHITE, Barry
☐ '74 Can't Get Enough Of Your Love, Babe ★
☐ '75 I'll Do For You Anything You Want Me To
☐ '73 I'm Gonna Love You Just A Little More Baby
☐ '73 I've Got So Much To Give
☐ '77 It's Ecstasy When You Lay Down Next To Me
☐ '75 Let The Music Play
☐ '73 Never, Never Gonna Give Ya Up
☐ '78 Oh What A Night For Dancing
☐ '94 Practice What You Preach
☐ '75 What Am I Gonna Do With You
☐ '74 You're The First, The Last, My Everything ★

☐ '78 Your Sweetness Is My Weakness

## WHITE, Bryan
☐ '95 Rebecca Lynn
☐ '97 Sittin' On Go
☐ '96 So Much For Pretending
☐ '95 Someone Else's Star

## WHITE, Karyn
☐ '86 Facts Of Love
*JEFF LORBER Feat. Karyn White*
☐ '89 Love Saw It
☐ '91 Romantic ★
☐ '89 Secret Rendezvous
☐ '89 Superwoman
☐ '91 Way I Feel About You, The
☐ '88 Way You Love Me, The

## WHITE, Tony Joe
☐ '69 Polk Salad Annie

## WHITE LION
☐ '88 Wait
☐ '88 When The Children Cry

## WHITE PLAINS
☐ '70 My Baby Loves Lovin'

## WHITESNAKE
☐ '90 Deeper The Love, The
☐ '89 Fool For Your Loving
☐ '87 Here I Go Again ★
☐ '87 Is This Love

## WHITE STRIPES, The
☐ '03 Seven Nation Army
☐ '02 We're Going To Be Friends

## WHITE TOWN
☐ '97 Your Woman

## WHITING, Margaret
☐ '56 Money Tree, The
☐ '66 Wheel Of Hurt, The

## WHITLEY, Keith
☐ '89 I'm No Stranger To The Rain
☐ '88 When You Say Nothing At All

## WHITTAKER, Roger
☐ '75 Last Farewell, The ★

## WHO, The
☐ '82 Athena
☐ '71 Baba O'Riley
☐ '71 Bargain
☐ '71 Behind Blue Eyes
☐ '67 Boris The Spider
☐ '68 Call Me Lightning
☐ '83 Eminence Front
☐ '73 5:15
☐ '71 Goin' Mobile
☐ '67 Happy Jack
☐ '67 I Can See For Miles ★
☐ '65 I Can't Explain
☐ '69 I'm Free
☐ '72 Join Together
☐ '71 Kids Are Alright

## WHO, The — cont'd
- ☐ '79 Long Live Rock
- ☐ '73 Love, Reign, O'er Me
- ☐ '68 Magic Bus
- ☐ '66 My Generation ★
- ☐ '71 My Wife
- ☐ '67 Pictures Of Lily
- ☐ '69 Pinball Wizard
- ☐ '73 Real Me
- ☐ '72 Relay, The
- ☐ '70 See Me, Feel Me
- ☐ '70 Seeker, The
- ☐ '75 Squeeze Box
- ☐ '66 Substitute
- ☐ '70 Summertime Blues
- ☐ '69 We're Not Gonna Take It
- ☐ '78 Who Are You
- ☐ '71 Won't Get Fooled Again ★
- ☐ '81 You Better You Bet

## WIEDLIN, Jane
- ☐ '88 Rush Hour

## WILCOX, Harlow, & The Oakies
- ☐ '69 Groovy Grubworm

## WILD CHERRY
- ☐ '76 Play That Funky Music ★

## WILDE, Eugene
- ☐ '85 Don't Say No Tonight
- ☐ '84 Gotta Get You Home Tonight

## WILDE, Kim
- ☐ '82 Kids In America
- ☐ '87 You Keep Me Hangin' On

## WILDER, Matthew
- ☐ '83 Break My Stride
- ☐ '84 Kid's American, The

## WILKINSONS, The
- ☐ '98 26¢

## WILLIAMS, Andy
- ☐ '65 And Roses And Roses
- ☐ '58 Are You Sincere
- ☐ '56 Baby Doll
- ☐ '68 Battle Hymn Of The Republic
- ☐ '61 Bilbao Song, The
- ☐ '57 Butterfly
- ☐ '63 Can't Get Used To Losing You ★
- ☐ '56 Canadian Sunset
- ☐ '63 Days Of Wine And Roses
- ☐ '64 Dear Heart
- ☐ '62 Don't You Believe It
- ☐ '64 Fool Never Learns, A
- ☐ '69 Happy Heart
- ☐ '58 Hawaiian Wedding Song, The
- ☐ '63 Hopeless
- ☐ '57 I Like Your Kind Of Love
- ☐ '66 In The Arms Of Love
- ☐ '57 Lips Of Wine
- ☐ '59 Lonely Street
- ☐ '72 Love Theme From "The Godfather"
- ☐ '63 May Each Day

- ☐ '62 Moon River
- ☐ '67 More And More
- ☐ '67 Music To Watch Girls By
- ☐ '64 On The Street Where You Live
- ☐ '70 One Day Of Your Life
- ☐ '58 Promise Me, Love
- ☐ '62 Stranger On The Shore
- ☐ '59 Village Of St. Bernadette, The
- ☐ '71 (Where Do I Begin) Love Story

## WILLIAMS, Billy
- ☐ '56 Crazy Little Palace, A
- ☐ '57 I'm Gonna Sit Right Down And Write Myself A Letter ★

## WILLIAMS, Christopher
- ☐ '91 I'm Dreamin'

## WILLIAMS, Danny
- ☐ '64 White On White

## WILLIAMS, Deniece
- ☐ '76 Free
- ☐ '82 It's Gonna Take A Miracle
- ☐ '84 Let's Hear It For The Boy ★
- ☐ '78 Too Much, Too Little, Too Late ★
  *JOHNNY MATHIS/DENIECE WILLIAMS*

## WILLIAMS, Don
- ☐ '80 I Believe In You
- ☐ '78 Tulsa Time

## WILLIAMS, Hank Jr.
- ☐ '84 All My Rowdy Friends Are Coming Over Tonight
- ☐ '82 Country Boy Can Survive, A
- ☐ '79 Family Tradition
- ☐ '86 Mind Your Own Business
- ☐ '89 There's A Tear In My Beer
  *HANK WILLIAMS, JR. with Hank Williams, Sr.*

## WILLIAMS, John
- ☐ '75 Main Title (Theme From "Jaws")
- ☐ '77 Star Wars (Main Title)
- ☐ '77 Theme From "Close Encounters Of The Third Kind"

## WILLIAMS, Larry
- ☐ '57 Bony Moronie
- ☐ '57 Short Fat Fannie

## WILLIAMS, Mason
- ☐ '68 Classical Gas ★

## WILLIAMS, Maurice, & The Zodiacs
- ☐ '60 Stay ★

## WILLIAMS, Roger
- ☐ '57 Almost Paradise
- ☐ '55 Autumn Leaves ★
- ☐ '66 Born Free
- ☐ '56 La Mer (Beyond The Sea)
- ☐ '66 Lara's Theme From "Dr. Zhivago"
- ☐ '67 Love Me Forever
- ☐ '67 More Than A Miracle
- ☐ '58 Near You
- ☐ '57 Till
- ☐ '55 Wanting You

172

## WILLIAMS, Vanessa
- [ ] '95 Colors Of The Wind ★
- [ ] '91 Comfort Zone, The
- [ ] '89 Dreamin'
- [ ] '92 Just For Tonight
- [ ] '93 Love Is ★
  *VANESSA WILLIAMS & BRIAN McKNIGHT*
- [ ] '91 Running Back To You
- [ ] '92 Save The Best For Last ★
- [ ] '94 Sweetest Days, The

## WILLIAMSON, "Sonny Boy"
- [ ] '55 Don't Start Me Talkin'

## WILLIS, Bruce
- [ ] '87 Respect Yourself

## WILLIS, Chuck
- [ ] '58 Betty And Dupree
- [ ] '57 C. C. Rider
- [ ] '58 Hang Up My Rock And Roll Shoes
- [ ] '56 It's Too Late
- [ ] '58 What Am I Living For

## WILLS, Mark
- [ ] '00 Back At One
- [ ] '98 Don't Laugh At Me
- [ ] '98 I Do [Cherish You]
- [ ] '02 19 Somethin'
- [ ] '99 Wish You Were Here

## WILL TO POWER
- [ ] '88 Baby, I Love Your Way/Freebird Medley (Free Baby) ★
- [ ] '90 I'm Not In Love

## WILSON, Al
- [ ] '76 I've Got A Feeling (We'll Be Seeing Each Other Again)
- [ ] '74 La La Peace Song
- [ ] '73 Show And Tell
- [ ] '68 Snake, The

## WILSON, Ann
- [ ] '84 Almost Paradise...Love Theme From Footloose
  *MIKE RENO & ANN WILSON*
- [ ] '88 Surrender To Me
  *ANN WILSON & ROBIN ZANDER*

## WILSON, Gretchen
- [ ] '04 Here For The Party
- [ ] '05 Homewrecker
- [ ] '04 Redneck Woman
- [ ] '04 When I Think About Cheatin'

## WILSON, J. Frank, & The Cavaliers
- [ ] '64 Last Kiss ★

## WILSON, Jackie
- [ ] '60 Alone At Last
- [ ] '60 Am I The Man
- [ ] '63 Baby Workout
- [ ] '60 Doggin' Around
- [ ] '59 I'll Be Satisfied
- [ ] '61 I'm Comin' On On Back To You
- [ ] '58 Lonely Teardrops ★
- [ ] '61 My Empty Arms

- [ ] '60 Night ★
- [ ] '61 Please Tell Me Why
- [ ] '57 Reet Petite
- [ ] '63 Shake! Shake! Shake!
- [ ] '59 Talk That Talk
- [ ] '59 That's Why (I Love You So)
- [ ] '58 To Be Loved
- [ ] '66 Whispers (Gettin' Louder)
- [ ] '60 Woman, A Lover, A Friend, A
- [ ] '59 You Better Know It
- [ ] '60 (You Were Made For) All My Love
- [ ] '67 (Your Love Keeps Lifting Me) Higher And Higher ★

## WILSON, Meri
- [ ] '77 Telephone Man

## WILSON, Nancy
- [ ] '68 Face It Girl, It's Over
- [ ] '64 (You Don't Know) How Glad I Am

## WILSON PHILLIPS
- [ ] '91 Dream Is Still Alive, The
- [ ] '92 Give It Up
- [ ] '90 Hold On ★
- [ ] '90 Impulsive
- [ ] '90 Release Me ★
- [ ] '92 You Won't See Me Cry
- [ ] '91 You're In Love ★

## WILTON PLACE STREET BAND
- [ ] '77 Disco Lucy (I Love Lucy Theme)

## WINANS, BeBe & CeCe
- [ ] '91 Addictive Love
- [ ] '89 Heaven
- [ ] '91 I'll Take You There

## WINANS, CeCe
- [ ] '96 Count On Me
  *WHITNEY HOUSTON & CECE WINANS*

## WINANS, Mario
- [ ] '04 I Don't Wanna Know ★

## WINBUSH, Angela
- [ ] '87 Angel
- [ ] '89 It's The Real Thing

## WINCHESTER, Jesse
- [ ] '81 Say What

## WINDING, Kai, & Orchestra
- [ ] '63 More

## WING & A PRAYER FIFE & DRUM CORPS.
- [ ] '75 Baby Face

## WINGER
- [ ] '89 Headed For A Heartbreak
- [ ] '90 Miles Away
- [ ] '89 Seventeen

## WINGFIELD, Pete
- [ ] '75 Eighteen With A Bullet

## WINSTONS, The
- ☐ '69 Color Him Father

## WINTER, Edgar, Group
- ☐ '73 Frankenstein ★
- ☐ '73 Free Ride
- ☐ '74 River's Risin'

## WINTERHALTER, Hugo, & His Orchestra with Eddie Heywood
- ☐ '56 Canadian Sunset ★

## WINWOOD, Steve
- ☐ '87 Back In The High Life Again
- ☐ '88 Don't You Know What The Night Can Do?
- ☐ '87 Finer Things, The
- ☐ '86 Freedom Overspill
- ☐ '86 Higher Love ★
- ☐ '88 Holding On
- ☐ '90 One And Only Man
- ☐ '88 Roll With It ★
- ☐ '86 Split Decision
- ☐ '87 Valerie [remix]
- ☐ '81 While You See A Chance

## WISEGUYS, The
- ☐ '01 Start The Commotion

## WITHERS, Bill
- ☐ '71 Ain't No Sunshine ★
- ☐ '81 Just The Two Of Us ★
  GROVER WASHINGTON, JR. (with Bill Withers)
- ☐ '73 Kissing My Love
- ☐ '72 Lean On Me ★
- ☐ '77 Lovely Day
- ☐ '72 Use Me

## WOLF, Peter
- ☐ '87 Come As You Are
- ☐ '84 I Need You Tonight
- ☐ '84 Lights Out

## WOMACK, Bobby
- ☐ '72 Harry Hippie
- ☐ '85 I Wish He Didn't Trust Me So Much
- ☐ '81 If You Think You're Lonely Now
- ☐ '74 Lookin' For A Love
- ☐ '84 Love Has Finally Come At Last
  BOBBY WOMACK & PATTI LaBELLE
- ☐ '73 Nobody Wants You When You're Down And Out
- ☐ '71 That's The Way I Feel About Cha
- ☐ '72 Woman's Gotta Have It

## WOMACK, Lee Ann
- ☐ '97 Fool, The
- ☐ '00 I Hope You Dance ★
- ☐ '99 I'll Think Of A Reason Later
- ☐ '98 Little Past Little Rock, A
- ☐ '97 You've Got To Talk To Me

## WONDER, Stevie
- ☐ '66 Blowin In The Wind
- ☐ '74 Boogie On Reggae Woman
- ☐ '82 Do I Do
- ☐ '74 Don't You Worry 'Bout A Thing
- ☐ '82 Ebony And Ivory ★
  PAUL McCARTNEY (with Stevie Wonder)
- ☐ '63 Fingertips ★
- ☐ '68 For Once In My Life ★
- ☐ '85 Go Home
- ☐ '70 Heaven Help Us All
- ☐ '64 Hey Harmonica Man
- ☐ '73 Higher Ground
- ☐ '80 I Ain't Gonna Stand For It
- ☐ '84 I Just Called To Say I Love You ★
- ☐ '67 I Was Made To Love Her
- ☐ '76 I Wish
- ☐ '67 I'm Wondering
- ☐ '71 If You Really Love Me
- ☐ '77 Isn't She Lovely
- ☐ '73 Living For The City
- ☐ '84 Love Light In Flight
- ☐ '80 Master Blaster (Jammin') ★
- ☐ '69 My Cherie Amour
- ☐ '70 Never Had A Dream Come True
- ☐ '66 Nothing's Too Good For My Baby
- ☐ '86 Overjoyed
- ☐ '85 Part-Time Lover ★
- ☐ '66 Place In The Sun, A
- ☐ '79 Send One Your Love ★
- ☐ '68 Shoo-Be-Doo-Be-Doo-Da-Day
- ☐ '70 Signed, Sealed, Delivered I'm Yours ★
- ☐ '77 Sir Duke ★
- ☐ '87 Skeletons
- ☐ '72 Superstition ★
- ☐ '72 Superwoman (Where Were You When I Needed You)
- ☐ '82 That Girl
- ☐ '65 Uptight (Everything's Alright)
- ☐ '71 We Can Work It Out
- ☐ '69 Yester-Me, Yester-You, Yesterday
- ☐ '73 You Are The Sunshine Of My Life ★
- ☐ '74 You Haven't Done Nothin
- ☐ '68 You Met Your Match
- ☐ '88 You Will Know

## WONDER, Wayne
- ☐ '03 No Letting Go

## WOOD, Brenton
- ☐ '67 Gimme Little Sign
- ☐ '67 Oogum Boogum Song, The

## WOOD, Lauren
- ☐ '79 Please Don't Leave

## WOODS, Stevie
- ☐ '82 Just Can't Win 'Em All
- ☐ '81 Steal The Night

## WOOLEY, Sheb
- ☐ '58 Purple People Eater, The ★

## WORLD PARTY
- ☐ '87 Ship Of Fools (Save Me From Tomorrow)

## WORLEY, Darryl
- ☐ '05 Awful, Beautiful Life ★
- ☐ '03 Have You Forgotten?
- ☐ '02 I Miss My Friend

## WRAY, Link, & His Ray Men
- ☐ '59 Raw-Hide
- ☐ '58 Rumble

## WRECKX-N-EFFECT
- ☐ '92 Rump Shaker ★

## WRIGHT, Betty
- ☐ '71 Clean Up Woman
- ☐ '78 Dance With Me
  - *PETER BROWN with Betty Wright*
- ☐ '68 Girls Can't Do What The Guys Do

## WRIGHT, Charles, & The Watts 103rd Street Rhythm Band
- ☐ '69 Do Your Thing
- ☐ '70 Express Yourself
- ☐ '70 Love Land

## WRIGHT, Chely
- ☐ '99 Single White Female

## WRIGHT, Dale
- ☐ '58 She's Neat

## WRIGHT, Gary
- ☐ '76 Dream Weaver ★
- ☐ '76 Love Is Alive
- ☐ '81 Really Wanna Know You

## WRIGHT, Priscilla
- ☐ '55 Man In The Raincoat, The

## WU-TANG CLAN
- ☐ '94 C.R.E.A.M.
- ☐ '93 Method Man

## WYATT, Keke
- ☐ '02 Nothing In This World

## WYNETTE, Tammy
- ☐ '68 D-I-V-O-R-C-E
- ☐ '67 I Don't Wanna Play House
- ☐ '67 My Elusive Dreams
  - *DAVID HOUSTON & TAMMY WYNETTE*
- ☐ '68 Stand By Your Man ★

## WYNONNA
- ☐ '93 Bad Goodbye, A
  - *CLINT BLACK with Wynonna*
- ☐ '92 I Saw The Light
- ☐ '92 No One Else On Earth
- ☐ '94 Rock Bottom
- ☐ '92 She Is His Only Need
- ☐ '96 To Be Loved By You

# X

## X
- ☐ '85 Burning House Of Love
- ☐ '87 4th Of July

## XSCAPE
- ☐ '98 Arms Of The One Who Loves You, The
- ☐ '95 Feels So Good
- ☐ '93 Just Kickin' It
- ☐ '98 My Little Secret
- ☐ '93 Understanding
- ☐ '95 Who Can I Run To?

## XTC
- ☐ '92 Ballad Of Peter Pumpkinhead, The
- ☐ '89 Mayor Of Simpleton, The

# Y

## YANKOVIC, "Weird Al"
- ☐ '84 Eat It
- ☐ '85 Like A Surgeon
- ☐ '92 Smells Like Nirvana

## YARBROUGH, Glenn
- ☐ '65 Baby The Rain Must Fall

## YARBROUGH & PEOPLES
- ☐ '81 Don't Stop The Music
- ☐ '84 Don't Waste Your Time

## YARDBIRDS, The
- ☐ '65 For Your Love
- ☐ '66 Happenings Ten Years Time Ago
- ☐ '65 Heart Full Of Soul
- ☐ '65 I'm A Man
- ☐ '67 Little Games
- ☐ '66 Over Under Sideways Down
- ☐ '66 Shapes Of Things
- ☐ '65 Train Kept A-Rollin'

## YAZ
- ☐ '82 Only You
- ☐ '82 Situation

## YEARWOOD, Trisha
- ☐ '96 Believe Me Baby (I Lied)
- ☐ '97 How Do I Live
- ☐ '97 In Another's Eyes
  - *TRISHA YEARWOOD & GARTH BROOKS*
- ☐ '98 Perfect Love, A
- ☐ '91 She's In Love With The Boy
- ☐ '93 Song Remembers When, The
- ☐ '98 There Goes My Baby
- ☐ '95 Thinkin' About You
- ☐ '92 Walkaway Joe
  - *TRISHA YEARWOOD with Don Henley*
- ☐ '94 XXX's And OOO's (An American Girl)

## YELLO
- ☐ '87 Oh Yeah

## YELLOW BALLOON, The
- ☐ '67 Yellow Balloon

## YELLOWCARD
- ☐ '04 Ocean Avenue

## YES
- ☐ '72 America
- ☐ '72 And You And I
- ☐ '72 Close To The Edge
- ☐ '69 Every Little Thing
- ☐ '77 Going For The One
- ☐ '84 Leave It
- ☐ '91 Lift Me Up
- ☐ '72 Long Distance Runaround
- ☐ '87 Love Will Find A Way
- ☐ '83 Owner Of A Lonely Heart ★
- ☐ '87 Rhythm Of Love
- ☐ '72 Roundabout

## YES — cont'd
- ☐ '71 Starship Trooper
- ☐ '71 Your Move/All Good People
- ☐ '71 Yours Is No Disgrace

## YING YANG TWINS
- ☐ '03 Salt Shaker
- ☐ '05 Wait (The Whisper Song) ★
- ☐ '04 Whats Happnin!

## YOAKAM, Dwight
- ☐ '93 Ain't That Lonely Yet
- ☐ '93 Fast As You
- ☐ '86 Guitars, Cadillacs
- ☐ '86 Honky Tonk Man
- ☐ '88 Streets Of Bakersfield
  *DWIGHT YOAKAM & BUCK OWENS*
- ☐ '93 Thousand Miles From Nowhere, A

## YOUNG, Barry
- ☐ '65 One Has My Name (The Other Has My Heart)

## YOUNG, Faron
- ☐ '58 Alone With You
- ☐ '61 Hello Walls
- ☐ '71 It's Four In The Morning

## YOUNG, John Paul
- ☐ '78 Love Is In The Air

## YOUNG, Kathy, with The Innocents
- ☐ '61 Happy Birthday Blues
- ☐ '60 Thousand Stars, A ★

## YOUNG, Neil
- ☐ '70 After The Gold Rush
- ☐ '69 Cinnamon Girl
- ☐ '78 Comes A Time
- ☐ '75 Cortez The Killer
- ☐ '69 Cowgirl In The Sand
- ☐ '69 Down By The River
- ☐ '78 Four Strong Winds
- ☐ '72 Heart Of Gold ★
- ☐ '77 Like A Hurricane
- ☐ '72 Needle And The Damage Done
- ☐ '72 Old Man
- ☐ '70 Only Love Can Break Your Heart
- ☐ '89 Rockin' In The Free World
- ☐ '79 Rust Never Sleeps (Hey Hey, My My)
- ☐ '70 Southern Man
- ☐ '74 Walk On
- ☐ '70 When You Dance I Can Really Love

## YOUNG, Paul
- ☐ '84 Come Back And Stay
- ☐ '85 Everytime You Go Away ★
- ☐ '85 I'm Gonna Tear Your Playhouse Down
- ☐ '90 Oh Girl
- ☐ '92 What Becomes Of The Brokenhearted

## YOUNG, Victor, & His Singing Strings
- ☐ '57 (Main Theme) Around The World

## YOUNGBLOODS, The
- ☐ '67 Get Together

## YOUNGBLOODZ
- ☐ '03 Damn!

## YOUNG BUCK
- ☐ '04 Let Me In
- ☐ '04 Shorty Wanna Ride

## YOUNG GUNZ
- ☐ '03 Can't Stop, Won't Stop
- ☐ '04 No Better Love

## YOUNG-HOLT UNLIMITED
- ☐ '68 Soulful Strut
- ☐ '66 Wack Wack

## YOUNG M.C.
- ☐ '89 Bust A Move ★
- ☐ '89 Principal's Office

## YOUNG RASCALS — see RASCALS

## YO-YO
- ☐ '91 You Can't Play With My Yo-Yo

## YURO, Timi
- ☐ '61 Hurt
- ☐ '63 Make The World Go Away
- ☐ '62 What's A Matter Baby (Is It Hurting You)

# Z

## ZACHARIAS, Helmut
- ☐ '56 When The White Lilacs Bloom Again

## ZACHERLE, John, "The Cool Ghoul"
- ☐ '58 Dinner With Drac

## ZAGER, Michael, Band
- ☐ '78 Let's All Chant

## ZAGER & EVANS
- ☐ '69 In The Year 2525 ★

## ZAHND, Ricky, & The Blue Jeaners
- ☐ '55 (I'm Gettin') Nuttin' For Christmas

## ZAPP
- ☐ '82 Dance Floor
- ☐ '80 More Bounce To The Ounce

## ZAPPA, Frank
- ☐ '74 Cosmik Debris
- ☐ '79 Dancin' Fool
- ☐ '74 Don't Eat The Yellow Snow
- ☐ '79 Joe's Garage
- ☐ '73 Montana
- ☐ '70 My Guitar Wants To Kill Your Mama
- ☐ '69 Peaches En Regalia
- ☐ '70 Transylvania Boogie
- ☐ '82 Valley Girl

## ZEVON, Warren
- ☐ '80 Certain Girl, A
- ☐ '78 Excitable Boy
- ☐ '78 Lawyers, Guns And Money
- ☐ '78 Werewolves Of London ★

## ZHANÉ
- ☐ '94 Groove Thang
- ☐ '93 Hey Mr. D.J. ★
- ☐ '97 Request Line
- ☐ '94 Sending My Love
- ☐ '94 Shame

## Z'LOOKE
- ☐ '88 Can U Read My Lips

## ZOMBIES, The
- ☐ '64 She's Not There ★
- ☐ '65 Tell Her No
- ☐ '69 Time Of The Season ★

## ZZ TOP
- ☐ '77 Arrested For Driving While Blind
- ☐ '80 Cheap Sunglasses
- ☐ '90 Concrete And Steel
- ☐ '90 Doubleback
- ☐ '72 Francene
- ☐ '83 Gimme All Your Lovin
- ☐ '90 Give It Up
- ☐ '75 Heard It On The X
- ☐ '80 I Thank You
- ☐ '80 I'm Bad, I'm Nationwide
- ☐ '77 It's Only Love
- ☐ '73 La Grange
- ☐ '84 Legs
- ☐ '90 My Head's In Mississippi
- ☐ '94 Pincushion
- ☐ '86 Rough Boy
- ☐ '83 Sharp Dressed Man
- ☐ '85 Sleeping Bag
- ☐ '85 Stages
- ☐ '81 Tube Snake Boogie
- ☐ '75 Tush
- ☐ '86 Velcro Fly
- ☐ '92 Viva Las Vegas
- ☐ '72 Waitin' For The Bus/Jesus Just Left Chicago

# SONG TITLE SECTION

Following are some basic guidelines for using this section:

All titles are listed in alphabetical order and are in bold type.
The year is listed to the left of the title.
The artist name is listed in italics to the right (or below) the title.

In this book, **songs with identical titles are listed together even if they are different compositions**. Listed below the song title, in chronological order, are the artists' names. The following artists recorded songs with the same title, but they are not the same composition:

**My First Love**
'89 *Atlantic Starr*
'00 *Avant*

Most of the listings in this book mirror the following:

'93 **All About Soul** *Billy Joel*

Abbreviated titles such as "C.C. Rider" and "S.O.S." are listed at the beginning of their respective first letters. Conversely, abbreviated titles which spell out a word, such as "T-R-O-U-B-L-E" and "D-I-V-O-R-C-E" are sorted along with the regular spellings of these words.

If any of the articles "A," "An," "The" or "Tha" is the first word of a title, it is not shown. However, if a title is made up of only one other word, then it is shown as follows:

'77 **Pride, The** *Isley Brothers*

On occasion, similar titles are combined.  Examples:

### Tonight, Tonight [Tonite, Tonite]
'57  *Mello-Kings*
'96  *Smashing Pumpkins*

In the above case, one artist spelled the title "Tonight, Tonight" and the other artist spelled it as "Tonite, Tonite."

### I Saw Her [Him] Standing There
'64  *Beatles*
'88  *Tiffany*

In the above case, one artist recorded the title "I Saw Her Standing There" and the other artist as "I Saw Him Standing There."

If [medley] follows either a title or an artist's name, that indicates that the title is part of a medley.  Go to the artist section to find out the other part of the medley.

# A

'70 **ABC** *Jackson 5*
'01 **AM To PM** *Christina Milian*
'96 **ATLiens** *OutKast*
'00 **Aaron's Party (Come Get It)**
  *Aaron Carter*
'81 **Abacab** *Genesis*
'64 **Abigail Beecher** *Freddy Cannon*
'63 **Abilene** *George Hamilton IV*
'94 **About A Girl** *Nirvana*
'60 **About This Thing Called Love**
  *Fabian*
'03 **Above All** *Michael W. Smith*
  **Abracadabra**
'73 *DeFranco Family*
'82 *Steve Miller Band*
  **Abraham, Martin And John**
'68 *Dion*
'69 *Moms Mabley*
'69 *Miracles*
'71 *Tom Clay [medley]*
'71 **Absolutely Right**
  *Five Man Electrical Band*
'00 **Absolutely (Story Of A Girl)**
  *Ninedays*
'04 **Accidentally In Love**
  *Counting Crows*
'79 **Accidents Will Happen**
  *Elvis Costello*
'92 **Achy Breaky Heart** *Billy Ray Cyrus*
'90 **Across The River** *Bruce Hornsby*
  **Across The Universe**
'70 *Beatles*
'05 *Various Artists*
'03 **Act A Fool** *Ludacris*
  **Act Naturally**
'63 *Buck Owens*
'65 *Beatles*
  **Action**
'65 *Freddy Cannon*
'76 *Sweet*
'00 **Adam's Song** *Blink 182*
'91 **Addams Groove** *Hammer*
'86 **Addicted To Love** *Robert Palmer*
'88 **Addicted To You** *Levert*
'02 **Addictive** *Truth Hurts*
'91 **Addictive Love**
  *BeBe & CeCe Winans*
'98 **Adia** *Sarah McLachlan*
'62 **Adios Amigo** *Jim Reeves*
'55 **Adorable** *Drifters*
'84 **Adult Education**
  *Daryl Hall - John Oates*
'02 **Aerials** *System Of A Down*
'83 **Affair Of The Heart** *Rick Springfield*
'57 **Affair To Remember (Our Love Affair)** *Vic Damone*
'82 **Africa** *Toto*
'62 **Afrikaan Beat** *Bert Kaempfert*
'89 **After All** *Cher & Peter Cetera*
'70 **After Midnight** *Eric Clapton*
'57 **After School** *Randy Starr*
'91 **After The Dance** *Fourplay*
'83 **After The Fall** *Journey*
'85 **After The Fire** *Roger Daltrey*
'82 **After The Glitter Fades** *Stevie Nicks*
  **After The Gold Rush**
'70 *Neil Young*
'74 *Prelude*
'56 **After The Lights Go Down Low**
  *Al Hibbler*
'79 **After The Love Has Gone**
  *Earth, Wind & Fire*
'76 **After The Lovin'**
  *Engelbert Humperdinck*
'90 **After The Rain** *Nelson*
'75 **After The Thrill Is Gone** *Eagles*
'76 **Afternoon Delight**
  *Starland Vocal Band*
  **Again**
'93 *Janet Jackson*
'00 *Lenny Kravitz*
'92 **Again Tonight** *John Mellencamp*
'84 **Against All Odds (Take A Look At Me Now)** *Phil Collins*

'80 **Against The Wind** *Bob Seger*
'65 **Agent Double-O-Soul** *Edwin Starr*
'75 **Agony And The Ecstasy**
  *Smokey Robinson*
'80 **Ah! Leah!** *Donnie Iris*
'62 **Ahab, The Arab** *Ray Stevens*
'81 **Ai No Corrida** *Quincy Jones*
'81 **Ain't Even Done With The Night**
  *John Cougar Mellencamp*
'93 **Ain't Going Down (Til The Sun Comes Up)** *Garth Brooks*
'77 **Ain't Gonna Bump No More (With No Big Fat Woman)** *Joe Tex*
'66 **Ain't Gonna Lie** *Keith*
  **Ain't Got No Home**
'56 *Clarence Henry*
'73 *Band*
'69 **Ain't It Funky Now** *James Brown*
'01 **Ain't It Funny** *Jennifer Lopez*
'79 **Ain't Love A Bitch** *Rod Stewart*
'88 **Ain't No Half-Steppin'**
  *Big Daddy Kane*
  **Ain't No Mountain High Enough**
'67 *Marvin Gaye & Tammi Terrell*
'70 *Diana Ross*
'79 **Ain't No Stoppin' Us Now**
  *McFadden & Whitehead*
'71 **Ain't No Sunshine** *Bill Withers*
'68 **Ain't No Way** *Aretha Franklin*
'75 **Ain't No Way To Treat A Lady**
  *Helen Reddy*
'73 **Ain't No Woman (Like The One I've Got)** *Four Tops*
  **Ain't Nobody**
'83 *Rufus & Chaka Khan*
'96 *Monica*
'92 **Ain't Nobody Like You** *Miki Howard*
'86 **Ain't Nothin' Goin' On But The Rent**
  *Gwen Guthrie*
'01 **Ain't Nothing 'Bout You**
  *Brooks & Dunn*
  **Ain't Nothing Like The Real Thing**
'68 *Marvin Gaye & Tammi Terrell*
'76 *Donny & Marie Osmond*
'64 **Ain't Nothing You Can Do**
  *Bobby Bland*
'95 **Ain't Nuthin' But A She Thing**
  *Salt-N-Pepa*
'89 **Ain't Nuthin' In The World**
  *Miki Howard*
'64 **Ain't She Sweet** *Beatles*
'78 **Ain't Talkin' 'Bout Love**
  *Van Halen*
  **Ain't That A Shame**
'55 *Pat Boone*
'55 *Fats Domino*
'63 *4 Seasons*
'79 *Cheap Trick*
'61 **Ain't That Just Like A Woman**
  *Fats Domino*
'93 **Ain't That Lonely Yet**
  *Dwight Yoakam*
'56 **Ain't That Lovin' You Baby**
  *Jimmy Reed*
'64 **Ain't That Loving You Baby**
  *Elvis Presley*
'65 **Ain't That Peculiar** *Marvin Gaye*
  **Ain't Too [2] Proud [2] Beg**
'66 *Temptations*
'74 *Rolling Stones*
'92 *TLC*
'71 **Ain't Understanding Mellow**
  *Jerry Butler & Brenda Lee Eager*
'72 **Ain't Wastin' Time No More** *Allman Brothers Band*
'02 **Air Force Ones** *Nelly*
'74 **Air That I Breathe** *Hollies*
'70 **Airport Love Theme** *Vincent Bell*
'77 **Aja** *Steely Dan*
  **Al Di La'**
'62 *Emilio Pericoli*
'64 *Ray Charles Singers*
'80 **Alabama Getaway**
  *Grateful Dead*
'55 **Alabama Jubilee** *Ferko String Band*
'67 **Alabama Song (Whiskey Bar)**
  *Doors*

'69 **Albatross** *Fleetwood Mac*
'71 **Albert Flasher** *Guess Who*
  **Alfie**
'66 *Cher*
'67 *Dionne Warwick*
  **Alibis**
'84 *Sergio Mendes*
'93 *Tracy Lawrence*
'63 **Alice In Wonderland** *Neil Sedaka*
'68 **Alice Long (You're Still My Favorite Girlfriend)**
  *Tommy Boyce & Bobby Hart*
'81 **Alien** *Atlanta Rhythm Section*
'77 **Alison** *Elvis Costello*
  **Alive**
'92 *Pearl Jam*
'01 *P.O.D.*
'78 **Alive Again** *Chicago*
'85 **Alive & Kicking** *Simple Minds*
'67 **All** *James Darren*
'93 **All About Soul** *Billy Joel*
'62 **All Alone Am I** *Brenda Lee*
  **All Along The Watchtower**
'68 *Jimi Hendrix*
'68 *Bob Dylan*
'58 **All American Boy** *Bill Parsons*
'81 **All American Girls** *Sister Sledge*
'93 **All Apologies** *Nirvana*
'90 **All Around The World**
  *Lisa Stansfield*
'55 **All At Once You Love Her**
  *Perry Como*
  **All By Myself**
'55 *Fats Domino*
'75 *Eric Carmen*
'97 *Celine Dion*
  **All Cried Out**
'86 *Lisa Lisa & Cult Jam*
'97 *Allure*
'64 **All Day And All Of The Night** *Kinks*
'71 **All Day Music** *War*
'04 **All Falls Down** *Kanye West*
'88 **All Fired Up** *Pat Benatar*
'80 **All For Leyna** *Billy Joel*
  **All For [4] Love**
'91 *Color Me Badd*
'93 *Bryan Adams/Rod Stewart/Sting*
  **All For You**
'97 *Sister Hazel*
'01 *Janet Jackson*
'71 **All Good People [medley]** *Yes*
'60 **All I Could Do Was Cry** *Etta James*
'90 **All I Do Is Think Of You** *Troop*
'71 **All I Ever Need Is You** *Sonny & Cher*
'02 **All I Have** *Jennifer Lopez*
  **All I Have To Do Is Dream**
'58 *Everly Brothers*
'63 *Richard Chamberlain*
'70 *Bobbie Gentry & Glen Campbell*
'99 **All I Have To Give** *Backstreet Boys*
'73 **All I Know** *Garfunkel*
  **All I Need**
'67 *Temptations*
'84 *Jack Wagner*
'86 **All I Need Is A Miracle**
  *Mike + The Mechanics*
  **All I Really Want To Do**
'65 *Byrds*
'65 *Cher*
'66 **All I See Is You** *Dusty Springfield*
'94 **All I Wanna Do** *Sheryl Crow*
'90 **All I Wanna Do Is Make Love To You** *Heart*
  **All I Want**
'92 *Toad The Wet Sprocket*
'97 *702*
'94 **All I Want For Christmas Is You**
  *Mariah Carey*
'89 **All I Want Is Forever** *James "J.T." Taylor & Regina Belle*
'89 **All I Want Is You** *U2*
'86 **All I Wanted** *Kansas*
'90 **All I'm Missing Is You**
  *Glenn Medeiros*
'60 **All In My Mind** *Maxine Brown*

'96 **All Mixed Up** *311*
'87 **All My Ex's Live In Texas**
    *George Strait*
    **All My Life**
'83   *Kenny Rogers*
'90   *Linda Ronstadt/Aaron Neville*
'98   *K-Ci & JoJo*
'02   *Foo Fighters*
    **All My Love**
'79   *Led Zeppelin*
'98   *Queen Pen*
'64 **All My Loving** *Beatles*
'84 **All My Rowdy Friends Are Coming**
    **Over Tonight** *Hank Williams Jr.*
    **All Night Long**
'80   *Joe Walsh*
'99   *Faith Evans*
'83 **All Night Long (All Night)**
    *Lionel Richie*
'58 **(All of a Sudden) My Heart Sings**
    *Paul Anka*
'89 **All Of My Love** *Gap Band*
'84 **All Of You**
    *Julio Iglesias & Diana Ross*
    **All Or Nothing**
'90   *Milli Vanilli*
'01   *O-Town*
'81 **All Our Tomorrows** *Eddie Schwartz*
'80 **All Out Of Love** *Air Supply*
'58 **All Over Again** *Johnny Cash*
'80 **All Over The World**
    *Electric Light Orchestra*
'95 **All Over You** *Live*
'83 **All Right** *Christopher Cross*
'70 **All Right Now** *Free*
'88 **All She Wants Is** *Duran Duran*
'85 **All She Wants To Do Is Dance**
    *Don Henley*
'57 **All Shook Up** *Elvis Presley*
'99 **All Star** *Smash Mouth*
    **All Strung Out**
'66   *Nino Tempo & April Stevens*
'77   *John Travolta*
'88 **All That Money Wants**
    *Psychedelic Furs*
'93 **All That She Wants** *Ace Of Base*
    **All The King's Horses**
'72   *Aretha Franklin*
'86   *Firm*
'86 **All The Love In The World** *Outfield*
'90 **All The Man That I Need**
    *Whitney Houston*
'98 **All The Places (I Will Kiss You)**
    *Aaron Hall*
'99 **All The Small Things** *Blink 182*
    **All The Things She Said**
'86   *Simple Minds*
'03   *t.A.T.u.*
'96 **All The Things (Your Man Won't Do)**
    *Joe*
'58 **All The Time** *Johnny Mathis*
    **All The Way**
'57   *Frank Sinatra*
'83   *Triumph*
'72 **All The Young Dudes**
    *Mott The Hoople*
'83 **All This Love** *DeBarge*
    **All This Time**
'88   *Tiffany*
'91   *Sting*
'81 **All Those Years Ago**
    *George Harrison*
'84 **All Through The Night** *Cyndi Lauper*
'83 **All Time High** *Rita Coolidge*
'92 **All Woman** *Lisa Stansfield*
'77 **All You Get From Love Is A Love**
    **Song** *Carpenters*
'67 **All You Need Is Love** *Beatles*
'02 **All You Wanted** *Michelle Branch*
'85 **All You Zombies** *Hooters*
'56 **Allegheny Moon** *Patti Page*
'82 **Allentown** *Billy Joel*
'62 **Alley Cat** *Bent Fabric*
    **Alley-Oop**
'60   *Danté & the Evergreens*
'60   *Hollywood Argyles*

'94 **Allison Road** *Gin Blossoms*
'70 **Almost Cut My Hair**
    *Crosby, Stills, Nash & Young*
'99 **Almost Doesn't Count** *Brandy*
'93 **Almost Goodbye** *Mark Chesnutt*
'59 **Almost Grown** *Chuck Berry*
'90 **Almost Hear You Sigh**
    *Rolling Stones*
'02 **Almost Home** *Craig Morgan*
'78 **Almost Like Being In Love**
    *Michael Johnson*
'83 **Almost Over You** *Sheena Easton*
'57 **Almost Paradise** *Roger Williams*
'84 **Almost Paradise...Love Theme**
    **From Footloose**
    *Mike Reno & Ann Wilson*
'66 **Almost Persuaded** *David Houston*
'75 **Almost Saturday Night**
    *John Fogerty*
'78 **Almost Summer** *Celebration*
    **Alone**
'87   *Heart*
'97   *Bee Gees*
'72 **Alone Again (Naturally)**
    *Gilbert O'Sullivan*
'68 **Alone Again Or** *Love*
'60 **Alone At Last** *Jackie Wilson*
    **Alone (Why Must I Be Alone)**
'57   *Shepherd Sisters*
'64   *4 Seasons*
    **Alone With You**
'58   *Faron Young*
'92   *Tevin Campbell*
    **Along Came Jones**
'59   *Coasters*
'69   *Ray Stevens*
'85 **Along Comes A Woman** *Chicago*
'66 **Along Comes Mary** *Association*
'88 **Alphabet St.** *Prince*
'74 **Already Gone** *Eagles*
    **Alright**
'90   *Janet Jackson*
'93   *Kris Kross*
'73 **Also Sprach Zarathustra (2001)**
    *Deodato*
'62 **Alvin Twist** *Chipmunks*
'59 **Alvin's Harmonica** *Chipmunks*
'60 **Alvin's Orchestra** *Chipmunks*
    **Always**
'59   *Sammy Turner*
'87   *Atlantic Starr*
'94   *Bon Jovi*
'94   *Erasure*
'02   *Saliva*
    **Always And Forever**
'78   *Heatwave*
'90   *Whistle*
'96 **Always Be My Baby** *Mariah Carey*
'94 **Always In My Heart** *Tevin Campbell*
'60 **Always It's You** *Everly Brothers*
    **Always On My Mind**
'82   *Willie Nelson*
'88   *Pet Shop Boys*
'01 **Always On Time** *Ja Rule*
'92 **Always The Last To Know**
    *Del Amitri*
    **Always Together**
'64   *Al Martino*
'68   *Dells*
'98 **Am I Dreaming** *Ol' Skool*
'60 **Am I Losing You** *Jim Reeves*
    **Am I That Easy To Forget**
'60   *Debbie Reynolds*
'67   *Engelbert Humperdinck*
'60 **Am I The Man** *Jackie Wilson*
'92 **Am I The Same Girl**
    *Swing Out Sister*
'86 **Amanda** *Boston*
'99 **Amazed** *Lonestar*
'93 **Amazing** *Aerosmith*
    **Amazing Grace**
'70   *Judy Collins*
'72   *Royal Scots Dragoon Guards*
'68 **Ame Caline (Soul Coaxing)**
    *Raymond Lefevre*

    **Amen**
'64   *Impressions*
'68   *Otis Redding*
    **America**
'61   *Chita Rivera*
'68   *Simon & Garfunkel*
'72   *Yes*
'81   *Neil Diamond*
'72 **America The Beautiful** *Ray Charles*
'05 **American Baby**
    *Dave Matthews Band*
'72 **American City Suite**
    *Cashman & West*
    **American Dream**
'79   *Dirt Band*
'88   *Crosby, Stills, Nash & Young*
'77 **American Girl** *Tom Petty*
'82 **American Heartbeat** *Survivor*
'93 **American Honky-Tonk Bar**
    **Association** *Garth Brooks*
'04 **American Idiot** *Green Day*
'03 **American Life** *Madonna*
'83 **American Made** *Oak Ridge Boys*
    **American Music**
'82   *Pointer Sisters*
'91   *Violent Femmes*
    **American Pie**
'71   *Don McLean*
'00   *Madonna*
'03 **American Soldier** *Toby Keith*
'86 **American Storm** *Bob Seger*
    **American Trilogy**
'71   *Mickey Newbury*
'72   *Elvis Presley*
'73 **American Tune** *Paul Simon*
    **American Woman**
'70   *Guess Who*
'99   *Lenny Kravitz*
    **Americans**
'74   *Byron MacGregor*
'74   *Gordon Sinclair*
'75 **Amie** *Pure Prairie League*
'59 **Among My Souvenirs**
    *Connie Francis*
'61 **Amor** *Ben E. King*
'70 **Amos Moses** *Jerry Reed*
'55 **Amukiriki (The Lord Willing)**
    *Les Paul & Mary Ford*
'88 **Ana Ng** *They Might Be Giants*
'77 **Anarchy In The U.K.**
    *Sex Pistols*
'95 **And Fools Shine On** *Brother Cane*
'67 **And Get Away** *Esquires*
'82 **And I Am Telling You I'm Not Going**
    *Jennifer Holliday*
'64 **And I Love Her** *Beatles*
'73 **And I Love You So** *Perry Como*
'94 **And On And On** *Janet Jackson*
'94 **And Our Feelings** *Babyface*
'65 **And Roses And Roses**
    *Andy Williams*
'85 **And She Was** *Talking Heads*
'90 **And So It Goes** *Billy Joel*
'95 **And Still** *Reba McEntire*
    **And That Reminds Me**
'57   *Della Reese*
'57   *Kay Starr*
'80 **And The Beat Goes On** *Whispers*
'80 **And The Cradle Will Rock...**
    *Van Halen*
'85 **And We Danced** *Hooters*
'69 **And When I Die**
    *Blood, Sweat & Tears*
'72 **And You And I** *Yes*
    **Angel**
'71   *Jimi Hendrix*
'72   *Rod Stewart*
'73   *Aretha Franklin*
'85   *Madonna*
'87   *Angela Winbush*
'88   *Aerosmith*
'93   *Jon Secada*
'98   *Sarah McLachlan*
'00   *Shaggy*
'03   *Amanda Perez*

**Angel Baby**
'58  Dean Martin
'60  Rosie & The Originals
'91  Angelica
'89  **Angel Eyes** Jeff Healey Band
'82  **Angel In Blue** J. Geils Band
'77  **Angel In Your Arms** Hot
'88  **Angel Of Harlem** U2
'98  **Angel Of Mine** Monica
**Angel Of The Morning**
'68  Merrilee Rush
'81  Juice Newton
'60  **Angel On My Shoulder** Shelby Flint
'80  **Angel Say No** Tommy Tutone
'58  **Angel Smile** Nat "King" Cole
'89  **Angel Song** Great White
'60  **Angela Jones** Johnny Ferguson
'89  **Angelia** Richard Marx
'85  **Angels** Amy Grant
'93  **Angels Among Us** Alabama
'55  **Angels In The Sky** Crew Cuts
'59  **Angels Listened In** Crests
'96  **Angels Of The Silences**
      Counting Crows
'73  **Angie** Rolling Stones
'74  **Angie Baby** Helen Reddy
'01  **Angry All The Time** Tim McGraw
'87  **Animal** Def Leppard
'99  **Animal Song** Savage Garden
'62  **Anna (Go To Him)**
      Arthur Alexander
'74  **Annie's Song** John Denver
'93  **Anniversary** Tony Toni Tone
'80  **Another Brick In The Wall**
      Pink Floyd
'71  **Another Day** Paul McCartney
'89  **Another Day In Paradise** Phil Collins
'00  **Another Dumb Blonde** Hoku
'88  **Another Lover** Giant Steps
**Another Night**
'86  Aretha Franklin
'94  Real McCoy
'80  **Another One Bites The Dust** Queen
'74  **Another Park, Another Sunday**
      Doobie Brothers
'88  **Another Part Of Me** Michael Jackson
'93  **Another Sad Love Song**
      Toni Braxton
**Another Saturday Night**
'63  Sam Cooke
'74  Cat Stevens
'60  **Another Sleepless Night**
      Jimmy Clanton
'58  **Another Time, Another Place**
      Patti Page
'97  **Another You** David Kersh
'80  **Answering Machine** Rupert Holmes
'71  **Anticipation** Carly Simon
'95  **Ants Marching** Dave Matthews Band
**Any Day Now**
'62  Chuck Jackson
'82  Ronnie Milsap
'88  **Any Love** Luther Vandross
'74  **Any Major Dude Will Tell You**
      Steely Dan
'95  **Any Man Of Mine** Shania Twain
'94  **Any Time, Any Place** Janet Jackson
**Any Way You Want It**
'64  Dave Clark Five
'80  Journey
'61  **Anybody But Me** Brenda Lee
'97  **Anybody Seen My Baby?**
      Rolling Stones
**Anymore**
'60  Teresa Brewer
'91  Travis Tritt
'99  **Anyone Else** Collin Raye
'63  **Anyone Who Had A Heart**
      Dionne Warwick
**Anything**
'94  SWV
'95  3T
'02  Jaheim
'05  **Anything But Mine** Kenny Chesney
'88  **Anything For You** Gloria Estefan

'90  **Anything I Want** Kevin Paige
'90  **Anything Is Possible** Debbie Gibson
'62  **Anything That's Part Of You**
      Elvis Presley
**Anytime**
'78  Journey
'98  Brian McKnight
'94  **Anytime You Need A Friend**
      Mariah Carey
'56  **Anyway You Want Me (That's How I
      Will Be)** Elvis Presley
'99  **Anywhere** 112
'61  **Apache** Jorgen Ingmann
'70  **Ape Call** Nervous Norvus
'70  **Apeman** Kinks
'60  **Apple Green** June Valli
'65  **Apple Of My Eye** Roy Head
'67  **Apples, Peaches, Pumpkin Pie**
      Jay & The Techniques
'56  **April In Paris** Count Basie
'57  **April Love** Pat Boone
'78  **Aqua Boogie** Parliament
'71  **Aqualung** Jethro Tull
'69  **Aquarius/Let The Sunshine In**
      5th Dimension
'98  **Are U Still Down** Jon B.
'84  **Are We Ourselves?** Fixx
'65  **Are You A Boy Or Are You A Girl**
      Barbarians
'67  **Are You Experienced?**
      Jimi Hendrix
'03  **Are You Gonna Be My Girl** Jet
'93  **Are You Gonna Go My Way**
      Lenny Kravitz
'68  **Are You Happy** Jerry Butler
'03  **Are You Happy Now?**
      Michelle Branch
'98  **Are You Jimmy Ray?** Jimmy Ray
**Are You Lonely For Me**
'66  Freddy Scott
'91  Rude Boys
**Are You Lonesome To-night?**
'60  Elvis Presley
'73  Donny Osmond
'73  **Are You Man Enough** Four Tops
'70  **Are You Ready?**
      Pacific Gas & Electric
'58  **Are You Really Mine**
      Jimmie Rodgers
'55  **Are You Satisfied?** Rusty Draper
'82  **Are You Serious** Tyrone Davis
'58  **Are You Sincere** Andy Williams
'98  **Are You That Somebody?** Aaliyah
'01  **Area Codes** Ludacris
'77  **Ariel** Dean Friedman
'69  **Arizona** Mark Lindsay
'88  **Armageddon It** Def Leppard
'73  **Armed And Extremely Dangerous**
      First Choice
'89  **Arms Of Orion**
      Prince with Sheena Easton
'98  **Arms Of The One Who Loves You**
      Xscape
'90  **Around The Way Girl** LL Cool J
**Around The World**
'57  Bing Crosby
'57  Mantovani
'57  Victor Young
'01  **Around The World (La La La La La)**
      ATC
'77  **Arrested For Driving While Blind**
      ZZ Top
'79  **Arrow Through Me** Wings
'81  **Arthur's Theme (Best That You Can
      Do)** Christopher Cross
'60  **Artificial Flowers** Bobby Darin
'94  **As Any Fool Can See**
      Tracy Lawrence
'95  **As I Lay Me Down**
      Sophie B. Hawkins
'61  **As If I Didn't Know** Adam Wade
'63  **As Long As I Know He's Mine**
      Marvelettes
'88  **As Long As You Follow**
      Fleetwood Mac
'97  **As Long As You Love Me**
      Backstreet Boys

**As Tears Go By**
'64  Marianne Faithfull
'65  Rolling Stones
'70  **As The Years Go By** Mashmakhan
'63  **As Usual** Brenda Lee
'87  **As We Lay** Shirley Murdock
'96  **Ascension (Don't Ever Wonder)**
      Maxwell
'80  **Ashes By Now** Rodney Crowell
'80  **Ashes To Ashes** David Bowie
'61  **Asia Minor** Kokomo
**Ask Me**
'56  Nat "King" Cole
'64  Elvis Presley
'71  **Ask Me No Questions** B.B. King
'72  **Ask Me What You Want**
      Millie Jackson
'95  **Ask Of You** Raphael Saadiq
**Ask The Lonely**
'65  Four Tops
'83  Journey
'61  **Astronaut, The** Jose Jimenez
'61  **At Last** Etta James
**At My Front Door**
'55  Pat Boone
'55  El Dorados
'75  **At Seventeen** Janis Ian
'97  **At The Beginning**
      Donna Lewis & Richard Marx
'57  **At The Hop** Danny & The Juniors
'66  **At The Scene** Dave Clark Five
'67  **At The Zoo** Simon & Garfunkel
'81  **At This Moment**
      Billy Vera & The Beaters
'94  **At Your Best (You Are Love)**
      Aaliyah
'82  **Athena** Who
'81  **Atlanta Lady (Something About
      Your Love)** Marty Balin
'69  **Atlantis** Donovan
'80  **Atomic** Blondie
'83  **Atomic Dog** George Clinton
'65  **Attack** Toys
'85  **Attack Me With Your Love** Cameo
'75  **Attitude Dancing** Carly Simon
'73  **Aubrey** Bread
'56  **Auctioneer** Leroy Van Dyke
'99  **Auld Lang Syne** Kenny G
'01  **Austin** Blake Shelton
'84  **Authority Song**
      John Cougar Mellencamp
'75  **Autobahn** Kraftwerk
'84  **Automatic** Pointer Sisters
'83  **Automatic Man** Michael Sembello
'55  **Autumn Leaves**
      Roger Williams
'68  **Autumn Of My Life**
      Bobby Goldsboro
'56  **Autumn Waltz** Tony Bennett
'98  **Ava Adore** Smashing Pumpkins
'82  **Avalon** Roxy Music
'00  **Awake** Godsmack
'03  **Away From Me** Puddle Of Mudd
'04  **Awful, Beautiful Life** Darryl Worley
'85  **Axel F** Harold Faltermeyer

# B

'90  **B.B.D. (I Thought It Was Me)?**
      Bell Biv DeVoe
'71  **Baba O'Riley** Who
'79  **Babe** Styx
'69  **Babe I'm Gonna Leave You**
      Led Zeppelin
'66  **B-A-B-Y** Carla Thomas
**Baby**
'95  Brandy
'02  Ashanti
'02  **Baby, The** Blake Shelton
'91  **Baby Baby** Amy Grant
'92  **Baby-Baby-Baby** TLC
'69  **Baby, Baby Don't Cry** Miracles
**Baby Blue**
'61  Echoes
'72  Badfinger

183

'03 **Baby Boy** Beyoncé
**Baby, Come Back**
'68 Equals
'77 Player
'73 **Baby Come Close**
Smokey Robinson
**Baby, Come To Me**
'82 Patti Austin (with James Ingram)
'89 Regina Belle
'56 **Baby Doll** Andy Williams
'89 **Baby Don't Forget My Number**
Milli Vanilli
'72 **Baby Don't Get Hooked On Me**
Mac Davis
'65 **Baby Don't Go** Sonny & Cher
'72 **Baby Don't You Do It** Band
'63 **Baby Don't You Weep**
Garnet Mimms
'62 **Baby Elephant Walk** Miniature Men
**Baby Face**
'58 Little Richard
'75 Wing & Prayer Fife & Drum Corps
'05 **Baby Girl** Sugarland
'92 **Baby Got Back** Sir Mix-A-Lot
'87 **Baby Grand** Billy Joel & Ray Charles
**Baby Hold On**
'70 Grass Roots
'78 Eddie Money
'92 **Baby Hold On To Me**
Gerald Levert (with Eddie Levert)
'83 **Baby I Lied** Deborah Allen
**Baby, I Love You**
'63 Ronettes
'67 Aretha Franklin
'69 Andy Kim
**Baby, I Love Your Way**
'76 Peter Frampton
'88 Will To Power [medley]
'94 Big Mountain
**Baby I Need Your Loving**
'64 Four Tops
'67 Johnny Rivers
'71 **Baby I'm - A Want You** Bread
'05 **Baby I'm Back** Baby Bash
'78 **Baby I'm Burnin'** Dolly Parton
'69 **Baby, I'm For Real** Originals
'91 **Baby I'm Ready** Levert
**Baby, I'm Yours**
'65 Barbara Lewis
'93 Shai
'04 **Baby, It's Cold Outside**
Rod Stewart with Dolly Parton
'90 **Baby, It's Tonight** Jude Cole
**Baby It's You**
'61 Shirelles
'69 Smith
'04 JoJo
'83 **Baby Jane** Rod Stewart
'71 **Baby Let Me Kiss You** King Floyd
'72 **Baby Let Me Take You (In My Arms)**
Detroit Emeralds
'68 **Baby Let's Wait** Royal Guardsmen
**Baby Love**
'64 Supremes
'86 Regina
'82 **Baby Makes Her Blue Jeans Talk**
Dr. Hook
'67 **Baby, Now That I've Found You**
Foundations
'60 **Baby Oh Baby** Shells
'98 **Baby One More Time** Britney Spears
'66 **Baby Scratch My Back** Slim Harpo
'61 **Baby Sittin' Boogie** Buzz Clifford
'82 **Baby Step Back** Gordon Lightfoot
'69 **Baby Take Me In Your Arms**
Jefferson
'59 **Baby Talk** Jan & Dean
'80 **Baby Talks Dirty** Knack
'75 **Baby That's Backatcha**
Smokey Robinson
'65 **Baby The Rain Must Fall**
Glenn Yarbrough
'91 **Baby Universal** Tin Machine
'77 **Baby, What A Big Surprise** Chicago
'60 **Baby What You Want Me To Do**
Jimmy Reed

'63 **Baby Workout** Jackie Wilson
'67 **Baby You're A Rich Man** Beatles
'61 **Baby, You're Right** James Brown
'60 **Baby (You've Got What It Takes)**
Dinah Washington & Brook Benton
'61 **Baby's First Christmas**
Connie Francis
'80 **Babylon Sisters** Steely Dan
**Back And Forth**
'87 Cameo
'94 Aaliyah
**Back At One**
'99 Brian McKnight
'00 Mark Wills
**Back Door Man**
'61 Howlin' Wolf
'67 Doors
'95 **Back For Good** Take That
'00 **Back Here** BBMak
'74 **Back Home Again** John Denver
'80 **Back In Black** AC/DC
'65 **Back In My Arms Again** Supremes
'85 **Back In Stride**
Maze Feat. Frankie Beverly
'94 **Back In The Day** Ahmad
'87 **Back In The High Life Again**
Steve Winwood
'77 **Back In The Saddle** Aerosmith
**Back In The U.S.A.**
'59 Chuck Berry
'78 Linda Ronstadt
'68 **Back In The U.S.S.R.** Beatles
'85 **Back In Time** Huey Lewis
'72 **Back Off Boogaloo** Ringo Starr
'88 **Back On Holiday** Robbie Nevil
'80 **Back On My Feet Again** Babys
'82 **Back On The Chain Gang**
Pretenders
'67 **Back On The Street Again**
Sunshine Company
'72 **Back Stabbers** O'Jays
'99 **Back That Azz Up** Juvenile
'98 **Back 2 Good** Matchbox 20
'89 **Back To Life** Soul II Soul
'92 **Back To The Hotel** N2Deep
'77 **Back Together Again**
Daryl Hall & John Oates
'04 **Back When** Tim McGraw
'73 **Back When My Hair Was Short**
Gunhill Road
'84 **Back Where You Belong** 38 Special
'69 **Backfield In Motion** Mel & Tim
'66 **Backstage** Gene Pitney
'80 **Backstrokin'** Fatback
'94 **Backwater** Meat Puppets
'97 **Backyard Boogie** Mack 10
'87 **Bad** Michael Jackson
'73 **Bad, Bad Leroy Brown** Jim Croce
'75 **Bad Blood** Neil Sedaka
**Bad Boy**
'57 Jive Bombers
'82 Ray Parker Jr.
'82 Luther Vandross [medley]
'86 Miami Sound Machine
'01 **Bad Boy For Life**
P. Diddy, Black Rob & Mark Curry
'93 **Bad Boys** Inner Circle
'79 **Bad Case Of Loving You (Doctor, Doctor)** Robert Palmer
'74 **Bad Company** Bad Company
**Bad Girl**
'63 Neil Sedaka
'93 Madonna
'79 **Bad Girls** Donna Summer
'93 **Bad Goodbye**
Clint Black (with Wynonna)
'89 **Bad Love** Eric Clapton
**Bad Luck**
'56 B.B. King
'75 Harold Melvin
'60 **Bad Man Blunder** Kingston Trio
'88 **Bad Medicine** Bon Jovi
'69 **Bad Moon Rising**
Creedence Clearwater Revival
'90 **Bad Of The Heart** George LaMond
'75 **Bad Time** Grand Funk

'64 **Bad To Me** Billy J. Kramer
With The Dakotas
'82 **Bad To The Bone**
George Thorogood
'69 **Badge** Cream
'78 **Badlands** Bruce Springsteen
'63 **Bag Lady** Erykah Badu
'99 **Bailamos** Enrique Iglesias
'63 **Baja** Astronauts
'78 **Baker Street** Gerry Rafferty
'62 **Balboa Blue** Marketts
'68 **Ball And Chain** Big Brother & The
Holding Company
'70 **Ball Of Confusion (That's What The
World Is Today)** Temptations
'69 **Ball Of Fire** Tommy James
'04 **Balla Baby** Chingy
'58 **Ballad Of A Teenage Queen**
Johnny Cash
'65 **Ballad Of A Thin Man**
Bob Dylan
'74 **Ballad Of Billy The Kid**
Billy Joel
'68 **Ballad Of Bonnie And Clyde**
Georgie Fame
**Ballad Of Davy Crockett**
'55 "Tennessee" Ernie Ford
'55 Bill Hayes
'55 Fess Parker
'66 **Ballad Of Irving** Frank Gallop
'90 **Ballad of Jayne** L.A. Guns
'69 **Ballad Of John And Yoko** Beatles
'62 **Ballad Of Paladin** Duane Eddy
'92 **Ballad Of Peter Pumpkinhead** XTC
'60 **Ballad Of The Alamo** Marty Robbins
'66 **Ballad Of The Green Berets**
SSgt Barry Sadler
'57 **Ballerina** Nat "King" Cole
'86 **Ballerina Girl** Lionel Richie
'91 **Ballerina Out Of Control**
Ocean Blue
'74 **Ballero** War
'75 **Ballroom Blitz** Sweet
**Banana Boat Song**
'56 Fontane Sisters
'56 Tarriers
'56 Sarah Vaughan
'57 Harry Belafonte
'57 Stan Freberg
**Band Of Gold**
'55 Kit Carson
'55 Don Cherry
'66 Mel Carter
'70 Freda Payne
'74 **Band On The Run** Paul McCartney
'67 **Banda, A** Herb Alpert
**Bang A Gong (Get It On)**
'72 T. Rex
'85 Power Station
'94 **Bang And Blame** R.E.M.
'66 **Bang Bang (My Baby Shot Me
Down)** Cher
'68 **Bang-Shang-A-Lang** Archies
'83 **Bang The Drum All Day**
Todd Rundgren
'84 **Bang Your Head (Metal Health)**
Quiet Riot
'71 **Bangla-Desh** George Harrison
'55 **Banjo's Back In Town**
Teresa Brewer
'90 **Banned In The U.S.A.**
Luke Feat. 2 Live Crew
'60 **Barbara** Temptations
**Barbara-Ann**
'61 Regents
'66 Beach Boys
'97 **Barbie Girl** Aqua
'66 **Barefootin'** Robert Parker
'96 **Barely Breathing** Duncan Sheik
'76 **Baretta's Theme ("Keep Your Eye
On The Sparrow")**
Rhythm Heritage
'71 **Bargain** Who
'77 **Barracuda** Heart
'94 **Basket Case** Green Day

'73 **Basketball Jones Featuring Tyrone Shoelaces** *Cheech & Chong*
'77 **Bat Out Of Hell** *Meat Loaf*
'89 **Batdance** *Prince*
'66 **Batman & His Grandmother** *Dickie Goodman*
**Batman Theme**
'66 *Neal Hefti*
'66 *Marketts*
'71 **Battle Hymn Of Lt. Calley** *C Company*
**Battle Hymn Of The Republic**
'59 *Mormon Tabernacle Choir*
'68 *Andy Williams*
'59 **Battle Of Kookamonga** *Homer & Jethro*
'59 **Battle Of New Orleans** *Johnny Horton*
'58 **Baubles, Bangles And Beads** *Kirby Stone Four*
'99 **Bawitdaba** *Kid Rock*
'73 **Be** *Neil Diamond*
'56 **Be-Bop-A-Lula** *Gene Vincent*
'57 **Be-Bop Baby** *Ricky Nelson*
'98 **Be Careful** *Sparkle*
'63 **Be Careful Of Stones That You Throw** *Dion*
'83 **Be Good Johnny** *Men At Work*
'86 **Be Good To Yourself** *Journey*
'94 **Be Happy** *Mary J. Blige*
'01 **Be Like That** *3 Doors Down*
**Be My Baby**
'63 *Ronettes*
'70 *Andy Kim*
'94 **Be My Baby Tonight** *John Michael Montgomery*
'61 **Be My Boy** *Paris Sisters*
'76 **Be My Girl** *Dramatics*
'59 **Be My Guest** *Fats Domino*
'82 **Be My Lady** *Jefferson Starship*
**Be My Lover**
'72 *Alice Cooper*
'95 *La Bouche*
'85 **Be Near Me** *ABC*
'88 **Be Still My Beating Heart** *Sting*
'74 **Be Thankful For What You Got** *William DeVaughn*
'63 **Be True To Your School** *Beach Boys*
**Be With You**
'89 *Bangles*
'00 *Enrique Iglesias*
'05 **Be Yourself** *Audioslave*
'74 **Beach Baby** *First Class*
'81 **Beach Boys Medley** *Beach Boys*
'95 **Beaches Of Cheyenne** *Garth Brooks*
'64 **Beans In My Ears** *Serendipity Singers*
'78 **Beast Of Burden** *Rolling Stones*
'67 **Beat Goes On** *Sonny & Cher*
'83 **Beat It** *Michael Jackson*
'85 **Beat's So Lonely** *Charlie Sexton*
'82 **Beatles' Movie Medley** *Beatles*
'60 **Beatnik Fly** *Johnny & The Hurricanes*
**Beautiful**
'02 *Christina Aguilera*
'03 *Snoop Dogg*
'80 **Beautiful Boy (Darling Boy)** *John Lennon*
'00 **Beautiful Day** *U2*
'79 **Beautiful Girls** *Van Halen*
'94 **Beautiful In My Eyes** *Joshua Kadison*
'95 **Beautiful Life** *Ace Of Base*
'75 **Beautiful Loser** *Bob Seger*
'02 **Beautiful Mess** *Diamond Rio*
'68 **Beautiful Morning** *Rascals*
**Beautiful People**
'67 *Kenny O'Dell*
'67 *Bobby Vee*
'05 **Beautiful Soul** *Jesse McCartney*
'99 **Beautiful Stranger** *Madonna*
'72 **Beautiful Sunday** *Daniel Boone*
'92 **Beauty And The Beast** *Celine Dion & Peabo Bryson*

'66 **Beauty Is Only Skin Deep** *Temptations*
'64 **Because** *Dave Clark Five*
'01 **Because I Got High** *Afroman*
'90 **Because I Love You (The Postman Song)** *Stevie B*
'94 **Because Of Love** *Janet Jackson*
**Because Of You**
'87 *Cover Girls*
'98 *98°*
**Because The Night**
'78 *Patti Smith Group*
'93 *10,000 Maniacs*
'60 **Because They're Young** *Duane Eddy*
'96 **Because You Loved Me** *Celine Dion*
'71 **Bed Of Rose's** *Statler Brothers*
'93 **Bed Of Roses** *Bon Jovi*
'88 **Beds Are Burning** *Midnight Oil*
'62 **Beechwood 4-5789** *Marvelettes*
'98 **Been Around The World** *Puff Daddy*
'90 **Been Caught Stealing** *Jane's Addiction*
'58 **Been So Long** *Pastels*
'72 **Been To Canaan** *Carole King*
'84 **Beep A Freak** *Gap Band*
'58 **Beep Beep** *Playmates*
'75 **Beer Barrel Polka** *Bobby Vinton*
'03 **Beer For My Horses** *Toby Keith with Willie Nelson*
'65 **Before And After** *Chad & Jeremy*
'94 **Before I Let You Go** *BLACKstreet*
'78 **Before My Heart Finds Out** *Gene Cotton*
'75 **Before The Next Teardrop Falls** *Freddy Fender*
'94 **Before You Kill Us All** *Randy Travis*
'95 **Before You Walk Out Of My Life** *Monica*
'67 **Beg, Borrow And Steal** *Ohio Express*
'67 **Beggin'** *4 Seasons*
'68 **Beginning Of My End** *Unifics*
'71 **Beginnings** *Chicago*
'71 **Behind Blue Eyes** *Who*
'73 **Behind Closed Doors** *Charlie Rich*
'87 **Behind The Wall Of Sleep** *Smithereens*
'05 **Behind These Hazel Eyes** *Kelly Clarkson*
'81 **Being With You** *Smokey Robinson*
**Believe**
'95 *Elton John*
'98 *Cher*
'04 *Josh Groban*
'73 **Believe In Humanity** *Carole King*
'84 **Believe In Me** *Dan Fogelberg*
'59 **Believe Me** *Royal Teens*
'96 **Believe Me Baby (I Lied)** *Trisha Yearwood*
'58 **Believe What You Say** *Ricky Nelson*
'70 **Bell Bottom Blues** *Derek & The Dominos*
'68 **Bella Linda** *Grassroots*
'84 **Belle Of St. Mark** *Sheila E.*
'70 **Bells, The** *Originals*
'58 **Belonging To Someone** *Patti Page*
'72 **Ben** *Michael Jackson*
'67 **Bend Me, Shape Me** *American Breed*
'74 **Bennie And The Jets** *Elton John*
'00 **Bent** *Matchbox Twenty*
'67 **Bernadette** *Four Tops*
'57 **Bernardine** *Pat Boone*
'71 **Bertha** *Grateful Dead*
'75 **Bertha Butt Boogie** *Jimmy Castor Bunch*
'89 **Best, The** *Tina Turner*
'00 **Best Day** *George Strait*
'76 **Best Disco In Town** *Ritchie Family*
'95 **Best Friend** *Brandy*
'64 **Best Is Yet To Come** *Frank Sinatra*
**Best Of Both Worlds**
'67 *Lulu*
'86 *Van Halen*
'00 **Best Of Intentions** *Travis Tritt*

**Best Of My Love**
'74 *Eagles*
'77 *Emotions*
'81 **Best Of Times** *Styx*
'05 **Best Of You** *Foo Fighters*
'74 **Best Thing That Ever Happened To Me** *Gladys Knight*
'92 **Best Things In Life Are Free** *Luther Vandross & Janet Jackson*
'72 **Betcha By Golly, Wow** *Stylistics*
'87 **Betcha Say That** *Gloria Estefan*
'82 **Betcha She Don't Love You** *Evelyn King*
'76 **Beth** *Kiss*
'81 **Bette Davis Eyes** *Kim Carnes*
'84 **Better Be Good To Me** *Tina Turner*
'91 **Better Class Of Losers** *Randy Travis*
'92 **Better Days** *Bruce Springsteen*
'99 **Better Days (And The Bottom Drops Out)** *Citizen King*
'91 **Better Love** *Londonbeat*
'79 **Better Love Next Time** *Dr. Hook*
**Better Man**
'89 *Clint Black*
'94 *Pearl Jam*
'97 **Better Man, Better Off** *Tracy Lawrence*
'00 **Better Off Alone** *Alice Deejay*
'61 **Better Tell Him No** *Starlets*
'93 **Better Than You** *Lisa Keith*
'95 **Better Things To Do** *Terri Clark*
'58 **Betty And Dupree** *Chuck Willis*
'58 **Betty Lou Got A New Pair Of Shoes** *Bobby Freeman*
'80 **Betty Lou's Gettin' Out Tonight** *Bob Seger*
'00 **Between Me And You** *Ja Rule*
'89 **Between Something And Nothing** *Ocean Blue*
'97 **Between The Devil And Me** *Alan Jackson*
'83 **Between The Sheets** *Isley Brothers*
'05 **Beverly Hills** *Weezer*
'03 **Beware Of The Boys (Mundian To Bach Ke)** *Pan'jabi MC*
'61 **Bewildered** *James Brown*
**Beyond The Sea**
'56 *Roger Williams*
'60 *Bobby Darin*
**Bible Tells Me So**
'55 *Don Cornell*
'55 *Nick Noble*
'78 **Bicycle Race** *Queen*
'61 **Big Bad John** *Jimmy Dean*
'96 **Big Bang Baby** *Stone Temple Pilots*
'57 **Big Beat** *Fats Domino*
'58 **Big Bopper's Wedding** *Big Bopper*
**Big Boss Man**
'61 *Jimmy Reed*
'67 *Elvis Presley*
'60 **Big Boy Pate** *Olympics*
'04 **Big Chips** *R. Kelly & Jay-Z*
'72 **Big City Miss Ruth Ann** *Gallery*
'61 **Big Cold Wind** *Pat Boone*
'97 **Big Daddy** *Heavy D*
'99 **Big Deal** *LeAnn Rimes*
'62 **Big Draft** *Four Preps*
'94 **Big Empty** *Stone Temple Pilots*
'82 **Big Fun** *Kool & The Gang*
'62 **Big Girls Don't Cry** *4 Seasons*
'93 **Big Gun** *AC/DC*
'59 **Big Hunk O' Love** *Elvis Presley*
'59 **Big Hurt** *Miss Toni Fisher*
'60 **Big Iron** *Marty Robbins*
'61 **Big John** *Shirelles*
'83 **Big Log** *Robert Plant*
**Big Love**
'87 *Fleetwood Mac*
'96 *Tracy Byrd*
'58 **Big Man** *Four Preps*
'64 **Big Man In Town** *4 Seasons*
'96 **Big Me** *Foo Fighters*
'85 **Big Money** *Rush*
'94 **Big One** *George Strait*

185

'00 **Big Pimpin'** *Jay-Z*
'95 **Big Poppa** *Notorious B.I.G.*
'79 **Big Shot** *Billy Joel*
'03 **Big Star** *Kenny Chesney*
'86 **Big Time** *Peter Gabriel*
'94 **Big Time Sensuality** *Björk*
**Big Yellow Taxi**
'70   *Joni Mitchell*
'70   *Neighborhood*
'74   *Joni Mitchell [live]*
'03 **Bigger Than My Body** *John Mayer*
'95 **Bigger Than The Beatles** *Joe Diffie*
'80 **Biggest Part Of Me** *Ambrosia*
'61 **Bilbao Song** *Andy Williams*
'83 **Billie Jean** *Michael Jackson*
'73 **Billion Dollar Babies**
  *Alice Cooper*
'99 **Bills, Bills, Bills** *Destiny's Child*
'58 **Billy** *Kathy Linden*
'66 **Billy And Sue** *B.J. Thomas*
'58 **Billy Bayou** *Jim Reeves*
'74 **Billy, Don't Be A Hero**
  *Bo Donaldson*
'58 **Bimbombey** *Jimmie Rodgers*
'71 **Bip Bop** *Paul McCartney*
'85 **Bird, The** *Time*
'64 **Bird Dance Beat** *Trashmen*
'58 **Bird Dog** *Everly Brothers*
'58 **Bird On My Head** *David Seville*
'90 **Birdhouse In Your Soul**
  *They Might Be Giants*
**Birdland**
'63   *Chubby Checker*
'79   *Manhattan Transfer*
'65 **Birds And The Bees** *Jewel Akens*
'71 **Birds Of A Feather** *Raiders*
'55 **Birth Of The Boogie** *Bill Haley*
**Birthday**
'68   *Beatles*
'69   *Underground Sunshine*
'63 **Birthday Party** *Pixies Three*
'89 **Birthday Suit** *Johnny Kemp*
**Bitch**
'71   *Rolling Stones*
'97   *Meredith Brooks*
'74 **Bitch Is Back** *Elton John*
'77 **Bite Your Lip (Get up and dance!)**
  *Elton John*
'64 **Bits And Pieces** *Dave Clark Five*
'73 **Bitter Bad** *Melanie*
'98 **Bitter Sweet Symphony** *Verve*
'86 **Bizarre Love Triangle**
  *New Order*
'01 **Bizounce** *Olivia*
'92 **Black** *Pearl Jam*
'88 **Black And Blue** *Van Halen*
'72 **Black & White** *Three Dog Night*
'99 **Black Balloon** *Goo Goo Dolls*
'77 **Black Betty** *Ram Jam*
'85 **Black Cars** *Gino Vannelli*
'90 **Black Cat** *Janet Jackson*
'82 **Black Coffee In Bed** *Squeeze*
'77 **Black Cow** *Steely Dan*
'55 **Black Denim Trousers** *Cheers*
'71 **Black Dog** *Led Zeppelin*
'75 **Black Friday** *Steely Dan*
'94 **Black Hole Sun** *Soundgarden*
'66 **Black Is Black** *Los Bravos*
'84 **Black Lassie** *Cheech & Chong*
**Black Magic Woman**
'69   *Fleetwood Mac*
'70   *Santana [medley]*
'70 **Black Night** *Deep Purple*
'91 **Black Or White** *Michael Jackson*
'69 **Black Pearl** *Sonny Charles*
  *& The Checkmates, Ltd.*
'70 **Black Sabbath** *Black Sabbath*
'57 **Black Slacks** *Joe Bennett*
'75 **Black Superman - "Muhammad Ali"**
  *Johnny Wakelin*
'89 **Black Velvet** *Alannah Myles*
'74 **Black Water** *Doobie Brothers*
'68 **Blackbird** *Beatles*
'78 **Blame It On The Boogie** *Jacksons*

'63 **Blame It On The Bossa Nova**
  *Eydie Gorme*
'89 **Blame It On The Rain** *Milli Vanilli*
'93 **Blame It On Your Heart**
  *Patty Loveless*
'90 **Blaze Of Glory** *Jon Bon Jovi*
'64 **Bless Our Love** *Gene Chandler*
'05 **Bless The Broken Road**
  *Rascal Flatts*
'61 **Bless You** *Tony Orlando*
**Blessed**
'95   *Elton John*
'02   *Martina McBride*
'81 **Blessed Are The Believers**
  *Anne Murray*
'69 **Blessed Is The Rain** *Brooklyn Bridge*
'94 **Blind Man** *Aerosmith*
**Blinded By The Light**
'73   *Bruce Springsteen*
'76   *Manfred Mann*
'99 **Bling Bling** *B.G.*
'82 **Blister In The Sun** *Violent Femmes*
'76 **Blitzkrieg Bop** *Ramones*
'58 **Blob, The** *Five Blobs*
'73 **Blood Red And Goin' Down**
  *Tanya Tucker*
'75 **Bloody Well Right** *Supertramp*
'55 **Blossom Fell** *Nat "King" Cole*
'79 **Blow Away** *George Harrison*
'96 **Blow Up The Outside World**
  *Soundgarden*
**Blowin' In The Wind**
'63   *Bob Dylan*
'63   *Peter, Paul & Mary*
'66   *Stevie Wonder*
'03 **Blowin' Me Up (With Her Love)**
  *JC Chasez*
'70 **Blowing Away** *5th Dimension*
'91 **Blowing Kisses In The Wind**
  *Paula Abdul*
'96 **Blue** *LeAnn Rimes*
'60 **Blue Angel** *Roy Orbison*
'66 **Blue Autumn** *Bobby Goldsboro*
**Blue Bayou**
'63   *Roy Orbison*
'77   *Linda Ronstadt*
'58 **Blue Blue Day** *Don Gibson*
'57 **Blue Christmas** *Elvis Presley*
'96 **Blue Clear Sky** *George Strait*
'73 **Blue Collar**
  *Bachman-Turner Overdrive*
'78 **Blue Collar Man (Long Nights)** *Styx*
'99 **Blue (Da Ba Dee)** *Eiffel 65*
'82 **Blue Eyes** *Elton John*
'75 **Blue Eyes Crying In The Rain**
  *Willie Nelson*
**Blue Hawaii**
'58   *Billy Vaughn*
'61   *Elvis Presley*
'84 **Blue Jean** *David Bowie*
**Blue Monday**
'57   *Fats Domino*
'83   *New Order*
'71 **Blue Money** *Van Morrison*
'61 **Blue Moon** *Marcels*
'78 **Blue Morning, Blue Day** *Foreigner*
'98 **Blue On Black**
  *Kenny Wayne Shepherd Band*
'63 **Blue On Blue** *Bobby Vinton*
'72 **Blue Sky** *Allman Brothers Band*
'90 **Blue Sky Mine** *Midnight Oil*
'55 **Blue Star** *Les Baxter*
**Blue Suede Shoes**
'56   *Carl Perkins*
'56   *Elvis Presley*
'73   *Johnny Rivers*
'60 **Blue Tango** *Bill Black's Combo*
'63 **Blue Velvet** *Bobby Vinton*
'59 **Blue Winter** *Connie Francis*
'67 **Blue's Theme** *Davie Allan*
**Blueberry Hill**
'56   *Louis Armstrong*
'56   *Fats Domino*

**Bluebird**
'67   *Buffalo Springfield*
'75   *Helen Reddy*
'56 **Bluejean Bop** *Gene Vincent*
'78 **Bluer Than Blue** *Michael Johnson*
'90 **Blues, The** *Tony! Toni! Toné!*
'89 **Blues From A Gun**
  *Jesus & Mary Chain*
'70 **Blues Power** *Eric Clapton*
'62 **Blues (Stay Away From Me)**
  *Ace Cannon*
'01 **Blurry** *Puddle Of Mudd*
'55 **Bo Diddley** *Bo Diddley*
**Bo Weevil**
'56   *Teresa Brewer*
'56   *Fats Domino*
'82 **Bobbie Sue** *Oak Ridge Boys*
'59 **Bobby Sox To Stockings**
  *Frankie Avalon*
'62 **Bobby's Girl** *Marcie Blane*
'73 **Bodhisattva** *Steely Dan*
'94 **Body & Soul** *Anita Baker*
'98 **Body Bumpin' Yippie-Yi-Yo**
  *Public Announcement*
'82 **Body Language** *Queen*
'83 **Body Talk** *Deele*
'76 **Bohemian Rhapsody** *Queen*
'61 **Boll Weevil Song** *Brook Benton*
'61 **Bonanza** *Al Caiola*
'59 **Bongo Rock** *Preston Epps*
'62 **Bongo Stomp** *Little Joey & The Flips*
'59 **Bonnie Came Back** *Duane Eddy*
'57 **Bony Moronie** *Larry Williams*
'67 **Boogaloo Down Broadway**
  *Fantastic Johnny C*
'77 **Boogie Child** *Bee Gees*
'74 **Boogie Down** *Eddie Kendricks*
'76 **Boogie Fever** *Sylvers*
'77 **Boogie Nights** *Heatwave*
'74 **Boogie On Reggae Woman**
  *Stevie Wonder*
'78 **Boogie Oogie Oogie**
  *Taste Of Honey*
'76 **Boogie Shoes**
  *KC & The Sunshine Band*
'79 **Boogie Wonderland** *Earth,*
  *Wind & Fire/The Emotions*
'73 **Boogie Woogie Bugle Boy**
  *Bette Midler*
'58 **Book Of Love** *Monotones*
'62 **Boom Boom** *John Lee Hooker*
'55 **Boom Boom Boomerang**
  *DeCastro Sisters*
'79 **Boom Boom (Out Go The Lights)**
  *Pat Travers Band*
'93 **Boom! Shake The Room**
  *Jazzy Jeff & Fresh Prince*
'95 **Boombastic** *Shaggy*
'92 **Boot Scootin' Boogie**
  *Brooks & Dunn*
'94 **Booti Call** *BLACKstreet*
'01 **Bootylicious** *Destiny's Child*
'78 **Bootzilla** *Bootsy's Rubber Band*
'86 **Bop** *Dan Seals*
'58 **Bop-A-Lena** *Ronnie Self*
'84 **Bop 'Til You Drop** *Rick Springfield*
'55 **Bop-Ting-A-Ling** *LaVern Baker*
'56 **Boppin' The Blues** *Carl Perkins*
'83 **Border, The** *America*
'70 **Border Song** *Elton John*
'84 **Borderline** *Madonna*
'85 **Borderlines, The** *Jeffrey Osborne*
'67 **Boris The Spider** *Who*
'66 **Born A Woman** *Sandy Posey*
'92 **Born Country** *Alabama*
**Born Free**
'66   *Roger Williams*
'68   *Hesitations*
'84 **Born In The U.S.A.**
  *Bruce Springsteen*
'69 **Born On The Bayou** *Creedence*
  *Clearwater Revival*
'79 **Born To Be Alive** *Patrick Hernandez*
'88 **Born To Be My Baby** *Bon Jovi*
'68 **Born To Be Wild** *Steppenwolf*
'56 **Born To Be With You** *Chordettes*

'00 **Born To Fly** Sara Evans
'62 **Born To Lose** Ray Charles
'94 **Born To Roll**
　　Masta Ace Incorporated
'75 **Born To Run** Bruce Springsteen
'70 **Born To Wander** Rare Earth
'58 **Born Too Late** Poni-Tails
'79 **Boss, The** Diana Ross
'63 **Boss Guitar** Duane Eddy
'63 **Bossa Nova Baby** Elvis Presley
　　**Both Sides Now**
'68 　Judy Collins
'69 　Joni Mitchell
'93 **Both Sides Of The Story** Phil Collins
'02 **Bother** Stone Sour
'66 **Bottle Let Me Down** Merle Haggard
'67 **Bottle Of Wine** Fireballs
'80 **Boulevard** Jackson Browne
'05 **Boulevard Of Broken Dreams**
　　Green Day
'63 **Bounce, The** Olympics
'00 **Bounce With Me** Lil Bow Wow
'01 **Bouncin' Back (Bumpin' Me Against
　　The Wall)** Mystikal
'69 **Bouree** Jethro Tull
'96 **Bow Down** Westside Connection
'00 **Bow Wow (That's My Name)**
　　Lil Bow Wow
'67 **Bowling Green** Everly Brothers
'70 **Box Of Rain** Grateful Dead
'69 **Boxer, The** Simon & Garfunkel
　　**Boy From New York City**
'65 　Ad Libs
'81 　Manhattan Transfer
'85 **Boy In The Box** Corey Hart
'98 **Boy Is Mine** Brandy & Monica
'63 **Boy Named Sue** Johnny Cash
'63 **Boy Next Door** Secrets
'59 **Boy Without A Girl** Frankie Avalon
'76 **Boys Are Back In Town** Thin Lizzy
'84 **Boys Do Fall In Love** Robin Gibb
'85 **Boys Don't Cry** Cure
'87 **Boys Night Out** Timothy B. Schmit
　　**Boys Of Summer**
'84 　Don Henley
'03 　Ataris
'73 **Brain Damage [medley]**
　　Pink Floyd
'95 **Brain Stew [medley]** Green Day
'71 **Brand New Key** Melanie
'86 **Brand New Lover** Dead Or Alive
'91 **Brand New Man** Brooks & Dunn
'69 **Brand New Me** Dusty Springfield
'72 **Brandy (You're A Fine Girl)**
　　Looking Glass
'80 **Brass In Pocket (I'm Special)**
　　Pretenders
'75 **Brazil** Ritchie Family
'64 **Bread And Butter** Newbeats
'75 **Break Away** Art Garfunkel
'93 **Break It Down Again**
　　Tears For Fears
　　**Break It To Me Gently**
'62 　Brenda Lee
'77 　Aretha Franklin
'82 　Juice Newton
'82 **Break It Up** Foreigner
'83 **Break My Stride** Matthew Wilder
'67 **Break On Through (To The Other
　　Side)** Doors
'73 **Break Up To Make Up** Stylistics
'01 **Break Ya Neck** Busta Rhymes
'68 **Break Your Promise** Delfonics
'04 **Breakaway** Kelly Clarkson
'84 **Breakdance** Irene Cara
　　**Breakdown**
'77 　Tom Petty
'77 　Alan Parsons Project
'01 　Tantric
'71 **Breakdown, The** Rufus Thomas
'80 **Breakdown Dead Ahead**
　　Boz Scaggs
'95 **Breakfast At Tiffany's**
　　Deep Blue Something
'79 **Breakfast In America** Supertramp

'61 **Breakin' In A Brand New Broken
　　Heart** Connie Francis
'92 **Breakin' My Heart (Pretty Brown
　　Eyes)** Mint Condition
'84 **Breakin'...There's No Stopping Us**
　　Ollie & Jerry
'66 **Breakin' Up Is Breakin' My Heart**
　　Roy Orbison
'97 **Breaking All The Rules** She Moves
'81 **Breaking Away** Balance
'83 **Breaking The Chains** Dokken
'04 **Breaking The Habit** Linkin Park
'80 **Breaking The Law** Judas Priest
　　**Breaking Up Is Hard To Do**
'62 　Neil Sedaka
'70 　Lenny Welch
'72 　Partridge Family
'75 　Neil Sedaka [slow version]
'83 **Breaking Us In Two** Joe Jackson
'87 **Breakout** Swing Out Sister
'80 **Breaks, The** Kurtis Blow
'81 **Breakup Song (They Don't Write
　　'Em)** Greg Kihn Band
　　**Breathe**
'73 　Pink Floyd [medley]
'99 　Faith Hill
'03 　Michelle Branch
'04 　Fabolous
'93 **Breathe Again** Toni Braxton
'04 **Breathe, Stretch, Shake** Mase
'02 **Breathe Your Name**
　　Sixpence None The Richer
　　**Breathless**
'58 　Jerry Lee Lewis
'01 　Corrs
'55 **Breeze And I** Caterina Valente
'97 **Brick** Ben Folds Five
'77 **Brick House** Commodores
'74 **Bridge Of Sighs** Robin Trower
　　**Bridge Over Troubled Water**
'70 　Simon & Garfunkel
'71 　Aretha Franklin
'03 **Bright Lights** Matchbox Twenty
'61 **Bright Lights Big City** Jimmy Reed
'87 **Brilliant Disguise** Bruce Springsteen
'68 **Bring A Little Lovin'** Los Bravos
'05 **Bring Em Out** T.I.
'99 **Bring It All To Me**
　　Blaque Feat. *NSYNC
　　**Bring It On Home To Me**
'62 　Sam Cooke
'65 　Animals
'68 　Eddie Floyd
'67 **Bring It Up** James Brown
'03 **Bring Me To Life** Evanescence
'86 **Bring On The Dancing Horses**
　　Echo & The Bunnymen
'01 **Bring On The Rain** Jo Dee
　　Messina with Tim McGraw
'71 **Bring The Boys Home** Freda Payne
'88 **Bring The Noise** Public Enemy
'84 **Bringin' On The Heartbreak** Def
　　Leppard
'61 **Bristol Stomp** Dovells
'62 **Bristol Twistin' Annie** Dovells
'00 **Broadway** Goo Goo Dolls
'04 **Broken** Seether
'91 **Broken Arrow** Rod Stewart
'79 **Broken Hearted Me** Anne Murray
'59 **Broken-Hearted Melody**
　　Sarah Vaughan
'97 **Broken Wing** Martina McBride
'85 **Broken Wings** Mr. Mister
'95 **Brokenhearted** Brandy
'03 **Brokenheartsville** Joe Nichols
'90 **Brother Jukebox** Mark Chesnutt
'73 **Brother Louie** Stories
'69 **Brother Love's Travelling Salvation
　　Show** Neil Diamond
'70 **Brother Rapp** James Brown
'67 **Brown Eyed Girl** Van Morrison
'56 **Brown Eyed Handsome Man**
　　Chuck Berry
'68 **Brown Eyed Woman** Bill Medley

　　**Brown Sugar**
'71 　Rolling Stones
'95 　D'Angelo
'84 **Bruce** Rick Springfield
'92 **Bubba Shot The Jukebox**
　　Mark Chesnutt
'65 **Buckaroo** Buck Owens
'94 **Buddy Holly** Weezer
'89 **Buffalo Stance** Neneh Cherry
'99 **Bug A Boo** Destiny's Child
'69 **Build Me Up Buttercup** Foundations
'97 **Building A Mystery**
　　Sarah McLachlan
'60 **Bulldog** Fireballs
'87 **Bullet The Blue Sky** U2
'95 **Bullet With Butterfly Wings**
　　Smashing Pumpkins
'96 **Bulls On Parade**
　　Rage Against The Machine
　　**Bumble Bee**
'60 　LaVern Baker
'65 　Searchers
'61 **Bumble Boogie**
　　B. Bumble & The Stingers
'02 **Bump, Bump, Bump** B2K & P. Diddy
'94 **Bump N' Grind** R. Kelly
'74 **Bungle In The Jungle** Jethro Tull
'96 **Burden In My Hand** Soundgarden
　　**Burn**
'00 　Jo Dee Messina
'04 　Usher
'71 **Burn Down The Mission**
　　Elton John
'80 **Burn Rubber (Why You Wanna Hurt
　　Me)** Gap Band
'55 **Burn That Candle** Bill Haley
'81 **Burnin' For You** Blue Öyster Cult
'77 **Burnin' Sky** Bad Company
　　**Burning Bridges**
'60 　Jack Scott
'70 　Mike Curb Congregation
'04 **Burning Bright** Shinedown
'82 **Burning Down One Side**
　　Robert Plant
'83 **Burning Down The House**
　　Talking Heads
　　**Burning Heart**
'83 　Vandenberg
'85 　Survivor
'85 **Burning House Of Love** X
'72 **Burning Love** Elvis Presley
'68 **Burning Of The Midnight Lamp**
　　Jimi Hendrix
'66 **Bus Stop** Hollies
'56 **Bus Stop Song (A Paper Of Pins)**
　　Four Lads
'89 **Bust A Move** Young MC
'63 **Bust Out** Busters
'63 **Busted** Ray Charles
'79 **Bustin' Loose** Chuck Brown
'98 **Busy Man** Billy Ray Cyrus
'96 **But Anyway** Blues Traveler
'00 **But For The Grace Of God**
　　Keith Urban
'61 **But I Do** Clarence Henry
'66 **But It's Alright** J.J. Jackson
'69 **But You Know I Love You**
　　First Edition
'65 **But You're Mine** Sonny & Cher
'97 **Butta Love** Next
'75 **Butter Boy** Fanny
'01 **Butterflies** Michael Jackson
　　**Butterfly**
'57 　Charlie Gracie
'57 　Andy Williams
'97 　Mariah Carey
'01 　Crazy Town
'63 **Butterfly Baby** Bobby Rydell
　　**Butterfly Kisses**
'97 　Bob Carlisle
'97 　Raybon Bros.
'00 **Buy Me A Rose** Kenny Rogers
'61 **Buzz Buzz A-Diddle-It**
　　Freddy Cannon
'57 **Buzz-Buzz-Buzz** Hollywood Flames

**By The Time I Get To Phoenix**
'67 *Glen Campbell*
'69 *Isaac Hayes*
'93 **By The Time This Night Is Over**
  *Kenny G with Peabo Bryson*
'02 **By The Way** *Red Hot Chili Peppers*
'98 **Bye-Bye** *Jo Dee Messina*
'65 **Bye, Bye, Baby (Baby, Goodbye)**
  *4 Seasons*
'00 **Bye Bye Bye** *\*NSYNC*
**Bye Bye Love**
'57 *Everly Brothers*
'78 *Cars*

# C

'97 **C U When U Get There** *Coolio*
**C.C. Rider**
'57 *Chuck Willis*
'62 *LaVern Baker*
'66 *Animals*
**C'est La Vie**
'55 *Sarah Vaughan*
'86 *Robbie Nevil*
'99 *B\*Witched*
'60 **C'est Si Bon (It's So Good)**
  *Conway Twitty*
'68 **Cab Driver** *Mills Brothers*
'81 **Cadillac Ranch**
  *Bruce Springsteen*
'91 **Cadillac Style** *Sammy Kershaw*
'62 **Cajun Queen** *Jimmy Dean*
'60 **Calcutta** *Lawrence Welk*
'76 **Caledonia** *Robin Trower*
'60 **Calendar Girl** *Neil Sedaka*
'66 **California Dreamin'**
  *Mama's & The Papa's*
**California Girls**
'65 *Beach Boys*
'85 *David Lee Roth*
'96 **California Love** *2 Pac*
'67 **California Nights** *Lesley Gore*
'68 **California Soul** *5th Dimension*
'64 **California Sun** *Rivieras*
'00 **Californication**
  *Red Hot Chili Peppers*
'89 **Call It Love** *Poco*
**Call Me**
'58 *Johnny Mathis*
'66 *Chris Montez*
'70 *Aretha Franklin*
'80 *Blondie*
'82 *Skyy*
'91 *Phil Perry*
'97 *Le Click*
'02 *Tweet*
'73 **Call Me (Come Back Home)**
  *Al Green*
'63 **Call Me Irresponsible** *Jack Jones*
'68 **Call Me Lightning** *Who*
'62 **Call Me Mr. In-Between** *Burl Ives*
'74 **Call Me The Breeze**
  *Lynyrd Skynyrd*
'71 **Call Me Up In Dreamland**
  *Van Morrison*
**Call On Me**
'63 *Bobby Bland*
'74 *Chicago*
'84 **Call To The Heart** *Giuffria*
'94 **Callin' Baton Rouge** *Garth Brooks*
'00 **Callin' Me** *Lil' Zane*
**Calling All Angels**
'93 *Jane Siberry with k.d. lang*
'03 *Train*
'86 **Calling America**
  *Electric Light Orchestra*
'77 **Calling Dr. Love** *Kiss*
'91 **Calling Elvis** *Dire Straits*
'77 **Calling Occupants Of Interplanetary
  Craft** *Carpenters*
'93 **Calling To You** *Robert Plant*
'75 **Calypso** *John Denver*
'68 **Can I Change My Mind**
  *Tyrone Davis*
'98 **Can I Get A...** *Jay-Z*

**Can I Get A Witness**
'63 *Marvin Gaye*
'71 *Lee Michaels*
'57 **Can I Steal A Little Love**
  *Frank Sinatra*
'95 **Can I Touch You...There?**
  *Michael Bolton*
'92 **Can I Trust You With My Heart**
  *Travis Tritt*
'74 **Can This Be Real** *Natural Four*
'88 **Can U Read My Lips** *Z'Looke*
**Can We Still Be Friends**
'78 *Todd Rundgren*
'79 *Robert Palmer*
'93 **Can We Talk** *Tevin Campbell*
'94 **Can You Feel The Love Tonight**
  *Elton John*
'56 **Can You Find It In Your Heart**
  *Tony Bennett*
'66 **Can You Please Crawl Out Your
  Window?** *Bob Dylan*
'88 **Can You Stand The Rain**
  *New Edition*
'91 **Can You Stop The Rain**
  *Peabo Bryson*
'93 **Can't Break It To My Heart**
  *Tracy Lawrence*
'64 **Can't Buy Me Love** *Beatles*
'95 **Can't Cry Anymore** *Sheryl Crow*
'01 **Can't Deny It** *Fabolous*
'00 **Can't Fight The Moonlight**
  *LeAnn Rimes*
'85 **Can't Fight This Feeling**
  *REO Speedwagon*
'69 **Can't Find My Way Home**
  *Blind Faith*
'91 **Can't Forget You** *Gloria Estefan*
'74 **Can't Get Enough** *Bad Company*
'98 **Can't Get Enough Of You Baby**
  *Smash Mouth*
**Can't Get Enough Of Your Love,
  Babe**
'74 *Barry White*
'93 *Taylor Dayne*
'74 **Can't Get It Out Of My Head**
  *Electric Light Orchestra*
'89 **Can't Get Over You** *Maze Feat.
  Frankie Beverly*
'63 **Can't Get Used To Losing You**
  *Andy Williams*
'02 **Can't Get You Out Of My Head**
  *Kylie Minogue*
**Can't Help Falling In Love**
'61 *Elvis Presley*
'86 *Corey Hart*
'93 *UB40*
'03 **Can't Hold Us Down**
  *Christina Aguilera*
'91 **Can't Let Go** *Mariah Carey*
'03 **Can't Let You Go** *Fabolous*
'90 **(Can't Live Without Your) Love And
  Affection** *Nelson*
'97 **Can't Nobody Hold Me Down**
  *Puff Daddy*
'83 **Can't Shake Loose**
  *Agnetha Fältskog*
'78 **Can't Smile Without You**
  *Barry Manilow*
'87 **Can't Stay Away From You**
  *Gloria Estefan*
**Can't Stop**
'90 *After 7*
'02 *Red Hot Chili Peppers*
'77 **Can't Stop Dancin'**
  *Captain & Tennille*
'90 **Can't Stop Fallin' Into Love**
  *Cheap Trick*
'95 **Can't Stop Lovin' You** *Van Halen*
**Can't Stop Loving You**
'70 *Tom Jones*
'02 *Phil Collins*
'91 **Can't Stop This Thing We Started**
  *Bryan Adams*
'03 **Can't Stop, Won't Stop** *Young Gunz*

**Can't Take My Eyes Off You**
'67 *Frankie Valli*
'67 *Lettermen [medley]*
'98 *Lauryn Hill*
'91 **Can't Truss It** *Public Enemy*
**Can't We Try**
'80 *Teddy Pendergrass*
'87 *Dan Hill/Vonda Sheppard*
'65 **Can't You Hear My Heartbeat**
  *Herman's Hermits*
'72 **Can't You Hear The Song?**
  *Wayne Newton*
**Can't You See**
'73 *Marshall Tucker Band*
'95 *Total*
'64 **Can't You See That She's Mine**
  *Dave Clark Five*
'87 **Can'tcha Say (You Believe In Me)
  [medley]** *Boston*
**Canadian Sunset**
'56 *Andy Williams*
'56 *Hugo Winterhalter with Eddie
  Heywood*
'70 **Candida** *Dawn*
**Candle In The Wind**
'73 *Elton John*
'87 *Elton John [live]*
'97 *Elton John [1997]*
**Candy**
'86 *Cameo*
'90 *Iggy Pop*
'99 *Mandy Moore*
**Candy Girl**
'63 *4 Seasons*
'83 *New Edition*
**Candy Man**
'61 *Roy Orbison*
'72 *Sammy Davis, Jr.*
'95 **Candy Rain** *Soul For Real*
'05 **Candy Shop** *50 Cent*
**Cannonball**
'58 *Duane Eddy*
'85 *Supertramp*
'93 *Breeders*
'93 **Cantaloop** *US3*
'74 **Captain Jack** *Billy Joel*
'86 **Captain Of Her Heart** *Double*
'95 **Car, The** *Jeff Carson*
'76 **Car Wash** *Rose Royce*
'65 **Cara-Lin** *Strangeloves*
'65 **Cara, Mia** *Jay & The Americans*
'01 **Caramel** *City High*
'85 **Caravan Of Love** *Isley Jasper Isley*
'74 **Carefree Highway** *Gordon Lightfoot*
'84 **Careless Whisper** *Wham!*
'71 **Carey** *Joni Mitchell*
'59 **Caribbean** *Mitchell Torok*
'91 **Caribbean Blue** *Enya*
'84 **Caribbean Queen (No More Love
  On The Run)** *Billy Ocean*
'68 **Carmen** *Herb Alpert*
'95 **Carnival** *Natalie Merchant*
'58 **Carol** *Chuck Berry*
'69 **Carolina In My Mind** *James Taylor*
'75 **Carolina In The Pines**
  *Michael Murphey*
'66 **Caroline, No** *Brian Wilson*
'68 **Carpet Man** *5th Dimension*
**Carrie**
'80 *Cliff Richard*
'87 *Europe*
'67 **Carrie-Anne** *Hollies*
'96 **Carried Away** *George Strait*
'69 **Carry Me Back** *Rascals*
'70 **Carry On**
  *Crosby, Stills, Nash & Young*
'76 **Carry On Wayward Son** *Kansas*
'69 **Carry That Weight [medley]** *Beatles*
'97 **Carrying Your Love With Me**
  *George Strait*
'80 **Cars** *Gary Numan*
'87 **Casanova** *Levert*
'00 **Case Of The Ex (Whatcha Gonna
  Do)** *Mya*
'70 **Casey Jones** *Grateful Dead*

'67 **Casino Royale** *Herb Alpert*
**Cast Your Fate To The Wind**
'62 *Vince Guaraldi Trio*
'65 *Sounds Orchestral*
'72 **Castles In The Air** *Don McLean*
'56 **Casual Look** *Six Teens*
'77 **Cat Scratch Fever** *Ted Nugent*
'74 **Cat's In The Cradle** *Harry Chapin*
'58 **Catch A Falling Star** *Perry Como*
**Catch Me I'm Falling**
'84 *Real Life*
'87 *Pretty Poison*
'65 **Catch The Wind** *Donovan*
'65 **Catch Us If You Can**
     *Dave Clark Five*
'62 **Caterina** *Perry Como*
'60 **Cathy's Clown** *Everly Brothers*
'55 **Cattle Call** *Eddy Arnold*
'93 **Cats In The Cradle** *Ugly Kid Joe*
'05 **Caught Up** *Usher*
'86 **Caught Up In The Rapture**
     *Anita Baker*
'82 **Caught Up In You** *38 Special*
'87 **Causing A Commotion** *Madonna*
'70 **Cecilia** *Simon & Garfunkel*
'70 **Celebrate** *Three Dog Night*
'85 **Celebrate Youth** *Rick Springfield*
'80 **Celebration** *Kool & The Gang*
'03 **Celebrity** *Brad Paisley*
'98 **Celebrity Skin** *Hole*
'95 **Cell Therapy** *Goodie Mob.*
'85 **Celluloid Heroes** *Kinks*
'85 **Centerfield** *John Fogerty*
'81 **Centerfold** *J. Geils Band*
'84 **Centipede** *Rebbie Jackson*
'80 **Certain Girl** *Warren Zevon*
'58 **Certain Smile** *Johnny Mathis*
'04 **Ch-Check It Out** *Beastie Boys*
'62 **Cha-Cha-Cha** *Bobby Rydell*
'58 **Cha-Hua-Hua** *Pets*
'77 **Chain, The** *Fleetwood Mac*
**Chain Gang**
'56 *Bobby Scott*
'60 *Sam Cooke*
'67 **Chain Of Fools** *Aretha Franklin*
'00 **Chain Of Love** *Clay Walker*
'68 **Chained** *Marvin Gaye*
**Chains**
'62 *Cookies*
'90 *Patty Loveless*
'96 *Tina Arena*
**Chains Of Love**
'56 *Pat Boone*
'88 *Erasure*
'78 **Champagne Jam**
     *Atlanta Rhythm Section*
'96 **Champagne Supernova** *Oasis*
'57 **Chances Are** *Johnny Mathis*
'91 **Change** *Lisa Stansfield*
'03 **Change Clothes** *Jay-Z*
'00 **Change (In The House Of Flies)**
     *Deftones*
'86 **Change In The Weather**
     *John Fogerty*
'65 **Change Is Gonna Come** *Sam Cooke*
**Change Of Heart**
'78 *Eric Carmen*
'83 *Tom Petty*
'86 *Cyndi Lauper*
'71 **Change Partners** *Stephen Stills*
'96 **Change The World** *Eric Clapton*
'97 **Change Would Do You Good**
     *Sheryl Crow*
**Changes**
'72 *David Bowie*
'98 *2Pac*
'77 **Changes In Latitudes, Changes In
     Attitudes** *Jimmy Buffett*
'89 **Channel Z** *B-52's*
**Chanson D'Amour (Song Of Love)**
'58 *Fontane Sisters*
'58 *Art & Dotty Todd*
'99 **Chanté's Got A Man** *Chanté Moore*
'57 **Chantez-Chantez** *Dinah Shore*

**Chantilly Lace**
'58 *Big Bopper*
'72 *Jerry Lee Lewis*
'95 **Chanukah Song** *Adam Sandler*
**Chapel In The Moonlight**
'65 *Bachelors*
'67 *Dean Martin*
'64 **Chapel Of Love** *Dixie Cups*
'63 **Charade** *Henry Mancini*
'81 **Chariots Of Fire** *Vangelis*
'71 **Charity Ball** *Fanny*
'04 **Charlene** *Anthony Hamilton*
'59 **Charlie Brown** *Coasters*
'63 **Charms** *Bobby Vee*
'79 **Chase** *Giorgio Moroder*
'90 **Chasin' That Neon Rainbow**
     *Alan Jackson*
'93 **Chattahoochee** *Alan Jackson*
**Chattanooga Choo Choo**
'62 *Floyd Cramer*
'67 *Harpers Bizarre*
'78 *Tuxedo Junction*
'60 **Chattanooga Shoe Shine Boy**
     *Freddy Cannon*
'80 **Cheap Sunglasses** *ZZ Top*
'73 **Cheaper To Keep Her**
     *Johnnie Taylor*
'66 **Cheater, The** *Bob Kuban*
**Check It Out**
'73 *Tavares*
'88 *John Cougar Mellencamp*
'70 **Check Out Your Mind** *Impressions*
'95 **Check Yes Or No** *George Strait*
'93 **Check Yo Self** *Ice Cube*
'98 **Cheers 2 U** *Playa*
'78 **Cheeseburger In Paradise**
     *Jimmy Buffett*
'69 **Chelsea Morning** *Joni Mitchell*
'99 **Chemicals Between Us** *Bush*
'76 **Cherchez La Femme [medley]**
     *Dr. Buzzard's Original "Savannah"
     Band*
**Cherish**
'66 *Association*
'71 *David Cassidy*
'85 *Kool & The Gang*
'89 *Madonna*
'82 **Cherokee Fiddle** *Johnny Lee*
'77 **Cherry Baby** *Starz*
'87 **Cherry Bomb**
     *John Cougar Mellencamp*
**Cherry, Cherry**
'66 *Neil Diamond*
'73 *Neil Diamond [live]*
'69 **Cherry Hill Park** *Billy Joe Royal*
**Cherry Pie**
'60 *Skip & Flip*
'90 *Warrant*
**Cherry Pink (And Apple Blossom
     White)**
'55 *Alan Dale*
'55 *Perez Prado*
'59 **Cherrystone** *Addrisi Brothers*
'68 **Chest Fever** *Band*
**(Chestnuts Roasting On An Open
     Fire) ..see: Christmas Song**
'75 **Chevy Van** *Sammy Johns*
'68 **Chewy Chewy** *Ohio Express*
**Chicago**
'57 *Frank Sinatra*
'71 *Graham Nash*
'71 **Chick-A-Boom (Don't Ya Jes' Love
     It)** *Daddy Dewdrop*
'67 **Child Of Clay** *Jimmie Rodgers*
'96 **Children** *Robert Miles*
'71 **Children Of The Grave**
     *Black Sabbath*
'90 **Children Of The Night** *Richard Marx*
**Children's Marching Song**
'59 *Mitch Miller*
'59 *Cyril Stapleton*
'60 **China Doll** *Ames Brothers*
'83 **China Girl** *David Bowie*
'73 **China Grove** *Doobie Brothers*
'62 **Chip Chip** *Gene McDaniels*

'58 **Chipmunk Song** *Chipmunks*
'79 **Chiquitita** *Abba*
'71 **Chirpy Chirpy Cheep Cheep**
     *Mac & Katie Kissoon*
'81 **Chloe** *Elton John*
'69 **Choice Of Colors** *Impressions*
'69 **Chokin' Kind** *Joe Simon*
'68 **Choo Choo Train** *Box Tops*
'94 **Choose** *Color Me Badd*
'55 **Chop Chop Boom** *Crew-Cuts*
'77 **Christine Sixteen** *Kiss*
'95 **Christmas Eve (Sarajevo 12/24)**
     *Trans-Siberian Orchestra*
'00 **Christmas Shoes** *Newsong*
'99 **Christmas Song (Chestnuts
     Roasting On An Open Fire)**
     *Christina Aguilera*
'79 **Chuck E.'s In Love** *Rickie Lee Jones*
'64 **Chug-A-Lug** *Roger Miller*
'56 **Church Bells May Ring** *Diamonds*
'83 **Church Of The Poison Mind**
     *Culture Club*
'92 **Church Of Your Heart** *Roxette*
'89 **Church On Cumberland Road**
     *Shenandoah*
'59 **Ciao, Ciao Bambina** *Jacky Noguez*
'93 **Cielito Lindo** *Brave Combo*
'58 **Cimarron (Roll On)** *Billy Vaughn*
'68 **Cinnamon** *Derek*
**Cinco Robles (Five Oaks)**
'57 *Russell Arms*
'57 *Les Paul & Mary Ford*
**Cinderella**
'62 *Jack Ross*
'77 *Firefall*
**Cindy, Oh Cindy**
'56 *Eddie Fisher*
'56 *Vince Martin/The Tarriers*
'62 **Cindy's Birthday** *Johnny Crawford*
'62 **Cinnamon Cinder (It's A Very Nice
     Dance)** *Pastel Six*
'69 **Cinnamon Girl** *Neil Young*
'88 **Circle In The Sand** *Belinda Carlisle*
'78 **Circle Is Small (I Can See It In Your
     Eyes)** *Gordon Lightfoot*
'94 **Circle Of Life** *Elton John*
'82 **Circles** *Atlantic Starr*
'73 **Cisco Kid** *War*
'69 **Cissy Strut** *Meters*
'85 **C-I-T-Y** *John Cafferty*
'58 **City Lights** *Ray Price*
'56 **City Of Angels** *Highlights*
**City Of New Orleans**
'72 *Arlo Guthrie*
'84 *Willie Nelson*
'72 **Clair** *Gilbert O'Sullivan*
'74 **Clap For The Wolfman** *Guess Who*
'65 **Clapping Song** *Shirley Ellis*
'59 **Class, The** *Chubby Checker*
'68 **Classical Gas** *Mason Williams*
'58 **Claudette** *Everly Brothers*
'71 **Clean Up Woman** *Betty Wright*
'69 **Clean Up Your Own Back Yard**
     *Elvis Presley*
'02 **Cleanin' Out My Closet** *Eminem*
'60 **Clementine** *Bobby Darin*
'98 **Cleopatra's Theme** *Cleopatra*
'58 **Click-Clack** *Dickey Doo & The Don'ts*
'60 **Climb Ev'ry Mountain** *Tony Bennett*
'64 **Clinging Vine** *Bobby Vinton*
'01 **Clint Eastwood** *Gorillaz*
'98 **Clock Strikes** *Timbaland & Magoo*
'03 **Clocks** *Coldplay*
'80 **Clones (We're All)** *Alice Cooper*
'89 **Close My Eyes Forever**
     *Lita Ford/Ozzy Osbourne*
'78 **Close The Door** *Teddy Pendergrass*
'62 **Close To Cathy** *Mike Clifford*
'80 **Close To The Borderline**
     *Billy Joel*
'72 **Close To The Edge** *Yes*
'90 **Close To You** *Maxi Priest*
**Close Your Eyes**
'67 *Peaches & Herb*
'73 *Edward Bear*

'94 **Closer** *Nine Inch Nails*
'78 **Closer I Get To You** *Roberta Flack with Donny Hathaway*
'86 **Closer Than Close** *Jean Carne*
'89 **Closer Than Friends** *Surface*
'89 **Closer To Fine** *Indigo Girls*
'96 **Closer To Free** *BoDeans*
'70 **Closer To Home [medley]** *Grand Funk Railroad*
'77 **Closer To The Heart** *Rush*
'83 **Closer You Get** *Alabama*
'98 **Closing Time** *Semisonic*
'68 **Cloud Nine** *Temptations*
'85 **Cloudbusting** *Kate Bush*
'73 **Clouds** *David Gates*
'59 **Clouds, The** *Spacemen*
'90 **Club At The End Of The Street** *Elton John*
'03 **Clubbin** *Marques Houston*
'70 **Coal Miner's Daughter** *Loretta Lynn*
'71 **Coat Of Many Colors** *Dolly Parton*
**Cocaine**
'77    *Eric Clapton*
'80    *Eric Clapton [live]*
'02 **Cochise** *Audioslave*
'97 **Coco Jamboo** *Mr. President*
'72 **Coconut** *Nilsson*
'57 **Cocoanut Woman** *Harry Belafonte*
**Cold**
'67    *John Gary*
'04    *Crossfade*
'77 **Cold As Ice** *Foreigner*
'83 **Cold Blooded** *Rick James*
'93 **Cold Fire** *Rush*
'74 **Cold Gin** *Kiss*
'04 **Cold Hard Bitch** *Jet*
'89 **Cold Hearted** *Paula Abdul*
'80 **Cold Love** *Donna Summer*
'96 **Cold Rock A Party** *MC Lyte*
'84 **Cold Shot** *Stevie Ray Vaughan*
'67 **Cold Sweat** *James Brown*
'88 **Coldsweat** *Sugarcubes*
'69 **Cold Turkey** *Plastic Ono Band*
'05 **Collide** *Howie Day*
'69 **Color Him Father** *Winstons*
'66 **Color My World** *Petula Clark*
'95 **Colors Of The Wind** *Vanessa Williams*
'71 **Colour My World** *Chicago*
'88 **Colour Of Love** *Billy Ocean*
'64 **Come A Little Bit Closer** *Jay & The Americans*
'70 **Come And Get It** *Badfinger*
'63 **Come And Get These Memories** *Martha & The Vandellas*
'98 **Come And Get With Me** *Keith Sweat*
**Come And Get Your Love**
'74    *Redbone*
'95    *Real McCoy*
'65 **Come And Stay With Me** *Marianne Faithfull*
'92 **Come & Talk To Me** *Jodeci*
'89 **Come Anytime** *Hoodoo Gurus*
**Come As You Are**
'87    *Peter Wolf*
'92    *Nirvana*
'93 **Come Baby Come** *K7*
**Come Back**
'60    *Jimmy Clanton*
'80    *J. Geils Band*
'84 **Come Back And Stay** *Paul Young*
'62 **Come Back Silly Girl** *Lettermen*
'90 **Come Back To Me** *Janet Jackson*
'67 **Come Back When You Grow Up** *Bobby Vee*
'04 **Come Clean** *Hilary Duff*
'58 **Come Closer To Me** *Nat "King" Cole*
'97 **Come Cryin' To Me** *Lonestar*
'83 **Come Dancing** *Kinks*
'58 **Come Fly With Me** *Frank Sinatra*
'73 **Come Get To This** *Marvin Gaye*
**Come Go With Me**
'57    *Dell-Vikings*
'81    *Beach Boys*
'87    *Exposé*

'65 **Come Home** *Dave Clark Five*
'93 **Come Inside** *Intro*
'59 **Come Into My Heart** *Lloyd Price*
'73 **Come Live With Me** *Roy Clark*
'74 **Come Monday** *Jimmy Buffett*
'90 **Come Next Monday** *K.T. Oslin*
'64 **Come On** *Tommy Roe*
'59 **Come On And Get Me** *Fabian*
'89 **C'mon And Get My Love** *D Mob/Cathy Dennis*
'64 **C'mon And Swim** *Bobby Freeman*
'90 **Come On Back** *Carlene Carter*
'67 **Come On Down To My Boat** *Every Mothers' Son*
'83 **Come On Eileen** *Dexys Midnight Runners*
'58 **C'mon Everybody** *Eddie Cochran*
**Come On Let's Go**
'58    *Ritchie Valens*
'66    *McCoys*
'87    *Los Lobos*
'62 **Come On Little Angel** *Belmonts*
'99 **Come On Over** *Shania Twain*
**C'mon Marianne**
'67    *4 Seasons*
'76    *Donny Osmond*
'96 **C'Mon N' Ride It (The Train)** *Quad City DJ's*
'76 **Come On Over** *Olivia Newton-John*
'00 **Come On Over Baby (all I want is you)** *Christina Aguilera*
'94 **Come Out And Play** *Offspring*
'03 **Come Over** *Aaliyah*
'66 **(Come 'Round Here) I'm The One You Need** *Miracles*
'70 **Come Running** *Van Morrison*
'66 **Come Running Back** *Dean Martin*
'77 **Come Sail Away** *Styx*
'69 **Come Saturday Morning** *Sandpipers*
'65 **Come See** *Major Lance*
**Come See About Me**
'64    *Supremes*
'67    *Jr. Walker*
'96 **Come See Me** *112*
'59 **Come Softly To Me** *Fleetwoods*
**Come To Me**
'58    *Johnny Mathis*
'59    *Marv Johnson*
'79    *France Joli*
'94 **Come To My Window** *Melissa Etheridge*
'67 **Come To The Sunshine** *Harpers Bizarre*
**Come Together**
'69    *Beatles*
'78    *Aerosmith*
'93 **Come Undone** *Duran Duran*
'58 **Come What May** *Clyde McPhatter*
'98 **Come With Me** *Puff Daddy*
'95 **Comedown** *Bush*
'78 **Comes A Time** *Neil Young*
'91 **Comfort Zone** *Vanessa Williams*
'80 **Comfortably Numb** *Pink Floyd*
'93 **Comforter** *Shai*
'70 **Comin' Home** *Delaney & Bonnie*
'62 **Comin' Home Baby** *Mel Torme*
'81 **Comin' In And Out Of Your Life** *Barbra Streisand*
'66 **Coming On Strong** *Brenda Lee*
'86 **Coming Around Again** *Carly Simon*
'89 **Coming Home** *Cinderella*
'66 **Coming Home Soldier** *Bobby Vinton*
'90 **Coming Of Age** *Damn Yankees*
'91 **Coming Out Of The Dark** *Gloria Estefan*
'80 **Coming Up** *Paul McCartney*
'69 **Commotion** *Creedence Clearwater Revival*
'85 **Communication** *Power Station*
'69 **Communication Breakdown** *Led Zeppelin*
'79 **Complete Control** *Clash*
'02 **Complicated** *Avril Lavigne*
'69 **Composer, The** *Supremes*

'65 **Concrete And Clay** *Eddie Rambeau*
'90 **Concrete And Steel** *ZZ Top*
'76 **Coney Island Baby** *Lou Reed*
'04 **Confessions Part II** *Usher*
'56 **Confidential** *Sonny Knight*
'79 **Confusion** *Electric Light Orchestra*
'85 **Conga** *Miami Sound Machine*
'93 **Connected** *Stereo MC's*
'95 **Connection** *Elastica*
'72 **Conquistador** *Procol Harum [live]*
'62 **Conscience** *James Darren*
'92 **Constant Craving** *k.d. lang*
'94 **Constantly** *Immature*
'01 **Contagious** *Isley Brothers*
'61 **Continental Walk** *Hank Ballard*
**Control**
'86    *Janet Jackson*
'01    *Puddle Of Mudd*
'81 **Controversy** *Prince*
'72 **Convention '72** *Delegates*
'75 **Convoy** *C.W. McCall*
'73 **Cook With Honey** *Judy Collins*
'71 **Cool Aid** *Paul Humphrey*
'79 **Cool Change** *Little River Band*
'84 **Cool It Now** *New Edition*
'66 **Cool Jerk** *Capitols*
'81 **Cool Love** *Pablo Cruise*
'81 **Cool Night** *Paul Davis*
'57 **Cool Shake** *Del Vikings*
'78 **Copacabana (At The Copa)** *Barry Manilow*
'73 **Corazón** *Carole King*
'60 **Corinna, Corinna** *Ray Peterson*
'72 **Corner Of The Sky** *Jackson 5*
'56 **Corrine Corrina** *Joe Turner*
'75 **Cortez The Killer** *Neil Young*
'74 **Cosmik Debris** *Frank Zappa*
'64 **Cotton Candy** *Al Hirt*
'95 **Cotton Eye Joe** *Rednex*
'61 **Cotton Fields** *Highwaymen*
'80 **Could I Have This Dance** *Anne Murray*
'00 **Could It Be** *Jaheim*
'72 **Could It Be Forever** *David Cassidy*
'72 **Could It Be I'm Falling In Love** *Spinners*
'75 **Could It Be Magic** *Barry Manilow*
'90 **Could This Be Love** *Seduction*
'57 **Could This Be Magic** *Dubs*
'80 **Could You Be Loved** *Bob Marley*
'87 **Could've Been** *Tiffany*
'92 **Could've Been Me** *Billy Ray Cyrus*
'77 **Couldn't Get It Right** *Climax Blues Band*
'00 **Couldn't Last A Moment** *Collin Raye*
'61 **Count Every Star** *Donnie & The Dreamers*
'65 **Count Me In** *Gary Lewis*
'85 **Count Me Out** *New Edition*
**Count On Me**
'78    *Jefferson Starship*
'96    *Whitney Houston & CeCe Winans*
'96 **Counting Blue Cars** *Dishwalla*
'60 **Country Boy** *Fats Domino*
'82 **Country Boy Can Survive** *Hank Williams Jr.*
'75 **Country Boy (You Got Your Feet In L.A.)** *Glen Campbell*
'68 **Country Girl - City Man** *Billy Vera & Judy Clay*
'71 **Country Road** *James Taylor*
'91 **Couple Days Off** *Huey Lewis*
'68 **Court Of Love** *Unifics*
'69 **Court Of The Crimson King** *King Crimson*
'02 **Courtesy Of The Red, White And Blue (The Angry American)** *Toby Keith*
'00 **Cousin Dupree** *Steely Dan*
'64 **Cousin Of Mine** *Sam Cooke*
'89 **Cover Girl** *New Kids On The Block*
'84 **Cover Me** *Bruce Springsteen*
'89 **Cover Of Love** *Michael Damian*
'72 **Cover Of "Rolling Stone"** *Dr. Hook*

'98 **Cover You In Kisses**
    *John Michael Montgomery*
'79 **Coward Of The County**
    *Kenny Rogers*
'99 **Cowboy** *Kid Rock*
'02 **Cowboy In Me** *Tim McGraw*
'99 **Cowboy Take Me Away** *Dixie Chicks*
'03 **Cowboys Like Us** *George Strait*
'68 **Cowboys To Girls** *Intruders*
'72 **Cowboys Work Is Never Done**
    *Sonny & Cher*
'69 **Cowgirl In The Sand**
    *Neil Young*
'77 **Crackerbox Palace** *George Harrison*
'70 **Cracklin' Rosie** *Neil Diamond*
**Cradle Of Love**
'60   *Johnny Preston*
'90   *Billy Idol*
'00 **Crash And Burn** *Savage Garden*
'97 **Crash Into Me** *Dave Matthews Band*
'01 **Crawling** *Linkin Park*
'01 **Crawling In The Dark** *Hoobastank*
'86 **Crazay** *Jesse Johnson*
**Crazy**
'61   *Patsy Cline*
'87   *Icehouse*
'90   *Boys*
'91   *Seal*
'94   *Aerosmith*
'00   *K-Ci & JoJo*
'89 **Crazy About Her** *Rod Stewart*
**Crazy Arms**
'56   *Ray Price*
'60   *Bob Beckham*
'58 **Crazy Eyes For You** *Bobby Hamilton*
'00 **Crazy For This Girl** *Evan & Jaron*
'85 **Crazy For You** *Madonna*
'72 **Crazy Horses** *Osmonds*
'03 **Crazy In Love** *Beyoncé*
'85 **Crazy In The Night (Barking At**
    **Airplanes)** *Kim Carnes*
'56 **Crazy Little Palace** *Billy Williams*
'79 **Crazy Little Thing Called Love**
    *Queen*
**Crazy Love**
'58   *Paul Anka*
'70   *Van Morrison*
'79   *Poco*
'79   *Allman Brothers Band*
'72 **Crazy Mama** *J.J. Cale*
'76 **Crazy On You** *Heart*
'55 **Crazy Otto [medley]** *Johnny Maddox*
'81 **Crazy Train** *Ozzy Osbourne*
'94 **C.R.E.A.M.** *Wu-Tang Clan*
'91 **Cream** *Prince & The N.P.G.*
'03 **Creatures (For A While)** *311*
**Creep**
'93   *Radiohead*
'93   *Stone Temple Pilots*
'94   *TLC*
'67 **Creeque Alley** *Mamas & The Papas*
'71 **Cried Like A Baby** *Bobby Sherman*
'97 **Criminal** *Fiona Apple*
**Crimson And Clover**
'68   *Tommy James*
'82   *Joan Jett*
'55 **Croce Di Oro (Cross Of Gold)**
    *Patti Page*
'72 **Crocodile Rock** *Elton John*
'71 **Cross-Eyed Mary** *Jethro Tull*
'87 **Cross My Broken Heart** *Jets*
**Cross Fire!**
'63   *Orlons*
'89   *Stevie Ray Vaughan*
'59 **Crossfire** *Johnny & The Hurricanes*
'69 **Crossroads** *Cream*
'96 **Crossroads, Tha**
    *Bone Thugs-N-Harmony*
'68 **Crosstown Traffic** *Jimi Hendrix*
'62 **Crowd, The** *Roy Orbison*
'68 **Crown Of Creation**
    *Jefferson Airplane*
**Cruel Summer**
'84   *Bananarama*
'98   *Ace Of Base*

'79 **Cruel To Be Kind** *Nick Lowe*
**Cruisin'**
'79   *Smokey Robinson*
'00   *Huey Lewis & Gwyneth Paltrow*
'90 **Cruising For Bruising** *Basia*
'83 **Crumblin' Down**
    *John Cougar Mellencamp*
'73 **Crunge, The** *Led Zeppelin*
'98 **Crush** *Jennifer Paige*
'86 **Crush On You** *Jets*
**Cry**
'66   *Ronnie Dove*
'85   *Godley & Creme*
'89   *Waterfront*
'02   *Faith Hill*
**Cry Baby**
'56   *Bonnie Sisters*
'63   *Garnet Mimms*
'71   *Janis Joplin*
'05   *Melissa Etheridge & Joss Stone*
    *[medley]*
'62 **Cry Baby Cry** *Angels*
'55 **Cry! Cry! Cry!** *Johnny Cash*
'91 **Cry For Help** *Rick Astley*
'93 **Cry For You** *Jodeci*
'68 **Cry Like A Baby** *Box Tops*
**Cry Me A River**
'55   *Julie London*
'70   *Joe Cocker*
'02   *Justin Timberlake*
**Cry To Me**
'62   *Solomon Burke*
'63   *Betty Harris*
'00 **Crybaby** *Mariah Carey*
**Cryin'**
'89   *Vixen*
'93   *Aerosmith*
**Crying**
'61   *Roy Orbison*
'66   *Jay & The Americans*
'81   *Don McLean*
'93 **Crying Game** *Boy George*
'65 **Crying In The Chapel** *Elvis Presley*
'62 **Crying In The Rain** *Everly Brothers*
'65 **Crying Time** *Ray Charles*
'76 **Crystal Ball** *Styx*
'69 **Crystal Blue Persuasion**
    *Tommy James*
'67 **Crystal Chandelier** *Charley Pride*
'67 **Crystal Ship** *Doors*
'67 **Cuando Sali De Cuba** *Sandpipers*
'89 **Cuddly Toy (Feel For Me)**
    *Roachford*
'04 **Culo** *Pitbull*
'89 **Cult Of Personality** *Living Colour*
**Cum On Feel The Noize**
'73   *Slade*
'83   *Quiet Riot*
'95 **Cumbersome** *7 Mary 3*
'98 **Cup Of Life** *Ricky Martin*
**Cupid**
'61   *Sam Cooke*
'69   *Johnny Nash*
'76   *Tony Orlando & Dawn*
'80   *Spinners [medley]*
'97   *112*
'83 **Curly Shuffle** *Jump 'N The Saddle*
**Cut Across Shorty**
'59   *Eddie Cochran*
'70   *Rod Stewart*
'75 **Cut The Cake** *AWB*
'90 **Cuts Both Ways** *Gloria Estefan*
'83 **Cuts Like A Knife** *Bryan Adams*
'90 **Cuts You Up** *Peter Murphy*
'68 **Cycles** *Frank Sinatra*

# D

'68 **D. W. Washburn** *Monkees*
'73 **D'yer Mak'er** *Led Zeppelin*
'71 **D.O.A.** *Bloodrock*
'88 **Da'Butt** *E.U.*
'82 **Da Da Da I Don't Love You You**
    **Don't Love Me** *Trio*

'97 **Da' Dip** *Freak Nasty*
**Da Doo Ron Ron**
'63   *Crystals*
'77   *Shaun Cassidy*
'78 **Da Ya Think I'm Sexy?** *Rod Stewart*
'73 **Daddy Could Swear, I Declare**
    *Gladys Knight*
'72 **Daddy Don't You Walk So Fast**
    *Wayne Newton*
**Daddy-O**
'55   *Bonnie Lou*
'55   *Fontane Sisters*
'69 **Daddy Sang Bass** *Johnny Cash*
'90 **Daddy's Come Around**
    *Paul Overstreet*
'86 **Daddy's Hands** *Holly Dunn*
**Daddy's Home**
'61   *Shep & The Limelites*
'72   *Jermaine Jackson*
'82   *Cliff Richard*
'67 **Daddy's Little Girl** *Al Martino*
'69 **Daddy's Little Man** *O.C. Smith*
'96 **Daddy's Money** *Ricochet*
'73 **Daisy A Day** *Jud Strunk*
'75 **Daisy Jane** *America*
'63 **Daisy Petal Pickin'**
    *Jimmy Gilmer/Fireballs*
'92 **Dallas** *Alan Jackson*
'03 **Damn!** *Youngbloodz*
'92 **Damn I Wish I Was Your Lover**
    *Sophie B. Hawkins*
'79 **Damned If I Do** *Alan Parsons Project*
'90 **Dance, The** *Garth Brooks*
'78 **Dance Across The Floor**
    *Jimmy "Bo" Horne*
**Dance, Dance, Dance**
'64   *Beach Boys*
'76   *Steve Miller Band*
'77 **Dance, Dance, Dance (Yowsah,**
    **Yowsah, Yowsah)** *Chic*
'78 **Dance (Disco Heat)** *Sylvester*
'58 **Dance Everyone Dance**
    *Betty Madigan*
'82 **Dance Floor** *Zapp*
'84 **Dance Hall Days** *Wang Chung*
'88 **Dance Little Sister**
    *Terence Trent D'Arby*
'61 **Dance On Little Girl** *Paul Anka*
'61 **(Dance The) Mess Around**
    *Chubby Checker*
'79 **Dance The Night Away** *Van Halen*
'79 **Dance This Mess Around** *B-52s*
'57 **Dance To The Bop** *Gene Vincent*
'68 **Dance To The Music**
    *Sly & The Family Stone*
'00 **Dance Tonight** *Lucy Pearl*
'82 **Dance Wit' Me** *Rick James*
**Dance With Me**
'59   *Drifters*
'75   *Orleans*
'78   *Peter Brown with Betty Wright*
'00   *Debelah Morgan*
'01   *112*
'55 **Dance With Me Henry (Wallflower)**
    *Georgia Gibbs*
'03 **Dance With My Father**
    *Luther Vandross*
'62 **(Dance With The) Guitar Man**
    *Duane Eddy*
'99 **Dancin'** *Guy*
**Dancin' Fool**
'74   *Guess Who*
'79   *Frank Zappa*
'77 **Dancin' Man** *Q*
'62 **Dancin' Party** *Chubby Checker*
'97 **Dancin', Shaggin' On The**
    **Boulevard** *Alabama*
'78 **Dancin' Shoes** *Nigel Olsson*
'79 **Dancing Barefoot** *Patti Smith*
**Dancing Days**
'73   *Led Zeppelin*
'95   *Stone Temple Pilots*
'84 **Dancing In The Dark**
    *Bruce Springsteen*
'72 **Dancing In The Moonlight**
    *King Harvest*

'84 **Dancing In The Sheets** *Shalamar*
**Dancing In The Street**
'64   *Martha & The Vandellas*
'82   *Van Halen*
'85   *Mick Jagger & David Bowie*
'74 **Dancing Machine** *Jackson 5*
'86 **Dancing On The Ceiling**
  *Lionel Richie*
'76 **Dancing Queen** *Abba*
'58 **Dancing With My Shadow**
  *Four Voices*
'81 **Dancing With Myself** *Billy Idol*
'67 **Dandelion** *Rolling Stones*
'66 **Dandy** *Herman's Hermits*
'64 **Dang Me** *Roger Miller*
'00 **Danger (Been So Long)** *Mystikal*
'55 **Danger! Heartbreak Ahead**
  *Jaye P. Morgan*
'86 **Danger Zone** *Kenny Loggins*
**Dangerous**
'89   *Roxette*
'91   *Doobie Brothers*
'98   *Busta Rhymes*
'79 **Dangerous Type** *Cars*
'66 **Dangling Conversation**
  *Simon & Garfunkel*
'73 **Daniel** *Elton John*
'63 **Danke Schoen** *Wayne Newton*
**Danny Boy**
'59   *Conway Twitty*
'67   *Ray Price*
**Danny's Song**
'72   *Loggins & Messina*
'73   *Anne Murray*
'85 **Dare Me** *Pointer Sisters*
'90 **Dare To Fall In Love**
  *Brent Bourgeois*
'04 **Dare You To Move** *Switchfoot*
'74 **Dark Horse** *George Harrison*
'74 **Dark Lady** *Cher*
**Dark Moon**
'57   *Bonnie Guitar*
'57   *Gale Storm*
**Dark Star**
'70   *Grateful Dead*
'77   *Crosby, Stills & Nash*
'78 **Darkness On The Edge Of Town**
  *Bruce Springsteen*
'67 **Darlin'** *Beach Boys*
'76 **Darlin' Darlin' Baby (Sweet, Tender,**
  **Love)** *O'Jays*
'67 **Darling Be Home Soon**
  *Lovin' Spoonful*
'55 **Darling Je Vous Aime Beaucoup**
  *Nat "King" Cole*
'59 **Darling Lorraine** *Knockouts*
'93 **Daughter** *Pearl Jam*
'70 **Daughter Of Darkness** *Tom Jones*
'05 **Daughters** *John Mayer*
'71 **Dave** *Cheech & Chong*
'64 **Dawn (Go Away)** *Four Seasons*
'65 **Dawn Of Correction** *Spokesmen*
'71 **Day After Day** *Badfinger*
**Day By Day**
'72   *Godspell*
'85   *Hooters*
'72 **Day Dreaming** *Aretha Franklin*
'66 **Day For Decision** *Johnny Sea*
'72 **Day I Found Myself** *Honey Cone*
'87 **Day-In Day-Out** *David Bowie*
'67 **Day In The Life** *Beatles*
'66 **Day In The Life Of A Fool** *Jack Jones*
'69 **Day Is Done** *Peter, Paul & Mary*
'74 **Day Of The Eagle** *Robin Trower*
**Day The Rains Came**
'58   *Raymond Lefevre*
'58   *Jane Morgan*
'99 **Day The World Went Away**
  *Nine Inch Nails*
'65 **Day Tripper** *Beatles*
**Daybreak**
'74   *Nilsson*
'77   *Barry Manilow*
'66 **Daydream** *Lovin' Spoonful*

**Daydream Believer**
'67   *Monkees*
'79   *Anne Murray*
'98 **Daydreamin'** *Tatyana Ali*
**Days Go By**
'02   *Dirty Vegas*
'04   *Keith Urban*
'79 **Days Gone Down (Still Got The**
  **Light In Your Eyes)**
  *Gerry Rafferty*
'90 **Days Like These** *Asia*
'96 **Days Of Our Livez**
  *Bone Thugs-N-Harmony*
'69 **Days Of Sand And Shovels**
  *Bobby Vinton*
**Days Of Wine And Roses**
'63   *Henry Mancini*
'63   *Andy Williams*
'77 **Daytime Friends** *Kenny Rogers*
'69 **Dazed And Confused**
  *Led Zeppelin*
'76 **Dazz** *Brick*
'93 **Dazzey Duks** *Duice*
'80 **De Do Do Do, De Da Da Da** *Police*
'78 **Deacon Blues** *Steely Dan*
'67 **Dead End Street** *Lou Rawls*
'83 **Dead Giveaway** *Shalamar*
'64 **Dead Man's Curve** *Jan & Dean*
'73 **Dead Skunk** *Loudon Wainwright III*
'90 **Deadbeat Club** *B-52's*
**Dear Heart**
'64   *Jack Jones*
'64   *Henry Mancini*
'64   *Andy Williams*
'62 **Dear Ivan** *Jimmy Dean*
'61 **Dear Lady Twist** *Gary (U.S.) Bonds*
'62 **Dear Lonely Hearts** *Nat King Cole*
'95 **Dear Mama** *2Pac*
'68 **Dear Mr. Fantasy** *Traffic*
'62 **Dear One** *Larry Finnegan*
'68 **Dear Prudence** *Beatles*
'95 **December** *Collective Soul*
'75 **December, 1963 (Oh, What a Night)**
  *4 Seasons*
'59 **Deck Of Cards** *Wink Martindale*
'58 **DeDe Dinah** *Frankie Avalon*
'93 **Dedicated** *R. Kelly*
'66 **Dedicated Follower Of Fashion**
  *Kinks*
**Dedicated To The One I Love**
'59   *Shirelles*
'67   *Mamas & The Papas*
'80 **Deep Inside My Heart**
  *Randy Meisner*
**Deep Purple**
'57   *Billy Ward*
'63   *Nino Tempo & April Stevens*
'75   *Donny & Marie Osmond*
**Deeper And [&] Deeper**
'70   *Freda Payne*
'84   *Fixx*
'92   *Madonna*
'90 **Deeper Shade Of Soul**
  *Urban Dance Squad*
'88 **Deeper Than The Holler**
  *Randy Travis*
'79 **Deeper Than The Night**
  *Olivia Newton-John*
'90 **Deeper The Love** *Whitesnake*
'79 **Deja Vu** *Dionne Warwick*
'97 **Deja Vu (Uptown Baby)**
  *Lord Tariq & Peter Gunz*
'60 **Delaware** *Perry Como*
'58 **Delicious!** *Jim Backus*
'68 **Delilah** *Tom Jones*
'83 **Delirious** *Prince*
**Delta Dawn**
'72   *Tanya Tucker*
'73   *Helen Reddy*
'69 **Delta Lady** *Joe Cocker*
'63 **Denise** *Randy & The Rainbows*
'79 **Dependin' On You** *Doobie Brothers*
'83 **Der Kommissar** *After The Fire*
'62 **Desafinado** *Stan Getz/Charlie Byrd*
'84 **Desert Moon** *Dennis DeYoung*
'63 **Desert Pete** *Kingston Trio*

'00 **Desert Rose** *Sting*
'71 **Desiderata** *Les Crane*
**Desire**
'80   *Andy Gibb*
'88   *U2*
'77 **Desirée** *Neil Diamond*
'65 **Desolation Row** *Bob Dylan*
'73 **Desperado** *Eagles*
'82 **Destination Unknown**
  *Missing Persons*
'81 **Destroyer** *Kinks*
**Detroit City**
'63   *Bobby Bare*
'67   *Tom Jones*
'76 **Detroit Rock City** *Kiss*
'74 **Deuce** *Kiss*
'94 **Deuces Are Wild** *Aerosmith*
'75 **Devil In The Bottle** *T.G. Sheppard*
'87 **Devil Inside** *INXS*
**Devil Or Angel**
'56   *Clovers*
'60   *Bobby Vee*
'79 **Devil Went Down To Georgia**
  *Charlie Daniels Band*
'66 **Devil With A Blue Dress On**
  **[medley]** *Mitch Ryder*
**Devil Woman**
'62   *Marty Robbins*
'76   *Cliff Richard*
'77 **Devil's Gun** *C.J. & Co.*
**Devoted To You**
'58   *Everly Brothers*
'78   *Carly Simon & James Taylor*
'74 **Devotion** *Earth, Wind & Fire*
'88 **Dial My Heart** *Boys*
'72 **Dialogue** *Chicago*
'74 **Diamond Dogs** *David Bowie*
'73 **Diamond Girl** *Seals & Crofts*
'65 **Diamond Head** *Ventures*
'87 **Diamonds** *Herb Alpert (with*
  *Janet Jackson)*
**Diamonds And Pearls**
'60   *Paradons*
'91   *Prince*
'75 **Diamonds And Rust** *Joan Baez*
'57 **Diana** *Paul Anka*
'64 **Diane** *Bachelors*
**Diary**
'72   *Bread*
'04   *Alicia Keys*
'58 **Diary, The** *Neil Sedaka*
'82 **Did It In A Minute**
  *Daryl Hall & John Oates*
'03 **Did My Time** *Korn*
'76 **Did You Boogie (With Your Baby)**
  *Flash Cadillac &*
  *The Continental Kids*
'66 **Did You Ever Have To Make Up**
  **Your Mind?** *Lovin' Spoonful*
'99 **Did You Ever Think** *R. Kelly*
'69 **Did You See Her Eyes** *Illusion*
**Didn't I (Blow Your Mind This Time)**
'70   *Delfonics*
'89   *New Kids On The Block*
'87 **Didn't We Almost Have It All**
  *Whitney Houston*
'02 **Die Another Day** *Madonna*
'97 **Difference, The** *Wallflowers*
'01 **Differences** *Ginuwine*
'86 **Different Corner** *George Michael*
'67 **Different Drum** *Linda Ronstadt*
'79 **Different Worlds**
  *Maureen McGovern*
'01 **Dig In** *Lenny Kravitz*
'95 **Diggin' On You** *TLC*
'92 **Digging In The Dirt** *Peter Gabriel*
'86 **Digging Your Scene** *Blow Monkeys*
'85 **Digital Display** *Ready For The World*
'02 **Dilemma** *Nelly*
'79 **Dim All The Lights** *Donna Summer*
'55 **Dim, Dim, The Lights** *Bill Haley*
'72 **Dinay Flo** *Boz Scaggs*
'60 **Ding-A-Ling** *Bobby Rydell*
'58 **Ding Dong** *McGuire Sisters*

'75 **Ding Dong; Ding Dong**
    *George Harrison*
'67 **Ding Dong! The Witch Is Dead**
    *Fifth Estate*
'58 **Dinner With Drac** *John Zacherle*
'04 **Dip It Low** *Christina Milian*
'04 **Dirt Off Your Shoulder** *Jay-Z*
'91 **Dirt Road** *Sawyer Brown*
'89 **Dirty Blvd.** *Lou Reed*
'90 **Dirty Cash (Money Talks)**
    *Adventures Of Stevie V*
'90 **Dirty Deeds** *Joan Jett*
'81 **Dirty Deeds Done Dirt Cheap**
    *AC/DC*
'88 **Dirty Diana** *Michael Jackson*
'82 **Dirty Laundry** *Don Henley*
'66 **Dirty Water** *Standells*
'79 **Dirty White Boy** *Foreigner*
'72 **Dirty Work** *Steely Dan*
'67 **Dis-Advantages Of You** *Brass Ring*
'90 **Disappear** *INXS*
'89 **Disappointed** *Public Image Ltd.*
'76 **Disco Duck** *Rick Dees*
    **Disco Inferno**
'77     *Trammps*
'05     *50 Cent*
'76 **Disco Lady** *Johnnie Taylor*
'77 **Disco Lucy (I Love Lucy Theme)**
    *Wilton Place Street Band*
'79 **Disco Nights (Rock-Freak)** *GQ*
'75 **Disco Queen** *Hot Chocolate*
'97 **Discothéque** *U2*
'02 **Disease** *Matchbox Twenty*
'94 **Dissident** *Pearl Jam*
'96 **Distance, The** *Cake*
'66 **Distant Drums** *Jim Reeves*
'84 **Distant Early Warning** *Rush*
'74 **Distant Lover** *Marvin Gaye*
'66 **Distant Shores** *Chad & Jeremy*
'92 **Ditty** *Paperboy*
'92 **Divine Thing** *Soup Dragons*
'68 **D-I-V-O-R-C-E** *Tammy Wynette*
'78 **Dixie Chicken** *Little Feat*
'55 **Dixie Danny** *Laurie Sisters*
'69 **Dizzy** *Tommy Roe*
'91 **Do Anything** *Natural Selection*
'98 **Do For Love** *2Pac*
'82 **Do I Do** *Stevie Wonder*
'92 **Do I Have To Say The Words?**
    *Bryan Adams*
'64 **Do I Love You?** *Ronettes*
'70 **Do It** *Neil Diamond*
    **Do It Again**
'68     *Beach Boys*
'72     *Steely Dan*
'85     *Kinks*
'67 **Do It Again A Little Bit Slower**
    *Jon & Robin & The In Crowd*
'75 **Do It Any Way You Wanna**
    *People's Choice*
'74 **Do It Baby** *Miracles*
    **Do It For Love**
'85     *Sheena Easton*
'02     *Daryl Hall & John Oates*
'79 **Do It Or Die** *Atlanta Rhythm Section*
'74 **Do It ('Til You're Satisfied)**
    *B.T. Express*
'92 **Do It To Me** *Lionel Richie*
'90 **Do Me!** *Bell Biv DeVoe*
'91 **Do Me Again** *Freddie Jackson*
'85 **Do Me Baby** *Meli'sa Morgan*
    **Do Me Right**
'71     *Detroit Emeralds*
'91     *Guy*
'61 **Do-Re-Mi** *Lee Dorsey*
'80 **Do Right** *Paul Davis*
'67 **Do Right Woman-Do Right Man**
    *Aretha Franklin*
'68 **Do Something To Me** *Tommy James*
'02 **Do That...** *Baby*
'79 **Do That To Me One More Time**
    *Captain & Tennille*
'90 **Do The Bartman** *Simpsons*
'63 **Do The Bird** *Dee Dee Sharp*
'65 **Do The Boomerang** *Jr. Walker*

'65 **Do The Clam** *Elvis Presley*
'65 **Do The Freddie**
    *Freddie & The Dreamers*
'70 **Do The Funky Chicken**
    *Rufus Thomas*
'62 **(Do The New) Continental** *Dovells*
'70 **(Do The) Push And Pull**
    *Rufus Thomas*
'84 **Do They Know It's Christmas?**
    *Band Aid*
'64 **Do-Wacka-Do** *Roger Miller*
'64 **Do Wah Diddy Diddy** *Manfred Mann*
'84 **Do What You Do** *Jermaine Jackson*
'70 **Do What You Wanna Do**
    *Five Flights Up*
'76 **Do What You Want, Be What You**
    **Are** *Daryl Hall & John Oates*
    **Do Ya**
'77     *Electric Light Orchestra*
'87     *K.T. Oslin*
'77 **Do Ya Wanna Get Funky With Me**
    *Peter Brown*
'82 **Do You Believe In Love** *Huey Lewis*
    **Do You Believe In Magic**
'65     *Lovin' Spoonful*
'78     *Shaun Cassidy*
'92 **Do You Believe In Us** *Jon Secada*
'76 **Do You Feel Like We Do**
    *Peter Frampton*
'86 **Do You Get Enough Love**
    *Shirley Jones*
'68 **Do You Know The Way To San José**
    *Dionne Warwick*
'78 **Do You Know You Are My Sunshine**
    *Statler Brothers*
'71 **Do You Know What I Mean**
    *Lee Michaels*
'97 **Do You Know (What It Takes)**
    *Robyn*
'97 **Do You Like This** *Rome*
    **Do You Love Me**
'62     *Contours*
'64     *Dave Clark Five*
'98 **Do You Really Want Me (Show**
    **Respect)** *Robyn*
'82 **Do You Really Want To Hurt Me**
    *Culture Club*
'90 **Do You Remember?** *Phil Collins*
'80 **Do You Remember Rock 'N' Roll**
    **Radio** *Ramones*
'72 **Do You Remember These**
    *Statler Brothers*
'70 **Do You See My Love (For You**
    **Growing)** *Jr. Walker*
'95 **Do You Sleep?** *Lisa Loeb*
'94 **Do You Wanna Get Funky**
    *C+C Music Factory*
'78 **Do You Wanna Dance** *Ramones*
'77 **Do You Wanna Make Love**
    *Peter McCann*
'82 **Do You Wanna Touch Me (Oh Yeah)**
    *Joan Jett*
'85 **Do You Want Crying**
    *Katrina & The Waves*
'91 **Do You Want Me** *Salt-N-Pepa*
    **Do You Want To Dance**
'58     *Bobby Freeman*
'65     *Beach Boys*
'72     *Bette Midler*
'64 **Do You Want To Know A Secret**
    *Beatles*
    **Do Your Thing**
'69     *Watts 103rd Street Rhythm Band*
'72     *Isaac Hayes*
'89 **Doctor, The** *Doobie Brothers*
'84 **Doctor! Doctor!** *Thompson Twins*
'89 **Dr. Feelgood** *Mötley Crüe*
'83 **Dr. Heckyll & Mr. Jive** *Men At Work*
'72 **Doctor My Eyes** *Jackson Browne*
'74 **Doctor's Orders** *Carol Douglas*
'68 **Does Anybody Know I'm Here** *Dells*
'70 **Does Anybody Really Know What**
    **Time It Is?** *Chicago*
'84 **Does Fort Worth Ever Cross Your**
    **Mind** *George Strait*
'93 **Does He Love You** *Reba McEntire*
    *(with Linda Davis)*

'82 **Does It Make You Remember**
    *Kim Carnes*
'67 **Does My Ring Hurt Your Finger**
    *Charley Pride*
'96 **Does That Blue Moon Ever Shine**
    **On You** *Toby Keith*
'61 **Does Your Chewing Gum Lose It's**
    **Flavor (On The Bedpost Over**
    **Night)** *Lonnie Donegan*
'68 **Does Your Mama Know About Me**
    *Bobby Taylor*
'79 **Does Your Mother Know** *Abba*
'00 **Doesn't Really Matter** *Janet Jackson*
'71 **Doesn't Somebody Want To Be**
    **Wanted** *Partridge Family*
'79 **Dog & Butterfly** *Heart*
'76 **Dog Eat Dog** *Ted Nugent*
'55 **Dogface Soldier** *Russ Morgan*
'60 **Doggin' Around** *Jackie Wilson*
'69 **Doggone Right** *Miracles*
'96 **Doin It** *LL Cool J*
'87 **Doing It All For My Baby**
    *Huey Lewis*
'73 **Doing It To Death** *JB's*
'60 **Doll House** *Donnie Brooks*
'94 **Doll Parts** *Hole*
'71 **Dolly Dagger** *Jimi Hendrix*
'99 **Dolphin's Cry** *Live*
'55 **Domani (Tomorrow)** *Julius LaRosa*
'63 **Dominique** *Singing Nun*
'70 **Domino** *Van Morrison*
'88 **Domino Dancing** *Pet Shop Boys*
'87 **Dominoes** *Robbie Nevil*
'58 **Don't** *Elvis Presley*
'84 **Don't Answer Me**
    *Alan Parsons Project*
'66 **Don't Answer The Door** *B.B. King*
'90 **Don't Ask Me** *Public Image Ltd.*
'74 **Don't Ask Me No Questions**
    *Lynyrd Skynyrd*
    **Don't Ask Me Why**
'58     *Elvis Presley*
'80     *Billy Joel*
'89     *Eurythmics*
'92 **Don't Be Afraid** *Aaron Hall*
'63 **Don't Be Afraid, Little Darlin'**
    *Steve Lawrence*
    **Don't Be Angry**
'55     *Nappy Brown*
'55     *Crew-Cuts*
    **Don't Be Cruel**
'56     *Elvis Presley*
'60     *Bill Black's Combo*
'88     *Cheap Trick*
'88     *Bobby Brown*
'97 **Don't Be Stupid (You Know I Love**
    **You)** *Shania Twain*
'88 **Don't Believe The Hype**
    *Public Enemy*
'61 **Don't Bet Money Honey** *Linda Scott*
'61 **Don't Blame Me** *Everly Brothers*
'67 **Don't Blame The Children**
    *Sammy Davis, Jr.*
'62 **Don't Break The Heart That Loves**
    **You** *Connie Francis*
    **Don't Bring Me Down**
'66     *Animals*
'79     *Electric Light Orchestra*
'74 **Don't Call Us, We'll Call You**
    *Sugarloaf/Jerry Corbetta*
'02 **Dontchange** *Musiq*
'74 **Don't Change Horses (In The**
    **Middle Of A Stream)**
    *Tower Of Power*
'89 **Don't Close Your Eyes** *Kix*
'85 **Don't Come Around Here No More**
    *Tom Petty*
'60 **Don't Come Knockin'** *Fats Domino*
'73 **Don't Cross The River** *America*
    **Don't Cry**
'83     *Asia*
'91     *Guns N' Roses*
'96     *Seal*
'61 **Don't Cry, Baby** *Etta James*
'69 **Don't Cry Daddy** *Elvis Presley*
'97 **Don't Cry For Me Argentina**
    *Madonna*

'61 **Don't Cry No More** *Bobby Bland*
'78 **Don't Cry Out Loud**
    *Melissa Manchester*
'87 **Don't Disturb This Groove** *System*
'79 **Don't Do Me Like That** *Tom Petty*
'87 **Don't Dream It's Over**
    *Crowded House*
'98 **Don't Drink The Water**
    *Dave Matthews Band*
'74 **Don't Eat The Yellow Snow**
    *Frank Zappa*
'72 **Don't Ever Be Lonely (A Poor Little**
    **Fool Like Me)** *Cornelius*
    *Brothers & Sister Rose*
'79 **Don't Ever Wanna Lose Ya**
    *New England*
'72 **Don't Expect Me To Be Your Friend**
    *Lobo*
'80 **Don't Fall In Love With A Dreamer**
    *Kenny Rogers with Kim Carnes*
'76 **(Don't Fear) The Reaper**
    *Blue Öyster Cult*
'82 **Don't Fight It**
    *Kenny Loggins/Steve Perry*
'56 **Don't Forbid Me** *Pat Boone*
'64 **Don't Forget I Still Love You**
    *Bobbi Martin*
'86 **Don't Forget Me (When I'm Gone)**
    *Glass Tiger*
'83 **Don't Forget To Dance** *Kinks*
'96 **Don't Get Me Started** *Rhett Akins*
'86 **Don't Get Me Wrong** *Pretenders*
'69 **Don't Give In To Him** *Gary Puckett*
'81 **Don't Give It Up** *Robbie Patton*
'87 **Don't Give Up**
    *Peter Gabriel & Kate Bush*
'77 **Don't Give Up On Us** *David Soul*
'91 **Don't Go** *En Vogue*
'97 **Don't Go Away** *Oasis*
'90 **Don't Go Away Mad (Just Go Away)**
    *Mötley Crüe*
'76 **Don't Go Breaking My Heart**
    *Elton John & Kiki Dee*
'58 **Don't Go Home** *Playmates*
'62 **Don't Go Near The Indians**
    *Rex Allen*
'67 **Don't Go Out Into The Rain (You're**
    **Going To Melt)** *Herman's Hermits*
    **Don't Go To Strangers**
'56     *Vaughn Monroe*
'60     *Etta Jones*
'62 **Don't Hang Up** *Orlons*
'01 **Don't Happen Twice**
    *Kenny Chesney*
'78 **Don't Hold Back** *Chanson*
'77 **Don't It Make My Brown Eyes Blue**
    *Crystal Gayle*
'69 **Don't It Make You Want To Go**
    **Home** *Joe South*
'65 **Don't Just Stand There** *Patty Duke*
'71 **Don't Knock My Love** *Wilson Pickett*
'89 **Don't Know Much**
    *Linda Ronstadt/Aaron Neville*
'88 **Don't Know What You Got (Till It's**
    **Gone)** *Cinderella*
'02 **Don't Know Why** *Norah Jones*
'98 **Don't Laugh At Me** *Mark Wills*
'97 **Don't Leave Me** *BLACKstreet*
'76 **Don't Leave Me This Way**
    *Thelma Houston*
    **Don't Let Go**
'58     *Roy Hamilton*
'79     *Isaac Hayes*
'84     *Wang Chung*
'96 **Don't Let Go (Love)** *En Vogue*
'77 **Don't Let It Show**
    *Alan Parsons Project*
'81 **Don't Let Him Go** *REO Speedwagon*
'82 **Don't Let Him Know** *Prism*
'83 **Don't Let It End** *Styx*
'72 **Don't Let Me Be Lonely Tonight**
    *James Taylor*
    **Don't Let Me Be Misunderstood**
'65     *Animals*
'77     *Santa Esmeralda*
'69 **Don't Let Me Down** *Beatles*
'02 **Don't Let Me Get Me** *P!nk*

'92 **Don't Let Our Love Start Slippin'**
    **Away** *Vince Gill*
'71 **Don't Let The Green Grass Fool**
    **You** *Wilson Pickett*
'69 **Don't Let The Joneses Get You**
    **Down** *Temptations*
'64 **Don't Let The Rain Come Down**
    **(Crooked Little Man)**
    *Serendipity Singers*
'67 **Don't Let The Rain Fall Down On**
    **Me** *Critters*
'64 **Don't Let The Sun Catch You**
    **Crying** *Gerry & The Pacemakers*
    **Don't Let The Sun Go Down On Me**
'74     *Elton John*
'91     *George Michael/Elton John [live]*
'87 **Don't Let's Start**
    *They Might Be Giants*
'84 **Don't Look Any Further**
    *Dennis Edwards*
    **Don't Look Back**
'78     *Boston*
'89     *Fine Young Cannibals*
'87 **Don't Look Down - The Sequel**
    *Go West*
'85 **Don't Lose My Number** *Phil Collins*
    **Don't Make Me Over**
'62     *Dionne Warwick*
'89     *Sybil*
'87 **Don't Make Me Wait For Love**
    *Kenny G*
'87 **Don't Mean Nothing** *Richard Marx*
'65 **Don't Mess Up A Good Thing**
    *Fontella Bass & Bobby McClure*
'66 **Don't Mess With Bill** *Marvelettes*
'02 **Don't Mess With My Man** *Nivea*
'87 **Don't Need A Gun** *Billy Idol*
'83 **Don't Pay The Ferryman**
    *Chris DeBurgh*
'05 **Don't Phunk With My Heart**
    *Black Eyed Peas*
'58 **Don't Pity Me** *Dion & The Belmonts*
    **Don't Play That Song**
'62     *Ben E. King*
'70     *Aretha Franklin*
'71 **Don't Pull Your Love**
    *Hamilton, Joe Frank & Reynolds*
'80 **Don't Push It Don't Force It**
    *Leon Haywood*
'64 **Don't Rain On My Parade**
    *Barbra Streisand*
'88 **Don't Rock The Boat** *Midnight Star*
'91 **Don't Rock The Jukebox**
    *Alan Jackson*
'88 **Don't Rush Me** *Taylor Dayne*
'63 **Don't Say Goodnight And Mean**
    **Goodbye** *Shirelles*
'80 **Don't Say Goodnight (It's Time For**
    **Love)** *Isley Brothers*
'85 **Don't Say No Tonight** *Eugene Wilde*
'63 **Don't Say Nothin' Bad (About My**
    **Baby)** *Cookies*
'71 **Don't Say You Don't Remember**
    *Beverly Bremers*
'99 **Don't Say You Love Me** *M2M*
'63 **Don't Set Me Free** *Ray Charles*
'87 **Don't Shed A Tear** *Paul Carrack*
'89 **Don't Shut Me Out** *Kevin Paige*
'67 **Don't Sleep In The Subway**
    *Petula Clark*
'96 **Don't Speak** *No Doubt*
'81 **Don't Stand So Close To Me** *Police*
'55 **Don't Start Me Talkin'**
    *"Sonny Boy" Williamson*
'77 **Don't Stop** *Fleetwood Mac*
    **Don't Stop Believin'**
'76     *Olivia Newton-John*
'81     *Journey*
'78 **Don't Stop Me Now** *Queen*
'81 **Don't Stop The Music**
    *Yarbrough & Peoples*
'79 **Don't Stop 'Til You Get Enough**
    *Michael Jackson*
'76 **Don't Take Away The Music**
    *Tavares*
'89 **Don't Take It Personal**
    *Jermaine Jackson*

'95 **Don't Take It Personal (just one of**
    **dem days)** *Monica*
'68 **Don't Take It So Hard**
    *Paul Revere & The Raiders*
'94 **Don't Take The Girl** *Tim McGraw*
'59 **Don't Take Your Guns To Town**
    *Johnny Cash*
'75 **Don't Take Your Love** *Manhattans*
'04 **Don't Take Your Love Away** *Avant*
'82 **Don't Talk To Strangers**
    *Rick Springfield*
'93 **Don't Tear Me Up** *Mick Jagger*
    **Don't Tell Me**
'00     *Madonna*
'04     *Avril Lavigne*
'75 **Don't Tell Me Goodnight** *Lobo*
'89 **Don't Tell Me Lies** *Breathe*
'95 **Don't Tell Me (What Love Can Do)**
    *Van Halen*
'83 **Don't Tell Me You Love Me**
    *Night Ranger*
'00 **Don't Think I'm Not** *Kandi*
    **Don't Think Twice, It's All Right**
'63     *Bob Dylan*
'63     *Peter, Paul & Mary*
'65     *4 Seasons*
'60 **Don't Throw Away All Those**
    **Teardrops** *Frankie Avalon*
'64 **Don't Throw Your Love Away**
    *Searchers*
'69 **Don't Touch Me** *Bettye Swann*
'92 **Don't Tread On Me** *Damn Yankees*
'91 **Don't Treat Me Bad** *Firehouse*
'80 **Don't Try Suicide** *Queen*
'94 **Don't Turn Around** *Ace Of Base*
    **Don't Walk Away**
'84     *Rick Springfield*
'92     *Jade*
'97 **Don't Wanna Be A Player** *Joe*
'91 **Don't Wanna Change The World**
    *Phyllis Hyman*
'90 **Don't Wanna Fall In Love**
    *Jane Child*
    **Don't Wanna Lose You**
'89     *Gloria Estefan*
'96     *Lionel Richie*
'03 **Don't Wanna Try** *Frankie J.*
'91 **Don't Want To Be A Fool**
    *Luther Vandross*
'78 **Don't Want To Live Without It**
    *Pablo Cruise*
'81 **Don't Want To Wait Anymore** *Tubes*
'70 **Don't Waste My Time**
    *John Mayall*
'84 **Don't Waste Your Time**
    *Yarbrough & Peoples*
'61 **Don't Worry** *Marty Robbins*
    **Don't Worry Baby**
'64     *Beach Boys*
'77     *B.J. Thomas*
'88 **Don't Worry Be Happy**
    *Bobby McFerrin*
'70 **(Don't Worry) If There's A Hell**
    **Below We're All Going To Go**
    *Curtis Mayfield*
'62 **Don't You Believe It** *Andy Williams*
'67 **Don't You Care** *Buckinghams*
'85 **Don't You (Forget About Me)**
    *Simple Minds*
'01 **Don't You Forget It** *Glenn Lewis*
'83 **Don't You Get So Mad**
    *Jeffrey Osborne*
'58 **Don't You Just Know It**
    *Huey (Piano) Smith*
'59 **Don't You Know** *Della Reese*
'88 **Don't You Know What The Night**
    **Can Do?** *Steve Winwood*
    **Don't You Want Me**
'82     *Human League*
'87     *Jody Watley*
'74 **Don't You Worry 'Bout A Thing**
    *Stevie Wonder*
'79 **Don't You Write Her Off**
    *McGuinn, Clark & Hillman*
'58 **Doncha' Think It's Time**
    *Elvis Presley*
'71 **Done Too Soon** *Neil Diamond*

'58 **Donna** *Ritchie Valens*
'63 **Donna The Prima Donna** *Dion*
'74 **Doo Doo Doo Doo Doo**
    **(Heartbreaker)** *Rolling Stones*
'98 **Doo Wop (That Thing)** *Lauryn Hill*
'73 **Doolin'-Dalton** *Eagles*
'64 **Door Is Still Open To My Heart**
    *Dean Martin*
'74 **Doraville** *Atlanta Rhythm Section*
'76 **Dose Of Rock 'N' Roll** *Ringo Starr*
'76 **Dottie** *Danny & The Juniors*
'71 **Double Barrel** *Dave & Ansil Collins*
'81 **Double Dutch Bus** *Frankie Smith*
'71 **Double Lovin'** *Osmonds*
'66 **Double Shot (Of My Baby's Love)**
    *Swingin' Medallions*
'76 **Double Trouble** *Lynyrd Skynyrd*
'78 **Double Vision** *Foreigner*
'90 **Doubleback** *ZZ Top*
'96 **Down** *311*
'02 **Down A\*\* Chick** *Ja Rule*
'68 **Down At Lulu's** *Ohio Express*
'63 **(Down At) Papa Joe's** *Dixiebelles*
'91 **Down At The Twist And Shout**
    *Mary-Chapin Carpenter*
'89 **Down Boys** *Warrant*
'72 **Down By The Lazy River** *Osmonds*
'69 **Down By The River** *Neil Young*
'59 **Down By The Station** *Four Preps*
'95 **Down By The Water** *PJ Harvey*
'02 **Down 4 U** *Inc.*
'91 **Down Home** *Alabama*
'65 **Down In The Boondocks**
    *Billy Joe Royal*
'96 **Down Low (Nobody Has To Know)**
    *R. Kelly*
'68 **Down On Me** *Big Brother & The*
    *Holding Company*
'69 **Down On The Corner**
    *Creedence Clearwater Revival*
'94 **Down On The Farm** *Tim McGraw*
'58 **Down The Aisle Of Love**
    *Quin-Tones*
'63 **Down The Aisle (Wedding Song)**
    *Patti LaBelle*
'91 **Down To My Last Teardrop**
    *Tanya Tucker*
'98 **Down Town** *Days Of The New*
'82 **Down Under** *Men At Work*
'93 **Down With The King** *Run-D.M.C.*
'60 **Down Yonder**
    *Johnny & The Hurricanes*
    **Downtown**
'64    *Petula Clark*
'89    *One 2 Many*
'88 **Downtown Life**
    *Daryl Hall/John Oates*
'89 **Downtown Train** *Rod Stewart*
'63 **Drag City** *Jan & Dean*
'71 **Draggin' The Line** *Tommy James*
'81 **Draw Of The Cards** *Kim Carnes*
'77 **Draw The Line** *Aerosmith*
'93 **Dre Day** *Dr. Dre/Snoop Dogg*
'58 **Dream** *Betty Johnson*
'68 **Dream A Little Dream Of Me**
    *Mama Cass*
'95 **Dream About You** *Stevie B*
    **Dream Baby (How Long Must I**
    **Dream)**
'62    *Roy Orbison*
'71    *Glen Campbell*
'91 **Dream Is Still Alive** *Wilson Phillips*
'59 **Dream Lover** *Bobby Darin*
    **Dream Merchant**
'67    *Jerry Butler*
'75    *New Birth*
    **Dream On**
'73    *Aerosmith*
'74    *Righteous Brothers*
'65 **Dream On Little Dreamer**
    *Perry Como*
'79 **Dream Police** *Cheap Trick*
'76 **Dream Weaver** *Gary Wright*
'76 **Dreamboat Annie** *Heart*

'75 **Dreamer**
'75    *Supertramp*
'80    *Supertramp [live]*
    **Dreamin'**
'60    *Johnny Burnette*
'89    *Vanessa Williams*
'83 **Dreamin' Is Easy** *Steel Breeze*
    **Dreaming**
'79    *Blondie*
'80    *Cliff Richard*
'88    *Orchestral Manoeuvres In The Dark*
'95 **Dreaming Of You** *Selena*
'94 **Dreaming With My Eyes Open**
    *Clay Walker*
'91 **Dreamline** *Rush*
'93 **Dreamlover** *Mariah Carey*
    **Dreams**
'70    *Allman Brothers Band*
'77    *Fleetwood Mac*
'86    *Van Halen*
'93    *Gabrielle*
'04    *Diana DeGarmo*
'68 **Dreams Of The Everyday**
    **Housewife** *Glen Campbell*
'86 **Dreamtime** *Daryl Hall*
    **Dreamy Eyes**
'56    *Four Preps*
'58    *Johnny Tillotson*
'72 **Dreidel** *Don McLean*
'85 **Dress You Up** *Madonna*
'89 **Dressed For Success** *Roxette*
'02 **Drift & Die** *Puddle Of Mudd*
    **Drift Away**
'73    *Dobie Gray*
'03    *Uncle Kracker with Dobie Gray*
'78 **Driftwood** *Moody Blues*
'97 **Drink, Swear, Steal & Lie**
    *Michael Peterson*
'73 **Drinking Wine Spo-Dee O'Dee**
    *Jerry Lee Lewis*
'63 **Drip Drop** *Dion*
    **Drive**
'84    *Cars*
'92    *R.E.M.*
'00    *Incubus*
'02 **Drive (For Daddy Gene)**
    *Alan Jackson*
'57 **Drive In Show** *Eddie Cochran*
'66 **Drive My Car** *Beatles*
'92 **Drive South** *Suzy Bogguss*
'89 **Driven Out** *Fixx*
'79 **Driver's Seat** *Sniff 'n' the Tears*
'80 **Drivin' My Life Away** *Eddie Rabbitt*
'76 **Drivin' Wheel** *Foghat*
'04 **Drop It Like It's Hot** *Snoop Dogg*
'01 **Drops Of Jupiter (Tell Me)** *Train*
'56 **Drown In My Own Tears**
    *Ray Charles*
'01 **Drowning** *Backstreet Boys*
'71 **Drowning In The Sea Of Love**
    *Joe Simon*
'71 **Drum, The** *Bobby Sherman*
'67 **Dry Your Eyes**
    *Brenda & The Tabulations*
'65 **Duck, The** *Jackie Lee*
'01 **Duck And Run** *3 Doors Down*
'04 **Dude** *Beenie Man*
'87 **Dude (Looks Like A Lady)**
    *Aerosmith*
'73 **Dueling Banjos** *Eric Weissberg &*
    *Steve Mandell*
'62 **Duke Of Earl** *Gene Chandler*
'61 **Dum Dum** *Brenda Lee*
'55 **Dungaree Doll** *Eddie Fisher*
'94 **Dunkie Butt (Please Please Please)**
    *12 Gauge*
'77 **Dusic** *Brick*
'78 **Dust In The Wind** *Kansas*
'95 **Dust On The Bottle**
    *David Lee Murphy*
'60 **Dutchman's Gold** *Walter Brennan*
'84 **Dynamite** *Jermaine Jackson*
'75 **Dynomite** *Bazuka*

# E

'96 **E-Bow The Letter** *R.E.M.*
'05 **E-Pro** *Beck*
'00 **E.I.** *Nelly*
'74 **Earache My Eye (Featuring Alice**
    **Bowie)** *Cheech & Chong*
    **Early In The Morning**
'58    *Bobby Darin*
'58    *Buddy Holly*
'69    *Vanity Fare*
'82    *Gap Band*
'88    *Robert Palmer*
'71 **Early 1970** *Ringo Starr*
    **Earth Angel**
'55    *Penguins*
'55    *Crew-Cuts*
'55    *Gloria Mann*
'86    *New Edition*
'96 **Earth, The Sun, The Rain**
    *Color Me Badd*
'63 **Easier Said Than Done** *Essex*
'66 **East West** *Herman's Hermits*
'77 **Easy** *Commodores*
    **Easy Come, Easy Go**
'70    *Bobby Sherman*
'93    *George Strait*
'72 **Easy Livin** *Uriah Heep*
'84 **Easy Lover**
    *Philip Bailey with Phil Collins*
'71 **Easy Loving** *Freddie Hart*
'69 **Easy To Be Hard** *Three Dog Night*
'77 **Easy To Love** *Leo Sayer*
'84 **Eat It** *Weird Al Yankovic*
    **Ebb Tide**
'64    *Lenny Welch*
'65    *Righteous Brothers*
'82 **Ebony And Ivory** *Paul McCartney*
    *(with Stevie Wonder)*
    **Ebony Eyes**
'61    *Everly Brothers*
'78    *Bob Welch*
'69 **Echo Park** *Keith Barbour*
'73 **Eclipse [medley]** *Pink Floyd*
'73 **Ecstasy** *Ohio Players*
    **Eddie My Love**
'56    *Chordettes*
'56    *Fontane Sisters*
'56    *Teen Queens*
    **Edge Of A Broken Heart**
'87    *Bon Jovi*
'88    *Vixen*
'86 **Edge Of Heaven** *Wham!*
'82 **Edge Of Seventeen (Just Like The**
    **White Winged Dove)** *Stevie Nicks*
'77 **Edge Of The Universe** *Bee Gees*
'78 **Ego** *Elton John*
'65 **Eight Days A Week** *Beatles*
'87 **853-5937** *Squeeze*
'66 **Eight Miles High** *Byrds*
'99 **808** *Blaque*
'81 **867-5309/Jenny** *Tommy Tutone*
'71 **Eighteen** *Alice Cooper*
'89 **18 And Life** *Skid Row*
'88 **Eighteen Wheels And A Dozen**
    **Roses** *Kathy Mattea*
'75 **Eighteen With A Bullet**
    *Pete Wingfield*
'63 **18 Yellow Roses** *Bobby Darin*
'87 **80's Ladies** *K.T. Oslin*
'94 **Einstein On The Beach (For An**
    **Eggman)** *Counting Crows*
'70 **El Condor Pasa** *Simon & Garfunkel*
'60 **El Matador** *Kingston Trio*
'59 **El Paso** *Marty Robbins*
'58 **El Rancho Rock** *Champs*
'86 **El Shaddai** *Amy Grant*
'63 **El Watusi** *Ray Barretto*
    **Eleanor Rigby**
'66    *Beatles*
'68    *Ray Charles*
'69    *Aretha Franklin*
'72 **Elected** *Alice Cooper*
'85 **Election Day** *Arcadia*
'83 **Electric Avenue** *Eddy Grant*

'88 **Electric Blue** *Icehouse*
'89 **Electric Slide (Boogie)**
    *Marcia Griffiths*
'89 **Electric Youth** *Debbie Gibson*
'82 **Electricland** *Bad Company*
'97 **Elegantly Wasted** *INXS*
'68 **Elenore** *Turtles*
'91 **Elevate My Mind** *Stereo MC's*
'96 **Elevators (me & you)** *OutKast*
'56 **11th Hour Melody** *Al Hibbler*
'69 **Eli's Coming** *Three Dog Night*
'56 **Eloise** *Kay Thompson*
'66 **Elusive Butterfly** *Bob Lind*
'81 **Elvira** *Oak Ridge Boys*
'85 **Emergency** *Kool & The Gang*
'83 **Eminence Front** *Who*
'75 **Emma** *Hot Chocolate*
**Emotion**
'75   *Helen Reddy*
'77   *Samantha Sang*
'01   *Destiny's Child*
'86 **Emotion In Motion** *Ric Ocasek*
'97 **Emotional Girl** *Terri Clark*
'80 **Emotional Rescue** *Rolling Stones*
'03 **Emotional Rollercoaster**
    *Vivian Green*
**Emotions**
'60   *Brenda Lee*
'91   *Mariah Carey*
'90 **Emperor's New Clothes**
    *Sinéad O'Connor*
'80 **Empire Strikes Back [medley]** *Meco*
**Empty Arms**
'57   *Teresa Brewer*
'57   *Ivory Joe Hunter*
'82 **Empty Garden (Hey Hey Johnny)**
    *Elton John*
'70 **Empty Pages** *Traffic*
'59 **Enchanted** *Platters*
'58 **Enchanted Island** *Four Lads*
**Enchanted Sea**
'59   *Martin Denny*
'59   *Islanders*
**Encore**
'83   *Cheryl Lynn*
'05   *Eminem*
    *(also see: Numb)*
**End, The**
'58   *Earl Grant*
'67   *Doors*
'69   *Beatles [medley]*
'68 **End Of Our Road** *Gladys Knight*
'89 **End Of The Innocence** *Don Henley*
**End Of The Line**
'89   *Traveling Wilburys*
'91   *Allman Brothers Band*
'92 **End of the Road** *Boyz II Men*
'63 **End Of The World** *Skeeter Davis*
**Endless Love**
'81   *Diana Ross & Lionel Richie*
'94   *Luther Vandross & Mariah Carey*
'87 **Endless Nights** *Eddie Money*
'58 **Endless Sleep** *Jody Reynolds*
'88 **Endless Summer Nights**
    *Richard Marx*
'59 **Endlessly** *Brook Benton*
'99 **Enemy** *Days Of The New*
'74 **Energy Crisis '74** *Dickie Goodman*
'65 **Engine Engine #9** *Roger Miller*
'70 **Engine Number 9** *Wilson Pickett*
'65 **England Swings** *Roger Miller*
'56 **English Muffins And Irish Stew**
    *Sylvia Syms*
'90 **Enjoy The Silence** *Depeche Mode*
'76 **Enjoy Yourself** *Jacksons*
'82 **Enough Is Enough** *April Wine*
'91 **Enter Sandman** *Metallica*
**Entertainer, The**
'74   *Marvin Hamlisch/"The Sting"*
'74   *Billy Joel*
'90 **Epic** *Faith No More*
'67 **Epistle To Dippy** *Donovan*
'74 **Eres Tu (Touch The Wind)**
    *Mocedades*
'92 **Erotica** *Madonna*

'90 **Escapade** *Janet Jackson*
'02 **Escape** *Enrique Iglesias*
'79 **Escape (The Pina Colada Song)**
    *Rupert Holmes*
'71 **Escape-ism** *James Brown*
'62 **Eso Beso (That Kiss!)** *Paul Anka*
'89 **Eternal Flame** *Bangles*
'60 **Eternally** *Sarah Vaughan*
'65 **Eve Of Destruction** *Barry McGuire*
'93 **Even A Fool Can See** *Peter Cetera*
'92 **Even Better Than The Real Thing**
    *U2*
'92 **Even Flow** *Pearl Jam*
'80 **Even It Up** *Heart*
**Even Now**
'78   *Barry Manilow*
'83   *Bob Seger*
'67 **Even The Bad Times Are Good**
    *Tremeloes*
'79 **Even The Losers** *Tom Petty*
'82 **Even The Nights Are Better**
    *Air Supply*
'78 **Ever Fallen In Love** *Buzzcocks*
'60 **Everglades** *Kingston Trio*
**Everlasting Love**
'67   *Robert Knight*
'74   *Carl Carlton*
'78   *Andy Gibb*
'81   *Rex Smith/Rachel Sweet*
'89   *Howard Jones*
'97 **Everlong** *Foo Fighters*
'61 **Everlovin'** *Rick Nelson*
'61 **Every Beat Of My Heart** *Pips*
**Every Breath You Take**
'61   *Gene Pitney*
'83   *Police*
'55 **Every Day** *Count Basie*
'55 **Every Day I Have The Blues**
    *B.B. King*
**Every Day Of My Life**
'56   *McGuire Sisters*
'72   *Bobby Vinton*
'94 **Every Day Of The Week** *Jade*
'91 **Every Heartbeat** *Amy Grant*
'78 **Every Kinda People** *Robert Palmer*
'96 **Every Light In The House**
    *Trace Adkins*
'64 **Every Little Bit Hurts**
    *Brenda Holloway*
'86 **Every Little Kiss** *Bruce Hornsby*
'89 **Every Little Step** *Bobby Brown*
**Every Little Thing**
'69   *Yes*
'93   *Carlene Carter*
**Every Little Thing I Do**
'59   *Dion & The Belmonts*
'95   *Soul For Real*
'81 **Every Little Thing She Does Is**
    **Magic** *Police*
'98 **Every Morning** *Sugar Ray*
'58 **Every Night (I Pray)** *Chantels*
'94 **Every Once In A While** *BlackHawk*
'78 **Every 1's A Winner** *Hot Chocolate*
'71 **Every Picture Tells A Story**
    *Rod Stewart*
'88 **Every Rose Has Its Thorn** *Poison*
**Every Step Of The Way**
'63   *Johnny Mathis*
'85   *John Waite*
'97 **Every Time I Close My Eyes**
    *Babyface*
'79 **Every Time I Think Of You** *Babys*
'77 **(Every Time I Turn Around) Back In**
    **Love Again** *L.T.D.*
'75 **Every Time You Touch Me (I Get**
    **High)** *Charlie Rich*
'79 **Every Which Way But Loose**
    *Eddie Rabbitt*
'80 **Every Woman In The World**
    *Air Supply*
'63 **Everybody** *Tommy Roe*
'98 **Everybody (Backstreet's Back)**
    *Backstreet Boys*
'77 **Everybody Be Dancin'** *Starbuck*
'85 **Everybody Dance**
    *Ta Mara & The Seen*

'90 **Everybody Everybody** *Black Box*
'86 **Everybody Have Fun Tonight**
    *Wang Chung*
'93 **Everybody Hurts** *R.E.M.*
'67 **Everybody Knows** *Dave Clark Five*
'64 **Everybody Knows (I Still Love You)**
    *Dave Clark Five*
'93 **Everybody Lay Down** *Pat Benatar*
'59 **Everybody Likes To Cha Cha Cha**
    *Sam Cooke*
'65 **Everybody Loves A Clown**
    *Gary Lewis*
**Everybody Loves A Lover**
'58   *Doris Day*
'62   *Shirelles*
'78 **Everybody Loves A Rain Song**
    *B.J. Thomas*
'62 **Everybody Loves Me But You**
    *Brenda Lee*
'64 **Everybody Loves Somebody**
    *Dean Martin*
**Everybody Needs Love**
'67   *Gladys Knight*
'78   *Stephen Bishop*
**Everybody Needs Somebody To**
    **Love**
'64   *Solomon Burke*
'67   *Wilson Pickett*
'72 **Everybody Plays The Fool**
'72   *Main Ingredient*
'91   *Aaron Neville*
'85 **Everybody Wants To Rule The**
    **World** *Tears For Fears*
'82 **Everybody Wants You** *Billy Squier*
'71 **Everybody's Everything** *Santana*
'92 **Everybody's Free (To Feel Good)**
    *Rozalla*
'55 **Everybody's Got A Home But Me**
    *Eddie Fisher*
'70 **Everybody's Got The Right To Love**
    *Supremes*
'80 **Everybody's Got To Learn**
    **Sometime** *Korgis*
'70 **Everybody's Out Of Town**
    *B.J. Thomas*
'60 **Everybody's Somebody's Fool**
    *Connie Francis*
'69 **Everybody's Talkin'** *Nilsson*
**Everyday**
'57   *Buddy Holly*
'85   *James Taylor*
'94   *Phil Collins*
'83 **Everyday I Write The Book**
    *Elvis Costello*
'97 **Everyday Is A Winding Road**
    *Sheryl Crow*
**Everyday People**
'68   *Sly & The Family Stone*
'83   *Joan Jett*
'69 **Everyday With You Girl** *Classics IV*
'65 **Everyone's Gone To The Moon**
    *Jonathan King*
**Everything**
'89   *Jody Watley*
'97   *Mary J. Blige*
'70 **Everything A Man Could Ever Need**
    *Glen Campbell*
'92 **Everything About You** *Ugly Kid Joe*
'92 **Everything Changes** *Kathy Troccoli*
'96 **Everything Falls Apart**
    *Dog's Eye View*
'91 **(Everything I Do) I Do It For You**
    *Bryan Adams*
'88 **Everything I Miss At Home**
    *Cherrelle*
'72 **Everything I Own** *Bread*
'85 **Everything In My Heart** *Corey Hart*
'70 **Everything Is Beautiful** *Ray Stevens*
'89 **Everything Is Broken**
    *Bob Dylan*
'99 **Everything Is Everything** *Lauryn Hill*
'89 **Everything Reminds Me Of My Dog**
    *Jane Siberry*
'85 **Everything She Wants** *Wham!*
'68 **Everything That Touches You**
    *Association*
'97 **Everything To Everyone** *Everclear*

'00 **Everything You Want**
   *Vertical Horizon*
'88 **Everything Your Heart Desires**
   *Daryl Hall & John Oates*
'94 **Everything Zen** *Bush*
'64 **Everything's Alright** *Newbeats*
'98 **Everything's Changed** *Lonestar*
'92 **Everything's Gonna Be Alright**
   *Father MC*
'70 **Everything's Tuesday**
   *Chairman Of The Board*
'04 **Everytime** *Britney Spears*
'85 **Everytime You Go Away**
   *Paul Young*
   **Everywhere**
'87   *Fleetwood Mac*
'97   *Tim McGraw*
'01   *Michelle Branch*
'70 **Evil Ways** *Santana*
'75 **Evil Woman** *Electric Light Orchestra*
'69 **Evil Woman Don't Play Your Games**
   **With Me** *Crow*
'99 **Ex-Factor** *Lauryn Hill*
'00 **Ex-Girlfriend** *No Doubt*
'78 **Excitable Boy** *Warren Zevon*
'91 **Exclusivity** *Damian Dame*
'03 **Excuse Me Miss** *Jay-Z*
'95 **Exhale (Shoop Shoop)**
   *Whitney Houston*
   **Exodus**
'60   *Ferrante & Teicher*
'60   *Mantovani*
'61   *Eddie Harris*
'77   *Bob Marley*
'55 **Experience Unnecessary**
   *Sarah Vaughan*
'67 **Explosion (In Your Soul)**
   *Soul Survivors*
'75 **Express** *B.T. Express*
   **Express Yourself**
'70   *Charles Wright*
'89   *Madonna*
'90 **Expression** *Salt-N-Pepa*
'67 **Expressway (To Your Heart)**
   *Soul Survivors*
'82 **Eye In The Sky** *Alan Parsons Project*
'82 **Eye Of The Tiger** *Survivor*
'86 **Eye Of The Zombie** *John Fogerty*
'70 **Eyes Of A Child** *Moody Blues*
'68 **Eyes Of A New York Woman**
   *B.J. Thomas*
'74 **Eyes Of Silver** *Doobie Brothers*
'84 **Eyes Without A Face** *Billy Idol*

# F

'78 **FM (No Static At All)** *Steely Dan*
'94 **Fa All Y'all** *Da Brat*
'66 **Fa-Fa-Fa-Fa-Fa (Sad Song)**
   *Otis Redding*
   **Fabulous**
'57   *Charlie Gracie*
'02   *Jaheim*
'56 **Fabulous Character** *Sarah Vaughan*
'68 **Face It Girl, It's Over** *Nancy Wilson*
'85 **Face The Face** *Pete Townshend*
'86 **Facts Of Love**
   *Jeff Lorber Feat. Karyn White*
'01 **Fade** *Staind*
'81 **Fade Away** *Bruce Springsteen*
'94 **Fade Into You** *Mazzy Star*
'86 **Fadeaway** *BoDeans*
'00 **Faded** *SoulDecision*
'98 **Faded Pictures** *Case & Joe*
'91 **Fading Like A Flower (Every Time**
   **You Leave)** *Roxette*
'03 **Faint** *Linkin Park*
'77 **Fair Game**
   *Crosby, Stills & Nash*
'90 **Fairweather Friend** *Johnny Gill*
'74 **Fairytale** *Pointer Sisters*
'87 **Faith** *George Michael*
'92 **Faithful** *Go West*
'83 **Faithfully** *Journey*
'87 **Fake** *Alexander O'Neal*
'83 **Fake Friends** *Joan Jett*

'95 **Fake Plastic Trees** *Radiohead*
'67 **Fakin' It** *Simon & Garfunkel*
'94 **Fall Down** *Toad The Wet Sprocket*
'83 **Fall In Love With Me**
   *Earth, Wind & Fire*
'02 **Fall Into Me** *Emerson Drive*
'04 **Fall To Pieces** *Velvet Revolver*
   **Fallen Angel**
'76   *Frankie Valli*
'88   *Poison*
   **Fallen Star**
'57   *Jimmy Newman*
'57   *Nick Noble*
'01 **Fallin'** *Alicia Keys*
   **Fallin' In Love**
'74   *Souther, Hillman, Furay Band*
'75   *Hamilton, Joe Frank & Reynolds*
'96   *La Bouche*
   **Falling**
'63   *Roy Orbison*
'77   *LeBlanc & Carr*
'86   *Melba Moore*
'96   *Montell Jordan*
'97 **Falling In Love (Is Hard On The**
   **Knees)** *Aerosmith*
'86 **Falling In Love (Uh-Oh)**
   *Miami Sound Machine*
'00 **Falls Apart (Run Away)** *Sugar Ray*
   **Fame**
'75   *David Bowie*
'80   *Irene Cara*
'60 **Fame And Fortune** *Elvis Presley*
   **Family Affair**
'71   *Sly & The Family Stone*
'01   *Mary J. Blige*
'83 **Family Man** *Daryl Hall & John Oates*
'72 **Family Of Man** *Three Dog Night*
'02 **Family Portrait** *P!nk*
'79 **Family Tradition** *Hank Williams Jr.*
'83 **Fanatic, The** *Felony*
   **Fancy**
'69   *Bobbie Gentry*
'91   *Reba McEntire*
'77 **Fanfare For The Common Man**
   *Emerson, Lake & Palmer*
'60 **Fannie Mae** *Buster Brown*
'75 **Fanny (Be Tender With My Love)**
   *Bee Gees*
   **Fantastic Voyage**
'80   *Lakeside*
'94   *Coolio*
   **Fantasy**
'78   *Earth, Wind & Fire*
'82   *Aldo Nova*
'95   *Mariah Carey*
'78 **Far Away Eyes** *Rolling Stones*
'94 **Far Behind** *Candlebox*
'83 **Far From Over** *Frank Stallone*
'84 **Farewell My Summer Love**
   *Michael Jackson*
'64 **Farmer John** *Premiers*
'57 **Farther Up The Road**
   *Bobby "Blue" Bland*
'87 **Fascinated** *Company B*
   **Fascination**
'57   *Dick Jacobs*
'57   *Jane Morgan*
'57   *Dinah Shore*
'89 **Fascination Street** *Cure*
'80 **Fashion** *David Bowie*
'93 **Fast As You** *Dwight Yoakam*
'88 **Fast Car** *Tracy Chapman*
'96 **Fastlove** *George Michael*
'78 **Fat Bottomed Girls** *Queen*
'01 **Fat Lip** *Sum 41*
'98 **Father** *LL Cool J*
'77 **Father Christmas** *Kinks*
'88 **Father Figure** *George Michael*
'96 **Fear Of Being Alone** *Reba McEntire*
'93 **Feed The Tree** *Belly*
'61 **Feel It** *Sam Cooke*
'86 **Feel It Again** *Honeymoon Suite*
'02 **Feel It Boy** *Beenie Man*
'78 **Feel Like A Number** *Bob Seger*

   **Feel Like Makin' Love**
'74   *Roberta Flack*
'75   *Bad Company*
'95 **Feel Me Flow** *Naughty By Nature*
'60 **Feel So Fine** *Johnny Preston*
   **Feel So Good**
'55   *Shirley & Lee*
'97   *Mase*
'94 **Feel The Pain** *Dinosaur Jr.*
'68 **Feelin' Alright?** *Traffic*
'01 **Feelin' On Yo Booty** *R. Kelly*
'78 **Feelin' Satisfied** *Boston*
'73 **Feelin' Stronger Every Day** *Chicago*
'04 **Feelin' Way Too Damn Good**
   *Nickelback*
'72 **Feeling Alright** *Joe Cocker*
'03 **Feeling This** *Blink-182*
'75 **Feelings** *Morris Albert*
'90 **Feels Good** *Tony! Toni! Toné!*
'77 **Feels Like The First Time** *Foreigner*
   **Feels So Good**
'67   *Bunny Sigler [medley]*
'78   *Chuck Mangione*
'89   *Van Halen*
'95   *Xscape*
'84 **Feels So Real (Won't Let Go)**
   *Patrice Rushen*
'81 **Feels So Right** *Alabama*
'94 **Feenin'** *Jodeci*
'70 **Feliz Navidad** *José Feliciano*
'61 **Fell In Love On Monday**
   *Fats Domino*
'94 **Fell On Black Days** *Soundgarden*
'76 **Fernando** *Abba*
'65 **Ferry Cross The Mersey**
   *Gerry & The Pacemakers*
   **Fever**
'56   *Little Willie John*
'58   *Peggy Lee*
'65   *McCoys*
'76 **Fez, The** *Steely Dan*
'77 **Ffun** *Con Funk Shun*
'93 **Fields Of Gold** *Sting*
'01 **Fiesta Remix** *R. Kelly*
'99 **15 Minutes** *Marc Nelson*
'76 **Fifth Of Beethoven** *Walter Murphy*
'67 **59th Street Bridge Song (Feelin'**
   **Groovy)** *Harpers Bizarre*
'75 **50 Ways To Leave Your Lover**
   *Paul Simon*
'83 **Fight Fire With Fire** *Kansas*
   **Fight The Power**
'75   *Isley Brothers*
'89   *Public Enemy*
'03 **Fighter** *Christina Aguilera*
'03 **Figured You Out** *Nickelback*
'01 **Fill Me In** *Craig David*
'87 **Final Countdown** *Europe*
'91 **Finally** *Ce Ce Peniston*
'74 **Finally Got Myself Together (I'm A**
   **Changed Man)** *Impressions*
'85 **Find A Way** *Amy Grant*
'82 **Find Another Fool** *Quarterflash*
'61 **Find Another Girl** *Jerry Butler*
'81 **Find Your Way Back**
   *Jefferson Starship*
'02 **Fine Again** *Seether*
'84 **Fine Fine Day** *Tony Carey*
'87 **Finer Things** *Steve Winwood*
'86 **Finest, The** *S.O.S. Band*
'60 **Finger Poppin' Time** *Hank Ballard*
'63 **Fingertips** *Stevie Wonder*
'88 **Finish What Ya Started** *Van Halen*
'79 **Fins** *Jimmy Buffett*
   **Fire**
'67   *Jimi Hendrix*
'68   *Arthur Brown*
'74   *Ohio Players*
'78   *Pointer Sisters*
'81 **Fire And Ice** *Pat Benatar*
'70 **Fire And Rain** *James Taylor*
'71 **Fire And Water** *Wilson Pickett*
'74 **Fire, Baby I'm On Fire** *Andy Kim*
'77 **Fire Down Below** *Bob Seger*

'80 **Fire In The Morning** *Melissa Manchester*
**Fire It Up ..see: Turn It Up**
'80 **Fire Lake** *Bob Seger*
'75 **Fire On High** *Electric Light Orchestra*
'75 **Fire On The Mountain** *Marshall Tucker Band*
'89 **Fire Woman** *Cult*
'58 **Firefly** *Tony Bennett*
'97 **Firestarter** *Prodigy*
**First Cut Is The Deepest**
'77    *Rod Stewart*
'03    *Sheryl Crow*
'57 **First Date, First Kiss, First Love** *Sonny James*
'84 **First Day Of Summer** *Tony Carey*
'59 **First Name Initial** *Annette*
'98 **First Night** *Monica*
'95 **1st Of Tha Month** *Bone Thugs-N-Harmony*
'63 **First Quarrel** *Paul & Paula*
'90 **First Time** *Surface*
'72 **First Time Ever I Saw Your Face** *Roberta Flack*
'80 **First Time Love** *Livingston Taylor*
'61 **Fish, The** *Bobby Rydell*
'74 **Fish Ain't Bitin'** *Lamont Dozier*
'88 **Fisherman's Blues** *Waterboys*
'87 **Fishin' In The Dark** *Nitty Gritty Dirt Band*
'88 **Fishnet** *Morris Day*
'73 **5:15** *Who*
'63 **500 Miles Away From Home** *Bobby Bare*
'97 **5 Miles To Empty** *Brownstone*
'90 **Five Minutes** *Lorrie Morgan*
'96 **5 O'Clock** *Nonchalant*
'65 **Five O'Clock World** *Vogues*
'78 **5.7.0.5.** *City Boy*
'70 **5-10-15-20 (25-30 Years Of Love)** *Presidents*
'68 **Five To One** *Doors*
'98 **Flagpole Sitta** *Harvey Danger*
'88 **Flame, The** *Cheap Trick*
'87 **Flames Of Paradise** *Jennifer Rush (with Elton John)*
'61 **Flaming Star** *Elvis Presley*
'76 **Flaming Youth** *Kiss*
'66 **Flamingo** *Herb Alpert*
'78 **Flash Light** *Parliament*
'83 **Flashdance...What A Feeling** *Irene Cara*
'94 **Flava In Ya Ear** *Craig Mack*
'84 **Flesh For Fantasy** *Billy Idol*
'92 **Flex** *Mad Cobra*
'55 **Flip Flop And Fly** *Joe Turner*
'88 **Flirt** *Evelyn King*
'79 **Flirtin' With Disaster** *Molly Hatchet*
**Float On**
'77    *Floaters*
'04    *Modest Mouse*
'96 **Flood** *Jars Of Clay*
'65 **Flowers On The Wall** *Statler Brothers*
'72 **Floy Joy** *Supremes*
**Fly, The**
'61    *Chubby Checker*
'91    *U2*
**Fly Away**
'75    *John Denver*
'98    *Lenny Kravitz*
'75 **Fly By Night** *Rush*
**Fly Like An Eagle**
'76    *Steve Miller*
'96    *Seal*
**Fly Me To The Moon**
'62    *Joe Harnell [Bossa Nova]*
'64    *Frank Sinatra*
'65    *Tony Bennett*
'75 **Fly, Robin, Fly** *Silver Convention*
'90 **Fly To The Angels** *Slaughter*
'81 **Flying High Again** *Ozzy Osbourne*
'56 **Flying Saucer** *Buchanan & Goodman*

'57 **Flying Saucer The 2nd** *Buchanan & Goodman*
'03 **Flying Without Wings** *Ruben Studdard*
'01 **Follow Me** *Uncle Kracker*
'62 **Follow That Dream** *Elvis Presley*
'63 **Follow The Boys** *Connie Francis*
'96 **Follow You Down** *Gin Blossoms*
'78 **Follow You Follow Me** *Genesis*
**Folsom Prison Blues**
'56    *Johnny Cash*
'68    *Johnny Cash [live]*
**Fool, The**
'56    *Sanford Clark*
'97    *Lee Ann Womack*
'75 **Fool For The City** *Foghat*
**Fool For You**
'55    *Ray Charles*
'68    *Impressions*
'89 **Fool For Your Loving** *Whitesnake*
'78 **Fool (If You Think It's Over)** *Chris Rea*
'60 **Fool In Love** *Ike & Tina Turner*
'81 **Fool In Love With You** *Jim Photoglo*
'79 **Fool In The Rain** *Led Zeppelin*
'64 **Fool Never Learns** *Andy Williams*
'61 **Fool #1** *Brenda Lee*
**Fool On The Hill**
'67    *Beatles*
'68    *Sergio Mendes*
**Fool Such As I**
'59    *Elvis Presley*
'73    *Bob Dylan*
'76 **Fool To Cry** *Rolling Stones*
'76 **Fooled Around And Fell In Love** *Elvin Bishop*
'83 **Foolin'** *Def Leppard*
'94 **Foolin' Around** *Changing Faces*
'78 **Fooling Yourself (The Angry Young Man)** *Styx*
'02 **Foolish** *Ashanti*
'88 **Foolish Beat** *Debbie Gibson*
'97 **Foolish Games** *Jewel*
'84 **Foolish Heart** *Steve Perry*
'63 **Foolish Little Girl** *Shirelles*
**Foolish Pride**
'86    *Daryl Hall*
'94    *Travis Tritt*
**Fools Rush In**
'60    *Brook Benton*
'63    *Rick Nelson*
'61 **Foot Stomping** *Flares*
'84 **Footloose** *Kenny Loggins*
'60 **Footsteps** *Steve Lawrence*
'72 **Footstompin' Music** *Grand Funk Railroad*
'76 **Fopp** *Ohio Players*
'59 **For A Penny** *Pat Boone*
'83 **For A Rocker** *Jackson Browne*
'71 **For All We Know** *Carpenters*
'86 **For America** *Jackson Browne*
'71 **(For God's Sake) Give More Power To The People** *Chi-Lites*
'65 **For Lovin' Me** *Peter, Paul & Mary*
'67 **For Loving You** *Bill Anderson & Jan Howard*
'61 **For Me And My Gal** *Judy Garland [live]*
'61 **For My Baby** *Brook Benton*
'91 **For My Broken Heart** *Reba McEntire*
'58 **For My Good Fortune** *Pat Boone*
**For Once In My Life**
'67    *Tony Bennett*
'68    *Stevie Wonder*
'97 **For The First Time** *Kenny Loggins*
'70 **For The Good Times** *Ray Price*
'70 **For The Love Of Him** *Bobbi Martin*
'74 **For The Love Of Money** *O'Jays*
'75 **For The Love Of You** *Isley Brothers*
'81 **For Those About To Rock (We Salute You)** *AC/DC*
'86 **For Tonight** *Nancy Martinez*
'67 **For What It's Worth** *Buffalo Springfield*

**For You**
'63    *Rick Nelson*
'73    *Bruce Springsteen*
'81    *Manfred Mann*
'90    *Outfield*
'97    *Kenny Lattimore*
'01    *Staind*
'97 **For You I Will** *Monica*
'81 **For Your Eyes Only** *Sheena Easton*
**For Your Love**
'58    *Ed Townsend*
'65    *Yardbirds*
'67    *Peaches & Herb*
**For Your Precious Love**
'58    *Jerry Butler & The Impressions*
'63    *Garnet Mimms*
'67    *Oscar Toney, Jr.*
**Forever [4 Ever]**
'60    *Little Dippers*
'64    *Peter Drake*
'85    *Kenny Loggins*
'90    *Kiss*
'96    *Mariah Carey*
'03    *Lil' Mo*
'87 **Forever And Ever, Amen** *Randy Travis*
'03 **Forever And For Always** *Shania Twain*
'68 **Forever Came Today** *Supremes*
'56 **Forever Darling** *Ames Brothers*
'79 **Forever In Blue Jeans** *Neil Diamond*
'92 **Forever In Love** *Kenny G*
'86 **(Forever) Live And Die** *Orchestral Manoeuvres In The Dark*
'92 **Forever Love** *Color Me Badd*
'85 **Forever Man** *Eric Clapton*
'79 **Forever Mine** *O'Jays*
'91 **Forever My Lady** *Jodeci*
'91 **Forever Together** *Randy Travis*
**Forever Young**
'74    *Bob Dylan*
'88    *Rod Stewart*
'89 **Forever Your Girl** *Paula Abdul*
'90 **Forever's As Far As I'll Go** *Alabama*
'63 **Forget Him** *Bobby Rydell*
**Forget Me Not**
'58    *Kalin Twins*
'89    *Bad English*
'82 **Forget Me Nots** *Patrice Rushen*
'79 **Forgive Me Girl [medley]** *Spinners*
'55 **Forgive My Heart** *Nat "King" Cole*
'00 **Forgot About Dre** *Dr. Dre*
'85 **Fortress Around Your Heart** *Sting*
'99 **Fortunate** *Maxwell*
'69 **Fortunate Son** *Creedence Clearwater Revival*
'83 **40** *U2*
'59 **Forty Days** *Ronnie Hawkins*
'03 **45** *Shinedown*
'85 **Forty Hour Week (For A Livin')** *Alabama*
'59 **Forty Miles Of Bad Road** *Duane Eddy*
'68 **Forty Thousand Headmen** *Traffic*
'79 **Found A Cure** *Ashford & Simpson*
'93 **Found Out About You** *Gin Blossoms*
'99 **4,5,6** *Solé*
'85 **Four In The Morning (I Can't Take Any More)** *Night Ranger*
'62 **409** *Beach Boys*
'97 **4 Seasons Of Loneliness** *Boyz II Men*
'78 **Four Strong Winds** *Neil Young*
**Four Walls**
'57    *Jim Lowe*
'57    *Jim Reeves*
'68 **1432 Franklin Pike Circle Hero** *Bobby Russell*
'87 **4th Of July** *X*
'73 **4th Of July, Asbury Park (Sandy)** *Bruce Springsteen*
'75 **Fox On The Run** *Sweet*
'67 **Foxey Lady** *Jimi Hendrix*
'72 **Francene** *ZZ Top*

'73 **Frankenstein** *Edgar Winter Group*
'59 **Frankie** *Connie Francis*
**Frankie And Johnny**
'61   *Brook Benton*
'63   *Sam Cooke*
'66   *Elvis Presley*
'75 **Franklin's Tower** *Grateful Dead*
'57 **Fraulein** *Bobby Helms*
'83 **Freak-A-Zoid** *Midnight Star*
'95 **Freak Like Me** *Adina Howard*
'93 **Freak Me** *Silk*
'84 **Freakshow On The Dance Floor**
  *Bar-Kays*
'81 **Freaky Dancin'** *Cameo*
'95 **Fred Bear** *Ted Nugent*
'72 **Freddie's Dead** *Curtis Mayfield*
**Free**
'56   *Tommy Leonetti*
'71   *Chicago*
'76   *Deniece Williams*
'95 **Free As A Bird** *Beatles*
**Free Bird**
'74   *Lynyrd Skynyrd*
'88   *Will To Power [medley]*
'89 **Free Fallin'** *Tom Petty*
'76 **Free-For-All** *Ted Nugent*
'74 **Free Man In Paris** *Joni Mitchell*
'73 **Free Ride** *Edgar Winter Group*
'92 **Free Your Mind** *En Vogue*
**Freedom**
'71   *Jimi Hendrix*
'85   *George Michael*
'90   *George Michael*
'86 **Freedom Overspill** *Steve Winwood*
'70 **Freedom Rider** *Traffic*
'05 **Freek-A-Leek** *Petey Pablo*
'95 **Freek 'n You** *Jodeci*
'85 **Freeway Of Love** *Aretha Franklin*
'80 **Freewill** *Rush*
'58 **Freeze, The** *Tony & Joe*
'82 **Freeze-Frame** *J. Geils Band*
**Freight Train**
'57   *Rusty Draper*
'57   *Chas. McDevitt*
'85 **Fresh** *Kool & The Gang*
'70 **Fresh Air**
  *Quicksilver Messenger Service*
'97 **Freshmen, The** *Verve Pipe*
'92 **Friday I'm In Love** *Cure*
'67 **Friday On My Mind** *Easybeats*
'66 **Friday's Child** *Nancy Sinatra*
'89 **Friend Is A Friend** *Pete Townshend*
'98 **Friend of Mine** *Kelly Price*
'70 **Friend Of The Devil** *Grateful Dead*
'56 **Friendly Persuasion (Thee I Love)**
  *Pat Boone*
**Friends**
'71   *Elton John*
'73   *Bette Midler*
'89   *Jody Watley*
'92   *Michael W. Smith*
'86 **Friends And Lovers**
  *Gloria Loring & Carl Anderson*
'82 **Friends In Love**
  *Dionne Warwick & Johnny Mathis*
'90 **Friends In Low Places** *Garth Brooks*
'69 **Friendship Train** *Gladys Knight*
'61 **Frogg** *Brothers Four*
'90 **From A Distance** *Bette Midler*
'62 **From A Jack To A King** *Ned Miller*
'64 **From A Window**
  *Billy J. Kramer With The Dakotas*
'97 **From Here To Eternity**
  *Michael Peterson*
'74 **From His Woman To You**
  *Barbara Mason*
**From Me To You**
'63   *Del Shannon*
'64   *Beatles*
'72 **From The Beginning**
  *Emerson, Lake & Palmer*
'00 **From The Bottom Of My Broken**
  **Heart** *Britney Spears*
'98 **From This Moment On**
  *Shania Twain*

'03 **Frontin'** *Pharrell*
'98 **Frozen** *Madonna*
'79 **Frustrated** *Knack*
'03 **F**k It (I Don't Want You Back)**
  *Eamon*
'89 **F*** Tha Police** *N.W.A.*
'95 **Fu-Gee-La** *Fugees*
'66 **Fugitive, The** *Merle Haggard*
'02 **Full Moon** *Brandy*
'75 **Full Of Fire** *Al Green*
'64 **Fun, Fun, Fun** *Beach Boys*
'73 **Funeral For A Friend [medley]**
  *Elton John*
'70 **Funk #49** *James Gang*
'94 **Funkdafied** *Da Brat*
'80 **Funkin' For Jamaica (N.Y.)**
  *Tom Browne*
'67 **Funky Broadway** *Wilson Pickett*
'89 **Funky Cold Medina** *Tone Loc*
'71 **Funky Nassau**
  *Beginning Of The End*
'68 **Funky Street** *Arthur Conley*
'73 **Funky Stuff** *Kool & The Gang*
'73 **Funky Worm** *Ohio Players*
'94 **Funky Y-2-C** *Puppies*
**Funkytown**
'80   *Lipps, Inc.*
'87   *Pseudo Echo*
'61 **Funny** *Maxine Brown*
'72 **Funny Face** *Donna Fargo*
'64 **Funny Girl** *Barbra Streisand*
**Funny How Time Slips Away**
'61   *Jimmy Elledge*
'64   *Joe Hinton*
'62 **Funny Way Of Laughin'** *Burl Ives*
'73 **Future Shock** *Curtis Mayfield*
'86 **Future's So Bright, I Gotta Wear**
  **Shades** *Timbuk 3*

# G

'97 **G.H.E.T.T.O.U.T.** *Changing Faces*
'64 **G.T.O.** *Ronny & The Daytonas*
'66 **Gallant Men** *Senator Everett*
  *McKinley Dirksen*
**Gallows Pole**
'70   *Led Zeppelin*
'94   *Jimmy Page & Robert Plant*
'69 **Galveston** *Glen Campbell*
'78 **Gambler, The** *Kenny Rogers*
**Game Of Love**
'65   *Wayne Fontana & The Mindbenders*
'02   *Santana feat. Michelle Branch*
'04 **Game Over (Flip)** *Lil' Flip*
**Games**
'70   *Redeye*
'92   *Chuckii Booker*
**Games People Play**
'69   *Joe South*
'80   *Alan Parsons Project*
'66 **Games That Lovers Play**
  *Eddie Fisher*
'80 **Games Without Frontiers**
  *Peter Gabriel*
'92 **Gangsta** *Bell Biv DeVoe*
'93 **Gangsta Lean** *D.R.S.*
'02 **Gangsta Lovin'** *Eve*
'03 **Gangsta Nation**
  *Westside Connection*
'95 **Gangsta's Paradise** *Coolio*
'97 **Gangstas Make The World Go**
  **Round** *Westside Connection*
'68 **Gangster Of Love**
  *Steve Miller Band*
'56 **Garden Of Eden** *Joe Valino*
'72 **Garden Party** *Rick Nelson*
'04 **Gasolina** *Daddy Yankee*
'58 **Gee, But It's Lonely** *Pat Boone*
'55 **Gee Whittakers!** *Pat Boone*
'60 **Gee Whiz** *Innocents*
**Gee Whiz (Look At His Eyes)**
'61   *Carla Thomas*
'80   *Bernadette Peters*
'95 **Geek Stink Breath** *Green Day*
'95 **Gel** *Collective Soul*

'81 **Gemini Dream** *Moody Blues*
'99 **Genie In A Bottle** *Christina Aguilera*
'82 **Genius Of Love** *Tom Tom Club*
'90 **Gentle** *Dino*
'68 **Gentle On My Mind** *Glen Campbell*
'71 **George Jackson** *Bob Dylan*
'78 **Georgia** *Boz Scaggs*
**Georgia On My Mind**
'60   *Ray Charles*
'78   *Willie Nelson*
'66 **Georgy Girl** *Seekers*
'72 **Geronimo's Cadillac**
  *Michael Murphey*
'93 **Get A Haircut** *George Thorogood*
**Get A Job**
'58   *Mills Brothers*
'58   *Silhouettes*
'91 **Get A Leg Up** *John Mellencamp*
'98 **Get At Me Dog** *DMX*
'93 **Get Away** *Bobby Brown*
**Get Back**
'69   *Beatles with Billy Preston*
'04   *Ludacris*
'03 **Get Busy** *Sean Paul*
**Get Closer**
'76   *Seals & Crofts*
'82   *Linda Ronstadt*
'74 **Get Dancin'**
  *Disco-Tex & The Sex-O-Lettes*
**Get Down**
'73   *Gilbert O'Sullivan*
'78   *Gene Chandler*
'94   *Craig Mack*
'75 **Get Down, Get Down (Get On The**
  **Floor)** *Joe Simon*
'82 **Get Down On It** *Kool & The Gang*
'75 **Get Down Tonight**
  *KC & The Sunshine Band*
'99 **Get Gone** *Ideal*
'90 **Get Here** *Oleta Adams*
'71 **Get It On** *Chase*
'99 **Get It On...Tonite** *Montell Jordan*
'83 **Get It Right** *Aretha Franklin*
'79 **Get It Right Next Time**
  *Gerry Rafferty*
**Get It Together**
'73   *Jackson 5*
'97   *702*
'71 **Get It While You Can**
  *Janis Joplin*
'03 **Get Low**
  *Lil Jon & The East Side Boyz*
'67 **Get Me To The World On Time**
  *Electric Prunes*
'96 **Get Money** *Junior M.A.F.I.A.*
'78 **Get Off** *Foxy*
'65 **Get Off Of My Cloud** *Rolling Stones*
'72 **Get On The Good Foot**
  *James Brown*
**Get On Up**
'67   *Esquires*
'96   *Jodeci*
'89 **Get On Your Feet** *Gloria Estefan*
'76 **Get Out Of Denver** *Bob Seger*
'88 **Get Outta My Dreams, Get Into My**
  **Car** *Billy Ocean*
'94 **Get Over It** *Eagles*
'01 **Get Over Yourself** *Eden's Crush*
**Get Ready**
'66   *Temptations*
'70   *Rare Earth*
'92 **Get Ready For This** *2 Unlimited*
'56 **Get Rhythm** *Johnny Cash*
'05 **Get Right** *Jennifer Lopez*
'87 **Get That Love** *Thompson Twins*
'76 **Get The Funk Out Ma Face**
  *Brothers Johnson*
'91 **Get The Message** *Electronic*
'01 **Get The Party Started** *P!nk*
**Get Together**
'65   *We Five*
'67   *Youngbloods*
'76 **Get Up And Boogie (That's Right)**
  *Silver Convention*
'90 **Get Up! (Before The Night Is Over)**
  *Technotronic*

'71 **Get Up, Get Into It, Get Involved** James Brown
'70 **Get Up (I Feel Like Being Like A) Sex Machine** James Brown
'75 **Get Up, Stand Up** Bob Marley
'01 **Get Ur Freak On** Missy Elliott
'79 **Get Used To It** Roger Voudouris
'76 **Getaway** Earth, Wind & Fire
'85 **Getcha Back** Beach Boys
'01 **Gets Me Through** Ozzy Osbourne
'91 **Gett Off** Prince
'98 **Gettin' Jiggy Wit It** Will Smith
'77 **Gettin' Ready For Love** Diana Ross
'67 **Gettin' Together** Tommy James
'90 **Getting Away With It** Electronic
'04 **Getting Away With Murder** Papa Roach
'79 **Getting Closer** Wings
'93 **Getto Jam** Domino
'73 **Ghetto Child** Spinners
'98 **Ghetto Cowboy** Mo Thugs Family & Bone Thugs-N-Harmony
'97 **Ghetto Love** Da Brat
'98 **Ghetto Supastar (That Is What You Are)** Pras Michel
'84 **Ghost In You** Psychedelic Furs
'91 **Ghost Of A Chance** Rush
**(Ghost) Riders In The Sky**
'61 Ramrods
'79 Johnny Cash
'80 Outlaws
**Ghost Town**
'56 Don Cherry
'88 Cheap Trick
'84 **Ghostbusters** Ray Parker Jr.
'65 **Giddyup Go** Red Sovine
'59 **Gidget** James Darren
'97 **Gift, The** Jim Brickman with Collin Raye & Susan Ashton
'03 **Gigolo** Nick Cannon
'82 **Gigolo, The** O'Bryan
'83 **Gimme All Your Lovin** ZZ Top
'76 **Gimme Back My Bullets** Lynyrd Skynyrd
'70 **Gimme Dat Ding** Pipkins
'69 **Gimme Gimme Good Lovin'** Crazy Elephant
'67 **Gimme Little Sign** Brenton Wood
'69 **Gimme Shelter** Rolling Stones
**Gimme Some Lovin'**
'66 Spencer Davis Group
'80 Blues Brothers
'79 **Gimme Some Water** Eddie Money
'02 **Gimme The Light** Sean Paul
'73 **Gimme Three Steps** Lynyrd Skynyrd
'94 **Gin & Juice** Snoop Doggy Dogg
'62 **Gina** Johnny Mathis
'58 **Ginger Bread** Frankie Avalon
'61 **Ginnie Bell** Paul Dino
'62 **Ginny Come Lately** Brian Hyland
'05 **Girl** Destiny's Child
**Girl Can't Help It**
'57 Little Richard
'86 Journey
'80 **Girl, Don't Let It Get You Down** O'Jays
'64 **Girl From Ipanema** Stan Getz/Astrud Gilberto
'89 **Girl I Got My Eyes On You** Today
'67 **Girl I Knew Somewhere** Monkees
'89 **Girl I'm Gonna Miss You** Milli Vanilli
'93 **Girl, I've Been Hurt** Snow
'66 **Girl In Love** Outsiders
'84 **Girl In Trouble (Is A Temporary Thing)** Romeo Void
'82 **Girl Is Mine** Michael Jackson/Paul McCartney
**Girl Like You**
'67 Young Rascals
'89 Smithereens
'95 Edwyn Collins
'61 **Girl Of My Best Friend** Ral Donner
'79 **Girl Of My Dreams** Bram Tchaikovsky

'66 **Girl On A Swing** Gerry & The Pacemakers
'99 **Girl On TV** LFO
'02 **Girl Talk** TLC
'68 **Girl Watcher** O'Kaysions
'64 **Girl (Why You Wanna Make Me Blue)** Temptations
'57 **Girl With The Golden Braids** Perry Como
'93 **Girl U For Me** Silk
'89 **Girl You Know It's True** Milli Vanilli
'67 **Girl, You'll Be A Woman Soon** Neil Diamond
'97 **Girl's Gotta Do (What A Girl's Gotta Do)** Mindy cCready
'05 **Girlfight** Brooke Valentine
**Girlfriend**
'86 Bobby Brown
'88 Pebbles
'02 *NSYNC
'03 B2K
'84 **Girls** Dwight Twilley
'85 **Girls Are More Fun** Ray Parker Jr.
'80 **Girls Can Get It** Dr. Hook
'68 **Girls Can't Do What The Guys Do** Betty Wright
**Girls, Girls, Girls**
'87 Mötley Crüe
'01 Jay-Z
'62 **(Girls, Girls, Girls) Made To Love** Eddie Hodges
'63 **Girls Grow Up Faster Than Boys** Cookies
'67 **Girls In Love** Gary Lewis
'83 **Girls Just Want To Have Fun** Cyndi Lauper
'04 **Girls Lie Too** Terri Clark
'90 **Girls Nite Out** Tyler Collins
'83 **Girls On Film** Duran Duran
'77 **Girls' School** Wings
'84 **Girls With Guns** Tommy Shaw
'69 **Gitarzan** Ray Stevens
**Give A Little Bit**
'77 Supertramp
'04 Goo Goo Dolls
'64 **Give Him A Great Big Kiss** Shangri-Las
'72 **Give Ireland Back To The Irish** Wings
'80 **Give It All You Got** Chuck Mangione
'91 **Give It Away** Red Hot Chili Peppers
'73 **Give It To Me** J. Geils Band
'81 **Give It To Me Baby** Rick James
'74 **Give It To The People** Righteous Brothers
**Give It To [2] You**
'95 Da Brat
'99 Jordan Knight
**Give It Up**
'83 KC
'90 ZZ Top
'92 Wilson Phillips
'94 Public Enemy
'69 **Give It Up Or Turnit A Loose** James Brown
**Give It Up, Turn It Loose**
'76 Tyrone Davis
'92 En Vogue
'75 **Give It What You Got** B.T. Express
'70 **Give Me Just A Little More Time** Chairmen Of The Board
'00 **Give Me Just One Night (Una Noche)** 98°
'73 **Give Me Love - (Give Me Peace On Earth)** George Harrison
'96 **Give Me One Reason** Tracy Chapman
'80 **Give Me The Night** George Benson
'86 **Give Me The Reason** Luther Vandross
'57 **Give My Love To Rose** Johnny Cash
'73 **Give Me Your Love** Barbara Mason
'69 **Give Peace A Chance** Plastic Ono Band
'75 **Give The People What They Want** O'Jays
'87 **Give To Live** Sammy Hagar

'92 **Give U My Heart** Babyface
'56 **Give Us This Day** Joni James
'65 **Give Us Your Blessings** Shangri-Las
'73 **Give Your Baby A Standing Ovation** Dells
'98 **Given To Fly** Pearl Jam
'80 **Giving It Up For Your Love** Delbert McClinton
'64 **Giving Up** Gladys Knight
'89 **Giving Up On Love** Rick Astley
'90 **Giving You The Benefit** Pebbles
'88 **Giving You The Best That I Got** Anita Baker
'64 **Glad All Over** Dave Clark Five
'67 **Glad To Be Unhappy** Mamas & The Papas
'84 **Glamorous Life** Sheila E.
'89 **Glamour Boys** Living Colour
'68 **Glass Onion** Beatles
'56 **Glendora** Perry Como
'91 **Globe, The** Big Audio Dynamite II
**Gloria**
'65 Them
'66 Shadows Of Knight
'75 Patti Smith
'77 Enchantment
'82 Laura Branigan
'72 **Glory Bound** Grass Roots
'85 **Glory Days** Bruce Springsteen
'86 **Glory Of Love** Peter Cetera
'96 **Glycerine** Bush
'93 **Go** Pearl Jam
'66 **Go Ahead And Cry** Righteous Brothers
'72 **Go All The Way** Raspberries
'97 **Go Away** Lorrie Morgan
**Go Away Little Girl**
'62 Steve Lawrence
'66 Happenings
'71 Donny Osmond
'70 **Go Back** Crabby Appleton
'58 **Go Chase A Moonbeam** Jerry Vale
'04 **Go D.J.** Lil Wayne
'98 **Go Deep** Janet Jackson
'71 **Go Down Gamblin'** Blood, Sweat & Tears
'85 **Go For Soda** Kim Mitchell
'85 **Go Home** Stevie Wonder
'84 **Go Insane** Lindsey Buckingham
'59 **Go, Jimmy, Go** Jimmy Clanton
'65 **Go Now!** Moody Blues
**Go On With The Wedding**
'56 Kitty Kallen & Georgie Shaw
'56 Patti Page
'95 **Go Rest High On That Mountain** Vince Gill
'97 **Go The Distance** Michael Bolton
'67 **Go Where You Wanna Go** 5th Dimension
'77 **Go Your Own Way** Fleetwood Mac
**God**
'70 John Lennon
'94 Tori Amos
'59 **God Bless America** Connie Francis
**God Bless The USA**
'84 Lee Greenwood
'03 American Idol Finalists
'93 **God Blessed Texas** Little Texas
'61 **God, Country And My Baby** Johnny Burnette
'70 **God, Love And Rock & Roll** Teegarden & Van Winkle
**(God Must Have Spent) A Little More Time On You**
'98 *NSYNC
'99 Alabama (feat. *NSYNC)
'66 **God Only Knows** Beach Boys
'77 **God Save The Queen** Sex Pistols
'05 **God's Will** Martina McBride
'77 **Godzilla** Blue Öyster Cult
'05 **Goin' Crazy** Natalie
'82 **Goin' Down** Greg Guidry
'71 **Goin' Mobile** Who

**Goin' Out Of My Head**
'64   *Little Anthony & The Imperials*
'67   *Lettermen [medley]*
'57   **Goin' Steady** *Tommy Sands*
'94   **Goin' Through The Big D**
     *Mark Chesnutt*
**Going Back To Cali**
'88   *LL Cool J*
'97   *Notorious B.I.G.*
'77   **Going For The One** *Yes*
'64   **Going Going Gone** *Brook Benton*
**Going In Circles**
'69   *Friends Of Distinction*
'86   *Gap Band*
**Going To A Go-Go**
'65   *Miracles*
'82   *Rolling Stones*
'71   **Going To California**
     *Led Zeppelin*
'70   **Going To The Country**
     *Steve Miller Band*
'68   **Going Up The Country**
     *Canned Heat*
**Gold**
'79   *John Stewart*
'83   *Spandau Ballet*
'77   **Gold Dust Woman**
     *Fleetwood Mac*
'74   **Golden Age Of Rock 'N' Roll**
     *Mott The Hoople*
'69   **Golden Slumbers [medley]** *Beatles*
'75   **Golden Years** *David Bowie*
'65   **Goldfinger** *Shirley Bassey*
'86   **Goldmine** *Pointer Sisters*
**Gone**
'57   *Ferlin Husky*
'72   *Joey Heatherton*
'01   *\*NSYNC*
'05   *Montgomery Gentry*
'75   **Gone At Last**
     *Paul Simon/Phoebe Snow*
'97   **Gone Away** *Offspring*
'94   **Gone Country** *Alan Jackson*
'82   **Gone Daddy Gone** *Violent Femmes*
'64   **Gone, Gone, Gone** *Everly Brothers*
'98   **Gone Till November** *Wyclef Jean*
'77   **Gone Too Far** *England Dan &*
     *John Ford Coley*
'57   **Gonna Find Me A Bluebird**
     *Marvin Rainwater*
**Gonna Fly Now (Theme From**
     **'Rocky')**
'77   *Bill Conti*
'77   *Maynard Ferguson*
'95   **Gonna Get A Life** *Mark Chesnutt*
'56   **Gonna Get Along Without Ya Now**
     *Patience & Prudence*
'67   **Gonna Give Her All The Love I've**
     **Got** *Jimmy Ruffin*
'90   **Gonna Make You Sweat (Everybody**
     **Dance Now)** *C & C Music Factory*
'60   **Gonzo** *James Booker*
'69   **Goo Goo Barabajagal (Love Is Hot)**
     *Donovan with The Jeff Beck Group*
'95   **Good** *Better Than Ezra*
'90   **Good Clean Fun**
     *Allman Brothers Band*
'66   **Good Day Sunshine** *Beatles*
'92   **Good Enough** *Bobby Brown*
'92   **Good For Me** *Amy Grant*
'79   **Good Friend** *Mary MacGregor*
'79   **Good Girls Don't** *Knack*
**Good Golly, Miss Molly**
'58   *Little Richard*
'66   *Mitch Ryder [medley]*
'76   **Good Hearted Woman**
     *Waylon Jennings & Willie Nelson*
'95   **Good Intentions**
     *Toad The Wet Sprocket*
'63   **Good Life** *Tony Bennett*
'66   **Good Lovin'** *Young Rascals*
'69   **Good Lovin' Ain't Easy To Come By**
     *Marvin Gaye & Tammi Terrell*
'75   **Good Lovin' Gone Bad**
     *Bad Company*
'62   **Good Luck Charm** *Elvis Presley*

'01   **Good Morning Beautiful** *Steve Holy*
'73   **Good Morning Heartache**
     *Diana Ross*
'69   **Good Morning Starshine** *Oliver*
'64   **Good News** *Sam Cooke*
'69   **Good Old Rock 'N Roll** *Cat Mother*
     *& the All Night News Boys*
'97   **Good Riddance (Time Of Your Life)**
     *Green Day*
'94   **Good Run Of Bad Luck** *Clint Black*
**Good Stuff**
'92   *B-52's*
'02   *Kenny Chesney*
'68   **Good, The Bad And The Ugly**
     *Hugo Montenegro*
**Good Thing**
'66   *Paul Revere & The Raiders*
'89   *Fine Young Cannibals*
'91   **Good Things** *BoDeans*
'61   **Good Time Baby** *Bobby Rydell*
'72   **Good Time Charlie's Got The Blues**
     *Danny O'Keefe*
**Good Times**
'64   *Sam Cooke*
'79   *Chic*
'87   *INXS & Jimmy Barnes*
'90   *Dan Seals*
'02   *Styles*
'69   **Good Times Bad Times**
     *Led Zeppelin*
'78   **Good Times Roll** *Cars*
'60   **Good Timin'** *Jimmy Jones*
**Good Vibrations**
'66   *Beach Boys*
'76   *Todd Rundgren*
'91   *Marky Mark & The Funky Bunch*
**Goodbye**
'69   *Mary Hopkin*
'85   *Night Ranger*
'92   *Tevin Campbell*
'98   *Spice Girls*
'58   **Goodbye Baby** *Jack Scott*
'64   **Goodbye Baby (Baby Goodbye)**
     *Solomon Burke*
'61   **Goodbye Cruel World**
     *James Darren*
'00   **Goodbye Earl** *Dixie Chicks*
'77   **Goodbye Girl** *David Gates*
'86   **Goodbye Is Forever** *Arcadia*
'59   **Goodbye Jimmy, Goodbye**
     *Kathy Linden*
'79   **Goodbye Stranger** *Supertramp*
'72   **Goodbye To Love** *Carpenters*
'98   **Goodbye To My Homies** *Master P*
'02   **Goodbye To You** *Michelle Branch*
'73   **Goodbye Yellow Brick Road**
     *Elton John*
'04   **Goodies** *Ciara*
'65   **Goodnight** *Roy Orbison*
**Goodnight My Love**
'56   *McGuire Sisters*
'56   *Ray Peterson*
'63   *Fleetwoods*
'69   *Paul Anka*
'79   **Goodnight Tonight** *Wings*
'54   **Goodnite Sweeheart, Goodnite**
     *Spaniels*
'57   **Goody Goody** *Frankie Lymon*
'82   **Goody Two Shoes** *Adam Ant*
'85   **Goonies 'R' Good Enough**
     *Cyndi Lauper*
'02   **Gossip Folks** *Missy Elliott*
'60   **Got A Girl** *Four Preps*
'84   **Got A Hold On Me** *Christine McVie*
'91   **Got A Love For You** *Jomanda*
'58   **Got A Match?** *Daddy-O's*
'88   **Got It Made**
     *Crosby, Stills, Nash & Young*
'94   **Got Me Waiting**
     *Heavy D & The Boyz*
'87   **Got My Mind Set On You**
     *George Harrison*
**Got My Mojo Working**
'57   *Muddy Waters*
'66   *Jimmy Smith*
'93   **Got No Shame** *Brother Cane*

'97   **Got 'Til It's Gone** *Janet Jackson*
'78   **Got To Be Real** *Cheryl Lynn*
'71   **Got To Be There** *Michael Jackson*
'99   **Got To Get It** *Sisqó*
**Got To Get You Into My Life**
'76   *Beatles*
'78   *Earth, Wind & Fire*
'65   **Got To Get You Off My Mind**
     *Solomon Burke*
'77   **Got To Give It Up** *Marvin Gaye*
'99   **Got Your Money** *Ol' Dirty Bastard*
'97   **Gotham City** *R. Kelly*
'02   **Gots Ta Be** *B2K*
'98   **Gotta Be** *Jagged Edge*
'02   **Gotta Get Thru This**
     *Daniel Bedingfield*
'84   **Gotta Get You Home Tonight**
     *Eugene Wilde*
'70   **Gotta Hold On To This Feeling**
     *Jr. Walker*
'99   **Gotta Man** *Eve*
'79   **Gotta Serve Somebody** *Bob Dylan*
'00   **Gotta Tell You** *Samantha Mumba*
'58   **Gotta Travel On** *Billy Grammer*
'86   **Graceland** *Paul Simon*
**Graduation Day**
'56   *Four Freshmen*
'56   *Rover Boys*
'00   **Graduation (Friends Forever)**
     *Vitamin C*
'61   **Graduation Song... Pomp And**
     **Circumstance** *Adrian Kimberly*
'59   **Graduation's Here** *Fleetwoods*
'77   **Grand Illusion** *Styx*
'86   **Grandpa (Tell Me 'Bout The Good**
     **Old Days)** *Judds*
'63   **Grass Is Greener** *Brenda Lee*
'62   **Gravy (For My Mashed Potatoes)**
     *Dee Dee Sharp*
**Grazing In The Grass**
'68   *Hugh Masekela*
'69   *Friends Of Distinction*
'78   **Grease** *Frankie Valli*
'96   **Grease Megamix** *John Travolta &*
     *Olivia Newton-John*
'68   **Greasy Heart** *Jefferson Airplane*
'66   **Great Airplane Strike**
     *Paul Revere & The Raiders*
'57   **Great Balls Of Fire** *Jerry Lee Lewis*
'88   **Great Commandment** *Camouflage*
'73   **Great Gig In The Sky**
     *Pink Floyd*
'55   **Great Pretender** *Platters*
'99   **Greatest, The** *Kenny Rogers*
**Greatest Love Of All**
'77   *George Benson*
'86   *Whitney Houston*
'92   **Greatest Man I Never Knew**
     *Reba McEntire*
'01   **Greed** *Godsmack*
'96   **Greedy Fly** *Bush*
'56   **Green Door** *Jim Lowe*
'70   **Green-Eyed Lady** *Sugarloaf*
'66   **Green Grass** *Gary Lewis*
'75   **Green Grass & High Tides** *Outlaws*
'70   **Green Grass Starts To Grow**
     *Dionne Warwick*
'63   **Green, Green** *New Christy Minstrels*
'66   **Green, Green Grass Of Home**
     *Tom Jones*
'68   **Green Light** *American Breed*
'62   **Green Onions** *Booker T. & The MG's*
'69   **Green River**
     *Creedence Clearwater Revival*
'67   **Green Tambourine** *Lemon Pipers*
'63   **Greenback Dollar** *Kingston Trio*
'60   **Greenfields** *Brothers Four*
'73   **Grey Seal** *Elton John*
'02   **Grindin'** *Clipse*
'90   **Groove Is In The Heart** *Deee-Lite*
'78   **Groove Line** *Heatwave*
'70   **Groove Me** *King Floyd*
'94   **Groove Thang** *Zhané*
**Groovin'**
'67   *Booker T. & The M.G.'s*
'67   *Young Rascals*

'69 **Groovy Grubworm** *Harlow Wilcox*
**Groovy Kind Of Love**
'66   *Mindbenders*
'88   *Phil Collins*
'70 **Groovy Situation** *Gene Chandler*
'76 **Grow Some Funk Of Your Own**
  *Elton John*
'01 **Grown Men Don't Cry** *Tim McGraw*
'66 **Guantanamera** *Sandpipers*
'58 **Guess Things Happen That Way**
  *Johnny Cash*
'59 **Guess Who** *Jesse Belvin*
'80 **Guilty** *Barbra Streisand & Barry Gibb*
'59 **Guitar Boogie Shuffle** *Virtues*
**Guitar Man**
'68   *Elvis Presley*
'72   *Bread*
'86 **Guitars, Cadillacs** *Dwight Yoakam*
'55 **Gum Drop** *Crew-Cuts*
'96 **Guys Do It All The Time**
  *Mindy McCready*
'82 **Gypsy** *Fleetwood Mac*
'63 **Gypsy Cried** *Lou Christie*
'73 **Gypsy Man** *War*
'70 **Gypsy Queen [medley]** *Santana*
**Gypsy Woman**
'61   *Impressions*
'70   *Brian Hyland*
'91 **Gypsy Woman (She's Homeless)**
  *Crystal Waters*
'71 **Gypsys, Tramps & Thieves** *Cher*

# H

'69 **Hair** *Cowsills*
'75 **Hair Of The Dog** *Nazareth*
'66 **Hair On My Chinny Chin Chin**
  *Sam The Sham & The Pharoahs*
'73 **Half-Breed** *Cher*
'02 **Halfcrazy** *Musiq*
'62 **Half Heaven - Half Heartache**
  *Gene Pitney*
'79 **Half The Way** *Crystal Gayle*
**Halfway To Paradise**
'61   *Tony Orlando*
'68   *Bobby Vinton*
**Hallelujah**
'71   *Sweathog*
'94   *Jeff Buckley*
'73 **Hallelujah Day** *Jackson 5*
'95 **Hand In My Pocket** *Alanis Morissette*
'70 **Hand Me Down World** *Guess Who*
'05 **Hand That Feeds** *Nine Inch Nails*
'82 **Hand To Hold On To**
  *John Cougar Mellencamp*
'69 **Handbags And Gladrags**
  *Rod Stewart*
'88 **Handle With Care** *Traveling Wilburys*
'98 **Hands** *Jewel*
'02 **Hands Clean** *Alanis Morissette*
'55 **Hands Off** *Jay McShann*
'88 **Hands To Heaven** *Breathe*
**Handy Man**
'59   *Jimmy Jones*
'64   *Del Shannon*
'77   *James Taylor*
'68 **Hang 'Em High**
  *Booker T. & The MG's*
'82 **Hang Fire** *Rolling Stones*
'90 **Hang In Long Enough** *Phil Collins*
'74 **Hang On In There Baby**
  *Johnny Bristol*
**Hang On Sloopy**
'64   *Vibrations [My Girl]*
'65   *Ramsey Lewis Trio*
'65   *McCoys*
'58 **Hang Up My Rock And Roll Shoes**
  *Chuck Willis*
'99 **Hanginaround** *Counting Crows*
'85 **Hangin' On A String**
  **(Contemplating)** *Loose Ends*
'89 **Hangin' Tough**
  *New Kids On The Block*
'01 **Hanging By A Moment** *Lifehouse*
'86 **Hanging On A Heart Attack** *Device*

'59 **Hanging Tree** *Marty Robbins*
**Hanky Panky**
'66   *Tommy James*
'90   *Madonna*
**Happening**
'67   *Herb Alpert*
'67   *Supremes*
'66 **Happenings Ten Years Time Ago**
  *Yardbirds*
'72 **Happiest Girl In The Whole U.S.A.**
  *Donna Fargo*
'99 **Happily Ever After** *Case*
'79 **Happiness** *Pointer Sisters*
'74 **Happiness Is Just Around The**
  **Bend** *Main Ingredient*
**Happiness Street (Corner Sunshine**
  **Square)**
'56   *Tony Bennett*
'56   *Georgia Gibbs*
**Happy**
'72   *Rolling Stones*
'87   *Surface*
'02   *Ashanti*
'05   *Mudvayne*
'77 **Happy Anniversary** *Little River Band*
'61 **Happy Birthday Blues** *Kathy Young*
'61 **Happy Birthday, Sweet Sixteen**
  *Neil Sedaka*
'76 **Happy Days** *Pratt & McClain*
'63 **Happy Days Are Here Again**
  *Barbra Streisand*
'98 **Happy Girl** *Martina McBride*
'60 **Happy-Go-Lucky-Me** *Paul Evans*
'57 **Happy, Happy Birthday Baby**
  *Tune Weavers*
'69 **Happy Heart** *Andy Williams*
'67 **Happy Jack** *Who*
'76 **Happy Music** *Blackbyrds*
'59 **Happy Organ** *Dave 'Baby' Cortez*
**Happy People**
'74   *Temptations*
'04   *R. Kelly*
'59 **Happy Reindeer**
  *Dancer, Prancer & Nervous*
'68 **Happy Song (Dum-Dum)**
  *Otis Redding*
'66 **Happy Summer Days** *Ronnie Dove*
'67 **Happy Together** *Turtles*
'87 **Happy Wanderer** *Brave Combo*
'56 **Happy Whistler** *Don Robertson*
'71 **Happy Xmas (War Is Over)** *John*
  *Lennon*
'60 **Harbor Lights** *Platters*
'95 **Hard As A Rock** *AC/DC*
**Hard Day's Night**
'64   *Beatles*
'66   *Ramsey Lewis Trio*
'84 **Hard Habit To Break** *Chicago*
'58 **Hard Headed Woman** *Elvis Presley*
'98 **Hard Knock Life (Ghetto Anthem)**
  *Jay-Z*
'76 **Hard Luck Woman** *Kiss*
'90 **Hard Rock Bottom Of Your Heart**
  *Randy Travis*
'77 **Hard Rock Cafe** *Carole King*
'55 **Hard To Get** *Gisele MacKenzie*
'90 **Hard To Handle** *Black Crowes*
'81 **Hard To Say** *Dan Fogelberg*
**Hard To Say I'm Sorry**
'82   *Chicago*
'97   *Az Yet*
'81 **Harden My Heart** *Quarterflash*
'75 **Harder They Come** *Jimmy Cliff*
'03 **Harder To Breathe** *Maroon5*
'99 **Hardest Thing** *98°*
'59 **Harlem Nocturne** *Viscounts*
**Harlem Shuffle**
'63   *Bob & Earl*
'86   *Rolling Stones*
'73 **Harmony** *Elton John*
'68 **Harper Valley P.T.A.**
  *Jeannie C. Riley*
'72 **Harry Hippie** *Bobby Womack*
'63 **Harry The Hairy Ape** *Ray Stevens*
'75 **Harry Truman** *Chicago*
'01 **Hash Pipe** *Weezer*

'93 **Hat 2 Da Back** *TLC*
'05 **Hate It Or Love It** *Game*
'88 **Hate To Lose Your Lovin'** *Little Feat*
'61 **Hats Off To Larry** *Del Shannon*
'64 **Haunted House** *Gene Simmons*
'75 **Have A Cigar** *Pink Floyd*
'62 **Have A Good Time** *Sue Thompson*
'90 **Have A Heart** *Bonnie Raitt*
'64 **Have I The Right?** *Honeycombs*
'93 **Have I Told You Lately**
  *Rod Stewart [live]*
'85 **Have Mercy** *Judds*
98 **Have You Ever?** *Brandy*
'03 **Have You Ever Been In Love**
  *Celine Dion*
'86 **Have You Ever Loved Somebody**
  *Freddie Jackson*
'92 **Have You Ever Needed Someone**
  **So Bad** *Def Leppard*
'95 **Have You Ever Really Loved A**
  **Woman?** *Bryan Adams*
'71 **Have You Ever Seen The Rain**
  *Creedence Clearwater Revival*
'03 **Have You Forgotten?** *Darryl Worley*
'89 **Have You Had Your Love Today**
  *O'Jays*
'63 **Have You Heard** *Duprees*
'64 **Have You Looked Into Your Heart**
  *Jerry Vale*
'75 **Have You Never Been Mellow**
  *Olivia Newton-John*
**Have You Seen Her**
'71   *Chi-Lites*
'90   *M.C. Hammer*
'66 **Have You Seen Your Mother, Baby,**
  **Standing In The Shadow?**
  *Rolling Stones*
'74 **Haven't Got Time For The Pain**
  *Carly Simon*
'79 **Haven't Stopped Dancing Yet**
  *Gonzalez*
'61 **Havin' Fun** *Dion*
**Having A Party**
'62   *Sam Cooke*
'82   *Luther Vandross [medley]*
'94   *Rod Stewart (with Ronnie Wood)*
'69 **Hawaii Five-O** *Ventures*
'64 **Hawaii Tattoo** *Waikikis*
'58 **Hawaiian Wedding Song**
  *Andy Williams*
'96 **Hay** *Crucial Conflict*
'92 **Hazard** *Richard Marx*
**Hazy Shade Of Winter**
'66   *Simon & Garfunkel*
'87   *Bangles*
**He**
'55   *Al Hibbler*
'55   *McGuire Sisters*
'66   *Righteous Brothers*
**He Ain't Heavy, He's My Brother**
'69   *Hollies*
'70   *Neil Diamond*
**He Can't Love You [U]**
'80   *Michael Stanley Band*
'99   *Jagged Edge*
'99 **He Didn't Have To Be** *Brad Paisley*
**He Don't Love You (Like I Love**
  **You)**
'60   *Jerry Butler*
'75   *Tony Orlando & Dawn*
'62 **He Knows I Love Him Too Much**
  *Paris Sisters*
'00 **He Loves U Not** *Dream*
'80 **He Stopped Loving Her Today**
  *George Jones*
'93 **He Thinks He'll Keep Her**
  *Mary Chapin Carpenter*
'65 **He Touched Me** *Barbra Streisand*
'90 **He Walked On Water** *Randy Travis*
'00 **He Wasn't Man Enough**
  *Toni Braxton*
**He Will Break Your Heart ..see: He**
  **Don't Love You (Like I Love You)**
**He'll Have To Go [Stay]**
'59   *Jim Reeves*
'60   *Jeanne Black*

'85 **He'll Never Love You (Like I Do)**
 *Freddie Jackson*
'76 **He's A Friend** *Eddie Kendricks*
'81 **He's A Liar** *Bee Gees*
'62 **He's A Rebel** *Crystals*
'57 **He's Gone** *Chantels*
'58 **He's Got The Whole World (In His**
 **Hands)** *Laurie London*
'97 **He's Got You** *Brooks & Dunn*
 **He's Mine**
'57  *Platters*
'95  *MoKenStef*
'61 **(He's My) Dreamboat**
 *Connie Francis*
 **He's So Fine**
'63  *Chiffons*
'71  *Jody Miller*
'80 **He's So Shy** *Pointer Sisters*
'62 **He's Sure The Boy I Love** *Crystals*
'61 **(He's) The Great Impostor**
 *Fleetwoods*
'79 **He's The Greatest Dancer**
 *Sister Sledge*
'79 **Head Games** *Foreigner*
'90 **Head On** *Jesus & Mary Chain*
'96 **Head Over Feet** *Alanis Morissette*
 **Head Over Heels**
'84  *Go-Go's*
'85  *Tears For Fears*
'97  *Allure*
'87 **Head To Toe** *Lisa Lisa & Cult Jam*
'80 **Headed For A Fall** *Firefall*
'89 **Headed For A Heartbreak** *Winger*
'86 **Headlines** *Midnight Star*
'96 **Heads Carolina, Tails California**
 *Jo Dee Messina*
'04 **Headsprung** *LL Cool J*
'02 **Headstrong** *Trapt*
'92 **Heal The World** *Michael Jackson*
'89 **Healing Hands** *Elton John*
'01 **Heard It All Before**
 *Sunshine Anderson*
'77 **Heard It In A Love Song**
 *Marshall Tucker Band*
'75 **Heard It On The X** *ZZ Top*
 **Heart**
'55  *Eddie Fisher*
'55  *Four Aces*
 **Heart And Soul**
'61  *Cleftones*
'61  *Jan & Dean*
'83  *Huey Lewis*
'87  *T'Pau*
'82 **Heart Attack** *Olivia Newton-John*
'65 **Heart Full Of Soul** *Yardbirds*
'80 **Heart Hotels** *Dan Fogelberg*
'62 **Heart In Hand** *Brenda Lee*
'95 **Heart Is A Lonely Hunter**
 *Reba McEntire*
 **Heart Like A Wheel**
'81  *Steve Miller Band*
'90  *Human League*
'79 **Heart Of Glass** *Blondie*
'72 **Heart Of Gold** *Neil Young*
'88 **Heart Of Mine** *Boz Scaggs*
'84 **Heart Of Rock & Roll** *Huey Lewis*
 **Heart Of Stone**
'65  *Rolling Stones*
'90  *Taylor Dayne*
'90  *Cher*
'90 **Heart Of The Matter** *Don Henley*
 **Heart Of The Night**
'79  *Poco*
'82  *Juice Newton*
'93 **Heart-Shaped Box** *Nirvana*
'82 **Heart To Heart** *Kenny Loggins*
'93 **Heart Won't Lie**
 *Reba McEntire & Vince Gill*
'79 **Heartache Tonight** *Eagles*
'61 **Heartaches** *Marcels*
 **Heartaches By The Number**
'59  *Guy Mitchell*
'65  *Johnny Tillotson*

 **Heartbeat**
'58  *Buddy Holly*
'86  *Don Johnson*
'90  *Seduction*
'73 **Heartbeat - It's A Lovebeat**
 *DeFranco Family*
'87 **Heartbreak Beat** *Psychedelic Furs*
 **Heartbreak Hotel**
'56  *Elvis Presley*
'56  *Stan Freberg*
'80  *Jacksons*
'98  *Whitney Houston*
'60 **Heartbreak (It's Hurtin' Me)**
 *Little Willie John*
'74 **Heartbreak Kid** *Bo Donaldson*
 **Heartbreaker**
'69  *Led Zeppelin*
'78  *Dolly Parton*
'79  *Pat Benatar*
'82  *Dionne Warwick*
'99  *Mariah Carey*
'93 **Heartland** *George Strait*
'78 **Heartless** *Heart*
'82 **Heartlight** *Neil Diamond*
'81 **Hearts** *Marty Balin*
'93 **Hearts Are Gonna Roll** *Hal Ketchum*
'91 **Hearts Don't Think (They Feel)!**
 *Natural Selection*
 **Hearts Of Stone**
'55  *Fontane Sisters*
'56  *Charms*
'61  *Bill Black's Combo*
'73  *John Fogerty*
 **Hearts On Fire**
'81  *Randy Meisner*
'87  *Bryan Adams*
'84 **Heat Is On** *Glenn Frey*
 **Heat Of The Moment**
'82  *Asia*
'89  *After 7*
'87 **Heat Of The Night** *Bryan Adams*
 **Heat Wave**
'63  *Martha & The Vandellas*
'75  *Linda Ronstadt*
'69 **Heather Honey** *Tommy Roe*
 **Heaven**
'69  *Rascals*
'85  *Bryan Adams*
'89  *Warrant*
'89  *BeBe & CeCe Winans*
'97  *Nu Flavor*
'02  *DJ Sammy & Yanou*
'04  *Los Lonely Boys*
'95 **Heaven Beside You** *Alice In Chains*
'89 **Heaven Help Me** *Deon Estus*
'70 **Heaven Help Us All** *Stevie Wonder*
'86 **Heaven In Your Eyes** *Loverboy*
'87 **Heaven Is A Place On Earth**
 *Belinda Carlisle*
 **Heaven Knows**
'69  *Grass Roots*
'79  *Donna Summer*
'88  *Robert Plant*
'90  *Lalah Hathaway*
'76 **Heaven Must Be Missing An Angel**
 *Tavares*
'79 **Heaven Must Have Sent You**
 *Bonnie Pointer*
'77 **Heaven On The 7th Floor**
 *Paul Nicholas*
'92 **Heaven Sent** *INXS*
'98 **Heaven's What I Feel** *Gloria Estefan*
'99 **Heavy** *Collective Soul*
'91 **Heavy Fuel** *Dire Straits*
'71 **Heavy Makes You Happy**
 **(Sha-Na-Boom Boom)**
 *Staple Singers*
'56 **Heebie-Jeebies** *Little Richard*
'70 **Heed The Call** *Kenny Rogers &*
 *The First Edition*
'73 **Helen Wheels** *Paul McCartney*
'87 **Hell In A Bucket** *Grateful Dead*
'80 **Hell Is For Children**
 *Pat Benatar*
'03 **Hell Yeah** *Ginuwine*

'02 **Hella Good** *No Doubt*
'84 **Hello** *Lionel Richie*
 **Hello Again**
'81  *Neil Diamond*
'84  *Cars*
'70 **Hello Darlin'** *Conway Twitty*
'64 **Hello, Dolly!** *Louis Armstrong*
'67 **Hello Goodbye** *Beatles*
'63 **Hello Heartache, Goodbye Love**
 *Little Peggy March*
'66 **Hello Hello** *Sopwith "Camel"*
'73 **Hello Hurray** *Alice Cooper*
'68 **Hello, I Love You** *Doors*
 **Hello It's Me**
'69  *Nazz*
'73  *Todd Rundgren*
'61 **Hello Mary Lou** *Ricky Nelson*
'63 **Hello Mudduh, Hello Fadduh!**
 *Allan Sherman*
'76 **Hello Old Friend** *Eric Clapton*
 **Hello Stranger**
'63  *Barbara Lewis*
'77  *Yvonne Elliman*
'61 **Hello Walls** *Faron Young*
'60 **Hello Young Lovers** *Paul Anka*
'65 **Help!** *Beatles*
'77 **Help Is On Its Way** *Little River Band*
'74 **Help Me** *Joni Mitchell*
 **Help Me Girl**
'66  *Animals*
'66  *Outsiders*
'90 **Help Me Hold On** *Travis Tritt*
 **Help Me Make It Through The Night**
'71  *Sammi Smith*
'72  *Gladys Knight*
 **Help Me, Rhonda**
'65  *Beach Boys*
'75  *Johnny Rivers*
'03 **Help Pour Out The Rain (Lacey's**
 **Song)** *Buddy Jewell*
'68 **Help Yourself** *Tom Jones*
'70 **Helpless**
 *Crosby, Stills, Nash & Young*
'69 **Helplessly Hoping**
 *Crosby, Stills, Nash & Young*
'68 **Helter Skelter** *Beatles*
'00 **Hemorrhage (In My Hands)** *Fuel*
'58 **Henrietta** *Jimmy Dee*
'69 **Her Majesty [medley]** *Beatles*
'62 **Her Royal Majesty** *James Darren*
'80 **Her Strut** *Bob Seger*
'81 **Her Town Too**
 *James Taylor & J.D. Souther*
'72 **Hercules** *Elton John*
'89 **Here And Now** *Luther Vandross*
'77 **Here Come Those Tears Again**
 *Jackson Browne*
'67 **Here Comes My Baby** *Tremeloes*
'79 **Here Comes My Girl** *Tom Petty*
'59 **Here Comes Summer** *Jerry Keller*
'71 **Here Comes That Rainy Day**
 **Feeling Again** *Fortunes*
'94 **Here Comes The Hotstepper**
 *Ini Kamoze*
 **Here Comes The Judge**
'68  *Shorty Long*
'68  *Pigmeat Markham*
'65 **Here Comes The Night** *Them*
'84 **Here Comes The Rain Again**
 *Eurythmics*
 **Here Comes The Sun**
'69  *Beatles*
'71  *Richie Havens*
'89 **Here Comes Your Man** *Pixies*
'04 **Here For The Party** *Gretchen Wilson*
 **Here I Am (Come And Take Me)**
'73  *Al Green*
'91  *UB40*
'81 **Here I Am (Just When I Thought I**
 **Was Over You)** *Air Supply*
 **Here I Go Again**
'69  *Miracles*
'87  *Whitesnake*
'92  *Glenn Jones*
'97 **Here In My Heart** *Chicago*

'90 **Here In The Real World**
    *Alan Jackson*
'02 **Here Is Gone** *Goo Goo Dolls*
'65 **Here It Comes Again** *Fortunes*
    **Here We Are**
'89   *Gloria Estefan*
'91   *Alabama*
'91 **Here We Go** *C + C Music Factory*
    **Here We Go Again**
'67   *Ray Charles*
'92   *Portrait*
'88 **Here With Me** *REO Speedwagon*
'03 **Here Without You** *3 Doors Down*
'77 **Here You Come Again** *Dolly Parton*
'91 **Here's A Quarter (Call Someone**
    **Who Cares)** *Travis Tritt*
'01 **Here's To The Night** *Eve 6*
'90 **Here's Where The Story Ends**
    *Sundays*
    **Hero**
'93   *Mariah Carey*
'93   *David Crosby & Phil Collins*
'01   *Enrique Iglesias*
'02   *Chad Kroeger*
'96 **Hero Of The Day** *Metallica*
    **Heroes**
'77   *David Bowie*
'98   *Wallflowers*
'67 **Heroes And Villains** *Beach Boys*
'67 **Heroin** *Velvet Underground*
    **Hey Baby**
'62   *Bruce Channel*
'75   *Ted Nugent*
'89   *Henry Lee Summer*
'01   *No Doubt*
'67 **Hey Baby (They're Playing Our**
    **Song)** *Buckinghams*
'79 **Hey Bartender** *Blues Brothers*
'71 **Hey Big Brother** *Rare Earth*
'64 **Hey, Bobba Needle** *Chubby Checker*
'77 **Hey Deanie** *Shaun Cassidy*
'91 **Hey Donna** *Rythm Syndicate*
    **Hey, Girl**
'63   *Freddie Scott*
'71   *Donny Osmond*
'73 **Hey Girl (I Like Your Style)**
    *Temptations*
'67 **Hey Grandma** *Moby Grape*
'64 **Hey Harmonica Man** *Stevie Wonder*
'56 **Hey! Jealous Lover** *Frank Sinatra*
'93 **Hey Jealousy** *Gin Blossoms*
'64 **Hey Jean, Hey Dean** *Dean & Jean*
    **Hey Joe**
'66   *Leaves*
'67   *Jimi Hendrix*
    **Hey Jude**
'68   *Beatles*
'68   *Wilson Pickett*
'89 **Hey Ladies** *Beastie Boys*
'70 **Hey Lawdy Mama** *Steppenwolf*
'99 **Hey Leonardo (she likes me for me)**
    *Blessid Union Of Souls*
'66 **Hey, Leroy, Your Mama's Callin'**
    **You** *Jimmy Castor*
'62 **Hey, Let's Twist** *Joey Dee*
'63 **Hey Little Cobra** *Rip Chords*
    **Hey Little Girl**
'57   *Techniques*
'59   *Dee Clark*
'61   *Del Shannon*
'63   *Major Lance*
    **Hey Lover**
'88   *Freddie Jackson*
'95   *LL Cool J*
'02 **Hey Ma** *Cam'ron*
'04 **Hey Mama** *Black Eyed Peas*
'95 **Hey Man Nice Shot** *Filter*
'55 **Hey, Mr. Banjo** *Sunnysiders*
'93 **Hey Mr. D.J.** *Zhané*
'70 **Hey, Mister Sun** *Bobby Sherman*
'80 **Hey Nineteen** *Steely Dan*
'62 **Hey Paula** *Paul & Paula*
'54 **Hey There** *Rosemary Clooney*

    **Hey There Lonely Girl [Boy]**
'63   *Ruby & The Romantics*
'69   *Eddie Holman*
'80   *Robert John*
'71 **Hey Tonight**
    *Creedence Clearwater Revival*
'68 **Hey, Western Union Man**
    *Jerry Butler*
'75 **(Hey Won't You Play) Another**
    **Somebody Done Somebody**
    **Wrong Song** *B.J. Thomas*
'03 **Hey Ya!** *OutKast*
    **Hey You**
'75   *Bachman-Turner Overdrive*
'80   *Pink Floyd*
'70 **Hi-De-Ho** *Blood, Sweat & Tears*
    **Hi-Heel Sneakers**
'64   *Tommy Tucker*
'68   *José Feliciano*
'72 **Hi, Hi, Hi** *Wings*
'62 **Hide & Go Seek** *Bunker Hill*
'55 **Hide And Seek** *Joe Turner*
'61 **Hide Away** *Freddy King*
'62 **Hide 'Nor Hair** *Ray Charles*
'58 **Hideaway** *Four Esquires*
'92 **High** *Cure*
'89 **High Cotton** *Alabama*
'90 **High Enough** *Damn Yankees*
'59 **High Hopes** *Frank Sinatra*
'84 **High On Emotion** *Chris DeBurgh*
'85 **High On You** *Survivor*
'58 **High School Confidential**
    *Jerry Lee Lewis*
'77 **High School Dance** *Sylvers*
'59 **High School U.S.A.** *Tommy Facenda*
'58 **High Sign** *Diamonds*
'71 **High Time We Went** *Joe Cocker*
'85 **Highwayman** *Waylon Jennings/*
    *Willie Nelson/Johnny Cash/*
    *Kris Kristofferson*
'91 **Highwire** *Rolling Stones*
'99 **Higher** *Creed*
    **Higher Ground**
'73   *Stevie Wonder*
'89   *Red Hot Chili Peppers*
'86 **Higher Love** *Steve Winwood*
'74 **Higher Plane** *Kool & The Gang*
'65 **Highway 61 Revisited**
    *Bob Dylan*
'79 **Highway Song** *Blackfoot*
'72 **Highway Star** *Deep Purple*
'79 **Highway To Hell** *AC/DC*
'75 **Hijack** *Herbie Mann*
'71 **Hill Where The Lord Hides**
    *Chuck Mangione*
'80 **Him** *Rupert Holmes*
'67 **Him Or Me - What's It Gonna Be?**
    *Paul Revere & The Raiders*
'68 **Hip City** *Jr. Walker*
'93 **Hip Hop Hooray** *Naughty By Nature*
'67 **Hip Hug-Her** *Booker T. & The M.G.'s*
'86 **Hip To Be Square** *Huey Lewis*
'64 **Hippy Hippy Shake**
    *Swinging Blue Jeans*
'90 **Hippychick** *Soho*
'66 **History Repeats Itself**
    *Buddy Starcher*
'92 **Hit** *Sugarcubes*
'01 **Hit 'Em Up Style (Oops!)**
    *Blu Cantrell*
'96 **Hit Me Off** *New Edition*
'80 **Hit Me With Your Best Shot**
    *Pat Benatar*
'03 **Hit That** *Offspring*
'86 **Hit That Perfect Beat** *Bronski Beat*
    **Hit The Road Jack**
'61   *Ray Charles*
'76   *Stampeders*
'76 **Hitch A Ride** *Boston*
'63 **Hitch Hike** *Marvin Gaye*
'68 **Hitch It To The Horse**
    *Fantastic Johnny C*
'70 **Hitchin' A Ride** *Vanity Fare*
'60 **Hither And Thither And Yon**
    *Brook Benton*
'73 **Hocus Pocus** *Focus*

'72 **Hoedown**
    *Emerson, Lake & Palmer*
    **Hold Back The Night**
'76   *Trammps*
'77   *Graham Parker*
'72 **Hold Her Tight** *Osmonds*
'58 **Hold It** *Bill Doggett*
    **Hold Me**
'82   *Fleetwood Mac*
'98   *Brian McKnight*
'84 **Hold Me Now** *Thompson Twins*
'65 **Hold Me, Thrill Me, Kiss Me**
    *Mel Carter*
'95 **Hold Me, Thrill Me, Kiss Me, Kill Me**
    *U2*
'68 **Hold Me Tight** *Johnny Nash*
'83 **Hold Me 'Til The Mornin' Comes**
    *Paul Anka*
'94 **Hold My Hand** *Hootie & The Blowfish*
    **Hold On**
'79   *Ian Gomm*
'79   *Triumph*
'80   *Kansas*
'82   *Santana*
'90   *Wilson Phillips*
'90   *En Vogue*
'95   *Jamie Walters*
'80 **Hold On Hold Out**
    *Jackson Browne*
'66 **Hold On! I'm A Comin'** *Sam & Dave*
'81 **Hold On Loosely** *.38 Special*
'92 **Hold On My Heart** *Genesis*
'81 **Hold On Tight** *ELO*
'98 **Hold On To Me**
    *John Michael Montgomery*
'80 **Hold On To My Love** *Jimmy Ruffin*
'88 **Hold On To The Nights**
    *Richard Marx*
'78 **Hold The Line** *Toto*
'64 **Hold What You've Got** *Joe Tex*
'91 **Hold You Tight** *Tara Kemp*
'72 **Hold Your Head Up** *Argent*
'93 **Holdin' Heaven** *Tracy Byrd*
'75 **Holdin' On To Yesterday** *Ambrosia*
'86 **Holding Back The Years**
    *Simply Red*
'88 **Holding On** *Steve Winwood*
'78 **Holding On (When Love Is Gone)**
    *L.T.D.*
'84 **Holding Out For A Hero**
    *Bonnie Tyler*
'91 **Hole Hearted** *Extreme*
'68 **Hole In My Shoe** *Traffic*
'98 **Holes In The Floor Of Heaven**
    *Steve Wariner*
'03 **Holidae In** *Chingy*
    **Holiday**
'67   *Bee Gees*
'83   *Madonna*
'87   *Other Ones*
'05   *Green Day*
'83 **Holiday Road**
    *Lindsey Buckingham*
'99 **Holla Holla** *Ja Rule*
'05 **Hollaback Girl** *Gwen Stefani*
'69 **Holly Holy** *Neil Diamond*
'78 **Hollywood Nights** *Bob Seger*
'74 **Hollywood Swinging**
    *Kool & The Gang*
'66 **Holy Cow** *Lee Dorsey*
'90 **Holy Water** *Bad Company*
'67 **Homburg** *Procol Harum*
    **Home**
'89   *Stephanie Mills*
'90   *Joe Diffie*
'90   *Iggy Pop*
'96   *Alan Jackson*
'05   *Three Days Grace*
'05   *Michael Bublé*
'78 **Home And Dry** *Gerry Rafferty*
'77 **Home Bound** *Ted Nugent*
'65 **Home Of The Brave** *Jody Miller*
'85 **Home Sweet Home**
    *Mötley Crüe*
'99 **Home To You**
    *John Michael Montgomery*

'66 **Homeward Bound**
    *Simon & Garfunkel*
'05 **Homewrecker** *Gretchen Wilson*
**Honest I Do**
'57   *Jimmy Reed*
'60   *Innocents*
'87 **Honestly** *Stryper*
'79 **Honesty** *Billy Joel*
**Honey**
'68   *Bobby Goldsboro*
'97   *Mariah Carey*
'55 **Honey-Babe** *Art Mooney*
**Honey Chile**
'56   *Fats Domino*
'67   *Martha & The Vandellas*
'70 **Honey Come Back** *Glen Campbell*
'56 **Honey Don't** *Carl Perkins*
'74 **Honey, Honey** *Abba*
'97 **Honey, I'm Home** *Shania Twain*
'92 **Honey Love** *R. Kelly*
'57 **Honeycomb** *Jimmie Rodgers*
'87 **Honeythief, The** *Hipsway*
'72 **Honky Cat** *Elton John*
'56 **Honky Tonk** *Bill Doggett*
'86 **Honky Tonk Man** *Dwight Yoakam*
'97 **Honky Tonk Truth** *Brooks & Dunn*
'69 **Honky Tonk Women** *Rolling Stones*
'63 **Honolulu Lulu** *Jan & Dean*
'98 **Hooch** *Everything*
'60 **Hoochi Coochi Coo** *Hank Ballard*
'54 **Hoochie Coochie Man**
    *Muddy Waters*
'95 **Hook** *Blues Traveler*
'63 **Hooka Tooka** *Chubby Checker*
**Hooked On A Feeling**
'68   *B.J. Thomas*
'74   *Blue Swede*
'81 **Hooked On Classics**
    *Royal Philharmonic Orchestra*
'82 **Hooked On Swing [medley]**
    *Larry Elgart*
**Hooked On You**
'77   *Bread*
'89   *Sweet Sensation [remix]*
'66 **Hooray For Hazel** *Tommy Roe*
'63 **Hootenanny** *Glencoves*
'05 **Hope** *Twista*
'75 **Hope That We Can Be Together**
    **Soon** *Sharon Paige/Harold Melvin*
'82 **Hope You Love Me Like You Say**
    **You Do** *Huey Lewis*
'63 **Hopeless** *Andy Williams*
'93 **Hopelessly** *Rick Astley*
'78 **Hopelessly Devoted To You**
    *Olivia Newton-John*
'80 **Horizontal Bop** *Bob Seger*
'68 **Horse, The** *Cliff Nobles & Co.*
'72 **Horse With No Name** *America*
'78 **Hot Blooded** *Foreigner*
'99 **Hot Boyz**
    *Missy "Misdemeanor" Elliott*
'78 **Hot Child In The City** *Nick Gilder*
'56 **Hot Diggity (Dog Ziggity Boom)**
    *Perry Como*
'79 **Hot Dog** *Led Zeppelin*
'84 **Hot For Teacher** *Van Halen*
'69 **Hot Fun In The Summertime**
    *Sly & The Family Stone*
'83 **Hot Girls In Love** *Loverboy*
'88 **Hot Hot Hot** *Buster Poindexter*
'02 **Hot In Herre** *Nelly*
'82 **Hot In The City** *Billy Idol*
'78 **Hot Legs** *Rod Stewart*
'76 **Hot Line** *Sylvers*
'78 **Hot Love, Cold World** *Bob Welch*
'72 **Hot 'N' Nasty** *Humble Pie*
'79 **Hot Number** *Foxy*
'71 **Hot Pants** *James Brown*
'63 **Hot Pastrami** *Dartells*
'80 **Hot Rod Hearts** *Robbie Dupree*
**Hot Rod Lincoln**
'60   *Johnny Bond*
'60   *Charlie Ryan*
'72   *Commander Cody*
'00 **(Hot S\*\*t) Country Grammar** *Nelly*

'69 **Hot Smoke & Sasafrass**
    *Bubble Puppy*
'79 **Hot Stuff** *Donna Summer*
'79 **Hot Summer Nights** *Night*
'03 **Hotel** *Cassidy*
'77 **Hotel California** *Eagles*
'62 **Hotel Happiness** *Brook Benton*
'92 **Hotel Illness** *Black Crowes*
'74 **Hotter Than Hell** *Kiss*
'56 **Hound Dog** *Elvis Presley*
'59 **Hound Dog Man** *Fabian*
'85 **Hounds Of Love** *Kate Bush*
'87 **Hourglass** *Squeeze*
'89 **House** *Psychedelic Furs*
'72 **House At Pooh Corner**
    *Loggins & Messina*
'55 **House Of Blue Lights** *Chuck Miller*
'94 **House Of Love**
    *Amy Grant with Vince Gill*
'90 **House Of Pain** *Faster Pussycat*
**House Of The Rising Sun**
'64   *Animals*
'70   *Frijid Pink*
'68 **House That Jack Built**
    *Aretha Franklin*
'88 **House We Used To Live In**
    *Smithereens*
'56 **House With Love In It** *Four Lads*
'91 **Housecall (Your Body Can't Lie To**
    **Me)** *Shabba Ranks*
'75 **Houses Of The Holy**
    *Led Zeppelin*
'65 **Houston** *Dean Martin*
**How About That**
'59   *Dee Clark*
'92   *Bad Company*
**How Am I Supposed To Live**
    **Without You**
'83   *Laura Branigan*
'89   *Michael Bolton*
'97 **How Bizarre** *OMC*
'91 **How 'Bout Us** *Champaign*
**How Can I Be Sure**
'67   *Young Rascals*
'72   *David Cassidy*
'91 **How Can I Ease The Pain**
    *Lisa Fischer*
'88 **How Can I Fall?** *Breathe*
'77 **How Can I Leave You Again**
    *John Denver*
'83 **How Can I Refuse** *Heart*
'73 **How Can I Tell Her** *Lobo*
'90 **How Can We Be Lovers**
    *Michael Bolton*
'71 **How Can You Mend A Broken Heart**
    *Bee Gees*
'04 **How Come** *D12*
**How Deep Is Your Love**
'77   *Bee Gees*
'98   *Dru Hill*
'97 **How Do I Get There** *Deana Carter*
**How Do I Live**
'97   *LeAnn Rimes*
'97   *Trisha Yearwood*
'80 **How Do I Make You** *Linda Ronstadt*
'80 **How Do I Survive** *Amy Holland*
'96 **How Do U Want It** *2 Pac*
'66 **How Do You Catch A Girl**
    *Sam The Sham & The Pharoahs*
'72 **How Do You Do?** *Mouth & MacNeal*
'64 **How Do You Do It?**
    *Gerry & The Pacemakers*
'98 **How Do You Fall In Love** *Alabama*
'00 **How Do You Like Me Now?!**
    *Toby Keith*
'92 **How Do You Talk To An Angel**
    *Heights*
'80 **How Does It Feel To Be Back**
    *Daryl Hall & John Oates*
'66 **How Does That Grab You, Darlin'?**
    *Nancy Sinatra*
'99 **How Forever Feels** *Kenny Chesney*
'95 **How High** *Redman/Method Man*
'60 **How High The Moon** *Ella Fitzgerald*

**How Important Can It Be?**
'55   *Joni James*
'55   *Sarah Vaughan*
'62 **How Is Julie?** *Lettermen*
'56 **(How Little It Matters) How Little We**
    **Know** *Frank Sinatra*
'75 **How Long** *Ace*
'75 **How Long (Betcha' Got A Chick On**
    **The Side)** *Pointer Sisters*
'98 **How Long Gone** *Brooks & Dunn*
'69 **How Many More Times**
    *Led Zeppelin*
'83 **How Many Times Can We Say**
    **Goodbye**
    *Dionne Warwick & Luther Vandross*
'78 **How Much I Feel** *Ambrosia*
'91 **How Much Is Enough** *Fixx*
'77 **How Much Love** *Leo Sayer*
'85 **How Soon Is Now?** *Smiths*
**How Sweet It Is (To Be Loved By**
    **You)**
'64   *Marvin Gaye*
'66   *Jr. Walker*
'75   *James Taylor*
'58 **How The Time Flies** *Jerry Wallace*
'86 **(How To Be A) Millionaire** *ABC*
'91 **How To Dance** *Bingoboys/Princessa*
**How Was I To Know**
'96   *Reba McEntire*
'97   *John Michael Montgomery*
'05 **How We Do** *Game*
'85 **How Will I Know** *Whitney Houston*
'03 **How You Gonna Act Like That**
    *Tyrese*
'78 **How You Gonna See Me Now**
    *Alice Cooper*
'01 **How You Remind Me** *Nickelback*
'97 **How Your Love Makes Me Feel**
    *Diamond Rio*
'68 **How'd We Ever Get This Way**
    *Andy Kim*
'97 **How's It Going To Be**
    *Third Eye Blind*
'60 **Hucklebuck, The** *Chubby Checker*
'58 **Hula Hoop Song** *Georgia Gibbs*
'57 **Hula Love** *Buddy Knox*
'62 **Hully Gully Baby** *Dovells*
'86 **Human** *Human League*
'93 **Human Behaviour** *Björk*
'83 **Human Nature** *Michael Jackson*
    *(also see: Right Here)*
**Human Touch**
'83   *Rick Springfield*
'92   *Bruce Springsteen*
'93 **Human Wheels** *John Mellencamp*
'96 **Humans Being** *Van Halen*
**Humming Bird**
'55   *Frankie Laine*
'55   *Les Paul & Mary Ford*
'73 **Hummingbird** *Seals & Crofts*
'92 **Humpin' Around** *Bobby Brown*
'90 **Humpty Dance** *Digital Underground*
'61 **Hundred Pounds Of Clay**
    *Gene McDaniels*
'65 **Hung On You** *Righteous Brothers*
'66 **Hungry** *Paul Revere & The Raiders*
'87 **Hungry Eyes** *Eric Carmen*
'80 **Hungry Heart** *Bruce Springsteen*
'82 **Hungry Like The Wolf** *Duran Duran*
'67 **Hunter Gets Captured By The Game**
    *Marvelettes*
'68 **Hurdy Gurdy Man** *Donovan*
'75 **Hurricane** *Bob Dylan*
**Hurt**
'61   *Timi Yuro*
'76   *Elvis Presley*
'95   *Nine Inch Nails*
'03   *Johnny Cash*
'73 **Hurt, The** *Cat Stevens*
**Hurt So Bad**
'65   *Little Anthony & The Imperials*
'69   *Lettermen*
'80   *Linda Ronstadt*
'72 **Hurting Each Other** *Carpenters*
'90 **Hurting Kind (I've Got My Eyes On**
    **You)** *Robert Plant*

**Hurt So Good**
'73   Millie Jackson
'82   John Cougar Mellencamp
**Husbands And Wives**
'66   Roger Miller
'98   Brooks & Dunn
**Hush**
'68   Deep Purple
'04   LL Cool J
'65   **Hush, Hush, Sweet Charlotte**
    Patti Page
'59   **Hushabye** Mystics
'75   **Hustle, The** Van McCoy
'71   **Hymn 43** Jethro Tull
'86   **Hyperactive** Robert Palmer
'97   **Hypnotize** Notorious B.I.G.
'87   **Hypnotize Me** Wang Chung
'96   **Hypnotize The Moon** Clay Walker
**Hypnotized**
'67   Linda Jones
'73   Fleetwood Mac
'88   **Hysteria** Def Leppard

**I**

'82   **I.G.Y. (What A Beautiful World)**
    Donald Fagen
'76   **I.O.U.** Jimmy Dean
'63   **I Adore Him** Angels
'91   **I Adore Mi Amor** Color Me Badd
'66   **I Ain't Gonna Eat Out My Heart**
    **Anymore** Rascals
'80   **I Ain't Gonna Stand For It**
    Stevie Wonder
**I Ain't Got Nobody [medley]**
'56   Louis Prima & Keely Smith
'85   David Lee Roth
'71   **I Ain't Got Time Anymore**
    Glass Bottle
'59   **I Ain't Never** Webb Pierce
'73   **I Ain't The One** Lynyrd Skynyrd
'56   **I Almost Lost My Mind** Pat Boone
'94   **I Alone** Live
'66   **I Am A Rock** Simon & Garfunkel
'91   **I Am A Simple Man**
    Ricky Van Shelton
'63   **I Am A Witness** Tommy Hunt
'86   **I Am By Your Side** Corey Hart
'71   **I Am...I Said** Neil Diamond
**I Am Love**
'75   Jackson 5
'83   Jennifer Holliday
'70   **I Am Somebody** Johnnie Taylor
'96   **I Am That Man** Brooks & Dunn
'03   **I Am The Highway** Audioslave
'67   **I Am The Walrus** Beatles
'72   **I Am Woman** Helen Reddy
'58   **I Beg Of You** Elvis Presley
'88   **I Beg Your Pardon** Kon Kan
**I Believe**
'64   Bachelors
'82   Chilliwack
'94   Sounds Of Blackness
'95   Blessid Union Of Souls
'02   Diamond Rio
'04   Fantasia
'96   **I Believe I Can Fly** R. Kelly
'75   **I Believe I'm Gonna Love You**
    Frank Sinatra
'72   **I Believe In Music** Gallery
'80   **I Believe In You** Don Williams
'96   **I Believe In You And Me**
    Whitney Houston
'73   **I Believe In You (You Believe In Me)**
    Johnnie Taylor
'75   **(I Believe) There's Nothing Stronger**
    **Than Our Love**
    Paul Anka/Odia Coates
'77   **I Believe You** Dorothy Moore
**I Belong To You**
'74   Love Unlimited
'94   Toni Braxton
'97   **I Belong To You (Every Time I See**
    **Your Face)** Rome

'02   **I Breathe In, I Breathe Out**
    Chris Cagle
'03   **I Can** Nas
'98   **I Can Do That** Montell Jordan
'84   **I Can Dream About You**
    Dan Hartman
'69   **I Can Hear Music** Beach Boys
'74   **I Can Help** Billy Swan
'97   **I Can Love You** Mary J. Blige
**I Can Love You Like That**
'95   All-4-One
'95   John Michael Montgomery
'66   **I Can Make It With You**
    Pozo-Seco Singers
'65   **I Can Never Go Home Anymore**
    Shangri-Las
'01   **I Can Only Imagine** MercyMe
**I Can See Clearly Now**
'72   Johnny Nash
'93   Jimmy Cliff
'67   **I Can See For Miles** Who
'69   **I Can Sing A Rainbow [medley]**
    Dells
'98   **I Can Still Feel You** Collin Raye
'80   **I Can Survive** Triumph
'81   **I Can Take Care Of Myself**
    Billy Vera & The Beaters
'68   **I Can Take Or Leave Your Loving**
    Herman's Hermits
'73   **I Can Understand It** New Birth
'91   **I Can't Dance** Genesis
'84   **I Can't Drive 55** Sammy Hagar
'65   **I Can't Explain** Who
'69   **I Can't Get Next To You**
    Temptations
**(I Can't Get No) Satisfaction**
'65   Rolling Stones
'66   Otis Redding
'81   **I Can't Go For That (No Can Do)**
    Daryl Hall & John Oates
'66   **I Can't Grow Peaches On A Cherry**
    **Tree** Just Us
'76   **I Can't Hear You No More**
    Helen Reddy
'80   **I Can't Help It**
    Andy Gibb & Olivia Newton-John
'62   **I Can't Help It (If I'm Still In Love**
    **With You)** Johnny Tillotson
**I Can't Help Myself**
'65   Four Tops
'72   Donnie Elbert
'79   Bonnie Pointer
'60   **(I Can't Help You) I'm Falling Too**
    Skeeter Davis
'84   **I Can't Hold Back** Survivor
'80   **I Can't Let Go** Linda Ronstadt
'56   **I Can't Love You Enough**
    LaVern Baker
'91   **I Can't Make You Love Me**
    Bonnie Raitt
'69   **I Can't Quit You Baby**
    Led Zeppelin
'94   **I Can't Reach Her Anymore**
    Sammy Kershaw
'96   **I Can't Sleep Baby (If I)** R. Kelly
'81   **I Can't Stand It** Eric Clapton
'79   **I Can't Stand It No More**
    Peter Frampton
'67   **I Can't Stand Myself (When You**
    **Touch Me)** James Brown
**I Can't Stand The Rain**
'73   Ann Peebles
'78   Eruption
'80   **I Can't Stand Up For Falling Down**
    Elvis Costello
'63   **I Can't Stay Mad At You**
    Skeeter Davis
'68   **I Can't Stop Dancing** Archie Bell
'62   **I Can't Stop Loving You**
    Ray Charles
'63   **I Can't Stop Talking About You**
    Steve & Eydie
'80   **I Can't Tell You Why** Eagles
'68   **I Can't Turn You Loose**
    Chambers Brothers

**I Can't Wait**
'86   Nu Shooz
'86   Stevie Nicks
'04   Sleepy Brown
'91   **I Can't Wait Another Minute** Hi-Five
'97   **I Care 'Bout You** Milestone
'02   **I Care 4 U** Aaliyah
'66   **I Chose To Sing The Blues**
    Ray Charles
'66   **I Confess** New Colony Six
'95   **I Could Fall In Love** Selena
**I Could Have Danced All Night**
'56   Sylvia Syms
'56   Julie Andrews
'68   **I Could Never Love Another (After**
    **Loving You)** Temptations
'81   **I Could Never Miss You (More Than**
    **I Do)** Lulu
'87   **I Could Never Take The Place Of**
    **Your Man** Prince
**I Could Not Ask For More**
'99   Edwin McCain
'01   Sara Evans
'92   **I Could Use A Little Love (Right**
    **Now)** Freddie Jackson
'66   **I Couldn't Live Without Your Love**
    Petula Clark
'60   **I Count The Tears** Drifters
'58   **I Cried A Tear** LaVern Baker
'92   **I Cross My Heart** George Strait
'01   **I Cry** Ja Rule
'01   **I Did It** Dave Matthews Band
'95   **I Didn't Know My Own Strength**
    Lorrie Morgan
'86   **I Didn't Mean To Turn You On**
    Robert Palmer
'90   **I Didn't Want To Need You** Heart
'67   **I Dig Rock And Roll Music**
    Peter, Paul & Mary
'00   **I Disappear** Metallica
**I Do**
'65   Marvelows
'82   J. Geils Band
'96   Paul Brandt
'97   Lisa Loeb
'01   Toya
**I Do [Cherish You]**
'98   Mark Wills
'99   98°
'76   **I Do, I Do, I Do, I Do, I Do** Abba
**I Do Love You**
'65   Billy Stewart
'79   GQ
'60   **(I Do The) Shimmy Shimmy**
    Bobby Freeman
'84   **I Do'wanna Know** REO Speedwagon
'87   **I Do You** Jets
'71   **I Don't Blame You At All** Miracles
'93   **I Don't Call Him Daddy**
    Doug Supernaw
'95   **I Don't Even Know Your Name**
    Alan Jackson
'97   **I Don't Ever Want To See You Again**
    Uncle Sam
'90   **I Don't Have The Heart**
    James Ingram
'02   **I Don't Have To Be Me ('Til Monday)**
    Steve Azar
'90   **I Don't Know Anybody Else**
    Black Box
**I Don't Know How To Love Him**
'71   Yvonne Elliman
'71   Helen Reddy
'79   **I Don't Know If It's Right**
    Evelyn "Champagne" King
'82   **I Don't Know Where To Start**
    Eddie Rabbitt
'61   **I Don't Know Why** Linda Scott
'80   **I Don't Like Mondays**
    Boomtown Rats
'75   **I Don't Like To Sleep Alone**
    Paul Anka/Odia Coates
'87   **I Don't Mind At All** Bourgeois Tagg
'71   **I Don't Need No Doctor** Humble Pie
'81   **I Don't Need You** Kenny Rogers
'00   **I Don't Wanna** Aaliyah

'64 I Don't Wanna Be A Loser
  Lesley Gore
'91 I Don't Wanna Cry  Mariah Carey
'93 I Don't Wanna Fight  Tina Turner
'88 I Don't Wanna Go On With You Like
  That  Elton John
'04 I Don't Wanna Know  Mario Winans
'88 I Don't Wanna Live Without Your
  Love  Chicago
'67 I Don't Wanna Play House
  Tammy Wynette
'95 I Don't Want To Grow Up  Ramones
'91 I Don't Want To Lose Your Love
  B Angie B
'69 I Don't Want Nobody To Give Me
  Nothing  James Brown
'97 I Don't Want To  Toni Braxton
'05 I Don't Want To Be  Gavin DeGraw
'88 I Don't Want To Be A Hero
  Johnny Hates Jazz
'64 I Don't Want To Be Hurt Anymore
  Nat King Cole
'61 I Don't Want To Cry  Chuck Jackson
'71 I Don't Want To Do Wrong
  Gladys Knight
'77 I Don't Want To Know  Fleetwood
  Mac
'88 I Don't Want To Live Without You
  Foreigner
'87 I Don't Want To Lose Your Love
  Freddie Jackson
  I Don't Want To Miss A Thing
'98  Aerosmith
'98  Mark Chesnutt
'64 I Don't Want To See Tomorrow
  Nat King Cole
'64 I Don't Want To See You Again
  Peter & Gordon
'65 I Don't Want To Spoil The Party
  Beatles
'61 I Don't Want To Take A Chance
  Mary Wells
'97 I Don't Want To Wait  Paula Cole
'80 I Don't Want To Walk Without You
  Barry Manilow
'88 I Don't Want Your Love
  Duran Duran
'56 I Dreamed  Betty Johnson
'75 I Dreamed Last Night  Moody Blues
'61 I Dreamed Of A Hill-Billy Heaven
  Tex Ritter
'85 I Drink Alone
  George Thorogood
'89 I Drove All Night  Cyndi Lauper
'83 I Eat Cannibals  Total Coelo
'61 I Fall To Pieces  Patsy Cline
'74 I Feel A Song (In My Heart)
  Gladys Knight
'64 I Feel Fine  Beatles
'84 I Feel For You  Chaka Khan
'67 I Feel Free  Cream
'56 I Feel Good  Shirley & Lee
'87 I Feel Good All Over  Stephanie Mills
'67 I-Feel-Like-I'm-Fixin'-To-Die-
  Rag  Country Joe & The Fish
'77 I Feel Love  Donna Summer
'92 I Feel Lucky  Mary Chapin Carpenter
'61 I Feel So Bad  Elvis Presley
  I Feel The Earth Move
'71  Carole King
'89  Martika
'93 I Feel You  Depeche Mode
'90 I Fell In Love  Carlene Carter
'96 I Finally Found Someone
  Barbra Streisand & Bryan Adams
'66 I Fooled You This Time
  Gene Chandler
'66 I Fought The Law  Bobby Fuller Four
'65 I Found A Girl  Jan & Dean
'67 I Found A Love  Wilson Pickett
'82 I Found Somebody  Glenn Frey
'87 I Found Someone  Cher
'62 I Get A Kick Out Of You
  Frank Sinatra
  I Get Around
'64  Beach Boys
'93  2Pac

'82 I Get Excited  Rick Springfield
'75 I Get Lifted  George McCrae
'98 I Get Lonely  Janet Jackson
'88 I Get Weak  Belinda Carlisle
'04 I Go Back  Kenny Chesney
'96 I Go Blind  Hootie & The Blowfish
'77 I Go Crazy  Paul Davis
'90 I Go To Extremes  Billy Joel
'65 I Go To Pieces  Peter & Gordon
'79 I Go To Rio  Pablo Cruise
'72 I Got A Bag Of My Own
  James Brown
'58 I Got A Feeling  Ricky Nelson
'69 I Got A Line On You  Spirit
'92 I Got A Man  Positive K
'73 I Got A Name  Jim Croce
'92 I Got A Thang 4 Ya!  Lo-Key?
'59 I Got A Wife  Mark IV
'62 I Got A Woman  Jimmy McGriff
'73 I Got Ants In My Pants
  James Brown
'95 I Got 5 On It  Luniz
'95 I Got Id  Pearl Jam
'79 I Got My Mind Made Up (You Can
  Get It Girl)  Instant Funk
'67 I Got Rhythm  Happenings
'75 I Got Stoned And I Missed It
  Jim Stafford
'59 I Got Stripes  Johnny Cash
'58 I Got Stung  Elvis Presley
'68 I Got The Feelin'  James Brown
'66 I Got The Feelin' (Oh No No)
  Neil Diamond
'98 I Got The Hook Up!  Master P
'63 I Got What I Wanted  Brook Benton
'80 I Got You  Split Enz
'65 I Got You Babe  Sonny & Cher
'65 I Got You (I Feel Good)
  James Brown
'72 I Gotcha  Joe Tex
'63 I Gotta Dance To Keep From Crying
  Miracles
'60 I Gotta Know  Elvis Presley
'83 I Guess That's Why They Call It The
  Blues  Elton John
'69 I Guess The Lord Must Be In New
  York City  Nilsson
'67 I Had A Dream
  Paul Revere & The Raiders
'64 I Had A Talk With My Man
  Mitty Collier
'66 I Had Too Much To Dream (Last
  Night)  Electric Prunes
'04 I Hate Everything  George Strait
'03 (I Hate) Everything About You
  Three Days Grace
'88 I Hate Myself For Loving You
  Joan Jett
'95 I Hate U  Prince
'63 I Have A Boyfriend  Chiffons
'86 I Have Learned To Respect The
  Power Of Love  Stephanie Mills
'93 I Have Nothing  Whitney Houston
'65 I Hear A Symphony  Supremes
'66 I Hear Trumpets Blow  Tokens
  I Hear You Knocking
'55  Smiley Lewis
'55  Gale Storm
'70  Dave Edmunds
'87 I Heard A Rumour  Bananarama
  I Heard It Through The Grapevine
'67  Gladys Knight
'68  Marvin Gaye
'70  Creedence Clearwater Revival
'81  Roger
'74 I Honestly Love You
  Olivia Newton-John
'00 I Hope You Dance  Lee Ann Womack
'84 I Just Called To Say I Love You
  Stevie Wonder
'70 I Just Can't Help Believing
  B.J. Thomas
'87 I Just Can't Stop Loving You
  Michael Jackson
'87 (I Just) Died In Your Arms
  Cutting Crew
'57 I Just Don't Know  Four Lads

'66 I Just Don't Know What To Do With
  Myself  Dionne Warwick
'61 I Just Don't Understand
  Ann-Margret
'79 I Just Fall In Love Again
  Anne Murray
'02 I Just Wanna Be Mad  Terri Clark
'00 I Just Wanna Love U (Give It 2 Me)
  Jay-Z
'78 I Just Wanna Stop  Gino Vannelli
'79 I Just Want To Be  Cameo
'77 I Just Want To Be Your Everything
  Andy Gibb
'71 I Just Want To Celebrate  Rare Earth
'98 I Just Want To Dance With You
  George Strait
'77 I Just Want To Make Love To You
  Foghat [live]
'93 I Just Wanted You To Know
  Mark Chesnutt
'82 I Keep Forgettin' (Every Time
  You're Near)  Michael McDonald
'02 I Keep Looking  Sara Evans
'99 I Knew I Loved You  Savage Garden
'87 I Knew You Were Waiting (For Me)
  Aretha Franklin & George Michael
  I Knew You When
'65  Billy Joe Royal
'82  Linda Ronstadt
'95 I Know  Dionne Farris
'79 I Know A Heartache When I See
  One  Jennifer Warnes
'65 I Know A Place  Petula Clark
'93 (I Know I Got) Skillz
  Shaquille O'Neal
  (I Know) I'm Losing You
'66  Temptations
'70  Rare Earth
'71  Rod Stewart With Faces
'82 I Know There's Something Going
  On  Frida
'87 I Know What I Like  Huey Lewis
'03 I Know What You Want  Busta
  Rhymes & Mariah Carey
'98 I Know Where It's At  All Saints
'61 I Know (You Don't Love Me No
  More)  Barbara George
'87 I Know You Got Soul
  Eric B & Rakim
'88 I Know You're Out There
  Somewhere  Moody Blues
'00 I Learned From The Best
  Whitney Houston
'62 I Left My Heart In San Francisco
  Tony Bennett
'97 I Left Something Turned On At
  Home  Trace Adkins
'98 I Lie In The Bed I Make
  Brother Cane
  I Like
'89  Guy
'95  Kut Klose
'96  Montell Jordan
'76 I Like Dreamin'  Kenny Nolan
'78 I Like Girls  Fatback
  I Like It
'64  Gerry & The Pacemakers
'83  DeBarge
'89  Dino
'96  Blackout Allstars
'00  Sammie
'95 I Like It, I Love It  Tim McGraw
  I Like It Like That
'61  Chris Kenner
'64  Miracles
'65  Dave Clark Five
'04 I Like That  Houston
'67 I Like The Way  Tommy James
'91 I Like The Way (The Kissing Game)
  Hi-Five
'76 I Like To Do It
  KC & The Sunshine Band
'73 I Like To Live The Love  B.B. King
'80 I Like To Rock  April Wine
'57 I Like Your Kind Of Love
  Andy Williams
'71 I Likes To Do It  People's Choice

'89 **I Live By The Groove** *Paul Carrack*
'80 **I Live For The Weekend** *Triumph*
'87 **I Live For Your Love** *Natalie Cole*
'95 **I Live My Life For You** *Firehouse*
'00 **I Lost It** *Kenny Chesney*
'73 **I Love** *Tom T. Hall*
'80 **I Love A Rainy Night** *Eddie Rabbitt*
**I Love How You Love Me**
'61   *Paris Sisters*
'68   *Bobby Vinton*
'75 **I Love Music** *O'Jays*
'56 **I Love My Baby (My Baby Loves Me)** *Jill Corey*
'74 **I Love My Friend** *Charlie Rich*
'82 **I Love Rock 'N Roll** *Joan Jett*
'78 **I Love The Nightlife (Disco 'Round)** *Alicia Bridges*
'60 **I Love The Way You Love** *Marv Johnson*
'93 **I Love The Way You Love Me** *John Michael Montgomery*
'03 **I Love This Bar** *Toby Keith*
**I Love You**
'62   *Volume's*
'68   *People*
'77   *Donna Summer*
'81   *Climax Blues Band*
'99   *Martina McBride*
'02   *Faith Evans*
'96 **I Love You Always Forever** *Donna Lewis*
'63 **I Love You Because** *Al Martino*
'63 **(I Love You) Don't You Forget It** *Perry Como*
'66 **I Love You Drops** *Vic Dana*
'71 **I Love You For All Seasons** *Fuzz*
'57 **(I Love You) For Sentimental Reasons** *Sam Cooke*
'55 **I Love You Madly** *Four Coins*
'64 **I Love You More And More Every Day** *Al Martino*
'66 **I Love You 1000 Times** *Platters*
'91 **I Love Your Smile** *Shanice*
'81 **I Loved 'Em Every One** *T.G. Sheppard*
'59 **I Loves You, Porgy** *Nina Simone*
'80 **I Made It Through The Rain** *Barry Manilow*
'67 **I Make A Fool Of Myself** *Frankie Valli*
'03 **I Melt** *Rascal Flatts*
'83 **I Melt With You** *Modern English*
'68 **I Met Her In Church** *Box Tops*
'58 **I Met Him On A Sunday** *Shirelles*
'02 **I Miss My Friend** *Darryl Worley*
'97 **I Miss My Homies** *Master P*
**I Miss You**
'85   *Klymaxx*
'94   *Aaron Hall*
'94   *NIIU*
'04   *Blink-182*
**I Miss You So**
'56   *Chris Connor*
'59   *Paul Anka*
'65   *Little Anthony & The Imperials*
'81 **I Missed Again** *Phil Collins*
'60 **I Missed Me** *Jim Reeves*
'65 **I Must Be Seeing Things** *Gene Pitney*
'02 **I Need A Girl (Part One)** *P. Diddy*
'02 **I Need A Girl (Part Two)** *P. Diddy & Ginuwine*
**I Need A Lover**
'79   *Pat Benatar*
'79   *John Cougar Mellencamp*
'87 **I Need Love** *LL Cool J*
'66 **I Need Somebody** *? (Question Mark) & The Mysterians*
'76 **I Need To Be In Love** *Carpenters*
**I Need To Know**
'78   *Tom Petty*
'99   *Marc Anthony*

**I Need You**
'72   *America*
'82   *Paul Carrack*
'00   *LeAnn Rimes*
'02   *Jars Of Clay*
'54 **I Need You Now** *Eddie Fisher*
'84 **I Need You Tonight** *Peter Wolf*
'59 **I Need Your Love Tonight** *Elvis Presley*
'80 **I Need Your Lovin'** *Teena Marie*
'62 **I Need Your Loving** *Don Gardner & Dee Dee Ford*
'76 **I Never Cry** *Alice Cooper*
'93 **I Never Knew Love** *Doug Stone*
'67 **I Never Loved A Man (The Way I Love You)** *Aretha Franklin*
'79 **I Never Said I Love You** *Orsa Lia*
'94 **I Never Seen A Man Cry (aka I Seen A Man Die)** *Scarface*
**I Only Have Eyes For You**
'59   *Flamingos*
'75   *Art Garfunkel*
'56 **I Only Know I Love You** *Four Aces*
**I Only Want To Be With You**
'64   *Dusty Springfield*
'76   *Bay City Rollers*
'89   *Samantha Fox*
'61 **I Pity The Fool** *Bobby Bland*
'71 **I Play And Sing** *Dawn*
'80 **I Pledge My Love** *Peaches & Herb*
**I Put A Spell On You**
'56   *Screamin' Jay Hawkins*
'68   *Creedence Clearwater Revival*
'82 **I Ran (So Far Away)** *Flock Of Seagulls*
'82 **I Really Don't Need No Light** *Jeffrey Osborne*
**I Really Don't Want To Know**
'60   *Tommy Edwards*
'66   *Ronnie Dove*
'70   *Elvis Presley*
'61 **I Really Love You** *Stereos*
'88 **I Remember Holding You** *Boys Club*
**I Remember You**
'62   *Frank Ifield*
'89   *Skid Row*
'64 **I Rise, I Fall** *Johnny Tillotson*
'77 **I Robot** *Alan Parsons Project*
'66 **I Saw Her Again** *Mamas & The Papas*
**I Saw Her [Him] Standing There**
'64   *Beatles*
'88   *Tiffany*
'62 **I Saw Linda Yesterday** *Dickey Lee*
'90 **I Saw Red** *Warrant*
**I Saw The Light**
'72   *Todd Rundgren*
'92   *Wynonna*
**I Say A Little Prayer**
'67   *Dionne Warwick*
'68   *Aretha Franklin*
'97   *Diana King*
'67 **I Second That Emotion** *Miracles*
'94 **I See It Now** *Tracy Lawrence*
'66 **I See The Light** *Five Americans*
'93 **I See Your Smile** *Gloria Estefan*
'68 **I Shall Be Released** *Band*
'73 **I Shall Sing** *Art Garfunkel*
**I Shot The Sheriff**
'73   *Bob Marley*
'74   *Eric Clapton*
'97   *Warren G*
'02 **I Should Be...** *Dru Hill*
'02 **I Should Be Sleeping** *Emerson Drive*
'88 **I Should Be So Lucky** *Kylie Minogue*
'64 **I Should Have Known Better** *Beatles*
'64 **I Stand Accused** *Jerry Butler*
'02 **I Stand Alone** *Godsmack*
'68 **I Started A Joke** *Bee Gees*
**I Still Believe**
'88   *Brenda K. Starr*
'99   *Mariah Carey*
'92 **I Still Believe In You** *Vince Gill*

'83 **I Still Can't Get Over Loving You** *Ray Parker Jr.*
'87 **I Still Haven't Found What I'm Looking For** *U2*
'98 **I Still Love You** *Next*
**I Swear**
'93   *John Michael Montgomery*
'94   *All-4-One*
'67 **I Take It Back** *Sandy Posey*
'94 **I Take My Chances** *Mary Chapin Carpenter*
'67 **I Thank The Lord For The Night Time** *Neil Diamond*
**I Thank You**
'68   *Sam & Dave*
'80   *ZZ Top*
'70 **I Think I Love You** *Partridge Family*
'59 **I Think I'm Gonna Kill Myself** *Buddy Knox*
'00 **I Think I'm In Love With You** *Jessica Simpson*
'86 **I Think It's Love** *Jermaine Jackson*
**I Think We're Alone Now**
'67   *Tommy James*
'87   *Tiffany*
'69 **I Threw It All Away** *Bob Dylan*
'91 **I Touch Myself** *Divinyls*
'00 **I Try** *Macy Gray*
'94 **I Try To Think About Elvis** *Patty Loveless*
'00 **I Turn To You** *Christina Aguilera*
'69 **I Turned You On** *Isley Brothers*
**I Understand (Just How You Feel)**
'61   *G-Clefs*
'65   *Freddie & The Dreamers*
'59 **I Waited Too Long** *LaVern Baker*
'56 **I Walk The Line** *Johnny Cash*
'86 **I Wanna Be A Cowboy** *Boys Don't Cry*
'63 **I Wanna Be Around** *Tony Bennett*
'01 **I Wanna Be Bad** *Willa Ford*
'94 **I Wanna Be Down** *Brandy*
'59 **I Wanna Be Loved** *Ricky Nelson*
'90 **I Wanna Be Rich** *Calloway*
'78 **I Wanna Be Sedated** *Ramones*
'89 **I Wanna Be The One** *Stevie B*
'97 **I Wanna Be There** *Blessid Union Of Souls*
'72 **I Wanna Be Where You Are** *Michael Jackson*
**I Wanna Be With You**
'72   *Raspberries*
'79   *Isley Brothers*
'00   *Mandy Moore*
'69 **I Wanna Be Your Dog** *Stooges*
'79 **I Wanna Be Your Lover** *Prince*
'75 **I Wanna Dance Wit' Choo** *Disco Tex & The Sex-O-Lettes*
'87 **I Wanna Dance With Somebody (Who Loves Me)** *Whitney Houston*
'03 **I Wanna Do It All** *Terri Clark*
'97 **I Wanna Fall In Love** *Lila McCann*
'77 **I Wanna Get Next To You** *Rose Royce*
'86 **I Wanna Go Back** *Eddie Money*
'88 **I Wanna Have Some Fun** *Samantha Fox*
'85 **I Wanna Hear It From Your Lips** *Eric Carmen*
'00 **I Wanna Know** *Joe*
'68 **I Wanna Live** *Glen Campbell*
'64 **I Wanna Love Him So Bad** *Jelly Beans*
'61 **(I Wanna) Love My Life Away** *Gene Pitney*
'92 **I Wanna Love You** *Jade*
'99 **I Wanna Love You Forever** *Jessica Simpson*
'91 **I Wanna Sex You Up** *Color Me Badd*
'01 **I Wanna Talk About Me** *Toby Keith*
**(I Wanna) Testify**
'67   *Parliaments*
'69   *Johnnie Taylor*
'61 **I Wanna Thank You** *Bobby Rydell*
'84 **I Want A New Drug** *Huey Lewis*

I Want Candy
'65 *Strangeloves*
'82 *Bow Wow Wow*
'88 I Want Her *Keith Sweat*
I Want It All
'89 *Queen*
'99 *Warren G*
'99 I Want It That Way *Backstreet Boys*
'60 I Want To Be Wanted *Brenda Lee*
'87 I Want To Be Your Man *Roger*
'96 I Want To Come Over
  *Melissa Etheridge*
'65 I Want To (Do Everything For You)
  *Joe Tex*
'55 I Want To Do More *Ruth Brown*
'66 I Want To Go With You *Eddy Arnold*
'64 I Want To Hold Your Hand *Beatles*
'84 I Want To Know What Love Is
  *Foreigner*
'86 I Want To Make The World Turn
  Around *Steve Miller Band*
'63 I Want To Stay Here *Steve & Eydie*
I Want To Take You Higher
'69 *Sly & The Family Stone*
'70 *Ike & Tina Turner*
'59 I Want To Walk You Home
  *Fats Domino*
I Want You
'66 *Bob Dylan*
'76 *Marvin Gaye*
'89 *Shana*
'91 *Robert Palmer [medley]*
'97 *Savage Garden*
'03 *Thalia*
I Want You Back
'69 *Jackson 5*
'98 *'N Sync*
'56 I Want You, I Need You, I Love You
  *Elvis Presley*
'55 I Want You To Be My Baby
  *Georgia Gibbs*
'56 I Want You To Be My Girl
  *Frankie Lymon*
'57 I Want You To Know *Fats Domino*
'64 I Want You To Meet My Baby
  *Eydie Gorme*
'79 I Want You To Want Me *Cheap Trick*
'79 I Want You Tonight *Pablo Cruise*
'79 I Want Your Love *Chic*
'87 I Want Your Sex *George Michael*
'75 I Want'a Do Something Freaky To
  You *Leon Haywood*
'62 (I Was) Born To Cry *Dion*
'73 I Was Checkin' Out She Was
  Checkin' In *Don Covay*
'81 I Was Country When Country
  Wasn't Cool *Barbara Mandrell*
'67 I Was Kaiser Bill's Batman
  *Whistling Jack Smith*
'78 I Was Made For Dancin' *Leif Garrett*
'79 I Was Made For Lovin' You *Kiss*
'67 I Was Made To Love Her
  *Stevie Wonder*
'78 I Was Only Joking *Rod Stewart*
'56 I Was The One *Elvis Presley*
'66 (I Washed My Hands In) Muddy
  Water *Johnny Rivers*
I (Who Have Nothing)
'63 *Ben E. King*
'70 *Tom Jones*
'79 *Sylvester*
'65 I Will *Dean Martin*
I Will Always Love You
'74 *Dolly Parton*
'92 *Whitney Houston*
'95 *Dolly Parton with Vince Gill*
'68 I Will Always Think About You
  *New Colony Six*
'92 I Will Be Here For You
  *Michael W. Smith*
'78 I Will Be In Love With You
  *Livingston Taylor*
'87 I Will Be There *Glass Tiger*
'00 I Will...But *SheDaisy*
'98 I Will Buy You A New Life *Everclear*
'97 I Will Come To You *Hanson*

'84 I Will Dare *Replacements*
I Will Follow
'81 *U2*
'83 *U2 [live]*
'63 I Will Follow Him *Little Peggy March*
'00 I Will Love Again *Lara Fabian*
'89 I Will Not Go Quietly *Don Henley*
I Will Remember You
'92 *Amy Grant*
'99 *Sarah McLachlan [live]*
'78 I Will Still Love You *Stonebolt*
I Will Survive
'78 *Gloria Gaynor*
'96 *Chantay Savage*
'98 I Will Wait *Hootie & The Blowfish*
I Wish
'76 *Stevie Wonder*
'95 *Skee-Lo*
'00 *R. Kelly*
'00 *Carl Thomas*
'85 I Wish He Didn't Trust Me So Much
  *Bobby Womack*
'88 I Wish I Had A Girl
  *Henry Lee Summer*
'63 I Wish I Were A Princess
  *Little Peggy March*
'68 I Wish It Would Rain *Temptations*
'90 I Wish It Would Rain Down
  *Phil Collins*
'62 I Wish That We Were Married
  *Ronnie & The Hi-Lites*
'92 I Wish The Phone Would Ring
  *Exposé*
'64 I Wish You Love *Gloria Lynne*
'71 I Woke Up In Love This Morning
  *Partridge Family*
'89 I Won't Back Down *Tom Petty*
'87 I Won't Forget You *Poison*
'83 I Won't Hold You Back *Toto*
'74 I Won't Last A Day Without You
  *Carpenters*
'83 I Won't Stand In Your Way
  *Stray Cats*
'63 I Wonder *Brenda Lee*
'85 I Wonder If I Take You Home
  *Lisa-Lisa & Cult Jam*
I Wonder What She's Doing Tonight
  [Tonite]
'63 *Barry & The Tamerlanes*
'67 *Tommy Boyce & Bobby Hart*
I Wonder Why
'58 *Dion & The Belmonts*
'91 *Curtis Stigers*
'84 I Would Die 4 U *Prince*
'81 I Wouldn't Have Missed It For The
  World *Ronnie Milsap*
'74 I Wouldn't Treat A Dog (The Way
  You Treated Me) *Bobby Bland*
'77 I Wouldn't Want To Be Like You
  *Alan Parsons*
'75 I Write The Songs *Barry Manilow*
'92 I'd Die Without You *PM Dawn*
'93 I'd Do Anything For Love (But I
  Won't Do That) *Meat Loaf*
'94 I'd Give Anything *Gerald Levert*
'95 I'd Lie For You (And That's The
  Truth) *Meat Loaf*
I'd Like To Teach The World To
  Sing
'71 *Hillside Singers*
'71 *New Seekers*
'71 I'd Love To Change The World
  *Ten Years After*
'91 I'd Love You All Over Again
  *Alan Jackson*
'72 I'd Love You To Want Me *Lobo*
'79 I'd Rather Leave While I'm In Love
  *Rita Coolidge*
'97 I'd Rather Ride Around With You
  *Reba McEntire*
'76 I'd Really Love To See You Tonight
  *England Dan & John Ford Coley*
'87 I'd Still Say Yes *Klymaxx*
'69 I'd Wait A Million Years *Grass Roots*
'97 I'll Always Be Right There
  *Bryan Adams*
'73 I'll Always Love My Mama *Intruders*

I'll Always Love You
'65 *Spinners*
'88 *Taylor Dayne*
I'll Be
'97 *Foxy Brown*
'98 *Edwin McCain*
'86 I'll Be Alright Without You *Journey*
I'll Be Around
'72 *Spinners*
'95 *Rappin' 4-Tay*
'91 I'll Be By Your Side *Stevie B*
'65 I'll Be Doggone *Marvin Gaye*
I'll Be Good To You
'76 *Brothers Johnson*
'89 *Quincy Jones/Ray Charles/Chaka
  Khan*
'56 I'll Be Home *Pat Boone*
'89 I'll Be Loving You (Forever)
  *New Kids On The Block*
'97 I'll Be Missing You
  *Puff Daddy & Faith Evans*
'86 I'll Be Over You *Toto*
'59 I'll Be Satisfied *Jackie Wilson*
'74 I'll Be The Other Woman
  *Soul Children*
I'll Be There
'61 *Damita Jo*
'64 *Gerry & The Pacemakers*
'70 *Jackson 5*
'91 *Escape Club*
'92 *Mariah Carey*
I'll Be There For You
'89 *Bon Jovi*
'89 *Ashford & Simpson*
'95 *Method Man ft. Mary J. Blige
  [medley]*
'95 I'll Be There For You (Theme from
  "Friends") *Rembrandts*
'59 (I'll Be With You In) Apple Blossom
  Time *Tab Hunter*
'89 I'll Be You *Replacements*
'90 I'll Be Your Everything
  *Tommy Page*
'90 I'll Be Your Shelter *Taylor Dayne*
'72 I'll Be Your Shelter (In Time Of
  Storm) *Luther Ingram*
'57 I'll Come Running Back To You
  *Sam Cooke*
'64 I'll Cry Instead *Beatles*
'91 I'll Do 4 U *Father M.C.*
'75 I'll Do For You Anything You Want
  Me To *Barry White*
'82 I'll Fall In Love Again *Sammy Hagar*
'65 I'll Feel A Whole Lot Better *Byrds*
'91 I'll Get By *Eddie Money*
'90 I'll Give All My Love To You
  *Keith Sweat*
'98 I'll Go On Loving You *Alan Jackson*
'74 I'll Have To Say I Love You In A
  Song *Jim Croce*
'65 I'll Keep Holding On *Marvelettes*
'64 I'll Keep You Satisfied
  *Billy J. Kramer With The Dakotas*
'88 I'll Leave This World Loving You
  *Ricky Van Shelton*
'65 I'll Make All Your Dreams Come
  True *Ronnie Dove*
'94 I'll Make Love To You *Boyz II Men*
'71 I'll Meet You Halfway
  *Partridge Family*
'98 I'll Never Break Your Heart
  *Backstreet Boys*
'62 I'll Never Dance Again *Bobby Rydell*
I'll Never Fall In Love Again
'67 *Tom Jones*
'69 *Dionne Warwick*
'65 I'll Never Find Another You *Seekers*
'93 I'll Never Get Over You (Getting
  Over Me) *Exposé*
'91 I'll Never Let You Go (Angel Eyes)
  *Steelheart*
'79 I'll Never Love This Way Again
  *Dionne Warwick*
'61 I'll Never Smile Again *Platters*
'55 I'll Never Stop Loving You
  *Doris Day*
'75 I'll Play For You *Seals & Crofts*

'94 **I'll Remember** *Madonna*
'57 **I'll Remember Today** *Patti Page*
'58 **I'll Remember Tonight** *Pat Boone*
'60 **I'll Save The Last Dance For You**
*Damita Jo*
'90 **I'll See You In My Dreams** *Giant*
'94 **I'll Stand By You** *Pretenders*
'87 **I'll Still Be Loving You**
*Restless Heart*
'78 **I'll Supply The Love** *Toto*
'59 **I'll Take Care Of You** *Bobby Bland*
'67 **I'll Take Care Of Your Cares**
*Frankie Laine*
'66 **I'll Take Good Care Of You**
*Garnet Mimms*
'63 **I'll Take You Home** *Drifters*
**I'll Take You There**
'72 *Staple Singers*
'91 *BeBe & CeCe Winans*
'94 *General Public*
'99 **I'll Think Of A Reason Later**
*Lee Ann Womack*
'92 **I'll Think Of Something**
*Mark Chesnutt*
'64 **I'll Touch A Star** *Terry Stafford*
'95 **I'll Try** *Alan Jackson*
'67 **I'll Try Anything** *Dusty Springfield*
**I'll Try Something New**
'62 *Miracles*
'69 *Supremes & Temptations*
'83 **I'll Tumble 4 Ya** *Culture Club*
'84 **I'll Wait** *Van Halen*
'58 **I'll Wait For You** *Frankie Avalon*
**I'm A Believer**
'66 *Monkees*
'01 *Smash Mouth*
'69 **I'm A Better Man**
*Engelbert Humperdinck*
'65 **I'm A Fool** *Dino, Desi & Billy*
'61 **I'm A Fool To Care** *Joe Barry*
'65 **I'm A Happy Man** *Jive Five*
'59 **I'm A Hog For You** *Coasters*
'05 **I'm A Hustla** *Cassidy*
'57 **I'm A King Bee** *Slim Harpo*
'65 **I'm A Loser** *Beatles*
**I'm A Man**
'55 *Bo Diddley*
'59 *Fabian*
'65 *Yardbirds*
'67 *Spencer Davis Group*
'69 *Chicago*
'68 **I'm A Midnight Mover** *Wilson Pickett*
'66 **(I'm A) Road Runner** *Jr. Walker*
'01 **I'm A Slave 4 U** *Britney Spears*
'01 **I'm A Survivor** *Reba McEntire*
'61 **I'm A Telling You** *Jerry Butler*
'01 **I'm A Thug** *Trick Daddy*
'74 **I'm A Train** *Albert Hammond*
'74 **I'm A Woman** *Maria Muldaur*
**I'm Alive**
'80 *Electric Light Orchestra*
'83 *Neil Diamond*
'80 **I'm Almost Ready**
*Pure Prairie League*
'99 **I'm Already Taken** *Steve Wariner*
'01 **I'm Already There** *Lonestar*
**I'm Alright**
'80 *Kenny Loggins*
'98 *Jo Dee Messina*
'55 **(I'm Always Hearing) Wedding Bells**
*Eddie Fisher*
'57 **I'm Available** *Margie Rayburn*
'80 **I'm Bad, I'm Nationwide**
*ZZ Top*
'62 **I'm Blue (The Gong-Gong Song)**
*Ikettes*
'71 **I'm Comin' Home** *Tommy James*
'66 **I'm Comin' Home, Cindy** *Trini Lopez*
'61 **I'm Comin' On On Back To You**
*Jackie Wilson*
**I'm Coming Home**
'73 *Johnny Mathis*
'74 *Spinners*
'80 **I'm Coming Out** *Diana Ross*
'64 **I'm Crying** *Animals*
'73 **I'm Doin' Fine Now** *New York City*

'91 **I'm Dreamin'** *Christopher Williams*
'76 **I'm Easy** *Keith Carradine*
**I'm Every Woman**
'78 *Chaka Khan*
'93 *Whitney Houston*
'86 **I'm For Real** *Howard Hewett*
**I'm Free**
'69 *Who*
'90 *Soup Dragons*
'93 *Jon Secada*
'84 **I'm Free (Heaven Helps The Man)**
*Kenny Loggins*
'98 **I'm From The Country** *Tracy Byrd*
'60 **I'm Gettin' Better** *Jim Reeves*
'03 **I'm Glad** *Jennifer Lopez*
**I'm Goin' Down**
'85 *Bruce Springsteen*
'95 *Mary J. Blige*
'59 **I'm Gonna Be A Wheel Some Day**
*Fats Domino*
'02 **I'm Gonna Be Alright** *Jennifer Lopez*
'93 **I'm Gonna Be (500 Miles)**
*Proclaimers*
'64 **I'm Gonna Be Strong** *Gene Pitney*
'62 **I'm Gonna' Be Warm This Winter**
*Connie Francis*
'59 **I'm Gonna Get Married** *Lloyd Price*
'02 **I'm Gonna Getcha Good!**
*Shania Twain*
'61 **I'm Gonna Knock On Your Door**
*Eddie Hodges*
'73 **I'm Gonna Love You Just A Little**
**More Baby** *Barry White*
'58 **I'm Gonna Love You Too**
*Buddy Holly*
**I'm Gonna Make You Love Me**
'68 *Madeline Bell*
'68 *Supremes & Temptations*
'69 **I'm Gonna Make You Mine**
*Lou Christie*
'02 **I'm Gonna Miss Her (The Fishin'**
**Song)** *Brad Paisley*
'57 **I'm Gonna Sit Right Down And**
**Write Myself A Letter**
*Billy Williams*
'78 **I'm Gonna Take Care Of Everything**
*Rubicon*
'85 **I'm Gonna Tear Your Playhouse**
**Down** *Paul Young*
'80 **I'm Happy That Love Has Found**
**You** *Jimmy Hall*
'65 **I'm Henry VIII, I Am**
*Herman's Hermits*
'60 **I'm Hurtin'** *Roy Orbison*
'92 **I'm In A Hurry (And Don't Know**
**Why)** *Alabama*
**I'm In Love**
'74 *Aretha Franklin*
'81 *Evelyn King*
'56 **I'm In Love Again** *Fats Domino*
'94 **I'm In The Mood** *Ce Ce Peniston*
'61 **I'm In The Mood For Love** *Chimes*
'77 **I'm In You** *Peter Frampton*
**I'm Into Somethin' Good**
'64 *Earl-Jean*
'64 *Herman's Hermits*
'73 **I'm Just A Singer (In A Rock And**
**Roll Band)** *Moody Blues*
'01 **I'm Just Talkin' About Tonight**
*Toby Keith*
'61 **I'm Learning About Love**
*Brenda Lee*
**I'm Leaving It Up To You**
'63 *Dale & Grace*
'74 *Donny & Marie Osmond*
'01 **I'm Like A Bird** *Nelly Furtado*
'69 **I'm Livin' In Shame** *Supremes*
'59 **I'm Movin' On** *Ray Charles*
'72 **I'm Never Gonna Be Alone**
**Anymore** *Cornelius*
*Brothers & Sister Rose*
'59 **I'm Never Gonna Tell**
*Jimmie Rodgers*
'87 **I'm No Angel** *Gregg Allman Band*
'89 **I'm No Stranger To The Rain**
*Keith Whitley*
'60 **I'm Not Afraid** *Ricky Nelson*

'96 **I'm Not Giving You Up**
*Gloria Estefan*
'78 **I'm Not Gonna Let It Bother Me**
**Tonight** *Atlanta Rhythm Section*
**I'm Not In Love**
'75 *10cc*
'90 *Will To Power*
'75 **I'm Not Lisa** *Jessi Colter*
'70 **I'm Not My Brothers Keeper**
*Flaming Ember*
'99 **I'm Not Ready** *Keith Sweat*
'99 **I'm Not Running Anymore** *John*
*Mellencamp*
'95 **I'm Not Strong Enough To Say No**
*BlackHawk*
'86 **I'm Not The One** *Cars*
'88 **I'm Not Your Man** *Tommy Conwell*
'66 **(I'm Not Your) Steppin' Stone**
*Monkees*
**I'm On Fire**
'75 *Dwight Twilley Band*
'75 *5000 Volts*
'85 *Bruce Springsteen*
'64 **I'm On The Outside (Looking In)**
*Little Anthony & The Imperials*
**I'm Ready**
'59 *Fats Domino*
'94 *Tevin Campbell*
'66 **I'm Ready For Love**
*Martha & The Vandellas*
**I'm Real**
'88 *James Brown*
'01 *Jennifer Lopez*
'82 **I'm So Excited** *Pointers Sisters*
**I'm So Happy I Can't Stop Crying**
'96 *Sting*
'97 *Toby Keith with Sting*
**I'm So Into You**
'78 *Peabo Bryson*
'93 *SWV*
'66 **I'm So Lonesome I Could Cry**
*B.J. Thomas*
'64 **I'm So Proud** *Impressions*
**I'm Sorry**
'57 *Platters*
'60 *Brenda Lee*
'75 *John Denver*
'57 **I'm Stickin' With You** *Jimmy Bowen*
**I'm Still In Love With You**
'72 *Al Green*
'96 *New Edition*
'04 *Sean Paul*
'88 **I'm Still Searching** *Glass Tiger*
'83 **I'm Still Standing** *Elton John*
'72 **I'm Stone In Love With You**
*Stylistics*
'65 **I'm Telling You Now**
*Freddie & The Dreamers*
'89 **I'm That Type Of Guy** *LL Cool J*
'62 **(I'm The Girl On) Wolverton**
**Mountain** *Jo Ann Campbell*
'92 **I'm The One You Need** *Jody Watley*
'94 **I'm The Only One** *Melissa Etheridge*
'91 **I'm Too Sexy**
*R*S*F (Right Said Fred)*
'67 **I'm Waiting For The Man**
*Velvet Underground*
**I'm Walkin'**
'57 *Fats Domino*
'57 *Ricky Nelson*
'02 **I'm With You** *Avril Lavigne*
'67 **I'm Wondering** *Stevie Wonder*
'98 **I'm Your Angel**
*R. Kelly & Celine Dion*
'90 **I'm Your Baby Tonight**
*Whitney Houston*
'77 **I'm Your Boogie Man**
*KC & The Sunshine Band*
'70 **I'm Your Captain [medley]**
*Grand Funk Railroad*
'85 **I'm Your Man** *Wham!*
'66 **I'm Your Puppet**
*James & Bobby Purify*
'65 **I'm Yours** *Elvis Presley*
'62 **I've Been Everywhere** *Hank Snow*
'69 **I've Been Hurt** *Bill Deal*

'87 I've Been In Love Before
  Cutting Crew
'72 I've Been Lonely For So Long
  Frederick Knight
'67 I've Been Lonely Too Long
  Young Rascals
'65 I've Been Loving You Too Long (To
  Stop Now) Otis Redding
'74 (I've Been) Searchin' So Long
  Chicago
'91 I've Been Thinking About You
  Londonbeat
'75 I've Been This Way Before
  Neil Diamond
'59 I've Come Of Age Billy Storm
'90 I've Come To Expect It From You
  George Strait
'90 I've Cried My Last Tear For You
  Ricky Van Shelton
'81 I've Done Everything For You
  Rick Springfield
'71 I've Found Someone Of My Own
  Free Movement
'76 I've Got A Feeling (We'll Be Seeing
  Each Other Again) Al Wilson
'91 I've Got A Lot To Learn About Love
  Storm
'83 I've Got A Rock N' Roll Heart
  Eric Clapton
'74 I've Got A Thing About You Baby
  Elvis Presley
'65 I've Got A Tiger By The Tail
  Buck Owens
'55 I've Got A Woman Ray Charles
'62 (I've Got) Bonnie Bobby Rydell
'77 I've Got Love On My Mind
  Natalie Cole
'64 I've Got Sand In My Shoes Drifters
'73 I've Got So Much To Give
  Barry White
'74 I've Got The Music In Me
  Kiki Dee Band
'56 I've Got The World On A String
  Frank Sinatra
'65 I've Got To Be Somebody
  Billy Joe Royal
'73 I've Got To Use My Imagination
  Gladys Knight
  I've Got You Under My Skin
'56  Frank Sinatra
'66  4 Seasons
'68 I've Gotta Be Me Sammy Davis, Jr.
'68 I've Gotta Get A Message To You
  Bee Gees
'78 I've Had Enough Wings
'59 I've Had It Bell Notes
'87 (I've Had) The Time Of My Life
  Bill Medley & Jennifer Warnes
'70 I've Lost You Elvis Presley
'80 I've Loved You For A Long Time
  [medley] Spinners
'82 I've Never Been To Me Charlene
'68 I've Never Found A Girl (To Love
  Me Like You Do) Eddie Floyd
'66 I've Passed This Way Before
  Jimmy Ruffin
'61 I've Told Every Little Star
  Linda Scott
'95 Ice Cream Raekwon
'78 Ice Cream Man Van Halen
'90 Ice Ice Baby Vanilla Ice
'91 Iesha Another Bad Creation
  If
'71  Bread
'93  Janet Jackson
'62 If A Man Answers Bobby Darin
'83 If Anyone Falls Stevie Nicks
'94 If Bubba Can Dance (I Can Too)
  Shenandoah
'58 If Dreams Came True Pat Boone
'78 If Ever I See You Again
  Roberta Flack
'84 If Ever You're In My Arms Again
  Peabo Bryson
'66 If Every Day Was Like Christmas
  Elvis Presley
'04 If I Ain't Got You Alicia Keys
'68 If I Can Dream Elvis Presley

'78 If I Can't Have You Yvonne Elliman
'67 If I Could Build My Whole World
  Around You
  Marvin Gaye & Tammi Terrell
'02 If I Could Go! Angie Martinez
'94 If I Could Make A Living
  Clay Walker
'72 If I Could Reach You 5th Dimension
'97 If I Could Teach The World
  Bone Thugs-N-Harmony
'99 If I Could Turn Back The Hands Of
  Time R. Kelly
'89 If I Could Turn Back Time Cher
  If I Didn't Care
'59  Connie Francis
'61  Platters
'62 If I Didn't Have A Dime (To Play The
  Jukebox) Gene Pitney
'92 If I Didn't Have You Randy Travis
'92 If I Ever Fall In Love Shai
'93 If I Ever Lose My Faith In You Sting
'75 If I Ever Lose This Heaven AWB
'01 If I Fall You're Going Down With Me
  Dixie Chicks
'64 If I Fell Beatles
'59 If I Give My Heart To You
  Kitty Kallen
'59 If I Had A Girl Rod Lauren
  If I Had A Hammer
'62  Peter, Paul & Mary
'63  Trini Lopez
'82 If I Had My Wish Tonight
  David Lasley
'93 If I Had No Loot Tony Toni Tone
'05 If Heaven Andy Griggs
'91 If I Know Me George Strait
'65 If I Loved You Chad & Jeremy
'55 If I May Nat "King" Cole/Four Knights
'70 If I Never Knew Your Name Vic Dana
'97 If I Never Stop Loving You
  David Kersh
'65 If I Ruled The World Tony Bennett
'79 If I Said You Have A Beautiful Body
  Would You Hold It Against Me
  Bellamy Brothers
'95 If I Wanted To Melissa Etheridge
  If I Were A Carpenter
'66  Bobby Darin
'68  Four Tops
'70  Johnny Cash & June Carter
'71 If I Were A Rich Man Topol
'70 If I Were Your Woman
  Gladys Knight
'83 If I'd Been The One 38 Special
'89 If I'm Not Your Lover Al B. Sure!
'82 If It Ain't One Thing...It's Another
  Richard "Dimples" Fields
'88 If It Isn't Love New Edition
'96 If It Makes You Happy Sheryl Crow
  (If Loving You Is Wrong) I Don't
  Want To Be Right
'72  Luther Ingram
'79  Barbara Mandrell
'01 If My Heart Had Wings Faith Hill
'63 If My Pillow Could Talk
  Connie Francis
'71 If Not For You Olivia Newton-John
'83 If Only You Knew Patti LaBelle
'86 If She Knew What She Wants
  Bangles
'87 If She Would Have Been Faithful...
  Chicago
'68 If 6 Was 9 Jimi Hendrix
'91 If The Devil Danced (In Empty
  Pockets) Joe Diffie
'94 If The Good Die Young
  Tracy Lawrence
'82 If The Love Fits Wear It Leslie Pearl
'95 If The World Had A Front Porch
  Tracy Lawrence
'92 If There Hadn't Been You Billy Dean
'91 (If There Was) Any Other Way
  Celine Dion
'84 If This Is It Huey Lewis
'93 If Tomorrow Never Comes
  Garth Brooks
'90 If U Were Mine U-Krew

'73 If We Make It Through December
  Merle Haggard
'88 If We Never Meet Again
  Tommy Conwell
'90 If Wishes Came True
  Sweet Sensation
'92 If You Asked Me To Celine Dion
'87 If You Can Do It: I Can Too!!
  Meli'sa Morgan
'68 If You Can Want Miracles
'97 If You Could Only See Tonic
'70 If You Could Read My Mind
  Gordon Lightfoot
'59 (If You Cry) True Love, True Love
  Drifters
  If You Don't Know Me By Now
'72  Harold Melvin & The Bluenotes
'89  Simply Red
'55 If You Don't Want My Love
  Jaye P. Morgan
'04 If You Ever Stop Loving Me
  Montgomery Gentry
'94 If You Go Jon Secada
'92 If You Go Away NKOTB
'61 If You Gotta Make A Fool Of
  Somebody James Ray
'99 If You Had My Love Jennifer Lopez
'76 If You Know What I Mean
  Neil Diamond
'86 If You Leave Orchestral
  Manoeuvres In The Dark
'76 If You Leave Me Now Chicago
'72 If You Leave Me Tonight I'll Cry
  Jerry Wallace
'70 (If You Let Me Make Love To You
  Then) Why Can't I Touch You?
  Ronnie Dyson
  If You Love Me
'94  Brownstone
'99  Mint Condition
'74 If You Love Me (Let Me Know)
  Olivia Newton-John
'85 If You Love Somebody Set Them
  Free Sting
'99 If You (Lovin' Me) Silk
'63 If You Need Me Solomon Burke
'90 If You Needed Somebody
  Bad Company
'71 If You Really Love Me
  Stevie Wonder
'79 If You Remember Me
  Chris Thompson & Night
'98 If You See Him/If You See Her
  Reba McEntire/Brooks & Dunn
'80 If You Should Sail Nielsen/Pearson
'74 If You Talk In Your Sleep
  Elvis Presley
'98 If You Think I'm Jiggy Lox
  If You Think You're Lonely Now
'81  Bobby Womack
'95  K-Ci Hailey
'63 If You Wanna Be Happy Jimmy Soul
'74 If You Wanna Get To Heaven
  Ozark Mountain Daredevils
'79 If You Want It Niteflyte
'90 If You Want Me To Joe Diffie
'73 If You Want Me To Stay
  Sly & The Family Stone
'00 If You're Gone Matchbox Twenty
'84 If You're Gonna Play In Texas (You
  Gotta Have A Fiddle In The Band)
  Alabama
'95 (If You're Not In It For Love) I'm
  Outta Here! Shania Twain
'03 If You're Not The One
  Daniel Bedingfield
'73 If You're Ready (Come Go With Me)
  Staple Singers
'94 If You've Got Love
  John Michael Montgomery
'96 If Your Girl Only Knew Aaliyah
'02 Ignition R. Kelly
  Iko Iko
'65  Dixie Cups
'89  Belle Stars
'60 Image Of A Girl Safaris
'78 Imaginary Lover
  Atlanta Rhythm Section

'98 **Imagination** *Tamia*
'71 **Imagine** *John Lennon*
'98 **Imagine That** *Diamond Rio*
'75 **Immigrant, The** *Neil Sedaka*
'70 **Immigrant Song** *Led Zeppelin*
'72 **Immigration Man**
    *Graham Nash & David Crosby*
'02 **Impossible, The** *Joe Nichols*
'66 **Impossible Dream** *Jack Jones*
'97 **Impression That I Get**
    *Mighty Mighty Bosstones*
'90 **Impulsive** *Wilson Phillips*
'83 **In A Big Country** *Big Country*
'91 **In A Different Light** *Doug Stone*
'68 **In-A-Gadda-Da-Vida** *Iron Butterfly*
'69 **In A Moment** *Intrigues*
'04 **In A Real Love** *Phil Vassar*
'56 **In A Shanty In Old Shanty Town**
    *Somethin' Smith & The Redheads*
'92 **In A Week Or Two** *Diamond Rio*
'80 **In America** *Charlie Daniels Band*
'67 **In And Out Of Love** *Supremes*
'97 **In Another's Eyes**
    *Trisha Yearwood & Garth Brooks*
'91 **In Bloom** *Nirvana*
    **"In" Crowd**
'65   *Dobie Gray*
'65   *Ramsey Lewis Trio*
'03 **In Da Club** *50 Cent*
'63 **In Dreams** *Roy Orbison*
'70 **In Memory Of Elizabeth Reed**
    *Allman Brothers Band*
'97 **In My Bed** *Dru Hill*
'04 **In My Daughter's Eyes**
    *Martina McBride*
    **In My Dreams**
'87   *REO Speedwagon*
'91   *Party*
'89 **In My Eyes** *Stevie B*
'85 **In My House** *Mary Jane Girls*
'65 **In My Life** *Beatles*
'60 **In My Little Corner Of The World**
    *Anita Bryant*
'63 **In My Room** *Beach Boys*
'84 **In Neon** *Elton John*
'81 **In The Air Tonight** *Phil Collins*
'66 **In The Arms Of Love** *Andy Williams*
    **In The City**
'79   *Eagles*
'83   *Jam*
'92 **In The Closet** *Michael Jackson*
'81 **In The Dark** *Billy Squier*
'01 **In The End** *Linkin Park*
'79 **In The Evening** *Led Zeppelin*
'69 **In The Ghetto** *Elvis Presley*
'93 **In The Heart Of A Woman**
    *Billy Ray Cyrus*
'94 **In The House Of Stone And Light**
    *Martin Page*
'55 **In The Jailhouse Now** *Webb Pierce*
'95 **In The Meantime** *Spacehog*
'61 **In The Middle Of A Heartache**
    *Wanda Jackson*
'57 **In The Middle Of An Island**
    *Tennessee Ernie Ford*
    **In The Middle Of The House**
'56   *Rusty Draper*
'56   *Vaughn Monroe*
    **In The Midnight Hour**
'65   *Wilson Pickett*
'73   *Cross Country*
    **In The Misty Moonlight**
'64   *Jerry Wallace*
'67   *Dean Martin*
.   **In The Mood**
'59   *Ernie Fields*
'77   *Henhouse Five Plus Too*
'83   *Robert Plant*
'79 **In The Navy** *Village People*
'72 **In The Rain** *Dramatics*
'86 **In The Shape Of A Heart**
    *Jackson Browne*
    **In The Still Of the Night [Nite]**
'56   *Five Satins*
'60   *Dion & The Belmonts*
'92   *Boyz II Men*

    **In The Summertime**
'70   *Mungo Jerry*
'95   *Shaggy*
'69 **In The Year 2525** *Zager & Evans*
'79 **In Thee** *Blue Öyster Cult*
'93 **In These Arms** *Bon Jovi*
'92 **In This Life** *Collin Raye*
'03 **In Those Jeans** *Ginuwine*
'87 **In Too Deep** *Genesis*
'86 **In Your Eyes** *Peter Gabriel*
'81 **In Your Letter** *REO Speedwagon*
'88 **In Your Room** *Bangles*
'88 **In Your Soul** *Corey Hart*
'67 **Incense And Peppermints**
    *Strawberry Alarm Clock*
    **Incomplete**
'00   *Sisqó*
'05   *Backstreet Boys*
'00 **Independent Women** *Destiny's Child*
'67 **Indescribably Blue** *Elvis Presley*
'88 **Indestructible** *Four Tops*
'69 **Indian Giver** *1910 Fruitgum Co.*
'68 **Indian Lake** *Cowsills*
'94 **Indian Outlaw** *Tim McGraw*
    **Indian Reservation**
'68   *Don Fardon*
'71   *Paul Revere & The Raiders*
'70 **Indiana Wants Me** *R. Dean Taylor*
'84 **Infatuation** *Rod Stewart*
'93 **Informer** *Snow*
    **Innamorata**
'56   *Dean Martin*
'56   *Jerry Vale*
'71 **Inner City Blues (Make Me Wanna**
    **Holler)** *Marvin Gaye*
'83 **Innocent Man** *Billy Joel*
'93 **Insane In The Brain** *Cypress Hill*
'96 **Insensitive** *Jann Arden*
'75 **Inseparable** *Natalie Cole*
'66 **Inside-Looking Out** *Animals*
'83 **Inside Love (So Personal)**
    *George Benson*
'98 **Inside Out** *Eve 6*
'70 **Instant Karma** *John Ono Lennon*
'78 **Instant Replay** *Dan Hartman*
'98 **Intergalactic** *Beastie Boys*
'94 **Interstate Love Song**
    *Stone Temple Pilots*
'91 **Into The Great Wide Open**
    *Tom Petty*
'85 **Into The Groove** *Madonna*
'70 **Into The Mystic** *Van Morrison*
'80 **Into The Night** *Benny Mardones*
'03 **Into You** *Fabolous*
'93 **Into Your Arms** *Lemonheads*
'03 **Intuition** *Jewel*
'85 **Invincible** *Pat Benatar*
    **Invisible**
'85   *Alison Moyet*
'03   *Clay Aiken*
'97 **Invisible Man** *98°*
'86 **Invisible Touch** *Genesis*
'98 **Iris** *Goo Goo Dolls*
'71 **Iron Man** *Black Sabbath*
'96 **Ironic** *Alanis Morissette*
'01 **Irresistible** *Jessica Simpson*
'61 **Irresistible You** *Bobby Darin*
'60 **Is A Blue Bird Blue** *Conway Twitty*
'70 **Is Anybody Goin' To San Antone**
    *Charley Pride*
'91 **Is It Good To You**
    *Heavy D & The Boyz*
'86 **Is It Love** *Mr. Mister*
'69 **Is It Something You've Got**
    *Tyrone Davis*
'64 **Is It True** *Brenda Lee*
'81 **Is It You** *Lee Ritenour*
'79 **Is She Really Going Out With Him?**
    *Joe Jackson*
'96 **Is That A Tear** *Tracy Lawrence*
'69 **Is That All There Is** *Peggy Lee*
'60 **Is There Any Chance** *Marty Robbins*
'92 **Is There Life Out There**
    *Reba McEntire*

'83 **Is There Something I Should Know**
    *Duran Duran*
    **Is This Love**
'78   *Bob Marley*
'86   *Survivor*
'87   *Whitesnake*
'76 **Isis** *Bob Dylan*
'75 **Island Girl** *Elton John*
'57 **Island In The Sun** *Harry Belafonte*
'82 **Island Of Lost Souls** *Blondie*
'83 **Islands In The Stream** *Kenny*
    *Rogers with Dolly Parton*
'70 **Isn't It A Pity** *George Harrison*
'77 **Isn't It Time** *Babys*
'72 **Isn't Life Strange** *Moody Blues*
'77 **Isn't She Lovely** *Stevie Wonder*
'69 **Israelites** *Desmond Dekker*
'84 **It Ain't Enough** *Corey Hart*
    **It Ain't Me Babe**
'64   *Bob Dylan*
'65   *Turtles*
'99 **It Ain't My Fault 2**
    *Silkk The Shocker & Mystikal*
'91 **It Ain't Over 'Til It's Over**
    *Lenny Kravitz*
'59 **It Doesn't Matter Anymore**
    *Buddy Holly*
'71 **It Don't Come Easy** *Ringo Starr*
'70 **It Don't Matter To Me** *Bread*
'00 **It Feels So Good** *Sonique*
'91 **It Hit Me Like A Hammer**
    *Huey Lewis*
'64 **It Hurts Me** *Elvis Presley*
    **It Hurts To Be In Love**
'57   *Annie Laurie*
'64   *Gene Pitney*
'56 **It Isn't Right** *Platters*
'61 **It Keeps Rainin'** *Fats Domino*
'62 **It Keeps Right On A-Hurtin'**
    *Johnny Tillotson*
'76 **It Keeps You Runnin'**
    *Doobie Brothers*
'95 **It Matters To Me** *Faith Hill*
'55 **It May Sound Silly** *McGuire Sisters*
'62 **It Might As Well Rain Until**
    **September** *Carole King*
'83 **It Might Be You** *Stephen Bishop*
'67 **It Must Be Him** *Vikki Carr*
    **It Must Be Love**
'79   *Alton McClain & Destiny*
'83   *Madness*
'98   *Ty Herndon*
'00   *Alan Jackson*
'90 **It Must Have Been Love** *Roxette*
    **It Never Rains In Southern California**
'72   *Albert Hammond*
'90   *Tony! Toni! Toné!*
'60 **It Only Happened Yesterday**
    *Jack Scott*
'56 **It Only Hurts For A Little While**
    *Ames Brothers*
'75 **It Only Takes A Minute** *Tavares*
'78 **It Seems To Hang On**
    *Ashford & Simpson*
'68 **It Should Have Been Me**
    *Gladys Knight*
'91 **It Should've Been You**
    *Teddy Pendergrass*
'62 **It Started All Over Again**
    *Brenda Lee*
'93 **It Sure Is Monday** *Mark Chesnutt*
'73 **It Sure Took A Long, Long Time**
    *Lobo*
    **It Takes Two**
'67   *Marvin Gaye & Kim Weston*
'88   *Rob Base & D.J. E-Z Rock*
'66 **It Tears Me Up** *Percy Sledge*
'93 **It Was A Good Day** *Ice Cube*
'65 **It Was A Very Good Year**
    *Frank Sinatra*
'77 **It Was Almost Like A Song**
    *Ronnie Milsap*
'59 **It Was I** *Skip & Flip*
'00 **It Wasn't Me** *Shaggy*
'61 **It Will Stand** *Showmen*

'88 **It Would Take A Strong Strong Man** *Rick Astley*
'77 **It's A Crazy World** *Mac McAnally*
'01 **It's A Great Day To Be Alive** *Travis Tritt*
'78 **It's A Heartache** *Bonnie Tyler*
'78 **It's A Laugh** *Daryl Hall & John Oates*
 **It's A Little Too Late**
'93 *Tanya Tucker*
'96 *Mark Chesnutt*
'76 **It's A Long Way There** *Little River Band*
'81 **It's A Love Thing** *Whispers*
'66 **It's A Man's Man's Man's World** *James Brown*
 **It's A Miracle**
'75 *Barry Manilow*
'84 *Culture Club*
'83 **It's A Mistake** *Men At Work*
'70 **It's A New Day** *James Brown*
'70 **It's A Shame** *Spinners*
'91 **It's A Shame (My Sister)** *Monie Love*
'87 **It's A Sin** *Pet Shop Boys*
'55 **It's A Sin To Tell A Lie** *Somethin' Smith & The Redheads*
'98 **It's All About Me** *Mya With Sisqo*
'97 **It's All About The Benjamins** *Puff Daddy*
'99 **It's All About You (Not About Me)** *Tracie Spencer*
'61 **It's All Because** *Linda Scott*
'99 **It's All Been Done** *Barenaked Ladies*
'96 **It's All Coming Back To Me Now** *Celine Dion*
'75 **It's All Down To Goodnight Vienna** *Ringo Starr*
'79 **It's All I Can Do** *Cars*
 **It's All In The Game**
'58 *Tommy Edwards*
'63 *Cliff Richard*
'70 *Four Tops*
'64 **It's All Over Now** *Rolling Stones*
'65 **It's All Over Now, Baby Blue** *Bob Dylan*
 **It's All Right**
'63 *Impressions*
'93 *Huey Lewis*
'98 *Candlebox*
'96 **It's All The Way Live (Now)** *Coolio*
 **It's Almost Tomorrow**
'55 *David Carroll*
'55 *Dream Weavers*
'55 *Jo Stafford*
'65 **It's Alright** *Adam Faith*
'00 **It's Always Somethin'** *Joe Diffie*
'58 **(It's Been A Long Time) Pretty Baby** *Gino & Gina*
'01 **It's Been Awhile** *Staind*
'77 **It's Ecstasy When You Lay Down Next To Me** *Barry White*
'03 **It's Five O'Clock Somewhere** *Alan Jackson & Jimmy Buffett*
'71 **It's Four In The Morning** *Faron Young*
'69 **It's Getting Better** *Mama Cass*
'05 **It's Getting Better All The Time** *Brooks & Dunn*
'72 **It's Going To Take Some Time** *Carpenters*
'92 **It's Gonna Be A Lovely Day** *S.O.U.L. S.Y.S.T.E.M.*
 **It's Gonna Be Alright**
'65 *Gerry & The Pacemakers*
'89 *Ruby Turner*
'00 **It's Gonna Be Me** *\*NSYNC*
'82 **It's Gonna Take A Miracle** *Deniece Williams*
'61 **It's Gonna Work Out Fine** *Ike & Tina Turner*
'65 **It's Growing** *Temptations*
'80 **It's Hard To Be Humble** *Mac Davis*
'70 **It's Impossible** *Perry Como*
'86 **It's In The Way That You Use It** *Eric Clapton*
'83 **It's Inevitable** *Charlie*
'59 **It's Just A Matter Of Time** *Brook Benton*

'89 **(It's Just) The Way That You Love Me** *Paula Abdul*
'59 **It's Late** *Ricky Nelson*
 **It's Like That**
'84 *Run-D.M.C.*
'05 *Mariah Carey*
'55 **It's Love Baby (24 Hours a Day)** *Louis Brooks*
'96 **It's Midnight Cinderella** *Garth Brooks*
'88 **It's Money That Matters** *Randy Newman*
 **It's My Life**
'65 *Animals*
'84 *Talk Talk*
'00 *Bon Jovi*
'03 *No Doubt*
'63 **It's My Party** *Lesley Gore*
'80 **It's My Turn** *Diana Ross*
'68 **It's Nice To Be With You** *Monkees*
'89 **It's No Crime** *Babyface*
'97 **It's No Good** *Depeche Mode*
'88 **It's No Secret** *Kylie Minogue*
'89 **It's Not Enough** *Starship*
'57 **It's Not For Me To Say** *Johnny Mathis*
'87 **It's Not Over ('Til It's Over)** *Starship*
'99 **It's Not Right But It's Okay** *Whitney Houston*
'65 **It's Not Unusual** *Tom Jones*
'60 **It's Now Or Never** *Elvis Presley*
'66 **It's Now Winters Day** *Tommy Roe*
'76 **It's O.K.** *Beach Boys*
'71 **It's One Of Those Nights (Yes Love)** *Partridge Family*
 **It's Only Love**
'66 *Tommy James*
'77 *ZZ Top*
'85 *Bryan Adams/Tina Turner*
 **It's Only Make Believe**
'58 *Conway Twitty*
'70 *Glen Campbell*
'74 **It's Only Rock 'N Roll (But I Like It)** *Rolling Stones*
'59 **It's Only The Beginning** *Kalin Twins*
 **It's Over**
'64 *Roy Orbison*
'66 *Jimmie Rodgers*
'76 *Boz Scaggs*
'00 **It's Over Now** *112*
'82 **It's Raining Again** *Supertramp*
'83 **It's Raining Men** *Weather Girls*
'77 **It's Sad To Belong** *England Dan & John Ford Coley*
 **It's So Easy**
'58 *Crickets*
'77 *Linda Ronstadt*
'91 **It's So Hard To Say Goodbye To Yesterday** *Boyz II Men*
'80 **It's Still Rock And Roll To Me** *Billy Joel*
'67 **It's Such A Pretty World Today** *Andy Russell*
'89 **It's The Real Thing** *Angela Winbush*
 **It's The Same Old Song**
'65 *Four Tops*
'78 *KC & The Sunshine Band*
'59 **It's Time To Cry** *Paul Anka*
 **It's Too Late**
'56 *Chuck Willis*
'66 *Bobby Goldsboro*
'71 *Carole King*
'58 **It's Too Soon To Know** *Pat Boone*
'62 **It's Up To You** *Rick Nelson*
'67 **It's Wonderful** *Young Rascals*
'57 **It's You I Love** *Fats Domino*
'78 **It's You That I Need** *Enchantment*
'97 **It's Your Love** *Tim McGraw with Faith Hill*
'69 **It's Your Thing** *Isley Brothers*
'82 **Italian Girls** *Daryl Hall & John Oates*
'56 **Italian Theme** *Cyril Stapleton*
'58 **Itchy Twitchy Feeling** *Bobby Hendricks*
'67 **Itchycoo Park** *Small Faces*

'60 **Itsy Bitsy Teenie Weenie Yellow Polkadot Bikini** *Brian Hyland*
 **Ivory Tower**
'56 *Cathy Carr*
'56 *Otis Williams/Charms*
'56 *Gale Storm*
'57 **Ivy Rose** *Perry Como*
'01 **Izzo (H.O.V.A.)** *Jay-Z*

# J

'95 **J.A.R. (Jason Andrew Relva)** *Green Day*
'82 **Jack & Diane** *John Cougar Mellencamp*
'78 **Jack And Jill** *Raydio*
'75 **Jackie Blue** *Ozark Mountain Daredevils*
'72 **Jackie Wilson Said (I'm In Heaven When You Smile)** *Van Morrison*
 **Jackson**
'67 *Johnny Cash & June Carter*
'67 *Nancy Sinatra & Lee Hazlewood*
'87 **Jacob's Ladder** *Huey Lewis*
 **Jaded**
'95 *Green Day [medley]*
'01 *Aerosmith*
'84 **Jail House Rap** *Fat Boys*
'57 **Jailhouse Rock** *Elvis Presley*
'92 **Jam** *Michael Jackson*
'62 **Jam, The** *Bobby Gregg*
'87 **Jam Tonight** *Freddie Jackson*
'69 **Jam Up Jelly Tight** *Tommy Roe*
 **Jamaica Farewell**
'56 *Harry Belafonte*
'60 *Mantovani*
'72 **Jambalaya (On The Bayou)** *John Fogerty*
'99 **Jamboree** *Naughty By Nature*
'89 **James Brown** *Big Audio Dynamite*
'74 **James Dean** *Eagles*
'62 **James (Hold The Ladder Steady)** *Sue Thompson*
 **Jamie**
'62 *Eddie Holland*
'84 *Ray Parker Jr.*
'78 **Jamie's Cryin'** *Van Halen*
'87 **Jammin' Me** *Tom Petty*
'77 **Jamming** *Bob Marley*
'79 **Jane** *Jefferson Starship*
'88 **Jane Says** *Jane's Addiction*
'89 **Janie's Got A Gun** *Aerosmith*
'64 **Java** *Al Hirt*
'74 **Jazzman** *Carole King*
'90 **Jealous** *Gene Loves Jezebel*
'69 **Jealous Kind Of Fella** *Garland Green*
'60 **Jealous Of You** *Connie Francis*
'96 **Jealousy** *Natalie Merchant*
'69 **Jean** *Oliver*
'73 **Jean Genie** *David Bowie*
'58 **Jeannie Jeannie Jeannie** *Eddie Cochran*
'76 **Jeans On** *David Dundas*
'58 **Jennie Lee** *Jan & Dean*
'68 **Jennifer Eccles** *Hollies*
'68 **Jennifer Juniper** *Donovan*
'70 **Jennifer Tomkins** *Street People*
'02 **Jenny From The Block** *Jennifer Lopez*
'57 **Jenny, Jenny** *Little Richard*
'65 **Jenny Take A Ride!** *Mitch Ryder*
'83 **Jeopardy** *Greg Kihn Band*
'61 **Jeremiah Peabody's Poly Unsaturated Pills** *Ray Stevens*
'92 **Jeremy** *Pearl Jam*
'64 **Jerk, The** *Larks*
'90 **Jerk-Out** *Time*
 **Jesse**
'73 *Roberta Flack*
'80 *Carly Simon*
'73 **Jessica** *Allman Brothers Band*
'93 **Jessie** *Joshua Kadison*
'81 **Jessie's Girl** *Rick Springfield*
95' **Jesus Freak** *DC Talk*

213

'92 **Jesus He Knows Me** *Genesis*
'69 **Jesus Is A Soul Man**
    *Lawrence Reynolds*
'72 **Jesus Is Just Alright**
    *Doobie Brothers*
'72 **Jesus Just Left Chicago [medley]**
    *ZZ Top*
'96 **Jesus To A Child** *George Michael*
'04 **Jesus Walks** *Kanye West*
'74 **Jet** *Paul McCartney*
'77 **Jet Airliner** *Steve Miller Band*
'99 **Jigga My Nigga** *Jay-Z*
**Jim Dandy**
'56   *LaVern Baker*
'73   *Black Oak Arkansas*
'86 **Jimmy Lee** *Aretha Franklin*
'73 **Jimmy Loves Mary-Anne**
    *Looking Glass*
'67 **Jimmy Mack**
    *Martha & The Vandellas*
'61 **Jimmy's Girl** *Johnny Tillotson*
**Jingle Bell Rock**
'57   *Bobby Helms*
'61   *Bobby Rydell/Chubby Checker*
'55 **Jingle Bells** *Singing Dogs*
'69 **Jingle Jangle** *Archies*
'69 **Jingo** *Santana*
'75 **Jive Talkin'** *Bee Gees*
'58 **Jo-Ann** *Playmates*
'80 **JoJo** *Boz Scaggs*
'83 **Joanna** *Kool & The Gang*
'70 **Joanne** *Michael Nesmith*
'97 **Jock Jam** *ESPN Presents*
'71 **Jody's Got Your Girl And Gone**
    *Johnnie Taylor*
'79 **Joe's Garage** *Frank Zappa*
'90 **Joey** *Concrete Blonde*
'70 **John Barleycorn** *Traffic*
'62 **Johnny Angel** *Shelley Fabares*
'87 **Johnny B** *Hooters*
**Johnny B. Goode**
'58   *Chuck Berry*
'83   *Peter Tosh*
'62 **Johnny Get Angry** *Joanie Sommers*
'62 **Johnny Jingo** *Hayley Mills*
'62 **Johnny Loves Me** *Shelley Fabares*
'69 **Johnny One Time** *Brenda Lee*
'61 **Johnny Will** *Pat Boone*
'72 **Join Together** *Who*
'73 **Joker, The** *Steve Miller Band*
**Joker (That's What They Call Me)**
'57   *Hilltoppers*
'57   *Billy Myles*
'66 **Joker Went Wild** *Brian Hyland*
'74 **Jolene** *Dolly Parton*
'65 **Jolly Green Giant** *Kingsmen*
'85 **Jolly Mon Sing** *Jimmy Buffett*
'81 **Jones Vs. Jones** *Kool & The Gang*
'60 **Josephine** *Bill Black's Combo*
'70 **Joshua** *Dolly Parton*
'78 **Josie** *Steely Dan*
'68 **Journey To The Center Of The Mind**
    *Amboy Dukes*
**Joy**
'72   *Apollo 100*
'73   *Isaac Hayes*
'88   *Teddy Pendergrass*
'89 **Joy And Pain** *Donna Allen*
'71 **Joy To The World** *Three Dog Night*
'91 **Joyride** *Roxette*
'65 **Ju Ju Hand** *Sam The Sham &*
    *the Pharaohs*
'00 **Judith** *Perfect Circle*
'67 **Judy In Disguise (With Glasses)**
    *John Fred*
'75 **Judy Mae** *Boomer Castleman*
'63 **Judy's Turn To Cry** *Lesley Gore*
'94 **Juicy** *Notorious B.I.G.*
'83 **Juicy Fruit** *Mtume*
'56 **Juke Box Baby** *Perry Como*
'81 **Juke Box Hero** *Foreigner*
'90 **Jukebox In My Mind** *Alabama*
'91 **Jukebox With A Country Song**
    *Doug Stone*

'70 **Julie, Do Ya Love Me**
    *Bobby Sherman*
**Jump**
'84   *Van Halen*
'92   *Kris Kross*
'92 **Jump Around** *House Of Pain*
'84 **Jump (For My Love)** *Pointer Sisters*
'72 **Jump Into The Fire** *Nilsson*
'98 **Jump Jive An' Wail**
    *Brian Setzer Orchestra*
'03 **Jump Off** *Lil' Kim*
'60 **Jump Over** *Freddy Cannon*
'87 **Jump Start** *Natalie Cole*
'82 **Jump To It** *Aretha Franklin*
'98 **Jumper** *Third Eye Blind*
**Jumpin' Jack Flash**
'68   *Rolling Stones*
'86   *Aretha Franklin*
'00 **Jumpin', Jumpin'** *Destiny's Child*
'57 **June Night** *Jimmy Dorsey*
'73 **Jungle Boogie** *Kool & The Gang*
'72 **Jungle Fever** *Chakachas*
**Jungle Love**
'77   *Steve Miller Band*
'84   *Time*
'75 **Jungleland** *Bruce Springsteen*
'74 **Junior's Farm** *Paul McCartney*
'76 **Junk Food Junkie** *Larry Groce*
'61 **Jura (I Swear I Love You)**
    *Les Paul & Mary Ford*
'58 **Just A Dream** *Jimmy Clanton*
'90 **Just A Friend** *Biz Markie*
'02 **Just A Friend 2002** *Mario*
**Just A Gigolo [medley]**
'56   *Louis Prima & Keely Smith*
'85   *David Lee Roth*
'95 **Just A Girl** *No Doubt*
'83 **Just A Job To Do** *Genesis*
'05 **Just A Lil Bit** *50 Cent*
**Just A Little**
'60   *Brenda Lee*
'65   *Beau Brummels*
**Just A Little Bit**
'60   *Rosco Gordon*
'65   *Roy Head*
'65 **Just A Little Bit Better**
    *Herman's Hermits*
'75 **Just A Little Bit Of You**
    *Michael Jackson*
'59 **Just A Little Too Much**
    *Ricky Nelson*
'77 **Just A Song Before I Go**
    *Crosby, Stills & Nash*
'92 **Just Another Day** *Jon Secada*
'00 **Just Another Day In Paradise**
    *Phil Vassar*
'90 **Just Another Dream** *Cathy Dennis*
'85 **Just Another Night** *Mick Jagger*
'85 **Just As I Am** *Air Supply*
**Just As Much As Ever**
'59   *Bob Beckham*
'67   *Bobby Vinton*
'59 **Just Ask Your Heart** *Frankie Avalon*
'00 **Just Be A Man About It**
    *Toni Braxton*
'83 **Just Be Good To Me** *S.O.S. Band*
'64 **Just Be True** *Gene Chandler*
**Just Because**
'57   *Lloyd Price*
'89   *Anita Baker*
'03   *Jane's Addiction*
**Just Between You And Me**
'57   *Chordettes*
'81   *April Wine*
'89   *Lou Gramm*
'96   *DC Talk*
'57 **Just Born (To Be Your Baby)**
    *Perry Como*
'82 **Just Can't Win 'Em All**
    *Stevie Woods*
'59 **Just Come Home** *Hugo & Luigi*
'89 **Just Coolin'** *Levert*
'74 **Just Don't Want To Be Lonely**
    *Main Ingredient*

'68 **Just Dropped In (To See What**
    **Condition My Condition Was In)**
    *First Edition*
'61 **Just For Old Time's Sake**
    *McGuire Sisters*
'92 **Just For Tonight** *Vanessa Williams*
'00 **Just Friends (Sunny)** *Musiq*
'83 **Just Got Lucky** *JoBoxers*
'88 **Just Got Paid** *Johnny Kemp*
'61 **Just Got To Know**
    *Jimmy McCracklin*
'56 **Just In Time** *Tony Bennett*
'59 **Just Keep It Up** *Dee Clark*
'93 **Just Kickin' It** *Xscape*
'02 **Just Like A Pill** *P!nk*
'66 **Just Like A Woman** *Bob Dylan*
'87 **Just Like Heaven** *Cure*
'89 **Just Like Jesse James** *Cher*
'65 **Just Like Me**
    *Paul Revere & The Raiders*
'88 **Just Like Paradise** *David Lee Roth*
'64 **(Just Like) Romeo & Juliet**
    *Reflections*
'80 **(Just Like) Starting Over**
    *John Lennon*
**Just Like You**
'91   *Robbie Nevil*
'04   *Three Days Grace*
'04 **Just Lose It** *Eminem*
'58 **Just Married** *Marty Robbins*
'71 **Just My Imagination** *Temptations*
'81 **Just Once**
    *Quincy Jones/James Ingram*
'65 **Just Once In My Life**
    *Righteous Brothers*
**Just One Look**
'63   *Doris Troy*
'64   *Hollies*
60 **Just One Time** *Don Gibson*
'61 **Just Out Of Reach (Of My Two**
    **Open Arms)** *Solomon Burke*
'88 **Just Play Music!**
    *Big Audio Dynamite*
'77 **Just Remember I Love You** *Firefall*
'92 **Just Take My Heart** *Mr. Big*
'79 **Just The Same** *Journey*
**Just The Two Of Us**
'81   *Grover Washington, Jr. (with Bill*
    *Withers)*
'98   *Will Smith*
'91 **Just The Way It Is, Baby**
    *Rembrandts*
'77 **Just The Way You Are** *Billy Joel*
'76 **Just To Be Close To You**
    *Commodores*
'98 **Just To Hear You Say That You**
    **Love Me**
    *Faith Hill (With Tim McGraw)*
'57 **Just To Hold My Hand**
    *Clyde McPhatter*
'87 **Just To See Her** *Smokey Robinson*
'97 **Just To See You Smile** *Tim McGraw*
'75 **Just Too Many People**
    *Melissa Manchester*
'56 **Just Walking In The Rain**
    *Johnnie Ray*
'91 **Just Want To Hold You**
    *Jasmine Guy*
'78 **Just What I Needed** *Cars*
'79 **Just When I Needed You Most**
    *Randy Vanwarmer*
'65 **Just You** *Sonny & Cher*
'76 **Just You And I** *Melissa Manchester*
'73 **Just You 'N' Me** *Chicago*
'92 **Justified & Ancient** *KLF*
'90 **Justify My Love** *Madonna*

# K

**Ka-Ding-Dong**
'56   *Diamonds*
'56   *G-Clefs*
'56   *Hilltoppers*
**Kansas City**
'59   *Wilbert Harrison*
'63   *Trini Lopez*

'65 **Kansas City Star** *Roger Miller*
**Karma**
'05   *Lloyd Banks*
'05   *Alicia Keys*
'83 **Karma Chameleon** *Culture Club*
'73 **Karn Evil 9**
    *Emerson, Lake & Palmer*
'75 **Kashmir** *Led Zeppelin*
'75 **Katmandu** *Bob Seger*
'58 **Kathy-O** *Diamonds*
'69 **Kaw-Liga** *Charley Pride [live]*
'69 **Keem-O-Sabe** *Electric Indian*
'57 **Keep A Knockin'** *Little Richard*
'91 **Keep Coming Back** *Richard Marx*
'89 **Keep Each Other Warm**
    *Barry Manilow*
'83 **(Keep Feeling) Fascination**
    *Human League*
'76 **Keep Holding On** *Temptations*
'91 **Keep It Between The Lines**
    *Ricky Van Shelton*
'91 **Keep It Comin'** *Keith Sweat*
'77 **Keep It Comin' Love**
    *KC & The Sunshine Band*
'90 **Keep It Together** *Madonna*
'76 **Keep Me Cryin'** *Al Green*
'65 **Keep On Dancing** *Gentrys*
'96 **Keep On, Keepin' On** *MC Lyte*
'68 **Keep On Lovin' Me Honey**
    *Marvin Gaye & Tammi Terrell*
'80 **Keep On Loving You**
    *REO Speedwagon*
'89 **Keep On Movin'** *Soul II Soul*
'64 **Keep On Pushing** *Impressions*
'74 **Keep On Singing** *Helen Reddy*
'74 **Keep On Smilin'** *Wet Willie*
'73 **Keep On Truckin'** *Eddie Kendricks*
'92 **Keep On Walkin'** *Ce Ce Peniston*
'64 **Keep Searchin'** *Del Shannon*
'94 **Keep Talking** *Pink Floyd*
'67 **Keep The Ball Rollin'**
    *Jay & The Techniques*
'92 **Keep The Faith** *Bon Jovi*
'80 **Keep The Fire** *Kenny Loggins*
'82 **Keep The Fire Burnin'**
    *REO Speedwagon*
'95 **Keep Their Heads Ringin'** *Dr. Dre*
'93 **Keep Ya Head Up** *2Pac*
'87 **Keep Your Eye On Me** *Herb Alpert*
'62 **Keep Your Hands Off My Baby**
    *Little Eva*
'86 **Keep Your Hands To Yourself**
    *Georgia Satellites*
'72 **Keeper Of The Castle** *Four Tops*
'95 **Keeper Of The Stars** *Tracy Byrd*
'85 **Keeping The Faith** *Billy Joel*
'55 **Kentuckian Song** *Hilltoppers*
'70 **Kentucky Rain** *Elvis Presley*
**Kentucky Woman**
'67   *Neil Diamond*
'68   *Deep Purple*
'58 **Kewpie Doll** *Perry Como*
'81 **Key Largo** *Bertie Higgins*
'96 **Key West Intermezzo (I Saw You First)** *John Mellencamp*
'94 **Kick A Little** *Little Texas*
'77 **Kick It Out** *Heart*
'69 **Kick Out The Jams** *MC5*
'98 **Kicking My Heart Around**
    *Black Crowes*
'66 **Kicks** *Paul Revere & The Raiders*
'89 **Kickstart My Heart** *Mötley Crüe*
'76 **Kid Charlemagne** *Steely Dan*
'84 **Kid's American** *Matthew Wilder*
'60 **Kiddio** *Brook Benton*
'71 **Kids Are Alright** *Who*
'82 **Kids In America** *Kim Wilde*
'63 **Killer Joe** *Rocky Fellers*
'75 **Killer Queen** *Queen*
**Killin' Time**
'80   *Fred Knoblock & Susan Anton*
'89   *Clint Black*
'65 **Killing Floor** *Howlin' Wolf*
**Killing Me Softly With His Song**
'73   *Roberta Flack*
'96   *Fugees*

'84 **Killing Moon** *Echo & The Bunnymen*
'77 **Killing Of Georgie** *Rod Stewart*
'98 **Kind & Generous** *Natalie Merchant*
'66 **Kind Of A Drag** *Buckinghams*
'63 **Kind Of Boy You Can't Forget**
    *Raindrops*
'58 **King Creole** *Elvis Presley*
'86 **King For A Day** *Thompson Twins*
'72 **King Heroin** *James Brown*
'77 **King Is Gone** *Ronnie McDowell*
'83 **King Of Pain** *Police*
'85 **King Of Rock** *Run-D.M.C.*
'65 **King Of The Road** *Roger Miller*
'62 **King Of The Whole Wide World**
    *Elvis Presley*
'90 **King Of Wishful Thinking** *Go West*
'78 **King Tut** *Steve Martin*
'77 **Kings And Queens** *Aerosmith*
'74 **Kings Of The Party**
    *Brownsville Station*
**Kiss**
'86   *Prince*
'88   *Art Of Noise*
'71 **Kiss An Angel Good Mornin'**
    *Charley Pride*
'76 **Kiss And Say Goodbye** *Manhattans*
'88 **Kiss And Tell** *Bryan Ferry*
'65 **Kiss Away** *Ronnie Dove*
'95 **Kiss From A Rose** *Seal*
'79 **Kiss In The Dark** *Pink Lady*
'98 **Kiss Me** *Sixpence None The Richer*
'56 **Kiss Me Another** *Georgia Gibbs*
'88 **Kiss Me Deadly** *Lita Ford*
'68 **Kiss Me Goodbye** *Petula Clark*
'80 **Kiss Me In The Rain**
    *Barbra Streisand*
'64 **Kiss Me Quick** *Elvis Presley*
'64 **Kiss Me Sailor** *Diane Renay*
'81 **Kiss On My List**
    *Daryl Hall & John Oates*
'83 **Kiss The Bride** *Elton John*
'97 **Kiss The Rain** *Billie Myers*
'91 **Kiss Them For Me**
    *Siouxsie & The Banshees*
'00 **Kiss This** *Aaron Tippin*
'90 **Kiss This Thing Goodbye** *Del Amitri*
'78 **Kiss You All Over** *Exile*
'91 **Kiss You Back** *Digital Underground*
'89 **Kisses On The Wind** *Neneh Cherry*
'57 **Kisses Sweeter Than Wine**
    *Jimmie Rodgers*
'64 **Kissin' Cousins** *Elvis Presley*
'59 **Kissin' Time** *Bobby Rydell*
'96 **Kissin' You** *Total*
'91 **Kissing You** *Keith Washington*
'88 **Kissing A Fool** *George Michael*
'73 **Kissing My Love** *Bill Withers*
'57 **Knee Deep In The Blues**
    *Guy Mitchell*
'66 **Knight In Rusty Armour**
    *Peter & Gordon*
**Knock On Wood**
'66   *Eddie Floyd*
'67   *Otis Redding & Carla Thomas*
'79   *Amii Stewart*
'70 **Knock Three Times** *Dawn*
'90 **Knockin' Boots** *Candyman*
'93 **Knockin' Da Boots** *H-Town*
**Knockin' On Heaven's Doo**
'73   *Bob Dylan*
'90   *Guns N' Roses*
'77 **Knowing Me, Knowing You** *Abba*
**Ko Ko Mo (I Love You So)**
'55   *Perry Como*
'55   *Crew-Cuts*
'73 **Kodachrome** *Paul Simon*
'88 **Kokomo** *Beach Boys*
'59 **Kookie, Kookie (Lend Me Your Comb)** *Edward Byrnes & Connie Stevens*
'60 **Kookie Little Paradise**
    *Jo Ann Campbell*
'69 **Kozmic Blues** *Janis Joplin*
'00 **Kryptonite** *3 Doors Down*
'69 **Kum Ba Yah** *Tommy Leonetti*
'74 **Kung Fu** *Curtis Mayfield*

'74 **Kung Fu Fighting** *Carl Douglas*
'85 **Kyrie** *Mr. Mister*

# L

'77 **L.A. Sunshine** *War*
'71 **L.A. Woman** *Doors*
**La Bamba**
'58   *Ritchie Valens*
'87   *Los Lobos*
'58 **La Dee Dah** *Billy & Lillie*
'58 **La-Do-Dada** *Dale Hawkins*
'73 **La Grange** *ZZ Top*
'87 **La Isla Bonita** *Madonna*
'69 **La La La (If I Had You)**
    *Bobby Sherman*
'68 **La-La Means I Love You** *Delfonics*
'74 **La La Peace Song** *Al Wilson*
'58 **La Paloma** *Billy Vaughn*
'90 **Ladies First** *Queen Latifah*
'79 **Ladies Night** *Kool & The Gang*
**Lady**
'67   *Jack Jones*
'74   *Styx*
'79   *Little River Band*
'80   *Kenny Rogers*
'80   *Whispers*
'96   *D'Angelo*
'04   *Lenny Kravitz*
'67 **Lady Bird** *Nancy Sinatra & Lee Hazlewood*
'75 **Lady Blue** *Leon Russell*
'66 **Lady Godiva** *Peter & Gordon*
'87 **Lady In Red** *Chris DeBurgh*
'66 **Lady Jane** *Rolling Stones*
'78 **Lady Love** *Lou Rawls*
'83 **Lady Love Me (One More Time)**
    *George Benson*
'60 **Lady Luck** *Lloyd Price*
'68 **Lady Madonna** *Beatles*
**Lady Marmalade**
'75   *LaBelle*
'01   *Christina Aguilera, Lil' Kim, Mya & P!nk*
'96 **Lady Picture Show**
    *Stone Temple Pilots*
'68 **Lady Willpower** *Gary Puckett*
'81 **Lady (You Bring Me Up)**
    *Commodores*
'93 **Laid** *James*
'97 **Lakini's Juice** *Live*
'68 **Lalena** *Donovan*
'75 **Lamb Lies Down On Broadway**
    *Genesis*
'86 **Land Of Confusion** *Genesis*
'66 **Land Of Milk And Honey** *Vogues*
**Land Of 1000 Dances**
'65   *Cannibal & The Headhunters*
'66   *Wilson Pickett*
'80 **Landlord** *Gladys Knight*
**Landslide**
'75   *Fleetwood Mac*
'94   *Smashing Pumpkins*
'02   *Dixie Chicks*
**Language Of Love**
'61   *John D. Loudermilk*
'84   *Dan Fogelberg*
'66 **Lara's Theme From "Dr. Zhivago"**
    *Roger Williams*
'99 **Larger Than Life** *Backstreet Boys*
'65 **Last Chance To Turn Around**
    *Gene Pitney*
'79 **Last Cheater's Waltz** *T.G. Sheppard*
'76 **Last Child** *Aerosmith*
'78 **Last Dance** *Donna Summer*
**Last Date**
'60   *Floyd Cramer*
'60   *Lawrence Welk*
'75 **Last Farewell** *Roger Whittaker*
'75 **Last Game Of The Season (A Blind Man In The Bleachers)**
    *David Geddes*
**Last Kiss**
'64   *J. Frank Wilson*
'99   *Pearl Jam*

'63 Last Leaf *Cascades*
'89 Last Mile *Cinderella*
Last Night
'61 *Mar-Keys*
'96 *Az Yet*
'01 *Strokes*
'72 (Last Night) I Didn't Get To Sleep At All *5th Dimension*
'89 Last Of The Famous International Playboys *Morrissey*
'00 Last Resort *Papa Roach*
Last Song
'72 *Edward Bear*
'92 *Elton John*
'65 Last Time *Rolling Stones*
'84 Last Time I Made Love *Joyce Kennedy & Jeffrey Osborne*
'74 Last Time I Saw Him *Diana Ross*
'03 Last Train Home *Lostprophets*
'66 Last Train To Clarksville *Monkees*
'79 Last Train To London *Electric Light Orchestra*
'67 Last Waltz *Engelbert Humperdinck*
'66 Last Word In Lonesome Is Me *Eddy Arnold*
'89 Last Worthless Evening *Don Henley*
'57 Lasting Love *Sal Mineo*
'74 Late For The Sky *Jackson Browne*
'80 Late In The Evening *Paul Simon*
Lately
'93 *Jodeci*
'98 *Divine*
'65 Laugh At Me *Sonny*
'65 Laugh, Laugh *Beau Brummels*
'69 Laughing *Guess Who*
'63 Laughing Boy *Mary Wells*
'74 Laughter In The Rain *Neil Sedaka*
'65 Laurie (Strange Things Happen) *Dickey Lee*
'59 Lavender-Blue *Sammy Turner*
'78 Lawyers, Guns And Money *Warren Zevon*
'83 Lawyers In Love *Jackson Browne*
'70 Lay A Little Lovin' On Me *Robin McNamara*
'70 Lay Down (Candles In The Rain) *Melanie/Edwin Hawkins Singers*
'78 Lay Down Sally *Eric Clapton*
'56 Lay Down Your Arms *Chordettes*
'85 Lay It Down *Ratt*
'79 Lay It On The Line *Triumph*
'69 Lay Lady Lay *Bob Dylan*
Lay Your Hands On Me
'85 *Thompson Twins*
'89 *Bon Jovi*
'94 (Lay Your Head On My) Pillow *Tony Toni Tone*
'91 Laying Down The Law *Law*
Layla
'72 *Derek & The Dominos*
'92 *Eric Clapton [live]*
'67 Lazy Day *Spanky & Our Gang*
'58 Lazy Mary *Lou Monte*
'61 Lazy River *Bobby Darin*
'58 Lazy Summer Night *Four Preps*
'78 Le Freak *Chic*
Lead Me On
'79 *Maxine Nightingale*
'88 *Amy Grant*
'81 Leader Of The Band *Dan Fogelberg*
'64 Leader Of The Laundromat *Detergents*
'64 Leader Of The Pack *Shangri-Las*
'62 Léah *Roy Orbison*
'04 Lean Back *Terror Squad*
Lean On Me
'72 *Bill Withers*
'87 *Club Nouveau*
'66 Leaning On The Lamp Post *Herman's Hermits*
'91 Leap Of Faith *Lionel Cartwright*
'99 Learn To Fly *Foo Fighters*
'55 Learnin' The Blues *Frank Sinatra*

Learning To Fly
'87 *Pink Floyd*
'91 *Tom Petty*
'93 Learning To Live Again *Garth Brooks*
'81 Leather And Lace *Stevie Nicks (with Don Henley)*
'89 Leave A Light On *Belinda Carlisle*
'84 Leave A Tender Moment Alone *Billy Joel*
'04 Leave (Get Out) *JoJo*
'84 Leave It *Yes*
'73 Leave Me Alone (Ruby Red Dress) *Helen Reddy*
'94 Leaving Las Vegas *Sheryl Crow*
'73 Leaving Me *Independents*
'59 Leaving My Kitten Alone *Little Willie John*
'69 Leaving On A Jet Plane *Peter, Paul & Mary*
'58 Left Right Out Of Your Heart *Patti Page*
'83 Legal Tender *B-52s*
'97 Legend Of A Cowgirl *Imani Coppola*
'68 Legend Of A Mind *Moody Blues*
'80 Legend Of Wooley Swamp *Charlie Daniels Band*
'84 Legs *ZZ Top*
Lemon Tree
'62 *Peter, Paul & Mary*
'65 *Trini Lopez*
'67 Leopard-Skin Pill-Box Hat *Bob Dylan*
'58 Leroy *Jack Scott*
'68 Les Bicyclettes De Belsize *Engelbert Humperdinck*
'67 Lesson, The *Vikki Carr*
'99 Lesson In Leavin' *Jo Dee Messina*
'87 Lessons In Love *Level 42*
'00 Lessons Learned *Tracy Lawrence*
'69 Let A Woman Be A Woman - Let A Man Be A Man *Dyke & The Blazers*
'76 Let 'Em In *Wings*
'95 Let Her Cry *Hootie & The Blowfish*
'76 Let Her In *John Travolta*
'85 Let Him Go *Animotion*
'70 Let It Be *Beatles*
Let It Be Me
'60 *Everly Brothers*
'64 *Betty Everett & Jerry Butler*
'69 *Glen Campbell & Bobbie Gentry*
'82 *Willie Nelson*
'97 Let It Go *Ray J*
'77 Let It Go, Let It Flow *Dave Mason*
'67 Let It Out (Let It All Hang Out) *Hombres*
'70 Let It Rain *Eric Clapton*
'74 Let It Ride *Bachman-Turner Overdrive*
'88 Let It Roll *Little Feat*
Let It Shine
'75 *Olivia Newton-John*
'76 *Santana*
'93 Let It Snow *Boyz II Men*
'82 Let It Whip *Dazz Band*
'67 Let Love Come Between Us *James & Bobby Purify*
'69 Let Me *Paul Revere & The Raiders*
'65 Let Me Be *Turtles*
'80 Let Me Be The Clock *Smokey Robinson*
Let Me Be The One
'85 *Five Star*
'87 *Exposé*
'95 *Blessid Union Of Souls*
'73 Let Me Be There *Olivia Newton-John*
'80 Let Me Be Your Angel *Stacy Lattisaw*
'61 Let Me Belong To You *Brian Hyland*
'01 Let Me Blow Ya Mind *Eve*
'97 Let Me Clear My Throat *DJ Kool*
'05 Let Me Go *3 Doors Down*
'80 Let Me Go, Love *Nicolette Larson*

Let Me Go, Lover!
'55 *Joan Weber*
'55 *Teresa Brewer*
'55 *Patti Page*
Let Me In
'62 *Sensations*
'04 *Young Buck*
'98 Let Me Let Go *Faith Hill*
'05 Let Me Love You *Mario*
'80 Let Me Love You Tonight *Pure Prairie League*
'93 Let Me Ride *Dr. Dre*
'73 Let Me Serenade You *Three Dog Night*
'76 Let Me Take You Home Tonight *Boston*
'82 Let Me Tickle Your Fancy *Jermaine Jackson*
'80 Let My Love Open The Door *Pete Townshend*
'91 Let The Beat Hit 'Em *Lisa Lisa & Cult Jam*
'58 Let The Bells Keep Ringing *Paul Anka*
'89 Let The Day Begin *Call*
Let The Four Winds Blow
'57 *Roy Brown*
'61 *Fats Domino*
Let The Good Times Roll
'56 *Shirley & Lee*
'67 *Bunny Sigler [medley]*
'60 Let The Little Girl Dance *Billy Bland*
Let The Music Play
'75 *Barry White*
'83 *Shannon*
Let The Sunshine In ..see: Aquarius
'05 Let Them Be Little *Billy Dean*
'61 Let There Be Drums *Sandy Nelson*
'73 Let Your Hair Down *Temptations*
'76 Let Your Love Flow *Bellamy Brothers*
'71 Let Your Love Go *Bread*
'78 Let's All Chant *Michael Zager Band*
'04 Let's Be Us Again *Lonestar*
'91 Let's Chill *Guy*
Let's Dance
'62 *Chris Montez*
'83 *David Bowie*
'75 Let's Do It Again *Staple Singers*
'66 Let's Fall In Love *Peaches & Herb*
'04 Let's Get Away *T.I.*
Let's Get Down
'96 *Tony Toni Toné*
'03 *Bow Wow*
'73 Let's Get It On *Marvin Gaye*
'04 Let's Get It Started *Black Eyed Peas*
Let's Get Married
'74 *Al Green*
'00 *Jagged Edge*
'92 Let's Get Rocked *Def Leppard*
'80 Let's Get Serious *Jermaine Jackson*
'61 Let's Get Together *Hayley Mills*
Let's Go!
'62 *Routers*
'79 *Cars*
'87 *Wang Chung*
'04 *Trick Daddy*
'57 Let's Go Calypso *Rusty Draper*
'85 Let's Go All The Way *Sly Fox*
'84 Let's Go Crazy *Prince*
'82 Let's Go Dancin' (Ooh La, La, La) *Kool & The Gang*
'66 Let's Go Get Stoned *Ray Charles*
'60 Let's Go, Let's Go, Let's Go *Hank Ballard*
'63 Let's Go Steady Again *Neil Sedaka*
'61 Let's Go Trippin' *Dick Dale*
'81 Let's Groove *Earth, Wind & Fire*
Let's Hang On!
'65 *4 Seasons*
'82 *Barry Manilow*
'66 Let's Have A Party *Wanda Jackson*
'84 Let's Hear It For The Boy *Deniece Williams*
'63 Let's Limbo Some More *Chubby Checker*

'67 **Let's Live For Today** *Grass Roots*
'75 **Let's Live Together** *Road Apples*
'64 **Let's Lock The Door**
   *Jay & The Americans*
'96 **Let's Make A Night To Remember**
   *Bryan Adams*
'73 **Let's Pretend** *Raspberries*
'74 **Let's Put It All Together** *Stylistics*
'98 **Let's Ride** *Montell Jordan*
'67 **Let's Spend The Night Together**
   *Rolling Stones*
'66 **Let's Start All Over Again**
   *Ronnie Dove*
   **Let's Stay Together** .
'71   *Al Green*
'84   *Tina Turner*
'74 **Let's Straighten It Out** *Latimore*
'91 **Let's Talk About Sex** *Salt-N-Pepa*
'60 **Let's Think About Living**
   *Bob Luman*
'63 **Let's Turkey Trot** *Little Eva*
'61 **Let's Twist Again** *Chubby Checker*
'87 **Let's Wait Awhile** *Janet Jackson*
'87 **Let's Work** *Mick Jagger*
   **Let's Work Together**
'69   *Wilbert Harrison*
'70   *Canned Heat*
'94 **Letitgo** *Prince*
   **Letter, The**
'67   *Box Tops*
'69   *Arbors*
'70   *Joe Cocker with Leon Russell*
'63 **Letter From Sherry** *Dale Ward*
'61 **Letter Full Of Tears** *Gladys Knight*
'58 **Letter To An Angel** *Jimmy Clanton*
'92 **Letter To Elise** *Cure*
'73 **Letter To Myself** *Chi-Lites*
'04 **Letters From Home**
   *John Michael Montgomery*
'75 **Letting Go** *Wings*
'71 **Levon** *Elton John*
   **Liar**
'71   *Three Dog Night*
'00   *Profyle*
'65 **Liar, Liar** *Castaways*
'89 **Licence To Chill** *Billy Ocean*
'68 **Licking Stick - Licking Stick**
   *James Brown*
'77 **Lido Shuffle** *Boz Scaggs*
'62 **Lie To Me** *Brook Benton*
'57 **Liechtensteiner Polka** *Will Glahé*
   **Lies**
'65   *Knickerbockers*
'83   *Thompson Twins*
'87   *Jonathan Butler*
'90   *En Vogue*
'91   *EMF*
'79 **Life During Wartime**
   *Talking Heads*
'91 **Life Goes On** *Poison*
'85 **Life In A Northern Town**
   *Dream Academy*
'85 **Life In One Day** *Howard Jones*
'77 **Life In The Fast Lane** *Eagles*
'71 **Life Is A Carnival** *Band*
'92 **Life Is A Highway** *Tom Cochrane*
'74 **Life Is A Rock (But The Radio**
   **Rolled Me)** *Reunion*
'56 **Life Is But A Dream** *Harptones*
'81 **Life Of Illusion** *Joe Walsh*
'92 **Life Of Riley** *Lightning Seeds*
'88 **Life Turned Her That Way**
   *Ricky Van Shelton*
'92 **Life's A Dance**
   *John Michael Montgomery*
'78 **Life's Been Good** *Joe Walsh*
'02 **Lifestyles Of The Rich And Famous**
   *Good Charlotte*
'01 **Lifetime** *Maxwell*
   **Lift Me Up**
'91   *Yes*
'92   *Howard Jones*
   **Light My Fire**
'67   *Doors*
'68   *Jose Feliciano*

'87 **Light Of Day** *Joan Jett*
'65 **Lightnin' Strikes** *Lou Christie*
'95 **Lightning Crashes** *Live*
'67 **Lightning's Girl** *Nancy Sinatra*
'78 **Lights** *Journey*
'01 **Lights, Camera, Action!** *Mr. Cheeks*
'84 **Lights Out** *Peter Wolf*
'67 **(Lights Went Out In) Massachusetts**
   *Bee Gees*
'66 **Like A Baby** *Len Barry*
'77 **Like A Hurricane** *Neil Young*
'89 **Like A Prayer** *Madonna*
'86 **Like A Rock** *Bob Seger*
'65 **Like A Rolling Stone** *Bob Dylan*
'03 **Like A Stone** *Audioslave*
'78 **Like A Sunday In Salem (The Amos**
   **& Andy Song)** *Gene Cotton*
'85 **Like A Surgeon** *"Weird Al" Yankovic*
'84 **Like A Virgin** *Madonna*
'67 **Like An Old Time Movie**
   *Scott McKenzie*
'03 **Like Glue** *Sean Paul*
'02 **Like I Love You** *Justin Timberlake*
'61 **Like, Long Hair**
   *Paul Revere & The Raiders*
'86 **Like No Other Night** *38 Special*
'60 **Like Strangers** *Everly Brothers*
'96 **Like The Rain** *Clint Black*
'95 **Like There Ain't No Yesterday**
   *BlackHawk*
'95 **Like This And Like That** *Monica*
'68 **Like To Get To Know You**
   *Spanky & Our Gang*
'05 **Like You Soldiers** *Eminem*
'91 **Lily Was Here** *David A. Stewart*
   *& Candy Dulfer*
   **Limbo Rock**
'62   *Champs*
'62   *Chubby Checker*
'63 **Linda** *Jan & Dean*
   **Ling, Ting, Tong**
'55   *Charms*
'55   *Five Keys*
'93 **Linger** *Cranberries*
   **Lion Sleeps Tonight**
'61   *Tokens*
'72   *Robert John*
'57 **Lips Of Wine** *Andy Williams*
'56 **Lipstick And Candy And**
   **Rubbersole Shoes** *Julius LaRosa*
'59 **Lipstick On Your Collar**
   *Connie Francis*
'00 **Liquid Dreams** *O-Town*
   **Lisbon Antigua**
'55   *Nelson Riddle*
'56   *Mitch Miller*
'97 **Listen** *Collective Soul*
'66 **Listen People** *Herman's Hermits*
'78 **Listen To Her Heart** *Tom Petty*
'69 **Listen To The Band** *Monkees*
'72 **Listen To The Music**
   *Doobie Brothers*
'75 **Listen To What The Man Said**
   *Wings*
'89 **Listen To Your Heart** *Roxette*
'99 **Lit Up** *Buckcherry*
'68 **Little Arrows** *Leapy Lee*
'63 **Little Band Of Gold** *James Gilreath*
'67 **Little Bit Me, A Little Bit You**
   *Monkees*
   **Little Bit More**
'76   *Dr. Hook*
'86   *Melba Moore (with Freddie Jackson)*
'67 **Little Bit O' Soul** *Music Explosion*
'65 **Little Bit Of Heaven** *Ronnie Dove*
'86 **Little Bit Of Love (Is All It Takes)**
   *New Edition*
   **Little Bit Of Soap**
'61   *Jarmels*
'79   *Nigel Olsson*
'74 **Little Bit Of Sympathy**
   *Robin Trower*
'96 **Little Bitty** *Alan Jackson*
'60 **Little Bitty Girl** *Bobby Rydell*

   **Little Bitty Pretty One**
'57   *Thurston Harris*
'62   *Clyde McPhatter*
'72   *Jackson 5*
'61 **Little Bitty Tear** *Burl Ives*
'62 **Little Black Book** *Jimmy Dean*
'58 **Little Blue Man** *Betty Johnson*
'61 **Little Boy Sad** *Johnny Burnette*
   **Little By Little**
'57   *Nappy Brown*
'85   *Robert Plant*
'64 **Little Children** *Billy J. Kramer*
   *With The Dakotas*
'60 **Little Coco Palm** *Jerry Wallace*
   **Little Darlin'**
'57   *Diamonds*
'57   *Gladiolas*
'63 **Little Deuce Coupe** *Beach Boys*
'61 **Little Devil** *Neil Sedaka*
'62 **Little Diane** *Dion*
'59 **Little Dipper** *Mickey Mozart Quintet*
'58 **Little Drummer Boy**
   *Harry Simeone Chorale*
'61 **Little Egypt (Ying-Yang)** *Coasters*
'67 **Little Games** *Yardbirds*
   **Little Girl**
'66   *Syndicate Of Sound*
'00   *John Michael Montgomery*
'65 **Little Girl I Once Knew** *Beach Boys*
'56 **Little Girl Of Mine** *Cleftones*
'99 **Little Good-Byes** *SheDaisy*
'83 **Little Good News** *Anne Murray*
   **Little Green Apples**
'68   *Roger Miller*
'68   *O.C. Smith*
'70 **Little Green Bag**
   *George Baker Selection*
'64 **Little Honda** *Hondells*
'80 **Little In Love** *Cliff Richard*
'89 **Little Jackie Wants To Be A Star**
   *Lisa Lisa & Cult Jam*
'80 **Little Jeannie** *Elton John*
   **Little Latin Lupe Lu**
'63   *Righteous Brothers*
'66   *Mitch Ryder*
'68 **Little Less Conversation**
   *Elvis Presley*
'93 **Little Less Talk And A Lot More**
   **Action** *Toby Keith*
'88 **Little Liar** *Joan Jett*
'87 **Little Lies** *Fleetwood Mac*
'90 **Little Love** *Corey Hart*
   **Little Man**
'66   *Sonny & Cher*
'99   *Alan Jackson*
'92 **Little Miss Can't Be Wrong**
   *Spin Doctors*
'95 **Little Miss Honky Tonk**
   *Brooks & Dunn*
'03 **Little Moments** *Brad Paisley*
   **Little More Love**
'78   *Olivia Newton-John*
'97   *Vince Gill*
'97 **Little More Time With You**
   *James Taylor*
'64 **Little Old Lady (From Pasadena)**
   *Jan & Dean*
'67 **Little Old Wine Drinker, Me**
   *Dean Martin*
'67 **Little Ole Man (Uptight- Every-**
   **thing's Alright)** *Bill Cosby*
'98 **Little Past Little Rock**
   *Lee Ann Womack*
'77 **Little Queen** *Heart*
'83 **Little Red Corvette** *Prince*
'62 **Little Red Rented Rowboat**
   *Joe Dowell*
'66 **Lil' Red Riding Hood** *Sam The*
   *Sham & The Pharoahs*
'97 **Little Red Rodeo** *Collin Raye*
'63 **Little Red Rooster** *Sam Cooke*
'88 **Little Respect** *Erasure*
   **Little Rock**
'86   *Reba McEntire*
'94   *Collin Raye*

**Little Sister**
'61 *Elvis Presley*
'05 *Queens Of The Stone Age*
'59 **Little Space Girl** *Jesse Lee Turner*
'58 **Little Star** *Elegants*
'65 **Little Things** *Bobby Goldsboro*
'59 **Little Things Mean A Lot**
 *Joni James*
'83 **Little Too Late** *Pat Benatar*
'62 **Little Town Flirt** *Del Shannon*
'88 **Little Walter** *Tony! Toni! Toné!*
'97 **Little White Lie** *Sammy Hagar*
'57 **Little White Lies** *Betty Johnson*
'73 **Little Willy** *Sweet*
'68 **Little Wing** *Jimi Hendrix*
'92 **Live And Learn** *Joe Public*
**Live And Let Die**
'73 *Wings*
'91 *Guns N' Roses*
'85 **Live Every Moment**
 *REO Speedwagon*
'91 **Live For Loving You** *Gloria Estefan*
'95 **Live Forever** *Oasis*
'86 **Live Is Life** *Opus*
'04 **Live Like You Were Dying**
 *Tim McGraw*
'87 **Live My Life** *Boy George*
'86 **Live To Tell** *Madonna*
'93 **Live Until I Die** *Clay Walker*
'75 **Lively Up Yourself** *Bob Marley*
'76 **Livin' For The Weekend** *O'Jays*
'73 **Livin' For You** *Al Green*
'84 **Livin' In Desperate Times**
 *Olivia Newton-John*
'77 **Livin' In The Life** *Isley Brothers*
'01 **Livin' It Up** *Ja Rule*
'79 **Livin' It Up (Friday Night)**
 *Bell & James*
'99 **Livin' La Vida Loca** *Ricky Martin*
'86 **Livin' On A Prayer** *Bon Jovi*
'94 **Livin' On Love** *Alan Jackson*
'93 **Livin' On The Edge** *Aerosmith*
'76 **Livin' Thing** *Electric Light Orchestra*
'63 **Living A Lie** *Al Martino*
'75 **Living A Little, Laughing A Little**
 *Spinners*
'80 **Living After Midnight**
 *Judas Priest*
'02 **Living And Living Well**
 *George Strait*
'59 **Living Doll** *Cliff Richard*
'73 **Living For The City** *Stevie Wonder*
'87 **Living In A Box** *Living In A Box*
'81 **Living In A Fantasy** *Leo Sayer*
'72 **Living In A House Divided** *Cher*
'96 **Living In A Moment** *Ty Herndon*
'85 **Living In America** *James Brown*
'94 **Living In Danger** *Ace Of Base*
'89 **Living In Sin** *Bon Jovi*
'72 **Living In The Past** *Jethro Tull*
'68 **Living In The U.S.A.**
 *Steve Miller Band*
'81 **Living Inside Myself** *Gino Vannelli*
'69 **Living Loving Maid (She's Just A
 Woman)** *Led Zeppelin*
'76 **Living Next Door To Alice** *Smokie*
'85 **Living On A Thin Line** *Kinks*
'83 **Living On The Edge**
 *Jim Capaldi*
'73 **Living Together, Growing Together**
 *5th Dimension*
'89 **Living Years** *Mike & The Mechanics*
'75 **Lizzie And The Rainman**
 *Tanya Tucker*
'68 **Lo Mucho Que Te Quiero**
 *Rene & Rene*
'78 **Load-Out, The [medley]**
 *Jackson Browne*
'04 **Locked Up** *Akon*
'04 **Loco** *David Lee Murphy*
**Loco-Motion, The**
'62 *Little Eva*
'74 *Grand Funk*
'88 *Kylie Minogue*
'71 **Locomotive Breath** *Jethro Tull*
'63 **Loddy Lo** *Chubby Checker*

'69 **Lodi**
 *Creedence Clearwater Revival*
'79 **Logical Song** *Supertramp*
'70 **Lola** *Kinks*
'58 **Lollipop** *Chordettes*
'62 **Lollipops And Roses** *Jack Jones*
'97 **Lollipop (Candyman)** *Aqua*
'80 **London Calling** *Clash*
'78 **London Town** *Wings*
'67 **(Loneliness Made Me Realize) It's
 You That I Need** *Temptations*
'65 **L-O-N-E-L-Y** *Bobby Vinton*
'05 **Lonely** *Akon*
'99 **Lonely And Gone**
 *Montgomery Gentry*
**Lonely Boy**
'59 *Paul Anka*
'59 *Conway Twitty*
'77 *Andrew Gold*
'62 **Lonely Bull (El Solo Torro)**
 *Herb Alpert*
'70 **Lonely Days** *Bee Gees*
'59 **Lonely For You** *Gary Stites*
'59 **Lonely Guitar** *Annette*
'87 **Lonely In Love** *Dan Fogelberg*
'58 **Lonely Island** *Sam Cooke*
'61 **Lonely Man** *Elvis Presley*
'76 **Lonely Night (Angel Face)**
 *Captain & Tennille*
'82 **Lonely Nights** *Bryan Adams*
'05 **Lonely No More** *Rob Thomas*
'85 **Lonely Ol' Night**
 *John Cougar Mellencamp*
'59 **Lonely One** *Duane Eddy*
'74 **Lonely People** *America*
'59 **Lonely Street** *Andy Williams*
'63 **Lonely Surfer** *Jack Nitzsche*
'58 **Lonely Teardrops** *Jackie Wilson*
'60 **Lonely Teenager** *Dion*
'96 **Lonely Too Long** *Patty Loveless*
'60 **Lonely Weekends** *Charlie Rich*
'79 **Lonesome Loser** *Little River Band*
'58 **Lonesome Town** *Ricky Nelson*
'71 **Long Ago And Far Away**
 *James Taylor*
'70 **Long And Winding Road** *Beatles*
'70 **Long As I Can See The Light**
 *Creedence Clearwater Revival*
'72 **Long Cool Woman (In A Black
 Dress)** *Hollies*
'72 **Long Dark Road** *Hollies*
'96 **Long December** *Counting Crows*
'72 **Long Distance Runaround** *Yes*
'01 **Long Goodbye** *Brooks & Dunn*
'77 **Long Haired Country Boy** *Charlie
 Daniels Band*
'72 **Long Haired Lover From Liverpool**
 *Little Jimmy Osmond*
'66 **Long Live Our Love** *Shangri-Las*
'79 **Long Live Rock** *Who*
**Long Lonely Nights**
'57 *Clyde McPhatter*
'65 *Bobby Vinton*
'70 **Long Lonesome Highway**
 *Michael Parks*
'70 **Long Long Time** *Linda Ronstadt*
'77 **Long, Long Way From Home**
 *Foreigner*
'79 **Long Run** *Eagles*
'75 **Long Tall Glasses (I Can Dance)**
 *Leo Sayer*
**Long Tall Sally**
'56 *Pat Boone*
'56 *Little Richard*
'77 **Long Time** *Boston*
'02 **Long Time Gone** *Dixie Chicks*
'73 **Long Train Runnin'** *Doobie Brothers*
'94 **Long View** *Green Day*
'79 **Longer** *Dan Fogelberg*
'84 **Longest Time** *Billy Joel*
'55 **Longest Walk** *Jaye P. Morgan*
'74 **Longfellow Serenade** *Neil Diamond*
'97 **Longneck Bottle** *Garth Brooks*
'89 **Look, The** *Roxette*
'75 **Look At Me (I'm In Love)** *Moments*
'88 **Look Away** *Chicago*

**Look For A Star**
'60 *Garry Miles*
'60 *Billy Vaughn*
'92 **Look Heart, No Hands** *Randy Travis*
'57 **Look Homeward, Angel**
 *Johnnie Ray*
'61 **Look In My Eyes** *Chantels*
'74 **Look In My Eyes Pretty Woman**
 *Tony Orlando & Dawn*
'97 **Look Into My Eyes**
 *Bone Thugs-N-Harmony*
**Look Of Love**
'64 *Lesley Gore*
'67 *Dusty Springfield*
'68 *Sergio Mendes*
'82 *ABC*
'88 **Look Out Any Window**
 *Bruce Hornsby*
'65 **Look Through Any Window** *Hollies*
'66 **Look Through My Window**
 *Mamas & The Papas*
'70 **Look What They've Done To My
 Song Ma** *New Seekers*
'72 **Look What You Done For Me**
 *Al Green*
**Look What You've Done**
'66 *Pozo Seco Singers*
'04 *Jet*
'80 **Look What You've Done To Me**
 *Boz Scaggs*
'98 **Lookin' At Me** *Mase*
**Lookin' For A Love**
'71 *J. Geils Band*
'74 *Bobby Womack*
**Lookin' For Love**
'66 *Ray Conniff*
'80 *Johnny Lee*
'70 **Lookin' Out My Back Door**
 *Creedence Clearwater Revival*
'72 **Lookin' Through The Windows**
 *Jackson 5*
'58 **Looking Back** *Nat "King" Cole*
'68 **Looking For A Fox** *Clarence Carter*
'87 **Looking For A New Love**
 *Jody Watley*
'83 **Looking For A Stranger** *Pat Benatar*
'76 **Looking For Space** *John Denver*
'93 **Looking Through Patient Eyes**
 *PM Dawn*
**Looking Through The Eyes Of Love**
'65 *Gene Pitney*
'72 *Partridge Family*
'98 **Looking Through Your Eyes**
 *LeAnn Rimes*
'77 **Looks Like We Made It**
 *Barry Manilow*
'62 **Loop De Loop** *Johnny Thunder*
'88 **Loosey's Rap** *Rick James*
'04 **Lord Have Mercy** *Michael W. Smith*
'74 **Lord's Prayer** *Sister Janet Mead*
'76 **Lorelei** *Styx*
'04 **Lose My Breath** *Destiny's Child*
'02 **Lose Yourself** *Eminem*
**Loser**
'93 *Beck*
'00 *3 Doors Down*
'91 **Losing My Religion** *R.E.M.*
'63 **Losing You** *Brenda Lee*
'79 **Lost Her In The Sun** *John Stewart*
'87 **Lost In Emotion**
 *Lisa Lisa & Cult Jam*
**Lost In Love**
'80 *Air Supply*
'85 *New Edition*
'85 **Lost In The Fifties Tonight (In The
 Still Of The Night)** *Ronnie Milsap*
**Lost In You**
'88 *Rod Stewart*
'99 *Garth Brooks As Chris Gaines*
'89 **Lost In Your Eyes** *Debbie Gibson*
'61 **Lost Love** *H.B. Barnum*
'61 **Lost Someone** *James Brown*
'76 **Lost Without Your Love** *Bread*
'78 **Lotta Love** *Nicolette Larson*
'57 **Lotta Lovin'** *Gene Vincent*

**Louie Louie**
'63 *Kingsmen*
'66 *Sandpipers*
'96 **Loungin** *LL Cool J*
**Love**
'71 *Lettermen*
'92 *Sundays*
'01 *Musiq Soulchild*
'94 **Love A Little Stronger** *Diamond Rio*
'57 **Love Affair** *Sal Mineo*
'89 **Love And Anger** *Kate Bush*
'90 **Love & Emotion** *Stevie B*
'72 **Love And Happiness** *Al Green*
**Love And Marriage**
'55 *Dinah Shore*
'55 *Frank Sinatra*
'91 **Love And Understanding** *Cher*
**Love At [@] First [1st] Sight**
'91 *Styx*
'02 *Kylie Minogue*
'03 *Mary J. Blige*
**Love Ballad**
'76 *L.T.D.*
'79 *George Benson*
'88 **Love Bites** *Def Leppard*
'85 **Love Bizarre** *Sheila E.*
'67 **Love Bug Leave My Heart Alone**
 *Martha & The Vandellas*
'62 **Love Came To Me** *Dion*
'69 **Love (Can Make You Happy)** *Mercy*
'92 **Love Can Move Mountains**
 *Celine Dion*
'87 **Love Changes**
 *Kashif & Meli'sa Morgan*
'88 **Love Changes (Everything)**
 *Climie Fisher*
**Love Child**
'68 *Supremes*
'90 *Sweet Sensation*
'82 **Love Come Down** *Evelyn King*
'00 **Love Don't Cost A Thing**
 *Jennifer Lopez*
'78 **Love Don't Live Here Anymore**
 *Rose Royce*
'74 **Love Don't Love Nobody** *Spinners*
'93 **Love Don't Love You** *En Vogue*
'67 **Love Eyes** *Nancy Sinatra*
'75 **Love Finds It's Own Way**
 *Gladys Knight*
'76 **Love Fire** *Jigsaw*
'97 **Love Gets Me Every Time**
 *Shania Twain*
'70 **Love Grows (Where My Rosemary**
 **Goes)** *Edison Lighthouse*
'77 **Love Gun** *Kiss*
'76 **Love Hangover** *Diana Ross*
'84 **Love Has Finally Come At Last**
 *Bobby Womack & Patti LaBelle*
'71 **Love Her Madly** *Doors*
**Love Hurts**
'60 *Everly Brothers*
'75 *Nazareth*
'73 **Love I Lost** *Harold Melvin*
'67 **Love I Saw In You Was Just A**
 **Mirage** *Miracles*
'89 **Love In An Elevator** *Aerosmith*
'77 **Love In 'C' Minor** *Cerrone*
'82 **Love In Store** *Fleetwood Mac*
'81 **Love In The First Degree** *Alabama*
'76 **Love In The Shadows** *Neil Sedaka*
'89 **Love In Your Eyes** *Eddie Money*
'93 **Love Is** *Vanessa Williams &*
 *Brian McKnight*
'83 **Love Is A Battlefield** *Pat Benatar*
'57 **Love Is A Golden Ring**
 *Frankie Laine*
'87 **Love Is A House** *Force M.D.'s*
'66 **Love Is A Hurtin' Thing** *Lou Rawls*
**Love Is A Many-Splendored Thing**
'55 *Don Cornell*
'55 *Four Aces*
'83 **Love Is A Stranger** *Eurythmics*
'91 **Love Is A Wonderful Thing**
 *Michael Bolton*
'76 **Love Is Alive** *Gary Wright*
'68 **Love Is All Around** *Troggs*

'58 **Love Is All We Need**
 *Tommy Edwards*
'81 **Love Is Alright Tonite**
 *Rick Springfield*
'00 **Love Is Blind** *Eve*
**Love Is Blue**
'68 *Al Martino*
'68 *Paul Mauriat*
'69 *Dells [medley]*
'86 **Love Is Forever** *Billy Ocean*
'67 **Love Is Here And Now You're Gone**
 *Supremes*
'82 **Love Is In Control (Finger On The**
 **Trigger)** *Donna Summer*
'78 **Love Is In The Air** *John Paul Young*
'68 **(Love Is Like A) Baseball Game**
 *Intruders*
'81 **Love Is Like A Rock** *Donnie Iris*
'66 **Love Is Like An Itching In My Heart**
 *Supremes*
'78 **Love Is Like Oxygen** *Sweet*
'92 **Love Is On The Way** *Saigon Kick*
**Love Is Strange**
'57 *Mickey & Sylvia*
'67 *Peaches & Herb*
'94 **Love Is Strong** *Rolling Stones*
'79 **Love Is The Answer**
 *England Dan & John Ford Coley*
'75 **Love Is The Drug** *Roxy Music*
'85 **Love Is The Seventh Wave** *Sting*
'55 **(Love Is) The Tender Trap**
 *Frank Sinatra*
'77 **(Love Is) Thicker Than Water**
 *Andy Gibb*
'72 **Love Jones**
 *Brighter Side Of Darkness*
'70 **Love Land** *Charles Wright*
**Love Letters**
'62 *Ketty Lester*
'66 *Elvis Presley*
'57 **Love Letters In The Sand**
 *Pat Boone*
'73 **Love Lies Bleeding [medley]**
 *Elton John*
'84 **Love Light In Flight** *Stevie Wonder*
'98 **Love Like This** *Faith Evans*
'75 **L-O-V-E (Love)** *Al Green*
**Love, Love, Love**
'55 *Webb Pierce*
'56 *Clovers*
'56 *Diamonds*
'75 **Love Machine** *Miracles*
'68 **Love Makes A Woman**
 *Barbara Acklin*
**Love Makes The World Go 'Round**
'58 *Perry Como*
'63 *Paul Anka*
'66 *Deon Jackson*
'90 **Love Makes Things Happen**
 *Pebbles*
**Love Me**
'56 *Elvis Presley*
'76 *Yvonne Elliman*
'91 *Collin Raye*
'92 *Tracie Spencer*
'98 *112*
'91 **Love Me All Up** *Stacy Earl*
'64 **Love Me Do** *Beatles*
'90 **Love Me Down** *Freddie Jackson*
'74 **Love Me For A Reason** *Osmonds*
'90 **Love Me For Life** *Stevie B*
**Love Me Forever**
'57 *Four Esquires*
'57 *Eydie Gorme*
'67 *Roger Williams*
'98 **Love Me Good** *Michael W. Smith*
**Love Me Or Leave Me**
'55 *Sammy Davis, Jr.*
'55 *Lena Horne*
'55 *Doris Day*
**Love Me Tender**
'56 *Elvis Presley*
'62 *Richard Chamberlain*
'67 *Percy Sledge*
'57 **Love Me To Pieces** *Jill Corey*
'82 **Love Me Tomorrow** *Chicago*

'69 **Love Me Tonight** *Tom Jones*
'67 **Love Me Two Times** *Doors*
'62 **Love Me Warm And Tender**
 *Paul Anka*
**Love Me With All Your Heart**
'64 *Ray Charles Singers*
'66 *Bachelors*
'71 **Love Means (You Never Have To**
 **Say You're Sorry)**
 *Sounds Of Sunshine*
'83 **Love My Way** *Psychedelic Furs*
'91 **Love Of A Lifetime** *Firehouse*
'01 **Love Of A Woman** *Travis Tritt*
'97 **Love Of My Life** *Sammy Kershaw*
'02 **Love Of My Life (An Ode To Hip**
 **Hop)** *Erykah Badu*
'63 **Love Of My Man** *Theola Kilgore*
**Love On A Two-Way Street**
'70 *Moments*
'81 *Stacy Lattisaw*
'90 **Love On Arrival** *Dan Seals*
'80 **Love On The Rocks** *Neil Diamond*
'75 **Love Or Leave** *Spinners*
'70 **Love Or Let Me Be Lonely**
 *Friends Of Distinction*
'78 **Love Or Something Like It**
 *Kenny Rogers*
'88 **Love Overboard** *Gladys Knight*
'79 **Love Pains** *Yvonne Elliman*
'86 **Love Parade** *Dream Academy*
'82 **Love Plus One** *Haircut One Hundred*
**Love Potion Number Nine**
'59 *Clovers*
'64 *Searchers*
**Love Power**
'67 *Sandpebbles*
'87 *Dionne Warwick & Jeffrey Osborne*
'91 *Luther Vandross [medley]*
'76 **Love Really Hurts Without You**
 *Billy Ocean*
'73 **Love, Reign, O'er Me** *Who*
**Love Rollercoaster**
'75 *Ohio Players*
'96 *Red Hot Chili Peppers*
'89 **Love Saw It** *Karyn White*
'89 **Love Shack** *B-52's*
'63 **Love She Can Count On** *Miracles*
'92 **Love Shoulda Brought You Home**
 *Toni Braxton*
'94 **Love Sneakin' Up On You**
 *Bonnie Raitt*
'63 **Love So Fine** *Chiffons*
'76 **Love So Right** *Bee Gees*
'84 **Love Somebody** *Rick Springfield*
**Love Song**
'73 *Anne Murray*
'89 *Cure*
'89 *Tesla*
'04 *311*
'95 **Love Song For A Savior** *Jars Of Clay*
'94 **Love Spreads** *Stone Roses*
'80 **Love Stinks** *J. Geils Band*
'80 **Love T.K.O.** *Teddy Pendergrass*
**Love Takes Time**
'79 *Orleans*
'90 *Mariah Carey*
**Love The One You're With**
'70 *Stephen Stills*
'71 *Isley Brothers*
'80 **Love The World Away**
 *Kenny Rogers*
'76 **Love Theme From A Star Is Born**
 **(Evergreen)** *Barbra Streisand*
'78 **Love Theme From Eyes Of Laura**
 **Mars (Prisoner)** *Barbra Streisand*
'61 **(Love Theme From) One Eyed**
 **Jacks** *Ferrante & Teicher*
'69 **Love Theme From Romeo & Juliet**
 *Henry Mancini*
'85 **Love Theme From St. Elmo's Fire**
 *David Foster*
'72 **Love Theme From The Godfather**
 *Andy Williams*
'91 **Love...Thy Will Be Done** *Martika*
'75 **Love To Love You Baby**
 *Donna Summer*

'86 **Love Touch** *Rod Stewart*
'73 **Love Train** *O'Jays*
'95 **Love U 4 Life** *Jodeci*
'92 **Love U More** *Sunscreem*
'90 **Love Under New Management**
*Miki Howard*
'60 **Love Walked In** *Dinah Washington*
'86 **Love Walks In** *Van Halen*
'71 **Love We Had (Stays On My Mind)**
*Dells*
'86 **Love Will Conquer All** *Lionel Richie*
**Love Will Find A Way**
'69 *Jackie DeShannon*
'78 *Pablo Cruise*
'87 *Yes*
'94 **Love Will Keep Us Alive** *Eagles*
'75 **Love Will Keep Us Together**
*Captain & Tennille*
'90 **Love Will Lead You Back**
*Taylor Dayne*
'90 **Love Will Never Do (Without You)**
*Janet Jackson*
'88 **Love Will Save The Day**
*Whitney Houston*
'84 **Love Will Show Us How**
*Christine McVie*
'80 **Love Will Tear Us Apart**
*Joy Division*
'82 **Love Will Turn You Around**
*Kenny Rogers*
'90 **Love Without End, Amen**
*George Strait*
'75 **Love Won't Let Me Wait**
*Major Harris*
**Love You Down**
'86 *Ready For The World*
'98 *Inoj*
'79 **Love You Inside Out** *Bee Gees*
'81 **Love You Like I Never Loved Before**
*John O'Banion*
'58 **Love You Most Of All** *Sam Cooke*
'03 **Love You Out Loud** *Rascal Flatts*
'70 **Love You Save** *Jackson 5*
'66 **Love You Save (May Be Your Own)**
*Joe Tex*
'60 **Love You So** *Ron Holden*
'86 **Love Zone** *Billy Ocean*
'82 **Love's Been A Little Bit Hard On Me**
*Juice Newton*
'04 **Love's Divine** *Seal*
'63 **Love's Gonna Live Here**
*Buck Owens*
"92 **Love's Got A Hold On You**
*Alan Jackson*
'77 **Love's Grown Deep** *Kenny Nolan*
'71 **Love's Lines, Angles And Rhymes**
*5th Dimension*
'66 **Love's Made A Fool Of You**
*Bobby Fuller Four*
'99 **Love's The Only House**
*Martina McBride*
'73 **Love's Theme**
*Love Unlimited Orchestra*
'97 **Loved Too Much** *Ty Herndon*
'96 **Lovefool** *Cardigans*
'84 **Lovelite** *O'Bryan*
'77 **Lovely Day** *Bill Withers*
**Lovely One**
'56 *Four Voices*
'80 *Jacksons*
'67 **Lovely Rita** *Beatles*
'88 **Lover In Me** *Sheena Easton*
'62 **Lover Please** *Clyde McPhatter*
'65 **Lover's Concerto** *Toys*
**Lover's Holiday**
'68 *Peggy Scott & Jo Jo Benson*
'80 *Change*
'61 **Lover's Island** *Blue Jays*
'58 **Lover's Question** *Clyde McPhatter*
**Loverboy**
'84 *Billy Ocean*
'01 *Mariah Carey*
'84 **Lovergirl** *Teena Marie*
'05 **Lovers And Friends**
*Lil Jon & The East Side Boyz*
'62 **Lovers By Night, Strangers By Day**
*Fleetwoods*

'59 **Lovers Never Say Goodbye**
*Flamingos*
'62 **Lovers Who Wander** *Dion*
'73 **Loves Me Like A Rock** *Paul Simon*
'60 **Lovey Dovey** *Buddy Knox*
'85 **Lovin' Every Minute Of It** *Loverboy*
'88 **Lovin' On Next To Nothin'**
*Gladys Knight*
'79 **Lovin', Touchin', Squeezin'** *Journey*
**Lovin' You**
'75 *Minnie Riperton*
'87 *O'Jays*
'91 **Loving Blind** *Clint Black*
'71 **Loving Her Was Easier (Than Anything I'll Ever Do Again)**
*Kris Kristofferson*
'57 **Loving You** *Elvis Presley*
'72 **Loving You Just Crossed My Mind**
*Sam Neely*
'93 **Low** *Cracker*
'79 **Low Budget** *Kinks*
'71 **Low Rider** *War*
'71 **Low Spark Of High Heeled Boys**
*Traffic*
**Lowdown**
'71 *Chicago*
'76 *Boz Scaggs*
'94 **Lucas With The Lid Off** *Lucas*
**Lucille**
'57 *Little Richard*
'60 *Everly Brothers*
'77 *Kenny Rogers*
'77 **Luckenbach, Texas**
*Waylon Jennings*
**Lucky**
'85 *Greg Kihn*
'00 *Britney Spears*
'89 **Lucky Charm** *Boys*
'59 **Lucky Devil** *Carl Dobkins, Jr.*
'85 **Lucky In Love** *Mick Jagger*
'58 **Lucky Ladybug** *Billy & Lillie*
'57 **Lucky Lips** *Ruth Brown*
'96 **Lucky Love** *Ace Of Base*
'71 **Lucky Man**
*Emerson, Lake & Palmer*
**Lucky One**
'84 *Laura Branigan*
'94 *Amy Grant*
'82 **Lucky Ones** *Loverboy*
'84 **Lucky Star** *Madonna*
'70 **Lucretia Mac Evil**
*Blood, Sweat & Tears*
**Lucy In The Sky With Diamonds**
'67 *Beatles*
'74 *Elton John*
'87 **Luka** *Suzanne Vega*
'98 **Lullaby** *Shawn Mullins*
'55 **Lullaby Of Birdland** *Blue Stars*
'61 **Lullaby Of Love** *Frank Gari*
'61 **Lullaby Of The Leaves** *Ventures*
'95 **Lump** *Presidents Of The United States Of America*
'77 **Lust For Life** *Iggy Pop*
'98 **Luv 2 Luv U** *Timbaland & Magoo*
'02 **Luv U Better** *LL Cool J*
'75 **Lyin' Eyes** *Eagles*
'90 **Lyin' To Myself** *David Cassidy*
'04 **Lying From You** *Linkin Park*

# M

'97 **MMMBop** *Hanson*
'59 **M.T.A.** *Kingston Trio*
'70 **Ma Belle Amie** *Tee Set*
**MacArthur Park**
'68 *Richard Harris*
'78 *Donna Summer*
'95 **Macarena (bayside boys mix)**
*Los Del Rio*
'74 **Machine Gun** *Commodores*
'78 **Macho Man** *Village People*
**Mack The Knife ..see: Moritat**
'86 **Mad About You** *Belinda Carlisle*
'02 **Made You Look** *Nas*
'76 **Mademoiselle** *Styx*

'60 **Madison, The** *Al Brown*
'60 **Madison Time** *Ray Bryant Combo*
'71 **Madman Across The Water**
*Elton John*
'89 **Madonna Of The Wasps**
*Robyn Hitchcock/Egyptians*
'71 **Maggie May** *Rod Stewart*
'65 **Maggie's Farm** *Bob Dylan*
'71 **Maggot Brain** *Funkadelic*
**Magic**
'75 *Pilot*
'80 *Olivia Newton-John*
'84 *Cars*
'68 **Magic Bus** *Who*
'68 **Magic Carpet Ride** *Steppenwolf*
'76 **Magic Man** *Heart*
'58 **Magic Moments** *Perry Como*
'03 **Magic Stick** *Lil' Kim*
'66 **Magic Town** *Vogues*
**Magical Mystery Tour**
'67 *Beatles*
'77 *Ambrosia*
'78 **Magnet And Steel** *Walter Egan*
'60 **Magnificent Seven** *Al Caiola*
'91 **Main Course** *Freddie Jackson*
'79 **Main Event/Fight** *Barbra Streisand*
'77 **Mainstreet** *Bob Seger*
'61 **Majestic, The** *Dion*
'83 **Major Tom (Coming Home)**
*Peter Schilling*
'80 **Make A Little Magic** *Dirt Band*
'82 **Make A Move On Me**
*Olivia Newton-John*
**Make Believe**
'69 *Wind*
'82 *Toto*
'98 **Make Em' Say Uhh!** *Master P*
**Make It Easy On Yourself**
'62 *Jerry Butler*
'65 *Walker Bros.*
'70 *Dionne Warwick*
'71 **Make It Funky** *James Brown*
'92 **Make It Happen** *Mariah Carey*
'98 **Make It Hot** *Nicole*
'88 **Make It Last Forever** *Keith Sweat*
'89 **Make It Like It Was** *Regina Belle*
'88 **Make It Real** *Jets*
'70 **Make It With You** *Bread*
'92 **Make Love Like A Man** *Def Leppard*
'83 **Make Love Stay** *Dan Fogelberg*
'58 **Make Me A Miracle** *Jimmie Rodgers*
'66 **Make Me Belong To You**
*Barbara Lewis*
'88 **Make Me Lose Control** *Eric Carmen*
'70 **Make Me Smile** *Chicago*
'71 **Make Me The Woman That You Go Home To** *Gladys Knight*
'65 **Make Me Your Baby** *Barbara Lewis*
'67 **Make Me Yours** *Bettye Swann*
**Make The World Go Away**
'63 *Timi Yuro*
'65 *Eddy Arnold*
'90 **Make You Sweat** *Keith Sweat*
'69 **Make Your Own Kind Of Music**
*Mama Cass Elliot*
'55 **Make Yourself Comfortable**
*Sarah Vaughan*
'02 **Makin' Good Love** *Avant*
'79 **Makin' It** *David Naughton*
'59 **Makin' Love** *Floyd Robinson*
'67 **Making Every Minute Count**
*Spanky & Our Gang*
'82 **Making Love** *Roberta Flack*
'87 **Making Love In The Rain**
*Herb Alpert*
'83 **Making Love Out Of Nothing At All**
*Air Supply*
'67 **Making Memories** *Frankie Laine*
'05 **Making Memories Of Us** *Keith Urban*
'76 **Making Our Dreams Come True**
*Cyndi Grecco*
'98 **Malibu** *Hole*
**Mama**
'60 *Connie Francis*
'66 *B.J. Thomas*
'83 *Genesis*

'79 **Mama Can't Buy You Love** *Elton John*
'63 **Mama Didn't Lie** *Jan Bradley*
'56 **Mama From The Train** *Patti Page*
'91 **Mama, I'm Coming Home** *Ozzy Osbourne*
'73 **Mama Kin** *Aerosmith*
'57 **Mama Look At Bubu** *Harry Belafonte*
'61 **Mama Said** *Shirelles*
'91 **Mama Said Knock You Out** *LL Cool J*
'56 **Mama, Teach Me To Dance** *Eydie Gorme*
'70 **Mama Told Me (Not To Come)** *Three Dog Night*
'68 **Mama Tried** *Merle Haggard*
'82 **Mama Used To Say** *Junior*
'72 **Mama Weer All Crazee Now** *Slade*
'71 **Mama's Pearl** *Jackson 5*
**Mamacita**
'88 *Troop*
'00 *Public Announcement*
'54 **Mambo Italiano** *Rosemary Clooney*
'99 **Mambo No. 5 (A Little Bit Of...)** *Lou Bega*
'55 **Mambo Rock** *Bill Haley*
**Mame**
'66 *Herb Alpert*
'66 *Bobby Darin*
'76 **Mamma Mia** *Abba*
'87 **Mammas Don't Let Your Babies Grow Up To Be Cowboys** *Waylon Jennings & Willie Nelson*
'55 **Man Chases A Girl** *Eddie Fisher*
'99 **Man! I Feel Like A Woman!** *Shania Twain*
'78 **Man I'll Never Be** *Boston*
'71 **Man In Black** *Johnny Cash*
'88 **Man In The Mirror** *Michael Jackson*
**Man In The Raincoat**
'55 *Marion Marlowe*
'55 *Priscilla Wright*
'82 **Man On The Corner** *Genesis*
'93 **Man On The Moon** *R.E.M.*
'82 **Man On Your Mind** *Little River Band*
'00 **Man Overboard** *Blink-182*
'86 **Man Size Love** *Klymaxx*
'96 **Man This Lonely** *Brooks & Dunn*
'03 **Man To Man** *Gary Allan*
'62 **(Man Who Shot) Liberty Valance** *Gene Pitney*
'95 **Man Who Sold The World** *Nirvana*
**Man With The Golden Arm**
'56 *Dick Jacobs [Main Title/Molly-O]*
'56 *Richard Maltby*
'56 *McGuire Sisters*
'68 **Man Without Love** *Engelbert Humperdinck*
'78 **Mañana** *Jimmy Buffett*
'87 **Mandolin Rain** *Bruce Hornsby*
'74 **Mandy** *Barry Manilow*
'82 **Maneater** *Daryl Hall & John Oates*
'57 **Mangos** *Rosemary Clooney*
'58 **Manhattan Spiritual** *Reg Owen*
'83 **Maniac** *Michael Sembello*
'67 **Manic Depression** *Jimi Hendrix*
'86 **Manic Monday** *Bangles*
'55 **Manish Boy** *Muddy Waters*
'69 **Many Rivers To Cross** *Jimmy Cliff*
'60 **Many Tears Ago** *Connie Francis*
'58 **March From The River Kwai and Colonel Bogey** *Mitch Miller*
'94 **March Of The Pigs** *Nine Inch Nails*
'97 **Marching To Mars** *Sammy Hagar*
'77 **Margaritaville** *Jimmy Buffett*
**Maria**
'60 *Johnny Mathis*
'99 *Blondie*
'63 **Maria Elena** *Los Indios Tabajaras*
'00 **Maria Maria** *Santana Feat. The Product G&B*
**Marianne**
'57 *Terry Gilkyson & The Easy Riders*
'57 *Hilltoppers*

'65 **Marie** *Bachelors*
'74 **Marie Laveau** *Bobby Bare*
'61 **(Marie's the Name) His Latest Flame** *Elvis Presley*
'59 **Marina** *Rocco Granata*
'63 **Marlena** *Four Seasons*
'77 **Marquee Moon** *Television*
'69 **Marrakesh Express** *Crosby, Stills & Nash*
'79 **Married Men** *Bette Midler*
'63 **Martian Hop** *Ran-Dells*
'62 **Mary Ann Regrets** *Burl Ives*
'72 **Mary Had A Little Lamb** *Wings*
'67 **Mary In The Morning** *Al Martino*
'78 **Mary Jane** *Rick James*
'93 **Mary Jane's Last Dance** *Tom Petty*
'59 **Mary Lou** *Ronnie Hawkins*
'67 **Mary, Mary** *Monkees*
'56 **Mary's Boy Child** *Harry Belafonte*
'62 **Mary's Little Lamb** *James Darren*
'87 **Mary's Prayer** *Danny Wilson*
'99 **Mas Tequila** *Sammy Hagar*
'62 **Mashed Potato Time** *Dee Dee Sharp*
'80 **Master Blaster (Jammin')** *Stevie Wonder*
'68 **Master Jack** *Four Jacks & A Jill*
'86 **Master Of Puppets** *Metallica*
**Masterpiece**
'73 *Temptations*
'92 *Atlantic Starr*
'64 **Matador, The** *Major Lance*
**Matchbox**
'57 *Carl Perkins*
'64 *Beatles*
'85 **Material Girl** *Madonna*
'86 **Matter Of Trust** *Billy Joel*
'67 **Maxwell's Silver Hammer** *Beatles*
'63 **May Each Day** *Andy Williams*
'69 **May I** *Bill Deal*
'65 **May The Bird Of Paradise Fly Up Your Nose** *"Little" Jimmy Dickens*
'59 **May You Always** *McGuire Sisters*
**Maybe**
'58 *Chantels*
'70 *Three Degrees*
'58 **Maybe Baby** *Crickets*
'01 **Maybe I Deserve** *Tank*
'64 **Maybe I Know** *Lesley Gore*
'79 **Maybe I'm A Fool** *Eddie Money*
**Maybe I'm Amazed**
'70 *Paul McCartney*
'77 *Wings [live]*
'91 **Maybe It Was Memphis** *Pam Tillis*
'71 **Maybe Tomorrow** *Jackson 5*
**Maybellene**
'55 *Chuck Berry*
'64 *Johnny Rivers*
'04 **Mayberry** *Rascal Flatts*
'89 **Mayor Of Simpleton** *XTC*
'98 **Me** *Paula Cole*
'03 **Me Against The Music** *Britney Spears*
'73 **Me And Baby Brother** *War*
**Me And Bobby McGee**
'71 *Janis Joplin*
'71 *Jerry Lee Lewis*
'72 **Me And Julio Down By The Schoolyard** *Paul Simon*
'72 **Me And Mrs. Jones** *Billy Paul*
'71 **Me And My Arrow** *Nilsson*
'96 **Me And You** *Kenny Chesney*
'71 **Me And You And A Dog Named Boo** *Lobo*
**Me, Myself And I**
'89 *De La Soul*
'03 *Beyoncé*
'89 **Me So Horny** *2 Live Crew*
'96 **Me Too** *Toby Keith*
'96 **Me Wise Magic** *Van Halen*
'73 **Meadows** *Joe Walsh*
'63 **Mean Woman Blues** *Roy Orbison*
'04 **Meant To Live** *Switchfoot*
'63 **Mecca** *Gene Pitney*
'69 **Medicine Man** *Buchanan Brothers*

'81 **Medley** *Stars On 45*
'91 **Meet In The Middle** *Diamond Rio*
'87 **Meet Me Half Way** *Kenny Loggins*
'85 **Meet Me In Montana** *Marie Osmond with Dan Seals*
'99 **Meet Virginia** *Train*
'04 **Megalomaniac** *Incubus*
'72 **Melissa** *Allman Brothers Band*
'66 **Mellow Yellow** *Donovan*
**Melody Of Love**
'55 *Billy Vaughn*
'55 *Four Aces*
'55 *David Carroll*
'55 *Ames Brothers [Melodie D'Amour]*
**Memories**
'69 *Elvis Presley*
'69 *Lettermen [medley]*
**Memories Are Made Of This**
'55 *Dean Martin*
'55 *Gale Storm*
'60 *Everly Brothers*
**Memories Of You**
'55 *Four Coins*
'56 *Rosemary Clooney*
**Memory**
'82 *Barry Manilow*
'82 *Barbra Streisand*
'97 **Memory Remains** *Metallica*
**Memphis**
'63 *Lonnie Mack*
'64 *Johnny Rivers*
'67 **Memphis Soul Stew** *King Curtis*
'69 **Memphis Underground** *Herbie Mann*
'91 **Men** *Gladys Knight*
'84 **Men All Pause** *Klymaxx*
'68 **Men Are Gettin' Scarce** *Joe Tex*
'97 **Men In Black** *Will Smith*
'65 **Men In My Little Girl's Life** *Mike Douglas*
'69 **Mendocino** *Sir Douglas Quintet*
'94 **Mental Picture** *Jon Secada*
'90 **Mentirosa** *Mellow Man Ace*
'71 **Mercedes Benz** *Janis Joplin*
'88 **Mercedes Boy** *Pebbles*
'93 **Mercury Blues** *Alan Jackson*
'64 **Mercy, Mercy** *Don Covay*
**Mercy Mercy Me (The Ecology)**
'71 *Marvin Gaye*
'91 *Robert Palmer [medley]*
**Mercy, Mercy, Mercy**
'67 *"Cannonball" Adderley*
'67 *Buckinghams*
'70 **Merry Christmas Darling** *Carpenters*
**Merry Go Round**
'90 *Replacements*
'90 *Keith Sweat*
'02 **Mesmerize** *Ja Rule*
'60 **Mess Of Blues** *Elvis Presley*
'82 **Message, The** *Grandmaster Flash*
'79 **Message In A Bottle** *Police*
'76 **Message In Our Music** *O'Jays*
'81 **Message Of Love** *Pretenders*
'66 **Message To Michael** *Dionne Warwick*
'93 **Method Man** *Wu-Tang Clan*
'84 **Method Of Modern Love** *Daryl Hall/John Oates*
'83 **Metro, The** *Berlin*
'90 **Metropolis** *Church*
'58 **Mexican Hat Rock** *Applejacks*
'83 **Mexican Radio** *Wall Of Voodoo*
'64 **Mexican Shuffle** *Herb Alpert*
'61 **Mexico** *Bob Moore*
'94 **Mi Vida Loca (My Crazy Life)** *Pam Tillis*
'98 **Miami** *Will Smith*
'85 **Miami Vice Theme** *Jan Hammer*
'61 **Michael** *Highwaymen*
**Michelle**
'65 *Beatles*
'66 *David & Jonathan*
'82 **Mickey** *Toni Basil*
'63 **Mickey's Monkey** *Miracles*

'02 **Middle, The** *Jimmy Eat World*
'83 **Middle Of The Road** *Pretenders*
'74 **Midnight At The Oasis**
    *Maria Muldaur*
    **Midnight Blue**
'75   *Melissa Manchester*
'87   *Lou Gramm*
'68 **Midnight Confessions** *Grass Roots*
'69 **Midnight Cowboy**
    *Ferrante & Teicher*
'92 **Midnight In Montgomery**
    *Alan Jackson*
'62 **Midnight In Moscow** *Kenny Ball*
'63 **Midnight Mary** *Joey Powers*
    **Midnight Rider**
'72   *Joe Cocker*
'73   *Gregg Allman*
'80 **Midnight Rocks** *Al Stewart*
    **Midnight Special**
'60   *Paul Evans*
'65   *Johnny Rivers*
'59 **Midnight Stroll** *Revels*
'73 **Midnight Train To Georgia**
    *Gladys Knight*
'79 **Midnight Wind** *John Stewart*
'74 **Might Just Take Your Life**
    *Deep Purple*
'71 **Mighty Clouds Of Joy** *B.J. Thomas*
'74 **Mighty Love** *Spinners*
'74 **Mighty Mighty** *Earth, Wind & Fire*
'68 **Mighty Quinn (Quinn The Eskimo)**
    *Manfred Mann*
'90 **Miles Away** *Winger*
'03 **Milkshake** *Kelis*
'64 **Miller's Cave** *Bobby Bare*
    **Million To One**
'60   *Jimmy Charles*
'73   *Donny Osmond*
'69 **Mind, Body and Soul**
    *Flaming Ember*
'73 **Mind Games** *John Lennon*
'91 **Mind Playing Tricks On Me**
    *Geto Boys*
'86 **Mind Your Own Business**
    *Hank Williams Jr.*
'74 **Mine For Me** *Rod Stewart*
'00 **Minority** *Green Day*
'69 **Minotaur, The** *Dick Hyman*
'75 **Minstrel In The Gallery**
    *Jethro Tull*
'79 **Minute By Minute** *Doobie Brothers*
    **Miracle**
'90   *Jon Bon Jovi*
'91   *Whitney Houston*
'56 **Miracle Of Love** *Eileen Rodgers*
    **Miracles**
'75   *Jefferson Starship*
'83   *Stacy Lattisaw*
'67 **Mirage** *Tommy James*
'83 **Mirror Man** *Human League*
'82 **Mirror Mirror** *Diana Ross*
'73 **Misdemeanor** *Foster Sylvers*
'99 **Miserable** *Lit*
'95 **Misery** *Soul Asylum*
'94 **Mishale** *Andru Donalds*
'62 **Misirlou** *Dick Dale*
    **Misled**
'84   *Kool & The Gang*
'94   *Celine Dion*
'03 **Miss Independent** *Kelly Clarkson*
'84 **Miss Me Blind** *Culture Club*
'80 **Miss Sun** *Boz Scaggs*
    **Miss You**
'78   *Rolling Stones*
'02   *Aaliyah*
'93 **Miss You In A Heartbeat**
    *Def Leppard*
'89 **Miss You Like Crazy** *Natalie Cole*
'89 **Miss You Much** *Janet Jackson*
'88 **Missed Opportunity**
    *Daryl Hall/John Oates*
'95 **Missing** *Everything But The Girl*

    **Missing You**
'61   *Ray Peterson*
'82   *Dan Fogelberg*
'84   *John Waite*
'84   *Diana Ross*
'96   *Brandy, Tamia, Gladys Knight &*
    *Chaka Khan*
'01   *Case*
'92 **Missing You Now** *Michael Bolton*
'60 **Mission Bell** *Donnie Brooks*
'86 **Missionary Man** *Eurythmics*
'70 **Mississippi Queen** *Mountain*
'90 **Missunderstanding** *Al B. Sure!*
'84 **Mistake No. 3** *Culture Club*
    **Misty**
'59   *Johnny Mathis*
'63   *Lloyd Price*
'75   *Ray Stevens*
'76 **Misty Blue** *Dorothy Moore*
'71 **Misty Mountain Hop**
    *Led Zeppelin*
'80 **Misunderstanding** *Genesis*
'89 **Mixed Emotions** *Rolling Stones*
'64 **Mixed-Up, Shook-Up, Girl**
    *Patty & The Emblems*
'94 **Mmm Mmm Mmm Mmm**
    *Crash Test Dummies*
'97 **Mo Money Mo Problems**
    *Notorious B.I.G.*
'58 **Mocking Bird, The** *Four Lads*
    **Mockingbird**
'63   *Inez Foxx*
'74   *Carly Simon & James Taylor*
'05   *Eminem*
'61 **Model Girl** *Johnny Mastro*
'84 **Modern Day Delilah**
    *Van Stephenson*
'81 **Modern Girl** *Sheena Easton*
'83 **Modern Love** *David Bowie*
'86 **Modern Woman** *Billy Joel*
'65 **Mohair Sam** *Charlie Rich*
    **Molly-O ..see: Man With The Golden**
    **Arm**
'95 **Molly (Sixteen Candles)** *Sponge*
'02 **Moment Like This** *Kelly Clarkson*
'55 **Moments To Remember** *Four Lads*
    **Mona Lisa**
'59   *Carl Mann*
'59   *Conway Twitty*
'72 **Mona Lisas And Mad Hatters**
    *Elton John*
'66 **Monday, Monday**
    *Mamas & The Papas*
'75 **Monday Morning**
    *Fleetwood Mac*
    **Money**
'73   *Pink Floyd*
'80   *Flying Lizards*
'92 **Money Can't Buy You Love**
    *Ralph Tresvant*
'84 **Money Changes Everything**
    *Cyndi Lauper*
'92 **Money Don't Matter 2 Night** *Prince*
'85 **Money For Nothing** *Dire Straits*
'76 **Money Honey** *Bay City Rollers*
'93 **Money In The Bank** *John Anderson*
'98 **Money, Power & Respect** *Lox*
    **Money (That's what I want)**
'60   *Barrett Strong*
'64   *Kingsmen*
'56 **Money Tree** *Margaret Whiting*
'86 **Money$ Too Tight (To Mention)**
    *Simply Red*
'90 **Moneytalks** *AC/DC*
'88 **Monkey** *George Michael*
'89 **Monkey Gone To Heaven** *Pixies*
'63 **Monkey Time** *Major Lance*
'69 **Monster** *Steppenwolf*
'62 **Monster Mash** *Bobby "Boris" Pickett*
'62 **Monsters' Holiday**
    *Bobby "Boris" Pickett*
'73 **Montana** *Frank Zappa*
'70 **Montego Bay** *Bobby Bloom*
'67 **Monterey** *Animals*

    **Mony Mony**
'68   *Tommy James*
'81   *Billy Idol*
'87   *Billy Idol [live]*
'76 **Moody Blue** *Elvis Presley*
'61 **Moody River** *Pat Boone*
'69 **Moody Woman** *Jerry Butler*
'65 **Moon Over Naples** *Bert Kaempfert*
    **Moon River**
'61   *Jerry Butler*
'61   *Henry Mancini*
'62   *Andy Williams*
'71 **Moon Shadow** *Cat Stevens*
'58 **Moon Talk** *Perry Como*
'70 **Moondance** *Van Morrison*
    **Moonglow And Theme From**
    **"Picnic"**
'56   *George Cates*
'56   *McGuire Sisters [Picnic]*
'56   *Morris Stoloff*
'67 **Moonlight Drive** *Doors*
'76 **Moonlight Feels Right** *Starbuck*
'56 **Moonlight Gambler** *Frankie Laine*
    **Moonlight Swim**
'57   *Nick Noble*
'57   *Tony Perkins*
'87 **Moonlighting (Theme)** *Al Jarreau*
    **More**
'56   *Perry Como*
'63   *Kai Winding*
    **More And More**
'67   *Andy Williams*
'93   *Captain Hollywood Project*
'80 **More Bounce To The Ounce** *Zapp*
'66 **More I See You** *Chris Montez*
    **More Love**
'67   *Miracles*
'80   *Kim Carnes*
'61 **More Money For You And Me**
    *Four Preps*
'76 **More, More, More**
    *Andrea True Connection*
'76 **More Than A Feeling** *Boston*
'67 **More Than A Miracle** *Roger Williams*
    **More Than A Woman**
'77   *Tavares*
'78   *Bee Gees*
'02   *Aaliyah*
'91 **More Than Ever** *Nelson*
'80 **More Than I Can Say** *Leo Sayer*
'81 **More Than Just The Two Of Us**
    *Sneaker*
'01 **More Than That** *Backstreet Boys*
'67 **More Than The Eye Can See**
    *Al Martino*
    **More Than This**
'83   *Roxy Music*
'97   *10,000 Maniacs*
'91 **More Than Words** *Extreme*
'90 **More Than Words Can Say** *Alias*
'88 **More Than You Know** *Martika*
'69 **More Today Than Yesterday**
    *Spiral Starecase*
'94 **More You Ignore Me, The Closer**
    **I Get** *Morrissey*
'59 **Morgen** *Ivo Robic*
    **Moritat (Theme From The**
    **Threepenny Opera)**
'56   *Louis Armstrong*
'56   *Richard Hayman & Jan August*
'56   *Dick Hyman*
'56   *Lawrence Welk*
'59   *Bobby Darin [Mack The Knife]*
'60   *Ella Fitzgerald*
'83 **Mornin'** *Al Jarreau*
'75 **Mornin' Beautiful**
    *Tony Orlando & Dawn*
'73 **Morning After** *Maureen McGovern*
'79 **Morning Dance** *Spyro Gyra*
'68 **Morning Dew** *Lulu*
'69 **Morning Girl** *Neon Philharmonic*
'72 **Morning Has Broken** *Cat Stevens*
    **Morning Side Of The Mountain**
'59   *Tommy Edwards*
'74   *Donny & Marie Osmond*

'81 **Morning Train (Nine To Five)**
   *Sheena Easton*
'73 **Most Beautiful Girl** *Charlie Rich*
'94 **Most Beautiful Girl In The World**
   *Prince*
'00 **Most Girls** *P!nk*
'98 **Most High**
   *Jimmy Page & Robert Plant*
'74 **Most Likely You Go Your Way (And
   I'll Go Mine)** *Bob Dylan*
'55 **Most Of All** *Don Cornell*
'62 **Most People Get Married** *Patti Page*
'55 **Mostly Martha** *Crew Cuts*
'70 **Mother** *John Lennon*
'72 **Mother And Child Reunion**
   *Paul Simon*
'71 **Mother Freedom** *Bread*
'61 **Mother-In-Law** *Ernie K-Doe*
'96 **Mother Mother** *Tracy Bonham*
'69 **Mother Popcorn** *James Brown*
'66 **Mothers Little Helper** *Rolling Stones*
'86 **Mothers Talk** *Tears For Fears*
'72 **Motorcycle Mama** *Sailcat*
'87 **Motortown** *Kane Gang*
'91 **Motown Song** *Rod Stewart (with
   The Temptations)*
'91 **Motownphilly** *Boyz II Men*
'82 **Mountain Music** *Alabama*
   **Mountain Of Love**
'60 *Harold Dorman*
'64 *Johnny Rivers*
'61 **Mountain's High** *Dick & DeeDee*
'86 **Mountains** *Prince*
'96 **Mouth** *Merril Bainbridge*
'91 **Move Any Mountain** *Shamen*
'86 **Move Away** *Culture Club*
'02 **Move B***h** *Ludacris*
   **Move Over**
'69 *Steppenwolf*
'71 *Janis Joplin*
'92 **Move This** *Technotronic*
'04 **Move Ya Body** *Nina Sky*
'79 **Move Your Boogie Body** *Bar-Kays*
'76 **Movin'** *Brass Construction*
'58 **Movin' N' Groovin'** *Duane Eddy*
   **Movin' On**
'75 *Bad Company*
'98 *Mya*
'78 **Movin' Out (Anthony's Song)**
   *Billy Joel*
'78 **Moving In Stereo** *Cars*
'94 **Moving On Up** *M People*
'76 **Mozambique** *Bob Dylan*
'63 **Mr. Bass Man** *Johnny Cymbal*
'71 **Mr. Big Stuff** *Jean Knight*
'59 **Mr. Blue** *Fleetwoods*
'78 **Mr. Blue Sky** *Electric Light Orchestra*
'70 **Mr. Bojangles** *Nitty Gritty Dirt Band*
'05 **Mr. Brightside** *Killers*
'68 **Mr. Businessman** *Ray Stevens*
'72 **Mister Can't You See**
   *Buffy Sainte-Marie*
'60 **Mr. Custer** *Larry Verne*
'89 **Mr. D.J.** *Joyce "Fenderella" Irby*
'66 **Mr. Dieingly Sad** *Critters*
'75 **Mr. Jaws** *Dickie Goodman*
'93 **Mr. Jones** *Counting Crows*
'57 **Mr. Lee** *Bobbettes*
'64 **Mr. Lonely** *Bobby Vinton*
'92 **Mr. Loverman** *Shabba Ranks*
'60 **Mr. Lucky** *Henry Mancini*
'04 **Mr. Mom** *Lonestar*
'92 **Mister Please** *Damn Yankees*
'83 **Mr. Roboto** *Styx*
   **Mister Sandman**
'55 *Chordettes*
'55 *Four Aces*
'81 *Emmylou Harris*
'67 **Mr. Soul** *Buffalo Springfield*
'66 **Mr. Spaceman** *Byrds*
'69 **Mr. Sun, Mr. Moon**
   *Paul Revere & The Raiders*
   **Mr. Tambourine Man**
'65 *Byrds*
'65 *Bob Dylan*

'84 **Mr. Telephone Man** *New Edition*
'93 **Mr. Vain** *Culture Beat*
'92 **Mr. Wendal** *Arrested Development*
   **Mr. Wonderful**
'56 *Teddi King*
'56 *Peggy Lee*
'56 *Sarah Vaughan*
'65 **Mrs. Brown You've Got A Lovely
   Daughter** *Herman's Hermits*
   **Mrs. Robinson**
'68 *Simon & Garfunkel*
'69 *Booker T. & The M.G.'s*
'00 **Ms. Jackson** *OutKast*
'89 **Much Too Young (To Feel This
   Damn Old)** *Garth Brooks*
'05 **Mud On The Tires** *Brad Paisley*
'69 **Muddy River** *Johnny Rivers*
'60 **Mule Skinner Blues** *Fendermen*
'77 **Mull Of Kintyre** *Paul McCartney*
'61 **Multiplication** *Bobby Darin*
'98 **Mummers' Dance**
   *Loreena McKennitt*
'59 **Mummy, The** *Bob McFadden & Dor*
'82 **Muscles** *Diana Ross*
   **Music**
'00 *Madonna*
'01 *Eric Sermon*
'79 **Music Box Dancer** *Frank Mills*
'72 **Music From Across The Way**
   *James Last*
'75 **Music Never Stopped**
   *Grateful Dead*
'99 **Music Of My Heart**
   *\*NSYNC & Gloria Estefan*
   **Music To Watch Girls By**
'66 *Bob Crewe Generation*
'67 *Andy Williams*
'76 **Muskrat Love** *Captain & Tennille*
'74 **Must Of Got Lost** *J. Geils Band*
'65 **Must To Avoid** *Herman's Hermits*
'66 **Mustang Sally** *Wilson Pickett*
'86 **My Adidas** *Run-D.M.C.*
'98 **My All** *Mariah Carey*
'78 **My Angel Baby** *Toby Beau*
'55 **My Babe** *Little Walter*
   **My Baby**
'65 *Temptations*
'86 *Pretenders*
'01 *Lil' Romeo*
'97 **MyBabyDaddy** *B-Rock & The Bizz*
'55 **(My Baby Don't Love Me) No More**
   *DeJohn Sisters*
'56 **My Baby Left Me** *Elvis Presley*
'70 **My Baby Loves Lovin'** *White Plains*
   **My Baby Loves Me**
'66 *Martha & The Vandellas*
'93 *Martina McBride*
'67 **My Baby Must Be A Magician**
   *Marvelettes*
   **My Back Pages**
'64 *Bob Dylan*
'67 *Byrds*
'04 **My Band** *D12*
'99 **My Best Friend** *Tim McGraw*
'78 **My Best Friend's Girl** *Cars*
'56 **My Blue Heaven** *Fats Domino*
'97 **My Body** *LSG*
'55 **My Bonnie Lassie** *Ames Brothers*
'64 **My Bonnie (My Bonnie Lies Over
   The Ocean)** *Beatles*
   **My Boo**
'96 *Ghost Town DJ's*
'04 *Usher & Alicia Keys*
'62 **My Boomerang Won't Come Back**
   *Charlie Drake*
'75 **My Boy** *Elvis Presley*
   **My Boy-Flat Top**
'55 *Boyd Bennett*
'55 *Dorothy Collins*
'64 **My Boy Lollipop** *Millie Small*
'63 **My Boyfriend's Back** *Angels*
'89 **My Brave Face** *Paul McCartney*
'58 **My Bucket's Got A Hole In It**
   *Ricky Nelson*
'69 **My Cherie Amour** *Stevie Wonder*

'82 **My City Was Hone** *Pretenders*
   **My Coloring Book**
'62 *Kitty Kallen*
'62 *Sandy Stewart*
'67 **My Cup Runneth Over** *Ed Ames*
'62 **My Dad** *Paul Petersen*
'60 **My Dearest Darling** *Etta James*
'72 **My Ding-A-Ling** *Chuck Berry*
'57 **My Dream** *Platters*
'61 **My Elusive Dreams**
   *David Houston & Tammy Wynette*
'61 **My Empty Arms** *Jackie Wilson*
'84 **My Ever Changing Moods**
   *Style Council*
'00 **My Everything** *98°*
'74 **My Eyes Adored You** *Frankie Valli*
'77 **My Fair Share** *Seals & Crofts*
'89 **My Fantasy** *Teddy Riley*
'98 **My Father's Eyes** *Eric Clapton*
'99 **My Favorite Girl** *Dave Hollister*
'98 **My Favorite Mistake** *Sheryl Crow*
'65 **My Favorite Things** *Julie Andrews*
   **My First Love**
'89 *Atlantic Starr*
'00 *Avant*
'99 **My First Night With You** *Mya*
'87 **My Forever Love** *Levert*
'95 **My Friends** *Red Hot Chili Peppers*
'03 **My Front Porch Looking In**
   *Lonestar*
'66 **My Generation** *Who*
   **My Girl**
'65 *Temptations*
'82 *Donnie Iris*
'85 *Daryl Hall & John Oates/David
   Ruffin/ Eddie Kendrick [medley]*
'88 *Suave'*
'74 **My Girl Bill** *Jim Stafford*
'81 **My Girl (Gone, Gone, Gone)**
   *Chilliwack*
'65 **My Girl Has Gone** *Miracles*
   **My Girl Josephine**
'60 *Fats Domino*
'67 *Jerry Jaye*
'05 **My Give A Damn's Busted**
   *Jo Dee Messina*
'70 **My Guitar Wants To Kill Your Mama**
   *Frank Zappa*
   **My Guy**
'64 *Mary Wells*
'82 *Sister Sledge*
'58 **My Happiness** *Connie Francis*
'04 **My Happy Ending** *Avril Lavigne*
'90 **My Head's In Mississippi** *ZZ Top*
'77 **My Heart Belongs To Me**
   *Barbra Streisand*
'64 **My Heart Belongs To Only You**
   *Bobby Vinton*
'91 **My Heart Belongs To You**
   *Russ Irwin*
'88 **My Heart Can't Tell You No**
   *Rod Stewart*
'60 **My Heart Has A Mind Of Its Own**
   *Connie Francis*
'59 **My Heart Is An Open Book**
   *Carl Dobkins, Jr.*
'91 **My Heart Is Failing Me** *Riff*
   **My Heart Skips A Beat**
'64 *Buck Owens*
'89 *Cover Girls*
'98 **My Heart Will Go On (Love Theme
   From 'Titanic')** *Celine Dion*
'66 **My Heart's Symphony** *Gary Lewis*
'80 **My Heroes Have Always Been
   Cowboys** *Willie Nelson*
'60 **My Home Town** *Paul Anka*
'85 **My Hometown** *Bruce Springsteen*
'04 **My Immortal** *Evanescence*
   **My Kind Of Girl**
'61 *Matt Monro*
'94 *Collin Raye*
'83 **My Kind Of Lady** *Supertramp*
'65 **My Kind Of Town** *Frank Sinatra*
'90 **My Kinda Girl** *Babyface*

**My Last Date (With You)**
'60    Skeeter Davis
'60    Joni James
'78  **My Life**  Billy Joel
'02  **My List**  Toby Keith
'56  **My Little Angel**  Four Lads
'66  **My Little Red Book**  Love
'98  **My Little Secret**  Xscape
'75  **My Little Town**  Simon & Garfunkel
     **My Love**
'65    Petula Clark
'73    Paul McCartney
'83    Lionel Richie
'94    Little Texas
'60  **My Love For You**  Johnny Mathis
'64  **My Love, Forgive Me**  Robert Goulet
'90  **My Love Is A Fire**  Donny Osmond
'95  **My Love Is For Real**  Paula Abdul
'03  **My Love Is Like...WO**  Mya
'97  **My Love Is The Shhh!**
       Somethin' For The People
'99  **My Love Is Your Love**
       Whitney Houston
'92  **My Lovin' (You're Never Gonna Get
     It)**  En Vogue
'67  **My Mammy**  Happenings
'65  **My Man**  Barbra Streisand
     **My Maria**
'73    B.W. Stevenson
'96    Brooks & Dunn
'70  **My Marie**  Engelbert Humperdinck
'59  **My Melancholy Baby**
       Tommy Edwards
'74  **My Melody Of Love**  Bobby Vinton
'74  **My Mistake (Was To Love You)**
       Diana Ross & Marvin Gaye
'80  **My Mother's Eyes**  Bette Midler
'73  **My Music**  Loggins & Messina
'90  **My, My, My**  Johnny Gill
'99  **My Name Is**  Eminem
'91  **My Name Is Not Susan**
       Whitney Houston
'92  **My Name Is Prince**  Prince
'91  **My Next Broken Heart**
       Brooks & Dunn
'00  **My Next Thirty Years**  Tim McGraw
'84  **My Oh My**  Slade
'73  **My Old School**  Steely Dan
'57  **My One Sin**  Four Coins
'97  **My Own Prison**  Creed
     **My Own True Love**
'59    Jimmy Clanton
'62    Duprees
'99  **My Own Worst Enemy**  Lit
'57  **My Personal Possession**
       Nat "King" Cole/Four Knights
'04  **My Place**  Nelly
'69  **My Pledge Of Love**
       Joe Jeffrey Group
'56  **My Prayer**  Platters
'88  **My Prerogative**  Bobby Brown
'01  **My Sacrifice**  Creed
'93  **My Second Home**  Tracy Lawrence
'79  **My Sharona**  Knack
'93  **My Sister**  Juliana Hatfield Three
     **My Special Angel**
'57    Bobby Helms
'68    Vogues
'63  **My Summer Love**
       Ruby & The Romantics
     **My Sweet Lady**
'74    Cliff DeYoung
'77    John Denver
'70  **My Sweet Lord**  George Harrison
'60  **My Tani**  Brothers Four
'74  **My Thang**  James Brown
     **My Town**
'83    Michael Stanley Band
'02    Montgomery Gentry
'65  **My Town, My Guy And Me**
       Lesley Gore
'55  **My Treasure**  Hilltoppers
'63  **My True Confession**  Brook Benton
'58  **My True Love**  Jack Scott
'61  **My True Story**  Jive Five

     **My Way**
'69    Frank Sinatra
'77    Elvis Presley
'98    Usher
'01    Limp Bizkit
'69  **My Whole World Ended (The
     Moment You Left Me)**
       David Ruffin
'63  **My Whole World Is Falling Down**
       Brenda Lee
'71  **My Wife**  Who
'59  **My Wish Came True**  Elvis Presley
'72  **My World**  Bee Gees
'66  **My World Is Empty Without You**
       Supremes
'91  **Mysterious Ways**  U2
'85  **Mystery Lady**  Billy Ocean
'55  **Mystery Train**  Elvis Presley
'65  **Mystic Eyes**  Them

# N

'70  **N.I.B.**  Black Sabbath
     **Na Na Hey Hey Kiss Him Goodbye**
'69    Steam
'87    Nylons
'76  **Nadia's Theme (The Young And The
     Restless)**
       Barry DeVorzon & Perry Botkin, Jr.
'64  **Nadine (Is It You?)**  Chuck Berry
'61  **"Nag"**  Halos
'96  **Naked Eye**  Luscious Jackson
'95  **Name**  Goo Goo Dolls
'64  **Name Game**  Shirley Ellis
'77  **Name Of The Game**  Abba
'66  **Nashville Cats**  Lovin' Spoonful
'86  **Nasty**  Janet Jackson
'71  **Nathan Jones**  Supremes
'94  **National Working Woman's Holiday**
       Sammy Kershaw
'77  **Native New Yorker**  Odyssey
'99  **Natural Blues**  Moby
'60  **Natural Born Lover**  Fats Domino
'73  **Natural High**  Bloodstone
'71  **Natural Man**  Lou Rawls
'95  **Natural One**  Folk Implosion
'67  **Natural Woman**  Aretha Franklin
'68  **Naturally Stoned**  Avant-Garde
'61  **Nature Boy**  Bobby Darin
'71  **Nature's Way**  Spirit
'04  **Naughty Girl**  Beyoncé
'88  **Naughty Girls (Need Love Too)**
       Samantha Fox
'84  **Naughty Naughty**  John Parr
'64  **Navy Blue**  Diane Renay
'70  **Neanderthal Man**  Hotlegs
'58  **Near You**  Roger Williams
'58  **Nee Nee Na Na Na Na Nu Nu**
       Dicky Doo & The Don'ts
'89  **Need A Little Taste Of Love**
       Doobie Brothers
'74  **Need To Be**  Jim Weatherly
'63  **Need To Belong**  Jerry Butler
'58  **Need You**  Donnie Owens
'78  **Need You Bad**  Ted Nugent
'87  **Need You Tonight**  INXS
'72  **Needle And The Damage Done**
       Neil Young
     **Needles And Pins**
'64    Searchers
'86    Tom Petty/Stevie Nicks
'73  **Neither One Of Us (Wants To Be
     The First To Say Goodbye)**
       Gladys Knight
'92  **Neon Moon**  Brooks & Dunn
'67  **Neon Rainbow**  Box Tops
'77  **Nether Lands**  Dan Fogelberg
'84  **Neutron Dance**  Pointer Sisters
'85  **Never**  Heart
'92  **Never A Time**  Genesis
'02  **Never Again**  Nickelback
'86  **Never As Good As The First Time**
       Sade
'59  **Never Be Anyone Else But You**
       Ricky Nelson

'80  **Never Be The Same**
       Christopher Cross
'75  **Never Been Any Reason**
       Head East
'82  **Never Been In Love**  Randy Meisner
'71  **Never Been To Spain**
       Three Dog Night
     **Never Can Say Goodbye**
'71    Isaac Hayes
'71    Jackson 5
'74    Gloria Gaynor
'87    Communards
'69  **Never Comes The Day**
       Moody Blues
'88  **Never Die Young**  James Taylor
'71  **Never Ending Song Of Love**
       Delaney & Bonnie
'85  **Never Ending Story**  Limahl
'90  **Never Enough**  Cure
'98  **Never Ever**  All Saints
'68  **Never Give You Up**  Jerry Butler
'77  **Never Going Back Again**
       Fleetwood Mac
'76  **Never Gonna Fall In Love Again**
       Eric Carmen
'87  **Never Gonna Give You Up**
       Rick Astley
'91  **Never Gonna Let You Down**
       Surface
     **Never Gonna Let You Go**
'83    Sergio Mendes
'99    Faith Evans
     **Never Had A Dream Come True**
'70    Stevie Wonder
'01    S Club 7
'93  **Never Keeping Secrets**  Babyface
'90  **Never Knew Lonely**  Vince Gill
'88  **Never Knew Love Like This**
       Alexander O'Neal/Cherrelle
'80  **Never Knew Love Like This Before**
       Stephanie Mills
'96  **Never Leave Me Alone**  Nate Dogg
'03  **Never Leave You - Uh Oooh, Uh
     Oooh!**  Lumidee
'75  **Never Let Her Go**  David Gates
'87  **Never Let Me Down**  David Bowie
'87  **Never Let Me Down Again**
       Depeche Mode
'00  **Never Let You Go**  Third Eye Blind
'94  **Never Lie**  Immature
'97  **Never Make A Promise**  Dru Hill
     **Never My Love**
'67    Association
'71    5th Dimension
'74    Blue Swede
'73  **Never, Never Gonna Give Ya Up**
       Barry White
     **Never On Sunday**
'60    Don Costa
'61    Chordettes
'87  **Never Say Goodbye**  Bon Jovi
'03  **Never Scared**  Bone Crusher
'93  **Never Should've Let You Go**
       Hi-Five
'91  **Never Stop**  Brand New Heavies
'85  **Never Surrender**  Corey Hart
'88  **Never Tear Us Apart**  INXS
'98  **Never There**  Cake
'87  **Never Thought (That I Could Love)**
       Dan Hill
'81  **Never Too Much**  Luther Vandross
'56  **Never Turn Back**  Al Hibbler
'94  **New Age Girl**  Deadeye Dick
'85  **New Attitude**  Patti LaBelle
'02  **New Day Has Come**  Celine Dion
'69  **New Day Yesterday**  Jethro Tull
'83  **New Frontier**  Donald Fagen
'64  **New Girl In School**  Jan & Dean
'76  **New Kid In Town**  Eagles
'63  **New Mexican Rose**  Four Seasons
'84  **New Moon On Monday**  Duran Duran
'70  **New Mother Nature [medley]**
       Guess Who
'60  **New Orleans**  U.S. Bonds
'80  **New Romance (It's A Mystery)**
       Spider

224

'88 **New Sensation** *INXS*
'84 **New Song** *Howard Jones*
'91 **New Way (To Light Up An Old Flame)** *Joe Diffie*
'82 **New World Man** *Rush*
'83 **New Year's Day** *U2*
'04 **New York** *Ja Rule*
'78 **New York Groove** *Ace Frehley*
'67 **New York Mining Disaster 1941** *Bee Gees*
'90 **New York Minute** *Don Henley*
'76 **New York State Of Mind** *Billy Joel*
'77 **New York, You Got Me Dancing** *Andrea True Connection*
'65 **New York's A Lonely Town** *Trade Winds*
'62 **Next Door To An Angel** *Neil Sedaka*
'00 **Next Episode** *Dr. Dre/Snoop Dogg*
'97 **Next Lifetime** *Erykah Badu*
'67 **Next Plane To London** *Rose Garden*
'86 **Next Time I Fall** *Peter Cetera with Amy Grant*
'90 **Next To You, Next To Me** *Shenandoah*
'98 **Nice & Slow** *Usher*
'82 **Nice Girls** *Eye To Eye*
'60 **Nice 'N' Easy** *Frank Sinatra*
'76 **Nice 'N' Naasty** *Salsoul Orchestra*
'88 **Nice 'N' Slow** *Freddie Jackson*
'72 **Nice To Be With You** *Gallery*
'90 **Nicety** *Michel'le*
'72 **Nickel Song** *Melanie*
'81 **Nicole** *Point Blank*
'60 **Night** *Jackie Wilson*
   **Night [Nite] And Day**
'88    *Al B. Sure!*
'90    *U2*
'74 **Night Chicago Died** *Paper Lace*
'78 **Night Fever** *Bee Gees*
'62 **Night Has A Thousand Eyes** *Bobby Vee*
'94 **Night In My Veins** *Pretenders*
'85 **Night Is Still Young** *Billy Joel*
'76 **Night Life** *Willie Nelson*
'56 **Night Lights** *Nat "King" Cole*
   **Night Moves**
'76    *Bob Seger*
'86    *Marilyn Martin*
'81 **Night Owls** *Little River Band*
'73 **Night The Lights Went Out In Georgia** *Vicki Lawrence*
   **Night They Drove Old Dixie Down**
'69    *Band*
'71    *Joan Baez*
'66 **Night Time** *Strangeloves*
'99 **Night To Remember** *Joe Diffie*
'62 **Night Train** *James Brown*
'83 **Nightbird** *Stevie Nicks/Sandy Stewart*
'75 **Nightime** *Pretty Poison*
'75 **Nightingale** *Carole King*
'88 **Nightmare On My Street** *DJ Jazzy Jeff & The Fresh Prince*
'89 **Nightmares** *Violent Femmes*
'76 **Nights Are Forever Without You** *England Dan & John Ford Coley*
'72 **Nights In White Satin** *Moody Blues*
'91 **Nights Like This** *After 7*
'75 **Nights On Broadway** *Bee Gees*
'85 **Nightshift** *Commodores*
'67 **Niki Hoeky** *P.J. Proby*
'86 **Nikita** *Elton John*
'00 **911** *Wyclef Jean*
'90 **911 Is A Joke** *Public Enemy*
'80 **9 To 5** *Dolly Parton*
'85 **19** *Paul Hardcastle*
'04 **1985** *Bowling For Soup*
'74 **Nineteen Hundred And Eighty Five** *Paul McCartney*
'70 **1900 Yesterday** *Liz Damon's Orient Express*
'82 **\*\*1999\*\*** *Prince*
'96 **1979** *Smashing Pumpkins*
'02 **19 Somethin'** *Mark Wills*

'66 **19th Nervous Breakdown** *Rolling Stones*
'66 **98.6** *Keith*
'79 **99** *Toto*
'83 **99 Luftballons** *Nena*
'75 **99 Miles From L.A.** *Albert Hammond*
'04 **99 Problems** *Jay-Z*
'57 **Ninety-Nine Ways** *Tab Hunter*
'56 • **Ninety Nine Years (Dead Or Alive)** *Guy Mitchell*
'66 **96 Tears** *? (Question Mark) & The Mysterians*
   **Nitty Gritty**
'63    *Shirley Ellis*
'69    *Gladys Knight*
   **No Other Arms**
'55    *Georgie Shaw*
'64    *Bachelors*
'04 **No Better Love** *Young Gunz*
'74 **No Charge** *Melba Montgomery*
'58 **No Chemise, Please** *Gerry Granahan*
'96 **No Diggity** *BLACKstreet*
'93 **No Doubt About It** *Neal McCoy*
'86 **No Easy Way Out** *Robert Tepper*
'94 **No Excuses** *Alice In Chains*
'93 **No Future In The Past** *Vince Gill*
'99 **No Leaf Clover** *Metallica*
'03 **No Letting Go** *Wayne Wonder*
'85 **No Lookin' Back** *Michael McDonald*
'71 **No Love At All** *B.J. Thomas*
'57 **No Love (But Your Love)** *Johnny Mathis*
'70 **No Matter What** *Badfinger*
'65 **No Matter What Shape (Your Stomach's In)** *T-Bones*
'69 **No Matter What Sign You Are** *Supremes*
'67 **No Milk Today** *Herman's Hermits*
'92 **No Mistakes** *Patty Smyth*
   **No More**
'55    *McGuire Sisters*
'00    *Ruff Endz*
'00 **No More (Baby I'ma Do Right)** *3LW*
'01 **No More Drama** *Mary J. Blige*
'95 **No More "I Love You's"** *Annie Lennox*
'89 **No More Lies** *Michel'le*
'84 **No More Lonely Nights** *Paul McCartney*
'73 **No More Mr. Nice Guy** *Alice Cooper*
'89 **No More Rhyme** *Debbie Gibson*
'79 **No More Tears (Enough Is Enough)** *Barbra Streisand/ Donna Summer*
'84 **No More Words** *Berlin*
'90 **No Myth** *Michael Penn*
'96 **No News** *Lonestar*
'80 **No Night So Long** *Dionne Warwick*
'97 **No, No, No** *Destiny's Child*
'75 **No No Song** *Ringo Starr*
   **No, Not Much!**
'56    *Four Lads*
'69    *Vogues*
'63 **No One** *Ray Charles*
'95 **No One Else** *Total*
'92 **No One Else On Earth** *Wynonna*
'86 **No One Is To Blame** *Howard Jones*
   **No One Knows**
'58    *Dion & The Belmonts*
'02    *Queens Of The Stone Age*
'82 **No One Like You** *Scorpions*
'96 **No One Needs To Know** *Shania Twain*
'72 **No One To Depend On** *Santana*
'92 **No Ordinary Love** *Sade*
'59 **No Other Arms, No Other Lips** *Chordettes*
'64 **No Particular Place To Go** *Chuck Berry*
'99 **No Pigeons** *Sporty Thievz*
'98 **No Place That Far** *Sara Evans*
'04 **No Problem** *Lil Scrappy*
'93 **No Rain** *Blind Melon*
'92 **No Regrets** *Tom Cochrane*
'65 **No Reply** *Beatles*
'81 **No Reply At All** *Genesis*

'99 **No Scrubs** *TLC*
'03 **No Shoes, No Shirt, No Problems** *Kenny Chesney*
'88 **No Smoke Without A Fire** *Bad Company*
'91 **No Son Of Mine** *Genesis*
'02 **No Such Thing** *John Mayer*
'70 **No Sugar Tonight [medley]** *Guess Who*
'78 **No Tell Lover** *Chicago*
   **No Time**
'69    *Guess Who*
'96    *Lil' Kim*
'84 **No Way Out** *Jefferson Starship*
   **No Woman, No Cry**
'75    *Bob Marley*
'96    *Fugees*
   **Nobody**
'82    *Sylvia*
'96    *Keith Sweat*
'67 **Nobody But Me** *Human Beinz*
'58 **Nobody But You** *Dee Clark*
'69 **Nobody But You Babe** *Clarence Reid*
   **Nobody Does It Better**
'77    *Carly Simon*
'98    *Nate Dogg*
'98 **Nobody Else** *Tyrese*
'64 **Nobody I Know** *Peter & Gordon*
   **Nobody Knows**
'95    *Tony Rich Project*
'96    *Kevin Sharp*
'60 **Nobody Loves Me Like You** *Flamingos*
'82 **Nobody Said It Was Easy** *Le Roux*
'84 **Nobody Told Me** *John Lennon*
'01 **Nobody Wants To Be Lonely** *Ricky Martin with Christina Aguilera*
'73 **Nobody Wants You When You're Down And Out** *Bobby Womack*
   **Nobody Wins**
'81    *Elton John*
'93    *Radney Foster*
'76 **Nobody's Fault But Mine** *Led Zeppelin*
   **Nobody's Fool**
'86    *Cinderella*
'88    *Kenny Loggins*
'90 **Nobody's Home** *Clint Black*
'88 **Nobody's Perfect** *Mike + The Mechanics*
'98 **Nobody's Supposed To Be Here** *Deborah Cox*
'04 **Nolia Clap** *Juvenile • Wacko • Skip*
'94 **None Of Your Business** *Salt-N-Pepa*
'99 **Nookie** *Limp Bizkit*
'92 **Norma Jean Riley** *Diamond Rio*
'61 **Norman** *Sue Thompson*
'60 **North To Alaska** *Johnny Horton*
'65 **Norwegian Wood (This Bird Has Flown)** *Beatles*
'02 **Not A Day Goes By** *Lonestar*
'94 **Not A Moment Too Soon** *Tim McGraw*
'90 **Not Counting You** *Garth Brooks*
'68 **Not Enough Indians** *Dean Martin*
'85 **Not Enough Love In The World** *Don Henley*
'92 **Not Enough Time** *INXS*
   **Not Fade Away**
'57    *Buddy Holly*
'64    *Rolling Stones*
'96 **Not Gon' Cry** *Mary J. Blige*
'88 **Not Just Another Girl** *Ivan Neville*
'79 **(not just) Knee Deep** *Funkadelic*
'63 **Not Me** *Orlons*
'95 **Not On Your Love** *Jeff Carson*
'59 **Not One Minute More** *Della Reese*
'67 **Not So Sweet Martha Lorraine** *Country Joe & The Fish*
'95 **Not That Different** *Collin Raye*
'65 **Not The Lovin' Kind** *Dino, Desi & Billy*
'92 **Not The Only One** *Bonnie Raitt*
'97 **Not Tonight** *Lil' Kim*

'02 **Nothin'** *N.O.R.E.*
'86 **Nothin' At All** *Heart*
'88 **Nothin' But A Good Time** *Poison*
'96 **Nothin' But The Cavi Hit**
    *Mack 10 & Tha Dogg Pound*
'97 **Nothin' But The Taillights**
    *Clint Black*
'93 **Nothin' My Love Can't Fix**
    *Joey Lawrence*
'89 **Nothin' To Hide** *Poco*
    **Nothin' To Lose**
'74    *Kiss*
'04    *Josh Gracin*
'00 **Nothing As It Seems** *Pearl Jam*
'92 **Nothing Broken But My Heart**
    *Celine Dion*
'69 **Nothing But A Heartache** *Flirtations*
'65 **Nothing But Heartaches** *Supremes*
'62 **Nothing Can Change This Love**
    *Sam Cooke*
'88 **Nothing Can Come Between Us**
    *Sade*
'65 **Nothing Can Stop Me**
    *Gene Chandler*
'90 **Nothing Compares 2 U**
    *Sinéad O'Connor*
'92 **Nothing Else Matters** *Metallica*
'74 **Nothing From Nothing** *Billy Preston*
'02 **Nothing In This World** *Keke Wyatt*
'04 **Nothing On But The Radio**
    *Gary Allan*
'87 **Nothing's Gonna Change My Love**
    **For You** *Glenn Medeiros*
'87 **Nothing's Gonna Stop Us Now**
    *Starship*
'66 **Nothing's Too Good For My Baby**
    *Stevie Wonder*
'90 **Notice Me** *Nikki*
    **Notorious**
'86    *Duran Duran*
'87    *Loverboy*
'92 **November Rain** *Guns N' Roses*
'96 **Novocaine For The Soul** *Eels*
'58 **Now And For Always**
    *George Hamilton IV*
'94 **Now and Forever** *Richard Marx*
'67 **Now I Know** *Jack Jones*
'92 **Now More Than Ever**
    *John Mellencamp*
'72 **Now Run And Tell That**
    *Denise LaSalle*
'98 **Now That I Found You** *Terri Clark*
    **Now That We Found Love**
'79    *Third World*
'91    *Heavy D & The Boyz*
'89 **Now You're In Heaven**
    *Julian Lennon*
'66 **Nowhere Man** *Beatles*
'96 **Nowhere To Go** *Melissa Etheridge*
'65 **Nowhere To Run**
    *Martha & The Vandellas*
'92 **Nu Nu** *Lidell Townsell & M.T.F.*
    **Numb**
'93    *U2*
'03    *Linkin Park*
'04 **Numb/Encore** *Jay-Z/Linkin Park*
'74 **#9 Dream** *John Lennon*
'01 **#1** *Nelly*
'96 **#1 Crush** *Garbage*
'05 **Number One Spot** *Ludacris*
'73 **Nutbush City Limits**
    *Ike & Tina Turner*
'93 **Nuthin' But A "G" Thang**
    *Dr. Dre/Snoop Dogg*
'62 **Nutrocker** *B. Bumble & The Stingers*
'94 **Nuttin' But Love**
    *Heavy D & The Boyz*
    **Nuttin' For Christmas**
'55    *Barry Gordon*
'55    *Joe Ward*
'55    *Ricky Zahnd*

**O**

'05 **O** *Omarion*
'60 **O Dio Mio** *Annette*

'02 **O Holy Night** *Josh Groban*
'82 **O Superman (For Massenet)**
    *Laurie Anderson*
'02 **'03 Bonnie & Clyde** *Jay-Z*
'91 **O.P.P.** *Naughty By Nature*
'85 **Oak Tree** *Morris Day*
'88 **Oasis** *Roberta Flack*
'85 **Object Of My Desire** *Starpoint*
'94 **Objects In The Rear View Mirror**
    **May Appear Closer Than They**
    **Are** *Meat Loaf*
'68 **Ob-La-Di, Ob-La-Da** *Beatles*
'84 **Obscene Phone Caller** *Rockwell*
'85 **Obsession** *Animotion*
'05 **Obsession [No Es Amor]** *Frankie J*
'73 **Ocean, The** *Led Zeppelin*
'04 **Ocean Avenue** *Yellowcard*
'87 **Ocean Front Property** *George Strait*
'69 **Octopus's Garden** *Beatles*
    **Ode To Billie Joe**
'67    *Bobbie Gentry*
'67    *Kingpins*
'95 **Ode To My Family** *Cranberries*
'88 **Off On Your Own (Girl)** *Al B. Sure!*
'80 **Off The Wall** *Michael Jackson*
'05 **Oh** *Ciara*
'72 **Oh, Babe, What Would You Say?**
    *Hurricane Smith*
'64 **Oh Baby Don't You Weep**
    *James Brown*
    **Oh Boy**
'57    *Crickets*
'02    *Cam'ron*
'59 **Oh! Carol** *Neil Sedaka*
'89 **Oh Daddy** *Adrian Belew*
    **Oh! Darling**
'69    *Beatles*
'78    *Robin Gibb*
'89 **Oh Father** *Madonna*
    **Oh Girl**
'72    *Chi-Lites*
'90    *Paul Young*
    **Oh Happy Day**
'69    *Edwin Hawkins' Singers*
'70    *Glen Campbell*
'66 **Oh How Happy** *Shades Of Blue*
    **Oh Julie**
'58    *Crescendos*
'82    *Barry Manilow*
'73 **Oh La De Da** *Staple Singers*
'60 **Oh, Little One** *Jack Scott*
'58 **Oh Lonesome Me** *Don Gibson*
'69 **Oh Me Oh My (I'm A Fool For You**
    **Baby)** *Lulu*
'74 **Oh My My** *Ringo Starr*
'81 **Oh No** *Commodores*
'64 **Oh No Not My Baby** *Maxine Brown*
'58 **Oh-Oh, I'm Falling In Love Again**
    *Jimmie Rodgers*
'86 **Oh, People** *Patti LaBelle*
    **Oh, Pretty Woman**
'64    *Roy Orbison*
'82    *Van Halen*
'85 **Oh Sheila** *Ready For The World*
'84 **Oh Sherrie** *Steve Perry*
'55 **Oh! Susanna** *Singing Dogs*
'74 **Oh Very Young** *Cat Stevens*
    **Oh Well**
'70    *Fleetwood Mac*
'79    *Rockets*
'69 **Oh, What A Night** *Dells*
'78 **Oh What A Night For Dancing**
    *Barry White*
    **Oh Yeah**
'66    *Shadows Of Knight*
'87    *Yello*
'70 **Ohio** *Crosby, Stills, Nash & Young*
'94 **Oíche Chiún (Silent Night)** *Enya*
'05 **Okay** *Nivea*
'69 **Okie From Muskogee**
    *Merle Haggard*
'55 **Oklahoma!** *Gordon MacRae*
'02 **Ol' Red** *Blake Shelton*
'69 **Old Brown Shoe** *Beatles*
'57 **Old Cape Cod** *Patti Page*

'75 **Old Days** *Chicago*
'94 **Old Enough To Know Better**
    *Wade Hayes*
'80 **Old-Fashion Love** *Commodores*
'77 **Old Fashioned Boy (You're The**
    **One)** *Stallion*
'71 **Old Fashioned Love Song**
    *Three Dog Night*
'88 **Old Folks**
    *Ronnie Milsap & Mike Reid*
'85 **Old Hippie** *Bellamy Brothers*
'60 **Old Lamplighter** *Browns*
'72 **Old Man** *Neil Young*
'96 **Old Man & Me (When I Get To**
    **Heaven)** *Hootie & The Blowfish*
'84 **Old Man Down The Road**
    *John Fogerty*
'56 **Old Philosopher** *Eddie Lawrence*
'62 **Old Rivers** *Walter Brennan*
'81 **Old Songs** *Barry Manilow*
'79 **Old Time Rock & Roll** *Bob Seger*
'61 **Ole Buttermilk Sky**
    *Bill Black's Combo*
'79 **Oliver's Army** *Elvis Costello*
'67 **Omaha** *Moby Grape*
'67 **On A Carousel** *Hollies*
'96 **On A Good Night** *Wade Hayes*
'74 **On A Night Like This**
    *Bob Dylan*
'91 **On A Sunday Afternoon**
    *Lighter Shade Of Brown*
    **On And [&] On**
'74    *Gladys Knight*
'77    *Stephen Bishop*
'97    *Erykah Badu*
'94 **On Bended Knee** *Boyz II Men*
    **On Broadway**
'63    *Drifters*
'78    *George Benson*
'04 **On Fire** *Lloyd Banks*
'56 **On London Bridge** *Jo Stafford*
    **On My Own**
'86    *Patti LaBelle & Michael McDonald*
'97    *Peach Union*
    **On My Word Of Honor**
'56    *B.B. King*
'56    *Platters*
'89 **On Our Own** *Bobby Brown*
'89 **On Second Thought** *Eddie Rabbitt*
'77 **On The Border** *Al Stewart*
'84 **On The Dark Side**
    *John Cafferty*
'82 **On The Loose** *Saga*
'86 **On The Other Hand** *Randy Travis*
'80 **On The Radio** *Donna Summer*
'61 **On The Rebound** *Floyd Cramer*
    **On The Road Again**
'68    *Canned Heat*
'80    *Willie Nelson*
'78 **On The Shelf**
    *Donny & Marie Osmond*
    **On The Street Where You Live**
'56    *Vic Damone*
'56    *Eddie Fisher*
'64    *Andy Williams*
'87 **On The Turning Away** *Pink Floyd*
'04 **On The Way Down** *Ryan Cabrera*
'82 **On The Way To The Sky**
    *Neil Diamond*
'90 **On The Way Up** *Elisa Fiorillo*
'82 **On The Wings Of Love**
    *Jeffrey Osborne*
'63 **On Top Of Spaghetti** *Tom Glazer*
'64 **Once A Day** *Connie Smith*
'89 **Once Bitten Twice Shy** *Great White*
'80 **Once In A Lifetime**
    *Talking Heads*
'60 **Once In Awhile** *Chimes*
    **Once Upon A Time**
'61    *Rochell & The Candles*
'64    *Marvin Gaye & Mary Wells*
'75 **Once You Get Started**
    *Rufus Feat. Chaka Khan*
'71 **Once You Understand** *Think*

**One**
'69 Three Dog Night
'89 Bee Gees
'89 Metallica
'92 U2
'98 Creed
**One, The**
'92 Elton John
'00 Backstreet Boys
'02 Gary Allan
'91 **One And Only** Chesney Hawkes
'90 **One And Only Man** Steve Winwood
'71 **One Bad Apple** Osmonds
'95 **One Boy, One Girl** Collin Raye
'63 **One Broken Heart For Sale**
     Elvis Presley
'04 **One Call Away** Chingy
**One Chain Don't Make No Prison**
'74 Four Tops
'78 Santana
'74 **One Day At A Time** Marilyn Sellars
'70 **One Day Of Your Life** Andy Williams
'65 **One Dyin' And A Buryin'**
     Roger Miller
'95 **One Emotion** Clint Black
**One Fine Day**
'63 Chiffons
'80 Carole King
'71 **One Fine Morning** Lighthouse
'57 **One For My Baby** Tony Bennett
'87 **One For The Mockingbird**
     Cutting Crew
'88 **One Good Reason** Paul Carrack
'88 **One Good Woman** Peter Cetera
'65 **One Has My Name (The Other Has
     My Heart)** Barry Young
'96 **One Headlight** Wallflowers
'87 **One Heartbeat** Smokey Robinson
'74 **One Hell Of A Woman** Mac Davis
'86 **One Hit (To The Body)**
     Rolling Stones
'94 **100% Pure Love** Crystal Waters
'81 **One Hundred Ways**
     Quincy Jones/James Ingram
'04 **100 Years** Five For Fighting
'97 **One I Gave My Heart To** Aaliyah
'87 **One I Love** R.E.M.
**One In A Million**
'56 Platters
'84 Romantics
'96 Aaliyah
'80 **One In A Million You** Larry Graham
'65 **One Kiss For Old Times' Sake**
     Ronnie Dove
'02 **One Last Breath** Creed
'93 **One Last Cry** Brian McKnight
'78 **One Last Kiss** J. Geils Band
'70 **One Less Bell To Answer**
     5th Dimension
'73 **One Less Set Of Footsteps**
     Jim Croce
'72 **One Life To Live** Manhattans
'85 **One Lonely Night**
     REO Speedwagon
'77 **One Love** Bob Marley
'76 **One Love In My Lifetime**
     Diana Ross
'70 **One Man Band** Three Dog Night
'73 **One Man Band (Plays All Alone)**
     Ronnie Dyson
'74 **One Man Woman/One Woman Man**
     Paul Anka/Odia Coates
'61 **One Mint Julep** Ray Charles
'01 **One Minute Man** Missy Elliott
'88 **One Moment In Time**
     Whitney Houston
'71 **One Monkey Don't Stop No Show**
     Honey Cone
'95 **One More Chance/Stay With Me**
     Notorious B.I.G.
'01 **One More Day** Diamond Rio
'93 **One More Last Chance** Vince Gill
'85 **One More Night** Phil Collins
'72 **One More Saturday Night**
     Grateful Dead
'97 **One More Time** Real McCoy

**One More Try**
'88 George Michael
'90 Timmy -T-
'99 Divine
**One Nation Under A Groove**
'78 Funkadelic
'94 Ice Cube [Bop Gun]
'58 **One Night** Elvis Presley
'97 **One Night At A Time** George Strait
'85 **One Night In Bangkok** Murray Head
'85 **One Night Love Affair** Bryan Adams
'99 **One Night Stand** J-Shin
'73 **One Of A Kind (Love Affair)**
     Spinners
'85 **One Of The Living** Tina Turner
**One Of These Days**
'71 Pink Floyd
'98 Tim McGraw
'75 **One Of These Nights** Eagles
'95 **One Of Us** Joan Osborne
'60 **One Of Us (Will Weep Tonight)**
     Patti Page
'83 **One On One** Daryl Hall & John Oates
'83 **One Particular Harbor** Jimmy Buffett
'76 **One Piece At A Time** Johnny Cash
'91 **One Shot** Tin Machine
'80 **One Step Closer** Doobie Brothers
'86 **One Step Closer To You**
     Gavin Christopher
'87 **One Step Up** Bruce Springsteen
**One Summer Night**
'58 Danleers
'61 Diamonds
'95 **One Sweet Day**
     Mariah Carey & Boyz II Men
'81 **One That You Love** Air Supply
**One [1] Thing**
'83 INXS
'04 Finger Eleven
'05 Amerie
'83 **One Thing Leads To Another** Fixx
**One Tin Soldier (The Legend Of
     Billy Jack)**
'69 Original Caste
'71 Coven
'71 **One Toke Over The Line**
     Brewer & Shipley
'61 **One Track Mind** Bobby Lewis
'80 **One-Trick Pony** Paul Simon
'05 **1,2 Step** Ciara
**1-2-3**
'65 Len Barry
'88 Gloria Estefan
'68 **1, 2, 3, Red Light** 1910 Fruitgum Co.
'96 **1,2,3,4 (Sumpin' New)** Coolio
'00 **One Voice** Billy Gilman
'79 **One Way Or Another** Blondie
'72 **One Way Out**
     Allman Brothers Band
'96 **One Way Ticket (Because I Can)**
     LeAnn Rimes
'98 **One Week** Barenaked Ladies
'62 **One Who Really Loves You**
     Mary Wells
'93 **One Woman** Jade
'82 **One You Love** Glenn Frey
'71 **One's On The Way** Loretta Lynn
'80 **Only A Lonely Heart Sees**
     Felix Cavaliere
'88 **Only A Memory** Smithereens
'00 **Only God Knows Why** Kid Rock
'90 **Only Here For A Little While**
     Billy Dean
'90 **Only Human** Jeffrey Osborne
**Only In America**
'63 Jay & The Americans
'01 Brooks & Dunn
'87 **Only In My Dreams** Debbie Gibson
'62 **Only Love Can Break A Heart**
     Gene Pitney
'70 **Only Love Can Break Your Heart**
     Neil Young
'76 **Only Love Is Real** Carole King
'57 **Only One Love** George Hamilton IV

**Only Sixteen**
'59 Sam Cooke
'76 Dr. Hook
'78 **Only The Good Die Young** Billy Joel
**Only The Lonely**
'60 Roy Orbison
'82 Motels
'69 **Only The Strong Survive**
     Jerry Butler
'85 **Only The Young** Journey
'01 **Only Time** Enya
**Only Time Will Tell**
'82 Asia
'91 Nelson
'95 **Only Wanna Be With You**
     Hootie & The Blowfish
'84 **Only When You Leave**
     Spandau Ballet
'75 **Only Women** Alice Cooper
'75 **Only Yesterday** Carpenters
**Only You [U]**
'55 Hilltoppers
'55 Platters
'59 Franck Pourcel
'74 Ringo Starr
'82 Yaz
'96 112
'04 Ashanti
**Only You Know And I Know**
'70 Dave Mason
'71 Delaney & Bonnie
'65 **Oo Wee Baby, I Love You**
     Fred Hughes
'56 **Ooby Dooby** Roy Orbison
'92 **Oochie Coochie** MC Brains
'01 **Oochie Wally** QB Finest
'67 **Oogum Boogum Song**
     Brenton Wood
'03 **Ooh!** Mary J. Blige
'96 **Ooh Aah...Just A Little Bit** Gina G
'73 **Ooh Baby** Gilbert O'Sullivan
**Ooh Baby Baby**
'65 Miracles
'78 Linda Ronstadt
'77 **Ooh Boy** Rose Royce
**O-o-h Child**
'70 5 Stairsteps
'93 Dino
'73 **Ooh La La** Faces
'90 **Ooh La La (I Can't Get Over You)**
     Perfect Gentlemen
'58 **Ooh! My Soul** Little Richard
'85 **Ooh Ooh Song** Pat Benatar
'60 **Ooh Poo Pah Doo** Jessie Hill
'88 **Ooo La La La** Teena Marie
'90 **Ooops Up** Snap!
'00 **Oops!...I Did It Again** Britney Spears
'02 **Oops (Oh My)** Tweet
'82 **Open Arms** Journey
'67 **Open Letter To My Teenage Son**
     Victor Lundberg
'66 **Open The Door To Your Heart**
     Darrell Banks
'96 **Open Up Your Eyes** Tonic
'55 **Open Up Your Heart (And Let The
     Sunshine In)** Cowboy
     Church Sunday School
'04 **Open Your Eyes** Alter Bridge
'86 **Open Your Heart** Madonna
**Operator**
'75 Manhattan Transfer
'84 Midnight Star
'72 **Operator (That's Not the Way it
     Feels)** Jim Croce
'76 **Ophelia** Band
'86 **Opportunities (Let's Make Lots Of
     Money)** Pet Shop Boys
'89 **Opposites Attract** Paula Abdul
'91 **Optimistic** Sounds Of Blackness
'66 **Opus 17 (Don't You Worry 'Bout
     Me)** 4 Seasons
'88 **Orange Crush** R.E.M.
'02 **Ordinary Day** Vanessa Carlton
'99 **Ordinary Life** Chad Brock
'05 **Ordinary People** John Legend
'93 **Ordinary World** Duran Duran

'00 **Original Prankster** *Offspring*
'89 **Orinoco Flow (Sail Away)** *Enya*
'83 **Other Arms** *Robert Plant*
'82 **Other Guy** *Little River Band*
**Other Side**
'90   *Aerosmith*
'00   *Red Hot Chili Peppers*
'91 **Other Side Of Summer**
  *Elvis Costello*
'82 **Other Woman** *Ray Parker Jr.*
'89 **Ouija Board, Ouija Board** *Morrissey*
**Our Day Will Come**
'63   *Ruby & The Romantics*
'75   *Frankie Valli*
'91 **Our Frank** *Morrissey*
**Our House**
'70   *Crosby, Stills, Nash & Young*
'83   *Madness*
'81 **Our Lips Are Sealed** *Go-Go's*
'78 **Our Love** *Natalie Cole*
'78 **(Our Love) Don't Throw It All Away**
  *Andy Gibb*
'63 **Our Winter Love** *Bill Pursell*
'80 **Out Here On My Own** *Irene Cara*
'91 **Out In The Cold** *Tom Petty*
'70 **Out In The Country** *Three Dog Night*
'63 **Out Of Limits** *Marketts*
'86 **Out Of Mind Out Of Sight** *Models*
'98 **Out Of My Bones** *Randy Travis*
'99 **Out Of My Head** *Fastball*
'63 **Out Of My Mind** *Johnny Tillotson*
'64 **Out Of Sight** *James Brown*
'56 **Out Of Sight, Out Of Mind**
  *Five Keys*
'88 **Out Of The Blue** *Debbie Gibson*
'73 **Out Of The Question**
  *Gilbert O'Sullivan*
'84 **Out Of Touch**
  *Daryl Hall & John Oates*
'82 **Out Of Work** *Gary U.S. Bonds*
'72 **Outa-Space** *Billy Preston*
'73 **Outlaw Man** *Eagles*
'00 **Outside** *Aaron Lewis with Fred Durst*
'60 **Outside My Window** *Fleetwoods*
'74 **Outside Woman** *Bloodstone*
'03 **Outsider, The** *Perfect Circle*
'82 **Outstanding** *Gap Band*
**Over And Over**
'58   *Bobby Day*
'65   *Dave Clark Five*
'04   *Nelly*
'75 **Over My Head** *Fleetwood Mac*
'73 **Over The Hills And Far Away**
  *Led Zeppelin*
**Over The Mountain; Across The**
  **Sea**
'57   *Johnnie & Joe*
'63   *Bobby Vinton*
**Over The Rainbow**
'60   *Demensions*
'61   *Judy Garland [live]*
'66 **Over Under Sideways Down**
  *Yardbirds*
'68 **Over You** *Gary Puckett*
'86 **Overjoyed** *Stevie Wonder*
'83 **Overkill** *Men At Work*
'04 **Overnight Celebrity** *Twista*
'74 **Overnight Sensation (Hit Record)**
  *Raspberries*
'70 **Overture From Tommy (A Rock**
  **Opera)** *Assembled Multitude*
'83 **Owner Of A Lonely Heart** *Yes*
'71 **Oye Como Va** *Santana*
'04 **Oye Mi Canto** *N.O.R.E.*

# P

'03 **P.I.M.P.** *50 Cent*
'64 **P.S. I Love You** *Beatles*
'62 **P.T. 109** *Jimmy Dean*
'83 **P.Y.T. (Pretty Young Thing)**
  *Michael Jackson*
'82 **Pac-Man Fever** *Buckner & Garcia*
'58 **Padre** *Toni Arden*
'88 **Paid In Full** *Eric B & Rakim*

'04 **Pain** *Jimmy Eat World*
'63 **Pain In My Heart** *Otis Redding*
'66 **Paint It, Black** *Rolling Stones*
'73 **Painted Ladies** *Ian Thomas*
'63 **Painted, Tainted Rose** *Al Martino*
'69 **Pale Blue Eyes** *Velvet Underground*
'62 **Palisades Park** *Freddy Cannon*
'75 **Paloma Blanca**
  *George Baker Selection*
'88 **Pamela** *Toto*
'84 **Panama** *Van Halen*
'83 **Pancho And Lefty**
  *Willie Nelson & Merle Haggard*
'66 **Pandora's Golden Heebie Jeebies**
  *Association*
'83 **Papa, Can You Hear Me?**
  *Barbra Streisand*
'86 **Papa Don't Preach** *Madonna*
'74 **Papa Don't Take No Mess**
  *James Brown*
'92 **Papa Loved Mama** *Garth Brooks*
'54 **Papa Loves Mambo** *Perry Como*
'62 **Papa-Oom-Mow-Mow** *Rivingtons*
'72 **Papa Was A Rollin' Stone**
  *Temptations*
**Papa's Got A Brand New Bag**
'65   *James Brown*
'68   *Otis Redding*
'67 **Paper Cup** *5th Dimension*
'92 **Paper Doll** *PM Dawn*
'87 **Paper In Fire**
  *John Cougar Mellencamp*
**Paper Roses**
'60   *Anita Bryant*
'73   *Marie Osmond*
'68 **Paper Sun** *Traffic*
'65 **Paper Tiger** *Sue Thompson*
'66 **Paperback Writer** *Beatles*
'82 **Paperlate** *Genesis*
**Paradise**
'88   *Sade*
'02   *LL Cool J*
'78 **Paradise By The Dashboard Light**
  *Meat Loaf*
'89 **Paradise City** *Guns N' Roses*
'71 **Paranoid** *Black Sabbath*
'97 **Paranoid Andoid** *Radiohead*
'86 **Paranoimia** *Art Of Noise*
'99 **Pardon Me** *Incubus*
'88 **Parents Just Don't Understand**
  *D.J. Jazzy Jeff & The Fresh Prince*
'58 **Part Of Me** *Jimmy Clanton*
'75 **Part Of The Plan** *Dan Fogelberg*
**Part Time Love**
'63   *Little Johnny Taylor*
'75   *Gladys Knight*
'78   *Elton John*
'85 **Part-Time Lover** *Stevie Wonder*
'85 **Party All The Time** *Eddie Murphy*
'98 **Party Continues** *JD & Da Brat*
**Party Doll**
'57   *Buddy Knox*
'57   *Steve Lawrence*
'74 **Party Down** *Little Beaver*
'62 **Party Lights** *Claudine Clark*
'81 **Party Time** *T.G. Sheppard*
'83 **Party Train** *Gap Band*
'00 **Party Up (Up In Here)** *DMX*
'81 **Party's Over (Hopelessly In Love)**
  *Journey*
'89 **Partyman** *Prince*
'90 **Pass It On Down** *Alabama*
'03 **Pass That Dutch** *Missy Elliott*
'02 **Pass The Courvoisier**
  *Busta Rhymes*
'82 **Pass The Dutchie** *Musical Youth*
'04 **Passenger Seat** *SheDaisy*
'91 **P.A.S.S.I.O.N** *Rythm Syndicate*
'80 **Passion** *Rod Stewart*
'93 **Passionate Kisses**
  *Mary Chapin Carpenter*
'92 **Past The Point Of Rescue**
  *Hal Ketchum*
'67 **Pata Pata** *Miriam Makeba*

**Patches**
'62   *Dickey Lee*
'70   *Clarence Carter*
'89 **Patience** *Guns N' Roses*
'58 **Patricia** *Perez Prado*
'74 **Payback, The** *James Brown*
'70 **Pay To The Piper**
  *Chairmen Of The Board*
'67 **Pay You Back With Interest** *Hollies*
'68 **Paying The Cost To Be The Boss**
  *B.B. King*
'89 **Peace In Our Time** *Eddie Money*
'57 **Peace In The Valley** *Elvis Presley*
'77 **Peace Of Mind** *Boston*
'75 **Peace Pipe** *B.T. Express*
'71 **Peace Train** *Cat Stevens*
'70 **Peace Will Come (According To**
  **Plan)** *Melanie*
'73 **Peaceful** *Helen Reddy*
'72 **Peaceful Easy Feeling** *Eagles*
'01 **Peaceful World**
  *John Mellencamp*
'96 **Peaches** *Presidents Of The*
  *United States Of America*
'01 **Peaches & Cream** *112*
'69 **Peaches En Regalia**
  *Frank Zappa*
'65 **Peaches "N" Cream** *Ikettes*
'79 **Peanut Butter** *Twennynine*
'57 **Peanuts** *Little Joe & The Thrillers*
**Peek-A-Boo**
'58   *Cadillacs*
'88   *Siouxsie & The Banshees*
'77 **Peg** *Steely Dan*
'57 **Peggy Sue** *Buddy Holly*
'64 **Penetration** *Pyramids*
'60 **Pennies From Heaven** *Skyliners*
'82 **Penny For Your Thoughts** *Tavares*
'67 **Penny Lane** *Beatles*
'84 **Penny Lover** *Lionel Richie*
**People**
'64   *Barbra Streisand*
'68   *Tymes*
'85 **People Are People** *Depeche Mode*
'91 **People Are Still Having Sex** *LaTour*
'67 **People Are Strange** *Doors*
'92 **People Everyday**
  *Arrested Development*
'65 **People Get Ready** *Impressions*
'68 **People Got To Be Free** *Rascals*
'74 **People Gotta Move** *Gino Vannelli*
'88 **People Have The Power** *Patti Smith*
'72 **People Make The World Go Round**
  *Stylistics*
'79 **People Of The South Wind** *Kansas*
'64 **People Say** *Dixie Cups*
'60 **"Pepe"** *Duane Eddy*
'62 **Pepino The Italian Mouse**
  *Lou Monte*
'96 **Pepper** *Butthole Surfers*
'55 **Pepper-Hot Baby** *Jaye P. Morgan*
'61 **Peppermint Twist**
  *Joey Dee & the Starliters*
'62 **Percolator (Twist)**
  *Billy Joe & The Checkmates*
**Perfect**
'98   *Smashing Pumpkins*
'03   *Sara Evans*
'03   *Simple Plan*
'72 **Perfect Day** *Lou Reed*
'85 **Perfect Kiss** *New Order*
'98 **Perfect Love** *Trisha Yearwood*
'85 **Perfect Way** *Scritti Politti*
'88 **Perfect World** *Huey Lewis*
'60 **Perfidia** *Ventures*
'95 **Perry Mason** *Ozzy Osbourne*
'89 **Personal Jesus** *Depeche Mode*
'59 **Personality** *Lloyd Price*
'73 **Personality Crisis**
  *New York Dolls*
'82 **Personally** *Karla Bonoff*
**Peter Gunn**
'59   *Ray Anthony*
'60   *Duane Eddy*
'86   *Art Of Noise*
'59 **Petite Fleur** *Chris Barber*

'93 **Pets** *Porno For Pyros*
'56 **Petticoats Of Portugal** *Dick Jacobs*
'75 **Philadelphia Freedom** *Elton John*
'58 **Philadelphia U.S.A.** *Nu Tornados*
'66 **Phoenix Love Theme (Senza Fine)**
    *Brass Ring*
**Photograph**
'73   *Ringo Starr*
'83   *Def Leppard*
'81 **Physical** *Olivia Newton-John*
'88 **Piano In The Dark** *Brenda Russell*
'74 **Piano Man** *Billy Joel*
'90 **Piccadilly Palare** *Morrissey*
'74 **Pick Up The Pieces** *AWB*
'68 **Pickin' Wild Mountain Berries**
    *Peggy Scott & Jo Jo Benson*
'94 **Pickup Man** *Joe Diffie*
'02 **Picture** *Kid Rock Feat. Sheryl Crow*
'67 **Pictures Of Lily** *Who*
**Pictures Of Matchstick Men**
'68   *Status Quo*
'89   *Camper Van Beethoven*
'90 **Pictures Of You** *Cure*
**Piece Of My Heart**
'68   *Big Brother & The Holding Company*
'91   *Tara Kemp*
'94   *Faith Hill*
'05   *Melissa Etheridge & Joss Stone*
    *[medley]*
'72 **Pieces Of April** *Three Dog Night*
'83 **Pieces Of Ice** *Diana Ross*
'04 **Pieces Of Me** *Ashlee Simpson*
'66 **Pied Piper** *Crispian St. Peters*
'73 **Pillow Talk** *Sylvia*
'80 **Pilot Of The Airwaves** *Charlie Dore*
**Pinball Wizard**
'69   *Who*
'73   *New Seekers [medley]*
'75   *Elton John*
'00 **Pinch Me** *Barenaked Ladies*
'94 **Pincushion** *ZZ Top*
'60 **Pineapple Princess** *Annette*
'98 **Pink** *Aerosmith*
**Pink Cadillac**
'84   *Bruce Springsteen*
'88   *Natalie Cole*
'60 **Pink Chiffon** *Mitchell Torok*
'83 **Pink Houses**
    *John Cougar Mellencamp*
'64 **Pink Panther Theme** *Henry Mancini*
'59 **Pink Shoe Laces** *Dodie Stevens*
'63 **Pipeline** *Chantay's*
'66 **Place In The Sun** *Stevie Wonder*
'91 **Place In This World**
    *Michael W. Smith*
'94 **Place Where You Belong** *Shai*
'59 **Plain Jane** *Bobby Darin*
'82 **Planet Rock** *Afrika Bambaataa*
'55 **Plantation Boogie** *Lenny Dee*
'67 **Plastic Fantastic Lover**
    *Jefferson Airplane*
'01 **Play** *Jennifer Lopez*
'55 **Play It Fair** *LaVern Baker*
'72 **Play Me** *Neil Diamond*
'55 **Play Me Hearts And Flowers**
    **(I Wanna Cry)** *Johnny Desmond*
'75 **Play On Love** *Jefferson Starship*
**Play That Funky Music**
'76   *Wild Cherry*
'90   *Vanilla Ice*
'80 **Play The Game** *Queen*
'82 **Play The Game Tonight** *Kansas*
'94 **Playaz Club** *Rappin' 4-Tay*
**Playboy**
'62   *Marvelettes*
'68   *Gene & Debbe*
'95 **Player's Anthem** *Junior M.A.F.I.A.*
'94 **Player's Ball** *OutKast*
'91 **Playground** *Another Bad Creation*
'73 **Playground In My Mind**
    *Clint Holmes*
'57 **Playing For Keeps** *Elvis Presley*
'71 **Playing In The Band**
    *Grateful Dead*
'67 **Pleasant Valley Sunday** *Monkees*

**Please Come Home For Christmas**
'60   *Charles Brown*
'78   *Eagles*
'74 **Please Come To Boston**
    *Dave Loggins*
'62 **Please Don't Ask About Barbara**
    *Bobby Vee*
**Please Don't Go**
'61   *Ral Donner*
'79   *KC & The Sunshine Band*
'92   *K.W.S.*
'96   *Immature*
'97   *No Mercy*
'88 **Please Don't Go Girl**
    *New Kids On The Block*
'79 **Please Don't Leave** *Lauren Wood*
'63 **Please Don't Talk To The Lifeguard**
    *Diane Ray*
'93 **Please Forgive Me** *Bryan Adams*
'60 **Please Help Me, I'm Falling**
    *Hank Locklin*
**Please Love Me Forever**
'61   *Cathy Jean & The Roommates*
'67   *Bobby Vinton*
'75 **Please Mr. Please**
    *Olivia Newton-John*
**Please Mr. Postman**
'61   *Marvelettes*
'74   *Carpenters*
'59 **Please Mr. Sun** *Tommy Edwards*
'64 **Please Please Me** *Beatles*
'56 **Please, Please, Please**
    *James Brown*
'99 **Please Remember Me** *Tim McGraw*
'68 **Please Return Your Love To Me**
    *Temptations*
'61 **Please Stay** *Drifters*
**Please Tell Me Why**
'61   *Jackie Wilson*
'66   *Dave Clark Five*
'87 **Pleasure Principle** *Janet Jackson*
**Pledge Of Love**
'57   *Ken Copeland*
'57   *Mitchell Torok*
**Pledging My Love**
'55   *Johnny Ace*
'55   *Teresa Brewer*
'93 **Plush** *Stone Temple Pilots*
'02 **Po' Folks** *Nappy Roots*
'96 **Po Pimp** *Do Or Die*
'61 **Pocketful Of Miracles** *Frank Sinatra*
'60 **Poetry In Motion** *Johnny Tillotson*
'75 **Poetry Man** *Phoebe Snow*
'69 **Point It Out** *Miracles*
'77 **Point Of Know Return** *Kansas*
**Point Of No Return**
'62   *Gene McDaniels*
'86   *Nu Shooz*
'87   *Exposé*
**Poison**
'89   *Alice Cooper*
'90   *Bell Biv DeVoe*
'83 **Poison Arrow** *ABC*
'59 **Poison Ivy** *Coasters*
'90 **Policy Of Truth** *Depeche Mode*
'72 **Political Science**
    *Randy Newman*
'83 **Politics Of Dancing** *Re-Flex*
'69 **Polk Salad Annie** *Tony Joe White*
'96 **Pony** *Ginuwine*
'61 **Pony Time** *Chubby Checker*
**Poor Boy**
'56   *Elvis Presley*
'58   *Royaltones*
'61 **Poor Fool** *Ike & Tina Turner*
'59 **Poor Jenny** *Everly Brothers*
'58 **Poor Little Fool** *Ricky Nelson*
'63 **Poor Little Rich Girl**
    *Steve Lawrence*
'57 **Poor Man's Roses (Or A Rich Man's**
    **Gold)** *Patti Page*
'81 **Poor Man's Son** *Survivor*
'55 **Poor Me** *Fats Domino*

**Poor People Of Paris**
'56   *Les Baxter*
'56   *Russ Morgan*
'56   *Lawrence Welk*
**Poor Poor Pitiful Me**
'78   *Linda Ronstadt*
'96   *Terri Clark*
'66 **Poor Side Of Town** *Johnny Rivers*
'01 **Pop** *\*NSYNC*
'99 **Pop A Top** *Alan Jackson*
'82 **Pop Goes The Movies** *Meco*
'91 **Pop Goes The Weasel** *3rd Bass*
'87 **Pop Goes The World**
    *Men Without Hats*
'85 **Pop Life** *Prince*
'79 **Pop Muzik** *M*
'62 **Pop Pop Pop - Pie** *Sherrys*
'86 **(Pop, Pop, Pop, Pop) Goes My Mind**
    *Levert*
'89 **Pop Singer**
    *John Cougar Mellencamp*
'72 **Pop That Thang** *Isley Brothers*
'72 **Popcorn** *Hot Butter*
'69 **Popcorn, The** *James Brown*
'55 **Popcorn Song** *Cliffie Stone*
'62 **Popeye (The Hitchhiker)**
    *Chubby Checker*
'66 **Popsicle** *Jan & Dean*
'63 **Popsicles And Icicles** *Murmaids*
'56 **Port Au Prince** *Nelson Riddle*
'77 **Portrait (He Knew)** *Kansas*
**Portrait Of My Love**
'61   *Steve Lawrence*
'67   *Tokens*
'56 **Portuguese Washerwomen**
    *Joe "Fingers" Carr*
'65 **Positively 4th Street** *Bob Dylan*
'90 **Possession** *Bad English*
'85 **Possession Obsession**
    *Daryl Hall/John Oates*
'95 **Possum Kingdom** *Toadies*
'91 **Poundcake** *Van Halen*
'88 **Pour Some Sugar On Me**
    *Def Leppard*
'90 **Power, The** *Snap!*
'78 **Power Of Gold**
    *Dan Fogelberg/Tim Weisberg*
'98 **Power Of Good-Bye** *Madonna*
**Power Of Love**
'72   *Joe Simon*
'85   *Huey Lewis*
'87   *Laura Branigan*
'91   *Luther Vandross [medley]*
'93   *Celine Dion*
'71 **Power To The People** *John Lennon*
'91 **Power Windows** *Billy Falcon*
'88 **Powerful Stuff**
    *Fabulous Thunderbirds*
'94 **Practice What You Preach**
    *Barry White*
'99 **Praise You** *Fatboy Slim*
'90 **Pray** *M.C. Hammer*
'02 **Prayer** *Disturbed*
'94 **Prayer For The Dying** *Seal*
'00 **Prayin' For Daylight** *Rascal Flatts*
'90 **Praying For Time** *George Michael*
'72 **Precious And Few** *Climax*
'97 **Precious Declaration**
    *Collective Soul*
'79 **Precious Love** *Bob Welch*
'70 **Precious, Precious** *Jackie Moore*
'81 **Precious To Me** *Phil Seymour*
'86 **Press** *Paul McCartney*
'82 **Pressure** *Billy Joel*
'73 **Pressure Drop**
    *Toots & The Maytals*
'76 **Pretender, The** *Jackson Browne*
'89 **Pretending** *Eric Clapton*
'71 **Pretty As You Feel**
    *Jefferson Airplane*
'67 **Pretty Ballerina** *Left Banke*
'59 **Pretty Blue Eyes** *Steve Lawrence*
'66 **Pretty Flamingo** *Manfred Mann*
'98 **Pretty Fly (For A White Guy)**
    *Offspring*
'95 **Pretty Girl** *Jon B.*

229

'79 **Pretty Girls** *Melissa Manchester*
'58 **Pretty Girls Everywhere**
    *Eugene Church*
'81 **Pretty In Pink** *Psychedelic Furs*
'96 **Pretty Little Adriana** *Vince Gill*
'61 **Pretty Little Angel Eyes** *Curtis Lee*
'96 **Pretty Noose** *Soundgarden*
'63 **Pretty Paper** *Roy Orbison*
'90 **Pretty Pink Rose**
    *Adrian Belew & David Bowie*
'77 **Pretty Vacant** *Sex Pistols*
'74 **Pretzel Logic** *Steely Dan*
'89 **Price Of Love** *Bad English*
'03 **Price To Play** *Staind*
'77 **Pride, The** *Isley Brothers*
**Pride And Joy**
'63    *Marvin Gaye*
'83    *Stevie Ray Vaughan*
'93    *Coverdale-Page*
'84 **Pride (In The Name Of Love)** *U2*
'84 **Prime Time** *Alan Parsons Project*
'59 **Primrose Lane** *Jerry Wallace*
'61 **Princess** *Frank Gari*
'89 **Principal's Office** *Young M.C.*
'56 **Priscilla** *Eddie Cooley*
'89 **Prisoner, The** *Howard Jones*
'63 **Prisoner Of Love** *James Brown*
'78 **Prisoner Of Your Love** *Player*
'85 **Private Dancer** *Tina Turner*
'81 **Private Eyes**
    *Daryl Hall & John Oates*
'80 **Private Idaho** *B-52's*
'91 **Private Line** *Gerald Levert*
'58 **Problems** *Everly Brothers*
**Promise**
'00    *Eve 6*
'00    *Jagged Edge*
'88 **Promise, The** *When In Rome*
'88 **Promise Me** *Cover Girls*
'58 **Promise Me, Love** *Andy Williams*
'91 **Promise Of A New Day** *Paula Abdul*
**Promised Land**
'74    *Elvis Presley*
'78    *Bruce Springsteen*
**Promises**
'78    *Eric Clapton*
'99    *Def Leppard*
'81 **Promises In The Dark** *Pat Benatar*
**Promises, Promises**
'68    *Dionne Warwick*
'83    *Naked Eyes*
'93 **Prop Me Up Beside The Jukebox**
    **(If I Die)** *Joe Diffie*
'63 **Proud** *Johnny Crawford*
**Proud Mary**
'69    *Creedence Clearwater Revival*
'71    *Ike & Tina Turner*
'75 **Proud One** *Osmonds*
'78 **Prove It All Night** *Bruce Springsteen*
'88 **Prove Your Love** *Taylor Dayne*
'70 **Psychedelic Shack** *Temptations*
'98 **Psycho Circus** *Kiss*
'77 **Psycho Killer** *Talking Heads*
'98 **Psycho Man** *Black Sabbath*
'66 **Psychotic Reaction** *Count Five*
'67 **Pucker Up Buttercup** *Jr. Walker*
'63 **Puff (The Magic Dragon)**
    *Peter, Paul & Mary*
'88 **Pull Over** *Levert*
**Pump It Up**
'78    *Elvis Costello*
'03    *Joe Budden*
'89 **Pump Up The Jam** *Technotronic*
'87 **Pump Up The Volume** *M/A/R/R/S*
'94 **Pumps And A Bump** *Hammer*
'62 **Punish Her** *Bobby Vee*
**Puppet Man**
'70    *5th Dimension*
'71    *Tom Jones*
'65 **Puppet On A String** *Elvis Presley*
**Puppy Love**
'60    *Paul Anka*
'64    *Barbara Lewis*
'72    *Donny Osmond*
'90 **Pure** *Lightning Seeds*

'00 **Purest Of Pain (A Puro Dolor)**
    *Son By Four*
**Purple Haze**
'67    *Jimi Hendrix*
'93    *Cure*
'01 **Purple Hills** *D-12*
'58 **Purple People Eater** *Sheb Wooley*
'84 **Purple Rain** *Prince*
'97 **Push** *Matchbox 20*
'62 **Push And Kick** *Mark Valentino*
'87 **Push It** *Salt-N-Pepa*
'68 **Pusher, The** *Steppenwolf*
'66 **Pushin' Too Hard** *Seeds*
'98 **Pushin' Weight** *Ice Cube*
'63 **Pushover** *Etta James*
'58 **Pussy Cat** *Ames Brothers*
'57 **Put A Light In The Window**
    *Four Lads*
**Put A Little Love In Your Heart**
'69    *Jackie DeShannon*
'88    *Annie Lennox & Al Green*
'58 **Put A Ring On My Finger**
    *Les Paul & Mary Ford*
'83 **Put It In A Magazine** *Sonny Charles*
'00 **Put It On Me** *Ja Rule*
'03 **Put That Woman First** *Jaheim*
'88 **Put This Love To The Test**
    *Jon Astley*
'60 **Put Your Arms Around Me Honey**
    *Fats Domino*
'58 **Put Your Dreams Away**
    *Frank Sinatra*
'71 **Put Your Hand In The Hand** *Ocean*
'73 **Put Your Hands Together** *O'Jays*
'97 **Put Your Hands Where My Eyes**
    **Could See** *Busta Rhymes*
'59 **Put Your Head On My Shoulder**
    *Paul Anka*
'89 **Put Your Mouth On Me**
    *Eddie Murphy*
'83 **Puttin' On The Ritz** *Taco*

## Q

'92 **Quality Time** *Hi-Five*
'68 **Quando, Quando, Quando**
    *Engelbert Humperdinck*
'61 **Quarter To Three** *U.S. Bonds*
'56 **Que Sera, Sera (Whatever Will Be,**
    **Will Be)** *Doris Day*
'81 **Queen Of Hearts** *Juice Newton*
'92 **Queen Of Memphis**
    *Confederate Railroad*
'76 **Queen Of My Soul**
    *Average White Band*
'83 **Queen Of The Broken Hearts**
    *Loverboy*
'58 **Queen Of The Hop** *Bobby Darin*
'65 **Queen Of The House** *Jody Miller*
'93 **Queen Of The Night**
    *Whitney Houston*
'57 **Queen Of The Senior Prom**
    *Mills Brothers*
'69 **Quentin's Theme** *Charles*
    *Randolph Grean Sounde*
**Question**
'60    *Lloyd Price*
'70    *Moody Blues*
'68 **Question Of Temperature**
    *Balloon Farm*
'71 **Questions 67 And 68** *Chicago*
'68 **Quick Joey Small (Run Joey Run)**
    *Kasenetz-Katz Singing Orchestral*
    *Circus*
'63 **Quicksand** *Martha & The Vandellas*
'59 **Quiet Village** *Martin Denny*
'97 **Quit Playing Games (With My Heart)**
    *Backstreet Boys*
'61 **Quite A Party** *Fireballs*

## R

**Race Is On**
'65    *Jack Jones*
'89    *Sawyer Brown*
'56 **Race With The Devil** *Gene Vincent*

'74 **Radar Love** *Golden Earring*
'83 **Radio Free Europe** *R.E.M.*
'84 **Radio Ga-Ga** *Queen*
'78 **Radio, Radio** *Elvis Costello*
'89 **Radio Romance** *Tiffany*
'85 **Radioactive** *Firm*
**Rag Doll**
'64    *4 Seasons*
'88    *Aerosmith*
'69 **Rag Mama Rag** *Band*
'59 **Ragtime Cowboy Joe** *Chipmunks*
**Rain**
'66    *Beatles*
'90    *Dan Fogelberg [medley]*
'93    *Madonna*
'98    *SWV*
'86 **Rain, The** *Oran "Juice" Jones*
'71 **Rain Dance** *Guess Who*
'68 **Rain In My Heart** *Frank Sinatra*
'03 **Rain On Me** *Ashanti*
'66 **Rain On The Roof** *Lovin' Spoonful*
'86 **Rain On The Scarecrow**
    *John Cougar Mellencamp*
'62 **Rain Rain Go Away** *Bobby Vinton*
'73 **Rain Song** *Led Zeppelin*
'97 **Rain (Supa Dupa Fly)** *Missy Elliott*
'67 **Rain, The Park & Other Things**
    *Cowsills*
**Rainbow**
'57    *Russ Hamilton*
'63    *Gene Chandler*
'65    *Gene Chandler ['65]*
'79 **Rainbow Connection**
    *Kermit (Jim Henson)*
'61 **Raindrops** *Dee Clark*
'69 **Raindrops Keep Fallin' On My Head**
    *B.J. Thomas*
**Raining In My Heart**
'59    *Buddy Holly*
'61    *Slim Harpo*
'03 **Raining On Sunday** *Keith Urban*
'66 **Rains Came** *Sir Douglas Quintet*
'75 **Rainy Day People** *Gordon Lightfoot*
'66 **Rainy Day Women #12 & 35**
    *Bob Dylan*
'71 **Rainy Days And Mondays**
    *Carpenters*
'02 **Rainy Dayz** *Mary J. Blige*
'70 **Rainy Night In Georgia**
    *Brook Benton*
'98 **Raise The Roof** *Luke*
'01 **Raise Up** *Petey Pablo*
'61 **Ram-Bunk-Shush** *Ventures*
'61 **Rama Lama Ding Dong** *Edsels*
'69 **Ramble On** *Led Zeppelin*
'68 **Ramblin' Gamblin' Man** *Bob Seger*
'73 **Ramblin Man** *Allman Brothers Band*
'62 **Ramblin' Rose** *Nat King Cole*
'58 **Ramrod** *Duane Eddy*
'67 **Randy Scouse Git** *Monkees*
'80 **Ranking Full Stop** *English Beat*
'70 **Rapper, The** *Jaggerz*
'79 **Rapper's Delight** *Sugarhill Gang*
'97 **Rappers' Ball** *E-40*
'81 **Rapture** *Blondie*
'85 **Raspberry Beret** *Prince*
**Raunchy**
'57    *Ernie Freeman*
'57    *Bill Justis*
'57    *Billy Vaughn*
'58 **Rave On** *Buddy Holly*
'76 **Raven, The**
    *Alan Parsons Project*
'59 **Raw-Hide** *Link Wray*
'98 **Ray Of Hope** *Rascals*
'98 **Ray Of Light** *Madonna*
'55 **Razzle-Dazzle** *Bill Haley*
'03 **Re-Align** *Godsmack*
'99 **Re-Arranged** *Limp Bizkit*
'77 **Reach For It** *George Duke*
'70 **Reach Out And Touch (Somebody's**
    **Hand)** *Diana Ross*
'64 **Reach Out For Me** *Dionne Warwick*

**Reach Out I'll Be There**
'66 Four Tops
'71 Diana Ross
'68 **Reach Out Of The Darkness**
Friend & Lover
'02 **React** Erick Sermon
'83 **Read 'Em And Weep** Barry Manilow
'03 **Read Your Mind** Avant
'74 **Ready** Cat Stevens
'74 **Ready For Love** Bad Company
'78 **Ready For The Times To Get Better**
Crystal Gayle
**Ready Or Not**
'90 After 7
'96 Fugees
'68 **Ready Or Not Here I Come (Can't Hide From Love)** Delfonics
'56 **Ready Teddy** Little Richard
'99 **Ready To Run** Dixie Chicks
'78 **Ready To Take A Chance Again**
Barry Manilow
'03 **Real Good Man** Tim McGraw
'87 **Real Life** John Cougar Mellencamp
**Real Love**
'80 Doobie Brothers
'89 Jody Watley
'89 Skyy
'91 Bob Seger
'92 Mary J. Blige
'96 Beatles
'73 **Real Me** Who
'91 **Real, Real, Real** Jesus Jones
'00 **Real Slim Shady** Eminem
'58 **Real Wild Child** Ivan
**Real World**
'93 Queensryche
'98 Matchbox 20
'81 **Really Wanna Know You**
Gary Wright
'04 **Reason, The** Hoobastank
**Reason To Believe**
'71 Rod Stewart
'93 Rod Stewart with Ronnie Wood [live]
'95 **Rebecca Lynn** Bryan White
'65 **Rebel Kind** Dino, Desi & Billy
'74 **Rebel Rebel** David Bowie
'58 **Rebel-'Rouser** Duane Eddy
'83 **Rebel Yell** Billy Idol
'93 **Rebirth Of Slick (Cool Like Dat)**
Digable Planets
'93 **Reckless** Alabama
'69 **Reconsider Me** Johnny Adams
'65 **Recovery** Fontella Bass
'02 **Red, The** Chevelle
'81 **Red Barchetta** Rush
'03 **Red Dirt Road** Brooks & Dunn
'69 **Red House** Jimi Hendrix
'95 **Red Light Special** TLC
'02 **Red Rag Top** Tim McGraw
'86 **Red Rain** Peter Gabriel
**Red Red Wine**
'68 Neil Diamond
'88 UB40 [rap by Astro]
'59 **Red River Rock**
Johnny & The Hurricanes
'58 **Red River Rose** Ames Brothers
'58 **Red Rooster** Howling' Wolf
**Red Roses For A Blue Lady**
'65 Vic Dana
'65 Bert Kaempfert
'65 Wayne Newton
'66 **Red Rubber Ball** Cyrkle
**Red Sails In The Sunset**
'60 Platters
'63 Fats Domino
'80 **Redemption Song** Bob Marley
'72 **Redneck Friend**
Jackson Browne
'82 **Redneck Girl** Bellamy Brothers
'04 **Redneck Woman** Gretchen Wilson
'72 **Redwood Tree** Van Morrison
**Reelin' And Rockin'**
'58 Chuck Berry
'65 Dave Clark Five
'72 Chuck Berry [live]

'73 **Reeling In The Years** Steely Dan
'57 **Reet Petite** Jackie Wilson
'67 **Reflections** Supremes
'70 **Reflections Of My Life** Marmalade
'84 **Reflex, The** Duran Duran
'80 **Refugee** Tom Petty
'89 **Regina** Sugarcubes
'93 **Regret** New Order
'94 **Regulate** Warren G. & Nate Dogg
'84 **Relax** Frankie Goes To Hollywood
'72 **Relay, The** Who
**Release Me**
'62 Esther Phillips
'67 Engelbert Humperdinck
'90 Wilson Phillips
'92 **Remedy** Black Crowes
'03 **Remedy (I Won't Worry)** Jason Mraz
**Remember Me**
'64 Rita Pavone
'70 Diana Ross
'65 **(Remember Me) I'm The One Who Loves You** Dean Martin
'77 **(Remember The Days Of The) Old Schoolyard** Cat Stevens
'89 **Remember (The First Time)**
Eric Gable
'83 **Remember The Nights** Motels
'92 **Remember The Time**
Michael Jackson
'62 **Remember Then** Earls
**Remember (Walkin' In The Sand)**
'64 Shangri-Las
'79 Aerosmith
'75 **Remember What I Told You To Forget** Tavares
**Remember When**
'59 Platters
'03 Alan Jackson
'57 **Remember You're Mine** Pat Boone
'78 **Reminiscing** Little River Band
'75 **Rendezvous** Hudson Brothers
'96 **Renee** Lost Boyz
**Renegade**
'76 Michael Murphey
'79 Styx
'97 **Request Line** Zhané
**Rescue Me**
'65 Fontella Bass
'88 Al B. Sure!
'91 Madonna
**Respect**
'65 Otis Redding
'67 Aretha Franklin
**Respect Yourself**
'71 Staple Singers
'87 Bruce Willis
'66 **Respectable** Outsiders
'92 **Rest In Peace** Extreme
'92 **Restless Heart** Peter Cetera
**Resurrection Shuffle**
'71 Ashton, Gardner & Dyke
'71 Tom Jones
'97 **Return Of The Mack** Mark Morrison
'67 **Return Of The Red Baron**
Royal Guardsmen
'94 **Return To Innocence** Enigma
'58 **Return To Me** Dean Martin
'62 **Return To Sender** Elvis Presley
'79 **Reunited** Peaches & Herb
'59 **Reveille Rock**
Johnny & The Hurricanes
'61 **Revenge** Brook Benton
'63 **Reverend Mr. Black** Kingston Trio
'70 **Revival (Love Is Everywhere** Allman Brothers Band
'68 **Revolution** Beatles
'66 **Rhapsody In The Rain** Lou Christie
'76 **Rhiannon (Will You Ever Win)**
Fleetwood Mac
'75 **Rhinestone Cowboy** Glen Campbell
'74 **Rhyme Tyme People**
Kool & The Gang
'64 **Rhythm** Major Lance
'99 **Rhythm Divine** Enrique Iglesias
'92 **Rhythm Is A Dancer** Snap!

'87 **Rhythm Is Gonna Get You**
Gloria Estefan
'89 **Rhythm Nation** Janet Jackson
'87 **Rhythm Of Love** Yes
'91 **Rhythm Of My Heart** Rod Stewart
**Rhythm Of The Night**
'85 DeBarge
'94 Corona
**Rhythm Of The Rain**
'63 Cascades
'90 Dan Fogelberg [medley]
**Rich Girl**
'77 Daryl Hall & John Oates
'05 Gwen Stefani
'91 **Rico Suave** Gerardo
'62 **Ride!** Dee Dee Sharp
'65 **Ride Away** Roy Orbison
'70 **Ride Captain Ride** Blues Image
'74 **Ride 'Em Cowboy** Paul Davis
'80 **Ride Like The Wind**
Christopher Cross
'68 **Ride My See-Saw** Moody Blues
'67 **Ride, Ride, Ride** Brenda Lee
'74 **Ride The Tiger**
Jefferson Starship
'64 **Ride The Wild Surf** Jan & Dean
'91 **Ride The Wind** Poison
'01 **Ride Wit Me** Nelly
'65 **Ride Your Pony** Lee Dorsey
'71 **Riders On The Storm** Doors
'74 **Ridin' The Storm Out**
REO Speedwagon
'01 **Riding With Private Malone**
David Ball
'76 **Right Back Where We Started From**
Maxine Nightingale
'84 **Right By Your Side** Eurythmics
'78 **Right Down The Line** Gerry Rafferty
'91 **Right Down To It** Damian Dame
'93 **Right Here** SWV [Human Nature]
'91 **Right Here, Right Now** Jesus Jones
'89 **Right Here Waiting** Richard Marx
'92 **Right Kind Of Love** Jeremy Jordan
**Right Now**
'91 Van Halen
'92 Al B. Sure!
'00 SR-71
'98 **Right On The Money** Alan Jackson
'71 **Right On The Tip Of My Tongue**
Brenda & The Tabulations
'87 **Right On Track** Breakfast Club
**Right Or Wrong**
'61 Wanda Jackson
'64 Ronnie Dove
'73 **Right Place Wrong Time** Dr. John
'87 **Right Thing** Simply Red
'73 **Right Thing To Do** Carly Simon
'03 **Right Thurr** Chingy
'77 **Right Time Of The Night**
Jennifer Warnes
'74 **Rikki Don't Lose That Number**
Steely Dan
'59 **Ring-A-Ling-A-Lario**
Jimmie Rodgers
'65 **Ring Dang Doo** Sam The Sham
& The Pharoahs
**Ring My Bell**
'79 Anita Ward
'91 D.J. Jazzy Jeff & The Fresh Prince
**Ring Of Fire**
'61 Duane Eddy
'63 Johnny Cash
'72 **Ring The Living Bell** Melanie
'64 **Ringo** Lorne Greene
'71 **Rings** Cymarron
'62 **Rinky Dink** Baby Cortez
'83 **Rio** Duran Duran
**Rip It Up**
'56 Bill Haley
'56 Little Richard
'72 **Rip Off** Laura Lee
'64 **Rip Van Winkle** Devotions
'70 **Ripple** Grateful Dead
'79 **Rise** Herb Alpert
'02 **Rising, The** Bruce Springsteen

'88 **Ritual** *Dan Reed Network*
'92 **River, The** *Garth Brooks*
**River Deep - Mountain High**
'66   *Ike & Tina Turner*
'69   *Deep Purple*
'70   *Supremes & Four Tops*
'69 **River Is Wide** *Grassroots*
'95 **River Of Deceit** *Mad Season*
'93 **River Of Dreams** *Billy Joel*
'74 **River's Risin'** *Edgar Winter*
'78 **Rivers Of Babylon** *Boney M*
'60 **Road Runner** *Bo Diddley*
**Road To Nowhere**
'85   *Talking Heads*
'92   *Ozzy Osbourne*
'70 **Roadhouse Blues** *Doors*
'76 **Roadrunner** *Modern Lovers*
'89 **Roam** *B-52's*
'84 **Robert DeNiro's Waiting**
  *Bananarama*
'59 **Robbin' The Cradle** *Tony Bellus*
'56 **R-O-C-K** *Bill Haley*
'55 **Rock-A-Beatin' Boogie** *Bill Haley*
'57 **Rock-A-Billy** *Guy Mitchell*
**Rock-A-Bye Your Baby With A Dixie**
  **Melody**
'56   *Jerry Lewis*
'61   *Aretha Franklin*
'61 **Rock-A-Hula Baby** *Elvis Presley*
'89 **Rock And A Hard Place**
  *Rolling Stones*
**Rock And Roll**
'71   *Led Zeppelin*
'72   *Gary Glitter*
'75 **Rock And Roll All Nite** *Kiss [live]*
'76 **Rock & Roll Band** *Boston*
**Rock And Roll Dreams Come**
  **Through**
'81   *Jim Steinman*
'94   *Meat Loaf*
'85 **Rock And Roll Girls** *John Fogerty*
'74 **Rock And Roll Heaven**
  *Righteous Brothers*
'74 **Rock And Roll, Hoochie Koo**
  *Rick Derringer*
'58 **Rock And Roll Is Here To Stay**
  *Danny & The Juniors*
'76 **Rock And Roll Love Letter**
  *Bay City Rollers*
'72 **Rock And Roll Lullaby** *B.J. Thomas*
'78 **Rock & Roll Machine** *Triumph*
**Rock And Roll Music**
'57   *Chuck Berry*
'64   *Beatles*
'76   *Beach Boys*
'77 **Rock And Roll Never Forgets**
  *Bob Seger*
'71 **Rock & Roll Stew** *Traffic*
'55 **Rock And Roll Waltz** *Kay Starr*
'68 **Rock And Soul Music**
  *Country Joe & The Fish*
'55 **Rock Around The Clock** *Bill Haley*
'94 **Rock Bottom** *Wynonna*
'86 **R.O.C.K. In The U.S.A. (A Salute To**
  **'60's Rock)**
  *John Cougar Mellencamp*
'56 **Rock Island Line** *Lonnie Donegan*
'79 **Rock Lobster** *B-52's*
'55 **Rock Love** *Fontane Sisters*
'69 **Rock Me** *Steppenwolf*
'86 **Rock Me Amadeus** *Falco*
**Rock Me Baby**
'64   *B.B. King*
'72   *David Cassidy*
'74 **Rock Me Gently** *Andy Kim*
'85 **Rock Me Tonight (For Old Times**
  **Sake)** *Freddie Jackson*
'84 **Rock Me Tonite** *Billy Squier*
'93 **Rock My World (Little Country Girl)**
  *Brooks & Dunn*
'69 **Rock 'N' Roll** *Velvet Underground*
**Rock 'N' Roll Fantasy**
'78   *Kinks*
'79   *Bad Company*
'80 **Rock 'N' Roll High School** *Ramones*

'74 **Rock N' Roll (I Gave You The Best**
  **Years Of My Life)** *Mac Davis*
'83 **Rock 'N' Roll Is King** *ELO*
'72 **Rock 'N Roll Soul**
  *Grand Funk Railroad*
'67 **Rock 'N' Roll Woman**
  *Buffalo Springfield*
'83 **Rock Of Ages** *Def Leppard*
'88 **Rock Of Life** *Rick Springfield*
**Rock On**
'73   *David Essex*
'89   *Michael Damian*
'72 **Rock Me On The Water**
  *Jackson Browne*
'56 **Rock Right** *Georgia Gibbs*
'01 **Rock Show** *Blink-182*
**Rock Steady**
'71   *Aretha Franklin*
'87   *Whispers*
'86 **Rock The Bells** *LL Cool J*
**Rock The Boat**
'74   *Hues Corporation*
'01   *Aaliyah*
'82 **Rock The Casbah** *Clash*
'87 **Rock The Night** *Europe*
'82 **Rock This Town** *Stray Cats*
'03 **Rock Wit U (Awww Baby)** *Ashanti*
'89 **Rock Wit'cha** *Bobby Brown*
'79 **Rock With You** *Michael Jackson*
'84 **Rock You Like A Hurricane**
  *Scorpions*
'74 **Rock Your Baby** *George McCrae*
'03 **Rock Your Body** *Justin Timberlake*
'57 **Rock Your Little Baby To Sleep**
  *Buddy Knox*
'58 **Rocka-Conga** *Applejacks*
'98 **Rockafeller Skank** *Fatboy Slim*
'78 **Rockaway Beach** *Ramones*
'89 **Rocket** *Def Leppard*
'72 **Rocket Man** *Elton John*
'78 **Rocket Ride** *Kiss*
'88 **Rocket 2 U** *Jets*
'75 **Rockford Files** *Mike Post*
'75 **Rockin' All Over The World**
  *John Fogerty*
'60 **Rockin' Around The Christmas Tree**
  *Brenda Lee*
'85 **Rockin' At Midnight** *Honeydrippers*
'75 **Rockin' Chair** *Gwen McCrae*
'72 **Rockin' Down The Highway**
  *Doobie Brothers*
'60 **Rockin' Good Way (To Mess**
  **Around And Fall In Love)**
  *Dinah Washington & Brook Benton*
'89 **Rockin' In The Free World**
  *Neil Young*
'80 **Rockin' Into The Night** *38 Special*
'60 **Rockin' Little Angel** *Ray Smith*
'76 **Rockin' Me** *Steve Miller*
**Rockin' Robin**
'58   *Bobby Day*
'72   *Michael Jackson*
'73 **Rockin' Roll Baby** *Stylistics*
'74 **Rockin' Soul** *Hues Corporation*
'91 **Rockin' Years** *Dolly Parton*
  *with Ricky Van Shelton*
'60 **Rocking Goose**
  *Johnny & The Hurricanes*
**Rocking Pneumonia And The**
  **Boogie Woogie Flu**
'57   *Huey Smith*
'72   *Johnny Rivers*
'83 **Rockit** *Herbie Hancock*
'75 **Rocky** *Austin Roberts*
'72 **Rocky Mountain High** *John Denver*
'73 **Rocky Mountain Way** *Joe Walsh*
'68 **Rocky Raccoon** *Beatles*
'91 **Rodeo** *Garth Brooks*
'79 **Rolene** *Moon Martin*
'83 **Roll Me Away** *Bob Seger*
'75 **Roll On Down The Highway**
  *Bachman-Turner Overdrive*
'84 **Roll On (Eighteen Wheeler)**
  *Alabama*

**Roll Over Beethoven**
'56   *Chuck Berry*
'64   *Beatles*
'73   *Electric Light Orchestsra*
'95 **Roll To Me** *del Amitri*
'88 **Roll With It** *Steve Winwood*
'78 **Roll With The Changes**
  *REO Speedwagon*
'79 **Roller** *April Wine*
'00 **Rollin'** *Limp Bizkit*
'55 **Rollin' Stone** *Fontane Sisters*
'77 **Rollin' With The Flow** *Charlie Rich*
'01 **Rollout (My Business)** *Ludacris*
'84 **Romancing The Stone** *Eddy Grant*
'91 **Romantic** *Karyn White*
'90 **Romeo** *Dino*
**Romeo And [&] Juliet**
'92   *Stacy Earl*
'98   *Sylk-E. Fyne*
'79 **Romeo's Tune** *Steve Forbert*
'89 **Roni** *Bobby Brown*
'64 **Ronnie** *4 Seasons*
'90 **Room At The Top** *Adam Ant*
**Room To Move**
'69   *John Mayall*
'89   *Animotion*
'89 **Rooms On Fire** *Stevie Nicks*
'93 **Rooster** *Alice In Chains*
'76 **Roots, Rock, Reggae** *Bob Marley*
'78 **Rosalinda's Eyes** *Billy Joel*
'73 **Rosalita (Come Out Tonight)**
  *Bruce Springsteen*
'82 **Rosanna** *Toto*
'80 **Rose, The** *Bette Midler*
'56 **Rose And A Baby Ruth**
  *George Hamilton IV*
'70 **Rose Garden** *Lynn Anderson*
'98 **Rose Is Still A Rose** *Aretha Franklin*
'04 **Roses** *OutKast*
'62 **Roses Are Red (My Love)**
  *Bobby Vinton*
'57 **Rosie Lee** *Mello-Tones*
'79 **Rotation** *Herb Alpert*
'86 **Rough Boy** *ZZ Top*
'80 **Rough Boys** *Pete Townshend*
'97 **Round About Way** *George Strait*
**Round And Round**
'57   *Perry Como*
'84   *Ratt*
'90   *Tevin Campbell*
'65 **Round Every Corner** *Petula Clark*
'94 **Round Here** *Counting Crows*
'72 **Roundabout** *Yes*
'82 **Route 101** *Herb Alpert*
'62 **Route 66 Theme** *Nelson Riddle*
'79 **Roxanne** *Police*
'74 **Rub It In** *Billy "Crash" Craddock*
'90 **Rub You The Right Way** *Johnny Gill*
'60 **Rubber Ball** *Bobby Vee*
'04 **Rubber Band Man** *T.I.*
'79 **Rubber Biscuit** *Blues Brothers*
'70 **Rubber Duckie** *Ernie (Jim Henson)*
'76 **Rubberband Man** *Spinners*
'69 **Rubberneckin'** *Elvis Presley*
'69 **Ruben James** *Kenny Rogers &*
  *The First Edition*
'60 **Ruby** *Ray Charles*
'62 **Ruby Ann** *Marty Robbins*
**Ruby Baby**
'63   *Dion*
'74   *Billy "Crash" Craddock*
'69 **Ruby, Don't Take Your Love To**
  **Town** *Kenny Rogers & The*
  *First Edition*
'60 **Ruby Duby Du** *Tobin Mathews & Co.*
'67 **Ruby Tuesday** *Rolling Stones*
'60 **Rudolph The Red Nosed Reindeer**
  *Chipmunks*
'75 **Rudy** *Supertramp*
'56 **Rudy's Rock** *Bill Haley*
'99 **Ruff Ryders' Anthem** *DMX*
'93 **RuffNeck** *MC Lyte*
'58 **Rumble** *Link Wray*
'86 **Rumbleseat**
  *John Cougar Mellencamp*

**Rumor Has It**
'90   *Reba McEntire*
'97   *Clay Walker*
**Rumors**
'62   *Johnny Crawford*
'86   *Timex Social Club*
'92   **Rump Shaker** *Wreckx-N-Effect*
'01   **Run** *George Strait*
'95   **Run Away** *Real McCoy*
'69   **Run Away Child, Running Wild**
    *Temptations*
'65   **Run, Baby Run (Back Into My**
    **Arms)** *Newbeats*
'78   **Run For Home** *Lindisfarne*
'82   **Run For The Roses** *Dan Fogelberg*
'75   **Run Joey Run** *David Geddes*
'80   **Run Like Hell** *Pink Floyd*
'59   **Run Red Run** *Coasters*
'66   **Run, Run, Look And See**
    *Brian Hyland*
'72   **Run Run Run** *Jo Jo Gunne*
'84   **Run Runaway** *Slade*
'60   **Run Samson Run** *Neil Sedaka*
'70   **Run Through The Jungle**
    *Creedence Clearwater Revival*
'61   **Run To Him** *Bobby Vee*
'72   **Run To Me** *Bee Gees*
**Run To You**
'84   *Bryan Adams*
'93   *Whitney Houston*
'76   **Run With The Pack**
    *Bad Company*
'95   **Run-Around** *Blues Traveler*
**Runaround**
'60   *Fleetwoods*
'61   *Regents*
'91   *Van Halen*
**Runaround Sue**
'61   *Dion*
'77   *Leif Garrett*
**Runaway**
'61   *Del Shannon*
'78   *Jefferson Starship*
'84   *Bon Jovi*
'95   *Janet Jackson*
'78   **Runaway Love** *Linda Clifford*
'93   **Runaway Train** *Soul Asylum*
'84   **Runner** *Manfred Mann*
'72   **Runnin' Away**
    *Sly & The Family Stone*
'89   **Runnin' Down A Dream** *Tom Petty*
'03   **Runnin (Dying To Live)** *2Pac*
'78   **Runnin' With The Devil**
    *Van Halen*
'02   **Running Away** *Hoobastank*
'91   **Running Back To You**
    *Vanessa Williams*
'59   **Running Bear** *Johnny Preston*
'04   **Running Blind** *Godsmack*
'78   **Running On Empty** *Jackson Browne*
'96   **Running Out Of Reasons To Run**
    *Rick Trevino*
'61   **Running Scared** *Roy Orbison*
'85   **Running Up That Hill** *Kate Bush*
'83   **Running With The Night**
    *Lionel Richie*
'72   **Runway, The** *Grass Roots*
'91   **Rush** *Big Audio Dynamite*
'88   **Rush Hour** *Jane Wiedlin*
'91   **Rush, Rush** *Paula Abdul*
'86   **Russians** *Sting*
'79   **Rust Never Sleeps (Hey Hey, My**
    **My)** *Neil Young*
'65   **Rusty Bells** *Brenda Lee*

# S

'75   **S.O.S.** *Abba*
'66   **S.Y.S.L.J.F.M. (The Letter Song)**
    *Joe Tex*
'94   **Sabotage** *Beastie Boys*
'61   **Sacred** *Castells*
'89   **Sacred Emotion** *Donny Osmond*
'90   **Sacrifice** *Elton John*
'79   **Sad Café** *Eagles*

'79   **Sad Eyes** *Robert John*
'97   **Sad Lookin' Moon** *Alabama*
'60   **Sad Mood** *Sam Cooke*
'61   **Sad Movies (Make Me Cry)**
    *Sue Thompson*
'65   **Sad, Sad Girl** *Barbara Mason*
'84   **Sad Songs (Say So Much)**
    *Elton John*
'75   **Sad Sweet Dreamer**
    *Sweet Sensation*
'91   **Sadeness** *Enigma*
'83   **Safety Dance** *Men Without Hats*
'93   **Said I Loved You...But I Lied**
    *Michael Bolton*
'57   **Sail Along Silvery Moon**
    *Billy Vaughn*
'72   **Sail Away** *Randy Newman*
'79   **Sail On** *Commodores*
**Sailing**
'75   *Rod Stewart*
'80   *Christopher Cross*
'60   **Sailor (Your Home Is The Sea)**
    *Lolita*
'74   **Sally Can't Dance** *Lou Reed*
'74   **Sally G** *Paul McCartney*
'63   **Sally, Go 'Round The Roses**
    *Jaynetts*
'83   **Salt In My Tears** *Martin Briley*
'03   **Salt Shaker** *Ying Yang Twins*
'72   **Salty Dog** *Procol Harum [live]*
'96   **Salvation** *Cranberries*
'77   **Sam** *Olivia Newton-John*
'80   **Same Old Lang Syne**
    *Dan Fogelberg*
'55   **Same Old Saturday Night**
    *Frank Sinatra*
'74   **Same Old Song And Dance**
    *Aerosmith*
'60   **Same One** *Brook Benton*
'75   **Same Thing It Took** *Impressions*
'61   **San Antonio Rose** *Floyd Cramer*
'67   **San Franciscan Nights** *Animals*
'67   **San Francisco (Be Sure To Wear**
    **Flowers In Your Hair)**
    *Scott McKenzie*
'68   **San Francisco Girls (Return Of The**
    **Native)** *Fever Tree*
'85   **Sanctified Lady** *Marvin Gaye*
'86   **Sanctify Yourself** *Simple Minds*
'55   **Sand And The Sea** *Nat "King" Cole*
'72   **Sandman** *America*
'01   **Sandstorm** *Darude*
**Sandy**
'59   *Larry Hall*
'63   *Dion*
'65   *Ronny & The Daytonas*
'57   **Santa And The Satellite**
    *Buchanan & Goodman*
**Santa Claus Is Coming To Town**
'62   *4 Seasons*
'75   *Bruce Springsteen*
'95   **Santa Monica (Watch The World**
    **Die)** *Everclear*
'97   **Santeria** *Sublime*
**Sara**
'79   *Fleetwood Mac*
'85   *Starship*
'76   **Sara Smile** *Daryl Hall & John Oates*
'80   **(Sartorial Eloquence) Don't Ya**
    **Wanna Play This Game No More?**
    *Elton John*
'73   **Satellite Of Love** *Lou Reed*
'65   **Satin Pillows** *Bobby Vinton*
'73   **Satin Sheets** *Jeanne Pruett*
'75   **Satin Soul** *Love Unlimited Orchestra*
'02   **Satisfaction** *Eve*
'89   **Satisfied** *Richard Marx*
'66   **Satisfied Mind** *Bobby Hebb*
'99   **Satisfy You** *Puff Daddy*
'72   **Saturday In The Park** *Chicago*
'86   **Saturday Love**
    *Cherrelle/Alexander O'Neal*
'71   **Saturday Morning Confusion**
    *Bobby Russell*

**Saturday Night [Nite]**
'63   *New Christy Minstrels*
'75   *Bay City Rollers*
'76   *Earth, Wind & Fire*
'64   **Saturday Night At The Movies**
    *Drifters*
'75   **Saturday Night Special**
    *Lynyrd Skynyrd*
'79   **Saturday Night, Sunday Morning**
    *Thelma Houston*
'73   **Saturday Night's Alright For**
    **Fighting** *Elton John*
'02   **Saturday (Oooh! Ooooh!)** *Ludacris*
'81   **Sausalito Summernight** *Diesel*
'79   **Savannah Nights** *Tom Johnston*
'85   **Save A Prayer** *Duran Duran*
'76   **Save It For A Rainy Day**
    *Stephen Bishop*
'82   **Save It For Later** *English Beat*
'64   **Save It For Me** *4 Seasons*
'90   **Save Me** *Fleetwood Mac*
'91   **Save Some Love** *Keedy*
'92   **Save The Best For Last**
    *Vanessa Williams*
'70   **Save The Country** *5th Dimension*
**Save The Last Dance For Me**
'60   *Drifters*
'74   *DeFranco Family*
'83   **Save The Overtime (For Me)**
    *Gladys Knight*
'98   **Save Tonight** *Eagle-Eye Cherry*
'65   **Save Your Heart For Me** *Gary Lewis*
'76   **Save Your Kisses For Me**
    *Brotherhood Of Man*
'85   **Save Your Love (For #1)**
    *René & Angela*
'61   **Saved** *LaVern Baker*
'83   **Saved By Zero** *Fixx*
'85   **Saving All My Love For You**
    *Whitney Houston*
'92   **Saving Forever For You** *Shanice*
'91   **Sax And Violins** *Talking Heads*
'90   **Say A Prayer** *Breathe*
'81   **Say Goodbye To Hollywood**
    *Billy Joel*
'73   **Say, Has Anybody Seen My Sweet**
    **Gypsy Rose** *Dawn*
'66   **Say I Am (What I Am)**
    *Tommy James*
'97   **Say...If You Feel Alright**
    *Crystal Waters*
'98   **Say It** *Voices Of Theory*
'88   **Say It Again** *Jermaine Stewart*
**Say It Isn't So**
'83   *Daryl Hall & John Oates*
'85   *Outfield*
'68   **Say It Loud - I'm Black And I'm**
    **Proud** *James Brown*
'59   **Say Man** *Bo Diddley*
'79   **Say Maybe** *Neil Diamond*
'99   **Say My Name** *Destiny's Child*
'83   **Say Say Say**
    *Paul McCartney & Michael Jackson*
'65   **Say Something Funny** *Patty Duke*
'81   **Say What** *Jesse Winchester*
'03   **Say Yes** *Floetry*
'64   **Say You** *Ronnie Dove*
'76   **Say You Love Me** *Fleetwood Mac*
'85   **Say You, Say Me** *Lionel Richie*
'87   **Say You Will** *Foreigner*
'81   **Say You'll Be Mine**
    *Christopher Cross*
'97   **Say You'll Be There** *Spice Girls*
'77   **Say You'll Stay Until Tomorrow**
    *Tom Jones*
'65   **(Say) You're My Girl** *Roy Orbison*
'85   **Say You're Wrong** *Julian Lennon*
'88   **Sayin' Sorry (Don't Make It Right)**
    *Denise Lopez*
'04   **Scandalous** *Mis-Teeq*
'99   **Scar Tissue** *Red Hot Chili Peppers*
**Scarborough Fair**
'68   *Sergio Mendes*
'68   *Simon & Garfunkel*
'59   **Scarlet Ribbons (For Her Hair)**
    *Browns*
'04   **Scars** *Papa Roach*

'77 **Scenes From An Italian Restaurant** *Billy Joel*
'01 **Schism** *Tool*
'75 **School** *Supertramp*
'75 **School Boy Crush** *AWB*
'57 **School Day** *Chuck Berry*
'61 **School Is In** *Gary (U.S.) Bonds*
'61 **School Is Out** *Gary (U.S.) Bonds*
'92 **School Me** *Gerald Levert*
'72 **School's Out** *Alice Cooper*
'71 **Scorpio** *Dennis Coffey*
'62 **Scotch And Soda** *Kingston Trio*
'64 **Scratchy** *Travis Wammack*
'95 **Scream** *Michael Jackson & Janet Jackson*
'87 **Se La** *Lionel Richie*
'76 **Se Si Bon [medley]** *Dr. Buzzard's Original "Savannah" Band*
'59 **Sea Cruise** *Frankie Ford*
'61 **Sea Of Heartbreak** *Don Gibson*
    **Sea Of Love**
'59     *Phil Phillips With The Twilights*
'81     *Del Shannon*
'84     *Honeydrippers*
    **Sealed With A Kiss**
'62     *Brian Hyland*
'68     *Gary Lewis*
'72     *Bobby Vinton*
'73 **Search And Destroy** *Stooges*
'85 **Search Is Over** *Survivor*
'57 **Searchin'** *Coasters*
'98 **Searchin' My Soul** *Vonda Shepard*
'66 **Searching For My Love** *Bobby Moore*
'87 **Seasons Change** *Exposé*
'74 **Seasons In The Sun** *Terry Jacks*
'69 **Seattle** *Perry Como*
'74 **Second Avenue** *Garfunkel*
'89 **Second Chance** *Thirty Eight Special*
'56 **Second Fiddle** *Kay Starr*
'62 **Second Hand Love** *Connie Francis*
'77 **Second Hand News** *Fleetwood Mac*
'65 **Second Hand Rose** *Barbra Streisand*
'85 **Second Nature** *Dan Hartman*
'98 **Second Round K.O.** *Canibus*
    **Second Time Around**
'61     *Frank Sinatra*
'79     *Shalamar*
'94 **Secret** *Madonna*
'58 **Secret, The** *Gordon MacRae*
    **Secret Agent Man**
'66     *Johnny Rivers*
'66     *Ventures*
'95 **Secret Garden** *Bruce Springsteen*
'90 **Secret Garden (Sweet Seduction Suite)** *Quincy Jones/Al B. Sure!/ James Ingram/El DeBarge/ Barry White*
    **Secret Love**
'66     *Billy Stewart*
'75     *Freddy Fender*
'85 **Secret Lovers** *Atlantic Starr*
'89 **Secret Rendezvous** *Karyn White*
'86 **Secret Separation** *Fixx*
'58 **Secretly** *Jimmie Rodgers*
'68 **Security** *Etta James*
'80 **Seduction, The** *James Last Band*
'69 **See** *Rascals*
'67 **See Emily Play** *Pink Floyd*
    **See Me, Feel Me**
'70     *Who*
'73     *New Seekers [medley]*
    **See Saw**
'56     *Moonglows*
'68     *Aretha Franklin*
'64 **See The Funny Little Clown** *Bobby Goldsboro*
'91 **See The Lights** *Simple Minds*
'85 **See What Love Can Do** *Eric Clapton*
    **See You In September**
'59     *Tempos*
'66     *Happenings*
'56 **See You Later, Alligator** *Bill Haley*

'90 **Seein' My Father In Me** *Paul Overstreet*
'02 **Seein' Red** *Unwritten Law*
'91 **Seeing Things** *Black Crowes*
'70 **Seeker, The** *Who*
'84 **Self Control** *Laura Branigan*
'94 **Self Esteem** *Offspring*
'64 **Selfish One** *Jackie Ross*
'94 **Selling The Drama** *Live*
'97 **Semi-Charmed Life** *Third Eye Blind*
'92 **Seminole Wind** *John Anderson*
'57 **Send For Me** *Nat "King" Cole*
'83 **Send Her My Love** *Journey*
'75 **Send In The Clowns** *Judy Collins*
'83 **Send Me An Angel** *Real Life*
    **Send Me Some Lovin'**
'57     *Little Richard*
'63     *Sam Cooke*
    **Send Me The Pillow You Dream On**
'62     *Johnny Tillotson*
'65     *Dean Martin*
'79 **Send One Your Love** *Stevie Wonder*
'03 **Send The Pain Below** *Chevelle*
'90 **Sending All My Love** *Linear*
'94 **Sending My Love** *Zhané*
'03 **Señorita** *Justin Timberlake*
'90 **Sensitivity** *Ralph Tresvant*
'95 **Sentimental** *Deborah Cox*
'77 **Sentimental Lady** *Bob Welch*
'61 **Sentimental Me** *Elvis Presley*
'85 **Sentimental Street** *Night Ranger*
'85 **Separate Lives** *Phil Collins & Marilyn Martin*
'72 **Separate Ways** *Elvis Presley*
'83 **Separate Ways (Worlds Apart)** *Journey*
'00 **Separated** *Avant*
'78 **September** *Earth, Wind & Fire*
'74 **September Gurls** *Big Star*
'61 **September In The Rain** *Dinah Washington*
'79 **September Morn'** *Neil Diamond*
'80 **Sequel** *Harry Chapin*
'87 **Serious** *Donna Allen*
'77 **Serpentine Fire** *Earth, Wind & Fire*
'91 **Set Adrift On Memory Bliss** *PM Dawn*
    **Set Me Free**
'65     *Kinks*
'80     *Utopia*
'91 **Set The Night To Music** *Roberta Flack with Maxi Priest*
'95 **Set U Free** *Planet Soul*
'99 **Set Your Eyes To Zion** *P.O.D.*
'92 **7** *Prince*
'66 **7 And 7 Is** *Love*
'80 **Seven Bridges Road** *Eagles*
'62 **Seven Day Weekend** *Gary (US) Bonds*
    **Seven [7] Days**
'56     *Dorothy Collins*
'56     *Crew Cuts*
'56     *Clyde McPhatter*
'97     *Mary J. Blige*
'01     *Craig David*
'58 **"7-11" (Mambo No. 5)** *Gone All Stars*
'59 **(Seven Little Girls) Sitting In The Back Seat** *Paul Evans*
'03 **Seven Nation Army** *White Stripes*
'67 **7 Rooms Of Gloom** *Four Tops*
'82 **777-9311** *Time*
'93 **Seven Whole Days** *Toni Braxton*
'87 **Seven Wonders** *Fleetwood Mac*
'81 **Seven Year Ache** *Rosanne Cash*
'65 **Seventh Son** *Johnny Rivers*
    **Seventeen [17]**
'55     *Boyd Bennett*
'55     *Rusty Draper*
'55     *Fontane Sisters*
'84     *Rick James*
'89     *Winger*
'62 **Seventy Six Trombones** *Robert Preston*
'98 **Sex and Candy** *Marcy Playground*

'85 **Sex As A Weapon** *Pat Benatar*
    **Sex Machine ..see: Get Up**
'93 **Sex Me** *R. Kelly*
'82 **Sexual Healing** *Marvin Gaye*
'80 **Sexy Eyes** *Dr. Hook*
'84 **Sexy Girl** *Glenn Frey*
'74 **Sexy Mama** *Moments*
'67 **Sgt. Pepper's Lonely Hearts Club Band** *Beatles*
'64 **Sha La La** *Manfred Mann*
'74 **Sha-La-La (Make Me Happy)** *Al Green*
'00 **Shackles (Praise You)** *Mary Mary*
'78 **Shadow Dancing** *Andy Gibb*
'65 **Shadow Of Your Smile, The** *Tony Bennett*
'79 **Shadows In The Moonlight** *Anne Murray*
'82 **Shadows Of The Night** *Pat Benatar*
'62 **Shadrack** *Brook Benton*
'97 **Shady Lane** *Pavement*
'64 **Shaggy Dog** *Mickey Lee Lane*
'65 **Shake** *Sam Cooke*
'97 **Shake, The** *Neal McCoy*
'67 **Shake A Tail Feather** *James & Bobby Purify*
'65 **Shake And Fingerpop** *Jr. Walker*
'88 **Shake For The Sheik** *Escape Club*
'78 **Shake It** *Ian Matthews*
'81 **Shake It Up** *Cars*
'66 **Shake, Wake Me (When It's Over)** *Four Tops*
    **Shake, Rattle & Roll**
'54     *Bill Haley*
'54     *Joe Turner*
'67     *Arthur Conley*
'63 **Shake! Shake! Shake!** *Jackie Wilson*
'76 **(Shake, Shake, Shake) Shake Your Booty** *KC & The Sunshine Band*
'00 **Shake Ya Ass** *Mystikal*
'03 **Shake Ya Tailfeather** *Nelly/P. Diddy/Murphy Lee*
'86 **Shake You Down** *Gregory Abbott*
'79 **Shake Your Body (Down To The Ground)** *Jacksons*
'99 **Shake Your Bon-Bon** *Ricky Martin*
'78 **Shake Your Groove Thing** *Peaches & Herb*
'87 **Shake Your Love** *Debbie Gibson*
'76 **Shake Your Rump To The Funk** *Bar-Kays*
'87 **Shakedown** *Bob Seger*
'79 **Shakedown Cruise** *Jay Ferguson*
'78 **Shakedown Street** *Grateful Dead*
'75 **Shakey Ground** *Temptations*
'82 **Shakin'** *Eddie Money*
'65 **Shakin' All Over** *Guess Who?*
'56 **Shall We Dance** *Yul Brynner & Deborah Kerr*
'73 **Shambala** *Three Dog Night*
    **Shame**
'78     *Evelyn "Champagne" King*
'85     *Motels*
'94     *Zhané*
'62 **Shame On Me** *Bobby Bare*
'82 **Shame On The Moon** *Bob Seger*
'68 **Shame, Shame** *Magic Lanterns*
'75 **Shame, Shame, Shame** *Shirley (& Company)*
'91 **Shameless** *Garth Brooks*
'82 **Shanghai Breezes** *John Denver*
    **Shangri-La**
'57     *Four Coins*
'64     *Vic Dana*
'64     *Robert Maxwell*
'76 **Shannon** *Henry Gross*
'70 **Shape I'm In** *Band*
'00 **Shape Of My Heart** *Backstreet Boys*
'68 **Shape Of Things To Come** *Max Frost*
'66 **Shapes Of Things** *Yardbirds*
'70 **Share The Land** *Guess Who*
    **Share Your Love With Me**
'69     *Aretha Franklin*
'81     *Kenny Rogers*

234

'78 **Sharing The Night Together** *Dr. Hook*
'62 **Sharing You** *Bobby Vee*
'84 **Sharkey's Day** *Laurie Anderson*
'83 **Sharp Dressed Man** *ZZ Top*
'78 **Shattered** *Rolling Stones*
'88 **Shattered Dreams** *Johnny Hates Jazz*
'75 **Shaving Cream** *Benny Bell*
'60 **Shazam!** *Duane Eddy*
'54 **Sh'Boom** *Chords*
**She**
'67   *Monkees*
'69   *Tommy James*
'90 **She Ain't Worth It** *Glenn Medeiros*
'95 **She Ain't Your Ordinary Girl** *Alabama*
'00 **She Bangs** *Ricky Martin*
'79 **She Believes In Me** *Kenny Rogers*
'69 **She Belongs To Me** *Rick Nelson*
'66 **She Blew A Good Thing** *Poets*
'83 **She Blinded Me With Science** *Thomas Dolby*
'84 **She Bop** *Cyndi Lauper*
**She Came In Through The Bathroom Window**
'69   *Beatles*
'69   *Joe Cocker*
'62 **She Can't Find Her Keys** *Paul Petersen*
'01 **She Couldn't Change Me** *Montgomery Gentry*
'62 **She Cried** *Jay & The Americans*
'77 **She Did It** *Eric Carmen*
'93 **She Don't Know She's Beautiful** *Sammy Kershaw*
'94 **She Don't Use Jelly** *Flaming Lips*
'89 **She Drives Me Crazy** *Fine Young Cannibals*
'02 **She Hates Me** *Puddle Of Mudd*
'92 **She Is His Only Need** *Wynonna*
'67 **She Is Still A Mystery** *Lovin' Spoonful*
'02 **She Loves Me Not** *Papa Roach*
'64 **She Loves You** *Beatles*
'96 **She Never Lets It Go To Her Heart** *Tim McGraw*
'59 **She Say (Oom Dooby Doom)** *Diamonds*
'91 **She Talks To Angels** *Black Crowes*
'62 **She Thinks I Still Care** *George Jones*
'00 **She Thinks My Tractor's Sexy** *Kenny Chesney*
'64 **She Understands Me** *Johnny Tillotson*
'93 **She Used To Be Mine** *Brooks & Dunn*
'88 **She Wants To Dance With Me** *Rick Astley*
'58 **She Was Only Seventeen (He Was One Year More)** *Marty Robbins*
'04 **She Will Be Loved** *Maroon5*
'83 **She Works Hard For The Money** *Donna Summer*
'67 **She'd Rather Be With Me** *Turtles*
'02 **She'll Leave You With A Smile** *George Strait*
'81 **She's A Bad Mama Jama (She's Built, She's Stacked)** *Carl Carlton*
'83 **She's A Beauty** *Tubes*
'63 **She's A Fool** *Lesley Gore*
'68 **She's A Heartbreaker** *Gene Pitney*
'71 **She's A Lady** *Tom Jones*
'67 **She's A Rainbow** *Rolling Stones*
'64 **She's A Woman** *Beatles*
'65 **She's About A Mover** *Sir Douglas Quintet*
'99 **She's All I Ever Had** *Ricky Martin*
**She's All I Got**
'71   *Freddie North*
'01   *Jimmy Cozier*
'78 **She's Always A Woman** *Billy Joel*
'95 **She's Every Woman** *Garth Brooks*
'61 **She's Everything (I Wanted You To Be)** *Ral Donner*

**She's Gone**
'74   *Tavares*
'74   *Daryl Hall & John Oates*
'97 **She's Gonna Make It** *Garth Brooks*
'81 **She's Got A Way** *Billy Joel*
'97 **She's Got It All** *Kenny Chesney*
'92 **She's Got The Rhythm (And I Got The Blues)** *Alan Jackson*
'62 **She's Got You** *Patsy Cline*
'91 **She's In Love With The Boy** *Trisha Yearwood*
'65 **She's Just My Style** *Gary Lewis*
'67 **She's Leaving Home** *Beatles*
'87 **She's Like The Wind** *Patrick Swayze*
'68 **She's Lookin' Good** *Wilson Pickett*
'84 **She's Mine** *Steve Perry*
'00 **She's More** *Andy Griggs*
'90 **She's My Baby** *Traveling Wilburys*
'67 **She's My Girl** *Turtles*
'03 **She's My Kind Of Rain** *Tim McGraw*
'58 **She's Neat** *Dale Wright*
'71 **She's Not Just Another Woman** *8th Day*
'94 **She's Not The Cheatin' Kind** *Brooks & Dunn*
**She's Not There**
'64   *Zombies*
'77   *Santana*
'62 **She's Not You** *Elvis Presley*
'88 **She's On The Left** *Jeffrey Osborne*
'80 **She's Out Of My Life** *Michael Jackson*
'92 **She's Playing Hard To Get** *Hi-Five*
'83 **(She's) Sexy + 17** *Stray Cats*
'80 **She's So Cold** *Rolling Stones*
'99 **She's So High** *Tal Bachman*
'84 **She's Strange** *Cameo*
'96 **She's Taken A Shine** *John Berry*
'64 **She's The One** *Chartbusters*
'85 **She's Waiting** *Eric Clapton*
'77 **Sheena Is A Punk Rocker** *Ramones*
'62 **Sheila** *Tommy Roe*
'98 **Shelf In The Room** *Days Of The New*
'90 **Shelter Me** *Cinderella*
'63 **Shelter Of Your Arms** *Sammy Davis Jr.*
'62 **Sherry** *4 Seasons*
**Shifting, Whispering Sands**
'55   *Rusty Draper*
'55   *Billy Vaughn*
'70 **Shilo** *Neil Diamond*
'98 **Shimmer** *Fuel*
'59 **Shimmy, Shimmy, Ko-Ko-Bop** *Little Anthony & The Imperials*
'94 **Shine** *Collective Soul*
'79 **Shine A Little Love** *Electric Light Orchestra*
'80 **Shine On** *L.T.D.*
'75 **Shine On You Crazy Diamond** *Pink Floyd*
'74 **Shinin' On** *Grand Funk*
**Shining Star**
'75   *Earth, Wind & Fire*
'80   *Manhattans*
'91 **Shiny Happy People** *R.E.M.*
'88 **Ship Of Fools** *Robert Plant*
'87 **Ship Of Fools (Save Me From Tomorrow)** *World Party*
'79 **Ships** *Barry Manilow*
'57 **Shish-Kebab** *Ralph Marterie*
'82 **Shock The Monkey** *Peter Gabriel*
'98 **Shoes You're Wearing** *Clint Black*
'75 **Shoeshine Boy** *Eddie Kendricks*
'68 **Shoo-Be-Doo-Be-Doo-Da-Day** *Stevie Wonder*
'93 **Shoop** *Salt-N-Pepa*
**Shoop Shoop Song (It's In His Kiss)**
'64   *Betty Everett*
'90   *Cher*
'68 **Shoot'em Up, Baby** *Andy Kim*
'75 **Shooting Star** *Bad Company*
**Shop Around**
'60   *Miracles*
'76   *Captain & Tennille*
'57 **Short Fat Fannie** *Larry Williams*

'77 **Short People** *Randy Newman*
'58 **Short Shorts** *Royal Teens*
'04 **Shorty Wanna Ride** *Young Buck*
'98 **Shorty (You Keep Playin' With My Mind)** *Imajin*
'86 **Shot In The Dark** *Ozzy Osbourne*
'65 **Shotgun** *Jr. Walker*
'82 **Should I Do It** *Pointer Sisters*
'82 **Should I Stay Or Should I Go** *Clash*
'95 **Should've Asked Her Faster** *Ty England*
'93 **Should've Been A Cowboy** *Toby Keith*
'87 **Should've Known Better** *Richard Marx*
'80 **Should've Never Let You Go** *Neil Sedaka & Dara Sedaka*
'89 **Shoulder To Cry On** *Tommy Page*
**Shout**
'59   *Isley Brothers*
'62   *Joey Dee*
'85   *Tears For Fears*
'76   **Shout It Out Loud** *Kiss*
'62 **Shout! Shout! (Knock Yourself Out)** *Ernie Maresca*
**Show And Tell**
'73   *Al Wilson*
'89   *Peabo Bryson*
'89 **Show Don't Tell** *Rush*
**Show Me**
'67   *Joe Tex*
'84   *Glenn Jones*
'84   *Pretenders*
'90   *Howard Hewett*
'03 **Show Me How To Live** *Audioslave*
**Show Me Love**
'93   *Robin S*
'97   *Robyn*
'00 **Show Me The Meaning Of Being Lonely** *Backstreet Boys*
**Show Me The Way**
'76   *Peter Frampton*
'87   *Regina Belle*
'90   *Styx*
'74 **Show Must Go On** *Three Dog Night*
'85 **Show Some Respect** *Tina Turner*
'77 **Show You The Way To Go** *Jacksons*
'73 **Showdown** *Electric Light Orchestra*
'87 **Showdown At Big Sky** *Robbie Robertson*
'89 **Shower Me With Your Love** *Surface*
'76 **Shower The People** *James Taylor*
'75 **(Shu-Doo-Pa-Poo-Poop) Love Being Your Fool** *Travis Wammack*
'61 **Shu Rah** *Fats Domino*
'63 **Shut Down** *Beach Boys*
'94 **Shut Up And Kiss Me** *Mary Chapin Carpenter*
'62 **Shutters And Boards** *Jerry Wallace*
'95 **Shy Guy** *Diana King*
'58 **Sick And Tired** *Fats Domino*
'02 **Sick Of Being Lonely** *Field Mob*
'95 **Sick Of Myself** *Matthew Sweet*
'74 **Sideshow** *Blue Magic*
'64 **Sidewalk Surfin'** *Jan & Dean*
'85 **Sidewalk Talk** *Jellybean*
'02 **Scientist, The** *Coldplay*
'94 **Sign, The** *Ace Of Base*
'83 **Sign Of Fire** *Fixx*
**Sign 'O' The Times**
'87   *Prince*
'97   *Queensrÿche*
'66 **Sign Of The Times** *Petula Clark*
'88 **Sign Your Name** *Terence Trent D'Arby*
**Signed, Sealed, Delivered I'm Yours**
'70   *Stevie Wonder*
'77   *Peter Frampton*
**Signs**
'71   *Five Man Electrical Band*
'91   *Tesla*
'67 **Silence Is Golden** *Tremeloes*
'92 **Silent All These Years** *Tori Amos*

'91 **Silent Lucidity** *Queensrÿche*
'04 **Silent Night** *Five For Fighting*
'92 **Silent Prayer**
   *Shanice feat. Johnny Gill*
'85 **Silent Running (On Dangerous Ground)** *Mike + The Mechanics*
'88 **Silhouette** *Kenny G*
   **Silhouettes**
'57   *Diamonds*
'57   *Rays*
'65   *Herman's Hermits*
'76 **Silly Love Songs** *Wings*
'70 **Silver Bird** *Mark Lindsay*
'76 **Silver, Blue & Gold**
   *Bad Company*
'77 **Silver Springs** *Fleetwood Mac*
'62 **Silver Threads And Golden Needles** *Springfields*
'68 **Simon Says** *1910 Fruitgum Co.*
'00 **Simple Kind Of Life** *No Doubt*
'93 **Simple Life** *Elton John*
'01 **Simple Things** *Jim Brickman*
'88 **Simply Irresistible** *Robert Palmer*
   **Since I Don't Have You**
'59   *Skyliners*
'81   *Don McLean*
'63 **Since I Fell For You** *Lenny Welch*
'65 **Since I Lost My Baby** *Temptations*
'56 **Since I Met You Baby**
   *Ivory Joe Hunter*
'70 **Since I've Been Loving You**
   , *Led Zeppelin*
   **Since You [U] Been Gone**
'79   *Rainbow*
'05   *Kelly Clarkson*
'82 **Since You're Gone** *Cars*
   **Since You've Been Gone**
'59   *Clyde McPhatter*
'78   *Head East*
'87   *Outfield*
   **Sincerely**
'55   *McGuire Sisters*
'55   *Moonglow's*
'89 **Sincerely Yours** *Sweet Sensation*
'73 **Sing** *Carpenters*
'75 **Sing A Song** *Earth, Wind & Fire*
'58 **Sing Boy Sing** *Tommy Sands*
'78 **Sing For The Day** *Styx*
'03 **Sing For The Moment** *Eminem*
   **Singing The Blues**
'56   *Guy Mitchell*
'56   *Marty Robbins*
'66 **Single Girl** *Sandy Posey*
'85 **Single Life** *Cameo*
'99 **Single White Female** *Chely Wright*
'60 **Sink The Bismarck** *Johnny Horton*
'77 **Sir Duke** *Stevie Wonder*
'84 **Sister Christian** *Night Ranger*
'75 **Sister Golden Hair** *America*
'73 **Sister Mary Elephant (Shudd-Up!)** *Cheech & Chong*
'85 **Sisters Are Doin' It For Themselves** *Eurythmics & Aretha Franklin*
'67 **Sit Down, I Think I Love You** *Mojo Men*
'71 **Sit Yourself Down** *Stephen Stills*
   **Sittin' In The Balcony**
'57   *Eddie Cochran*
'57   *Johnny Dee*
'90 **Sittin' In The Lap Of Luxury** *Louie Louie*
'97 **Sittin' On Go** *Bryan White*
   **(Sittin' On) The Dock Of The Bay**
'68   *Otis Redding*
'88   *Michael Bolton*
'96 **Sittin' On Top Of The World** *Da Brat*
'95 **Sittin' Up In My Room** *Brandy*
'72 **Sitting** *Cat Stevens*
'83 **Sitting At The Wheel** *Moody Blues*
'65 **Sitting In The Park** *Billy Stewart*
'82 **Situation** *Yaz*
   **Six Days On The Road**
'63   *Dave Dudley*
'97   *Sawyer Brown*
'93 **Six Feet Deep** *Geto Boys*

'82 **Six Months In A Leaky Boat**
   *Split Enz*
'59 **Six Nights A Week** *Crests*
'67 **Six O'Clock** *Lovin' Spoonful*
'01 **Six-Pack Summer** *Phil Vassar*
'66 **634-5789 (Soulsville, U.S.A.)**
   *Wilson Pickett*
'58 **16 Candles** *Crests*
'60 **Sixteen Reasons** *Connie Stevens*
   **Sixteen Tons**
'55   *Johnny Desmond*
'55   *"Tennessee" Ernie Ford*
'96 **6th Avenue Heartache** *Wallflowers*
'82 **'65 Love Affair** *Paul Davis*
'02 **Sk8er Boi** *Avril Lavigne*
'74 **Skating Away On The Thin Ice Of A New Day** *Jethro Tull*
'87 **Skeletons** *Stevie Wonder*
'74 **Skin Tight** *Ohio Players*
'87 **Skin Trade** *Duran Duran*
'67 **Skinny Legs And All** *Joe Tex*
'58 **Skinny Minnie** *Bill Haley*
'67 **Skip A Rope** *Henson Cargill*
'75 **Sky High** *Jigsaw*
'91 **Sky Is Crying** *Stevie Ray Vaughan*
'68 **Sky Pilot** *Animals*
'93 **Slam** *Onyx*
'64 **Slaughter On Tenth Avenue**
   *Ventures*
'85 **Slave To Love** *Bryan Ferry*
'86 **Sledgehammer** *Peter Gabriel*
'60 **Sleep** *Little Willie John*
'59 **Sleep Walk** *Santo & Johnny*
'85 **Sleeping Bag** *ZZ Top*
'93 **Sleeping Satellite** *Tasmin Archer*
'78 **Sleeping Single In A Double Bed**
   *Barbara Mandrell*
'77 **Sleepwalker** *Kinks*
   **Slide**
'77   *Slave*
'98   *Goo Goo Dolls*
'68 **Slip Away** *Clarence Carter*
'77 **Slip Slidin' Away** *Paul Simon*
'75 **Slippery When Wet** *Commodores*
'56 **Slippin' And Slidin'** *Little Richard*
'72 **Slippin' Into Darkness** *War*
'83 **Slipping Away** *Dave Edmunds*
'04 **Slither** *Velvet Revolver*
'66 **Sloop John B** *Beach Boys*
'92 **Slow And Sexy**
   *Shabba Ranks feat. Johnny Gill*
'92 **Slow Dance (Hey Mr. DJ)** *R. Kelly*
'77 **Slow Dancin' Don't Turn Me On**
   *Addrisi Bros.*
'77 **Slow Dancin' (Swayin' To The Music)** *Johnny Rivers*
   **Slow Down**
'64   *Beatles*
'86   *Loose Ends*
'05   *Bobby Valentino*
   **Slow Hand**
'81   *Pointer Sisters*
'82   *Conway Twitty*
'03 **Slow Jamz** *Twista*
   **Slow Motion**
'90   *Gerald Alston*
'92   *Color Me Badd*
'04   *Juvenile*
'75 **Slow Ride** *Foghat*
'62 **Slow Twistin'** *Chubby Checker*
   *(with Dee Dee Sharp)*
   **Slow Walk**
'56   *Sil Austin*
'56   *Bill Doggett*
'77 **Slowdown** *John Miles*
'70 **Sly, Slick, And The Wicked**
   *Lost Generation*
'72 **Small Beginnings** *Flash*
'61 **Small Sad Sam** *Phil McLean*
'85 **Small Town**
   *John Cougar Mellencamp*
'91 **Small Town Saturday Night**
   *Hal Ketchum*
   **Small World**
'59   *Johnny Mathis*
'88   *Huey Lewis*

'85 **Smalltown Boys** *Bronski Beat*
'95 **Smashing Young Man**
   *Collective Soul*
'92 **Smells Like Nirvana**
   *"Weird Al" Yankovic*
'91 **Smells Like Teen Spirit** *Nirvana*
   **Smile**
'59   *Tony Bennett*
'97   *Scarface*
'99   *Vitamin C*
'99   *Lonestar*
'69 **Smile A Little Smile For Me**
   *Flying Machine*
'83 **Smile Has Left Your Eyes** *Asia*
'71 **Smiling Faces Sometimes**
   *Undisputed Truth*
'83 **Smiling Islands** *Robbie Patton*
'77 **Smoke From A Distant Fire**
   *Sanford/Townsend Band*
   **Smoke Gets In Your Eyes**
'58   *Platters*
'72   *Blue Haze*
'73 **Smoke On The Water** *Deep Purple*
   **Smoke Stack Lightning**
'56   *Howlin' Wolf*
'91   *Lynyrd Skynyrd*
'55 **Smokey Joe's Cafe** *Robins*
'59 **Smokie** *Bill Black's Combo*
'76 **Smokin'** *Boston*
   **Smokin' In The Boy's Room**
'73   *Brownsville Station*
'85   *Mötley Crüe*
'97 **Smokin' Me Out** *Warren G*
'86 **Smoking Gun** *Robert Cray Band*
'80 **Smoky Mountain Rain**
   *Ronnie Milsap*
'61 **Smoky Places** *Corsairs*
'99 **Smooth** *Santana Feat. Rob Thomas*
   **Smooth Criminal**
'88   *Michael Jackson*
'01   *Alien Ant Farm*
   **Smooth Operator**
'59   *Sarah Vaughan*
'85   *Sade*
'85 **Smuggler's Blues** *Glenn Frey*
'03 **Snake** *R. Kelly*
'68 **Snake, The** *Al Wilson*
'62 **Snap Your Fingers** *Joe Henderson*
'69 **Snatching It Back** *Clarence Carter*
'66 **Snoopy Vs. The Red Baron**
   *Royal Guardsmen*
'67 **Snoopy's Christmas**
   *Royal Guardsmen*
'70 **Snowbird** *Anne Murray*
'89 **So Alive** *Love & Rockets*
'93 **So Alone** *Men At Large*
'99 **So Anxious** *Ginuwine*
'83 **So Bad** *Paul McCartney*
'90 **So Close** *Daryl Hall/John Oates*
'04 **So Cold** *Breaking Benjamin*
'62 **So Deep** *Brenda Lee*
'87 **So Emotional** *Whitney Houston*
   **So Far Away**
'71   *Carole King*
'86   *Dire Straits*
'96   *Rod Stewart*
'03   *Staind*
'59 **So Fine** *Fiestas*
'01 **So Fresh, So Clean** *OutKast*
'03 **So Gone** *Monica*
'88 **So Good** *Al Jarreau*
'79 **So Good, So Right** *Brenda Russell*
'69 **So Good Together** *Andy Kim*
'95 **So Help Me Girl** *Joe Diffie*
'77 **So High (Rock Me Baby And Roll Me Away)** *Dave Mason*
'69 **So I Can Love You** *Emotions*
'85 **So In Love** *Orchestral Manoeuvres In The Dark*
'00 **So In Love With Two** *Mikaila*
'77 **So In To You**
   *Atlanta Rhythm Section*
'98 **So Into You** *Tamia*
'61 **So Long Baby** *Del Shannon*
'59 **So Many Ways** *Brook Benton*

**236**

'96 **So Much For Pretending**
  *Bryan White*
**So Much In Love**
'63 *Tymes*
'94 *All-4-One*
'91 **So Much Love** *B Angie B*
'57 **So Rare** *Jimmy Dorsey*
'76 **So Sad The Song** *Gladys Knight*
'60 **So Sad (To Watch Good Love Go Bad)** *Everly Brothers*
'04 **So Sexy** *Twista*
'62 **So This Is Love** *Castells*
'73 **So Very Hard To Go**
  *Tower Of Power*
'83 **So Wrong** *Patrick Simmons*
'74 **So You Are A Star** *Hudson Brothers*
'90 **So You Like What You See**
  *Samuelle*
'91 **So You Think You're In Love**
  *Robyn Hitchcock/Egyptians*
'67 **So You Want To Be A Rock 'N' Roll Star** *Byrds*
'77 **So You Win Again** *Hot Chocolate*
'02 **Soak Up The Sun** *Sheryl Crow*
'67 **Society's Child (Baby I've Been Thinking)** *Janis Ian*
'97 **Sock It 2 Me**
  *Missy "Misdemeanor" Elliott*
'67 **Sock It To Me-Baby!** *Mitch Ryder*
'57 **Soft** *Bill Doggett*
**Soft Summer Breeze**
'56 *Diamonds*
'56 *Eddie Heywood*
'64 **Softly, As I Leave You** *Frank Sinatra*
'55 **Softly, Softly** *Jaye P. Morgan*
'72 **Softly Whispering I Love You**
  *English Congregation*
'89 **Sold Me Down The River** *Alarm*
'95 **Sold (The Grundy County Auction Incident)**
  *John Michael Montgomery*
'05 **Soldier** *Destiny's Child*
'62 **Soldier Boy** *Shirelles*
'89 **Soldier Of Love** *Donny Osmond*
'84 **Solid** *Ashford & Simpson*
**Solitaire**
'75 *Carpenters*
'83 *Laura Branigan*
'04 *Clay Aiken*
'66 **Solitary Man** *Neil Diamond*
'77 **Solsbury Hill** *Peter Gabriel*
'04 **Some Beach** *Blake Shelton*
'05 **Some Cut** *Trillville*
'64 **Some Day We're Gonna Love Again**
  *Searchers*
'81 **Some Days Are Diamonds (Some Days Are Stone)** *John Denver*
'65 **Some Enchanted Evening**
  *Jay & The Americans*
'92 **Some Girls Do** *Sawyer Brown*
**Some Guys Have All The Luck**
'73 *Persuaders*
'84 *Rod Stewart*
'59 **Some Kind-A Earthquake**
  *Duane Eddy*
'83 **Some Kind Of Friend** *Barry Manilow*
'88 **Some Kind Of Lover** *Jody Watley*
**Some Kind Of Wonderful**
'61 *Drifters*
'74 *Grand Funk*
'85 **Some Like It Hot** *Power Station*
'85 **Some Things Are Better Left Unsaid** *Daryl Hall/John Oates*
'68 **Some Things You Never Get Used To** *Supremes*
'68 **Some Velvet Morning**
  *Nancy Sinatra & Lee Hazlewood*
**Somebody**
'85 *Bryan Adams*
'04 *Reba McEntire*
'84 **Somebody Else's Guy**
  *Jocelyn Brown*
'62 **Somebody Have Mercy** *Sam Cooke*
'02 **Somebody Like You** *Keith Urban*
'91 **Somebody Loves You Baby (You Know Who It Is)** *Patti LaBelle*

**Somebody To Love**
'67 *Jefferson Airplane*
'76 *Queen*
'93 *George Michael & Queen [live]*
'92 **Somebody To Shove** *Soul Asylum*
'04 **Somebody Told Me** *Killers*
'58 **Somebody Touched Me**
  *Buddy Knox*
'56 **Somebody Up There Likes Me**
  *Perry Como*
'82 **Somebody's Baby** *Jackson Browne*
'70 **Somebody's Been Sleeping**
  *100 Proof Aged in Soul*
'76 **Somebody's Gettin' It**
  *Johnnie Taylor*
'81 **Somebody's Knockin'** *Terri Gibbs*
'86 **Somebody's Out There** *Triumph*
'84 **Somebody's Watching Me** *Rockwell*
'70 **Somebody's Watching You**
  *Little Sister*
**Someday**
'86 *Glass Tiger*
'91 *Alan Jackson*
'91 *Mariah Carey*
'96 *All-4-One*
'99 *Sugar Ray*
'03 *Nickelback*
'72 **Someday Never Comes**
  *Creedence Clearwater Revival*
'82 **Someday, Someway**
  *Marshall Crenshaw*
'69 **Someday We'll Be Together**
  *Supremes*
**Someone**
'59 *Johnny Mathis*
'97 *SWV*
'81 **Someone Could Lose A Heart Tonight** *Eddie Rabbitt*
'96 **Someone Else's Dream** *Faith Hill*
'95 **Someone Else's Star** *Bryan White*
'75 **Someone Saved My Life Tonight**
  *Elton John*
'80 **Someone That I Used To Love**
  *Natalie Cole*
'01 **Someone To Call My Lover**
  *Janet Jackson*
'92 **Someone To Hold** *Trey Lorenz*
'95 **Someone To Love** *Jon B.*
'55 **Someone You Love** *Nat "King" Cole*
'77 **Somethin' 'Bout 'Cha** *Latimore*
'59 **Somethin Else** *Eddie Cochran*
'95 **Somethin' 4 Da Honeyz**
  *Montell Jordan*
'67 **Somethin' Stupid**
  *Nancy Sinatra & Frank Sinatra*
**Something**
'69 *Beatles*
'02 *Lasgo*
'97 **Something About The Way You Look Tonight** *Elton John*
**Something About You**
'65 *Four Tops*
'76 *Boston*
'86 *Level 42*
'75 **Something Better To Do**
  *Olivia Newton-John*
'91 **Something Got Me Started**
  *Simply Red*
'90 **Something Happened On The Way To Heaven** *Phil Collins*
'92 **Something He Can Feel** *En Vogue*
'93 **Something In Common** *Bobby Brown With Whitney Houston*
'91 **Something In My Heart** *Michel'le*
'69 **Something In The Air**
  *Thunderclap Newman*
'89 **Something In The Way (You Make Me Feel)** *Stephanie Mills*
'93 **Something In Your Eyes**
  *Bell Biv DeVoe*
'88 **Something Just Ain't Right**
  *Keith Sweat*
'99 **Something Like That** *Tim McGraw*
'87 **Something Real (Inside Me/Inside You)** *Mr. Mister*
'87 **Something So Strong**
  *Crowded House*

'97 **Something That We Do** *Clint Black*
'90 **Something To Believe In** *Poison*
'86 **Something To Grab For** *Ric Ocasek*
'91 **Something To Talk About**
  *Bonnie Raitt*
'70 **Something's Burning**
  *Kenny Rogers & The First Edition*
'93 **Something's Goin' On** *U.N.V.*
'62 **Something's Got A Hold On Me**
  *Etta James*
**Something's Gotta Give**
'55 *Sammy Davis, Jr.*
'55 *McGuire Sisters*
'72 **Something's Wrong With Me**
  *Austin Roberts*
**Sometimes**
'77 *Facts Of Life*
'99 *Britney Spears*
'80 **Sometimes A Fantasy** *Billy Joel*
'92 **Sometimes Love Just Ain't Enough**
  *Patty Smyth with Don Henley*
'90 **Sometimes She Cries** *Warrant*
'77 **Sometimes When We Touch**
  *Dan Hill*
**Somewhere**
'63 *Tymes*
'66 *Len Barry*
'85 *Barbra Streisand*
'81 **Somewhere Down The Road**
  *Barry Manilow*
'03 **Somewhere I Belong** *Linkin Park*
'91 **Somewhere In My Broken Heart**
  *Billy Dean*
**Somewhere In The Night**
'75 *Helen Reddy*
'78 *Barry Manilow*
'64 **Somewhere In Your Heart**
  *Frank Sinatra*
'66 **Somewhere, My Love** *Ray Conniff*
'92 **Somewhere Other Than The Night**
  *Garth Brooks*
'86 **Somewhere Out There**
  *Linda Ronstadt & James Ingram*
'66 **Somewhere There's A Someone**
  *Dean Martin*
'01 **Son Of A Gun (I Betcha Think This Song Is About You)**
  *Janet Jackson*
'68 **Son Of A Preacher Man**
  *Dusty Springfield*
'68 **Son Of Hickory Holler's Tramp**
  *O.C. Smith*
'72 **Son Of My Father** *Giorgio Moroder*
'74 **Son Of Sagittarius** *Eddie Kendricks*
'56 **Song For A Summer Night**
  *Mitch Miller*
'97 **Song For Mama** *Boyz II Men*
'70 **Song Of Joy** *Miguel Rios*
**(Song Of Love) ..see: Chanson D'Amour**
'55 **Song Of The Dreamer** *Eddie Fisher*
'79 **Song On The Radio** *Al Stewart*
'89 **Song Of The South** *Alabama*
'73 **Song Remains The Same**
  *Led Zeppelin*
'93 **Song Remembers When**
  *Trisha Yearwood*
'72 **Song Sung Blue** *Neil Diamond*
'97 **Song 2** *Blur*
**Songbird**
'78 *Barbra Streisand*
'87 *Kenny G*
'70 **Soolaimón (African Trilogy II)**
  *Neil Diamond*
'93 **Soon** *Tanya Tucker*
'95 **Soon As I Get Home** *Faith Evans*
**Sooner Or Later**
'71 *Grass Roots*
'75 *Impressions*
'05 *Breaking Benjamin*
'69 **Sophisticated Cissy** *Meters*
'76 **Sophisticated Lady (She's A Different Lady)** *Natalie Cole*
'59 **Sorry (I Ran All the Way Home)**
  *Impalas*
'76 **Sorry Seems To Be The Hardest Word** *Elton John*

'04 **Sorry 2004** *Ruben Studdard*
'87 **Soul City** *Partland Brothers*
'69 **Soul Deep** *Box Tops*
'67 **Soul Finger** *Bar-Kays*
'85 **Soul Kiss** *Olivia Newton-John*
'68 **Soul-Limbo** *Booker T. & The M.G.'s*
'73 **Soul Makossa** *Manu Dibango*
**Soul Man**
'67   *Sam & Dave*
'78   *Blues Brothers*
'71 **Soul Power** *James Brown*
'89 **Soul Provider** *Michael Bolton*
'68 **Soul Serenade** *Willie Mitchell*
'70 **Soul Shake** *Delaney & Bonnie*
'73 **Soul Song** *Joe Stampley*
'93 **Soul To Squeeze**
  *Red Hot Chili Peppers*
'62 **Soul Twist** *King Curtis*
'68 **Soulful Strut** *Young-Holt Unlimited*
'83 **Souls** *Rick Springfield*
'69 **Soulshake**
  *Peggy Scott & Jo Jo Benson*
'67 **Sound Of Love** *Five Americans*
'91 **Sound Of Your Voice** *38 Special*
'65 **Sounds Of Silence**
  *Simon & Garfunkel*
'00 **Sour Girl** *Stone Temple Pilots*
'73 **South City Midnight Lady** *Doobie Brothers*
'00 **South Side** *Moby*
'63 **South Street** *Orlons*
'75 **South's Gonna Do It**
  *Charlie Daniels Band*
'82 **Southern Cross**
  *Crosby, Stills & Nash*
'01 **Southern Hospitality** *Ludacris*
'70 **Southern Man** *Neil Young*
'77 **Southern Nights** *Glen Campbell*
'04 **Southside** *Lloyd*
'64 **Southtown, U.S.A.** *Dixiebelles*
'89 **Sowing The Seeds Of Love**
  *Tears For Fears*
'82 **Space Age Love Song**
  *Flock Of Seagulls*
'01 **Space Between**
  *Dave Matthews Band*
'73 **Space Cowboy**
  *Steve Miller Band*
'96 **Space Jam** *Quad City DJ's*
'98 **Space Lord** *Monster Magnet*
'73 **Space Oddity** *David Bowie*
'73 **Space Race** *Billy Preston*
'72 **Space Truckin'** *Deep Purple*
'72 **Spaceman** *Nilsson*
'65 **Spanish Eyes** *Al Martino*
'66 **Spanish Flea** *Herb Alpert*
**Spanish Harlem**
'60   *Ben E. King*
'71   *Aretha Franklin*
'62 **Spanish Lace** *Gene McDaniels*
'73 **Speak To Me [medley]**
  *Pink Floyd*
'72 **Speak To The Sky** *Rick Springfield*
'80 **Special Lady**
  *Ray, Goodman, & Brown*
'68 **Special Occasion** *Miracles*
'05 **Speed Of Sound** *Coldplay*
'55 **Speedoo** *Cadillacs*
'62 **Speedy Gonzales** *Pat Boone*
'90 **Spend My Life** *Slaughter*
'99 **Spend My Life With You** *Eric Benét*
'91 **Spending My Time** *Roxette*
'83 **Spice Of Life** *Manhattan Transfer*
'97 **Spice Up Your Life** *Spice Girls*
'73 **Spiders & Snakes** *Jim Stafford*
'96 **Spiderwebs** *No Doubt*
'85 **Spies Like Us** *Paul McCartney*
'70 **Spill The Wine** *Eric Burdon & War*
'94 **Spin The Black Circle** *Pearl Jam*
'69 **Spinning Wheel**
  *Blood, Sweat & Tears*
'66 **Spinout** *Elvis Presley*
'70 **Spirit In The Dark** *Aretha Franklin*
**Spirit In The Night**
'73   *Bruce Springsteen*
'77   *Manfred Mann*

'70 **Spirit In The Sky**
  *Norman Greenbaum*
'98 **Spirit Of A Boy - Wisdom Of A Man**
  *Randy Travis*
'80 **Spirit Of Radio** *Rush*
'75 **Spirit Of The Boogie**
  *Kool & The Gang*
'82 **Spirits In The Material World** *Police*
'98 **Splackavellie** *Pressha*
'04 **Splash Waterfalls** *Ludacris*
'58 **Splish Splash** *Bobby Darin*
'86 **Split Decision** *Steve Winwood*
**Spooky**
'67   *Classics IV*
'79   *Atlanta Rhythm Section*
**Spoonful**
'60   *Howlin' Wolf*
'68   *Cream*
'94 **Spoonman** *Soundgarden*
'88 **Spotlight** *Madonna*
'90 **Spread My Wings** *Troop*
'76 **Springtime Mama** *Henry Gross*
'88 **Spy In The House Of Love**
  *Was (Not Was)*
'81 **Square Biz** *Teena Marie*
'75 **Squeeze Box** *Who*
'85 **St. Elmo's Fire (Man In Motion)**
  *John Parr*
'69 **St. Stephen** *Grateful Dead*
'56 **St. Therese Of The Roses**
  *Billy Ward*
'03 **Stacy's Mom** *Fountains Of Wayne*
'86 **Stages** *ZZ Top*
**Stagger Lee**
'58   *Lloyd Price*
'67   *Wilson Pickett*
'71   *Tommy Roe*
**Stairway To Heaven**
'60   *Neil Sedaka*
'71   *Led Zeppelin*
'00 **Stan** *Eminem*
**Stand**
'69   *Sly & The Family Stone*
'88   *R.E.M.*
'83 **Stand Back** *Stevie Nicks*
'98 **Stand Beside Me** *Jo Dee Messina*
**Stand By Me**
'61   *Ben E. King*
'66   *Spyder Turner*
'75   *John Lennon*
'80   *Mickey Gilley*
**Stand By Your Man**
'68   *Tammy Wynette*
'70   *Candi Staton*
'00 **Stand Inside Your Love**
  *Smashing Pumpkins*
'76 **Stand Tall** *Burton Cummings*
'03 **Stand Up** *Ludacris*
'92 **Stand Up (Kick Love Into Motion)**
  *Def Leppard*
'74 **Standing At The End Of The Line**
  *Lobo*
'66 **Standing In The Shadows Of Love**
  *Four Tops*
'87 **Standing On Higher Ground**
  *Alan Parsons Project*
**Standing On The Corner**
'56   *Four Lads*
'56   *Dean Martin*
'95 **Standing On The Edge Of Goodbye**
  *John Berry*
'96 **Standing Outside A Broken Phone Booth With Money In My Hand**
  *Primitive Radio Gods*
'93 **Standing Outside The Fire**
  *Garth Brooks*
'01 **Standing Still** *Jewel*
'74 **Star** *Stealers Wheel*
'74 **Star Baby** *Guess Who*
**Star Spangled Banner**
'71   *Jimi Hendrix*
'91   *Whitney Houston*
**Star Wars Theme**
'77   *Meco*
'77   *John Williams*
'60 **Starbright** *Johnny Mathis*

**Stardust**
'57   *Billy Ward*
'57   *Nat "King" Cole*
'64   *Nino Tempo & April Stevens*
'72 **Starman** *David Bowie*
'97 **Staring At The Sun** *U2*
'96 **Stars Over Texas** *Tracy Lawrence*
'71 **Starship Trooper** *Yes*
'81 **Start Me Up** *Rolling Stones*
'57 **Start Movin' (In My Direction)**
  *Sal Mineo*
'89 **Start Of A Romance** *Skyy*
'92 **Start The Car** *Jude Cole*
'01 **Start The Commotion** *Wiseguys*
'72 **Starting All Over Again** *Mel & Tim*
'80 **Starting Over Again** *Dolly Parton*
'93 **State Of Mind** *Clint Black*
'84 **State Of Shock** *Jacksons*
'85 **State Of The Heart** *Rick Springfield*
'91 **State Of The World** *Janet Jackson*
'71 **Statesboro Blues**
  *Allman Brothers Band*
**Stay**
'60   *Maurice Williams*
'64   *4 Seasons*
'78   *Jackson Browne [medley]*
'91   *Jodeci*
'92   *Shakespear's Sister*
'94   *Eternal*
'98 **Stay (Awasting Time)**
  *Dave Matthews Band*
**Stay Awhile**
'64   *Dusty Springfield*
'71   *Bells*
'03 **Stay Gone** *Jimmy Wayne*
'94 **Stay (I Missed You)** *Lisa Loeb*
'68 **Stay In My Corner** *Dells*
**Stay The Night**
'84   *Chicago*
'86   *Benjamin Orr*
'99   *Immature*
'99 **Stay The Same** *Joey McIntyre*
**Stay With Me**
'66   *Lorraine Ellison*
'72   *Faces*
  *(also see: One More Chance)*
'83 **Stay With Me Tonight**
  *Jeffrey Osborne*
'77 **Stayin' Alive** *Bee Gees*
'61 **Stayin' In** *Bobby Vee*
'88 **Staying Together** *Debbie Gibson*
'81 **Staying With It** *Firefall*
'04 **Stays In Mexico** *Toby Keith*
**Steal Away**
'64   *Jimmy Hughes*
'70   *Johnnie Taylor*
'80   *Robbie Dupree*
'99 **Steal My Sunshine** *Len*
'81 **Steal The Night** *Stevie Woods*
'73 **Stealin'** *Uriah Heep*
'92 **Steam** *Peter Gabriel*
'73 **Steamroller Blues** *Elvis Presley*
'89 **Steamy Windows** *Tina Turner*
'92 **Steel Bars** *Michael Bolton*
'62 **Steel Guitar And A Glass Of Wine**
  *Paul Anka*
'62 **Steel Men** *Jimmy Dean*
'96 **Steelo** *702*
'00 **Stellar** *Incubus*
**Step By Step**
'60   *Crests*
'73   *Joe Simon*
'81   *Eddie Rabbitt*
'90   *New Kids On The Block*
'97   *Whitney Houston*
'03 **Step In The Name Of Love** *R. Kelly*
'73 **Step Into Christmas**
  *Elton John*
'67 **Step Out Of Your Mind**
  *American Breed*
'85 **Step That Step** *Sawyer Brown*
'67 **Step To The Rear** *Marilyn Maye*
'78 **Steppin' In A Slide Zone**
  *Moody Blues*

238

**Steppin' Out**
'76   *Neil Sedaka*
'82   *Joe Jackson*
'74   **Steppin' Out (Gonna Boogie Tonight)** *Tony Orlando & Dawn*
'73   **Stepping Razor** *Peter Tosh*
'02   **Steve McQueen** *Sheryl Crow*
'63   **Stewball** *Peter, Paul & Mary*
'86   **Stick Around** *Julian Lennon*
'93   **Stick It Out** *Rush*
'61   **Stick Shift** *Duals*
'71   **Stick-Up** *Honey Cone*
'61   **Stick With Me Baby** *Everly Brothers*
'91   **Sticks And Stones** *Tracy Lawrence*
'00   **Stiff Upper Lip** *AC/DC*
**Still**
'63   *Bill Anderson*
'79   *Commodores*
'98   **Still A G Thang** *Snoop Dogg*
'87   **Still A Thrill** *Jody Watley*
'76   **Still Crazy After All These Years** *Paul Simon*
'02   **Still Fly** *Big Tymers*
'03   **Still Frame** *Trapt*
'87   **Still In Love [medley]** *Boston*
'82   **Still In Saigon** *Charlie Daniels Band*
'98   **Still Not A Player** *Big Punisher*
'81   **Still Right Here In My Heart** *Pure Prairie League*
'76   **Still The One** *Orleans*
'78   **Still The Same** *Bob Seger*
'82   **Still They Ride** *Journey*
'70   **Still Water (Love)** *Four Tops*
'92   **Sting Me** *Black Crowes*
'02   **Stingy** *Ginuwine*
'73   **Stir It Up** *Johnny Nash*
'02   **Stole** *Kelly Rowland*
**Stomp**
'80   *Brothers Johnson*
'97   *God's Property*
'78   **Stone Blue** *Foghat*
'82   **Stone Cold** *Rainbow*
'71   **Stone Cold Fever** *Jimi Hendrix*
'91   **Stone Cold Gentleman** *Ralph Tresvant*
'69   **Stone Free** *Jimi Hendrix*
'87   **Stone Love** *Kool & The Gang*
'70   **Stoned Love** *Supremes*
'73   **Stoned Out Of My Mind** *Chi-Lites*
**Stoned Soul Picnic**
'68   *5th Dimension*
'68   *Laura Nyro*
'71   **Stones** *Neil Diamond*
'70   **Stoney End** *Barbra Streisand*
'57   **Stood Up** *Ricky Nelson*
**Stop!**
'90   *Jane's Addiction*
'98   *Spice Girls*
'74   **Stop And Smell The Roses** *Mac Davis*
**Stop And Think It Over**
'64   *Dale & Grace*
'67   *Perry Como*
'83   **Stop Doggin' Me Around** *Klique*
'81   **Stop Draggin' My Heart Around** *Stevie Nicks (with Tom Petty)*
**Stop! In The Name Of Love**
'65   *Supremes*
'83   *Hollies*
'71   **Stop, Look, Listen (To Your Heart)** *Stylistics*
'66   **Stop Stop Stop** *Hollies*
'62   **Stop The Music** *Shirelles*
'70   **Stop The War Now** *Edwin Starr*
'62   **Stop The Wedding** *Etta James*
'86   **Stop To Love** *Luther Vandross*
'80   **Stop Your Sobbing** *Pretenders*
**Stormy**
'68   *Classics IV*
'79   *Santana*
'71   **Story In Your Eyes** *Moody Blues*
'57   **Story Of My Life** *Marty Robbins*
**Story Of My Love**
'59   *Conway Twitty*
'61   *Paul Anka*

**Story Untold**
'55   *Crew-Cuts*
'55   *Nutmegs*
'67   **Stout-Hearted Men** *Barbra Streisand*
**Straight From The Heart**
'81   *Allman Brothers Band*
'83   *Bryan Adams*
'68   **Straight Life** *Bobby Goldsboro*
'78   **Straight On** *Heart*
'03   **Straight Out Of Line** *Godsmack*
'74   **Straight Shootin' Woman** *Steppenwolf*
'91   **Straight Tequila Night** *John Anderson*
'88   **Straight Up** *Paula Abdul*
'90   **Stranded** *Heart*
**Stranded In The Jungle**
'56   *Cadets*
'56   *Gadabouts*
'56   *Jayhawks*
'67   **Strange Brew** *Cream*
'88   **Strange But True** *Times Two*
'67   **Strange Days** *Doors*
'71   **Strange Kind Of Woman** *Deep Purple*
'76   **Strange Magic** *Electric Light Orchestra*
'78   **Strange Way** *Firefall*
'87   **Strangelove** *Depeche Mode*
'77   **Stranger, The** *Billy Joel*
**Stranger In My House**
'83   *Ronnie Milsap*
'01   *Tamia*
**Stranger In Town**
'65   *Del Shannon*
'84   *Toto*
**Stranger On The Shore**
'62   *Mr. Acker Bilk*
'62   *Andy Williams*
'66   **Strangers In The Night** *Frank Sinatra*
'67   **Strawberry Fields Forever** *Beatles*
'77   **Strawberry Letter 23** *Brothers Johnson*
'68   **Strawberry Shortcake** *Jay & The Techniques*
'96   **Strawberry Wine** *Deana Carter*
'82   **Stray Cat Strut** *Stray Cats*
'74   **Streak, The** *Ray Stevens*
'77   **Street Corner Serenade** *Wet Willie*
'96   **Street Dreams** *Nas*
'68   **Street Fighting Man** *Rolling Stones*
'78   **Street Hassle** *Lou Reed*
'79   **Street Life** *Crusaders*
**Street Of Dreams**
'83   *Rainbow*
'91   *Nia Peeples*
'76   **Street Singin'** *Lady Flash*
'88   **Streets Of Bakersfield** *Dwight Yoakam & Buck Owens*
'94   **Streets Of Philadelphia** *Bruce Springsteen*
'91   **Strike It Up** *Black Box*
**String Along**
'60   *Fabian*
'63   *Rick Nelson*
'62   **Stripper, The** *David Rose*
'81   **Stroke, The** *Billy Squier*
'94   **Stroke You Up** *Changing Faces*
'89   **Strokin'** *Clarence Carter*
'57   **Stroll, The** *Diamonds*
'94   **Strong Enough** *Sheryl Crow*
'00   **Stronger** *Britney Spears*
'81   **Stronger Than Before** *Carole Bayer Sager*
'84   **Strung Out** *Steve Perry*
'84   **Strut** *Sheena Easton*
'74   **Strutter** *Kiss*
'74   **Struttin'** *Billy Preston*
'62   **Stubborn Kind Of Fellow** *Marvin Gaye*
'73   **Stuck In The Middle With You** *Stealers Wheel*
'66   **Stuck Inside Of Mobile With The Memphis Blues Again** *Bob Dylan*

**Stuck On You**
'60   *Elvis Presley*
'84   *Lionel Richie*
'86   **Stuck With You** *Huey Lewis*
'78   **Stuff Like That** *Quincy Jones*
'79   **Stumblin' In** *Suzi Quatro & Chris Norman*
'03   **Stunt 101** *G-Unit*
'58   **Stupid Cupid** *Connie Francis*
'96   **Stupid Girl** *Garbage*
'01   **Stutter** *Joe*
'72   **Suavecito** *Malo*
'93   **Sublime** *Ocean Blue*
'66   **Substitute** *Who*
'65   **Subterranean Homesick Blues** *Bob Dylan*
'64   **Such A Night** *Elvis Presley*
'79   **Such A Woman** *Tycoon*
'65   **(Such An) Easy Question** *Elvis Presley*
**Suddenly**
'80   *Olivia Newton-John & Cliff Richard*
'85   *Billy Ocean*
'83   **Suddenly Last Summer** *Motels*
**Suddenly There's A Valley**
'55   *Gogi Grant*
'55   *Julius LaRosa*
'55   *Jo Stafford*
'04   **Suds In The Bucket** *Sara Evans*
'72   **Suffragette City** *David Bowie*
'03   **Suga Suga** *Baby Bash*
'74   **Sugar Baby Love** *Rubettes*
**Sugar Daddy**
'71   *Jackson 5*
'89   *Thompson Twins*
'84   **Sugar Don't Bite** *Sam Harris*
'65   **Sugar Dumpling** *Sam Cooke*
'95   **Sugar Hill** *AZ*
'64   **Sugar Lips** *Al Hirt*
'70   **Sugar Magnolia** *Grateful Dead*
'58   **Sugar Moon** *Pat Boone*
'69   **Sugar On Sunday** *Clique*
'63   **Sugar Shack** *Jimmy Gilmer/Fireballs*
**Sugar, Sugar**
'69   *Archies*
'70   *Wilson Pickett*
'66   **Sugar Town** *Nancy Sinatra*
'84   **Sugar Walls** *Sheena Easton*
'57   **Sugartime** *McGuire Sisters*
'90   **Suicide Blonde** *INXS*
'69   **Suite: Judy Blue Eyes** *Crosby, Stills & Nash*
'76   **Suite Madame Blue** *Styx*
**Sukiyaki**
'63   *Kyu Sakamoto*
'81   *Taste Of Honey*
'94   *4 P.M. (For Positive Music)*
'79   **Sultans Of Swing** *Dire Straits*
'76   **Summer** *War*
'92   **Summer Babe** *Pavement*
'72   **Summer Breeze** *Seals & Crofts*
'99   **Summer Girls** *LFO*
'66   **Summer In The City** *Lovin' Spoonful*
**Summer Nights**
'65   *Marianne Faithull*
'78   *John Travolta & Olivia Newton-John*
'85   **Summer Of '69** *Bryan Adams*
**Summer Rain**
'67   *Johnny Rivers*
'90   *Belinda Carlisle*
'66   **Summer Samba (So Nice)** *Walter Wanderley*
'71   **Summer Sand** *Dawn*
'60   **Summer Set** *Monty Kelly*
**Summer Song**
'64   *Chad & Jeremy*
'92   *Joe Satriani*
'73   **Summer (The First Time)** *Bobby Goldsboro*
'90   **Summer Vacation** *Party*
'66   **Summer Wind** *Frank Sinatra*
'69   **Summer Wine** *Nancy Sinatra with Lee Hazelwood*
'95   **Summer's Comin'** *Clint Black*
'60   **Summer's Gone** *Paul Anka*

**239**

**Summertime**
'57  *Sam Cooke*
'66  *Billy Stewart*
'91  *D.J. Jazzy Jeff & The Fresh Prince*
**Summertime Blues**
'58  *Eddie Cochran*
'68  *Blue Cheer*
'70  *Who*
'94  *Alan Jackson*
'58  **Summertime, Summertime** *Jamies*
'66  **Sun Ain't Gonna Shine (Anymore)**
       *Walker Bros.*
'85  **Sun Always Shines On T.V.** *A-Ha*
'85  **Sun City**
       *Artists United Against Apartheid*
'65  **Sunday And Me**
       *Jay & The Americans*
'83  **Sunday Bloody Sunday** *U2*
'67  **Sunday For Tea** *Peter & Gordon*
'68  **Sunday Mornin'** *Spanky & Our Gang*
**Sunday Morning**
'67  *Velvet Underground*
'05  *Maroon5*
'67  **Sunday Will Never Be The Same**
       *Spanky & Our Gang*
'74  **Sundown** *Gordon Lightfoot*
'77  **Sunflower** *Glen Campbell*
'84  **Sunglasses At Night** *Corey Hart*
'66  **Sunny** *Bobby Hebb*
'66  **Sunny Afternoon** *Kinks*
'97  **Sunny Came Home** *Shawn Colvin*
'72  **Sunny Days** *Lighthouse*
'76  **Sunrise** *Eric Carmen*
'85  **Sunset Grill** *Don Henley*
**Sunshine**
'71  *Jonathan Edwards*
'75  *O'Jays*
'77  *Enchantment*
'89  *Dino*
'04  *Lil' Flip*
'67  **Sunshine Girl** *Parade*
'65  **Sunshine, Lollipops And Rainbows**
       *Lesley Gore*
'68  **Sunshine Of Your Love** *Cream*
'74  **Sunshine On My Shoulders**
       *John Denver*
'66  **Sunshine Superman** *Donovan*
'70  **Super Bad** *James Brown*
'73  **Super Fly Meets Shaft**
       *John & Ernest*
'81  **Super Freak** *Rick James*
'98  **SuperThug (What What)** *Noreaga*
'86  **Superbowl Shuffle**
       *Chicago Bears Shufflin' Crew*
'72  **Superfly** *Curtis Mayfield*
**Superman**
'79  *Herbie Mann*
'03  *Eminem*
'01  **Superman (It's Not Easy)**
       *Five For Fighting*
'75  **Supernatural Thing** *Ben E. King*
'94  **Supernova** *Liz Phair*
'88  **Supersonic** *J.J. Fad*
**Superstar**
'70  *Murray Head*
'71  *Carpenters*
'76  *Paul Davis*
'03  *Ruben Studdard*
'71  **Superstar (Remember How You Got**
       **Where You Are)** *Temptations*
**Superstition**
'72  *Stevie Wonder*
'87  *Stevie Ray Vaughan*
'88  **Superstitious** *Europe*
**Superwoman**
'89  *Karyn White*
'01  *Lil' Mo*
'72  **Superwoman (Where Were You**
       **When I Needed You)**
       *Stevie Wonder*
'74  **Sure As I'm Sittin' Here**
       *Three Dog Night*
'66  **Sure Gonna Miss Her** *Gary Lewis*
'79  **Sure Know Something** *Kiss*
'92  **Sure Love** *Hal Ketchum*
'63  **Surf City** *Jan & Dean*

'63  **Surfer Girl** *Beach Boys*
'62  **Surfer's Stomp** *Mar-Kets*
'63  **Surfin' Bird** *Trashmen*
'62  **Surfin' Safari** *Beach Boys*
**Surfin' U.S.A.**
'63  *Beach Boys*
'77  *Leif Garrett*
**Surrender**
'61  *Elvis Presley*
'71  *Diana Ross*
'78  *Cheap Trick*
'88  **Surrender To Me**
       *Ann Wilson & Robin Zander*
'01  **Survivor** *Destiny's Child*
'67  **Susan** *Buckinghams*
**Susie Darlin'**
'58  *Robin Luke*
'62  *Tommy Roe*
**Suspicion**
'62  *Elvis Presley*
'64  *Terry Stafford*
'79  **Suspicions** *Eddie Rabbitt*
'69  **Suspicious Minds** *Elvis Presley*
'85  **Sussudio** *Phil Collins*
'86  **Suzanne** *Journey*
'59  **Suzie Baby** *Bobby Vee*
**Suzie-Q**
'57  *Dale Hawkins*
'68  *Creedence Clearwater Revival*
'96  **Swallowed** *Bush*
'73  **Swamp Witch** *Jim Stafford*
'55  **Swanee** *Jaye P. Morgan*
'57  **Swanee River Rock (Talkin' 'Bout**
       **That River)** *Ray Charles*
'60  **Sway** *Bobby Rydell*
'00  **Swear It Again** *Westlife*
'75  **Swearin' To God** *Frankie Valli*
'93  **Sweat (A La La La La Long)**
       *Inner Circle*
**Sweet And Gentle**
'55  *Alan Dale*
'55  *Georgia Gibbs*
'71  **Sweet And Innocent** *Donny Osmond*
'81  **Sweet Baby**
       *Stanley Clarke/George Duke*
'68  **Sweet Blindness** *5th Dimension*
'69  **Sweet Caroline** *Neil Diamond*
'69  **Sweet Cherry Wine** *Tommy James*
'88  **Sweet Child O' Mine** *Guns N' Roses*
'71  **Sweet City Woman** *Stampeders*
'68  **Sweet Cream Ladies, Forward**
       **March** *Box Tops*
**Sweet Dreams**
'66  *Tommy McLain*
'81  *Air Supply*
'96  *La Bouche*
'83  **Sweet Dreams (Are Made of This)**
       *Eurythmics*
'63  **Sweet Dreams (Of You)** *Patsy Cline*
'75  **Sweet Emotion** *Aerosmith*
'86  **Sweet Freedom** *Michael McDonald*
'71  **Sweet Hitch-Hiker**
       *Creedence Clearwater Revival*
'74  **Sweet Home Alabama**
       *Lynyrd Skynyrd*
**Sweet Inspiration**
'68  *Sweet Inspirations*
'72  *Barbra Streisand [medley]*
**Sweet Jane**
'70  *Velvet Underground*
'74  *Lou Reed*
'99  **Sweet Lady** *Tyrese*
'78  **Sweet Life** *Paul Davis*
'58  **Sweet Little Sixteen** *Chuck Berry*
**Sweet Love**
'75  *Commodores*
'86  *Anita Baker*
'79  **Sweet Lui-Louise** *Ironhorse*
'70  **Sweet Mary** *Wadsworth Mansion*
'75  **Sweet Maxine** *Doobie Brothers*
'59  **Sweet Nothin's** *Brenda Lee*
'92  **Sweet November** *Troop*
'56  **Sweet Old Fashioned Girl**
       *Teresa Brewer*
'66  **Sweet Pea** *Tommy Roe*

'94  **Sweet Potatoe Pie** *Domino*
'72  **Sweet Seasons** *Carole King*
'80  **Sweet Sensation** *Stephanie Mills*
**Sweet Sixteen**
'60  *B.B. King*
'87  *Billy Idol*
'67  **Sweet Soul Music** *Arthur Conley*
'03  **Sweet Southern Comfort**
       *Buddy Jewell*
'75  **Sweet Sticky Thing** *Ohio Players*
**Sweet Surrender**
'72  *Bread*
'74  *John Denver*
'98  *Sarah McLachlan*
'68  **(Sweet Sweet Baby) Since You've**
       **Been Gone** *Aretha Franklin*
'66  **Sweet Talkin' Guy** *Chiffons*
'78  **Sweet Talkin' Woman**
       *Electric Light Orchestra*
**Sweet Thing**
'76  *Rufus Feat. Chaka Khan*
'93  *Mary J. Blige*
'82  **Sweet Time** *REO Speedwagon*
'73  **Sweet Understanding Love**
       *Four Tops*
'64  **Sweet William** *Millie Small*
'65  **Sweet Woman Like You** *Joe Tex*
'59  **Sweeter Than You** *Ricky Nelson*
'94  **Sweetest Days** *Vanessa Williams*
'85  **Sweetest Taboo** *Sade*
**Sweetest Thing**
'97  *Fugees*
'98  *U2*
'81  **Sweetest Thing (I've Ever Known)**
       *Juice Newton*
'67  **Sweetest Thing This Side Of**
       **Heaven** *Chris Bartley*
**Sweetheart**
'70  *Engelbert Humperdinck*
'81  *Franke & The Knockouts*
'02  **Sweetness** *Jimmy Eat World*
'61  **Sweets For My Sweet** *Drifters*
'84  **Swept Away** *Diana Ross*
'97  **Swing My Way** *K.P. & Envyi*
'89  **Swing The Mood [medley]**
       *Jive Bunny & the Mastermixers*
'83  **Swingin'** *John Anderson*
'62  **Swingin' Gently** *Earl Grant*
'62  **Swingin' Safari** *Billy Vaughn*
'60  **Swingin' School** *Bobby Rydell*
'58  **Swingin' Shepherd Blues**
       *Moe Koffman Quartette*
'66  **Swinging Doors** *Merle Haggard*
'63  **Swinging On A Star**
       *Big Dee Irwin/Little Eva*
'77  **Swingtown** *Steve Miller Band*
'62  **Swiss Maid** *Del Shannon*
'05  **Switch** *Will Smith*
'80  **Switchin' To Glide [medley]** *Kings*
'72  **Sylvia's Mother** *Dr. Hook*
'68  **Sympathy For The Devil**
       *Rolling Stones*
'66  **Symphony For Susan** *Arbors*
'88  **Symptoms Of True Love**
       *Tracie Spencer*
'83  **Synchronicity II** *Police*
'76  **(System Of) Doctor Tarr And**
       **Professor Fether**
       *Alan Parsons Project*
'87  **System Of Survival**
       *Earth, Wind & Fire*

# T

'92  **T.L.C.** *Linear*
'60  **T.L.C. Tender Love And Care**
       *Jimmie Rodgers*
'76  **T.N.T.** *AC/DC*
'74  **TSOP (The Sound Of Philadelphia)**
       *MFSB feat. The Three Degrees*
'82  **TV Party** *Black Flag*
'76  **TVC 15** *David Bowie*
'60  **Ta Ta** *Clyde McPhatter*
'82  **Tainted Love** *Soft Cell*
'94  **Take A Bow** *Madonna*
'78  **Take A Chance On Me** *Abba*

'69 Take A Letter Maria *R.B. Greaves*
'80 Take A Little Rhythm *Ali Thomson*
'59 Take A Message To Mary
    *Everly Brothers*
'99 Take A Picture *Filter*
'69 Take Care Of Your Homework
    *Johnnie Taylor*
'61 Take Five *Dave Brubeck Quartet*
'61 Take Good Care Of Her *Adam Wade*
    Take Good Care Of My Baby
'61   *Bobby Vee*
'68   *Bobby Vinton*
'82 Take It Away *Paul McCartney*
    Take It Easy
'72   *Eagles*
'86   *Andy Taylor*
'93   *Travis Tritt*
'81 Take It Easy On Me *Little River Band*
'76 Take It Like A Man
    *Bachman-Turner Overdrive*
'81 Take It On The Run
    *REO Speedwagon*
'88 Take It So Hard *Keith Richards*
'75 Take It To The Limit *Eagles*
'97 Take It To The Streets *Rampage*
'94 Take Me As I Am *Faith Hill*
'65 Take Me Back
    *Little Anthony & The Imperials*
'82 Take Me Down *Alabama*
'68 Take Me For A Little While
    *Vanilla Fudge*
    Take Me Home
'79   *Cher*
'86   *Phil Collins*
'71 Take Me Home, Country Roads
    *John Denver*
'86 Take Me Home Tonight
    *Eddie Money*
'78 Take Me I'm Yours
    *Michael Henderson*
'75 Take Me In Your Arms (Rock Me)
    *Doobie Brothers*
'04 Take Me Out *Franz Ferdinand*
'98 Take Me There *BLACKstreet & Mya*
'83 Take Me To Heart *Quarterflash*
'78 Take Me To The Next Phase
    *Isley Brothers*
'70 Take Me To The Pilot
    *Elton John*
    Take Me To The River
'74   *Al Green*
'78   *Talking Heads*
'85 Take Me With U *Prince*
    Take My Breath Away
'86   *Berlin*
'04   *Jessica Simpson*
'81 Take My Heart (You Can Have It If
    You Want It) *Kool & The Gang*
'82 Take Off *Bob & Doug McKenzie*
'85 Take On Me *A-Ha*
'79 Take The Long Way Home
    *Supertramp*
'76 Take The Money And Run
    *Steve Miller*
'63 Take These Chains From My Heart
    *Ray Charles*
'92 Take This Heart *Richard Marx*
'92 Take Time *Chris Walker*
'68 Take Time To Know Her
    *Percy Sledge*
'01 Take You Out *Luther Vandross*
'92 Take Your Memory With You
    *Vince Gill*
    Take Your Time (Do It Right)
'80   *S.O.S. Band*
'88   *Pebbles*
'86 Taken In *Mike + The Mechanics*
'97 Takes A Little Time *Amy Grant*
'74 Takin' Care Of Business
    *Bachman-Turner Overdrive*
'76 Takin' It To The Streets
    *Doobie Brothers*
'99 Taking Everything *Gerald Levert*
'00 Taking You Home *Don Henley*
'04 Talk About Our Love *Brandy*
'63 Talk Back Trembling Lips
    *Johnny Tillotson*

'87 Talk Dirty To Me *Poison*
'89 Talk It Over *Grayson Hugh*
'04 Talk Shows On Mute *Incubus*
'66 Talk Talk *Music Machine*
'59 Talk That Talk *Jackie Wilson*
    Talk To Me
'59   *Frank Sinatra*
'85   *Stevie Nicks*
'86   *Chico DeBarge*
'90   *Anita Baker*
    Talk To Me, Talk To Me
'58   *Little Willie John*
'63   *Sunny & The Sunglows*
81 Talk To Ya Later *Tubes*
'57 Talkin' To The Blues *Jim Lowe*
'64 Talking About My Baby *Impressions*
    Talking In Your Sleep
'78   *Crystal Gayle*
'83   *Romantics*
'72 Talking Loud And Saying Nothing
    *James Brown*
    Tall Cool One
'59   *Wailers*
'88   *Robert Plant*
'59 Tall Paul *Annette*
'95 Tall, Tall Trees *Alan Jackson*
'59 Tallahassee Lassie *Freddy Cannon*
    Tammy
'57   *Ames Brothers*
'57   *Debbie Reynolds*
'76 Tangerine *Salsoul Orchestra*
'75 Tangled Up In Blue *Bob Dylan*
'68 Tapioca Tundra *Monkees*
'66 Tar And Cement *Verdelle Smith*
'85 Tarzan Boy *Baltimora*
'65 Taste Of Honey *Herb Alpert*
'97 Taste Of India *Aerosmith*
'86 Tasty Love *Freddie Jackson*
'72 Taurus *Dennis Coffey*
'72 Taxi *Harry Chapin*
'66 Taxman *Beatles*
'58 Tchaikovsky: Piano Concerto No. 1
    *Van Cliburn*
'58 Tea For Two (Cha Cha)
    *Tommy Dorsey Orchestra*
    Teach Me Tonight
'55   *DeCastro Sisters*
'55   *Jo Stafford*
'62   *George Maharis*
'70 Teach Your Children
    *Crosby, Stills, Nash & Young*
'70 Teacher *Jethro Tull*
    Teacher, Teacher
'58   *Johnny Mathis*
'84   *38 Special*
'61 Tear, A *Gene McDaniels*
'59 Tear Drop *Santo & Johnny*
'57 Tear Drops *Lee Andrews*
'56 Tear Fell *Teresa Brewer*
'76 Tear The Roof Off The Sucker (Give
    Up The Funk) *Parliament*
'98 Tearin' Up My Heart *\*NSYNC*
'84 Tears *John Waite*
'64 Tears And Roses *Al Martino*
'92 Tears In Heaven *Eric Clapton*
'70 Tears Of A Clown *Miracles*
'58 Tears On My Pillow
    *Little Anthony & The Imperials*
'59 Teasable, Pleasable You
    *Buddy Knox*
'60 Teddy *Connie Francis*
    Teddy Bear
'57   *Elvis Presley*
'76   *Red Sovine*
'73 Teddy Bear Song *Barbara Fairchild*
'57 Teen-Age Crush *Tommy Sands*
'62 Teen Age Idol *Rick Nelson*
    Teen Age Prayer
'55   *Gloria Mann*
'55   *Gale Storm*
'59 Teen Angel *Mark Dinning*
'59 Teen Beat *Sandy Nelson*
'59 Teenager In Love
    *Dion & The Belmonts*

    Teenage Heaven
'59   *Eddie Cochran*
'63   *Johnny Cymbal*
'57 Teenager's Romance *Ricky Nelson*
'83 Telefone (Long Distance Love
    Affair) *Sheena Easton*
'77 Telephone Line
    *Electric Light Orchestra*
'77 Telephone Man *Meri Wilson*
'69 Tell All The People *Doors*
'00 Tell Her *Lonestar*
'83 Tell Her About It *Billy Joel*
    Tell Her No
'65   *Zombies*
'83   *Juice Newton*
'73 Tell Her She's Lovely *El Chicano*
'62 Tell Him *Exciters*
'59 Tell Him No *Travis & Bob*
'70 Tell It All Brother *Kenny Rogers &*
    *The First Edition*
    Tell It Like It Is
'66   *Aaron Neville*
'80   *Heart*
'87 Tell It To My Heart *Taylor Dayne*
'66 Tell It To The Rain *4 Seasons*
'60 Tell Laura I Love Her *Ray Peterson*
'67 Tell Mama *Etta James*
    Tell Me
'62   *Dick & DeeDee*
'95   *Groove Theory*
'96   *Dru Hill*
'74 Tell Me A Lie *Sami Jo*
'84 Tell Me I'm Not Dreamin' (Too Good
    To Be True) *Jermaine Jackson &*
    *Michael Jackson*
'99 Tell Me It's Real *K-Ci & JoJo*
'90 Tell Me Something
    *Indecent Obsession*
'74 Tell Me Something Good *Rufus*
'67 Tell Me To My Face *Keith*
'82 Tell Me Tomorrow
    *Smokey Robinson*
'93 Tell Me What You Dream
    *Restless Heart*
'91 Tell Me What You Want Me To Do
    *Tevin Campbell*
'95 Tell Me When *Human League*
    Tell Me Why
'61   *Belmonts*
'64   *Bobby Vinton*
'66   *Elvis Presley*
'89   *Exposé*
'64 Tell Me (You're Coming Back)
    *Rolling Stones*
'62 Telstar *Tornadoes*
'70 Temma Harbour *Mary Hopkin*
    Temptation
'61   *Everly Brothers*
'91   *Corina*
'70 Temptation Eyes *Grass Roots*
'81 Tempted *Squeeze*
'04 Tempted To Touch *Rupee*
'58 Ten Commandments Of Love
    *Harvey & The Moonglows*
'63 Ten Little Indians *Beach Boys*
'84 10-9-8 *Face To Face*
'02 Ten Rounds With José Cuervo
    *Tracy Byrd*
'83 Tender Is The Night
    *Jackson Browne*
'91 Tender Kisses *Tracie Spencer*
'86 Tender Love *Force M.D.'s*
'89 Tender Lover *Babyface*
    Tender Years
'61   *George Jones*
'84   *John Cafferty*
'61 Tenderly *Bert Kaempfert*
'84 Tenderness *General Public*
'92 Tennessee *Arrested Development*
'70 Tennessee Bird Walk
    *Jack Blanchard & Misty Morgan*
'75 Tenth Avenue Freeze-Out *Bruce*
    *Springsteen*
'58 Tequila *Champs*
'73 Tequila Sunrise *Eagles*
'77 Terrapin Station *Grateful Dead*

**241**

'96 **Test For Echo** *Rush*
'95 **Texas Tornado** *Tracy Lawrence*
'90 **Texas Twister** *Little Feat*
'97 **Thank God For Believers**
  *Mark Chesnutt*
'93 **Thank God For You** *Sawyer Brown*
'99 **Thank God I Found You**
  *Mariah Carey*
'75 **Thank God I'm A Country Boy**
  *John Denver*
'78 **Thank God It's Friday** *Love & Kisses*
'58 **Thank Heaven For Little Girls**
  *Maurice Chevalier*
 **Thank You [U]**
'69 *Led Zeppelin*
'98 *Alanis Morissette*
'01 *Dido*
'70 **Thank You (Falettinme Be Mice Elf
  Agin)** *Sly & The Family Stone*
'78 **Thank You For Being A Friend**
  *Andrew Gold*
'64 **Thank You Girl** *Beatles*
'59 **Thank You Pretty Baby**
  *Brook Benton*
'88 **Thanks For My Child**
  *Cheryl Pepsii Riley*
'74 **Thanks For Saving My Life**
  *Billy Paul*
'87 **That Ain't Love** *REO Speedwagon*
'95 **That Ain't My Truck** *Rhett Akins*
'94 **That Ain't No Way To Go**
  *Brooks & Dunn*
'99 **That Don't Impress Me Much**
  *Shania Twain*
 **That Girl**
'82 *Stevie Wonder*
'96 *Maxi Priest*
'80 **That Girl Could Sing**
  *Jackson Browne*
'73 **That Lady** *Isley Brothers*
'63 **That Lucky Old Sun** *Ray Charles*
 **That Old Black Magic**
'55 *Sammy Davis, Jr.*
'58 *Louis Prima & Keely Smith*
'61 *Bobby Rydell*
'60 **That Old Feeling** *Kitty Kallen*
'81 **That Old Song** *Ray Parker Jr.*
'77 **That Smell** *Lynyrd Skynyrd*
'62 **That Stranger Used To Be My Girl**
  *Trade Martin*
'93 **That Summer** *Garth Brooks*
'63 **That Sunday, That Summer**
  *Nat King Cole*
'86 **That Was Then, This Is Now**
  *Monkees*
'85 **That Was Yesterday** *Foreigner*
'02 **That'd Be Alright** *Alan Jackson*
 **That'll Be The Day**
'57 *Crickets*
'76 *Linda Ronstadt*
 **That's All**
'56 *"Tennessee" Ernie Ford*
'83 *Genesis*
55 **That's All I Want From You**
  *Jaye P. Morgan*
'54 **That's All Right** *Elvis Presley*
'56 **That's All There Is To That**
  *Nat "King" Cole/Four Knights*
'60 **That's All You Gotta Do** *Brenda Lee*
'95 **That's As Close As I'll Get To
  Loving You** *Aaron Tippin*
'81 **That's Entertainment** *Jam*
'63 **That's How Heartaches Are Made**
  *Baby Washington*
'61 **That's It - I Quit - I'm Movin' On**
  *Sam Cooke*
'66 **That's Life** *Frank Sinatra*
'83 **That's Love** *Jim Capaldi*
'87 **That's My Job** *Conway Twitty*
'59 **That's My Little Suzie** *Ritchie Valens*
'94 **That's My Story** *Collin Raye*
'62 **That's Old Fashioned (That's The
  Way Love Should Be)**
  *Everly Brothers*
'77 **That's Rock 'N' Roll** *Shaun Cassidy*
'01 **That's The Joint** *Funky 4 + 1*

 **That's The Way**
'89 *Katrina & The Waves*
'00 *Jo Dee Messina*
'64 **That's The Way Boys Are**
  *Lesley Gore*
'71 **That's The Way I Feel About Cha**
  *Bobby Womack*
'75 **That's The Way (I Like It)**
  *KC & The Sunshine Band*
'71 **That's The Way I've Always Heard It
  Should Be** *Carly Simon*
'99 **That's The Way It Is** *Celine Dion*
'93 **That's The Way Love Goes**
  *Janet Jackson*
 **That's The Way Love Is**
'63 *Bobby Bland*
'69 *Marvin Gaye*
'75 **That's The Way Of The World**
  *Earth, Wind & Fire*
'85 **That's What Friends Are For**
  *Dionne Warwick*
'61 **That's What Girls Are Made For**
  *Spinners*
'05 **That's What I Love About Sunday**
  *Craig Morgan*
'04 **That's What It's All About**
  *Brooks & Dunn*
'93 **That's What Love Can Do**
  *Boy Krazy*
'87 **That's What Love Is All About**
  *Michael Bolton*
'91 **That's What Love Is For** *Amy Grant*
'64 **That's What Love Is Made Of**
  *Miracles*
'02 **That's When I Love You** *Phil Vassar*
'75 **That's When The Music Takes Me**
  *Neil Sedaka*
'57 **That's When Your Heartaches
  Begin** *Elvis Presley*
'70 **That's Where I Went Wrong**
  *Poppy Family*
'76 **That's Where The Happy People Go**
  *Trammps*
'59 **That's Why (I Love You So)**
  *Jackie Wilson*
'98 **That's Why I'm Here** *Kenny Chesney*
'60 **Theme For Young Lovers**
  *Percy Faith*
 **Theme From A Summer Place**
'60 *Percy Faith*
'65 *Lettermen*
'62 **Theme From Ben Casey** *Valjean*
'73 **Theme From Cleopatra Jones**
  *Joe Simon*
 **Theme From Close Encounters**
'77 *John Williams*
'78 *Meco*
'61 **Theme From Dixie** *Duane Eddy*
'62 **Theme From Dr. Kildare (Three
  Stars Will Shine Tonight)**
  *Richard Chamberlain*
'81 **Theme From Greatest American
  Hero (Believe It Or Not)**
  *Joey Scarbury*
'81 **Theme From Hill Street Blues**
  *Mike Post*
'75 **Theme From Jaws (Main Title)**
  *John Williams*
 **Theme From Love Story**
'71 *Francis Lai*
'71 *Henry Mancini*
'71 *Andy Williams [Where Do I Begin)]*
'82 **(Theme From) Magnum P.I.**
  *Mike Post*
'75 **Theme From Mahogany (Do You
  Know Where You're Going To)**
  *Diana Ross*
'96 **Theme From Mission: Impossible**
  *Adam Clayton & Larry Mullen*
'80 **Theme From New York, New York**
  *Frank Sinatra*
'71 **Theme From Shaft** *Isaac Hayes*
'71 **Theme From Summer Of '42**
  *Peter Nero*
'75 **Theme From S.W.A.T.**
  *Rhythm Heritage*
'60 **Theme From The Apartment**
  *Ferrante & Teicher*

'80 **Theme From The Dukes Of Hazzard
  (Good Ol' Boys)** *Waylon Jennings*
'72 **Theme From The Men** *Isaac Hayes*
'66 **Theme From The Monkees** *Monkees*
'56 **Theme From The Proud Ones**
  *Nelson Riddle*
 **Theme From The Three Penny
  Opera ..see: Moritat**
'60 **Theme From The Unforgiven (The
  Need For Love)** *Don Costa*
'68 **Theme From Valley Of The Dolls**
  *Dionne Warwick*
'78 **Theme From Which Way Is Up**
  *Stargard*
'78 **Themes From The Wizard Of Oz**
  *Meco*
'74 **Then Came You**
  *Dionne Warwick & Spinners*
'63 **Then He Kissed Me** *Crystals*
'99 **Then The Morning Comes**
  *Smash Mouth*
'97 **Then What?** *Clay Walker*
'67 **Then You Can Tell Me Goodbye**
  *Casinos*
'92 **There Ain't Nothin' Wrong With The
  Radio** *Aaron Tippin*
'97 **There Goes** *Alan Jackson*
'75 **There Goes Another Love Song**
  *Outlaws*
 **There Goes My Baby**
'59 *Drifters*
'84 *Donna Summer*
'98 *Trisha Yearwood*
 **There Goes My Everything**
'67 *Engelbert Humperdinck*
'70 *Elvis Presley*
'58 **There Goes My Heart** *Joni James*
'03 **There Goes My Life** *Kenny Chesney*
'63 **There! I've Said It Again**
  *Bobby Vinton*
'68 **There Is** *Dells*
'67 **There Is A Mountain** *Donovan*
'00 **There Is No Arizona** *Jamie O'Neal*
'73 **There It Is** *Tyrone Davis*
'59 **There Must Be A Way** *Joni James*
'85 **There Must Be An Angel (Playing
  With My Heart)** *Eurythmics*
 **There She Goes**
'60 *Jerry Wallace*
'91 *La's*
'99 *Sixpence None The Richer*
'01 *Babyface*
'60 **(There Was A) Tall Oak Tree**
  *Dorsey Burnette*
'68 **There Was A Time** *James Brown*
'91 **There Will Never Be Another
  Tonight** *Bryan Adams*
'66 **There Will Never Be Another You**
  *Chris Montez*
'74 **There Won't Be Anymore**
  *Charlie Rich*
'00 **There You Go** *P!nk*
'01 **There You'll Be** *Faith Hill*
'86 **There'll Be Sad Songs (To Make
  You Cry)** *Billy Ocean*
'69 **There'll Come A Time** *Betty Everett*
'78 **There'll Never Be** *Switch*
'57 **There's A Gold Mine In The Sky**
  *Pat Boone*
 **There's A Kind Of Hush (All Over
  The World)**
'67 *Herman's Hermits*
'76 *Carpenters*
'60 **There's A Moon Out Tonight** *Capris*
'89 **There's A Tear In My Beer** *Hank
  Williams Jr. with Hank Williams Sr.*
 **(There's) Always Something There
  To Remind Me**
'70 *R.B. Greaves*
'83 *Naked Eyes*
'68 **There's Gonna Be A Showdown**
  *Archie Bell*
'03 **(there's gotta be) More To Life**
  *Stacie Orrico*
'81 **(There's) No Gettin' Over Me**
  *Ronnie Milsap*

'73 **There's No Me Without You** Manhattans
'61 **There's No Other (Like My Baby)** Crystals
'85 **There's No Way** Alabama
'87 **There's Nothing Better Than Love** Luther Vandross with Gregory Hines
'58 **There's Only One Of You** Four Lads
'60 **There's Something On Your Mind** Bobby Marchan
'87 **There's The Girl** Heart
'98 **There's Your Trouble** Dixie Chicks
'92 **These Are Days** 10,000 Maniacs
'98 **These Are The Times** Dru Hill
'63 **These Arms Of Mine** Otis Redding
'66 **These Boots Are Made For Walkin'** Nancy Sinatra
'02 **These Days** Rascal Flatts
'86 **These Dreams** Heart
**These Eyes**
'69 Guess Who?
'69 Jr. Walker
'68 **They Can't Take That Away From Me** Tony Bennett
'96 **They Don't Care About Us** Michael Jackson
**They Don't Know**
'84 Tracey Ullman
'98 Jon B
'75 **They Just Can't Stop It the (Games People Play)** Spinners
'97 **They Like It Slow** H-Town
'70 **(They Long To Be) Close To You** Carpenters
'92 **They Want EFX** Das EFX
'89 **They Want Money** Kool Moe Dee
'66 **They're Coming To Take Me Away, Ha-Haaa!** Napoleon XIV
'72 **Thick As A Brick** Jethro Tull
'90 **Thieves In The Temple** Prince
**Thin Line Between Love & Hate**
'71 Persuaders
'96 H-Town
'72 **Thing Called Love** Johnny Cash
'62 **Things** Bobby Darin
'85 **Things Can Only Get Better** Howard Jones
'67 **Things I Should Have Said** Grass Roots
'68 **Things I'd Like To Say** New Colony Six
'91 **Things That Make You Go Hmmmm...** C + C Music Factory
'77 **Things We Do For Love** 10 CC
'97 **Things'll Never Change** E-40
**Think**
'60 James Brown
'64 Brenda Lee
'68 Aretha Franklin
'90 Information Society
'80 **Think About Me** Fleetwood Mac
'66 **Think I'll Go Somewhere And Cry Myself To Sleep** Al Martino
'82 **Think I'm In Love** Eddie Money
**Think It Over**
'58 Crickets
'78 Cheryl Ladd
'83 **Think Of Laura** Christopher Cross
'61 **Think Twice** Brook Benton
'95 **Thinkin' About You** Trisha Yearwood
'92 **Thinkin' Back** Color Me Badd
'98 **Thinkin' Bout It** Gerald Levert
'94 **Thinkin' Problem** David Ball
**Thinking Of You**
'73 Loggins & Messina
'88 Earth, Wind & Fire
'89 Sa-Fire
'97 Tony Toni Toné
**Third Rate Romance**
'75 Amazing Rhythm Aces
'94 Sammy Kershaw
'94 **Third Rock From The Sun** Joe Diffie
'67 **Third Stone From The Sun** Jimi Hendrix

'79 **Third Time Lucky (First Time I Was A Fool)** Foghat
'72 **Thirteen** Big Star
'72 **30 Days In The Hole** Jimi Hendrix
'55 **Thirty Days (To Come Back Home)** Chuck Berry
'96 **Thirty-Three** Smashing Pumpkins
'97 **32 Flavors** Alana Davis
'95 **This Ain't A Love Song** Bon Jovi
'97 **(This Ain't) No Thinkin' Thing** Trace Adkins
'80 **This Beat Goes On** [medley] Kings
'60 **This Bitter Earth** Dinah Washington
'86 **This Could Be The Night** Loverboy
'65 **This Diamond Ring** Gary Lewis
'94 **This DJ** Warren G
'66 **This Door Swings Both Ways** Herman's Hermits
'74 **This Flight Tonight** Nazareth
'59 **This Friendly World** Fabian
'69 **This Girl Is A Woman Now** Gary Puckett
**This Guy's [Girl's] In Love With You**
'68 Herb Alpert
'69 Dionne Warwick
'74 **This Heart** Gene Redding
'90 **This House** Tracie Spencer
'00 **This I Promise You** *NSYNC
'59 **This I Swear** Skyliners
'95 **This Is A Call** Foo Fighters
'63 **This Is All I Ask** Tony Bennett
'96 **This Is For The Lover In You** Babyface
'95 **This Is How We Do It** Montell Jordan
'79 **This Is It** Kenny Loggins
'01 **This Is Me** Dream
'68 **This Is My Country** Impressions
'67 **This Is My Song** Petula Clark
'84 **This Is Not A Love Song** Public Image Ltd.
'85 **This Is Not America** David Bowie & Pat Metheny Group
'03 **This Is The Night** Clay Aiken
'90 **This Is The Right Time** Lisa Stansfield
'86 **This Is The Time** Billy Joel
'77 **This Is The Way That I Feel** Marie Osmond
'04 **This Is Your Life** Switchfoot
'96 **This Is Your Night** Amber
'99 **This Is Your Time** Michael W. Smith
'98 **This Kiss** Faith Hill
'95 **This Lil' Game We Play** Subway
'65 **This Little Bird** Marianne Faithull
**This Little Girl**
'63 Dion
'81 Gary U.S. Bonds
'58 **This Little Girl Of Mine** Everly Brothers
'58 **This Little Girl's Gone Rockin'** Ruth Brown
'04 **This Love** Maroon5
**This Magic Moment**
'60 Drifters
'68 Jay & The Americans
'82 **This Man Is Mine** Heart
'76 **This Masquerade** George Benson
'78 **This Moment In Time** Engelbert Humperdinck
**This Night Won't Last Forever**
'79 Michael Johnson
'97 Sawyer Brown
'66 **This Old Heart Of Mine** Isley Brothers
'54 **This Ole House** Rosemary Clooney
'89 **This One's For The Children** New Kids On The Block
'03 **This One's For The Girls** Martina McBride
'76 **This One's For You** Barry Manilow
'59 **This Should Go On Forever** Rod Bernard
'76 **This Song** George Harrison

**This Time**
'61 Troy Shondell
'80 John Cougar Mellencamp
'83 Bryan Adams
'88 Kiara (with Shanice)
'94 Sawyer Brown
'00 **This Time Around** Hanson
'89 **This Time I Know It's For Real** Donna Summer
'78 **This Time I'm In It For Love** Player
'92 **This Used To Be My Playground** Madonna
'68 **This Wheel's On Fire** Band
'75 **This Will Be** Natalie Cole
'84 **This Woman** Kenny Rogers
'95 **This Woman And This Man** Clay Walker
'72 **This World** Staple Singers
'03 **Thoia Thoing** R. Kelly
'00 **Thong Song** Sisqó
'92 **Thorn In My Pride** Black Crowes
'63 **Those Lazy-Hazy-Crazy Days Of Summer** Nat King Cole
'61 **Those Oldies But Goodies (Remind Me Of You)** Little Caesar & The Romans
'79 **Those Shoes** Eagles
'68 **Those Were The Days** Mary Hopkin
'64 **Thou Shalt Not Steal** Dick & DeeDee
'92 **Thought I'd Died And Gone To Heaven** Bryan Adams
'02 **Thousand Miles** Vanessa Carlton
'56 **Thousand Miles Away** Heartbeats
'93 **Thousand Miles From Nowhere** Dwight Yoakam
'60 **Thousand Stars** Kathy Young
'97 **3 AM** Matchbox 20
'91 **3 A.M. Eternal** KLF
'59 **Three Bells** Browns
'61 **Three Hearts In A Tangle** Roy Drusky
'77 **Three Little Birds** Bob Marley
'67 **Three Little Fishes** [medley] Mitch Ryder
**Three Little Pigs**
'74 Cheech & Chong
'93 Green Jelly
'60 **Three Nights A Week** Fats Domino
'65 **Three O'Clock In The Morning** Bert Kaempfert
'74 **Three Ring Circus** Blue Magic
'59 **Three Stars** Tommy Dee with Carol Kay
'60 **Three Steps To Heaven** Eddie Cochran
'78 **Three Times A Lady** Commodores
'80 **Three Times In Love** Tommy James
'64 **Three Window Coupe** Rip Chords
'03 **Three Wooden Crosses** Randy Travis
'69 **Thrill Is Gone** B.B. King
'84 **Thriller** Michael Jackson
'89 **Through The Storm** Aretha Franklin & Elton John
'03 **Through The Wire** Kanye West
'81 **Through The Years** Kenny Rogers
'86 **Throwing It All Away** Genesis
'94 **thuggish-ruggish-Bone** Bone Thugs-N-Harmony
'02 **Thugz Mansion** 2Pac
'72 **Thunder And Lightning** Chi Coltrane
'77 **Thunder In My Heart** Leo Sayer
'77 **Thunder Island** Jay Ferguson
'75 **Thunder Road** Bruce Springsteen
'91 **Thunder Rolls** Garth Brooks
'65 **Thunderball** Tom Jones
'90 **Thunderstruck** AC/DC
'85 **Thy Word** Amy Grant
'90 **Tic-Tac-Toe** Kyper
'65 **Ticket To Ride** Beatles
'80 **Tide Is High** Blondie
'73 **Tie A Yellow Ribbon Round The Ole Oak Tree** Dawn

'63 **Tie Me Kangaroo Down, Sport** *Rolf Harris*
'77 **Tie Your Mother Down** *Queen*
'60 **Ties That Bind** *Brook Benton*
'59 **Tiger** *Fabian*
'72 **Tight Rope** *Leon Russell*
'68 **Tighten Up** *Archie Bell*
'70 **Tighter, Tighter** *Alive & Kicking*
'59 **Tijuana Jail** *Kingston Trio*
'65 **Tijuana Taxi** *Herb Alpert*
'96 **Til I Hear It From You** *Gin Blossoms*
'59 **('Til) I Kissed You** *Everly Brothers*
'85 **'Til My Baby Comes Home** *Luther Vandross*
'95 **'Til You Do Me Right** *After 7*
'57 **Till**
    *Roger Williams*
'61    *Angels*
'68    *Vogues*
'62 **Till Death Do Us Part** *Bob Braun*
'88 **Till I Loved You** *Barbra Streisand & Don Johnson*
'63 **Till Then** *Classics*
'59 **Till There Was You** *Anita Bryant*
'94 **Till You Love Me** *Reba McEntire*
'89 **Timber, I'm Falling In Love** *Patty Loveless*
    **Time**
'66    *Pozo-Seco Singers*
'73    *Pink Floyd*
'81    *Alan Parsons Project*
'95    *Hootie & The Blowfish*
    **Time After Time**
'66    *Chris Montez*
'84    *Cyndi Lauper*
'90    *Timmy -T-*
'98    *Inoj*
'93 **Time And Chance** *Color Me Badd*
'71 **Time And Love** *Barbra Streisand*
'60 **Time And The River** *Nat King Cole*
'88 **Time And Tide** *Basia*
'83 **Time (Clock Of The Heart)** *Culture Club*
'90 **Time For Letting Go** *Jude Cole*
    **Time For Livin'**
'68    *Association*
'74    *Sly & The Family Stone*
'66 **Time For Love** *Tony Bennett*
'78 **Time For Me To Fly** *REO Speedwagon*
'68 **Time Has Come Today** *Chambers Brothers*
'73 **Time In A Bottle** *Jim Croce*
'64 **Time Is On My Side** *Rolling Stones*
'69 **Time Is Tight** *Booker T. & The M.G.'s*
'80 **Time Is Time** *Andy Gibb*
'91 **Time, Love And Tenderness** *Michael Bolton*
'96 **Time Marches On** *Tracy Lawrence*
'69 **Time Of The Season** *Zombies*
'81 **Time Out Of Mind** *Steely Dan*
'78 **Time Passages** *Al Stewart*
'67 **Time, Time** *Ed Ames*
'73 **Time To Get Down** *O'Jays*
'70 **Time To Kill** *Band*
'83 **Time Will Reveal** *DeBarge*
'66 **Time Won't Let Me** *Outsiders*
'75 **Times Of Your Life** *Paul Anka*
'64 **Times They Are A-Changin'** *Bob Dylan*
'71 **Timothy** *Buoys*
'74 **Tin Man** *America*
'55 **Tina Marie** *Perry Como*
'71 **Tiny Dancer** *Elton John*
'68 **Tip-Toe Thru' The Tulips With Me** *Tiny Tim*
'04 **Tipsy** *J-Kwon*
'71 **Tired Of Being Alone** *Al Green*
'80 **Tired Of Toein' The Line** *Rocky Burnette*
'65 **Tired Of Waiting For You** *Kinks*
'62 **To A Sleeping Beauty** *Jimmy Dean*
'84 **To All The Girls I've Loved Before** *Julio Iglesias & Willie Nelson*
'86 **To Be A Lover** *Billy Idol*

'58 **To Be Loved** *Jackie Wilson*
'96 **To Be Loved By You** *Wynonna*
'91 **To Be With You** *Mr. Big*
    **To Each His Own**
'60    *Platters*
'68    *Frankie Laine*
'75    *Faith Hope & Charity*
'67 **To Give (The Reason I Live)** *Frankie Valli*
    **To Know You [Him] Is To Love You [Him]**
'58    *Teddy Bears*
'65    *Peter & Gordon*
'69    *Bobby Vinton*
'73    *B.B. King*
    **To Love Somebody**
'67    *Bee Gees*
'92    *Michael Bolton*
'98 **To Love You More** *Celine Dion*
'98 **To Make You Feel My Love** *Garth Brooks*
'87 **To Prove My Love** *Michael Cooper*
'67 **To Sir With Love** *Lulu*
'69 **To Susan On The West Coast Waiting** *Donovan*
'57 **To The Aisle** *Five Satins*
'74 **To The Door Of The Sun (Alle Porte Del Sole)** *Al Martino*
'56 **To The Ends Of The Earth** *Nat "King" Cole*
'97 **To The Moon And Back** *Savage Garden*
'68 **To Wait For Love** *Herb Alpert*
'02 **To Where You Are** *Josh Groban*
'56 **To You, My Love** *Nick Noble*
'71 **Toast And Marmalade For Tea** *Tin Tin*
'64 **Tobacco Road** *Nashville Teens*
    **Today**
'64    *New Christy Minstrels*
'93    *Smashing Pumpkins*
'63 **(Today I Met) The Boy I'm Gonna Marry** *Darlene Love*
'76 **Today's The Day** *America*
    **Together**
'61    *Connie Francis*
'80    *Tierra*
    **Together Again**
'64    *Buck Owens*
'66    *Ray Charles*
'97    *Janet Jackson*
    **Together Forever**
'88    *Rick Astley*
'91    *Lisette Melendez*
'72 **Together Let's Find Love** *5th Dimension*
'60 **Togetherness** *Frankie Avalon*
'63 **Tom Cat** *Rooftop Singers*
'58 **Tom Dooley** *Kingston Trio*
'81 **Tom Sawyer** *Rush*
'90 **Tom's Diner** *D.N.A. Feat. Suzanne Vega*
    **Tomorrow**
'67    *Strawberry Alarm Clock*
'92    *Morrissey*
'95    *Silverchair*
'90 **Tomorrow (A Better You, Better Me)** *Quincy Jones/Tevin Campbell*
'86 **Tomorrow Doesn't Matter Tonight** *Starship*
'88 **Tomorrow People** *Ziggy Marley*
    **Tonight**
'61    *Ferrante & Teicher*
'84    *Kool & The Gang*
'90    *New Kids On The Block*
'61 **Tonight (Could Be The Night)** *Velvets*
'83 **Tonight, I Celebrate My Love** *Peabo Bryson/Roberta Flack*
'61 **Tonight I Fell In Love** *Tokens*
'82 **Tonight I'm Yours (Don't Hurt Me)** *Rod Stewart*
'61 **Tonight My Love, Tonight** *Paul Anka*
'85 **Tonight She Comes** *Cars*

    **Tonight, Tonight [Tonite, Tonite]**
'57    *Mello-Kings*
'96    *Smashing Pumpkins*
'87 **Tonight, Tonight, Tonight** *Genesis*
    **Tonight You Belong To Me**
'56    *Patience & Prudence*
'56    *Lennon Sisters*
    **Tonight's The [Tonite's Tha] Night**
'60    *Shirelles*
'65    *Solomon Burke*
'76    *Rod Stewart*
'95 **Tonite's Tha Night** *Kris Kross*
'01 **Too Bad** *Nickelback*
'92 **Too Busy Being In Love** *Doug Stone*
'69 **Too Busy Thinking About My Baby** *Marvin Gaye*
'98 **Too Close** *Next*
'56 **Too Close For Comfort** *Eydie Gorme*
'90 **Too Cold At Home** *Mark Chesnutt*
'92 **Too Funky** *George Michael*
'97 **Too Gone, Too Long** *En Vogue*
    **Too Hot**
'80    *Kool & The Gang*
'95    *Coolio*
'77 **Too Hot Ta Trot** *Commodores*
'85 **Too Late For Goodbyes** *Julian Lennon*
'90 **Too Late To Say Goodbye** *Richard Marx*
'72 **Too Late To Turn Back Now** *Cornelius Brothers & Sister Rose*
'91 **2 Legit 2 Quit** *Hammer*
    **Too Many Fish In The Sea**
'64    *Marvelettes*
'67    *Mitch Ryder [medley]*
'65 **Too Many Rivers** *Brenda Lee*
'91 **Too Many Walls** *Cathy Dennis*
'92 **Too Many Ways To Fall** *Arc Angels*
    **Too Much**
'57    *Elvis Presley*
'96    *Dave Matthews Band*
'98    *Spice Girls*
'88 **Too Much Ain't Enough Love** *Jimmy Barnes*
'78 **Too Much Heaven** *Bee Gees*
'67 **Too Much Of Nothing** *Peter, Paul & Mary*
'92 **Too Much Passion** *Smithereens*
'68 **Too Much Talk** *Paul Revere & The Raiders*
'60 **Too Much Tequila** *Champs*
'81 **Too Much Time On My Hands** *Styx*
'78 **Too Much, Too Little, Too Late** *Johnny Mathis/ Deniece Williams*
'76 **Too Old To Rock 'N' Roll: Too Young To Die** *Jethro Tull*
'74 **Too Rolling Stoned** *Robin Trower*
'83 **Too Shy** *Kajagoogoo*
'81 **Too Tight** *Con Funk Shun*
'68 **Too Weak To Fight** *Clarence Carter*
'72 **Too Young** *Donny Osmond*
'56 **Too Young To Go Steady** *Nat "King" Cole*
'78 **Took The Last Train** *David Gates*
'94 **Tootsee Roll** *69 Boyz*
'91 **Top Of The Pops** *Smithereens*
    **Top Of The World**
'73    *Carpenters*
'91    *Van Halen*
'58 **Topsy II** *Cozy Cole*
    **Torero**
'58    *Renato Carosone*
'58    *Julius LaRosa*
    **Torn**
'98    *Creed*
'98    *Natalie Imbruglia*
'76 **Torn Between Two Lovers** *Mary MacGregor*
'59 **Torquay** *Fireballs*
    **Torture**
'62    *Kris Jensen*
'84    *Jacksons*
'61 **Tossin' And Turnin'** *Bobby Lewis*

244

**Total Eclipse Of The Heart**
'83 *Bonnie Tyler*
'95 *Nicki French*
'74 **Touch A Hand, Make A Friend**
*Staple Singers*
'80 **Touch And Go** *Cars*
'98 **Touch It** *Monifah*
**Touch Me**
'68 *Doors*
'74 *Fancy*
'91 **Touch Me (All Night Long)**
*Cathy Dennis*
'86 **Touch Me (I Want Your Body)**
*Samantha Fox*
'73 **Touch Me In The Morning**
*Diana Ross*
'96 **Touch Me Tease Me** *Case*
'81 **Touch Me When We're Dancing**
*Carpenters*
'87 **Touch Of Grey** *Grateful Dead*
'97 **Touch, Peel And Stand**
*Days Of The New*
'61 **Touchables In Brooklyn**
*Dickie Goodman*
'85 **Tough All Over** *John Cafferty*
'03 **Tough Little Boys** *Gary Allan*
'61 **Tower Of Strength** *Gene McDaniels*
'61 **Town Without Pity** *Gene Pitney*
'04 **Toxic** *Britney Spears*
'02 **Toxicity** *System Of A Down*
'89 **Toy Soldiers** *Martika*
'56 **Tra La La** *Georgia Gibbs*
'63 **Tra La La La Suzy** *Dean & Jean*
**Traces**
'69 *Classics IV*
'69 *Lettermen [medley]*
**Tracks Of My Tears**
'65 *Miracles*
'67 *Johnny Rivers*
'75 *Linda Ronstadt*
'69 **Tracy** *Cuff Links*
'60 **Tracy's Theme** *Spencer Ross*
'02 **Trade It All** *Fabolous*
**Tragedy**
'59 *Thomas Wayne*
'61 *Fleetwoods*
'79 *Bee Gees*
'84 *John Hunter*
'80 **Train In Vain (Stand By Me)** *Clash*
**Train Kept A Rollin'**
'56 *Johnny Burnette Trio*
'65 *Yardbirds*
'74 · *Aerosmith*
'60 **Train Of Love** *Annette*
'74 **Train Of Thought** *Cher*
'79 **Train, Train** *Blackfoot*
'66 **Trains And Boats And Planes**
*Dionne Warwick*
'67 **Tramp** *Otis Redding & Carla Thomas*
'75 **Trampled Under Foot** *Led Zeppelin*
'56 **Transfusion** *Nervous Norvus*
'70 **Transylvania Boogie**
*Frank Zappa*
'61 **Transistor Sister** *Freddy Cannon*
'85 **Trapped** *Bruce Springsteen*
'71 **Trapped By A Thing Called Love**
*Denise LaSalle*
'93 **Trashy Woman**
*Confederate Railroad*
'70 **Travelin' Band**
*Creedence Clearwater Revival*
**Travelin' Man**
'61 *Ricky Nelson*
'75 *Bob Seger*
'02 **Travelin' Soldier** *Dixie Chicks*
'56 **Treasure Of Love** *Clyde McPhatter*
'58 **Treasure Of Your Love**
*Eileen Rodgers*
**Treat Her Like A Lady**
'71 *Cornelius Brothers & Sister Rose*
'84 *Temptations*
**Treat Her Right**
'65 *Roy Head*
'96 *Sawyer Brown*
'57 **Treat Me Nice** *Elvis Presley*
'81 **Treat Me Right** *Pat Benatar*

'94 **Tremor Christ** *Pearl Jam*
'96 **Tres Delinquentes**
*Delinquent Habits*
'61 **Triangle** *Janie Grant*
'80 **Trickle Trickle** *Manhattan Transfer*
**Tricky**
'56 *Gus Jinkins*
'57 *Ralph Marterie*
'98 **Trippin'** *Total*
'96 **Trippin' On A Hole In A Paper Heart**
*Stone Temple Pilots*
'72 **Troglodyte (Cave Man)**
*Jimmy Castor Bunch*
'61 **Trolley Song** *Judy Garland [live]*
'85 **Trommeltanz (Din Daa Daa)**
*George Kranz*
'75 **T-R-O-U-B-L-E** *Elvis Presley*
**Trouble**
'81 *Lindsey Buckingham*
'88 *Nia Peeples*
'60 **Trouble In Paradise** *Crests*
'72 **Trouble Man** *Marvin Gaye*
'89 **Trouble Me** *10,000 Maniacs*
'70 **Truckin'** *Grateful Dead*
**True**
'83 *Spandau Ballet*
'04 *Ryan Cabrera*
'86 **True Blue** *Madonna*  •
'90 **True Blue Love** *Lou Gramm*
**True Colors**
'86 *Cyndi Lauper*
'98 *Phil Collins*
'87 **True Faith** *New Order*
'69 **True Grit** *Glen Campbell*
**True Love**
'56 *Bing Crosby & Grace Kelly*
'56 *Jane Powell*
'88 *Glenn Frey*
'63 **True Love Never Runs Smooth**
*Gene Pitney*
**True Love Ways**
'59 *Buddy Holly*
'65 *Peter & Gordon*
'82 **Truly** *Lionel Richie*
'97 **Truly Madly Deeply** *Savage Garden*
'61 **Trust In Me** *Etta James*
'91 **Truth, The** *TAMI Show*
'05 **Truth Is** *Fantasia*
'69 **Try A Little Kindness**
*Glen Campbell*
**Try A Little Tenderness**
'66 *Otis Redding*
'69 *Three Dog Night*
**Try Again**
'83 *Champaign*
'00 *Aaliyah*
'64 **Try It Baby** *Marvin Gaye*
'69 **Try (Just A Little Bit Harder)** *Janis
Joplin*
'58 **Try Me** *James Brown*
'58 **Try The Impossible** *Lee Andrews*
'75 **Try To Remember [medley]**
*Gladys Knight*
'66 **Try Too Hard** *Dave Clark Five*
'94 **Tryin' To Get Over You** *Vince Gill*
'76 **Tryin' To Get The Feeling Again**
*Barry Manilow*
'81 **Tryin' To Live My Life Without You**
*Bob Seger*
'77 **Tryin' To Love Two** *William Bell*
'73 **Trying To Hold On To My Woman**
*Lamont Dozier*
'70 **Trying To Make A Fool Of Me**
*Delfonics*
'81 **Tube Snake Boogie** *ZZ Top*
'97 **Tubthumping** *Chumbawamba*
'74 **Tubular Bells** *Mike Oldfield*
'96 **Tucker's Town**
*Hootie & The Blowfish*
'59 **Tucumcari** *Jimmie Rodgers*
'68 **Tuesday Afternoon (Forever
Afternoon)** *Moody Blues*
'61 **Tuff** *Ace Cannon*
'86 **Tuff Enuff** *Fabulous Thunderbirds*

**Tulsa Time**
'78 *Don Williams*
'80 *Eric Clapton*
'88 **Tumblin' Down** *Ziggy Marley*
**Tumbling Dice**
'72 *Rolling Stones*
'78 *Linda Ronstadt*
'58 **Tumbling Tumbleweeds**
*Billy Vaughn*
'87 **Tunnel Of Love** *Bruce Springsteen*
'71 **Tupelo Honey** *Van Morrison*
'63 **Turn Around** *Dick & DeeDee*
'68 **Turn Around, Look At Me** *Vogues*
'70 **Turn Back The Hands Of Time**
*Tyrone Davis*
'66 **Turn-Down Day** *Cyrkle*
'80 **Turn It On Again** *Genesis*
'98 **Turn It Up [Remix]/Fire It Up**
*Busta Rhymes*
**Turn Me Loose**
'59 *Fabian*
'81 *Loverboy*
'04 **Turn Me On** *Kevin Lyttle*
'97 **Turn My Head** *Live*
'01 **Turn Off The Light** *Nelly Furtado*
'79 **Turn Off The Lights**
*Teddy Pendergrass*
**Turn On Your Love Light**
'61 *Bobby Bland*
'70 *Grateful Dead*
**Turn The Beat Around**
'76 *Vicki Sue Robinson*
'94 *Gloria Estefan*
**Turn The Page**
'76 *Bob Seger*
'98 *Metallica*
'67 **Turn The World Around**
*Eddy Arnold*
'77 **Turn To Stone**
*Electric Light Orchestra*
'84 **Turn To You** *Go-Go's*
'65 **Turn! Turn! Turn!** *Byrds*
'84 **Turn Up The Radio** *Autograph*
'81 **Turn Your Love Around**
*George Benson*
'89 **Turned Away** *Chuckii Booker*
'80 **Turning Japanese** *Vapors*
'75 **Turning Point** *Tyrone Davis*
'90 **Turtle Power!** *Partners In Kryme*
'58 **Turvy II** *Cozy Cole*
'75 **Tush** *ZZ Top*
'79 **Tusk** *Fleetwood Mac*
**Tutti' Frutti**
'56 *Pat Boone*
'56 *Little Richard*
**Tweedlee Dee**
'55 *LaVern Baker*
'55 *Georgia Gibbs*
**Twelfth Of Never**
'57 *Johnny Mathis*
'73 *Donny Osmond*
'67 **Twelve Thirty (Young Girls Are
Coming To The Canyon)**
*Mamas & The Papas*
'69 **Twenty-Five Miles** *Edwin Starr*
'70 **25 Or 6 To 4** *Chicago*
'57 **Twenty Flight Rock** *Eddie Cochran*
'63 **Twenty Four Hours From Tulsa**
*Gene Pitney*
'99 **24/7** *Kevon Edmonds*
'63 **Twenty Miles** *Chubby Checker*
'03 **21 Questions** *50 Cent*
'64 **20-75** *Willie Mitchell*
'98 **26¢** *Wilkinsons*
'58 **26 Miles (Santa Catalina)**
*Four Preps*
'81 **Twilight** *ELO*
'58 **Twilight Time** *Platters*
'87 **Twilight World** *Swing Out Sister*
'82 **Twilight Zone** *Golden Earring*
'80 **Twilight Zone/Twilight Tone**
*Manhattan Transfer*
'65 **Twine Time**
*Alvin Cash & The Crawlers*
'66 **Twinkle Toes** *Roy Orbison*

**Twist, The**
'60 *Chubby Checker*
'60 *Hank Ballard*
'88 *Fat Boys/Chubby Checker*
     *[Yo, Twist!]*
**Twist And Shout**
'62 *Isley Brothers*
'64 *Beatles*
'63 **Twist It Up** *Chubby Checker*
'83 **Twist Of Fate** *Olivia Newton-John*
'62 **Twist, Twist Senora**
     *Gary (U.S.) Bonds*
'96 **Twisted** *Keith Sweat*
'62 **Twistin' Matilda** *Jimmy Soul*
'62 **Twistin' Postman** *Marvelettes*
'62 **Twistin' The Night Away**
     *Sam Cooke*
'60 **Twistin' U.S.A.** *Danny & The Juniors*
'59 **Twixt Twelve And Twenty**
     *Pat Boone*
'88 **2 A.M.** *Teddy Pendergrass*
'97 **2 Become 1** *Spice Girls*
'56 **Two Different Worlds** *Don Rondo*
'71 **Two Divided By Love** *Grass Roots*
'78 **Two Doors Down** *Dolly Parton*
'63 **Two Faces Have I** *Lou Christie*
'75 **Two Fine People** *Cat Stevens*
**Two Hearts**
'55 *Pat Boone*
'81 *Stephanie Mills/Teddy Pendergrass*
'88 *Phil Collins*
'83 **Two Hearts Beat As One** *U2*
'82 **Two Less Lonely People In The**
     **World** *Air Supply*
'67 **Two Little Kids** *Peaches & Herb*
'62 **Two Lovers** *Mary Wells*
'88 **Two Occasions** *Deele*
'91 **Two Of A Kind, Workin' On A Full**
     **House** *Garth Brooks*
'86 **Two Of Hearts** *Stacey Q*
'78 **Two Out Of Three Ain't Bad**
     *Meat Loaf*
'86 **Two People** *Tina Turner*
'01 **Two People Fell In Love**
     *Brad Paisley*
'97 **Two Piña Coladas** *Garth Brooks*
'80 **Two Places At The Same Time**
     *Ray Parker Jr.*
'93 **Two Princes** *Spin Doctors*
'84 **Two Sides Of Love** *Sammy Hagar*
'92 **Two Sparrows In A Hurricane**
     *Tanya Tucker*
'93 **Two Steps Behind** *Def Leppard*
'99 **Two Teardrops** *Steve Wariner*
'84 **2000 Miles** *Pretenders*
**Two Tickets To Paradise**
'63 *Brook Benton*
'78 *Eddie Money*
'89 **Two To Make It Right** *Seduction*
'84 **Two Tribes**
     *Frankie Goes To Hollywood*
'02 **Two Wrongs** *Wyclef Jean*
'90 **Type** *Living Colour*
'86 **Typical Male** *Tina Turner*
'97 **Tyrone** *Erykah Badu*

# U

'05 **U Already Know** *112*
'90 **U Can't Touch This** *M.C. Hammer*
'02 **U Don't Have To Call** *Usher*
'05 **U Don't Know Me** *T.I.*
'01 **U Got It Bad** *Usher*
'87 **U Got The Look** *Prince*
'99 **U Know What's Up** *Donell Jones*
'04 **U Make Me Wanna** *Jadakiss*
'01 **U Remind Me** *Usher*
'94 **U Send Me Swingin'** *Mint Condition*
'04 **U Should've Known Better** *Monica*
'94 **U Will Know**
     *BMU (Black Men United)*
'68 **U.S. Male** *Elvis Presley*
'01 **Ugly** *Bubba Sparxxx*
'02 **Uh Huh** *B2K*
'59 **Uh! Oh!** *Nutty Squirrels*

'64 **Um, Um, Um, Um, Um, Um**
     *Major Lance*
'90 **Unanswered Prayers** *Garth Brooks*
**Unbelievable**
'91 *EMF*
'98 *Diamond Rio*
'89 **Unborn Heart** *Dan Hill*
'96 **Un-Break My Heart** *Toni Braxton*
'02 **Unbroken** *Tim McGraw*
'61 **Unchain My Heart** *Ray Charles*
'81 **Unchained** *Van Halen*
**Unchained Melody**
'55 *Les Baxter*
'55 *Roy Hamilton*
'55 *Al Hibbler*
'65 *Righteous Brothers*
'96 *LeAnn Rimes*
'71 **Uncle Albert/Admiral Halsey**
     *Paul & Linda McCartney*
'70 **Uncle John's Band**
     *Grateful Dead*
'00 **Unconditional** *Clay Davidson*
'66 **Under My Thumb**
     *Rolling Stones*
'72 **Under My Wheels** *Alice Cooper*
'81 **Under Pressure**
     *Queen & David Bowie*
'64 **Under The Boardwalk** *Drifters*
'92 **Under The Bridge**
     *Red Hot Chili Peppers*
'88 **Under The Milky Way** *Church*
'65 **Under Your Spell Again**
     *Johnny Rivers*
'77 **Undercover Angel** *Alan O'Day*
'83 **Undercover Of The Night**
     *Rolling Stones*
'02 **Underneath It All** *No Doubt*
'02 **Underneath Your Clothes** *Shakira*
'64 **Understand Your Man** *Johnny Cash*
**Understanding**
'84 *Bob Seger*
'93 *Xscape*
'94 **Undone-The Sweather Song**
'69 **Undun** *Guess Who*
'73 **Uneasy Rider** *Charlie Daniels*
**Unforgettable**
'59 *Dinah Washington*
'91 *Natalie Cole with Nat "King" Cole*
'91 **Unforgiven, The** *Metallica*
'97 **Unforgiven II** *Metallica*
'68 **Unicorn, The** *Irish Rovers*
'98 **Uninvited** *Alanis Morissette*
'76 **Union Man** *Cate Bros.*
'83 **Union Of The Snake** *Duran Duran*
'80 **United Together** *Aretha Franklin*
'70 **United We Stand**
     *Brotherhood Of Man*
'93 **U.N.I.T.Y.** *Queen Latifah*
'68 **Unknown Soldier** *Doors*
'99 **Unpretty** *TLC*
'90 **Unskinny Bop** *Poison*
'94 **Until I Fall Away** *Gin Blossoms*
'97 **Until I Find You Again** *Richard Marx*
'96 **Until It Sleeps** *Metallica*
'72 **Until It's Time For You To Go**
     *Elvis Presley*
'91 **Until She Comes** *Psychedelic Furs*
**Until You Come Back To Me (That's**
     **What I'm Gonna Do)**
'73 *Aretha Franklin*
'90 *Miki Howard*
'92 **Until Your Love Comes Back**
     **Around** *RTZ*
'00 **Untitled (How Does It Feel)**
     *D'Angelo*
'03 **Unwell** *Matchbox Twenty*
**Up All Night**
'81 *Boomtown Rats*
'90 *Slaughter*
'70 **Up Around The Bend**
     *Creedence Clearwater Revival*
'68 **Up From The Skies**
     *Jimi Hendrix*
'75 **Up In A Puff Of Smoke** *Polly Brown*
'97 **Up Jumps Da Boogie**
     *Magoo & Timbaland*

'69 **Up On Cripple Creek** *Band*
**Up On The Roof**
'62 *Drifters*
'79 *James Taylor*
'70 **Up The Ladder To The Roof**
     *Supremes*
'60 **Up Town** *Roy Orbison*
'67 **Up-Up And Away** *5th Dimension*
'82 **Up Where We Belong**
     *Joe Cocker & Jennifer Warnes*
'67 **Ups And Downs**
     *Paul Revere & The Raiders*
'80 **Upside Down** *Diana Ross*
'65 **Uptight (Everything's Alright)**
     *Stevie Wonder*
'62 **Uptown** *Crystals*
'77 **Uptown Festival (Motown Medley)**
     *Shalamar*
'83 **Uptown Girl** *Billy Joel*
'81 **Urgent** *Foreigner*
'73 **Us And Them** *Pink Floyd*
'72 **Use Me** *Bill Withers*
'78 **Use Ta Be My Girl** *O'Jays*
'65 **Use Your Head** *Mary Wells*
'96 **Use Your Heart** *SWV*
'60 **Utopia** *Frank Gari*

# V

**Vacation**
'62 *Connie Franics*
'82 *Go-Go's*
'97 **Valentine** *Martina McBride*
'87 **Valerie** *Steve Winwood [remix]*
'68 **Valleri** *Monkees*
'82 **Valley Girl** *Frank Zappa*
'57 **Valley Of Tears** *Fats Domino*
'88 **Valley Road** *Bruce Hornsby*
'84 **Valotte** *Julian Lennon*
'60 **Vaquero** *Fireballs*
'94 **Vasoline** *Stone Temple Pilots*
'70 **Vehicle** *Ides Of March*
'86 **Velcro Fly** *ZZ Top*
'72 **Ventura Highway** *America*
**Venus**
'59 *Frankie Avalon*
'69 *Shocking Blue*
'86 *Bananarama*
'75 **Venus And Mars Rock Show** *Wings*
'62 **Venus In Blue Jeans** *Jimmy Clanton*
'89 **Veronica** *Elvis Costello*
'05 **Vertigo** *U2*
'58 **Very Precious Love** *Ames Brothers*
'93 **Very Special** *Big Daddy Kane*
**Very Special Love**
'57 *Johnny Nash*
'58 *Debbie Reynolds*
'74 **Very Special Love Song**
     *Charlie Rich*
'92 **Vibeology** *Paula Abdul*
**Victim Of Love**
'77 *Eagles*
'79 *Elton John*
'87 *Bryan Adams*
'80 **Victims Of The Fury**
     *Robin Trower*
'70 **Victoria** *Kinks*
**Victory**
'86 *Kool & The Gang*
'98 *Puff Daddy*
'01 **Video** *India.Arie*
'79 **Video Killed The Radio Star**
     *Buggles*
'86 **Vienna Calling** *Falco*
'85 **View To A Kill** *Duran Duran*
'62 **Village Of Love** *Nathaniel Mayer*
'59 **Village Of St. Bernadette**
     *Andy Williams*
'72 **Vincent** *Don McLean*
'04 **Vindicated** *Dashboard Confessional*
'90 **Vision Of Love** *Mariah Carey*
'66 **Visions Of Johanna** *Bob Dylan*
'04 **Vitamin R (Leading Us Along)**
     *Chevelle*

**Viva Las Vegas**
'64   *Elvis Presley*
'92   *ZZ Top*
'70  **Viva Tirado** *El Chicano*
'99  **Vivrant Thing** *Q-Tip*
'90  **Vogue** *Madonna*
'81  **Voice, The** *Moody Blues*
'03  **Voice Within** *Christina Aguilera*
'79  **Voices** *Cheap Trick*
'85  **Voices Carry** *'Til Tuesday*
'89  **Voices Of Babylon** *Outfield*
'91  **Voices That Care** *Voices That Care*
    **Volare (Nel Blu Dipinto Di Blu)**
'58   *Dean Martin*
'58   *Domenico Modugno*
'60   *Bobby Rydell*
'75   *Al Martino*
'80  **Volcano** *Jimmy Buffett*
'69  **Volunteers** *Jefferson Airplane*
'68  **Voodoo Child (Slight Return)**
    *Jimi Hendrix*
'65  **Voodoo Woman** *Bobby Goldsboro*
'85  **Vox Humana** *Kenny Loggins*
'82  **Voyeur** *Kim Carnes*

# W

'74  **WOLD** *Harry Chapin*
'66  **Wack Wack** *Young Holt Trio*
    **Wade In The Water**
'66   *Ramsey Lewis*
'67   *Herb Alpert*
'62  **Wah Watusi** *Orlons*
'88  **Wait** *White Lion*
    **Wait A Minute**
'61   *Coasters*
'01   *Ray-J*
'57  **Wait And See** *Fats Domino*
    **Wait For Me**
'60   *Playmates*
'79   *Daryl Hall & John Oates*
'05  **Wait (The Whisper Song)**
    *Ying Yang Twins*
'63  **Wait Til' My Bobby Gets Home**
    *Darlene Love*
'72  **Waitin' For The Bus [medley]**
    *ZZ Top*
'57  **Waitin' In School** *Ricky Nelson*
'81  **Waiting, The** *Tom Petty*
'81  **Waiting For A Girl Like You**
    *Foreigner*
'88  **Waiting For A Star To Fall**
    *Boy Meets Girl*
'91  **Waiting For Love** *Alias*
'91  **Waiting For That Day**
    *George Michael*
'99  **Waiting For Tonight** *Jennifer Lopez*
'81  **Waiting On A Friend** *Rolling Stones*
'84  **Wake Me Up Before You Go-Go**
    *Wham!*
    **Wake The Town And Tell The People**
'55   *Les Baxter*
'55   *Mindy Carson*
'75  **Wake Up Everybody** *Harold Melvin*
    **Wake Up Little Susie**
'57   *Everly Brothers*
'82   *Simon & Garfunkel*
'85  **Wake Up (Next To You)**
    *Graham Parker*
    **Walk, The**
'58   *Jimmy McCracklin*
'91   *Sawyer Brown*
'70  **Walk A Mile In My Shoes** *Joe South*
    **Walk Away**
'64   *Matt Monro*
'71   *James Gang*
'80   *Donna Summer*
'75  **Walk Away From Love** *David Ruffin*
    **Walk Away Renee**
'66   *Left Banke*
'68   *Four Tops*
    **Walk Don't Run**
'60   *Ventures*
'64   *Ventures ['64]*

'56  **Walk Hand In Hand** *Tony Martin*
'65  **Walk In The Black Forest**
    *Horst Jankowski*
    **Walk Like A Man**
'63   *4 Seasons*
'73   *Grand Funk*
'86  **Walk Like An Egyptian** *Bangles*
'85  **Walk Of Life** *Dire Straits*
    **Walk On**
'74   *Neil Young*
'90   *Reba McEntire*
    **Walk On By**
'61   *Leroy Van Dyke*
'64   *Dionne Warwick*
'69   *Isaac Hayes*
'89   *Sybil*
'90  **Walk On Faith** *Mike Reid*
'92  **Walk On The Ocean**
    *Toad The Wet Sprocket*
    **Walk On The Wild Side**
'62   *Jimmy Smith*
'73   *Lou Reed*
    **Walk On Water**
'72   *Neil Diamond*
'88   *Eddie Money*
'61  **Walk Right Back** *Everly Brothers*
'63  **Walk Right In** *Rooftop Singers*
'89  **Walk The Dinosaur** *Was (Not Was)*
    **Walk This Way**
'76   *Aerosmith*
'86   *Run-D.M.C.*
'91  **Walk Through Fire** *Bad Company*
'92  **Walkaway Joe** *Trisha Yearwood*
    *with Don Henley*
'03  **Walked Outta Heaven** *Jagged Edge*
'57  **Walkin' After Midnight** *Patsy Cline*
    **Walkin' Away**
'90   *Clint Black*
'95   *Diamond Rio*
    **Walkin' In The Rain**
'64   *Ronettes*
'69   *Jay & The Americans*
'72  **Walkin' In The Rain With The One I Love** *Love Unlimited*
'67  **Walkin' In The Sunshine**
    *Roger Miller*
'63  **Walkin' Miracle** *Essex*
'66  **Walkin' My Cat Named Dog**
    *Norma Tanega*
'97  **Walkin' On The Sun** *Smash Mouth*
'61  **Walkin' With My Angel** *Bobby Vee*
'58  **Walking Along** *Diamonds*
'88  **Walking Away** *Information Society*
'94  **Walking Away A Winner**
    *Kathy Mattea*
'87  **Walking Down Your Street** *Bangles*
'91  **Walking In Memphis** *Marc Cohn*
'93  **Walking In My Shoes**
    *Depeche Mode*
'75  **Walking In Rhythm** *Blackbyrds*
'84  **Walking On A Thin Line** *Huey Lewis*
'92  **Walking On Broken Glass**
    *Annie Lennox*
'85  **Walking On Sunshine**
    *Katrina & The Waves*
'63  **Walking Proud** *Steve Lawrence*
'63  **Walking The Dog** *Rufus Thomas*
'60  **Walking To New Orleans**
    *Fats Domino*
'80  **Walks Like A Lady** *Journey*
'55  **Wallflower, The** *Etta James*
'60  **Waltzing Matilda** *Jimmie Rodgers*
    **Wanderer, The**
'61   *Dion*
'80   *Donna Summer*
'77  **Wang Dang Sweet Poontang**
    *Ted Nugent*
'80  **Wango Tango** *Ted Nugent*
'02  **Wanksta** *50 Cent*
'83  **Wanna Be Startin' Somethin'**
    *Michael Jackson*
'04  **Wanna Get To Know You** *G-Unit*
'97  **Wannabe** *Spice Girls*
'93  **Wannagirl** *Jeremy Jordan*
'71  **Want Ads** *Honey Cone*
'90  **Wanted** *Alan Jackson*

'87  **Wanted Dead Or Alive** *Bon Jovi*
'55  **Wanting You** *Roger Williams*
    **War**
'70   *Edwin Starr*
'86   *Bruce Springsteen*
'82  **War Is Hell (On The Homefront Too)**
    *T.G. Sheppard*
'71  **War Pigs** *Black Sabbath*
'84  **War Song** *Culture Club*
'66  **Warm And Tender Love**
    *Percy Sledge*
'92  **Warm It Up** *Kris Kross*
'78  **Warm Ride** *Rare Earth*
'62  **Warmed Over Kisses (Left Over Love)** *Brian Hyland*
    **Warning**
'00   *Green Day*
'02   *Incubus*
'84  **Warrior, The** *Scandal*
'89  **Was It Nothing At All**
    *Michael Damian*
'63  **Washington Square**
    *Village Stompers*
'81  **Wasn't That A Party** *Irish Rovers*
'75  **Wasted Days And Wasted Nights**
    *Freddy Fender*
'82  **Wasted On The Way**
    *Crosby, Stills & Nash*
'77  **Wasted Time** *Eagles*
'01  **Wasting My Time** *Default*
'03  **Wat Da Hook Gon Be** *Murphy Lee*
'92  **Watch Me** *Lorrie Morgan*
'97  **Watch Me Do My Thing** *Immature*
'79  **Watch Out For Lucy** *Eric Clapton*
'67  **Watch The Flowers Grow**
    *4 Seasons*
'03  **Watch The Wind Blow By**
    *Tim McGraw*
'70  **Watching Scotty Grow**
    *Bobby Goldsboro*
'77  **Watching The Detectives**
    *Elvis Costello*
'71  **Watching The River Flow**
    *Bob Dylan*
'81  **Watching The Wheels** *John Lennon*
'88  **Watching You** *Loose Ends*
'61  **Water Boy** *Don Shirley Trio*
'95  **Water Runs Dry** *Boyz II Men*
'95  **Waterfalls** *TLC*
    **Waterloo**
'59   *Stonewall Jackson*
'74   *Abba*
'68  **Waterloo Sunset** *Kinks*
'63  **Watermelon Man**
    *Mongo Santamaria Band*
'61  **Watusi, The** *Vibrations*
'03  **Wave On Wave** *Pat Green*
'78  **Wavelength** *Van Morrison*
'98  **Way, The** *Fastball*
'77  **Way Down** *Elvis Presley*
'59  **Way Down Yonder In New Orleans**
    *Freddie Cannon*
'83  **Way He Makes Me Feel**
    *Barbra Streisand*
'91  **Way I Feel About You** *Karyn White*
'77  **Way I Feel Tonight** *Bay City Rollers*
'59  **Way I Walk** *Jack Scott*
'75  **Way I Want To Touch You**
    *Captain & Tennille*
'86  **Way It Is** *Bruce Hornsby*
'72  **Way Of Love** *Cher*
'94  **Way She Loves Me** *Richard Marx*
    **Way We Were**
'73   *Barbra Streisand*
'75   *Gladys Knight [medley]*
    **Way You Do The Things You Do**
'64   *Temptations*
'78   *Rita Coolidge*
'85   *Daryl Hall & John Oates/David Ruffin/ Eddie Kendrick [medley]*
'90   *UB40*
'61  **Way You Look Tonight** *Lettermen*
    **Way You Love Me**
'88   *Karyn White*
'00   *Faith Hill*

'87 **Way You Make Me Feel**
　　*Michael Jackson*
'03 **Way You Move** *OutKast*
'58 **Ways Of A Woman In Love**
　　*Johnny Cash*
'56 **Wayward Wind** *Gogi Grant*
'66 **(We Ain't Got) Nothin' Yet**
　　*Blues Magoos*
'88 **We All Sleep Alone** *Cher*
'79 **We Are Family** *Sister Sledge*
'77 **We Are The Champions [medley]**
　　*Queen*
'85 **We Are The World** *USA for Africa*
'84 **We Are The Young** *Dan Hartman*
'84 **We Belong** *Pat Benatar*
　　**We Belong Together**
'58 　*Robert & Johnny*
'05 　*Mariah Carey*
'85 **We Built This City** *Starship*
'68 **We Can Fly** *Cowsills*
　　**We Can Work It Out**
'65 　*Beatles*
'71 　*Stevie Wonder*
'99 **We Can't Be Friends**
　　*Deborah Cox with R.L.*
'89 **We Can't Go Wrong** *Cover Girls*
'76 **We Can't Hide It Anymore**
　　*Larry Santos*
'85 **We Close Our Eyes** *Go West*
'86 **We Connect** *Stacey Q*
'00 **We Danced** *Brad Paisley*
'96 **We Danced Anyway** *Deana Carter*
'89 **We Didn't Start The Fire** *Billy Joel*
'86 **We Don't Have To Take Our Clothes
　　Off** *Jermaine Stewart*
'85 **We Don't Need Another Hero
　　(Thunderdome)** *Tina Turner*
'79 **We Don't Talk Anymore**
　　*Cliff Richard*
　　**We Go Together**
'56 　*Moonglows*
'60 　*Jan & Dean*
'92 **We Got A Love Thang**
　　*Ce Ce Peniston*
'95 **We Got It** *Immature*
'59 **We Got Love** *Bobby Rydell*
'69 **We Got More Soul**
　　*Dyke & The Blazers*
'82 **We Got The Beat** *Go-Go's*
'65 **We Gotta Get Out Of This Place**
　　*Animals*
'70 **We Gotta Get You A Woman** *Runt*
'92 **We Hate It When Our Friends
　　Become Successful** *Morrissey*
'77 **We Just Disagree** *Dave Mason*
'99 **We Like To Party!** *Vengaboys*
'80 **We Live For Love** *Pat Benatar*
'64 **We Love You Beatles** *Carefrees*
'73 **We May Never Pass This Way
　　(Again)** *Seals & Crofts*
'63 **We Shall Overcome** *Joan Baez*
'92 **We Tell Ourselves** *Clint Black*
'01 **We Thuggin** *Fat Joe*
'83 **We Two** *Little River Band*
'91 **We Want The Funk** *Gerardo*
'97 **We Were In Love** *Toby Keith*
'80 **We Were Meant To Be Lovers**
　　*Photoglo*
'77 **We Will Rock You [medley]** *Queen*
'87 **We'll Be Together** *Sting*
'93 **We'll Burn That Bridge**
　　*Brooks & Dunn*
'78 **We'll Never Have To Say Goodbye
　　Again**
　　*England Dan & John Ford Coley*
'64 **We'll Sing In The Sunshine**
　　*Gale Garnett*
'67 **We're A Winner** *Impressions*
'77 **We're All Alone** *Rita Coolidge*
'90 **We're All In The Same Gang**
　　*West Coast Rap All-Stars*
'73 **We're An American Band**
　　*Grand Funk*
'74 **We're Getting Careless With Our
　　Love** *Johnnie Taylor*
'02 **We're Going To Be Friends**
　　*White Stripes*

'65 **We're Gonna Make It** *Little Milton*
'81 **We're In This Love Together**
　　*Al Jarreau*
　　**We're Not Gonna Take It**
'69 　*Who*
'84 　*Twisted Sister*
'97 **We're Not Making Love No More**
　　*Dru Hill*
'86 **We're Ready** *Boston*
'72 **We've Got To Get It On Again**
　　*Addrisi Brothers*
　　**We've Got Tonite**
'78 　*Bob Seger*
'83 　*Kenny Rogers & Sheena Easton*
'70 **We've Only Just Begun** *Carpenters*
'87 **We've Only Just Begun (The
　　Romance Is Not Over)**
　　*Glenn Jones*
'93 **Weak** *SWV*
'03 **Weak And Powerless** *Perfect Circle*
'58 **Wear My Ring Around Your Neck**
　　*Elvis Presley*
'67 **Wear Your Love Like Heaven**
　　*Donovan*
'56 **Weary Blues** *McGuire Sisters*
'64 **Wedding, The** *Julie Rogers*
　　**Wedding Bell Blues**
'66 　*Laura Nyro*
'69 　*5th Dimension*
'71 **Wedding Song (There Is Love)**
　　*Paul Stookey*
'79 **Weekend** *Wet Willie*
'76 **Weekend In New England**
　　*Barry Manilow*
　　**Weight, The**
'68 　*Band*
'69 　*Aretha Franklin*
　　**Welcome Back**
'76 　*John Sebastian*
'04 　*Mase*
'62 **Welcome Home Baby** *Shirelles*
'60 **(Welcome) New Lovers** *Pat Boone*
'01 **Welcome To Atlanta**
　　*Jermaine Dupri & Ludacris*
'83 **Welcome To Heartlight**
　　*Kenny Loggins*
'04 **Welcome To My Life** *Simple Plan*
'75 **Welcome To My Nightmare**
　　*Alice Cooper*
'86 **Welcome To The Boomtown**
　　*David & David*
'88 **Welcome To The Jungle**
　　*Guns N' Roses*
'75 **Welcome To The Machine**
　　*Pink Floyd*
'61 **Well. I Told You** *Chantels*
'65 **Well Respected Man** *Kinks*
'78 **Werewolves Of London**
　　*Warren Zevon*
'86 **West End Girls** *Pet Shop Boys*
'62 **West Of The Wall** *Toni Fisher*
'70 **Westbound #9** *Flaming Ember*
'58 **Western Movies** *Olympics*
'67 **Western Union** *Five Americans*
'98 **Westside** *TQ*
'63 **Wham!** *Lonnie Mack*
'76 **Wham Bam (Shang-A-Lang)** *Silver*
　　**What A Diff'rence A Day Makes**
'59 　*Dinah Washington*
'75 　*Esther Phillips*
'79 **What A Fool Believes**
　　*Doobie Brothers*
'99 **What A Girl Wants**
　　*Christina Aguilera*
'63 **What A Guy** *Raindrops*
'61 **What A Party** *Fats Domino*
'61 **What A Price** *Fats Domino*
'62 **(What A Sad Way) To Love
　　Someone** *Ral Donner*
'61 **What A Surprise** *Johnny Maestro*
'67 **What A Woman In Love Won't Do**
　　*Sandy Posey*
'88 **What A Wonderful World**
　　*Louis Armstrong*
　　**What About Love**
'85 　*Heart*
'86 　*'Til Tuesday*

　　**What About Me**
'82 　*Moving Pictures*
'84 　*Kenny Rogers with Kim Carnes &
　　　James Ingram*
'00 **What About Now** *Lonestar*
　　**What About Us**
'97 　*Total*
'02 　*Brandy*
'92 **What About Your Friends** *TLC*
'72 **What Am I Crying For?** *Classics IV*
'61 **What Am I Gonna Do**
　　*Jimmy Clanton*
'83 **What Am I Gonna Do (I'm So In
　　Love With You)** *Rod Stewart*
'75 **What Am I Gonna Do With You**
　　*Barry White*
　　**What Am I Living For**
'58 　*Chuck Willis*
'60 　*Conway Twitty*
'81 **What Are We Doin' In Love**
　　*Dottie West (with Kenny Rogers)*
　　**What Becomes Of The
　　Brokenhearted**
'66 　*Jimmy Ruffin*
'92 　*Paul Young*
'55 **What'cha Gonna Do** *Drifters*
'81 **What Cha' Gonna Do For Me**
　　*Chaka Khan*
'79 **What Cha Gonna Do With My Lovin'**
　　*Stephanie Mills*
'91 **What Comes Naturally**
　　*Sheena Easton*
'78 **What Do I Get?** *Buzzcocks*
'99 **What Do You Say** *Reba McEntire*
'69 **What Does It Take (To Win Your
　　Love)** *Jr. Walker*
'90 **What Goes Around** *Regina Belle*
'78 **What Goes Up**
　　*Alan Parsons Project*
'87 **What Have I Done To Deserve This?**
　　*Pet Shop Boys/ Dusty Springfield*
'65 **What Have They Done To The Rain**
　　*Searchers*
'86 **What Have You Done For Me Lately**
　　*Janet Jackson*
'88 **What I Am** *Edie Brickell*
'96 **What I Got** *Sublime*
　　**What I Like About You**
'80 　*Romantics*
'89 　*Michael Morales*
'01 **What I Really Meant To Say**
　　*Cyndi Thomson*
'00 **What If** *Creed*
'93 **What If I Came Knocking**
　　*John Mellencamp*
'97 **What If I Said**
　　*Anita Cochran with Steve Wariner*
'01 **What If She's An Angel**
　　*Tommy Shane Steiner*
'84 **(What) In The Name Of Love**
　　*Naked Eyes*
'60 **What In The World's Come Over
　　You** *Jack Scott*
'69 **What Is And What Should Never Be**
　　*Led Zeppelin*
'71 **What Is Life** *George Harrison*
　　**What Is Love**
'59 　*Playmates*
'84 　*Howard Jones*
'93 　*Haddaway*
'70 **What Is Truth** *Johnny Cash*
'01 **What It Feels Like For A Girl**
　　*Madonna*
'90 **What It Takes** *Aerosmith*
'98 **What It's Like** *Everlast*
'81 **What Kind Of Fool**
　　*Barbra Streisand & Barry Gibb*
　　**What Kind Of Fool Am I**
'62 　*Sammy Davis Jr.*
'82 　*Rick Springfield*
　　**What Kind Of Fool Do You Think I
　　Am**
'63 　*Tams*
'69 　*Bill Deal*
'62 **What Kind Of Love Is This**
　　*Joey Dee*

248

**What Kind Of Man Would I Be**
'89   *Chicago*
'96   *Mint Condition*
'95   **What Mattered Most** *Ty Herndon*
'93   **What Might Have Been** *Little Texas*
'64   **What Now** *Gene Chandler*
    **What Now My Love**
'66   *Herb Alpert*
'66   *Sonny & Cher*
'92   **What Part Of No** *Lorrie Morgan*
'92   **What She's Doing Now**
    *Garth Brooks*
'94   **What The Cowgirls Do** *Vince Gill*
    **What The World Needs Now Is Love**
'65   *Jackie DeShannon*
'71   *Tom Clay [medley]*
'97   **What They Do** *Roots*
'04   **What U Gon' Do**
    *Lil Jon & The East Side Boyz*
'03   **What Was I Thinkin'** *Dierks Bentley*
'63   **What Will Mary Say** *Johnny Mathis*
'01   **What Would You Do?** *City High*
'95   **What Would You Say**
    *Dave Matthews Band*
'99   **What Ya Want** *Eve & Nokio*
'89   **What You Don't Know** *Exposé*
'87   **What You Get Is What You See**
    *Tina Turner*
'86   **What You Need** *INXS*
'88   **What You See Is What You Get**
    *Brenda K. Starr*
'98   **What You Want** *Mase*
    **What You Won't Do For Love**
'78   *Bobby Caldwell*
'93   *Go West*
'00   **What'Chu Like** *Da Brat*
    **What'd I Say**
'59   *Ray Charles*
'61   *Jerry Lee Lewis*
'62   *Bobby Darin*
'64   *Elvis Presley*
'05   **What's A Guy Gotta Do** *Joe Nichols*
'62   **What's A Matter Baby** *Timi Yuro*
'63   **What's Easy For Two Is So Hard**
    **For One** *Mary Wells*
'82   **What's Forever For**
    *Michael Murphey*
    **What's Going On**
'71   *Marvin Gaye*
'87   *Cyndi Lauper*
'01   *Artists Against AIDS*
'81   **What's He Got** *Producers*
'99   **What's It Gonna Be?!**
    *Busta Rhymes*
'93   **What's It To You** *Clay Walker*
    **What's Love Got To Do With It**
'84   *Tina Turner*
'96   *Warren G*
'02   **What's Luv?** *Fat Joe*
'99   **What's My Age Again?** *Blink 182*
'93   **What's My Name?**
    *Snoop Doggy Dog*
'65   **What's New Pussycat?** *Tom Jones*
'97   **What's On Tonight** *Montell Jordan*
'88   **What's On Your Mind (Pure Energy)**
    *Information Society*
'79   **(What's So Funny 'Bout) Peace,**
    **Love And Happiness**
    *Elvis Costello*
'62   **What's So Good About Good-by**
    *Miracles*
'94   **What's The Frequency, Kenneth?**
    *R.E.M.*
'64   **What's The Matter With You Baby**
    *Marvin Gaye & Mary Wells*
'69   **What's The Use Of Breaking Up**
    *Jerry Butler*
'98   **What's This Life For** *Creed*
'93   **What's Up** *4 Non Blondes*
'93   **What's Up Doc? (Can We Rock?)**
    *Fu-Schnickens*
'00   **What's Your Fantasy** *Ludacris*
'73   **What's Your Mama's Name**
    *Tanya Tucker*

    **What's Your Name**
'62   *Don & Juan*
'77   *Lynyrd Skynyrd*
'98   **Whatcha Gone Do?** *Link*
'77   **Whatcha Gonna Do** *Pablo Cruise*
'71   **Whatcha See Is Whatcha Get**
    *Dramatics*
'97   **Whatever** *En Vogue*
'74   **Whatever Gets You Thru The Night**
    *John Lennon*
    **Whatever Lola Wants (Lola Gets)**
'55   *Dinah Shore*
'55   *Sarah Vaughan*
'74   **Whatever You Got, I Want**
    *Jackson 5*
'99   **Whatever You Say** *Martina McBride*
'91   **Whatever You Want**
    *Tony! Toni! Toné!*
'04   **Whats Happnin!** *Ying Yang Twins*
'94   **Whatta Man**
    *Salt 'N' Pepa with En Vogue*
'78   **Wheel In The Sky** *Journey*
'66   **Wheel Of Hurt** *Margaret Whiting*
'61   **Wheels** *String-A-Longs*
'96   **Wheelz Of Steel** *OutKast*
'58   **When** *Kalin Twins*
    **When A Man Loves A Woman**
'66   *Percy Sledge*
'80   *Bette Midler*
'91   *Michael Bolton*
'98   **When A Woman's Fed Up** *R. Kelly*
'82   **When All Is Said And Done** *Abba*
'95   **When Boy Meets Girl** *Terri Clark*
'94   **When Can I See You** *Babyface*
'84   **When Doves Cry** *Prince*
'82   **When He Shines** *Sheena Easton*
'90   **When I Call Your Name** *Vince Gill*
    **When I Close My Eyes**
'96   *Kenny Chesney*
'99   *Shanice*
'94   **When I Come Around** *Green Day*
'69   **When I Die** *Motherlode*
    **When I Fall In Love**
'61   *Lettermen*
'93   *Celine Dion & Clive Griffin*
'64   **When I Grow Up (To Be A Man)**
    *Beach Boys*
'92   **When I Look Into Your Eyes**
    *Firehouse*
'89   **When I Looked At Him** *Exposé*
'77   **When I Need You** *Leo Sayer*
'99   **When I Said I Do**
    *Clint Black (w/Lisa Hartman Black)*
'57   **When I See You** *Fats Domino*
'89   **When I See You Smile** *Bad English*
'01   **When I Think About Angels**
    *Jamie O'Neal*
'04   **When I Think About Cheatin'**
    *Gretchen Wilson*
'86   **When I Think Of You** *Janet Jackson*
'79   **When I Wanted You** *Barry Manilow*
'67   **When I Was Young** *Animals*
'90   **When I'm Back On My Feet Again**
    *Michael Bolton*
    **When I'm Gone**
'65   *Brenda Holloway*
'02   *3 Doors Down*
'67   **When I'm Sixty-Four** *Beatles*
'83   **When I'm With You** *Sheriff*
'88   **When It's Love** *Van Halen*
    **When I'ts Over**
'82   *Loverboy*
'01   *Sugar Ray*
'66   **When Liking Turns To Loving**
    *Ronnie Dove*
'88   **When Love Comes To Town**
    *U2 with B.B. King*
'94   **When Love Finds You** *Vince Gill*
'56   **When My Blue Moon Turns To Gold**
    **Again** *Elvis Presley*
'56   **When My Dreamboat Comes Home**
    *Fats Domino*
'62   **When My Little Girl Is Smiling**
    *Drifters*
'93   **When My Ship Comes In** *Clint Black*
'92   **When She Cries** *Restless Heart*

'66   **(When She Needs Good Lovin') She**
    **Comes To Me** *Chicago Loop*
'81   **When She Was My Girl** *Four Tops*
'87   **When Smokey Sings** *ABC*
'67   **When Something Is Wrong With My**
    **Baby** *Sam & Dave*
'61   **When The Boy In Your Arms (Is The**
    **Boy In Your Heart)**
    *Connie Francis*
'58   **When The Boys Talk About The**
    **Girls** *Valerie Carr*
'88   **When The Children Cry** *White Lion*
'85   **When The Going Gets Tough, The**
    **Tough Get Going** *Billy Ocean*
'86   **When The Heart Rules The Mind**
    *GTR*
'02   **When The Last Time** *Clipse*
71   **When The Levee Breaks**
    *Led Zeppelin*
    **When The Lights Go Out**
'83   *Naked Eyes*
'98   *Five*
'63   **When The Lovelight Starts Shining**
    **Through His Eyes** *Supremes*
'67   **When The Music's Over** *Doors*
'89   **When The Night Comes** *Joe Cocker*
'56   **When The Saints Go Marching In**
    *Bill Haley*
'67   **When The Snow Is On The Roses**
    *Ed Ames*
'04   **When The Sun Goes Down**
    *Kenny Chesney & Uncle Kracker*
    **When The White Lilacs Bloom**
    **Again**
'56   *Billy Vaughn*
'56   *Helmut Zacharias*
'71   **When There's No You**
    *Engelbert Humperdinck*
'94   **When We Dance** *Sting*
'61   **When We Get Married** *Dreamlovers*
'88   **When We Kiss** *Bardeux*
'87   **When We Was Fab** *George Harrison*
    **When Will I Be Loved**
'60   *Everly Brothers*
'75   *Linda Ronstadt*
'90   **When Will I See You Smile Again?**
    *Bell Biv DeVoe*
'74   **When Will I See You Again**
    *Three Degrees*
'98   **When You Believe** *Whitney*
    *Houston & Mariah Carey*
'84   **When You Close Your Eyes**
    *Night Ranger*
'55   **When You Dance** *Turbans*
'70   **When You Dance I Can Really Love**
    *Neil Young*
'96   **When You Love A Woman** *Journey*
'72   **When You Say Love** *Sonny & Cher*
    **When You Say Nothing At All**
'88   *Keith Whitley*
'95   *Alison Krauss & Union Station*
'05   **When You Tell Me That You Love**
    **Me** *American Idol Season 4*
    **When You Walk In The Room**
'64   *Searchers*
'94   *Pam Tillis*
'60   **When You Wish Upon A Star**
    *Dion & The Belmonts*
'96   **When You're Gone** *Cranberries*
'71   **When You're Hot, You're Hot**
    *Jerry Reed*
'79   **When You're In Love With A**
    **Beautiful Woman** *Dr. Hook*
'67   **When You're Young And In Love**
    *Marvelettes*
'85   **When Your Heart Is Weak**
    *Cock Robin*
'64   **Whenever He Holds You**
    *Bobby Goldsboro*
'78   **Whenever I Call You "Friend"**
    *Kenny Loggins*
'01   **Whenever, Wherever** *Shakira*
'94   **Whenever You Come Around**
    *Vince Gill*
'59   **Where** *Platters*
    **Where Are You**
'60   *Frankie Avalon*
'62   *Dinah Washington*

'02 **Where Are You Going** *Dave Matthews Band*
**Where Are You Now?**
'86 *Synch*
'91 *Clint Black*
'93 *Janet Jackson*
**Where Did Our Love Go**
'64 *Supremes*
'71 *Donnie Elbert*
'71 **Where Did They Go, Lord** *Elvis Presley*
'88 **Where Do Broken Hearts Go** *Whitney Houston*
'86 **Where Do The Children Go** *Hooters*
'89 **Where Do We Go From Here** *Stacy Lattisaw with Johnny Gill*
**Where Do You Go**
'65 *Cher*
'96 *No Mercy*
'90 **Where Does My Heart Beat Now** *Celine Dion*
'97 **Where Have All The Cowboys Gone?** *Paula Cole*
**Where Have All The Flowers Gone**
'62 *Kingston Trio*
'65 *Johnny Rivers*
'01 **Where I Come From** *Alan Jackson*
'00 **Where I Wanna Be** *Donell Jones*
**Where Is The Love**
'72 *Roberta Flack & Donny Hathaway*
'03 *Black Eyed Peas*
'96 **Where It's At** *Beck*
'99 **Where My Girls At?** *702*
'59 **Where Or When** *Dion & The Belmonts*
'73 **Where Peaceful Waters Flow** *Gladys Knight*
'01 **Where The Blacktop Ends** *Keith Urban*
'61 **Where The Boys Are** *Connie Francis*
'98 **Where The Green Grass Grows** *Tim McGraw*
'01 **Where The Party At** *Jagged Edge*
'96 **Where The River Flows** *Collective Soul*
'01 **Where The Stars And Stripes And The Eagle Fly** *Aaron Tippin*
'87 **Where The Streets Have No Name** *U2*
'59 **Where Were You (On Our Wedding Day)?** *Lloyd Price*
'66 **Where Were You When I Needed You** *Grass Roots*
'79 **Where Were You When I Was Falling In Love** *Lobo*
'01 **Where Were You (When The World Stopped Turning)** *Alan Jackson*
'66 **Where Will The Words Come From** *Gary Lewis*
'02 **Where Would You Be** *Martina McBride*
'92 **Where You Goin' Now** *Damn Yankees*
'71 **Where You Lead [medley]** *Barbra Streisand*
'97 **Where's The Love** *Hanson*
'69 **Where's The Playground Susie** *Glen Campbell*
'98 **Wherever You Go** *Voices Of Theory*
'01 **Wherever You Will Go** *Calling*
'70 **Which Way You Goin' Billy?** *Poppy Family*
'68 **While My Guitar Gently Weeps** *Beatles*
'81 **While You See A Chance** *Steve Winwood*
'87 **Willie The Wimp** *Stevie Ray Vaughan*
'90 **Whip Appeal** *Babyface*
'80 **Whip It** *Devo*
'70 **Whipping Post** *Allman Brothers Band*
'83 **Whirly Girl** *Oxo*
'04 **Whiskey Girl** *Toby Keith*
'99 **Whiskey In The Jar** *Metallica*
'04 **Whiskey Lullaby** *Brad Paisley*
'94 **Whisper My Name** *Randy Travis*

'84 **Whisper To A Scream (Birds Fly)** *Icicle Works*
**Whispering**
'63 *Nino Tempo & April Stevens*
'76 *Dr. Buzzard's Original "Savannah" Band [medley]*
'57 **Whispering Bells** *Dell-Vikings*
'66 **Whispers (Gettin' Louder)** *Jackie Wilson*
'69 **White Bird** *It's A Beautiful Day*
**White Christmas**
'54 *Drifters*
'55 *Bing Crosby*
'03 **White Flag** *Dido*
'84 **White Horse** *Laid Back*
'75 **White Knight** *Cledus Maggard*
'71 **White Lies, Blue Eyes** *Bullet*
'74 **White Light/White Heat** *Lou Reed*
'59 **White Lightning** *George Jones*
'83 **White Lines (Don't Don't Do It)** *Grandmaster & Melle Mel*
'79 **White Man In Hammersmith Palais** *Clash*
'64 **White On White** *Danny Williams*
'67 **White Rabbit** *Jefferson Airplane*
'79 **White Riot** *Clash*
'68 **White Room** *Cream*
'62 **White Rose Of Athens** *David Carroll*
**White Silver Sands**
'57 *Owen Bradley Quintet*
'57 *Don Rondo*
'60 *Bill Black's Combo*
'57 **White Sport Coat (And A Pink Carnation)** *Marty Robbins*
'83 **White Wedding** *Billy Idol*
'67 **Whiter Shade Of Pale** *Procol Harum*
'66 **Who Am I** *Petula Clark*
'98 **Who Am I "Sim Simma"** *Beenie Man*
'78 **Who Are You** *Who*
'95 **Who Can I Run To?** *Xscape*
'64 **Who Can I Turn To** *Tony Bennett*
'82 **Who Can It Be Now?** *Men At Work*
'99 **Who Dat** *JT Money*
'89 **Who Do You Give Your Love To?** *Michael Morales*
**Who Do You [U] Love**
'57 *Bo Diddley*
'64 *Sapphires*
'96 *Deborah Cox*
'74 **Who Do You Think You Are** *Bo Donaldson*
'87 **Who Found Who** *Jellybean/Elisa Fiorillo*
'01 **Who I Am** *Jessica Andrews*
'93 **Who Is It** *Michael Jackson*
'00 **Who Let The Dogs Out** *Baha Men*
'75 **Who Loves You** *Four Seasons*
'76 **Who Loves You Better** *Isley Brothers*
'57 **Who Needs You** *Four Lads*
'86 **Who Owns This Place** *Don Henley*
'61 **Who Put The Bomp (In The Bomp, Bomp, Bomp)** *Barry Mann*
'84 **Who Wears These Shoes?** *Elton John*
'67 **Who Will Answer?** *Ed Ames*
'96 **Who Will Save Your Soul** *Jewel*
'87 **Who Will You Run To** *Heart*
'03 **Who Wouldn't Wanna Be Me** *Keith Urban*
'96 **Who You Are** *Pearl Jam*
'76 **Who'd She Coo?** *Ohio Players*
'80 **Who'll Be The Fool Tonight** *Larsen-Feiten Band*
'65 **Who'll Be The Next In Line** *Kinks*
'70 **Who'll Stop The Rain** *Creedence Clearwater Revival*
'97 **Who's Cheatin' Who** *Alan Jackson*
'81 **Who's Crying Now** *Journey*
'92 **Who's Gonna Ride Your Wild Horses** *U2*
'85 **Who's Holding Donna Now** *DeBarge*

'73 **Who's In The Strawberry Patch With Sally** *Tony Orlando & Dawn*
'86 **Who's Johnny** *El DeBarge*
**Who's Making Love**
'68 *Johnnie Taylor*
'80 *Blues Brothers*
**Who's Sorry Now**
'58 *Connie Francis*
'75 *Marie Osmond*
**Who's That Girl**
'84 *Eurythmics*
'87 *Madonna*
'94 **Who's That Man** *Toby Keith*
'02 **Who's Your Daddy?** *Toby Keith*
'85 **Who's Zoomin' Who** *Aretha Franklin*
'77 **Whodunit** *Tavares*
'86 **Whoever's In New England** *Reba McEntire*
'57 **Whole Lot Of Shakin' Going On** *Jerry Lee Lewis*
'69 **Whole Lotta Love** *Led Zeppelin*
'58 **Whole Lotta Loving** *Fats Domino*
'77 **Whole Lotta Rosie** *AC/DC*
'92 **Whole New World (Aladdin's Theme)** *Peabo Bryson & Regina Belle*
'90 **Whole Wide World** *A'me Lorain*
'01 **Whole World** *OutKast*
'93 **Whoomp! (There It Is)** *Tag Team*
'93 **Whoot, There It Is** *95 South*
'95 **Whose Bed Have Your Boots Been Under?** *Shania Twain*
**Why**
'59 *Frankie Avalon*
'72 *Donny Osmond*
'92 *Annie Lennox*
'00 *Collective Soul*
'04 *Jadakiss*
'57 **Why Baby Why** *Pat Boone*
'03 **Why Can't I?** *Liz Phair*
'85 **Why Can't I Have You** *Cars*
'86 **Why Can't This Be Love** *Van Halen*
'75 **Why Can't We Be Friends?** *War*
'72 **Why Can't We Live Together** *Timmy Thomas*
'93 **Why Didn't I Think Of That** *Doug Stone*
**Why Do Fools Fall In Love**
'56 *Diamonds*
'56 *Frankie Lymon*
'56 *Gale Storm*
'81 *Diana Ross*
'60 **Why Do I Love You So** *Johnny Tillotson*
'63 **Why Do Lovers Break Each Other's Heart?** *Bob B. Soxx & The Blue Jeans*
'96 **Why Does It Hurt So Bad** *Whitney Houston*
'57 **Why Don't They Understand** *George Hamilton IV*
'02 **Why Don't We Fall In Love** *Amerie*
'03 **Why Don't You & I** *Santana Feat. Alex Band or Chad Kroeger*
'63 **Why Don't You Believe Me** *Duprees*
'99 **Why Don't You Get A Job?** *Offspring*
'55 **Why Don't You Write Me?** *Jacks*
'96 **Why I Love You So Much** *Monica*
'99 **Why I'm Here** *Oleander*
**Why Me**
'73 *Kris Kristofferson*
'79 *Styx*
'83 *Irene Cara*
'92 **Why Me Baby?** *Keith Sweat*
**Why Not Me**
'80 *Fred Knoblock*
'84 *Judds*
'87 **Why You Treat Me So Bad** *Club Nouveau*
'68 **Wichita Lineman** *Glen Campbell*
'92 **Wicked As It Seems** *Keith Richards*
'90 **Wicked Game** *Chris Isaak*
'98 **Wide Open Spaces** *Dixie Chicks*
'93 **Wide River** *Steve Miller Band*
'66 **Wiederseh'n** *Al Martino*

250

'00 **Wifey** *Next*
'90 **Wiggle It** *2 In A Room*
'62 **Wiggle Wobble** *Les Cooper*
'63 **Wild!** *Dee Dee Sharp*
'95 **Wild Angels** *Martina McBride*
'84 **Wild Boys** *Duran Duran*
'56 **Wild Cherry** *Don Cherry*
'67 **Wild Honey** *Beach Boys*
**Wild Horses**
'71    *Rolling Stones*
'87    *Gino Vannelli*
'61 **Wild In The Country** *Elvis Presley*
'57 **Wild Is The Wind** *Johnny Mathis*
**Wild Night**
'71    *Van Morrison*
'94    *John Mellencamp & Me'Shell*
   *Ndegéocello*
**Wild One**
'60    *Bobby Rydell*
'64    *Martha & The Vandellas*
'93    *Faith Hill*
**Wild Thing**
'66    *Troggs*
'67    *Senator Bobby*
'74    *Fancy*
'88    *Tone Loc*
'62 **Wild Weekend** *Rebels*
'86 **Wild Wild Life** *Talking Heads*
**Wild, Wild West**
'88    *Escape Club*
'99    *Will Smith*
'90 **Wild Women Do** *Natalie Cole*
**Wild World**
'71    *Cat Stevens*
'88    *Maxi Priest*
'93    *Mr. Big*
'75 **Wildfire** *Michael Murphey*
'73 **Wildflower** *Skylark*
'91 **Wildside** *Marky Mark & The*
   *Funky Bunch*
'63 **Wildwood Days** *Bobby Rydell*
'74 **Wildwood Weed** *Jim Stafford*
'73 **Will It Go Round In Circles**
   *Billy Preston*
'99 **Will 2K** *Will Smith*
'69 **Will You Be Staying After Sunday**
   *Peppermint Rainbow*
'93 **Will You Be There** *Michael Jackson*
'93 **Will You Be There (In The Morning)**
   *Heart*
**Will You Love Me Tomorrow**
'60    *Shirelles*
'68    *4 Seasons*
'78    *Dave Mason*
'92 **Will You Marry Me?** *Paula Abdul*
'86 **Will You Still Love Me?** *Chicago*
'84 **William, It Was Really Nothing**
   *Smiths*
**Willie And The Hand Jive**
'58    *Johnny Otis Show*
'74    *Eric Clapton*
'94 **Willing To Forgive** *Aretha Franklin*
'64 **Willow Weep For Me**
   *Chad & Jeremy*
'58 **Win Your Love For Me** *Sam Cooke*
'66 **Winchester Cathedral**
   *New Vaudeville Band*
'89 **Wind Beneath My Wings**
   *Bette Midler*
'67 **Wind Cries Mary** *Jimi Hendrix*
'83 **Wind Him Up** *Saga*
'57 **Wind In The Willow** *Jo Stafford*
'91 **Wind Of Change** *Scorpions*
'69 **Windmills Of Your Mind**
   *Dusty Springfield*
'67 **Windows Of The World**
   *Dionne Warwick*
'83 **Winds Of Change** *Jefferson Starship*
'67 **Windy** *Association*
'60 **Wings Of A Dove** *Ferlin Husky*
'94 **Wink** *Neal McCoy*
**Winner Takes It All**
'80    *Abba*
'87    *Sammy Hagar*

'75 **Winners And Losers**
   *Hamilton, Joe Frank & Reynolds*
'81 **Winning** *Santana*
'69 **Winter World Of Love**
   *Engelbert Humperdinck*
**Wipe Out**
'63    *Surfaris*
'87    *Fat Boys (with The Beach Boys)*
'56 **Wisdom Of A Fool** *Five Keys*
'79 **(Wish I Could Fly Like) Superman**
   *Kinks*
'94 **Wish I Didn't Know Now** *Toby Keith*
'66 **Wish Me A Rainbow**
   *Gunter Kallmann Chorus*
'64 **Wish Someone Would Care**
   *Irma Thomas*
**Wish You Were Here**
'75    *Pink Floyd*
'99    *Mark Wills*
'01    *Incubus*
'69 **Wishful Sinful** *Doors*
'64 **Wishin' And Hopin'**
   *Dusty Springfield*
'58 **Wishing For Your Love** *Voxpoppers*
'98 **Wishing I Was There**
   *Natalie Imbruglia*
'83 **Wishing (If I Had A Photograph Of**
   **You)** *Flock Of Seagulls*
'92 **Wishing On A Star** *Cover Girls*
'88 **Wishing Well** *Terence Trent D'Arby*
'74 **Wishing You Were Here** *Chicago*
'58 **Witch Doctor** *David Seville*
'71 **Witch Queen Of New Orleans**
   *Redbone*
**Witchcraft**
'58    *Frank Sinatra*
'63    *Elvis Presley*
'72 **Witchy Woman** *Eagles*
'66 **With A Girl Like You** *Troggs*
**With A Little Help From My Friends**
'67    *Beatles*
'69    *Joe Cocker*
'78 **With A Little Luck** *Wings*
'57 **With All My Heart** *Jodie Sands*
'00 **With Arms Wide Open** *Creed*
'89 **With Every Beat Of My Heart**
   *Taylor Dayne*
'59 **With Open Arms** *Jane Morgan*
'87 **With Or Without You** *U2*
'69 **With Pen In Hand** *Vikki Carr*
**With The Wind And The Rain In**
   **Your Hair** *Pat Boone*
'65 **With These Hands** *Tom Jones*
'67 **With This Ring** *Platters*
**With You**
'91    *Tony Terry*
'03    *Jessica Simpson*
'79 **With You I'm Born Again**
   *Billy Preston & Syreeta*
'57 **With You On My Mind**
   *Nat "King" Cole*
**With Your Love**
'58    *Jack Scott*
'76    *Jefferson Starship*
**Without Love (There Is Nothing)**
'57    *Clyde McPhatter*
'63    *Ray Charles*
'69    *Tom Jones*
'02 **Without Me** *Eminem*
**Without You**
'61    *Johnny Tillotson*
'71    *Nilsson*
'90    *Mötley Crüe*
'94    *Mariah Carey*
00    *Dixie Chicks*
'82 **Without You (Not Another Lonely**
   **Night)** *Franke & The Knockouts*
'91 **(Without You) What Do I Do With**
   **Me** *Tanya Tucker*
**Without Your Love**
'80    *Roger Daltrey*
'86    *Toto*
'63 **Wives And Lovers** *Jack Jones*
'00 **Wobble Wobble** *504 Boyz*
'62 **Wolverton Mountain** *Claude King*

**Woman**
'66    *Peter & Gordon*
'81    *John Lennon*
'60 **Woman, A Lover, A Friend**
   *Jackie Wilson*
'72 **Woman Don't Go Astray** *King Floyd*
'73 **Woman From Tokyo**
   *Deep Purple*
'89 **Woman In Chains** *Tears For Fears*
**Woman In Love**
'55    *Four Aces*
'55    *Frankie Laine*
'80    *Barbra Streisand*
'82 **Woman In Me** *Donna Summer*
'83 **Woman In You** *Bee Gees*
'72 **Woman Is The Nigger Of The World**
   *John Lennon*
'81 **Woman Needs Love (Just Like You**
   **Do)** *Ray Parker Jr.*
'74 **Woman To Woman** *Shirley Brown*
'04 **Woman With You** *Kenny Chesney*
'67 **Woman, Woman**
   *Union Gap feat. Gary Puckett*
'65 **Woman's Got Soul** *Impressions*
'72 **Woman's Gotta Have It**
   *Bobby Womack*
'01 **Woman's Worth** *Alicia Keys*
'71 **Women's Love Rights** *Laura Lee*
'71 **Won't Get Fooled Again** *Who*
'60 **Won't You Come Home Bill Bailey**
   *Bobby Darin*
'95 **Wonder** *Natalie Merchant*
'61 **Wonder Like You** *Rick Nelson*
**Wonder Of You**
'59    *Ray Peterson*
'70    *Elvis Presley*
**Wonderful**
'95    *Adam Ant*
'00    *Everclear*
'04    *Ja Rule*
'75 **Wonderful Baby** *Don McLean*
'62 **Wonderful Dream** *Majors*
'63 **Wonderful Summer** *Robin Ward*
'58 **Wonderful Time Up There**
   *Pat Boone*
'78 **Wonderful Tonight** *Eric Clapton*
**Wonderful! Wonderful!**
'57    *Johnny Mathis*
'63    *Tymes*
**Wonderful World**
'60    *Sam Cooke*
'65    *Herman's Hermits*
'78    *Art Garfunkel with James Taylor &*
   *Paul Simon*
'69 **Wonderful World, Beautiful People**
   *Jimmy Cliff*
'57 **Wondering** *Patti Page*
'80 **Wondering Where The Lions Are**
   *Bruce Cockburn*
'79 **Wonderland** *Commodores*
**Wonderland By Night**
'60    *Anita Bryant*
'60    *Bert Kaempfert*
'60    *Louis Prima*
'96 **Wonderwall** *Oasis*
'96 **Woo-Hah!! Got You All In Check**
   *Busta Rhymes*
'59 **Woo-Hoo** *Rock-A-Teens*
**Wooden Heart**
'60    *Elvis Presley*
'61    *Joe Dowell*
'69 **Wooden Ships**
   *Crosby, Stills, Nash & Young*
**Woodstock**
'70    *Crosby, Stills & Nash*
'70    *Joni Mitchell*
'71    *Matthews' Southern Comfort*
'98 **Woof Woof** *69 Boyz*
'65 **Wooly Bully**
   *Sam The Sham & the Pharaohs*
'88 **Word In Spanish** *Elton John*
'04 **Word Of God Speak** *MercyMe*
'91 **Word To The Mutha!** *Bell Biv DeVoe*
'86 **Word Up** *Cameo*

**Words**
'67 *Monkees*
'68 *Bee Gees*
'82 *Missing Persons*
'86 **Words Get In The Way**
    *Miami Sound Machine*
**Words Of Love**
'57 *Diamonds*
'57 *Buddy Holly*
'66 *Mamas & The Papas*
'02 **Work In Progress** *Alan Jackson*
'02 **Work It** *Missy Elliott*
'66 **Work Song** *Herb Alpert*
'74 **Workin' At The Car Wash Blues**
    *Jim Croce*
'82 **Workin' For A Livin'**
    *Huey Lewis*
'74 **Workin' For MCA**
    *Lynyrd SKynyrd*
'62 **Workin' For The Man** *Roy Orbison*
'69 **Workin' On A Groovy Thing**
    *5th Dimension*
'81 **Working For The Weekend**
    *Loverboy*
**Working In The Coal Mine**
'66 *Lee Dorsey*
'81 *Devo*
**Working My Way Back To You**
'66 *4 Seasons*
'79 *Spinners [medley]*
'95 **World I Know** *Collective Soul*
'72 **World Is A Ghetto** *War*
'65 **World Of Our Own** *Seekers*
'58 **World Outside** *Four Coins*
'87 **World Shut Your Mouth** *Julian Cope*
'67 **World We Knew (Over And Over)**
    *Frank Sinatra*
'64 **World Without Love** *Peter & Gordon*
'01 **World's Greatest** *R. Kelly*
'64 **Worried Guy** *Johnny Tillotson*
'59 **Worried Man** *Kingston Trio*
'59 **Worryin' Kind** *Tommy Sands*
'68 **Worst That Could Happen**
    *Brooklyn Bridge*
'87 **Wot's It To Ya** *Robbie Nevil*
**Would I Lie To You?**
'85 *Eurythmics*
'92 *Charles & Eddie*
'74 **Would You Lay With Me (In A Field**
    **Of Stone)** *Tanya Tucker*
'66 **Wouldn't It Be Nice** *Beach Boys*
'81 **Wrack My Brain** *Ringo Starr*
'85 **Wrap Her Up** *Elton John*
'86 **Wrap It Up** *Fabulous Thunderbirds*
'91 **Wrap My Body Tight** *Johnny Gill*
'01 **Wrapped Around** *Brad Paisley*
'84 **Wrapped Around Your Finger**
    *Police*
'02 **Wrapped Up In You** *Garth Brooks*
'76 **Wreck Of The Edmund Fitzgerald**
    *Gordon Lightfoot*
**Wringle, Wrangle**
'57 *Bill Hayes*
'57 *Fess Parker*
'99 **Write This Down** *George Strait*
'61 **Writing On The Wall** *Adam Wade*
'91 **Written All Over Your Face**
    *Rude Boys*
'99 **Written In The Stars**
    *Elton John & LeAnn Rimes*
'98 **Wrong Again** *Martina McBride*
'97 **Wrong Way** *Sublime*
'57 **Wun'erful, Wun'erful!** *Stan Freberg*
'78 **Wuthering Heights** *Kate Bush*

# X

'94 **XXX's And OOO's (An American**
    **Girl)** *Trisha Yearwood*
'80 **Xanadu** *Olivia Newton-John/*
    *Electric Light Orchestra*

# Y

'78 **Y.M.C.A.** *Village People*

'61 **Ya Ya** *Lee Dorsey*
'83 **Yah Mo B There** *James Ingram*
    *(with Michael McDonald)*
'63 **Yakety Sax (Axe)** *Boots Randolph*
'58 **Yakety Yak** *Coasters*
'78 **Yank Me, Crank Me**
    *Ted Nugent*
'86 **Yankee Rose** *David Lee Roth*
'59 **Yea-Yea (Class Cutter)**
    *Dale Hawkins*
'04 **Yeah!** *Usher*
'88 **Yeah, Yeah, Yeah** *Judson Spence*
'76 **Year Of The Cat** *Al Stewart*
'80 **Years** *Wayne Newton*
'65 **Yeh, Yeh** *Georgie Fame*
'01 **Yellow** *Coldplay*
'67 **Yellow Balloon** *Yellow Balloon*
'61 **Yellow Bird** *Arthur Lyman Group*
'00 **Yellow Ledbetter** *Pearl Jam*
'70 **Yellow River** *Christie*
**Yellow Rose Of Texas**
'55 *Johnny Desmond*
'55 *Stan Freberg*
'55 *Mitch Miller*
'66 **Yellow Submarine** *Beatles*
'59 **"Yep!"** *Duane Eddy*
'00 **Yes!** *Chad Brock*
**Yes, I'm Ready**
'65 *Barbara Mason*
'79 *Teri DeSario with K.C.*
'57 **Yes Tonight, Josephine**
    *Johnnie Ray*
'73 **Yes We Can Can** *Pointer Sisters*
'68 **Yester Love** *Miracles*
'69 **Yester-Me, Yester-You, Yesterday**
    *Stevie Wonder*
**Yesterday**
'65 *Beatles*
'67 *Ray Charles*
'68 **Yesterday I Heard The Rain**
    *Tony Bennett*
'73 **Yesterday Once More** *Carpenters*
'69 **Yesterday, When I Was Young**
    *Roy Clark*
'64 **Yesterday's Gone** *Chad & Jeremy*
'81 **Yesterday's Songs** *Neil Diamond*
'71 **Yo-Yo** *Osmonds*
'60 **Yogi** *Ivy Three*
**You ..also see: U**
**You**
'58 *Aquatones*
'75 *George Harrison*
'78 *Rita Coolidge*
'96 *Monifah*
'99 *Jesse Powell*
'95 **You Ain't Much Fun** *Toby Keith*
'74 **You Ain't Seen Nothing Yet**
    *Bachman-Turner Overdrive*
'61 **You Always Hurt The One You Love**
    *Clarence Henry*
**You And I**
'78 *Rick James*
'82 *Eddie Rabbitt with Crystal Gayle*
**You And Me**
'77 *Alice Cooper*
'05 *Lifehouse*
'74 **You And Me Against The World**
    *Helen Reddy*
'87 **You And Me Tonight** *Déja*
'74 **You Angel You** *Bob Dylan*
'83 **You Are** *Lionel Richie*
'71 **You Are Everything** *Stylistics*
'62 **You Are Mine** *Frankie Avalon*
'58 **You Are My Destiny** *Paul Anka*
'89 **You Are My Everything** *Surface*
'85 **You Are My Lady** *Freddie Jackson*
'55 **You Are My Love** *Joni James*
'76 **You Are My Starship**
    *Norman Connors*
'62 **You Are My Sunshine** *Ray Charles*
'95 **You Are Not Alone** *Michael Jackson*
'75 **You Are So Beautiful** *Joe Cocker*
'87 **You Are The Girl** *Cars*
'60 **You Are The Only One** *Ricky Nelson*
'73 **You Are The Sunshine Of My Life**
    *Stevie Wonder*

'76 **You Are The Woman** *Firefall*
'66 **You Baby** *Turtles*
'86 **You Be Illin'** *Run-D.M.C.*
'62 **You Beat Me To The Punch**
    *Mary Wells*
**You Belong To Me**
'62 *Duprees*
'77 *Doobie Brothers*
'78 *Carly Simon*
'85 **You Belong To The City** *Glenn Frey*
'59 **You Better Know It** *Jackie Wilson*
'62 **You Better Move On**
    *Arthur Alexander*
**You Better Run**
'66 *Young Rascals*
'80 *Pat Benatar*
'67 **You Better Sit Down Kids** *Cher*
'95 **You Better Think Twice** *Vince Gill*
'94 **You Better Wait** *Steve Perry*
'81 **You Better You Bet** *Who*
'97 **You Bring Me Up** *K-Ci & JoJo*
'68 **You Can All Join In** *Traffic*
'86 **You Can Call Me Al** *Paul Simon*
**You Can Depend On Me**
'61 *Brenda Lee*
'91 *Restless Heart*
**You Can Do It**
'78 *Dobie Gray*
'99 *Ice Cube*
'82 **You Can Do Magic** *America*
'95 **You Can Feel Bad** *Patty Loveless*
'75 **You Can Get It If You Really Want It**
    *Jimmy Cliff*
**You Can Have Her**
'61 *Roy Hamilton*
'74 *Sam Neely*
'57 **You Can Make It If You Try**
    *Gene Allison*
'63 **You Can Never Stop Me Loving You**
    *Johnny Tillotson*
'69 **You Can't Always Get What You**
    **Want** *Rolling Stones*
'79 **You Can't Change That** *Raydio*
'90 **You Can't Deny It** *Lisa Stansfield*
'64 **You Can't Do That** *Beatles*
'84 **You Can't Get What You Want (Till**
    **You Know What You Want)**
    *Joe Jackson*
'02 **You Can't Hide Beautiful**
    *Aaron Lines*
**You Can't Hurry Love**
'66 *Supremes*
'82 *Phil Collins*
'62 **You Can't Judge A Book By The**
    **Cover** *Bo Diddley*
'94 **You Can't Make A Heart Love**
    **Somebody** *George Strait*
'91 **You Can't Play With My Yo-Yo**
    *Yo-Yo*
'66 **You Can't Roller Skate In A Buffalo**
    **Herd** *Roger Miller*
'56 **You Can't Run Away From It**
    *Four Aces*
'83 **You Can't Run From Love**
    *Eddie Rabbitt*
**You Can't Sit Down**
'61 *Philip Upchurch Combo*
'63 *Dovells*
'03 **You Can't Take The Honky Tonk**
    **Out Of The Girl** *Brooks & Dunn*
'77 **You Can't Turn Me Off (In The**
    **Middle Of Turning Me On)**
    *High Inergy*
'58 **You Cheated** *Shields*
'91 **You Could Be Mine** *Guns N' Roses*
'72 **You Could Have Been A Lady**
    *April Wine*
'81 **You Could Have Been With Me**
    *Sheena Easton*
'81 **You Could Take My Heart Away**
    *Silver Condor*
'79 **You Decorated My Life**
    *Kenny Rogers*
'65 **You Didn't Have To Be So Nice**
    *Lovin' Spoonful*
'78 **You Don't Bring Me Flowers**
    *Barbra Streisand & Neil Diamond*

'63 You Don't Have To Be A Baby To
 Cry *Caravelles*
'76 You Don't Have To Be A Star
 *Marilyn McCoo & Billy Davis, Jr.*
'86 You Don't Have To Cry
 *René & Angela*
'91 You Don't Have To Go Home
 Tonight *Triplets*
'97 You Don't Have To Hurt No More
 *Mint Condition*
'66 (You Don't Have To) Paint Me A
 Picture *Gary Lewis*
 You Don't Have To Say You Love
 Me
'66 *Dusty Springfield*
'70 *Elvis Presley*
'90 You Don't Have To Worry *En Vogue*
'88 You Don't Know *Scarlett & Black*
'64 (You Don't Know) How Glad I Am
 *Nancy Wilson*
'94 You Don't Know How It Feels
 *Tom Petty*
 You Don't Know Me
'56 *Jerry Vale*
'60 *Lenny Welch*
'62 *Ray Charles*
'03 You Don't Know My Name
 *Alicia Keys*
'61 You Don't Know What You've Got
 (Until You Lose It) *Ral Donner*
'72 You Don't Mess Around With Jim
 *Jim Croce*
'57 You Don't Owe Me A Thing
 *Johnnie Ray*
'63 You Don't Own Me *Lesley Gore*
'82 You Don't Want Me Anymore
 *Steel Breeze*
'99 (You Drive Me) Crazy
 *Britney Spears*
'82 You Dropped A Bomb On Me
 *Gap Band*
'69 You Gave Me A Mountain
 *Frankie Laine*
'98 You Get What You Give
 *New Radicals*
'01 You Gets No Love *Faith Evans*
'85 You Give Good Love
 *Whitney Houston*
'86 You Give Love A Bad Name
 *Bon Jovi*
'79 You Gonna Make Me Love
 Somebody Else *Jones Girls*
 You Got It
'89 *Roy Orbison*
'95 *Bonnie Raitt*
'86 You Got It All *Jets*
'88 You Got It (The Right Stuff)
 *New Kids On The Block*
'82 You Got Lucky *Tom Petty*
'99 You Got Me *Roots*
'94 You Got Me Rocking *Rolling Stones*
'77 You Got That Right
 *Lynyrd Skynyrd*
'74 You Got The Love
 *Rufus feat. Chaka Khan*
'67 You Got To Me *Neil Diamond*
 You Got What It Takes
'59 *Marv Johnson*
'67 *Dave Clark Five*
'69 You Got Yours And I'll Get Mine
 *Delfonics*
'94 You Gotta Be *Des'ree*
'86 (You Gotta) Fight For Your Right
 (To Party!) *Beastie Boys*
'90 You Gotta Love Someone
 *Elton John*
'99 You Had Me From Hello
 *Kenny Chesney*
'74 You Haven't Done Nothin
 *Stevie Wonder*
'69 You, I *Rugbys*
 You Keep Me Hangin' On
'66 *Supremes*
'67 *Vanilla Fudge*
'68 *Joe Simon*
'87 *Kim Wilde*
'82 You Keep Runnin' Away *38 Special*
'67 You Keep Running Away *Four Tops*

'94 You Know How We Do It *Ice Cube*
'86 You Know I Love You...Don't You?
 *Howard Jones*
'91 You Know Me Better Than That
 *George Strait*
'79 You Know That I Love You *Santana*
'67 You Know What I Mean *Turtles*
'02 You Know You're Right *Nirvana*
'96 You Learn *Alanis Morissette*
'90 You Lie *Reba McEntire*
'92 You Lied To Me *Cathy Dennis*
 You Light Up My Life
'77 *Debby Boone*
'97 *LeAnn Rimes*
'74 You Little Trustmaker *Tymes*
'63 You Lost The Sweetest Boy
 *Mary Wells*
'78 You Love The Thunder
 *Jackson Browne*
'67 You Made It That Way (Watermelon
 Summer) *Perry Como*
'77 You Made Me Believe In Magic
 *Bay City Rollers*
'61 You Made Me Love You
 *Judy Garland [live]*
'77 You Make Loving Fun
 *Fleetwood Mac*
'74 You Make Me Feel Brand New
 *Stylistics*
'76 You Make Me Feel Like Dancing
 *Leo Sayer*
'79 You Make Me Feel (Mighty Real)
 *Sylvester*
'56 You Make Me Feel So Young
 *Frank Sinatra*
'01 You Make Me Sick *P!nk*
'97 You Make Me Wanna... *Usher*
'81 You Make My Dreams
 *Daryl Hall & John Oates*
'80 You May Be Right *Billy Joel*
'60 You Mean Everything To Me
 *Neil Sedaka*
'94 You Mean The World To Me
 *Toni Braxton*
'68 You Met Your Match *Stevie Wonder*
'84 You Might Think *Cars*
'98 You Move Me *Garth Brooks*
'64 You Must Believe Me *Impressions*
 You Must Have Been A Beautiful
 Baby
'61 *Bobby Darin*
'67 *Dave Clark Five*
'96 You Must Love Me *Madonna*
'58 You Need Hands *Eydie Gorme*
'70 You Need Love Like I Do (Don't
 You) *Gladys Knight*
'78 You Needed Me *Anne Murray*
'64 You Never Can Tell *Chuck Berry*
'78 You Never Done It Like That
 *Captain & Tennille*
'67 You Only Live Twice *Nancy Sinatra*
'72 You Ought To Be With Me *Al Green*
'95 You Oughta Know *Alanis Morissette*
'03 You Raise Me Up *Josh Groban*
 You Really Got Me
'64 *Kinks*
'78 *Van Halen*
'90 You Really Had Me Going
 *Holly Dunn*
'65 You Really Know How To Hurt A
 Guy *Jan & Dean*
'92 You Remind Me *Mary J. Blige*
'95 You Remind Me Of Something
 *R. Kelly*
'01 You Rock My World
 *Michael Jackson*
'00 You Sang To Me *Marc Anthony*
'81 You Saved My Soul
 *Burton Cummings*
 You Send Me
'57 *Teresa Brewer*
'57 *Sam Cooke*
'75 You Sexy Thing *Hot Chocolate*
'80 You Shook Me All Night Long
 *AC/DC*
'76 You Should Be Dancing *Bee Gees*

'97 You Should Be Mine (Don't Waste
 Your Time) *Brian McKnight*
'86 You Should Be Mine (The Woo Woo
 Song) *Jeffrey Osborne*
'64 You Should Have Seen The Way He
 Looked At Me *Dixie Cups*
'82 You Should Hear How She Talks
 About You *Melissa Manchester*
'57 You Shouldn't Do That *Sal Mineo*
'00 You Shouldn't Kiss Me Like This
 *Toby Keith*
'69 You Showed Me *Turtles*
'85 You Spin Me Round (Like A
 Record) *Dead Or Alive*
'79 You Take My Breath Away
 *Rex Smith*
'60 You Talk Too Much *Joe Jones*
'92 You Think You Know Her
 *Cause & Effect*
'78 You Thrill Me *Exile*
'78 You Took The Words Right Out Of
 My Mouth *Meat Loaf*
'65 You Turn Me On *Ian Whitcomb*
'72 You Turn Me On, I'm A Radio
 *Joni Mitchell*
'95 You Used To Love Me *Faith Evans*
'72 You Want It, You Got It
 *Detroit Emeralds*
'94 You Want This *Janet Jackson*
'72 You Wear It Well *Rod Stewart*
'60 (You Were Made For) All My Love
 *Jackie Wilson*
 You Were Made For Me
'58 *Sam Cooke*
'65 *Freddie & The Dreamers*
'96 You Were Meant For Me *Jewel*
 You Were Mine
'59 *Fireflies*
'99 *Dixie Chicks*
 You Were On My Mind
'65 *We Five*
'67 *Crispian St. Peters*
'65 You Were Only Fooling (While I
 Was Fooling In Love) *Vic Damone*
'88 You Will Know *Stevie Wonder*
 You Win Again
'58 *Jerry Lee Lewis*
'62 *Fats Domino*
'96 You Win My Love *Shania Twain*
'99 You Won't Ever Be Lonely
 *Andy Griggs*
'74 You Won't See Me *Anne Murray*
'92 You Won't See Me Cry
 *Wilson Phillips*
'94 You Wreck Me *Tom Petty*
'65 You'd Better Come Home
 *Petula Clark*
'80 You'll Accomp'ny Me *Bob Seger*
'99 You'll Be In My Heart *Phil Collins*
 You'll Lose A Good Thing
'62 *Barbara Lynn*
'76 *Freddy Fender*
'76 You'll Never Find Another Love
 Like Mine *Lou Rawls*
 You'll Never Get To Heaven (If You
 Break My Heart)
'64 *Dionne Warwick*
'73 *Stylistics*
'56 You'll Never Never Know *Platters*
'64 You'll Never Walk Alone
 *Patti LaBelle*
'95 You'll See *Madonna*
'03 You'll Think Of Me *Keith Urban*
'85 You're A Friend Of Mine *Clarence
 Clemons & Jackson Browne*
'00 You're A God *Vertical Horizon*
'78 You're A Part Of Me
 *Gene Cotton with Kim Carnes*
'73 You're A Special Part Of Me
 *Diana Ross & Marvin Gaye*
'64 You're A Wonderful One
 *Marvin Gaye*
 You're All I Need To Get By
'68 *Marvin Gaye & Tammi Terrell*
'71 *Aretha Franklin*
'95 *Method Man ft. Mary J. Blige
 [medley]*

253

'78 **You're All I've Got Tonight** *Cars*
'90 **You're Amazing** *Robert Palmer*
'98 **You're Beginning To Get To Me**
    *Clay Walker*
'83 **You're Driving Me Out Of My Mind**
    *Little River Band*
'98 **You're Easy On The Eyes**
    *Terri Clark*
'65 **You're Going To Lose That Girl**
    *Beatles*
'95 **You're Gonna Miss Me When I'm**
    **Gone** *Brooks & Dunn*
'63 **You're Good For Me** *Solomon Burke*
'74 **(You're) Having My Baby**
    *Paul Anka/Odia Coates*
'91 **You're In Love** *Wilson Phillips*
'77 **You're In My Heart (The Final**
    **Acclaim)** *Rod Stewart*
'96 **You're Makin' Me High** *Toni Braxton*
'76 **You're My Best Friend** *Queen*
'04 **You're My Better Half** *Keith Urban*
'67 **You're My Everything** *Temptations*
'81 **You're My Girl**
    *Franke & The Knockouts*
'57 **You're My One And Only Love**
    *Ricky Nelson*
'89 **You're My One And Only (True**
    **Love)** *Seduction*
    **(You're My) Soul And Inspiration**
'66    *Righteous Brothers*
'77    *Donny & Marie Osmond*
    **You're My World**
'64    *Cilla Black*
'77    *Helen Reddy*
'74 **You're No Good** *Linda Ronstadt*
'64 **You're Nobody Till Somebody**
    **Loves You** *Dean Martin*
'89 **You're Not Alone** *Chicago*
'85 **You're Only Human (Second Wind)**
    *Billy Joel*
'79 **You're Only Lonely** *J.D. Souther*
'87 **(You're Puttin') A Rush On Me**
    *Stephanie Mills*
    **You're Sixteen**
'60    *Johnny Burnette*
'73    *Ringo Starr*
'59 **You're So Fine** *Falcons*
'72 **You're So Vain** *Carly Simon*
'72 **You're Still A Young Man**
    *Tower Of Power*
'98 **You're Still The One** *Shania Twain*
'80 **You're Supposed To Keep Your**
    **Love For Me** *Jermaine Jackson*
'63 **(You're the) Devil In Disguise**
    *Elvis Presley*
'74 **You're The First, The Last, My**
    **Everything** *Barry White*
'84 **You're The Inspiration** *Chicago*
'78 **You're The Love** *Seals & Crofts*
    **You're The One**
'65    *Vogues*
'70    *Little Sister*
'96    *SWV*
'78 **You're The One That I Want** *John*
    *Travolta & Olivia Newton-John*
'80 **You're The Only Woman (You & I)**
    *Ambrosia*
'61 **You're The Reason** *Bobby Edwards*
'63 **You're The Reason I'm Living**
    *Bobby Darin*

'65 **You've Been Cheatin'** *Impressions*
'65 **You've Been In Love Too Long**
    *Martha & The Vandellas*
    **You've Got A Friend**
'71    *Roberta Flack & Donny Hathaway*
'71    *James Taylor*
'82 **You've Got Another Thing Comin'**
    *Judas Priest*
'70 **(You've Got Me) Dangling On A**
    **String** *Chairmen Of The Board*
'56 **You've Got Me Dizzy** *Jimmy Reed*
'76 **You've Got Me Runnin'** *Gene Cotton*
'56 **(You've Got) The Magic Touch**
    *Platters*
'71 **You've Got To Crawl (Before You**
    **Walk)** *8th Day*
    **You've Got To Hide Your Love**
    **Away**
'65    *Beatles*
'65    *Silkie*
'60 **(You've Got To) Move Two**
    **Mountains** *Marv Johnson*
'90 **You've Got To Stand For**
    **Something** *Aaron Tippin*
'97 **You've Got To Talk To Me**
    *Lee Ann Womack*
'65 **You've Got Your Troubles** *Fortunes*
    **You've Lost That Lovin' Feelin'**
'64    *Righteous Brothers*
'69    *Dionne Warwick*
'80    *Daryl Hall & John Oates*
    **You've Made Me So Very Happy**
'67    *Brenda Holloway*
'69    *Blood, Sweat & Tears*
'73 **You've Never Been This Far Before**
    *Conway Twitty*
'62 **You've Really Got A Hold On Me**
    *Miracles*
    **Young**
'02    *Kenny Chesney*
'55 **Young Abe Lincoln** *Don Cornell*
'75 **Young Americans** *David Bowie*
'63 **Young And In Love** *Dick & DeeDee*
'58 **Young And Warm And Wonderful**
    *Tony Bennett*
    **Young Blood**
'57    *Coasters*
'76    *Bad Company*
'79    *Rickie Lee Jones*
'60 **Young Emotions** *Ricky Nelson*
'68 **Young Girl**
    *Union Gap feat. Gary Puckett*
'76 **Young Hearts Run Free**
    *Candi Staton*
    **Young Love**
'56    *Sonny James*
'57    *Crew-Cuts*
'57    *Tab Hunter*
'73    *Donny Osmond*
'82    *Air Supply*
'63 **Young Lovers** *Paul & Paula*
'80 **Young Lust** *Pink Floyd*
'81 **Young Turks** *Rod Stewart*
'62 **Young World** *Rick Nelson*
'66 **Younger Girl** *Critters*
'01 **Young'n (Holla Back)** *Fabolous*
'90 **Your Baby Never Looked Good In**
    **Blue** *Exposé*
'02 **Your Body Is A Wonderland**
    *John Mayer*

'94 **Your Body's Callin'** *R. Kelly*
'74 **Your Bulldog Drinks Champagne**
    *Jim Stafford*
'73 **Your Cash Ain't Nothin' But Trash**
    *Steve Miller Band*
'62 **Your Cheating Heart** *Ray Charles*
'01 **Your Disease** *Saliva*
'61 **Your Friends** *Dee Clark*
'69 **Your Good Thing (Is About To End)**
    *Lou Rawls*
'82 **Your Imagination**
    *Daryl Hall & John Oates*
'98 **Your Life Is Now**
    *John Mellencamp*
    **Your Love**
'77    *Marilyn McCoo & Billy Davis Jr.*
'86    *Outfield*
'94 **Your Love Amazes Me** *John Berry*
'91 **Your Love Is A Miracle**
    *Mark Chesnutt*
'82 **Your Love Is Driving Me Crazy**
    *Sammy Hagar*
    **(Your Love Keeps Lifting Me)**
    **Higher And Higher**
'67    *Jackie Wilson*
'77    *Rita Coolidge*
'61 **Your Ma Said You Cried In Your**
    **Sleep Last Night** *Kenny Dino*
    **Your Mama Don't Dance**
'72    *Loggins & Messina*
'89    *Poison*
'71 **Your Move [medley]** *Yes*
'62 **Your Nose Is Gonna Grow**
    *Johnny Crawford*
'63 **Your Old Stand By** *Mary Wells*
    **Your Other Love**
'60    *Flamingos*
'63    *Connie Francis*
'67 **Your Precious Love**
    *Marvin Gaye & Tammi Terrell*
'85 **Your Smile** *René & Angela*
'77 **Your Smiling Face** *James Taylor*
'70 **Your Song** *Elton John*
'78 **Your Sweetness Is My Weakness**
    *Barry White*
'68 **Your Time Hasn't Come Yet, Baby**
    *Elvis Presley*
'70 **Your Time To Cry** *Joe Simon*
'63 **Your Used To Be** *Brenda Lee*
'57 **Your Wild Heart** *Joy Layne*
'86 **Your Wildest Dreams** *Moody Blues*
'97 **Your Woman** *White Town*
'71 **Yours Is No Disgrace** *Yes*
'01 **Youth Of The Nation** *P.O.D.*
'68 **Yummy Yummy Yummy**
    *Ohio Express*

# Z

'72 **Ziggy Stardust** *David Bowie*
'62 **Zip-A-Dee Doo-Dah** *Bob B.*
    *Soxx & The Blue Jeans*
'67 **Zip Code** *Five Americans*
'57 **Zip Zip** *Diamonds*
'94 **Zombie** *Cranberries*
'65 **Zorba The Greek** *Herb Alpert*
'58 **Zorro** *Chordettes*

# THE PLAYLISTS

## CLASSIC SONGS

| | |
|---|---|
| 1955-1959 | 1985-1989 |
| 1960-1964 | 1990-1994 |
| 1965-1969 | 1995-1999 |
| 1970-1974 | 2000-2004 |
| 1975-1979 | 2005 |
| 1980-1984 | |

Each of the above playlists consists of 200 of the hottest hits of each half-decade of the rock era, except for the 2005 playlist which covers 50 of the year's top hits from January to June.

Classic Rock (50 songs)

Road Trip! (100 songs)

The British Invasion 1964-65 (50 songs)

We're An American Band '60s & '70s (50 songs)

Retro Radio Early '80s (50 songs)

The Motown Sound Of The '60s (50 songs)

A Classic Christmas:

A Holly Jolly Christmas (55 songs)

Joy To The World (36 songs)

Ain't That A Shame...*Fats Domino*
All American Boy, The...*Bill Parsons*
All I Have To Do Is Dream...*Everly Brothers*
All Shook Up...*Elvis Presley*
All The Way...*Frank Sinatra*
Allegheny Moon...*Patti Page*
April Love...*Pat Boone*
At The Hop...*Danny & The Juniors*
Autumn Leaves...*Roger Williams*
Ballad Of Davy Crockett, The...*Bill Hayes*
Banana Boat (Day-O)...*Harry Belafonte*
Band Of Gold...*Don Cherry*
Battle Of New Orleans, The...*Johnny Horton*
Be-Bop-A-Lula...*Gene Vincent*
Believe What You Say...*Ricky Nelson*
Big Hunk O' Love, A...*Elvis Presley*
Big Hurt, The...*Miss Toni Fisher*
Bird Dog...*Everly Brothers*
Black Denim Trousers...*Cheers*
Blossom Fell, A...*Nat "King" Cole*
Blue Monday...*Fats Domino*
Blue Suede Shoes...*Carl Perkins*
Blueberry Hill...*Fats Domino*
Bo Diddley...*Bo Diddley*
Book Of Love...*Monotones*
Butterfly...*Charlie Gracie*
Bye Bye Love...*Everly Brothers*
Canadian Sunset...*Hugo Winterhalter/Eddie Heywood*
Catch A Falling Star...*Perry Como*
Chances Are...*Johnny Mathis*
Chantilly Lace...*Big Bopper*
Charlie Brown...*Coasters*
Cherry Pink And Apple Blossom White ...*Perez Prado*
C'mon Everybody...*Eddie Cochran*
Come Go With Me...*Dell-Vikings*
Come Softly To Me...*Fleetwoods*
Diana...*Paul Anka*
Donna...*Ritchie Valens*
Don't...*Elvis Presley*
Don't Be Cruel...*Elvis Presley*
Don't You Know...*Della Reese*
Dream Lover...*Bobby Darin*
Earth Angel...*Penguins*
Endless Sleep...*Jody Reynolds*
Fever...*Peggy Lee*
Fool, The...*Sanford Clark*
Get A Job...*Silhouettes*
Good Golly, Miss Molly...*Little Richard*
Great Balls Of Fire...*Jerry Lee Lewis*
Great Pretender, The...*Platters*
Green Door, The...*Jim Lowe*
Happy, Happy Birthday Baby...*Tune Weavers*
Happy Organ, The...*Dave 'Baby' Cortez*
Hard Headed Woman...*Elvis Presley*
Heartbreak Hotel...*Elvis Presley*

He's Got The Whole World (In His Hands) ...*Laurie London*
Hey! Jealous Lover...*Frank Sinatra*
Honeycomb...*Jimmie Rodgers*
Honky Tonk...*Bill Doggett*
Hot Diggity...*Perry Como*
Hound Dog...*Elvis Presley*
I Almost Lost My Mind...*Pat Boone*
I Only Have Eyes For You...*Flamingos*
I Walk The Line...*Johnny Cash*
I Want You, I Need You, I Love You...*Elvis Presley*
I'm Gonna Get Married...*Lloyd Price*
I'm Gonna Sit Right Down And Write Myself A Letter...*Billy Williams*
In The Still Of The Nite...*Five Satins*
It's All In The Game...*Tommy Edwards*
It's Just A Matter Of Time...*Brook Benton*
It's Only Make Believe...*Conway Twitty*
Ivory Tower...*Cathy Carr*
Jailhouse Rock...*Elvis Presley*
Jim Dandy...*LaVern Baker*
Johnny B. Goode...*Chuck Berry*
Just Walking In The Rain...*Johnnie Ray*
Kansas City...*Wilbert Harrison*
Kisses Sweeter Than Wine...*Jimmie Rodgers*
La Bamba...*Ritchie Valens*
La Dee Dah...*Billy & Lillie*
Learnin' The Blues...*Frank Sinatra*
(Let Me Be Your) Teddy Bear...*Elvis Presley*
Let Me Go Lover...*Joan Weber*
Lisbon Antigua...*Nelson Riddle*
Little Darlin'...*Diamonds*
Little Star...*Elegants*
Lollipop...*Chordettes*
Lonely Boy...*Paul Anka*
Lonely Teardrops...*Jackie Wilson*
Long Tall Sally...*Little Richard*
Love And Marriage...*Frank Sinatra*
Love Is A Many-Splendored Thing...*Four Aces*
Love Is Strange...*Mickey & Sylvia*
Love Letters In The Sand...*Pat Boone*
Love Me...*Elvis Presley*
Love Me Tender...*Elvis Presley*
Lover's Question, A...*Clyde McPhatter*
Lucille...*Little Richard*
Mack The Knife...*Bobby Darin*
Maybe...*Chantels*
Maybellene...*Chuck Berry*
Memories Are Made Of This...*Dean Martin*
Mr. Blue...*Fleetwoods*
Mr. Lee...*Bobbettes*
Mr. Sandman...*Chordettes*
Moments To Remember...*Four Lads*
Moonglow And Theme From "Picnic"...*Morris Stoloff/Columbia Pictures Orch.*
Moonlight Gambler...*Frankie Laine*

My Happiness...*Connie Francis*
My Prayer...*Platters*
My True Love...*Jack Scott*
Mystery Train...*Elvis Presley*
Nel Blu Dipinto Di Blu (Volaré)...*Domenico Modugno*
No, Not Much!...*Four Lads*
Oh, Boy!...*Buddy Holly & The Crickets*
Oh Lonesome Me...*Don Gibson*
Old Cape Cod...*Patti Page*
On The Street Where You Live...*Vic Damone*
Only You (And You Alone)...*Platters*
Party Doll...*Buddy Knox*
Patricia...*Perez Prado*
Peggy Sue...*Buddy Holly*
Personality...*Lloyd Price*
Pink Shoe Laces...*Dodie Stevens*
Please, Please, Please...*James Brown*
Poor Little Fool...*Ricky Nelson*
Poor People Of Paris, The...*Les Baxter*
Problems...*Everly Brothers*
Purple People Eater, The...*Sheb Wooley*
Put Your Head On My Shoulder...*Paul Anka*
Queen Of The Hop...*Bobby Darin*
Raunchy...*Bill Justis*
Rave On...*Buddy Holly*
Rebel-'Rouser...*Duane Eddy*
Red River Rock...*Johnny & The Hurricanes*
Rock & Roll Music...*Chuck Berry*
Rock And Roll Waltz...*Kay Starr*
Rock Around The Clock...*Bill Haley & His Comets*
Rock-In Robin...*Bobby Day*
Rock Island Line...*Lonnie Donegan*
Roll Over Beethoven...*Chuck Berry*
Round And Round...*Perry Como*
School Day...*Chuck Berry*
Sea Of Love...*Phil Phillips*
Searchin'...*Coasters*
See You Later, Alligator...*Bill Haley & His Comets*
Shifting Whispering Sands, The...*Billy Vaughn*
Short Shorts...*Royal Teens*
Shout...*Isley Brothers*
Silhouettes...*Rays*
Since I Met You Baby...*Ivory Joe Hunter*
Sincerely...*Moonglows*
Singing The Blues...*Guy Mitchell*
16 Candles...*Crests*
Sixteen Tons...*"Tennessee" Ernie Ford*

Sleep Walk...*Santo & Johnny*
Smoke Gets In Your Eyes...*Platters*
So Rare...*Jimmy Dorsey*
Sorry (I Ran All The Way Home)...*Impalas*
Splish Splash...*Bobby Darin*
Stagger Lee...*Lloyd Price*
Standing On The Corner...*Four Lads*
Stood Up...*Ricky Nelson*
Sugartime...*McGuire Sisters*
Summertime Blues...*Eddie Cochran*
Sweet Little Sixteen...*Chuck Berry*
Tammy...*Debbie Reynolds*
Tears On My Pillow...*Little Anthony & The Imperials*
Teen-Age Crush...*Tommy Sands*
Teenager In Love...*Dion & The Belmonts*
Tequila...*Champs*
That'll Be The Day...*Buddy Holly & The Crickets*
There Goes My Baby...*Drifters*
Three Bells, The...*Browns*
Tiger...*Fabian*
('Til) I Kissed You...*Everly Brothers*
To Know Him, Is To Love Him...*Teddy Bears*
Tom Dooley...*Kingston Trio*
Too Much...*Elvis Presley*
Topsy II...*Cozy Cole*
True Love...*Bing Crosby & Grace Kelly*
Tutti-Fruitti...*Little Richard*
26 Miles (Santa Catalina)...*Four Preps*
Twilight Time...*Platters*
Unchained Melody...*Al Hibbler*
Venus...*Frankie Avalon*
Wake Up Little Susie...*Everly Brothers*
Wayward Wind, The...*Gogi Grant*
What'd I Say...*Ray Charles*
Whatever Will Be, Will Be (Que Sera, Sera)...*Doris Day*
White Sport Coat (And A Pink Carnation) ...*Marty Robbins*
Whole Lot Of Shakin' Going On...*Jerry Lee Lewis*
Why Do Fools Fall In Love...*Frankie Lymon & The Teenagers*
Witch Doctor...*David Seville*
Wonderful! Wonderful!...*Johnny Mathis*
Yakety Yak...*Coasters*
Yellow Rose Of Texas, The...*Mitch Miller*
You Send Me...*Sam Cooke*
Young Blood...*Coasters*
Young Love...*Sonny James*

Alley-Oop...*Hollywood Argyles*
Apache...*Jorgen Ingmann*
Are You Lonesome To-night?...*Elvis Presley*
Baby Love...*Supremes*
Baby (You've Got What It Takes)...*Dinah Washington & Brook Benton*
Be My Baby...*Ronettes*
Because They're Young...*Duane Eddy*
Big Bad John...*Jimmy Dean*
Big Girls Don't Cry...*4 Seasons*
Blowin' In The Wind...*Bob Dylan*
Blue Moon...*Marcels*
Blue Velvet...*Bobby Vinton*
Bobby's Girl...*Marcie Blane*
Bread And Butter...*Newbeats*
Breaking Up Is Hard To Do...*Neil Sedaka*
Bristol Stomp...*Dovells*
Burning Bridges...*Jack Scott*
Can't Buy Me Love...*Beatles*
Can't Get Used To Losing You...*Andy Williams*
Can't Help Falling In Love...*Elvis Presley*
Cathy's Clown...*Everly Brothers*
Chain Gang...*Sam Cooke*
Chapel Of Love...*Dixie Cups*
Come See About Me...*Supremes*
Crazy...*Patsy Cline*
Crying...*Roy Orbison*
Da Doo Ron Ron...*Crystals*
Daddy's Home...*Shep & The Limelites*
Dancing In The Street...*Martha & The Vandellas*
Dawn (Go Away)...*4 Seasons*
Dedicated To The One I Love...*Shirelles*
Do Wah Diddy Diddy...*Manfred Mann*
Do You Love Me...*Contours*
Do You Want To Know A Secret...*Beatles*
Dominique...*Singing Nun*
Don't Break The Heart That Loves You...*Connie Francis*
Don't Worry...*Marty Robbins*
Duke Of Earl...*Gene Chandler*
Easier Said Than Done...*Essex*
El Paso...*Marty Robbins*
End Of The World, The...*Skeeter Davis*
Everybody Loves Somebody...*Dean Martin*
Everybody's Somebody's Fool...*Connie Francis*
Exodus...*Ferrante & Teicher*
Fingertips...*Stevie Wonder*
Fun, Fun, Fun...*Beach Boys*
G.T.O....*Ronny & The Daytonas*
Georgia On My Mind...*Ray Charles*
Go Away Little Girl...*Steve Lawrence*
Good Luck Charm...*Elvis Presley*
Good Timin'...*Jimmy Jones*
Green Onions...*Booker T. & The MG's*

Greenfields...*Brothers Four*
Handy Man...*Jimmy Jones*
Hard Day's Night, A...*Beatles*
He'll Have To Go...*Jim Reeves*
Hello, Dolly!...*Louis Armstrong*
Hello Mary Lou...*Ricky Nelson*
Hello Mudduh, Hello Fadduh!...*Allan Sherman*
He's A Rebel...*Crystals*
He's So Fine...*Chiffons*
Hey! Baby...*Bruce Channel*
Hey Little Cobra...*Rip Chords*
Hey Paula...*Paul & Paula*
Hit The Road Jack...*Ray Charles*
House Of The Rising Sun, The...*Animals*
Hundred Pounds Of Clay, A...*Gene McDaniels*
I Can't Stop Loving You...*Ray Charles*
I Fall To Pieces...*Patsy Cline*
I Feel Fine...*Beatles*
I Get Around...*Beach Boys*
I Left My Heart In San Francisco...*Tony Bennett*
I Like It Like That...*Chris Kenner*
I Love How You Love Me...*Paris Sisters*
I Saw Her Standing There...*Beatles*
I Want To Be Wanted...*Brenda Lee*
I Want To Hold Your Hand...*Beatles*
I Will Follow Him...*Little Peggy March*
I'm Sorry...*Brenda Lee*
I've Told Every Little Star...*Linda Scott*
If You Wanna Be Happy...*Jimmy Soul*
In My Room...*Beach Boys*
It's My Party...*Lesley Gore*
It's Now Or Never...*Elvis Presley*
Itsy Bitsy Teenie Weenie Yellow Polkadot Bikini...*Brian Hyland*
Johnny Angel...*Shelley Fabares*
Last Date...*Floyd Cramer*
Last Kiss...*J. Frank Wilson & The Cavaliers*
Leader Of The Pack...*Shangri-Las*
Let's Dance...*Chris Montez*
Limbo Rock...*Chubby Checker*
Lion Sleeps Tonight, The...*Tokens*
Little Honda...*Hondells*
Little Old Lady (From Pasadena)...*Jan & Dean*
Loco-Motion, The...*Little Eva*
Louie Louie...*Kingsmen*
Love Me Do...*Beatles*
(Man Who Shot) Liberty Valance, The...*Gene Pitney*
Mashed Potato Time...*Dee Dee Sharp*
Memphis...*Johnny Rivers*
Michael...*Highwaymen*
Midnight In Moscow...*Kenny Ball*
Monster Mash...*Bobby "Boris" Pickett*
Moody River...*Pat Boone*
Moon River...*Henry Mancini*

Mother-In-Law...*Ernie K-Doe*
Mountain's High, The...*Dick & Dee Dee*
Mr. Custer...*Larry Verne*
Mr. Lonely...*Bobby Vinton*
Mule Skinner Blues...*Fendermen*
My Boy Lollipop...*Millie Small*
My Boyfriend's Back...*Angels*
My Guy...*Mary Wells*
My True Story...*Jive Five*
Night...*Jackie Wilson*
North To Alaska...*Johnny Horton*
Oh, Pretty Woman...*Roy Orbison*
Only Love Can Break A Heart...*Gene Pitney*
Only The Lonely...*Roy Orbison*
Our Day Will Come...*Ruby & The Romantics*
Out Of Limits...*Marketts*
Palisades Park...*Freddy Cannon*
Peppermint Twist...*Joey Dee & The Starliters*
Pipeline...*Chantay's*
Please Mr. Postman...*Marvelettes*
Please Please Me...*Beatles*
Poetry In Motion...*Johnny Tillotson*
Pony Time...*Chubby Checker*
Popsicles And Icicles...*Murmaids*
Puff (The Magic Dragon)...*Peter, Paul & Mary*
Puppy Love...*Paul Anka*
Quarter To Three...*Gary (U.S.) Bonds*
Rag Doll...*4 Seasons*
Raindrops...*Dee Clark*
Ramblin' Rose...*Nat King Cole*
Return To Sender...*Elvis Presley*
Rhythm Of The Rain...*Cascades*
Ring Of Fire...*Johnny Cash*
Roses Are Red (My Love)...*Bobby Vinton*
Ruby Baby...*Dion*
Runaround Sue...*Dion*
Runaway...*Del Shannon*
Running Bear...*Johnny Preston*
Running Scared...*Roy Orbison*
Sally, Go 'Round The Roses...*Jaynetts*
Save The Last Dance For Me...*Drifters*
She Loves You...*Beatles*
Sheila...*Tommy Roe*
Sherry...*4 Seasons*
She's Not There...*Zombies*
Shop Around...*Miracles*
So Much In Love...*Tymes*
Soldier Boy...*Shirelles*
Spanish Harlem...*Ben E. King*

Stand By Me...*Ben E. King*
Stay...*Maurice Williams & The Zodiacs*
Stranger On The Shore...*Mr. Acker Bilk*
Stripper, The...*David Rose*
Stuck On You...*Elvis Presley*
Sugar Shack...*Jimmy Gilmer & The Fireballs*
Sukiyaki...*Kyu Sakamoto*
Surf City...*Jan & Dean*
Surfin' U.S.A....*Beach Boys*
Surrender...*Elvis Presley*
Suspicion...*Terry Stafford*
Take Good Care Of My Baby...*Bobby Vee*
Teen Angel...*Mark Dinning*
Tell Laura I Love Her...*Ray Peterson*
Telstar...*Tornadoes*
Theme From "A Summer Place"...*Percy Faith*
There's A Moon Out Tonight...*Capris*
Thousand Stars, A...*Kathy Young with The Innocents*
Times They Are A-Changin', The...*Bob Dylan*
Tossin' And Turnin'...*Bobby Lewis*
Travelin' Man...*Ricky Nelson*
Twist, The...*Chubby Checker*
Twist And Shout...*Beatles*
Up On The Roof...*Drifters*
Wah Watusi, The...*Orlons*
Walk -- Don't Run...*Ventures*
Walk Like A Man...*4 Seasons*
Walk On By...*Dionne Warwick*
Walk On By...*Leroy Van Dyke*
Walk Right In...*Rooftop Singers*
Walking To New Orleans...*Fats Domino*
Wanderer, The...*Dion*
Washington Square...*Village Stompers*
What In The World's Come Over You...*Jack Scott*
Wheels...*String-A-Longs*
Where Did Our Love Go...*Supremes*
Wild One...*Bobby Rydell*
Will You Love Me Tomorrow...*Shirelles*
Wipe Out...*Surfaris*
Wonderland By Night...*Bert Kaempfert*
Wooden Heart...*Joe Dowell*
World Without Love, A...*Peter & Gordon*
Yellow Bird...*Arthur Lyman Group*
You Really Got Me...*Kinks*
You're Sixteen...*Johnny Burnette*
(You're The) Devil In Disguise...*Elvis Presley*

All Along The Watchtower...*Jimi Hendrix*
All You Need Is Love...*Beatles*
Aquarius/Let The Sunshine In...*5th Dimension*
Bad Moon Rising...*Creedence Clearwater Revival*
Ballad Of The Green Berets, The...*SSgt Barry Sadler*
Barbara Ann...*Beach Boys*
Birds And The Bees, The...*Jewel Akens*
Born To Be Wild...*Steppenwolf*
Boy From New York City, The...*Ad Libs*
Boy Named Sue, A...*Johnny Cash*
Brown Eyed Girl...*Van Morrison*
California Dreamin'...*Mamas & Papas*
California Girls...*Beach Boys*
Chain Of Fools...*Aretha Franklin*
Change Is Gonna Come, A...*Sam Cooke*
Cherish...*Association*
Classical Gas...*Mason Williams*
Come On Down To My Boat...*Every Mothers' Son*
Come Together...*Beatles*
Crimson And Clover...*Tommy James & The Shondells*
Cry Like A Baby...*Box Tops*
Crying In The Chapel...*Elvis Presley*
Dance To The Music...*Sly & The Family Stone*
Daydream...*Lovin' Spoonful*
Daydream Believer...*Monkees*
Devil With A Blue Dress On & Good Golly Miss Molly...*Mitch Ryder*
Dizzy...*Tommy Roe*
Do You Believe In Magic...*Lovin' Spoonful*
Down On The Corner...*Creedence Clearwater Revival*
Downtown...*Petula Clark*
Eight Days A Week...*Beatles*
Eight Miles High...*Byrds*
Eleanor Rigby...*Beatles*
Eve Of Destruction...*Barry McGuire*
Everyday People...*Sly & The Family Stone*
For Once In My Life...*Stevie Wonder*
For What It's Worth...*Buffalo Springfield*
Game Of Love...*Wayne Fontana & The Mindbenders*
Georgy Girl...*Seekers*
Get Back...*Beatles*
Get Off Of My Cloud...*Rolling Stones*
Gimme Some Lovin'...*Spencer Davis Group*
Gloria...*Them*
God Only Knows...*Beach Boys*
Good Lovin'...*Young Rascals*
Good Morning Starshine...*Oliver*
Good, The Bad And The Ugly, The...*Hugo Montenegro*
Good Vibrations...*Beach Boys*
Grazing In The Grass...*Hugh Masekela*

Green River...*Creedence Clearwater Revival*
Green Tambourine...*Lemon Pipers*
Groovin'...*Young Rascals*
Groovy Kind Of Love, A...*Mindbenders*
Hang On Sloopy...*McCoys*
Hanky Panky...*Tommy James & The Shondells*
Happy Together...*Turtles*
Harper Valley P.T.A....*Jeannie C. Riley*
Hello Goodbye...*Beatles*
Hello, I Love You...*Doors*
Help!...*Beatles*
Help Me, Rhonda...*Beach Boys*
Hey Jude...*Beatles*
Honey...*Bobby Goldsboro*
Honky Tonk Women...*Rolling Stones*
Horse, The...*Cliff Nobles*
Hot Fun In The Summertime...*Sly & The Family Stone*
Hush, Hush Sweet Charlotte...*Patti Page*
I Can See For Miles...*Who*
I Can't Get Next To You...*Temptations*
(I Can't Get No) Satisfaction...*Rolling Stones*
I Can't Help Myself...*Four Tops*
I Fought The Law...*Bobby Fuller Four*
I Got You Babe...*Sonny & Cher*
I Got You (I Feel Good)...*James Brown*
I Heard It Through The Grapevine...*Marvin Gaye*
I'm A Believer...*Monkees*
I'm Henry VIII, I Am...*Herman's Hermits*
I'm Telling You Now...*Freddie & The Dreamers*
In-A-Gadda-Da-Vida...*Iron Butterfly*
In My Life...*Beatles*
In The Ghetto...*Elvis Presley*
In The Midnight Hour...*Wilson Pickett*
In The Year 2525...*Zager & Evans*
Incense And Peppermints...*Strawberry Alarm Clock*
It's Your Thing...*Isley Brothers*
Judy In Disguise (With Glasses)...*John Fred & His Playboy Band*
Jumpin' Jack Flash...*Rolling Stones*
Kicks...*Paul Revere & The Raiders*
Kind Of A Drag...*Buckinghams*
King Of The Road...*Roger Miller*
Lady Madonna...*Beatles*
Last Train To Clarksville...*Monkees*
Leaving On A Jet Plane...*Peter, Paul & Mary*
Letter, The...*Box Tops*
Light My Fire...*Doors*
Lightnin' Strikes...*Lou Christie*
Like A Rolling Stone...*Bob Dylan*
Lil' Red Riding Hood...*Sam The Sham & The Pharaohs*
Little Bit O' Soul...*Music Explosion*
Little Girl...*Syndicate Of Sound*
Little Latin Lupe Lu...*Mitch Ryder*

Love Child...*Supremes*
Love Is Blue...*Paul Mauriat*
Love Theme From Romeo & Juliet...*Henry Mancini*
Lover's Concerto, A...*Toys*
Mellow Yellow...*Donovan*
Monday, Monday...*Mamas & Papas*
Mony Mony...*Tommy James & The Shondells*
Mr. Tambourine Man...*Byrds*
Mrs. Brown You've Got A Lovely Daughter ...*Herman's Hermits*
Mrs. Robinson...*Simon & Garfunkel*
My Generation...*Who*
My Girl...*Temptations*
My Love...*Petula Clark*
Na Na Hey Hey Kiss Him Goodbye...*Steam*
Never My Love...*Association*
19th Nervous Breakdown...*Rolling Stones*
96 Tears...*? & The Mysterians*
Nowhere Man...*Beatles*
Ode To Billie Joe...*Bobbie Gentry*
Over And Over...*Dave Clark Five*
Paint It, Black...*Rolling Stones*
Papa's Got A Brand New Bag...*James Brown*
Paperback Writer...*Beatles*
Penny Lane...*Beatles*
People Get Ready...*Impressions*
People Got To Be Free...*Rascals*
Piece Of My Heart...*Big Brother & The Holding Co. (Janis Joplin)*
Pied Piper, The...*Crispian St. Peters*
Poor Side Of Town...*Johnny Rivers*
Proud Mary...*Creedence Clearwater Revival*
Purple Haze...*Jimi Hendrix*
Rain, The Park & Other Things, The...*Cowsills*
Rainy Day Women #12 & 35...*Bob Dylan*
Reach Out I'll Be There...*Four Tops*
Red Rubber Ball...*Cyrkle*
Respect...*Aretha Franklin*
River Deep-Mountain High...*Ike & Tina Turner*
Ruby Tuesday...*Rolling Stones*
Secret Agent Man...*Johnny Rivers*
She's Just My Style...*Gary Lewis & The Playboys*
(Sittin' On) The Dock Of The Bay...*Otis Redding*
Sloop John B...*Beach Boys*
Snoopy Vs. The Red Baron...*Royal Guardsmen*
Somethin' Stupid...*Nancy Sinatra & Frank Sinatra*
Something...*Beatles*
Soul Man...*Sam & Dave*
Sounds Of Silence, The...*Simon & Garfunkel*
Spinning Wheel...*Blood, Sweat & Tears*
Spooky...*Classics IV*
Stand By Your Man...*Tammy Wynette*
Stop! In The Name Of Love...*Supremes*

Strangers In The Night...*Frank Sinatra*
Strawberry Fields Forever...*Beatles*
Sugar, Sugar...*Archies*
Summer In The City...*Lovin' Spoonful*
Sunny...*Bobby Hebb*
Sunshine Of Your Love...*Cream*
Sunshine Superman...*Donovan*
Suspicious Minds...*Elvis Presley*
Sweet Caroline...*Neil Diamond*
Sweet Soul Music...*Arthur Conley*
Sympathy For The Devil...*Rolling Stones*
Take A Letter Maria...*R.B. Greaves*
Tell It Like It Is...*Aaron Neville*
(Theme From) Valley Of The Dolls...*Dionne Warwick*
These Boots Are Made For Walkin'...*Nancy Sinatra*
This Diamond Ring...*Gary Lewis & The Playboys*
This Guy's In Love With You...*Herb Alpert*
Those Were The Days...*Mary Hopkin*
Ticket To Ride...*Beatles*
Tighten Up...*Archie Bell & The Drells*
Time Of The Season...*Zombies*
To Sir With Love...*Lulu*
Treat Her Right...*Roy Head*
Turn! Turn! Turn!...*Byrds*
Unchained Melody...*Righteous Brothers*
Walk In The Black Forest...*Horst Jankowski*
We Can Work It Out...*Beatles*
Wedding Bell Blues...*5th Dimension*
Weight, The...*Band*
What's New Pussycat?...*Tom Jones*
When A Man Loves A Woman...*Percy Sledge*
White Rabbit...*Jefferson Airplane*
Whiter Shade Of Pale...*Procol Harum*
Wichita Lineman...*Glen Campbell*
Wild Thing...*Troggs*
Winchester Cathedral...*New Vaudeville Band*
Windy...*Association*
Woman, Woman...*Gary Puckett & The Union Gap*
Wooly Bully...*Sam The Sham & The Pharaohs*
Yellow Submarine...*Beatles*
Yesterday...*Beatles*
You Can't Hurry Love...*Supremes*
You Keep Me Hangin' On...*Supremes*
You Were On My Mind...*We Five*
(You're My) Soul And Inspiration...*Righteous Brothers*
You've Lost That Lovin' Feelin'...*Righteous Brothers*
You've Made Me So Very Happy...*Blood, Sweat & Tears*
Your Love Keeps Lifting Me Higher And Higher...*Jackie Wilson*

**ABC**...*Jackson 5*
**Ain't No Mountain High Enough**...*Diana Ross*
**Ain't No Sunshine**...*Bill Withers*
**Air That I Breathe**...*Hollies*
**Alone Again (Naturally)**...*Gilbert O'Sullivan*
**Amazing Grace**...*Judy Collins*
**American Pie**...*Don McLean*
**American Woman**...*Guess Who*
**Angie**...*Rolling Stones*
**Angie Baby**...*Helen Reddy*
**Annie's Song**...*John Denver*
**Baby Don't Get Hooked On Me**...*Mac Davis*
**Back Stabbers**...*O'Jays*
**Bad, Bad Leroy Brown**...*Jim Croce*
**Band Of Gold**...*Freda Payne*
**Band On The Run**...*Paul McCartney*
**Bennie And The Jets**...*Elton John*
**Billy, Don't Be A Hero**...*Bo Donaldson*
**Black & White**...*Three Dog Night*
**Black Magic Woman**...*Santana*
**Boogie Down**...*Eddie Kendricks*
**Brand New Key**...*Melanie*
**Brandy (You're A Fine Girl)**...*Looking Glass*
**Bridge Over Troubled Water**...*Simon & Garfunkel*
**Brother Louie**...*Stories*
**Brown Sugar**...*Rolling Stones*
**Burning Love**...*Elvis Presley*
**Candy Man, The**...*Sammy Davis, Jr.*
**Can't Get Enough Of Your Love, Babe**...*Barry White*
**Cat's In The Cradle**...*Harry Chapin*
**China Grove**...*Doobie Brothers*
**Cisco Kid, The**...*War*
**Cracklin' Rosie**...*Neil Diamond*
**Crocodile Rock**...*Elton John*
**Daniel**...*Elton John*
**Day After Day**...*Badfinger*
**Do It ('Til You're Satisfied)**...*B.T. Express*
**Don't Let The Sun Go Down On Me**...*Elton John*
**Dueling Banjos**...*Eric Weissberg & Steve Mandell*
**Everything Is Beautiful**...*Ray Stevens*
**Family Affair**...*Sly & The Family Stone*
**Fire And Rain**...*James Taylor*
**First Time Ever I Saw Your Face, The** ...*Roberta Flack*
**Frankenstein**...*Edgar Winter Group*
**Free Bird**...*Lynyrd Skynyrd*
**Give Me Love - (Give Me Peace On Earth)** ...*George Harrison*
**Go All The Way**...*Raspberries*
**Goodbye Yellow Brick Road**...*Elton John*
**Green-Eyed Lady**...*Sugarloaf*
**Gypsys, Tramps & Thieves**...*Cher*
**Have You Ever Seen The Rain**...*Creedence Clearwater Revival*

**Have You Seen Her**...*Chi-Lites*
**Heart Of Gold**...*Neil Young*
**Hey There Lonely Girl**...*Eddie Holman*
**Hold Your Head Up**...*Argent*
**Hooked On A Feeling**...*Blue Swede*
**Horse With No Name, A**...*America*
**How Can You Mend A Broken Heart**...*Bee Gees*
**I Am Woman**...*Helen Reddy*
**I Can Help**...*Billy Swan*
**I Can See Clearly Now**...*Johnny Nash*
**I Gotcha**...*Joe Tex*
**I Honestly Love You**...*Olivia Newton-John*
**I Shot The Sheriff**...*Eric Clapton*
**I Think I Love You**...*Partridge Family*
**I Want You Back**...*Jackson 5*
**I'd Love You To Want Me**...*Lobo*
**I'll Be There**...*Jackson 5*
**I'll Take You There**...*Staple Singers*
**If You Don't Know Me By Now**...*Harold Melvin & The Bluenotes*
**Imagine**...*John Lennon*
**Immigrant Song**...*Led Zeppelin*
**In The Summertime**...*Mungo Jerry*
**Indian Reservation**...*Raiders*
**Instant Karma (We All Shine On)**...*John Lennon & Yoko Ono*
**It's Too Late**...*Carole King*
**Joker, The**...*Steve Miller Band*
**Joy To The World**...*Three Dog Night*
**Just My Imagination (Running Away With Me)**...*Temptations*
**Keep On Truckin'**...*Eddie Kendricks*
**Killing Me Softly With His Song**...*Roberta Flack*
**King Fu Fighting**...*Carl Douglas*
**Knock Three Times**...*Tony Orlando & Dawn*
**Kodachrome**...*Paul Simon*
**Layla**...*Derek & The Dominos (Eric Clapton)*
**Lean On Me**...*Bill Withers*
**Let It Be**...*Beatles*
**Let's Get It On**...*Marvin Gaye*
**Let's Stay Together**...*Al Green*
**Live And Let Die**...*Paul McCartney*
**Lola**...*Kinks*
**Lonely Days**...*Bee Gees*
**Long And Winding Road, The**...*Beatles*
**Long Cool Woman (In A Black Dress)**...*Hollies*
**Lookin' Out My Back Door**...*Creedence Clearwater Revival*
**Love On A Two-Way Street**...*Moments*
**Love Train**...*O'Jays*
**Love You Save, The**...*Jackson 5*
**Love's Theme**...*Love Unlimited Orchestra*
**Maggie May**...*Rod Stewart*
**Make It With You**...*Bread*
**Mama Told Me (Not To Come)**...*Three Dog Night*

Me And Bobby McGee...*Janis Joplin*
Me And Mrs. Jones...*Billy Paul*
Midnight Train To Georgia...*Gladys Knight & The Pips*
Money...*Pink Floyd*
Morning Has Broken...*Cat Stevens*
Most Beautiful Girl, The...*Charlie Rich*
Mr. Big Stuff...*Jean Knight*
Mr. Bojangles...*Nitty Gritty Dirt Band*
My Ding-A-Ling...*Chuck Berry*
My Love...*Paul McCartney*
My Sweet Lord...*George Harrison*
Night Chicago Died, The...*Paper Lace*
Night The Lights Went Out In Georgia, The...*Vicki Lawrence*
Night They Drove Old Dixie Down, The...*Joan Baez*
Nights In White Satin...*Moody Blues*
Nothing From Nothing...*Billy Preston*
Oh Girl...*Chi-Lites*
Ohio...*Crosby, Stills, Nash & Young*
One Bad Apple...*Osmonds*
One Less Bell To Answer...*5th Dimension*
O-o-h Child...*5 Stairsteps*
Papa Was A Rollin' Stone...*Temptations*
Patches...*Clarence Carter*
Photograph...*Ringo Starr*
Playground In My Mind...*Clint Holmes*
Proud Mary...*Ike & Tina Turner*
Put Your Hand In The Hand...*Ocean*
Raindrops Keep Fallin' On My Head...*B.J. Thomas*
Rainy Days And Mondays...*Carpenters*
Rainy Night In Georgia...*Brook Benton*
Ramblin Man...*Allman Brothers Band*
Rapper, The...*Jaggerz*
Ride Captain Ride...*Blues Image*
Rings...*Cymarron*
Rock And Roll Part 2...*Gary Glitter*
Rock Me Gently...*Andy Kim*
Rock The Boat...*Hues Corporation*
Rock Your Baby...*George McCrae*
Rocket Man...*Elton John*
Rose Garden...*Lynn Anderson*
Saturday In The Park...*Chicago*
Seasons In The Sun...*Terry Jacks*
She's A Lady...*Tom Jones*
Signed, Sealed, Delivered I'm Yours...*Stevie Wonder*
Signs...*Five Man Electrical Band*
Smiling Faces Sometimes...*Undisputed Truth*
Smoke On The Water...*Deep Purple*
Song Sung Blue...*Neil Diamond*
Spill The Wine...*Eric Burdon & War*
Spirit In The Sky...*Norman Greenbaum*
Stairway To Heaven...*Led Zeppelin*
Streak, The...*Ray Stevens*
Sundown...*Gordon Lightfoot*

Sunshine On My Shoulders...*John Denver*
Superstar...*Carpenters*
Superstition...*Stevie Wonder*
Sweet Home Alabama...*Lynyrd Skynyrd*
TSOP (The Sound Of Philadelphia)...*MFSB feat. The Three Degrees*
Take Me Home, Country Roads...*John Denver*
Tears Of A Clown, The...*Smokey Robinson & The Miracles*
Thank You (Falettinme Be Mice Elf Agin)...*Sly & The Family Stone*
Theme From Shaft...*Isaac Hayes*
Then Came You...*Dionne Warwicke & Spinners*
(They Long To Be) Close To You...*Carpenters*
Thrill Is Gone...*B.B. King*
Tie A Yellow Ribbon Round The Ole Oak Tree...*Tony Orlando & Dawn*
Time In A Bottle...*Jim Croce*
Too Late To Turn Back Now...*Cornelius Brothers & Sister Rose*
Top Of The World...*Carpenters*
Travelin' Band...*Creedence Clearwater Revival*
Treat Her Like A Lady...*Cornelius Brothers & Sister Rose*
25 Or 5 To 4...*Chicago*
Uncle Albert/Admiral Halsey...*Paul & Linda McCartney*
Up Around The Bend...*Creedence Clearwater Revival*
Vehicle...*Ides Of March*
Venus...*Shocking Blue*
Want Ads...*Honey Cone*
War...*Edwin Starr*
Way We Were, The...*Barbra Streisand*
We're An American Band...*Grand Funk*
We've Only Just Begun...*Carpenters*
Whatcha See Is Whatcha Get...*Dramatics*
Whatever Gets You Thru The Night...*John Lennon*
What's Going On...*Marvin Gaye*
Which Way You Goin' Billy?...*Poppy Family*
Who'll Stop The Rain...*Creedence Clearwater Revival*
Whole Lotta Love...*Led Zeppelin*
Will It Go Round In Circles...*Billy Preston*
Without You...*Nilsson*
Won't Get Fooled Again...*Who*
You Ain't Seen Nothing Yet...*Bachman-Turner Overdrive*
You Are The Sunshine Of My Life...*Stevie Wonder*
You Make Me Feel Brand New...*Stylistics*
(You're) Having My Baby...*Paul Anka with Odia Coates*
You're Sixteen...*Ringo Starr*
You're So Vain...*Carly Simon*
You've Got A Friend...*James Taylor*
Your Song...*Elton John*

**After The Love Has Gone**...*Earth, Wind & Fire*
**Afternoon Delight**...*Starland Vocal Band*
**All By Myself**...*Eric Carmen*
**Babe**...*Styx*
**Baby Come Back**...*Player*
**Bad Blood**...*Neil Sedaka*
**Bad Girls**...*Donna Summer*
**Baker Street**...*Gerry Rafferty*
**Before The Next Teardrop Falls**...*Freddy Fender*
**Best Of My Love**...*Eagles*
**Best Of My Love**...*Emotions*
**Black Water**...*Doobie Brothers*
**Blinded By The Light**...*Manfred Mann*
**Blitzkrieg Bop**...*Ramones*
**Blue Eyes Crying In The Rain**...*Willie Nelson*
**Bohemian Rhapsody**...*Queen*
**Boogie Fever**...*Sylvers*
**Boogie Nights**...*Heatwave*
**Boogie Oogie Oogie**...*Taste Of Honey*
**Born To Be Alive**...*Patrick Hernandez*
**Born To Run**...*Bruce Springsteen*
**Car Wash**...*Rose Royce*
**Convoy**...*C.W. McCall*
**Da Ya Think I'm Sexy?**...*Rod Stewart*
**Dancing Queen**...*Abba*
**December, 1963 (Oh, What A Night)** ...*4 Seasons*
**Devil Went Down To Georgia, The**...*Charlie Daniels Band*
**Disco Lady**...*Johnnie Taylor*
**Don't Bring Me Down**...*Electric Light Orchestra*
**Don't Fear The Reaper**...*Blue Öyster Cult*
**Don't Go Breaking My Heart**...*Elton John & Kiki Dee*
**Don't It Make My Brown Eyes Blue**...*Crystal Gayle*
**Don't Leave Me This Way**...*Thelma Houston*
**Don't Stop**...*Fleetwood Mac*
**Don't Stop 'Til You Get Enough**...*Michael Jackson*
**Dream Weaver**...*Gary Wright*
**Dreams**...*Fleetwood Mac*
**Escape (The Pina Colada Song)**...*Rupert Holmes*
**Every Which Way But Loose**...*Eddie Rabbitt*
**Fallin' In Love**...*Hamilton, Joe Frank & Reynolds*
**Fame**...*David Bowie*
**50 Ways To Leave Your Lover**...*Paul Simon*
**Fire**...*Pointer Sisters*
**Float On**...*Floaters*
**Fly Like An Eagle**...*Steve Miller*
**Fly, Robin, Fly**...*Silver Convention*
**Fooled Around And Fell In Love**...*Elvin Bishop*
**Fox On The Run**...*Sweet*
**Get Down Tonight**...*KC & The Sunshine Band*
**Get Up, Stand Up**...*Bob Marley*

**Go Your Own Way**...*Fleetwood Mac*
**Good Times**...*Chic*
**Got To Give It Up**...*Marvin Gaye*
**Grease**...*Frankie Valli*
**Have You Never Been Mellow**...*Olivia Newton-John*
**He Don't Love You (Like I Love You)**...*Tony Orlando & Dawn*
**Heart Of Glass**...*Blondie*
**Heartache Tonight**...*Eagles*
**Heaven Knows**...*Donna Summer & Brooklyn Dreams*
**Here You Come Again**...*Dolly Parton*
**Heroes**...*David Bowie*
**Hopelessly Devoted To You**...*Olivia Newton-John*
**Hot Blooded**...*Foreigner*
**Hot Child In The City**...*Nick Gilder*
**Hot Stuff**...*Donna Summer*
**Hotel California**...*Eagles*
**How Deep Is Your Love**...*Bee Gees*
**Hustle, The**...*Van McCoy*
**I Just Want To Be Your Everything**...*Andy Gibb*
**I Want You To Want Me**...*Cheap Trick*
**I Will Survive**...*Gloria Gaynor*
**I Write The Songs**...*Barry Manilow*
**I'd Really Love To See You Tonight**...*England Dan & John Ford Coley*
**I'm In You**...*Peter Frampton*
**I'm Not In Love**...*10cc*
**I'm Your Boogie Man**...*KC & The Sunshine Band*
**If I Can't Have You**...*Yvonne Elliman*
**If You Leave Me Now**...*Chicago*
**In The Navy**...*Village People*
**Island Girl**...*Elton John*
**It's A Heartache**...*Bonnie Tyler*
**Jive Talkin'**...*Bee Gees*
**Junior's Farm**...*Paul McCartney*
**Just The Way You Are**...*Billy Joel*
**Just When I Needed You Most**...*Randy Vanwarmer*
**Kiss And Say Goodbye**...*Manhattans*
**Kiss You All Over**...*Exile*
**Knock On Wood**...*Amii Stewart*
**Lady Marmalade**...*LaBelle*
**Last Dance**...*Donna Summer*
**Last Farewell, The**...*Roger Whittaker*
**Laughter In The Rain**...*Neil Sedaka*
**Lay Down Sally**...*Eric Clapton*
**Le Freak**...*Chic*
**Let Your Love Flow**...*Bellamy Brothers*
**Let's Do It Again**...*Staple Singers*
**Let's Go**...*The Cars*
**Listen To What The Man Said**...*Paul McCartney*
**Logical Song, The**...*Supertramp*

Love Hangover...*Diana Ross*
(Love Is) Thicker Than Water...*Andy Gibb*
Love Machine...*Miracles*
Love Rollercoaster...*Ohio Players*
Love Theme From "A Star Is Born" (Evergreen)...*Barbra Streisand*
Love To Love You Baby...*Donna Summer*
Love Will Keep Us Together...*Captain & Tennille*
Lovin' You...*Minnie Riperton*
Lucille...*Kenny Rogers*
Lucy In The Sky With Diamonds...*Elton John*
Lyin' Eyes...*Eagles*
MacArthur Park...*Donna Summer*
Macho Man...*Village People*
Mandy...*Barry Manilow*
Margaritaville...*Jimmy Buffett*
Miss You...*Rolling Stones*
More Than A Feeling...*Boston*
Music Box Dancer...*Frank Mills*
My Eyes Adored You...*Frankie Valli*
My Life...*Billy Joel*
My Sharona...*Knack*
New Kid In Town...*Eagles*
Night Fever...*Bee Gees*
Night Moves...*Bob Seger*
No More Tears (Enough Is Enough)...*Barbra Streisand & Donna Summer*
No Woman No Cry (live)...*Bob Marley*
Nobody Does It Better...*Carly Simon*
One Of These Nights...*Eagles*
Philadelphia Freedom...*Elton John*
Pick Up The Pieces...*AWB*
Play That Funky Music...*Wild Cherry*
Pop Muzik...*M*
Rapper's Delight...*Sugarhill Gang*
Reunited...*Peaches & Herb*
Rhinestone Cowboy...*Glen Campbell*
Rich Girl...*Daryl Hall & John Oates*
Right Back Where We Started From...*Maxine Nightingale*
Ring My Bell...*Anita Ward*
Rise...*Herb Alpert*
Rock & Roll All Nite (live)...*Kiss*
Rock'n Me...*Steve Miller*
Roxanne...*Police*
Rubberband Man, The...*Spinners*
Saturday Night...*Bay City Rollers*
Send One Your Love...*Stevie Wonder*
Shadow Dancing...*Andy Gibb*
(Shake, Shake, Shake) Shake Your Booty ...*KC & The Sunshine Band*
Shining Star...*Earth, Wind & Fire*
Short People...*Randy Newman*
Show Me The Way...*Peter Frampton*
Silly Love Songs...*Paul McCartney*
Sir Duke...*Stevie Wonder*
Sister Golden Hair...*America*

Sometimes When We Touch...*Dan Hill*
Southern Nights...*Glen Campbell*
Star Wars Theme/Cantina Band...*Meco*
Stayin' Alive...*Bee Gees*
Sultans Of Swing...*Dire Straits*
Sweet Emotion...*Aerosmith*
Take A Chance On Me...*Abba*
Take It To The Limit...*Eagles*
Take Me To The River...*Talking Heads*
Take The Money And Run...*Steve Miller Band*
Thank God I'm A Country Boy...*John Denver*
That's The Way (I Like It)...*KC & The Sunshine Band*
Theme From Mahogany (Do You Know Where You're Going To)...*Diana Ross*
Theme From S.W.A.T....*Rhythm Heritage*
Three Times A Lady...*Commodores*
Thunder Road...*Bruce Springsteen*
Tonight's The Night (Gonna Be Alright)...*Rod Stewart*
Too Much Heaven...*Bee Gees*
Too Much, Too Little, Too Late...*Johnny Mathis & Deniece Williams*
Torn Between Two Lovers...*Mary MacGregor*
Tragedy...*Bee Gees*
Tusk...*Fleetwood Mac*
Undercover Angel...*Alan O'Day*
Walk This Way...*Aerosmith*
Watching The Detectives...*Elvis Costello*
We Are Family...*Sister Sledge*
We Will Rock You/We Are The Champions ...*Queen*
Welcome Back...*John Sebastian*
Werewolves Of London...*Warren Zevon*
What A Fool Believes...*Doobie Brothers*
When I Need You...*Leo Sayer*
When Will I Be Loved...*Linda Ronstadt*
Who Loves You...*4 Seasons*
Why Can't We Be Friends...*War*
With A Little Luck...*Paul McCartney*
Wreck Of The Edmund Fitzgerald, The ...*Gordon Lightfoot*
Y.M.C.A....*Village People*
You Don't Bring Me Flowers...*Barbra Streisand & Neil Diamond*
You Light Up My Life...*Debby Boone*
You Make Me Feel Like Dancing...*Leo Sayer*
You Needed Me...*Anne Murray*
You Sexy Thing...*Hot Chocolate*
You Should Be Dancing...*Bee Gees*
You'll Never Find Another Love Like Mine...*Lou Rawls*
You're In My Heart...*Rod Stewart*
You're No Good...*Linda Ronstadt*
You're The First, The Last, My Everything ...*Barry White*
You're The One That I Want...*John Travolta & Olivia Newton-John*

Abracadabra...*Steve Miller Band*
Africa...*Toto*
Against All Odds (Take A Look At Me Now)...*Phil Collins*
Against The Wind...*Bob Seger*
All Night Long (All Night)...*Lionel Richie*
All Out Of Love...*Air Supply*
All Those Years Ago...*George Harrison*
Always On My Mind...*Willie Nelson*
Another Brick In The Wall...*Pink Floyd*
Another One Bites The Dust...*Queen*
Arthur's Theme (Best That You Can Do)...*Christopher Cross*
Baby, Come To Me...*Patti Austin with James Ingram*
Back On The Chain Gang...*Pretenders*
Beat It...*Michael Jackson*
Best Of Times, The...*Styx*
Bette Davis Eyes...*Kim Carnes*
Billie Jean...*Michael Jackson*
Burning Down The House...*Talking Heads*
Call Me...*Blondie*
Caribbean Queen (No More Love On The Run)...*Billy Ocean*
Cars...*Gary Numan*
Celebration...*Kool & The Gang*
Centerfold...*J. Geils Band*
Chariots Of Fire...*Vangelis*
Come Dancing...*Kinks*
Come On Eileen...*Dexys Midnight Runners*
Coming Up (Live At Glasgow)...*Paul McCartney*
Coward Of The County...*Kenny Rogers*
Crazy Little Thing Called Love...*Queen*
Cum On Feel The Noize...*Quiet Riot*
Dance Hall Days...*Wang Chung*
Dancing In The Dark...*Bruce Springsteen*
De Do Do Do, De Da Da Da...*Police*
Der Kommissar...*After The Fire*
Dirty Laundry...*Don Henley*
Do That To Me One More Time...*Captain & Tennille*
Do You Really Want To Hurt Me...*Culture Club*
Don't Talk To Strangers...*Rick Springfield*
Don't You Want Me...*Human League*
Down Under...*Men At Work*
Drive...*Cars*
Drivin' My Life Away...*Eddie Rabbitt*
Ebony And Ivory...*Paul McCartney with Stevie Wonder*
867-5309/Jenny...*Tommy Tutone*
Electric Avenue...*Eddy Grant*
Elvira...*Oak Ridge Boys*
Emotional Rescue...*Rolling Stones*
Endless Love...*Diana Ross & Lionel Richie*
Every Breath You Take...*Police*
Every Little Thing She Does Is Magic...*Police*

Eye In The Sky...*Alan Parsons Project*
Eye Of The Tiger...*Survivor*
Eyes Without A Face...*Billy Idol*
Fame...*Irene Cara*
Flashdance...What A Feeling...*Irene Cara*
Fool In The Rain...*Led Zeppelin*
Footloose...*Kenny Loggins*
For Your Eyes Only...*Sheena Easton*
Freeze-Frame...*J. Geils Band*
Funkytown...*Lipps, Inc.*
Ghostbusters...*Ray Parker Jr.*
Girl Is Mine, The...*Michael Jackson & Paul McCartney*
Girls Just Want To Have Fun...*Cyndi Lauper*
Gloria...*Laura Branigan*
Goody Two Shoes...*Adam Ant*
Hard To Say I'm Sorry...*Chicago*
Harden My Heart...*Quarterflash*
He Stopped Loving Her Today...*George Jones*
He's So Shy...*Pointer Sisters*
Heat Of The Moment...*Asia*
Here Comes The Rain Again...*Eurythmics*
Hit Me With Your Best Shot...*Pat Benatar*
Hold Me...*Fleetwood Mac*
Hold Me Now...*Thompson Twins*
Hungry Heart...*Bruce Springsteen*
Hungry Like The Wolf...*Duran Duran*
Hurts So Good...*John Cougar Mellencamp*
I Can't Tell You Why...*Eagles*
I Feel For You...*Chaka Khan*
I Just Called To Say I Love You...*Stevie Wonder*
I Love A Rainy Night...*Eddie Rabbitt*
I Love Rock 'N Roll...*Joan Jett & The Blackhearts*
I Melt With You...*Modern English*
I Ran (So Far Away)...*Flock Of Seagulls*
I Want Candy...*Bow Wow Wow*
Islands In The Stream...*Kenny Rogers with Dolly Parton*
It's Raining Again...*Supertramp*
It's Still Rock And Roll To Me...*Billy Joel*
Jack & Diane...*John Cougar Mellencamp*
Jeopardy...*Greg Kihn Band*
Jessie's Girl...*Rick Springfield*
Joanna...*Kool & The Gang*
Jump...*Van Halen*
Jump (For My Love)...*Pointer Sisters*
(Just Like) Starting Over...*John Lennon*
Just The Two Of Us...*Grover Washington, Jr. with Bill Withers*
Karma Chameleon...*Culture Club*
Keep On Loving You...*REO Speedwagon*
King Of Pain...*Police*
Kiss On My List...*Daryl Hall & John Oates*
Lady...*Kenny Rogers*
Let It Whip...*Dazz Band*

Let's Dance...*David Bowie*
Let's Go Crazy...*Prince*
Let's Groove...*Earth, Wind & Fire*
Let's Hear It For The Boy...*Deniece Williams*
Like A Virgin...*Madonna*
Little Jeannie...*Elton John*
Little Red Corvette...*Prince*
London Calling...*Clash*
Lost In Love...*Air Supply*
Love On The Rocks...*Neil Diamond*
Magic...*Olivia Newton-John*
Maneater...*Daryl Hall & John Oates*
Maniac...*Michael Sembello*
Master Blaster (Jammin')...*Stevie Wonder*
Message, The...*Grand Master Flash*
Mickey...*Toni Basil*
Missing You...*John Waite*
More Than I Can Say...*Leo Sayer*
Morning Train (Nine To Five)...*Sheena Easton*
Mr. Roboto...*Styx*
Never Knew Love Like This Before... *Stephanie Mills*
New Year's Day...*U2*
9 To 5...*Dolly Parton*
99 Luftballons...*Nena*
Oh Sherrie...*Steve Perry*
On The Road Again...*Willie Nelson*
One Thing Leads To Another...*Fixx*
Open Arms...*Journey*
Our Lips Are Sealed...*Go-Go's*
Out Of Touch...*Daryl Hall & John Oates*
Owner Of A Lonely Heart...*Yes*
Physical...*Olivia Newton-John*
Planet Rock...*Afrika Bambaataa*
Please Don't Go...*KC & The Sunshine Band*
Private Eyes...*Daryl Hall & John Oates*
Purple Rain...*Prince*
Puttin' On The Ritz...*Taco*
Queen Of Hearts...*Juice Newton*
Rapture...*Blondie*
Rebel Yell...*Billy Idol*
Redemption Song...*Bob Marley*
Reflex, The...*Duran Duran*
Relax...*Frankie Goes To Hollywood*
Ride Like The Wind...*Christopher Cross*
Rock The Casbah...*Clash*
Rock This Town...*Stray Cats*
Rock With You...*Michael Jackson*
Rosanna...*Toto*
Rose, The...*Bette Midler*
Safety Dance, The...*Men Without Hats*
Sailing...*Christopher Cross*
Say Say Say...*Paul McCartney & Michael Jackson*

Sexual Healing...*Marvin Gaye*
Shake It Up...*Cars*
Shame On The Moon...*Bob Seger*
She Works Hard For The Money...*Donna Summer*
Shining Star...*Manhattans*
Sister Christian...*Night Ranger*
Slow Hand...*Pointer Sisters*
Start Me Up...*Rolling Stones*
Stop Draggin' My Heart Around...*Stevie Nicks with Tom Petty*
Stray Cat Strut...*Stray Cats*
Sukiyaki...*Taste Of Honey*
Sweet Dreams (Are Made Of This)...*Eurythmics*
Switchin' To Glide...*The Kings*
Tainted Love...*Soft Cell*
Take It On The Run...*REO Speedwagon*
Take Your Time (Do It Right)...*S.O.S. Band*
Talking In Your Sleep...*Romantics*
Tell Her About It...*Billy Joel*
Theme From New York, New York...*Frank Sinatra*
Thriller...*Michael Jackson*
Tide Is High, The...*Blondie*
Time After Time...*Cyndi Lauper*
To All The Girls I've Loved Before...*Julio Iglesias & Willie Nelson*
Total Eclipse Of The Heart...*Bonnie Tyler*
True...*Spandau Ballet*
Truly...*Lionel Richie*
Under Pressure...*Queen & David Bowie*
Up Where We Belong....*Joe Cocker & Jennifer Warnes*
Upside Down...*Diana Ross*
Uptown Girl...*Billy Joel*
Waiting For A Girl Like You...*Foreigner*
Wake Me Up Before You Go-Go...*Wham!*
Wanderer, The...*Donna Summer*
We Got The Beat...*Go-Go's*
What's Love Got To Do With It...*Tina Turner*
When Doves Cry...*Prince*
Whip It...*Devo*
Who Can It Be Now?...*Men At Work*
Wild Boys, The...*Duran Duran*
Woman...*John Lennon*
Woman In Love...*Barbra Streisand*
Working For The Weekend...*Loverboy*
Xanadu...*Olivia Newton-John/Electric Light Orchestra*
You Shook Me All Night Long...*AC/DC*
You Should Hear How She Talks About You...*Melissa Manchester*
Young Turks...*Rod Stewart*

Addicted To Love...*Robert Palmer*
All I Need...*Jack Wagner*
Alone...*Heart*
Always...*Atlantic Starr*
Amanda...*Boston*
Another Day In Paradise...*Phil Collins*
Anything For You...*Gloria Estefan*
At This Moment...*Billy Vera & The Beaters*
Axel F...*Harold Faltermeyer*
Baby Don't Forget My Number...*Milli Vanilli*
Baby, I Love Your Way/Freebird Medley...*Will To Power*
Back To Life...*Soul II Soul*
Bad...*Michael Jackson*
Bad Medicine...*Bon Jovi*
Batdance...*Prince*
Blame It On The Rain...*Milli Vanilli*
Born In The U.S.A. ...*Bruce Springsteen*
Boys Of Summer, The...*Don Henley*
Broken Wings...*Mr. Mister*
Buffalo Stance...*Neneh Cherry*
Bust A Move...*Young MC*
Can't Fight This Feeling...*REO Speedwagon*
Careless Whisper...*Wham!/George Michael*
Causing A Commotion...*Madonna*
Cherish...*Kool & The Gang*
Crazy For You...*Madonna*
Dancing On The Ceiling...*Lionel Richie*
Danger Zone...*Kenny Loggins*
Devil Inside...*INXS*
Didn't We Almost Have It All...*Whitney Houston*
Dirty Diana...*Michael Jackson*
Don't Come Around Here No More...*Tom Petty*
Don't Dream It's Over...*Crowded House*
Don't Forget Me (When I'm Gone)...*Glass Tiger*
Don't Know Much...*Linda Ronstadt with Aaron Neville*
Don't Wanna Lose You...*Gloria Estefan*
Don't Worry Be Happy...*Bobby McFerrin*
Don't You (Forget About Me)...*Simple Minds*
Eternal Flame...*Bangles*
Every Rose Has Its Thorn...*Poison*
Everybody Have Fun Tonight...*Wang Chung*
Everybody Wants To Rule The World...*Tears For Fears*
Everything She Wants...*Wham!*
Everytime You Go Away...*Paul Young*
Express Yourself...*Madonna*
Faith...*George Michael*
Fast Car...*Tracy Chapman*
Father Figure...*George Michael*
Final Countdown, The...*Europe*
Flame, The...*Cheap Trick*
Forever Your Girl...*Paula Abdul*
Freedom...*Wham!/George Michael*
Get Outta My Dreams, Get Into My Car...*Billy Ocean*

Girl I'm Gonna Miss You...*Milli Vanilli*
Glory Of Love...*Peter Cetera*
Good Thing...*Fine Young Cannibals*
Got My Mind Set On You...*George Harrison*
Graceland...*Paul Simon*
Greatest Love Of All...*Whitney Houston*
Groovy Kind Of Love...*Phil Collins*
Hands To Heaven...*Breathe*
Hangin' Tough...*New Kids On The Block*
Hazy Shade Of Winter...*Bangles*
Head To Toe...*Lisa Lisa & Cult Jam*
Heat Is On, The...*Glenn Frey*
Heaven...*Bryan Adams*
Heaven Is A Place On Earth...*Belinda Carlisle*
Here I Go Again...*Whitesnake*
Higher Love...*Steve Winwood*
Hold On To The Nights...*Richard Marx*
Holding Back The Years...*Simply Red*
How Will I Know...*Whitney Houston*
Human...*Human League*
I Just Can't Stop Loving You...*Michael Jackson*
(I Just) Died In Your Arms...*Cutting Crew*
I Knew You Were Waiting (For Me)...*Aretha Franklin & George Michael*
I Still Haven't Found What I'm Looking For ...*U2*
I Think We're Alone Now...*Tiffany*
I Wanna Dance With Somebody (Who Loves Me)...*Whitney Houston*
I Want To Know What Love Is...*Foreigner*
(I've Had) The Time Of My Life...*Bill Medley & Jennifer Warnes*
I'll Be Loving You (Forever)...*New Kids On The Block*
I'll Be There For You...*Bon Jovi*
If I Could Turn Back Time...*Cher*
If You Don't Know Me By Now...*Simply Red*
If You Leave...*Orchestral Manoeuvres In The Dark*
If You Love Somebody Set Them Free...*Sting*
Invisible Touch...*Genesis*
Jacob's Ladder...*Huey Lewis*
Keep Your Hands To Yourself...*Georgia Satellites*
Kiss...*Prince*
Kokomo...*Beach Boys*
Kyrie...*Mr. Mister*
La Bamba...*Los Lobos*
Lady In Red, The...*Chris DeBurgh*
Lean On Me...*Club Nouveau*
Life In A Northern Town...*Dream Academy*
Like A Prayer...*Madonna*
Listen To Your Heart...*Roxette*
Livin' On A Prayer...*Bon Jovi*
Living Years, The...*Mike & The Mechanics*

Look, The...*Roxette*
Looking For A New Love....*Jody Watley*
Lost In Emotion...*Lisa Lisa & Cult Jam*
Lost In Your Eyes...*Debbie Gibson*
Love Shack...*B-52's*
Loverboy...*Billy Ocean*
Luka...*Suzanne Vega*
Man In The Mirror...*Michael Jackson*
Manic Monday...*Bangles*
Material Girl...*Madonna*
Mercedes Boy...*Pebbles*
Miami Vice Theme...*Jan Hammer*
Miss You Much...*Janet Jackson*
Money For Nothing...*Dire Straits*
Monkey...*George Michael*
Mony Mony "Live"...*Billy Idol*
My Hometown...*Bruce Springsteen*
My Prerogative...*Bobby Brown*
Need You Tonight...*INXS*
Never Gonna Give You Up...*Rick Astley*
Nothing's Gonna Stop Us Now...*Starship*
Notorious...*Duran Duran*
Oh Sheila...*Ready For The World*
On My Own...*Patti LaBelle & Michael McDonald*
On Our Own...*Bobby Brown*
One More Night...*Phil Collins*
One More Try...*George Michael*
One Night In Bangkok...*Murray Head*
Orinoco Flow (Sail Away)...*Enya*
Papa Don't Preach...*Madonna*
Part-Time Lover...*Stevie Wonder*
Patience...*Guns N' Roses*
People Are People...*Depeche Mode*
Pour Some Sugar On Me...*Def Leppard*
Power Of Love, The...*Huey Lewis*
Pump Up The Volume...*M/A/R/R/S*
Raspberry Beret...*Prince*
Red Red Wine...*UB40*
Rhythm Of The Night...*DeBarge*
Right Here Waiting...*Richard Marx*
R.O.C.K. In The U.S.A....*John Cougar Mellencamp*
Rock Me Amadeus...*Falco*
Roll With It...*Steve Winwood*
St. Elmo's Fire (Man In Motion)...*John Parr*
Saving All My Love For You...*Whitney Houston*
Say You, Say Me...*Lionel Richie*
Sea Of Love...*Honeydrippers*
Seasons Change...*Exposé*
Separate Lives...*Phil Collins & Marilyn Martin*
Shake You Down...*Gregory Abbott*
Shakedown...*Bob Seger*
She Drives Me Crazy...*Fine Young Cannibals*
Shout...*Tears For Fears*

Simply Irresistible...*Robert Palmer*
Sledgehammer...*Peter Gabriel*
Smooth Operator...*Sade*
Somewhere Out There...*Linda Ronstadt & James Ingram*
Straight Up...*Paula Abdul*
Summer Of '69...*Bryan Adams*
Sussudio...*Phil Collins*
Sweet Child O' Mine...*Guns N' Roses*
Take My Breath Away...*Berlin*
Take On Me...*A-Ha*
That's What Friends Are For...*Dionne Warwick & Friends*
There'll Be Sad Songs (To Make You Cry) ...*Billy Ocean*
These Dreams...*Heart*
Touch Of Grey...*Grateful Dead*
Toy Soldiers...*Martika*
True Colors...*Cyndi Lauper*
Two Hearts...*Phil Collins*
Venus...*Bananarama*
View To A Kill, A...*Duran Duran*
Walk Like An Egyptian...*Bangles*
Walk Of Life...*Dire Straits*
Walk This Way...*Run-D.M.C.*
Way It Is, The...*Bruce Hornsby*
Way You Make Me Feel, The...*Michael Jackson*
We Are The World...*USA For Africa*
We Belong...*Pat Benatar*
We Built This City...*Starship*
We Didn't Start The Fire...*Billy Joel*
We Don't Need Another Hero (Thunderdome) ...*Tina Turner*
West End Girls...*Pet Shop Boys*
What Have I Done To Deserve This?...*Pet Shop Boys & Dusty Springfield*
When I See You Smile...*Bad English*
When I Think Of You...*Janet Jackson*
When I'm With You...*Sheriff*
Where Do Broken Hearts Go...*Whitney Houston*
Why Can't This Be Love...*Van Halen*
Wild Thing...*Tone Loc*
Wild, Wild West...*Escape Club*
Wind Beneath My Wings...*Bette Midler*
Wishing Well...*Terence Trent D'Arby*
With Or Without You...*U2*
Word Up...*Cameo*
You Belong To The City...*Glenn Frey*
You Give Love A Bad Name...*Bon Jovi*
You Gotta Fight For Your Right To Party! ...*Beastie Boys*
You're The Inspiration...*Chicago*

Achy Breaky Heart...*Billy Ray Cyrus*
Again...*Janet Jackson*
All 4 Love...*Color Me Badd*
All For Love...*Bryan Adams/Rod Stewart/Sting*
All I Wanna Do...*Sheryl Crow*
All I Wanna Do Is Make Love To You...*Heart*
All That She Wants...*Ace Of Base*
All The Man That I Need...*Whitney Houston*
Always...*Bon Jovi*
Another Night...*Real McCoy*
Baby Baby...*Amy Grant*
Baby-Baby-Baby...*TLC*
Baby Got Back...*Sir Mix-A-Lot*
Baby, I Love Your Way...*Big Mountain*
Back & Forth...*Aaliyah*
Bad Boys...*Inner Circle*
Beauty And The Beast...*Celine Dion & Peabo Bryson*
Because I Love You (The Postman Song) ...*Stevie B*
Black Cat...*Janet Jackson*
Black Or White...*Michael Jackson*
Black Velvet...*Alannah Myles*
Blaze Of Glory...*Jon Bon Jovi*
Boot Scootin' Boogie...*Brooks & Dunn*
Breathe Again...*Toni Braxton*
Bump N' Grind...*R. Kelly*
Can You Feel The Love Tonight...*Elton John*
Can't Help Falling In Love...*UB40*
(Can't Live Without Your) Love And Affection ...*Nelson*
Can't Stop This Thing We Started...*Bryan Adams*
Chattahoochee...*Alan Jackson*
Close To You...*Maxi Priest*
Coming Out Of The Dark...*Gloria Estefan*
Cradle Of Love...*Billy Idol*
Crazy...*Seal*
Cream...*Prince*
Dangerous...*Roxette*
Diamonds And Pearls...*Prince*
Do Anything...*Natural Selection*
Don't Let The Sun Go Down On Me...*George Michael & Elton John*
Don't Take The Girl...*Tim McGraw*
Downtown Train...*Rod Stewart*
Dreamlover...*Mariah Carey*
Electric Slide (Boogie)...*Marcia Griffiths*
Emotions...*Mariah Carey*
End Of The Road...*Boyz II Men*
Escapade...*Janet Jackson*
Every Heartbeat...*Amy Grant*
Everything About You...*Ugly Kid Joe*
(Everything I Do) I Do It For You...*Bryan Adams*
Fantastic Voyage...*Coolio*

Fields Of Gold...*Sting*
First Time, The...*Surface*
Free Fallin'...*Tom Petty*
Friends In Low Places...*Garth Brooks*
From A Distance...*Bette Midler*
Gonna Make You Sweat (Everybody Dance Now)...*C & C Music Factory*
Good Vibrations...*Marky Mark with Loleatta Holloway*
Have I Told You Lately...*Rod Stewart*
Hazard...*Richard Marx*
Here Come The Hotstepper...*Ini Kamoze*
Hero...*Mariah Carey*
Hey Mr. D.J....*Zhané*
High Enough...*Damn Yankees*
Hippychick...*Soho*
Hold On...*Wilson Phillips*
Hold You Tight...*Tara Kemp*
How Am I Supposed To Live Without You ...*Michael Bolton*
How Do You Talk To An Angel...*Heights*
Humpty Dance...*Digital Underground*
I Adore Mi Amor...*Color Me Badd*
I Don't Have The Heart...*James Ingram*
I Like The Way (The Kissing Game)...*Hi-Five*
I Love Your Smile...*Shanice*
I Swear...*All-4-One*
I Wanna Be Down...*Brandy*
I Wanna Be Rich...*Calloway*
I Will Always Love You...*Whitney Houston*
I Wish It Would Rain Down...*Phil Collins*
I'd Die Without You...*PM Dawn*
I'll Be There...*Mariah Carey*
I'll Be Your Everything...*Tommy Page*
I'll Make Love To You...*Boyz II Men*
I'll Never Let You Go (Angel Eyes)...*Steelheart*
I'll Stand By You...*Pretenders*
I'm Gonna Be (500 Miles)...*Proclaimers*
I'm Too Sexy...*R*S*F (Right Said Fred)*
I'm Your Baby Tonight...*Whitney Houston*
I've Been Thinking About You...*Londonbeat*
Ice Ice Baby...*Vanilla Ice*
If I Ever Fall In Love...*Shai*
If I Had No Loot...*Tony! Toni! Toné!*
If Wishes Came True...*Sweet Sensation*
If You Asked Me To...*Celine Dion*
Indian Outlaw...*Tim McGraw*
Informer...*Snow*
It Ain't Over 'Til It's Over...*Lenny Kravitz*
It Must Have Been Love...*Roxette*
It's So Hard To Say Goodbye To Yesterday ...*Boyz II Men*
Janie's Got A Gun...*Aerosmith*
Jeremy...*Pearl Jam*
Joey...*Concrete Blonde*
Joyride...*Roxette*

**Jump**...*Kris Kross*
**Jump Around**...*House Of Pain*
**Just A Friend**...*Biz Markie*
**Just Another Day**...*Jon Secada*
**Justified & Ancient**...*KLF with Tammy Wynette*
**Justify My Love**...*Madonna*
**Lately**...*Jodeci*
**Let's Get Rocked**...*Def Leppard*
**Linger**...*The Cranberries*
**Live And Learn**...*Joe Public*
**Looking Through Patient Eyes**...*PM Dawn*
**Loser**...*Beck*
**Losing My Religion**...*R.E.M.*
**Love Is**...*Vanessa Williams & Brian McKnight*
**Love Takes Time**...*Mariah Carey*
**Love Will Lead You Back**...*Taylor Dayne*
**Love Will Never Do (Without You)**...*Janet Jackson*
**Masterpiece**...*Atlantic Starr*
**Mmm Mmm Mmm Mmm**...*Crash Test Dummies*
**More Than Words**...*Extreme*
**More Than Words Can Say**...*Alias*
**Most Beautiful Girl In The World, The**...*Prince*
**Mr. Jones**...*Counting Crows*
**Mr. Wendal**...*Arrested Development*
**My Lovin' (You're Never Gonna Get It)**...*En Vogue*
**Nothing Compares 2 U**...*Sinéad O'Connor*
**November Rain**...*Guns N' Roses*
**Now And Forever**...*Richard Marx*
**Nuthin' But A "G" Thang**...*Dr. Dre*
**On Bended Knee**...*Boyz II Men*
**One**...*U2*
**One More Try**...*Timmy -T-*
**O.P.P.**...*Naughty By Nature*
**Opposites Attract**...*Paula Abdul*
**Ordinary World**...*Duran Duran*
**Personal Jesus**...*Depeche Mode*
**Poison**...*Bell Biv DeVoe*
**Power, The**...*Snap!*
**Power Of Love, The**...*Celine Dion*
**Pray**...*MC Hammer*
**Praying For Time**...*George Michael*
**Promise Of A New Day, The**...*Paula Abdul*
**Pump Up The Jam**...*Technotronic*
**Regulate**...*Warren G. & Nate Dogg*
**Release Me**...*Wilson Phillips*
**Remember The Time**...*Michael Jackson*
**Return To Innocence**...*Enigma*
**Rhythm Is A Dancer**...*Snap!*
**Rhythm Nation**...*Janet Jackson*
**Rhythm Of My Heart**...*Rod Stewart*

**Right Here/Human Nature**...*SWV*
**Right Here, Right Now**...*Jesus Jones*
**River Of Dreams, The**...*Billy Joel*
**Romantic**...*Karyn White*
**Rump Shaker**...*Wreckx-N-Effect*
**Runaway Train**...*Soul Asylum*
**Rush, Rush**...*Paula Abdul*
**Save The Best For Last**...*Vanessa Williams*
**Set Adrift On Memory Bliss**...*PM Dawn*
**7**...*Prince*
**She Ain't Worth It**...*Glenn Medeiros*
**Shoop**...*Salt-N-Pepa*
**Show Me Love**...*Robin S*
**Show Me The Way**...*Styx*
**Sign, The**...*Ace Of Base*
**Smells Like Teen Spirit**...*Nirvana*
**So Much In Love**...*All-4-One*
**Someday**...*Mariah Carey*
**Something To Talk About**...*Bonnie Raitt*
**Sometimes Love Just Ain't Enough**...*Patty Smyth with Don Henley*
**Stay**...*Shakespear's Sister*
**Stay (I Missed You)**...*Lisa Loeb & Nine Stories*
**Step By Step**...*New Kids On The Block*
**Streets Of Philadelphia**...*Bruce Springsteen*
**Tears In Heaven**...*Eric Clapton*
**Tennessee**...*Arrested Development*
**That's The Way Love Goes**...*Janet Jackson*
**This Used To Be My Playground**...*Madonna*
**To Be With You**...*Mr. Big*
**2 Legit 2 Quit**...*MC Hammer*
**Two To Make It Right**...*Seduction*
**U Can't Touch This**...*M.C. Hammer*
**Unbelievable**...*EMF*
**Under The Bridge**...*Red Hot Chili Peppers*
**Unskinny Bop**...*Poison*
**Vision Of Love**...*Mariah Carey*
**Vogue**...*Madonna*
**Walking On Broken Glass**...*Annie Lennox*
**Weak**...*SWV*
**What Is Love**...*Haddaway*
**What's Up**...*4 Non Blondes*
**Whatta Man**...*Salt 'N' Pepa with En Vogue*
**Where Does My Heart Beat Now**...*Celine Dion*
**Whole New World (Aladdin's Theme)**...*Peabo Bryson & Regina Belle*
**Whoomp! (There It Is)**...*Tag Team*
**Wicked Game**...*Chris Isaak*
**Wild Night**...*John Mellencamp & Me'Shell Ndegéocello*
**You're In Love**...*Wilson Phillips*

# CLASSIC 1995-1999 SONGS

Adia...*Sarah McLachlan*
All My Life...*K-Ci & JoJo*
All Star...*Smash Mouth*
Always Be My Baby...*Mariah Carey*
Angel...*Sarah McLachlan*
Angel Of Mine...*Monica*
Are You That Somebody?...*Aaliyah*
As I Lay Me Down...*Sophie B. Hawkins*
As Long As You Love Me...*Backstreet Boys*
Baby...*Brandy*
Baby One More Time...*Britney Spears*
Back At One...*Brian McKnight*
Back For Good...*Take That*
Bailamos...*Enrique Iglesias*
Basket Case...*Green Day*
Be My Lover...*La Bouche*
Because Of You...*98°*
Because You Loved Me...*Celine Dion*
Believe...*Cher*
Better Man...*Pearl Jam*
Big Poppa...*Notorious B.I.G.*
Bills, Bills, Bills...*Destiny's Child*
Bitch...*Meredith Brooks*
Boombastic...*Shaggy*
Boy Is Mine, The...*Brandy & Monica*
Breakfast At Tiffany's...*Deep Blue Something*
Buddy Holly...*Weezer*
Butterfly Kisses...*Bob Carlisle*
California Love...*2Pac*
Can't Nobody Hold Me Down...*Puff Daddy with Mase*
Candle In The Wind 1997...*Elton John*
Candy Rain...*Soul For Real*
Change The World...*Eric Clapton*
Colors Of The Wind...*Vanessa Williams*
C'Mon N' Ride It (The Train)...*Quad City DJ's*
Come With Me...*Puff Daddy*
Cotton Eye Joe...*Rednex*
Crash Into Me...*Dave Matthews Band*
Creep...*TLC*
Crossroads, Tha...*Bone Thugs-N-Harmony*
Crush...*Jennifer Paige*
Don't Let Go (Love)...*En Vogue*
Don't Speak...*No Doubt*
Don't Take It Personal...*Monica*
Doo Wop (That Thing)...*Lauryn Hill*
Every Morning...*Sugar Ray*
Everybody (Backstreet's Back)...*Backstreet Boys*
Exhale (Shoop Shoop)...*Whitney Houston*
Fantasy...*Mariah Carey*
Feel So Good...*Mase*
First Night, The...*Monica*
Fly...*Sugar Ray*
Follow You Down...*Gin Blossoms*
4 Seasons Of Loneliness...*Boyz II Men*
Freak Like Me...*Adina Howard*

Freshmen, The...*Verve Pipe*
From This Moment On...*Shania Twain*
Gangsta's Paradise...*Coolio*
Genie In A Bottle...*Christina Aguilera*
Gettin' Jiggy Wit It...*Will Smith*
Give Me One Reason...*Tracy Chapman*
Glycerine...*Bush*
God Must Have Spent A Little More Time On You...*\*NSYNC*
Hands...*Jewel*
Have You Ever?...*Brandy*
Have You Ever Really Loved A Woman?...*Bryan Adams*
Heartbreak Hotel...*Whitney Houston*
Hold My Hand...*Hootie & The Blowfish*
Honey...*Mariah Carey*
How Bizarre...*OMC*
How Deep Is Your Love...*Dru Hill with Redman*
How Do I Live...*LeAnn Rimes*
How Do U Want It...*2Pac with K-Ci & JoJo*
How's It Going To Be...*Third Eye Blind*
Hypnotize...*Notorious B.I.G.*
I Believe...*Blessid Union Of Souls*
I Believe I Can Fly...*R. Kelly*
I Can't Sleep Baby (If I)...*R. Kelly*
I Could Fall In Love...*Selena*
I Don't Want To Miss A Thing...*Aerosmith*
I Know...*Dionne Farris*
I Love You Always Forever...*Donna Lewis*
I Need To Know...*Marc Anthony*
I Wanna Love You Forever...*Jessica Simpson*
I Want It That Way...*Backstreet Boys*
I Want You...*Savage Garden*
I'll Be Missing You...*Puff Daddy & Faith Evans*
I'll Be There For You/You're All I Need To Get By...*Method Man with Mary J. Blige*
I'll Never Break Your Heart...*Backstreet Boys*
I'm The Only One...*Melissa Etheridge*
I'm Your Angel...*R. Kelly & Celine Dion*
If I Could Turn Back The Hands Of Time...*R. Kelly*
If It Makes You Happy...*Sheryl Crow*
If You Had My Love...*Jennifer Lopez*
Iris...*Goo Goo Dolls*
Ironic...*Alanis Morissette*
It's All About The Benjamins...*Puff Daddy*
It's All Coming Back To Me Now...*Celine Dion*
It's Not Right But It's Okay...*Whitney Houston*
It's Your Love...*Tim McGraw & Faith Hill*
Jumper...*Third Eye Blind*
Killing Me Softly...*Fugees feat. Lauryn Hill*
Kiss From A Rose...*Seal*
Kiss Me...*Sixpence None The Richer*
Last Kiss...*Pearl Jam*
Lately...*Divine*
Let's Ride...*Montell Jordan*
Livin' La Vida Loca...*Ricky Martin*

Long December, A...*Counting Crows*
Look Into My Eyes...*Bone Thugs-N-Harmony*
Loungin...*LL Cool J*
Lovefool...*Cardigans*
Lullaby...*Shawn Mullins*
Macarena...*Los Del Rio*
Mambo No. 5 (A Little Bit Of...)...*Lou Bega*
Men In Black...*Will Smith*
Missing...*Everything But The Girl*
MMMBop...*Hanson*
Mo Money Mo Problems...*Notorious B.I.G.*
Mouth...*Merril Bainbridge*
Music Of My Heart...*\*NSYNC & Gloria Estefan*
My All...*Mariah Carey*
My Body...*LSG*
My Heart Will Go On (Love Theme From 'Titanic')...*Celine Dion*
My Love Is The Shhh!...*Somethin' For The People*
My Way...*Usher*
Name...*Goo Goo Dolls*
Never Ever...*All Saints*
Nice & Slow...*Usher*
No Diggity...*Blackstreet with Dr. Dre*
No, No, No...*Destiny's Child with Wyclef Jean*
No Scrubs...*TLC*
Nobody...*Keith Sweat with Athena Cage*
Nobody Knows...*Tony Rich Project*
Nobody's Supposed To Be Here...*Deborah Cox*
Not Gon' Cry...*Mary J. Blige*
One Headlight...*Wallflowers*
One I Gave My Heart To...*Aaliyah*
One More Chance/Stay With Me...*Notorious B.I.G.*
One Of Us...*Joan Osborne*
One Sweet Day...*Mariah Carey & Boyz II Men*
One Week...*Barenaked Ladies*
Only Wanna Be With You...*Hootie & The Blowfish*
Please Remember Me...*Tim McGraw*
Pony...*Ginuwine*
Push...*Matchbox 20*
Quit Playing Games (With My Heart)...*Backstreet Boys*
Ray Of Light...*Madonna*
Real World...*Matchbox 20*
Return Of The Mack...*Mark Morrison*
Rhythm Of The Night...*Corona*
Run-Around...*Blues Traveler*

Run Away...*Real McCoy*
Runaway...*Janet Jackson*
Satisfy You...*Puff Daddy with R. Kelly*
Save Tonight...*Eagle-Eye Cherry*
Scar Tissue...*Red Hot Chili Peppers*
Semi-Charmed Life...*Third Eye Blind*
She's All I Ever Had...*Ricky Martin*
Sittin' Up In My Room...*Brandy*
Slide...*Goo Goo Dolls*
Smooth...*Santana Feat. Rob Thomas*
Something About The Way You Look Tonight...*Elton John*
Strong Enough...*Sheryl Crow*
Summer Girls...*LFO*
Sunny Came Home...*Shawn Colvin*
Take A Bow...*Madonna*
Tell Me It's Real...*K-Ci & JoJo*
Thank U...*Alanis Morissette*
This Is For The Lover In You...*Babyface*
This Is How We Do It...*Montell Jordan*
This Kiss...*Faith Hill*
3 AM...*Matchbox 20*
Together Again...*Janet Jackson*
Too Close...*Next*
Torn...*Natalie Imbruglia*
Total Eclipse Of The Heart...*Nicki French*
Truly Madly Deeply...*Savage Garden*
Tubthumping...*Chumbawamba*
Twisted...*Keith Sweat*
2 Become 1...*Spice Girls*
Un-Break My Heart...*Toni Braxton*
Unpretty...*TLC*
Walkin' On The Sun...*Smash Mouth*
Wannabe...*Spice Girls*
Waterfalls...*TLC*
Way, The...*Fastball*
What's It Gonna Be?!...*Busta Rhymes with Janet Jackson*
When I Come Around...*Green Day*
Where Do You Go...*No Mercy*
Where My Girls At?...*702*
Who Dat...*JT Money*
Wild Wild West...*Will Smith*
Wonderwall...*Oasis*
You Gotta Be...*Des'ree*
You Make Me Wanna......*Usher*
You Oughta Know...*Alanis Morissette*
You Were Meant For Me...*Jewel*
You're Makin' Me High...*Toni Braxton*
You're Still The One...*Shania Twain*

**Absolutely (Story Of A Girl)**...*Ninedays*
**Addictive**...*Truth Hurts with Rakim*
**Again**...*Lenny Kravitz*
**Air Force Ones**...*Nelly*
**All For You**...*Janet Jackson*
**All I Have**...*Jennifer Lopez with LL Cool J*
**All Or Nothing**...*O-Town*
**All The Small Things**...*Blink 182*
**All You Wanted**...*Michelle Branch*
**Always On Time**...*Ja Rule with Ashanti*
**Amazed**...*Lonestar*
**Angel**...*Shaggy with Rayvon*
**Baby Boy**...*Beyoncé with Sean Paul*
**Be With You**...*Enrique Iglesias*
**Beautiful**...*Christina Aguilera*
**Beautiful Day**...*U2*
**Bent**...*Matchbox Twenty*
**Blue (Da Ba Dee)**...*Eiffel 65*
**Blurry**...*Puddle Of Mudd*
**Bootylicious**...*Destiny's Child*
**Breakaway**...*Kelly Clarkson*
**Breathe**...*Faith Hill*
**Bring It All To Me**...*Blaque with *NSYNC*
**Bring Me To Life**...*Evanescence*
**Bump, Bump, Bump**...*B2K & P. Diddy*
**Burn**...*Usher*
**Butterfly**...*Crazy Town*
**Bye Bye Bye**...**NSYNC*
**Can't Let You Go**...*Fabolous*
**Case Of The Ex (Whatcha Gonna Do)**...*Mya*
**Cleanin' Out My Closet**...*Eminem*
**Clocks**...*Coldplay*
**Come On Over Baby (All I Want Is You)**...
 *Christina Aguilera*
**Complicated**...*Avril Lavigne*
**Confessions Part II**...*Usher*
**Crazy In Love**...*Beyoncé with Jay-Z*
**Cry Me A River**...*Justin Timberlake*
**Dance With Me**...*Debelah Morgan*
**Days Go By**...*Dirty Vegas*
**Dilemma**...*Nelly with Kelly Rowland*
**Doesn't Really Matter**...*Janet Jackson*
**Drift Away**...*Uncle Kracker with Dobie Gray*
**Drop It Like It's Hot**...*Snoop Dogg with Pharrell*
**Drops Of Jupiter (Tell Me)**...*Train*
**Everything You Want**...*Vertical Horizon*
**Fallin'**...*Alicia Keys*
**Family Affair**...*Mary J. Blige*
**Fiesta Remix**...*R. Kelly with Jay-Z*
**Flying Without Wings**...*Ruben Studdard*
**Follow Me**...*Uncle Kracker*
**Foolish**...*Ashanti*
**Freek-A-Leek**...*Petey Pablo*
**Frontin'**...*Pharrell with Jay-Z*
**Game Of Love, The**...*Santana Feat. Michelle Branch*

**Gangsta Lovin'**...*Eve with Alicia Keys*
**Get Busy**...*Sean Paul*
**Get It On...Tonite**...*Montell Jordan*
**Get Low**...*Lil Jon & The East Side Boyz*
**Get The Party Started**...*P!nk*
**Get Ur Freak On**...*Missy "Misdemeanor" Elliott*
**Gimme The Light**...*Sean Paul*
**Girlfriend**...**NSYNC with Nelly*
**Give Me Just One Night (Una Noche)**...*98°*
**Goodies**...*Ciara with Petey Pablo*
**Gotta Tell You**...*Samantha Mumba*
**Hanging By A Moment**...*Lifehouse*
**He Loves U Not**...*Dream*
**He Wasn't Man Enough**...*Toni Braxton*
**Heaven**...*DJ Sammy & Yannou*
**Here Without You**...*3 Doors Down*
**Hero**...*Chad Kroeger with Josey Scott*
**Hero**...*Enrique Iglesias*
**Hey Baby**...*No Doubt with Bounty Killer*
**Hey Ma**...*Cam'ron*
**Hey Ya!**...*OutKast*
**Higher**...*Creed*
**Hit 'Em Up Style (Oops!)**...*Blu Cantrell*
**Holidae In**...*Chingy with Ludacris & Snoop Dogg*
**Hot Boyz**...*Missy "Misdemeanor" Elliott*
**Hot In Herre**...*Nelly*
**Hotel**...*Cassidy with R. Kelly*
**How You Remind Me**...*Nickelback*
**I Believe**...*Fantasia*
**I Don't Wanna Know**...*Mario Winans with Enya & P. Diddy*
**I Hope You Dance**...*Lee Ann Womack*
**I Knew I Loved You**...*Savage Garden*
**I Know What You Want**...*Busta Rhymes & Mariah Carey*
**I Need A Girl (Part One)**...*P. Diddy with Usher & Loon*
**I Need A Girl (Part Two)**...*P. Diddy & Ginuwine*
**I Try**...*Macy Gray*
**I Wanna Know**...*Joe*
**I'm Real**...*Jennifer Lopez with Ja Rule*
**I'm With You**...*Avril Lavigne*
**If I Ain't Got You**...*Alicia Keys*
**If You're Gone**...*Matchbox Twenty*
**Ignition**...*R. Kelly*
**In Da Club**...*50 Cent*
**In The End**...*Linkin Park*
**Incomplete**...*Sisqó*
**Independent Women**...*Destiny's Child*
**Into You**...*Fabolous*
**It Wasn't Me**...*Shaggy with Ricardo Ducent*
**It's Been Awhile**...*Staind*
**It's Gonna Be Me**...**NSYNC*
**Izzo (H.O.V.A.)**...*Jay-Z*
**Jenny From The Block**...*Jennifer Lopez*
**Jesus Walks**...*Kanye West*

**Jumpin', Jumpin'**...*Destiny's Child*
**Just A Friend 2002**...*Mario*
**Just Lose It**...*Eminem*
**Kryptonite**...*3 Doors Down*
**Lady Marmalade**...*Christina Aguilera, Lil' Kim, Mya & P!nk*
**Lean Back**...*Terror Squad with Fat Joe & Remy*
**Let Me Blow Ya Mind**...*Eve with Gwen Stefani*
**Livin' It Up**...*Ja Rule with Case*
**Lose My Breath**...*Destiny's Child*
**Lose Yourself**...*Eminem*
**Magic Stick**...*Lil' Kim with 50 Cent*
**Maria Maria**...*Santana Feat. The Product G&B*
**Mesmerize**...*Ja Rule with Ashanti*
**Middle, The**...*Jimmy Eat World*
**Milkshake**...*Kelis*
**Miss You**...*Aaliyah*
**Missing You**...*Case*
**Moment Like This, A**...*Kelly Clarkson*
**Most Girls**...*P!nk*
**Move Ya Body**...*Nina Sky with Jabba*
**Ms. Jackson**...*OutKast*
**Music**...*Madonna*
**My Baby**...*Lil' Romeo*
**My Band**...*D12*
**My Boo**...*Usher & Alicia Keys*
**My Immortal**...*Evanescence*
**My Love Is Your Love**...*Whitney Houston*
**My Sacrifice**...*Creed*
**Naughty Girl**...*Beyoncé*
**Never Leave You – Uh Oooh, Uh Oooh!**...*Lumidee*
**'03 Bonnie & Clyde**...*Jay-Z with Beyoncé*
**Oh Boy**...*Cam'ron with Juelz Santana*
**One Call Away**...*Chingy*
**Only Time**...*Enya*
**Over And Over**...*Nelly with Tim McGraw*
**Peaches & Cream**...*112*
**Picture**...*Kid Rock with Sheryl Crow*
**Pieces Of Me**...*Ashlee Simpson*
**P.I.M.P.**...*50 Cent*
**Real Slim Shady, The**...*Eminem*
**Reason, The**...*Hoobastank*
**Ride Wit Me**...*Nelly*
**Right Thurr**...*Chingy*
**Rock Wit U (Awww Baby)**...*Ashanti*
**Roses**...*OutKast*
**Say My Name**...*Destiny's Child*
**Shake Ya Tailfeather**...*Nelly/P. Diddy/Murphy Lee*

**She Will Be Loved**...*Maroon5*
**Show Me The Meaning Of Being Lonely**...*Backstreet Boys*
**Slow Jamz**...*Twista with Kanye West & Jamie Foxx*
**Someday**...*Nickelback*
**Someone To Call My Lover**...*Janet Jackson*
**Stan**...*Eminem with Dido*
**Stand Up**...*Ludacris with Shawnna*
**Stutter**...*Joe with Mystikal*
**Sunshine**...*Lil' Flip*
**Survivor**...*Destiny's Child*
**Thank God I Found You**...*Mariah Carey with Joe & 98°*
**Thankyou**...*Dido*
**There You Go**...*P!nk*
**This I Promise You**...*\*NSYNC*
**This Is The Night**...*Clay Aiken*
**This Love**...*Maroon5*
**Thong Song**...*Sisqó*
**Thousand Miles, A**...*Vanessa Carlton*
**Tipsy**...*J-Kwon*
**Toxic**...*Britney Spears*
**Try Again**...*Aaliyah*
**Turn Me On**...*Kevin Lyttle*
**Turn Off The Light**...*Nelly Furtado*
**21 Questions**...*50 Cent with Nate Dogg*
**U Got It Bad**...*Usher*
**U Remind Me**...*Usher*
**Underneath It All**...*No Doubt*
**Unwell**...*Matchbox Twenty*
**Walked Outta Heaven**...*Jagged Edge*
**Way You Love Me, The**...*Faith Hill*
**Way You Move, The**...*OutKast*
**What A Girl Wants**...*Christina Aguilera*
**What's Luv?**...*Fat Joe with Ashanti*
**When I'm Gone**...*3 Doors Down*
**Whenever, Wherever**...*Shakira*
**Where Is The Love?**...*Black Eyed Peas*
**Where The Party At**...*Jagged Edge with Nelly*
**Wherever You Will Go**...*Calling*
**Who Let The Dogs Out**...*Baha Men*
**With Arms Wide Open**...*Creed*
**Without Me**...*Eminem*
**Wonderful**...*Ja Rule with R. Kelly & Ashanti*
**Work It**...*Missy "Misdemeanor" Elliott*
**Yeah!**...*Usher with Lil' Jon& Ludacris*
**You Don't Know My Name**...*Alicia Keys*
**You Sang To Me**...*Marc Anthony*

## CLASSIC 2005 SONGS

American Baby...*Dave Matthews Band*
Anything But Mine...*Kenny Chesney*
Awful, Beautiful Life...*Darryl Worley*
Be Yourself...*Audioslave*
Beautiful Soul...*Jesse McCartney*
Behind These Hazel Eyes...*Kelly Clarkson*
Best Of You...*Foo Fighters*
Beverly Hills...*Weezer*
Bless The Broken Road...*Rascal Flatts*
Boulevard Of Broken Dreams...*Green Day*
Bring Em Out...*T.I.*
Candy Shop...*50 Cent with Olivia*
Caught Up...*Usher*
Daughters...*John Mayer*
Disco Inferno...*50 Cent*
Don't Phunk With My Heart...*Black Eyed Peas*
Get Right...*Jennifer Lopez*
Goin' Crazy...*Natalie*
Hate It Or Love It...*The Game with 50 Cent*
Holiday...*Green Day*
Hollaback Girl...*Gwen Stefani*
Home...*Michael Bublé*
How We Do...*The Game with 50 Cent*
I Don't Want To Be...*Gavin DeGraw*
Incomplete...*Backstreet Boys*
Just A Lil Bit...*50 Cent*
Karma...*Alicia Keys*
Let Me Go...*3 Doors Down*
Let Me Love You...*Mario*
Lonely...*Akon*
Lonely No More...*Rob Thomas*
Lovers And Friends...*Lil Jon & The East Side Boyz*
Mr. Brightside...*The Killers*
Mockingbird...*Eminem*
Mud On The Tires...*Brad Paisley*
My Give A Damn's Busted...*Jo Dee Messina*
Obsession [No Es Amor]...*Frankie J with Baby Bash*
Oh...*Ciara with Ludacris*
1 Thing...*Amerie*
1,2 Step...*Ciara with Missy Elliott*
Rich Girl...*Gwen Stefani with Eve*
Since U Been Gone...*Kelly Clarkson*
Slow Down...*Bobby Valentino*
Soldier...*Destiny's Child*
Speed Of Sound...*Coldplay*
Switch...*Will Smith*
That's What I Love About Sunday...*Craig Morgan*
Truth Is...*Fantasia*
Wait (The Whisper Song)...*Ying Yang Twins*
We Belong Together...*Mariah Carey*

## CLASSIC ROCK

All Right Now...*Free*
American Pie...*Don McLean*
American Woman...*The Guess Who*
Blinded By The Light...*Manfred Mann*
Bohemian Rhapsody...*Queen*
Born In The U.S.A. ...*Bruce Springsteen*
Casey Jones...*Grateful Dead*
Changes...*David Bowie*
Crocodile Rock...*Elton John*
Do You Feel Like We Do...*Peter Frampton*
Don't Stop...*Fleetwood Mac*
For What It's Worth...*Buffalo Springfield*
Free Bird...*Lynyrd Skynyrd*
Heart Of Gold...*Neil Young*
Hey Jude...*The Beatles*
Honky Tonk Women...*The Rolling Stones*
Hotel California...*Eagles*
Imagine...*John Lennon*
In-A-Gadda-Da-Vida...*Iron Butterfly*
Iron Man...*Black Sabbath*
Layla...*Derek & The Dominos*
Light My Fire...*The Doors*
Like A Rolling Stone...*Bob Dylan*
Maggie May...*Rod Stewart*
Magic Carpet Ride...*Steppenwolf*
Maybe I'm Amazed...*Paul McCartney*
Money...*Pink Floyd*
More Than A Feeling...*Boston*
Mr. Tambourine Man...*The Byrds*
Night Moves...*Bob Seger*
Nights In White Satin...*The Moody Blues*
Piece Of My Heart...*Big Brother & The Holding Company*
Proud Mary...*Creedence Clearwater Revival*
Purple Haze...*Jimi Hendrix*
Runnin' With The Devil...*Van Halen*
Slow Ride...*Foghat*
Smoke On The Water...*Deep Purple*
Somebody To Love...*Jefferson Airplane*
Stairway To Heaven...*Led Zeppelin*
Suite: Judy Blue Eyes...*Crosby, Stills & Nash*
Sunshine Of Your Love...*Cream*
Takin' Care Of Business...*Bachman-Turner Overdrive*
Tom Sawyer...*Rush*
Walk On The Wild Side...*Lou Reed*
Walk This Way...*Aerosmith*
Weight, The...*The Band*
Whiter Shade Of Pale, A...*Procol Harum*
With A Little Help From My Friends...*Joe Cocker*
Won't Get Fooled Again...*The Who*
You Shook Me All Night Long...*AC/DC*

**Arrested For Driving While Blind**...*ZZ Top*
**Baby Please Don't Go**...*Them*
**Bad Case Of Loving You**...*Robert Palmer*
**Bad Moon Rising**...*Creedence Clearwater Revival*
**Barbara Ann**...*The Beach Boys*
**Barracuda**...*Heart*
**Be My Baby**...*The Ronettes*
**Beautiful Day**...*U2*
**Born To Be Wild**...*Steppenwolf*
**Born To Run**...*Bruce Springsteen*
**Brown Eyed Girl**...*Van Morrison*
**Burning Love**...*Elvis Presley*
**Call Me**...*Blondie*
**Chattahoochee**...*Alan Jackson*
**China Grove**...*The Doobie Brothers*
**Country Road**...*James Taylor*
**Crazy Little Thing Called Love**...*Queen*
**Da Doo Ron Ron**...*The Crystals*
**De Do Do Do, De Da Da Da**...*The Police*
**Desire**...*U2*
**Devil Went Down To Georgia**...*Charlie Daniels Band*
**Don't Get Me Wrong**...*The Pretenders*
**Don't Look Back**...*Fine Young Cannibals*
**Dream Police**...*Cheap Trick*
**Drive My Car**...*The Beatles*
**Drivin' My Life Away**...*Eddie Rabbitt*
**Drops Of Jupiter (Tell Me)**...*Train*
**Electric Avenue**...*Eddy Grant*
**Escapade**...*Janet Jackson*
**Fly Away**...*Lenny Kravitz*
**Free Ride**...*Edgar Winter Group*
**Friends In Low Places**...*Garth Brooks*
**Fun, Fun, Fun**...*The Beach Boys*
**Gear Jammer**...*George Thorogood*
**Gimme Some Lovin'**...*Spencer Davis Group*
**Go Your Own Way**...*Fleetwood Mac*
**Good Lovin'**...*The Young Rascals*
**Great Balls Of Fire**...*Jerry Lee Lewis*
**Highway 61 Revisited**...*Bob Dylan*
**Hit The Road Jack**...*Ray Charles*
**Holiday**...*Green Day*
**Holiday Road**...*Lindsey Buckingham*
**Hollywood Nights**...*Bob Seger*
**I Can't Drive 55**...*Sammy Hagar*
**I Drove All Night**...*Roy Orbison*
**I Fought The Law**...*Bobby Fuller Four*
**I'm Alright**...*Kenny Loggins*
**I'm Gonna Be (500 Miles)**...*The Proclaimers*
**I've Been Everywhere**...*Johnny Cash*
**Interstate Love Song**...*Stone Temple Pilots*
**Johnny B. Goode**...*Chuck Berry*
**Jump**...*Van Halen*

**Kansas City**...*Wilbert Harrison*
**Keep Your Hands To Yourself**...*Georgia Satellites*
**King Of The Road**...*Roger Miller*
**Let's Go**...*The Cars*
**Letter, The**...*The Box Tops*
**Life In The Fast Lane**...*Eagles*
**Life Is A Highway**...*Tom Cochrane*
**Little Bit O' Soul**...*The Music Explosion*
**Logical Song, The**...*Supertramp*
**London Calling**...*The Clash*
**Love Train**...*The O'Jays*
**Margaritaville**...*Jimmy Buffett*
**Memphis**...*Johnny Rivers*
**Middle, The**...*Jimmy Eat World*
**Mustang Sally**...*Wilson Pickett*
**No Particular Place To Go**...*Chuck Berry*
**On The Road Again**...*Willie Nelson*
**One Headlight**...*The Wallflowers*
**Open Road Song**...*Eve 6*
**Pride And Joy**...*Stevie Ray Vaughan*
**Radar Love**...*Golden Earring*
**Ramblin' Man**...*Allman Brothers Band*
**Rhythm Of My Heart**...*Rod Stewart*
**Road Runner**...*Bo Diddley*
**Road To Nowhere**...*Talking Heads*
**Road Trippin'**...*Red Hot Chili Peppers*
**Roadhouse Blues**...*The Doors*
**Roadrunner**...*Modern Lovers*
**R.O.C.K. In The U.S.A.** ...*John Cougar Mellencamp*
**Rock Of Ages**...*Def Leppard*
**Roll On Down The Highway**...*Bachman-Turner Overdrive*
**Runaway**...*Del Shannon*
**Runnin' Down A Dream**...*Tom Petty*
**Running On Empty**...*Jackson Browne*
**Spirit In The Sky**...*Norman Greenbaum*
**Switchin' To Glide**...*The Kings*
**Take It Easy**...*Eagles*
**Take Me Home Country Roads**...*Toots & The Maytals*
**Take The Money And Run**...*Steve Miller Band*
**Truckin'**...*Grateful Dead*
**Vacation**...*The Go-Go's*
**Ventura Highway**...*America*
**Walk Of Life**...*Dire Straits*
**Watching The Detectives**...*Elvis Costello*
**What I Like About You**...*The Romantics*
**Whole Lotta Love**...*Led Zeppelin*
**Working For The Weekend**...*Loverboy*
**You Ain't Seen Nothing Yet**...*Bachman-Turner Overdrive*

## THE BRITISH INVASION 1964-65

All Day And All Of The Night...*The Kinks*
As Tears Go By...*Marianne Faithfull*
Bad To Me...*Billy J. Kramer*
Can't Buy Me Love...*The Beatles*
Catch The Wind...*Donovan*
Do Wah Diddy Diddy...*Manfred Mann*
Don't Let The Sun Catch You Crying...*Gerry & The Pacemakers*
Downtown...*Petula Clark*
Everyone's Gone To The Moon...*Jonathan King*
Ferry Cross The Mersey...*Gerry & The Pacemakers*
For Your Love...*The Yardbirds*
Game Of Love...*Wayne Fontana & The Mindbenders*
Girl Don't Come...*Sandie Shaw*
Glad All Over...*Dave Clark Five*
Go Now!...*The Moody Blues*
Goldfinger...*Shirley Bassey*
Have I The Right?...*The Honeycombs*
Heart Full Of Soul...*The Yardbirds*
Hippy Hippy Shake...*The Swinging Blue Jeans*
House Of The Rising Sun, The...*The Animals*
I Can't Explain...*The Who*
(I Can't Get No) Satisfaction...*The Rolling Stones*
I Go To Pieces...*Peter & Gordon*
I Want To Hold Your Hand...*The Beatles*
I'm Gonna Love You Too...*The Hullaballoos*
I'm Into Something Good...*Herman's Hermits*
I'm Telling You Now...*Freddie & The Dreamers*
It's Alright...*Adam Faith & The Roulettes*
It's Not Unusual...*Tom Jones*
Just One Look...*The Hollies*
Last Time, The...*The Rolling Stones*
Little Children...*Billy J. Kramer*
Mrs. Brown You've Got A Lovely Daughter...*Herman's Hermits*
My Generation...*The Who*
Needles And Pins...*The Searchers*
Over And Over...*Dave Clark Five*
She Loves You...*The Beatles*
She's Not There...*The Zombies*
Tobacco Road...*The Nashville Teens*
We Gotta Get Out Of This Place...*The Animals*
What's New Pussycat?...*Tom Jones*
Wishin' And Hopin'...*Dusty Springfield*
World Without Love, A...*Peter & Gordon*
Yeh, Yeh...*Georgie Fame*
Yesterday's Gone...*Chad & Jeremy*
You Really Got Me...*The Kinks*
You Turn Me On...*Ian Whitcomb & Bluesville*
You're My World...*Cilla Black*
You've Got To Hide Your Love Away...*The Silkie*
You've Got Your Troubles...*The Fortunes*

## WE'RE AN AMERICAN BAND '60S & '70S

Along Comes Mary...*The Association*
And When I Die...*Blood, Sweat & Tears*
Black Magic Woman...*Santana*
Carry On Wayward Son...*Kansas*
Come Sail Away...*Styx*
Crazy Love...*Allman Brothers Band*
Cry Like A Baby...*The Box Tops*
Dance The Night Away...*Van Halen*
Do You Believe In Magic...*The Lovin' Spoonful*
Don't Look Back...*Boston*
Dream On...*Aerosmith*
Eight Miles High...*The Byrds*
Fire Lake...*Bob Seger*
Good Thing...*Paul Revere & The Raiders*
Green River...*Creedence Clearwater Revival*
Heart Of Glass...*Blondie*
Heart Of The Night...*Poco*
Hold The Line...*Toto*
I Get Around...*The Beach Boys*
I Was Made For Lovin' You...*Kiss*
Imaginary Lover...*Atlanta Rhythm Section*
It Don't Matter To Me...*Bread*
Jenny Take A Ride...*Mitch Ryder & The Detroit Wheels*
Kind Of A Drag...*The Buckinghams*
Last Train To Clarksville...*The Monkees*
Let's Live For Today...*The Grass Roots*
Long Train Runnin'...*The Doobie Brothers*
Looking For A Love...*J. Geils Band*
Lovin', Touchin', Squeezin'...*Journey*
Make Me Smile...*Chicago*
Money...*The Kingsmen*
One...*Three Dog Night*
People Got To Be Free...*The Rascals*
Refugee...*Tom Petty & The Heartbreakers*
Riders On The Storm...*The Doors*
Rock Me...*Steppenwolf*
Rock 'N' Roll Woman...*The Buffalo Springfield*
Rockaway Beach...*Ramones*
Rock'n Me...*Steve Miller*
She'd Rather Be With Me...*The Turtles*
Sugar Magnolia...*Grateful Dead*
Surrender...*Cheap Trick*
Sweet Home Alabama...*Lynyrd Skynyrd*
Take It To The Limit...*Eagles*
Take Me To The River...*Talking Heads*
Time For Me To Fly...*REO Speedwagon*
Tush...*ZZ Top*
We're An American Band...*Grand Funk Railroad*
White Rabbit...*Jefferson Airplane*
You Might Think...*The Cars*

# RETRO RADIO EARLY '80S

**Always Something There To Remind Me**...*Naked Eyes*
**Blister In The Sun**...*Violent Femmes*
**Blue Monday**...*New Order*
**Da Da Da I Don't Love You You Don't Love Me**...*Trio*
**Dancing With Myself**...*Billy Idol*
**Der Kommissar**...*After The Fire*
**Destination Unknown**...*Missing Persons*
**Doctor! Doctor!**...*Thompson Twins*
**Forever Mine**...*The Motels*
**Genius Of Love**...*Tom Tom Club*
**Goody Two Shoes**...*Adam Ant*
**I Melt With You**...*Modern English*
**I Want Candy**...*Bow Wow Wow*
**In A Big Country**...*Big Country*
**In Between Days (Without You)**...*The Cure*
**Just Got Lucky**...*JoBoxers*
**(Keep Feeling) Fascination**...*Human League*
**Let Me Go**...*Heaven 17*
**Love My Way**...*Psychedelic Furs*
**Love Plus One**...*Haircut 100*
**Make A Circuit With Me**...*The Polecats*
**Metro, The**...*Berlin*
**Mexican Radio**...*Wall Of Voodoo*
**99 Luftballons**...*Nena*
**Our House**...*Madness*
**People Are People**...*Depeche Mode*
**Politics Of Dancing, The**...*Re-Flex*
**Reap The Wild Wind**...*Ultravox*
**Red Skies**...*The Fixx*
**Rock Lobster**...*The B-52's*
**Safety Dance, The**...*Men Without Hats*
**Save It For Later**...*English Beat*
**She Blinded Me With Science**...*Thomas Dolby*
**Situation**...*Yaz*
**Six Months In A Leaky Boat**...*Split Enz*
**So In Love**...*Orchestral Manoeuvres In The Dark*
**Space Age Love Song**...*A Flock Of Seagulls*
**Tainted Love**...*Soft Cell*
**Tempted**...*Squeeze*
**Tenderness**...*General Public*
**Too Shy**...*Kajagoogoo*
**Trommeltanz (Din Daa Daa)**...*George Kranz*
**Turning Japanese**...*The Vapors*
**Up All Night**...*The Boomtown Rats*
**Weird Science**...*Oingo Boingo*
**What Do All The People Know**...*The Monroes*
**What I Like About You**...*The Romantics*
**What's He Got?**...*The Producers*
**Whip It**...*Devo*
**Whisper To A Scream (Birds Fly)**...*Icicle Works*

# THE MOTOWN SOUND OF THE '60s

**Ain't Nothing Like The Real Thing**...*Marvin Gaye & Tammi Terrell*
**Ain't Too Proud To Beg**...*The Temptations*
**Baby I Need Your Loving**...*Four Tops*
**Baby Love**...*The Supremes*
**Beauty Is Only Skin Deep**...*The Temptations*
**Beechwood 4-5789**...*The Marvelettes*
**Bernadette**...*Four Tops*
**Cloud Nine**...*The Temptations*
**Dancing In The Street**...*Martha & The Vandellas*
**Do You Love Me**...*The Contours*
**Don't Mess With Bill**...*The Marvelettes*
**Every Little Bit Hurts**...*Brenda Holloway*
**Fingertips – Pt. 2**...*Little Stevie Wonder*
**For Once In My Life**...*Stevie Wonder*
**Heat Wave**...*Martha & The Vandellas*
**Hot Sweet It Is To Be Loved By You**...*Marvin Gaye*
**I Can't Help Myself**...*Four Tops*
**I Second That Emotion**...*Smokey Robinson & The Miracles*
**I Want You Back**...*The Jackson 5*
**I Was Made To Love Her**...*Stevie Wonder*
**I'll Be Doggone**...*Marvin Gaye*
**It Takes Two**...*Marvin Gaye & Kim Weston*
**Jimmy Mack**...*Martha & The Vandellas*
**Love Child**...*Diana Ross & The Supremes*
**Mickey's Monkey**...*The Miracles*
**My Girl**...*The Temptations*
**My Guy**...*Mary Wells*
**Nowhere To Run**...*Martha & The Vandellas*
**Opce Upon A Time**...*Marvin Gaye & Mary Wells*
**One Who Really Loves You, The**...*Mary Wells*
**Playboy**...*The Marvelettes*
**Please Mr. Postman**...*The Marvelettes*
**Pride And Joy**...*Marvin Gaye*
**Quicksand**...*Martha & The Vandellas*
**Reach Out I'll Be There**...*Four Tops*
**Shop Around**...*The Miracles*
**Stop! In The Name Of Love**...*The Supremes*
**This Old Heart Of Mine (Is Weak For You)**...*The Isley Brothers*
**Tracks Of My Tears**...*The Miracles*
**Twenty-Five Miles**...*Edwin Starr*
**Two Lovers**...*Mary Wells*
**Uptight (Everything's Alright)**...*Stevie Wonder*
**War**...*Edwin Starr*
**Way You Do The Things You Do, The**...*The Temptations*
**Where Did Our Love Go**...*The Supremes*
**You Beat Me To The Punch**...*Mary Wells*
**You Can't Hurry Love**...*The Supremes*
**You Keep Me Hangin' On**...*The Supremes*
**You've Really Got A Hold On Me**...*The Miracles*
**Your Precious Love**...*Marvin Gaye & Tammi Terrell*

# A CLASSIC CHRISTMAS

## A HOLLY JOLLY CHRISTMAS:

All I Want For Christmas (Is My Two Front Teeth)...*Spike Jones*
All I Want For Christmas Is You...*Mariah Carey*
Blue Christmas...*Elvis Presley*
Carol Of The Bells...*Johnny Mathis*
Chipmunk Song, The...*Chipmunks*
Christmas (Baby Please Come Home)...*Darlene Love*
Christmas Island...*Leon Redbone*
Christmas Song, The...*Nat "King" Cole*
Christmas Time's A-Coming...*Emmylou Harris*
Christmas Waltz, The...*Frank Sinatra*
Deck The Halls...*Mitch Miller*
Feliz Navidad...*Jose Feliciano*
Frosty The Snow Man...*Gene Autry*
Good King Wenceslas...*Judy Collins*
Grandma Got Run Over By A Reindeer...*Elmo & Patsy*
Happy Holiday...*Barry Manilow*
Happy Xmas (War Is Over)...*John & Yoko*
Have Yourself A Merry Little Christmas...*Judy Garland*
Here Comes Santa Claus...*Gene Autry*
Here We Come A-Caroling...*Ray Conniff Singers*
Holly Jolly Christmas, A...*Burl Ives*
Home For The Holidays...*Perry Como*
I Saw Mommy Kissing Santa Claus...*Jimmy Boyd*
I'll Be Home For Christmas...*Bing Crosby*
If Every Day Was Like Christmas...*Elvis Presley*
It's Beginning To Look Like Christmas...*Perry Como*
It's The Most Wonderful Time Of The Year...*Andy Williams*
Jingle Bell Rock...*Bobby Helms*

Jingle Bells...*Bing Crosby & The Andrews Sisters*
Jolly Old St. Nicholas...*Eddy Arnold*
Let It Snow! Let It Snow! Let It Snow!...*Vaughn Monroe*
Little Saint Nick...*Beach Boys*
Marshmallow World, A...*Dean Martin*
Merry Christmas Baby...*Charles Brown*
Merry Christmas Darling...*Carpenters*
My Favorite Things...*Tony Bennett*
Nuttin' For Christmas...*Barry Gordon*
O Christmas Tree (O Tannenbaum)...*Aretha Franklin*
Please Come Home For Christmas...*Charles Brown*
Pretty Paper...*Roy Orbison*
Rockin' Around The Christmas Tree...*Brenda Lee*
Rudolph, The Red-Nosed Reindeer...*Gene Autry*
Santa Baby...*Eartha Kitt*
Santa Claus Is Comin' To Town...*Bruce Springsteen*
Silver Bells...*Bing Crosby & Carol Richards*
Sleigh Ride...*Boston Pops Orchestra*
Snoopy's Christmas...*Royal Guardsmen*
Step Into Christmas...*Elton John*
'Twas The Night Before Christmas...*Harry Simeone Chorale*
Twelve Days Of Christmas...*Harry Belafonte*
Up On The Housetop...*Gene Autry*
We Wish You A Merry Christmas...*Andre Kostelanetz Orch.*
White Christmas...*Bing Crosby*
Winter Wonderland...*Perry Como*
Wonderful Christmastime...*Paul McCartney*

## JOY TO THE WORLD:

Angels From The Realms Of Glory
Angels We Have Heard On High
Ave Maria (Schubert and Bach/Gounod versions)
Away In A Manger
Bring A Torch, Jeannette, Isabella
Caroling, Caroling
Coventry Carol
Ding Dong! Merrily On High
Do You Hear What I Hear
First Noel, The
Gesu Bambino
Go Tell It On The Mountain
God Rest Ye Merry Gentlemen
Good Christian Men, Rejoice
Hallelujah Chorus
Hark! The Herald Angels Sing
Holly And The Ivy, The
I Heard The Bells On Christmas Day

I Saw Three Ships
I Wonder As I Wander
It Came Upon A Midnight Clear
Jesu, Joy Of Man's Desiring
Joy To The World
Little Drummer Boy, The
Lo, How A Rose E'er Blooming
Mary, Did You Know?
Mary's Boy Child
O Come All Ye Faithful
O Come, O Come, Emmanuel
O Holy Night
O Little Town Of Bethlehem
Silent Night
Sweet Little Jesus Boy
We Three Kings Of Orient Are
What Child Is This?
While By My Sheep (Joy, Joy, Joy)

# *Joel Whitburn's*
# TOP POP SINGLES

Our all-time bestseller has never been a more useful, convenient and valuable addition to your music library! From vinyl 45s to CD singles to album tracks, here—and only here—are the more than 25,000 titles and 6,000 artists that appeared on Billboard's Pop music charts from 1955-2002…all arranged by artist for fast, easy reference! With key facts, hot hits and informative features highlighted in red. Bigger, beefier artist bios. Expanded, more accurate title notes. And updated record and CD pricing.

**1,024 pages**
**Size: 7" x 9"**
**Hardcover**

**$64⁹⁵**

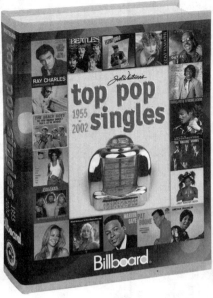

# *Joel Whitburn's*
# TOP POP ALBUMS

This colossal chronicle lists, by artist, over 22,000 charted albums…and over 225,000 album tracks…by more than 5,200 artists! It's packed with essential chart data…plus vinyl and CD album pricing…charted albums' availability on CD…photos of intriguing albums…updated artist bios and title notes… and, for each artist, a master A-Z index of all tracks from all of their albums! Only here will you find every album from 1955-2001 that made this 200-position chart.

**1,208 pages**
**Size: 7" x 9"**
**Hardcover**

**$79⁹⁵**

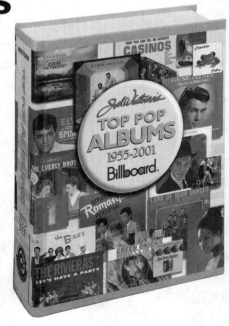

Visit www.recordresearch.com for book descriptions, sample pages and shipping terms.

# Joel Whitburn's
# POP ANNUAL

Count 'em down and download 'em to your digital player—45 year-by-year rankings, in numerical order according to the highest chart position reached, of the 23,070 singles that peaked on Billboard's Pop singles charts from 1955-1999. Includes comprehensive, essential chart data and more—all conveniently arranged for fast, easy reference. A must for every music enthusiast's bookshelf and the perfect companion to *Top Pop Singles*!

**912 pages**
**Size: 7" x 9"**

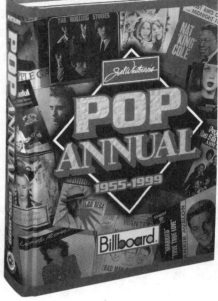

**$49⁹⁵**
**Softcover**

**$59⁹⁵**
**Hardcover**

# 'S
# S &
# ALBUMS
# 1940-1954

The big bands. The classic crooners. The classy female vocalists. The smooth vocal groups. The dynamic duos. Here's the complete history of pre-Rock Pop in four big books in one! An artist-by-artist singles anthology; a year-by-year ranking of classic Pop hits; the complete story of early Pop albums; plus the weekly "Best Sellers" Top 10 singles charts of 1940-1954.

**576 pages**
**Size: 7" x 9"**
**Hardcover**

**$49⁹⁵**

## *Joel Whitburn's*
# TOP R&B/HIP-HOP SINGLES

From R&B's early pioneers...to today's hottest Hip-Hop stars! Over 4,400 artists and nearly 20,000 song titles from Billboard's Rhythm & Blues/Soul/Black/Hip-Hop Singles charts from 1942-2004—all arranged by artist! With complete R&B chart data...R&B record and artist info... and much more.

**816 pages**
**Size: 7" x 9"**
**Hardcover**

**$59⁹⁵**

## *Joel Whitburn's*
# TOP R&B ALBUMS

Covers every artist and album to appear on Billboard's "Top R&B Albums" chart from 1965-1998, with complete chart info... features highlighting each artist's hit albums and hot chart eras...complete track listings for Top 10 albums...and more!

**360 pages**
**Size: 7" x 9"**
**Hardcover**

**$34⁹⁵**

# BILLBOARD "HOT 100" SINGLES CHART BOOKS

Straight from the pages of Billboard -- each decade's "Hot 100" and Pop singles music charts, with every weekly chart reproduced in black and white at about 70% of its original size. **Various page lengths. Size: 9" x 12". Hardcover.**

$59 ⁹⁵    $79 ⁹⁵    $79 ⁹⁵    $79 ⁹⁵    $79 ⁹⁵

**Billboard Pop Charts 1955-1959**

**Billboard Hot 100 Charts The Sixties**

**Billboard Hot 100 Charts The Seventies**

**Billboard Hot 100 Charts The Eighties**

**Billboard Hot 100 Charts The Nineties**

Visit www.recordresearch.com for book descriptions, sample pages and shipping terms.

# *Joel Whitburn's*
# TOP COUNTRY SONGS

An artist-by-artist listing of all charted Country hits, covering the complete chart careers of legendary Country greats and introducing fresh Country voices, with the chart data lowdown and songwriter(s) for every "Country" single from 1944-2005!

**Over 600 pages**
**Size: 7" x 9"**
**Hardcover**

$59⁹⁵

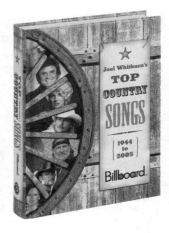

# *Joel Whitburn's*
# COUNTRY ANNUAL

54 complete, year-by-year rankings of over 16,000 records that peaked on Billboard's Country singles charts from 1944-1997, with each song ranked according to its highest chart position.

**704 pages**
**Size: 7" x 9"**
**Hardcover**

$44⁹⁵

# *Joel Whitburn's*
# TOP COUNTRY ALBUMS

The album chart histories of Country's greats—an artist-by-artist chronicle of every album to appear on Billboard's "Top Country Albums" chart from 1964-1997, with complete chart data, Top 10 album track listings, and more.

**304 pages**
**Size: 7" x 9"**
**Hardcover**

$34⁹⁵

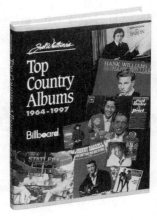

## 2000/2001/2002/2003/2004 BILLBOARD MUSIC YEARBOOKS

Each Yearbook is a comprehensive annual recap of each year's music, in complete artist-by-artist sections covering Billboard's major singles and albums charts. With complete chart data on every single, track and album that debuted during the year...plus artist biographical info, Time Capsules, entertainment obituaries and more!

**Over 200 pages each**
**Size: 6" x 9"**
**Softcover**

$29⁹⁵ each

# ROCK TRACKS

Billboard's two greatest Rock charts—now covered individually in this one book! A total of 22 years of every track and every artist that ever hit Billboard's "Mainstream Rock Tracks" and "Modern Rock Tracks" charts, with comprehensive data on every track from 1981-2002!

**336 pages**
**Size: 7" x 9"**
**Hardcover**

$39⁹⁵

# CHRISTMAS IN THE CHARTS

Charted holiday classics cover to cover—a jolly, joyous celebration of America's favorite holiday music from 1920-2004! This complete history of every charted Christmas single and album is drawn from a diversity of Billboard charts and music genres. Arranged by artist, with full chart data and all the trimmings for every Christmas hit!

**272 pages**
**Size: 7" x 9"**
**Softcover**

$29⁹⁵

# HOT DANCE/DISCO

Lists every artist and hit to appear on Billboard's national "Dance/Disco Club Play" chart from 1974-2003. All charted titles, album cuts—even complete albums that made the Dance chart in their entirety. Loaded with basic chart facts...intriguing Info on artists and recordings...Top Artists' pix...plus much more!

**368 pages**
**Size: 7" x 9"**
**Hardcover**

$39⁹⁵

## TOP ADULT CONTEMPORARY

The definitive work on the softer side of Pop music—an artist-by-artist compilation listing the nearly 8,000 singles and over 1,900 artists that appeared on Billboard's "Easy Listening" and "Hot Adult Contemporary" singles charts from 1961-2001.

**352 pages   Size: 7" x 9"   Hardcover**

## BILLBOARD TOP 10 SINGLES CHARTS

Includes every weekly Top 10 chart from rock and roll's formative years on Billboard's "Best Sellers" charts (1955-1958), followed by weekly Top 10's drawn from the "Hot 100" (1958-2000).

**712 pages   Size: 6" x 9"   Hardcover**

## BILLBOARD TOP 10 ALBUM CHARTS

More than 1800 individual Top 10 charts from over 35 years of weekly Billboard Top Album charts, beginning with the August 17, 1963 "Top LP's" chart right through "The Billboard 200" of December 26, 1998.

**536 pages   Size: 6" x 9"   Hardcover**

## #1 POP PIX

Picture this: 1,045 full-color photos of picture sleeves, sheet music covers or Billboard ads representing every #1 Pop hit from Billboard's Pop/Hot 100 charts, with selected chart data, from 1953-2003.

**112 pages   Size: 6" x 9"   Softcover**

## #1 ALBUM PIX

1,651 full-color photos—in three separate sections—of album covers of every #1 Pop, Country & R&B album in Billboard chart history, with selected chart data, from 1945-2004.

**176 pages   Size: 6" x 9"   Softcover**

## BUBBLING UNDER THE BILLBOARD HOT 100

Bursting with over 6,100 titles by more than 3,500 artists who appeared on Billboard's "Bubbling Under" chart—long the home to regional hits that lacked the sales and airplay to hit the Hot 100. Includes recordings by legendary artists before they hit the mainstream...rock's top stars...famous non-music celebrities...and classic one-shot "Bubbling"-only artists in this comprehensive chronology from 1959-2004.

**352 pages   Size: 7" x 9"   Hardcover**

# A CENTURY OF POP MUSIC 1900-1999

100 rankings of the 40 biggest hits of each year of the past century, based on America's weekly popular record charts—with complete chart data on every hit!

**256 pages**    **Size: 7" x 9"**    **Softcover**

# POP MEMORIES 1890-1954

An artist-by-artist account of the 65 formative years of recorded popular music—over 1,600 artists and 12,000 recordings in all—with data from popular music charts, surveys and listings.

**660 pages**    **Size: 6" x 9"**    **Hardcover**

# ALBUM CUTS

Nearly 1/4 million cuts from over 22,000 Pop albums that charted from 1955-2001, listed alphabetically, with the artist's name and chart debut year for each cut. The perfect partner for *Songs & Artists 2006*!

**720 pages**    **Size: 7" x 9"**    **Hardcover**

# BILLBOARD POP ALBUM CHARTS 1965-1969

A complete collection of actual reproductions of every weekly Billboard "Top LP's" Pop albums chart from January 2, 1965 through December 27, 1969— each shown in its entirety, in black-and-white, at about 70% of original size.

**496 pages**    **Size: 9" x 12"**    **Hardcover**

# TOP 1000 X 5

Five complete separate rankings—from #1 right down through #1,000—of the all-time top charted hits of Pop music 1940-1954, Pop music 1955-1996, Country music 1944-1996, R&B music 1942-1996 and Adult Contemporary music 1961-1996.

**288 pages**    **Size: 7" x 9"**    **Softcover**

# BILLBOARD #1s

See in seconds which record held the top spot each and every week for 42 years (1950-1991) on Billboard's Pop, R&B and Country singles and albums charts and Adult Contemporary singles chart.

**336 pages**    **Size: 7" x 9"**    **Softcover**